Brief Contents

Contents

Dedications

Talya Bauer

To my fantastic family, Horst, Nicholas, and Alexander.

Berrin Erdogan

To Emre and Devin, for being so lovely every day.

Jeremy Short

To my beautiful wife, Tessa; son, Jack; and daughter, Ella. You entertain and inspire me daily.

About the Authors

Talya Bauer

Talya Bauer (Ph.D., Purdue University) is the Cameron Professor of Management and Affiliated Professor of Psychology at Portland State University. She is an award-winning teacher and researcher and recipient of the Academy of Management Human Resource division's Innovations in Teaching Award as well as the Society for Industrial and Organizational Psychology (SIOP) Distinguished Teaching Contributions Award. She conducts research about relationships at work throughout the employee lifecycle, including leadership, organizational justice, HR analytics, recruitment, applicant and candidate experiences during selection, and new employee onboarding. Her work has been supported by grants from the National Science Foundation (NSF) and the National Institutes of Health (NIH) as well as the Society for Human Resource Management (SHRM) and SIOP foundations and has been published in research outlets such as the *Academy of Management Journal, Academy of Management Learning and Education, Academy of Management Perspectives, Journal of Applied Psychology, Journal of Management, Journal of Organizational Behavior*, and *Personnel Psychology*. She has worked with dozens of government, Fortune 1000, and start-up organizations and has been a Visiting Scholar in France, Italy, Singapore, Spain, the UK, and at Google Headquarters, and she has delivered keynote addresses in Australia, France, Greece, Norway, Spain, the UK, and the United States. She has served in elected positions, including the HRM Executive Committee of the Academy of Management and SIOP President. She is currently an Associate Editor for the *Journal of Applied Psychology* (and the former Editor-in-Chief of *Journal of Management*). Her work has been discussed in *Bloomberg Businessweek, Harvard Business Review*, the *New York Times, USA Today, Wall Street Journal*, and NPR's *All Things Considered*, and her work has been referenced 16,000+ times by scholars in their own work. She is a Fellow of SIOP, the American Psychological Association, the Association for Psychological Science, and the International Association of Applied Psychology.

Berrin Erdogan

Berrin Erdogan (Ph.D., University of Illinois at Chicago) is the Express Employment Professionals Professor of Management and Affiliated Professor of Psychology at Portland State University where she was recognized with the Innovative Teaching Award. She also holds a Distinguished Research Professor position at the University of Exeter, UK. Berrin's research focuses on two themes. First, she examines how leaders lead through the relationships they build with their employees; and the implications of manager-employee relationships for employee effectiveness, retention, and well-being. Second, she is interested in understanding person-job fit and misfit, with a focus on why and how employees find themselves overqualified for their jobs and the consequences of being overqualified. She conducted studies and shared results with organizations in manufacturing, retail, health care, education, information technology, construction, and banking among others, in the US, the UK, China, Turkey, Vietnam, France, and India. To date, she has published over 70 journal articles and book chapters, in journals including *Academy of Management Journal, Journal of Applied Psychology, Personnel Psychology, and Journal of Management*. She has also coauthored *Organizational Behavior: Bridging Science and Practice* published by FlatWorld, *Psychology and Work* published by Routledge, and *Human Resource Management: People, Data, and Analytics* by Sage Press. She co-edited the *Oxford Handbook of Leader-Member Exchange*, published by Oxford University Press. Her work has been discussed in media outlets, including the *New York Times, Harvard Business Review*, CNBC, BBC Capital, and *Wall Street Journal*, among others. She was elected a Fellow of the Society for Industrial and Organizational Psychology (SIOP) and the Association for Psychological Science (APS) for unique and unusual contributions to the field of applied psychology. She is the Editor-in-Chief of *Personnel Psychology*. Previously, she served as an associate editor for *European Journal of Work and Organizational Psychology* and *Personnel Psychology*. Berrin is a frequent speaker at national and international conferences and has served as a visiting scholar and given invited talks in Australia, Canada, Greece, Iceland, Singapore, Spain, Turkey, the UK, and the US.

Jeremy Short

Jeremy Short (PhD, 2000, Louisiana State University) is the G. Brint Ryan Chair in Entrepreneurship at the University of North Texas. His award-winning teaching includes classes on principles of management, strategic management, entrepreneurship, and research methods. Dr. Short's research focuses on the determinants of performance in organizations ranging from startups, social ventures, family firms, and large organizations. He has published more than eighty articles in journals such as *Strategic Management Journal*, *Strategic Entrepreneurship Journal*, *Organization Science*, *Personnel Psychology*, *Organizational Behavior and Human Decision Processes*, *Journal of Business Venturing*, *Academy of Management Learning and Education*, and *Journal of Management Education*, among others. He served as an associate editor for the *Journal of Management* and serves on the editorial boards of *Strategic Entrepreneurship Journal*, *Journal of Business Venturing*, *Journal of Management*, *Family Business Review*, and *Organizational Research Methods*. He also coauthored the first Harvard Business School case in graphic novel format as well as other graphic texts such as *Atlas Black: The Complete Adventure*. Jeremy's work has been highlighted in outlets such as *Forbes*, the *Wall Street Journal*, *USA Today*, *Scientific American Mind*, and *Franchise Times*. A recent study highlighting the citation count of scholarly publications placed Jeremy's scholarly impact among the top 2% of all management scholars in the world.

Preface

Principles of management is likely to be one of the first management or business courses that students take. Consequently, our objective when developing material for each chapter was to provide students and instructors with a solid and comprehensive foundation on the fundamentals of management. Each of the 15 chapters is comprehensive, succinct, and action-oriented. The book and available supplements have also been written in a direct, active style that we hope students and instructors find both readily accessible and immediately relevant.

So how are we delivering on these promises?

First, this principles of management book is organized around the well-established **planning**, **organizing**, **leading**, and **controlling** framework (or, simply, P-O-L-C). The P-O-L-C structure provides a number of benefits. Each chapter opens with a brief discussion of how the chapter topic fits in P-O-L-C. For instructors, the use of P-O-L-C as an overarching framework helps with organizing class material, developing the class calendar, and making choices about adding or removing readings and real-life examples. It also provides instructors with an invaluable reference point at the beginning and conclusion of each class session to share with students "where we've been, and where we're going next." Pedagogically, this is a simple yet powerful tool to aid and promote student learning. For students, the P-O-L-C typology provides both instructors and students with an enduring framework for processing and organizing just about everything they will learn and experience, during and beyond their classroom-based education, related to the management of organizations.

Second, there are **three underlying themes** carried through all the chapters. These themes are *strategic thinking*, *entrepreneurial thinking*, and *active management*. Strategy, for instance, is explicitly concerned with the determinants of superior organizational success. We treat organizational performance using the notion of the triple bottom line—the idea that economic performance allows individuals and organizations to perform positively in social and environmental ways as well. The triple bottom line includes financial, social, and environmental performance. The entrepreneurial dimension reflects an underlying and growing trend showing that students and instructors see themselves as entrepreneurs and active change agents, not just as managers. By starting fresh with an entrepreneurial/change management orientation, we provide a perspective on the principles of management that is relevant for the decisions students will make as they move into the types of decisions relevant in the competitive job market. Starting with the opening chapter, we incorporate an active management perspective to show how leaders and leadership are essential to personal and organizational effectiveness and effective organizational change. Moreover, the concluding section of each chapter is focused on the assessment and development of particular management skills.

Third, we incorporate a truly **interdisciplinary perspective** to your principles of management course. We are energized to write a text where mastery of the content has important implications for key skills such as effective decision making, coupled with the strategic, entrepreneurial, and leadership orientations. Your authors are award-winning teachers who have collectively been teaching classes for over half a century and harbor a deep knowledge and appreciation for the book's conceptual underpinnings with a sincere appreciation for experiential teaching approaches.

In an era with increasing concerns over higher-education costs, we are pleased to offer a competitively priced text without sacrificing author and content quality. In addition, an extensive instructors' manual and excellent set of PowerPoint slides provide teaching support for instructors. A test item file developed using state-of-the-art assessment techniques supports faculty in evaluating student performance.

What's New in Version 5.0?

In this edition, you'll find a number of updates since our last revision published nearly three years ago, including new examples, a greater focus on application, as well as many new and updated end-of-chapter cases, which bring course concepts to life for students and stimulate classroom discussions in which every student may participate.

In summary, the following changes have been made:

- This edition reflects a substantive overhaul to reflect more diversity of examples, and to incorporate the great changes globally that have occurred in the past years since our last revision. A specific focus embraces new challenges in regard to managing social media that are relevant to students today.
- All end-of-chapter cases were either written or rewritten to include the latest content or new content. Other new cases focus on contemporary management challenges such as how to best communicate given the current social media landscape.
- This edition is streamlined to make key points more quickly and powerfully than ever before. Chapters have been updated to include the most relevant information while removing distractions.
- All facts and figures have been updated with the most current information.
- New businesses are featured throughout the book.
- New business examples are included throughout the book.

What hasn't changed is our commitment to writing in a concise, accessible, and engaging manner to communicate the latest findings and best practices related to mastering the principles of management.

Support for Instructors

Principles of Management, v5.0 is accompanied by a robust supplements program that augments and enriches both the teaching and student learning experiences. All supplements were created to ensure accuracy and full alignment with the book's narrative. Faculty should contact their FlatWorld sales representative or FlatWorld support at support@flatworld.com for more information or to obtain access to the supplements upon adoption.

Instructor's Manual

The instructor's manual (IM) includes Learning Objectives and an outline for each chapter. The IM also features possible responses to case discussion questions which encourage students to more deeply engage with course material.

PowerPoint Slides

PowerPoint lecture slides provide a concise but thorough outline for each chapter and include relevant tables, figures, and images from the text to enliven lectures and stimulate class discussions. These PowerPoint slides also include a list of Learning Objectives by chapter. Instructors can use the slides as composed to support lectures or customize and build upon them to suit their particular teaching needs.

Online Quizzes

Quiz questions for student self-evaluation are available by section and by chapter in the online version of this text. Students can use the quizzes to test themselves on their comprehension as they move through the different sections of the text or once they have completed a chapter.

FlatWorld Homework

Accompanying FlatWorld Homework for this text is provided in an easy-to-use interface. Multiple choice, fill-in-the-blank, matching, and other question types are available for use and are all auto-gradable. Students who utilize the homework questions should see their performance improve on examinations that are given using the Test Item File questions provided to adopters via Word documents or LMS packages.

Test Item File

The Test Item File (TIF) includes more than fifty multiple-choice, fill-in-the-blank, and essay-question questions. All answers are provided, including possible responses to the essay questions. The items have been written specifically to reinforce the major topics covered in each chapter and to align with FlatWorld Homework and in-text quiz items. The Test Item File questions are also available in pre-formatted form for easy export into popular learning management systems such as Canvas or Blackboard.

Test Generator—Powered by Cognero

FlatWorld is pleased to provide a computer-generated test program powered by the leading assessment provider Cognero to assist instructors with selecting, randomizing, formatting, loading online, or printing exams. Please contact your local FlatWorld representative or FlatWorld support (support@fwk.com) for more information or to request the program.

Sample Syllabi

Sample syllabi based on either 16-week or 10-week terms provide useful templates that help new adopters transition from their current course textbook to Mastering Human Resource Management. Faculty can download the syllabi from the FlatWorld website or they can be obtained by contacting your local FlatWorld representative or FlatWorld support (support@flatworld.com).

We hope you and your students enjoy this edition as much as we enjoyed writing it!

Acknowledgments

Version 5.0

We would like to thank the following colleagues whose comprehensive feedback and suggestions for improving the material in this book over the course of its evolution has helped make this edition of *Principles of Management* the best version yet:

- Lynn Addison, Brewton-Parker College
- Martha Andrews, University of North Carolina, Wilmington
- Jay Azriel, York College of Pennsylvania
- Kevin Cavanagh, Bismarck State College
- Anjali Chaudhry, Saint Xavier University
- Linda Davenport, Klamath Community College
- John Girard, Minot State University
- Jeff Haynie, Nicholls State University
- Ghadir Ishqaidef, University of Wisconsin, Green Bay
- George Klemic, Lewis University
- William Laing, Brenau University
- Anita Leffel, University of Texas at San Antonio
- Gregory Luce, Bucks County Community College
- Bryan Jon Maciewski, Fond du Lac Tribal and Community College
- Angelia McQuade, Lanier Technical College
- Lorrie Mowry, McCook Community College
- Dr. Clara E. Munson, Albertus Magnus College
- Arlene Nicholas, Salve Regina University
- Marvin (Tony) Parker, Fort Valley State University
- Dr. Carla Patalano, New England Institute at Cambridge College
- Anthony Racka, Oakland Community College
- Sherry Robinson, Penn State University, Hazleton
- Renee Rogers, Forsyth Technical Community College
- Kelly Sell, Bucks County Community College
- P. Gerard Shaw, Dean College
- Wayne Smith, California State University, Northridge
- Karel Sovak, University of Mary
- Bradford Strand, North Dakota State University
- Atul Teckchandani, California State University, Fullerton
- Dennis Veit, University of Texas, Arlington

CHAPTER 1

Introduction to Principles of Management

Check please! Due to a high-stress environment and frequent turnover, the restaurant industry poses many challenges to the successful management of individuals and groups. This dynamic has only increased with analysts predicting 1 in 5 restaurants may close permanently in the wake of the COVID-19 pandemic.

Source: Shutterstock.com

Chapter Learning Objectives

Reading this chapter will help you accomplish the following:

1. Learn about managers and the nature of managerial work.
2. Understand the importance of psychology, leadership, entrepreneurship, and strategy within organizations.
3. Know the dimensions of management articulated in the planning-organizing-leading-controlling (P-O-L-C) framework.
4. Understand the relationship between economic, social, and environmental performance.
5. Understand how the concept of performance is understood at the individual and group levels.
6. Create your personal survivor's guide to learning and developing principles of management.

Thomas Edison once quipped, "There is a way to do it better—find it." This simple challenge is at the heart of the study and practice of management. Most of us have pondered better ways to manage others at work or considered ways to manage tasks better at home. As you've visited or worked at restaurants, coffee shops, schools, or other organizations—and talked with friends and family in numerous settings—it's likely you've encountered many instances where different personal interactions would have led to better experiences.

Chief Bogo's bigotry against small mammals in Disney's Zootopia is an example of a potential bias against management positions common in films that may hinder children from effective organizational readiness as they prepare for their future careers.

Source: Shutterstock.com

This book focuses on a number of skills that are critical to business success. For example, a recent article by *Forbes* magazine noted a number of skills that managers desperately need but often lack. Examples include learning to accept feedback, being able to empathize with the perspectives of others, and understanding how different aspects of individual efforts contribute to greater organizational goals.[1] These kinds of "soft skills" are critically important to employers, and demonstrating skills such as effective communication through body language, highlighting the ability to process feedback by nodding, and other active listening activities, and asserting strategic thinking in an interview such as proactively learning key facts about a potential employer is key to successfully landing a job.[2] By simply reading the first paragraph of this chapter you have, at some level, managed a soft skill such as the challenge of time management and procrastination that plagues many individuals (especially if you are taking a largely self-paced or online class).[3] The *need* for managerial talent is so large that a recent study by Burning Glass Technologies estimated 1.3 management or supervisor roles available for every worker.[4] However, scholars that study **organizational readiness** examined over fifty Disney films and found that common themes of manipulation and deception often paint managers in a bad light creating potential biases against management positions.[5] Whether you're a Disney villain plotting a scheme of world domination or a benevolent social entrepreneur hoping to change the world for good, you need strong management skills to continually master organizational challenges.

Management is the art and science of managing others. Knowledge of management will help you identify and develop the skills to better manage your career, relationships, and the behavior of others in organizations. A manager's primary challenge is to solve problems creatively, and **management** often refers to "the art of getting things done through the efforts of other people."[6] The **principles of management** are the means by which you work to accomplish tasks through others individually, in groups, or in organizations. Formally defined, the principles of management are the activities that "plan, organize, and control the operations of the basic elements of [people], materials, machines, methods, money, and markets, providing direction and coordination, and giving leadership to human efforts, so as to achieve the sought objectives of the enterprise."[7] For nearly a century, principles of management have been discussed using the P-O-L-C framework, which refers to the management functions of planning, organizing, leading, and controlling. While managers do not necessarily spend all their time managing, everyone employed in an organization is affected by management principles, processes, policies, and practices. Consequently, finding a "way to do it better" is a challenge that helps all individuals to meet their personal and professional goals.

organizational readiness

The expectations surrounding future organizational life based on cultural influences from childhood.

management

The art and science of accomplishing individual and organizational goals through the efforts of individuals and groups using planning, organizing, leading, and controlling.

principles of management

The concepts managers use in an effort to accomplish management goals.

1.1 Who Are Managers?

Learning Objectives

1. Know what is meant by the term "manager."
2. Describe the types of managers.
3. Understand the nature of managerial work.

Types of Managers

The term *manager* relates to both a position in an organization as well as the nature of different roles and responsibilities. Figure 1.1 summarizes classic and contemporary views of organizations with respect to managerial roles.[8] In contrast to the traditional view of management where the manager is seen as the "boss" who wields unquestioned power over employees, the contemporary view casts top managers as individuals that support and serve other managers and employees through a process called empowerment just as the organization ultimately exists to serve its customers and clients. **Empowerment** is the process of enabling or authorizing an individual to think, behave, take action, and control work and decision-making in autonomous ways.

A number of different types of managers can be found in organizations. *Top managers* are responsible for developing the organization's strategy and acting as a steward for[9] its vision and mission. An example is found in Microsoft CEO Satya Nadella outlining their mission to "empower every person and every organization on the planet to achieve more."[10] *Functional managers* are responsible for the efficiency and effectiveness of a specific area of the business, such as accounting or marketing. *Supervisory managers*, or *team managers*, are responsible for coordinating a subgroup of a particular division or a team composed of members from different parts of the organization.

Line and staff managers serve two distinct functions. A *line manager*, often called a product or service manager, leads a team that contributes directly to the products or services the organization creates. For example, a line manager at Apple Inc. might be responsible for the production, marketing, and profitability of the Apple watch. In contrast, a *staff manager* leads a function that creates indirect inputs. For example, finance and accounting are critical organizational functions but do not typically provide a clear input into the final product or service a customer buys. Instead, they serve a supporting role. A *project manager* is responsible for the planning, execution, and closing of a specific project. For example, the HGTV show *Home Town* depicts the husband and wife team of Erin and Ben Napier as they transform homes in Laurel, Mississippi.[11] Project managers are often found in construction, architecture, consulting, computer networking, telecommunications, and software development.

A *general manager* is responsible for managing a clearly identifiable revenue-producing unit, such as a store, business unit, or product line. Typically, general managers make decisions across various functions and have rewards tied to the performance of the entire unit. General managers take direction from their top executives and must first understand the executives' overall plan for the company. Then they set specific goals for their own departments to fit in with the plan. The general manager of production, for example, might have to increase certain product lines and phase out others. Moreover, general managers must describe their goals clearly to their support staff. Supervisory managers see that the goals are met.

Restaurants often empower employees to offer free dessert to dissatisfied patrons to maintain long-term customer allegiance. That might be particularly effective at Chick-fil-A, whose chocolate chip cookie was highlighted as the favorite fast food offering by "Eat This, Not That!" in 2020.

Source: Shutterstock.com

empowerment

The process of enabling or authorizing an individual to think, behave, take action, and control work and decision-making in autonomous ways.

FIGURE 1.1 Types of Managers

We illustrate the different types of managers using examples drawn from fact and fiction.

Top managers are responsible for developing the organization's strategy and acting as a steward for its vision and mission. Michael Dell showed this type of visionary leadership by founding Dell, Inc. after successfully selling computers out of his dorm room as a freshman student at the University of Texas.

Functional managers are responsible for the efficiency and effectiveness of a specific area such as accounting or marketing. Functional managers at marketing-intensive companies such as Kellogg's, General Mills, and Post must carefully manage many similar but competing brands. In fact, these individuals are typically called brand managers.

Supervisory managers, or team managers, are responsible for coordinating a subgroup with a particular function or a team composed of members from different parts of the organization. Hotel managers are responsible for all aspects of their hotel, from staffing and customer service to the flowers on display in the hotel lobby.

Line managers, often referred to as product or service managers, lead a team that contributes directly to the products or services the organization creates. Line managers often serve critical roles in keeping assembly line manufacturing on track to meet the organization's production goals as in the auto industry.

A staff manager leads a group that creates indirect inputs. Staff managers usually provide an advisory role. The White House chief of staff (an office held by Jacob Lew among others during the Obama administration) provides a high-profile example of this important managerial type.

Project managers are responsible for the planning, execution, and completion of projects. Project managers are found in industries such as construction, architecture, consulting, computer networking, telecommunications, or software development. General contractors often serve as project managers in new housing construction.

General managers are responsible for managing a clearly identifiable, revenue-producing unit, such as a store, business unit, or product line. Michael Scott served as a general manager of the Scranton branch of paper merchant Dunder-Mifflin in the first several seasons of the popular TV series *The Office*.

Source: Shutterstock.com, https://en.wikipedia.org/wiki/Michael_Dell#/media/File:Michael_Dell_2010.jpg, https://commons.wikimedia.org/wiki/File:Jacob_Lew_official_portrait.jpg, Featureflash Photo Agency/Shutterstock.com.

FIGURE 1.2 The Changing Roles of Management and Managers

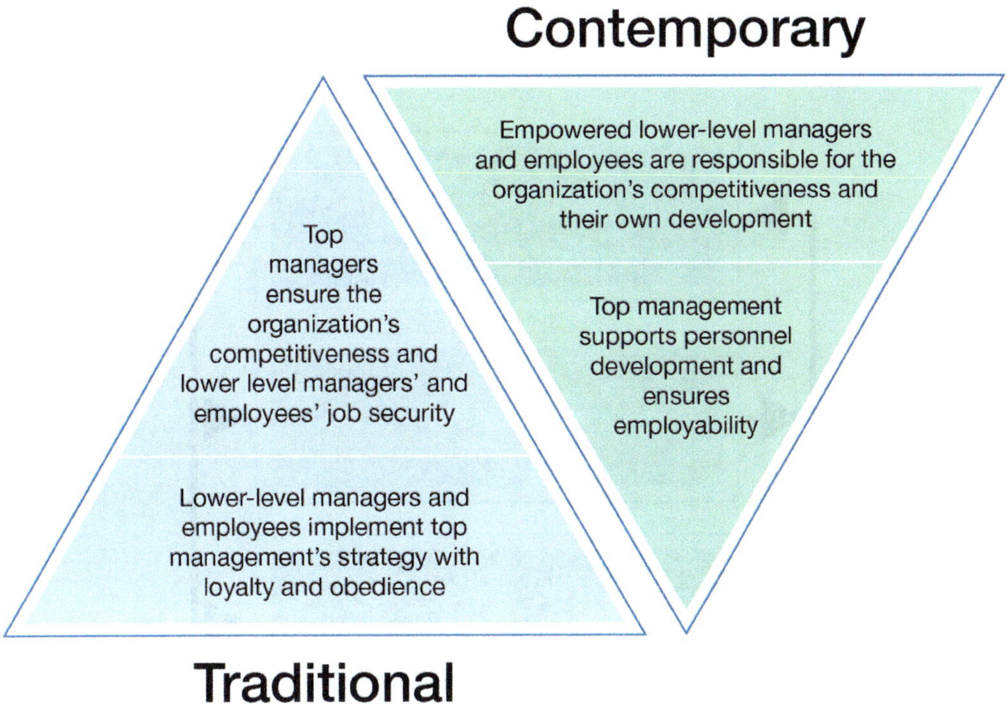

The Nature of Managerial Work

Managers are responsible for the processes of getting activities completed effectively and efficiently with other people while setting and achieving the firm's goals through the execution of four basic management functions: planning, organizing, leading, and controlling. Both sets of processes utilize human, financial, and material resources.

Why are some managers more effective than others? There have been a number of studies on what managers actually do, with one of the most famous conducted by Professor Henry Mintzberg in the early 1970s.[12] After following managers around and observing their behaviors for several weeks, Mintzberg concluded that to meet the many demands of performing their functions, managers assume multiple roles (a role is an organized set of behaviors). Mintzberg identified ten roles common to the work of all managers. As summarized in Figure 1.3, the 10 roles are divided into three groups: interpersonal, informational, and decisional. The informational roles link all managerial work together, while the interpersonal roles ensure that information is provided. The decisional roles make significant use of the information. The performance of managerial roles and the requirements of these roles can be played at different times by the same manager and to different degrees, depending on the level and function of management. The ten roles are described below.

The three interpersonal roles are primarily concerned with interpersonal relationships. In the figurehead role, the manager represents the organization in all matters of formality. The top-level manager represents the company legally and socially to those outside of the organization. The supervisor represents the work group to higher management and higher management to the work group. In the liaison role, the manager interacts with peers and people outside the organization. The top-level manager uses the liaison role to gain favors and information, while the supervisor uses it to maintain the routine flow of work. The leader role defines the relationships between the manager and employees.

FIGURE 1.3 Ten Managerial Roles

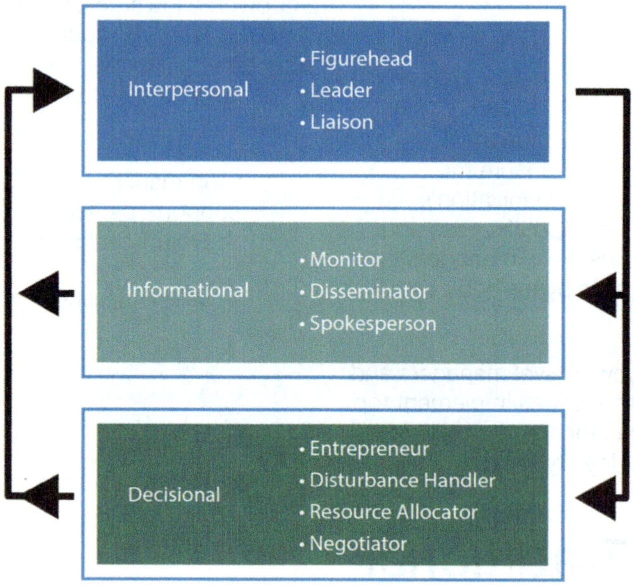

The unique relationships between individuals in their interpersonal roles place the manager in a position to handle information in different ways. Thus, the three informational roles are primarily concerned with the information aspects of managerial work. In the monitor role, the manager receives and collects information. In the role of disseminator, the manager transmits special information into the organization. The top-level manager receives and transmits more information from people outside the organization than the supervisor. In the role of spokesperson, the manager disseminates the organization's information into its environment. Thus, the top-level manager is seen as an industry expert, while the supervisor is seen as a unit or departmental expert.

The unique access to information places the manager at the center of organizational decision making. There are four decisional roles managers play. In the entrepreneur role, the manager initiates change. An example of such change is found at Hello Sunshine, the production company founded by Reese Witherspoon to place the voices of women at the forefront of the film industry.[13] In the disturbance handler role, the manager deals with threats to the organization. Such skills were critical for Volkswagen in the wake of the resignation of their CEO, Martin Winterkorn, following the revelation that the auto manufacturer had manipulated emissions tests with several of the diesel vehicles in 2015.[14] In the resource allocator role, the manager chooses where the organization will expend its efforts. Such skills are critical for managers such as Lawrence Culp, CEO of General Electric, due to their involvement in a number of diverse industries ranging from aviation to healthcare and home appliances. In the negotiator role, the manager negotiates on behalf of the organization. Such skills are as valuable to small business owners, corporate CEOs, and politicians charged with negotiating peace between disputing nations. The top-level manager makes the decisions about the organization as a whole, while the supervisor makes decisions about his or her particular work unit.

A master of interpersonal roles, Chris Paul has served as the NBA Player's Association President since 2013.

Source: Featureflash Photo Agency/ Shutterstock.com

The supervisor performs these managerial roles but with different emphasis than higher managers. Supervisory management is more focused and short-term in outlook. Thus, the figurehead role becomes less significant and the disturbance handler and negotiator roles increase in importance for the supervisor. Since leadership permeates all activities, the leader role is among the most important of all roles at all levels of management.

Key Takeaway

Managers are responsible for accomplishing work through others by using the key managerial functions of planning, organizing, leading, and controlling. The nature of management has evolved from the traditional hierarchical relationship between managers and employees to a climate better characterized as an upside-down pyramid, where top executives support middle managers and middle managers, in turn, support the employees, who innovate and fulfill the needs of customers and clients. Through all four managerial functions, the work of managers ranges across 10 roles, from figurehead to negotiator. While actual managerial work can seem challenging, the skills you gain through principles of management—consisting of the functions of planning, organizing, leading, and controlling—will help you to meet these challenges.

Discussion Questions

1. Why do organizations need managers? Can you imagine an organization without managers? What are some different types of managers and how do they differ? What types of managers do you prefer to work for personally?
2. Reflect on Mintzberg's ten managerial roles. What are they? Which have you personally held? Which seem easier and which seem harder for individuals to do effectively?
3. Imagine you are designing a new restaurant or retail store. Which managerial roles do you think you'll need in this new management position? What friends would you want to hire or avoid hiring and why? Are any jobs less important, or are they all important at different times?
4. What four managerial functions are the focus of principles of management? Think of an effective organization you know about in some depth as either an employee or a customer. Do you think they do a good job in all four of these managerial functions? Why or why not?

1.2 Psychology, Leadership, Entrepreneurship, and Strategy

Learning Objectives

1. Know the roles and importance of psychology, leadership, entrepreneurship, and strategic management (strategy) in principles of management.
2. Understand how psychology, leadership, entrepreneurship, and strategy are interrelated.

Management principles are drawn from a number of academic fields such as psychology, leadership, entrepreneurship, and strategy. We outline key issues culled from each field below.

Psychology

psychology

Psychology refers to the study of how individuals act and behave as individuals and in groups in different situations.

Psychology refers to the study of how individuals act and behave as individuals and in groups in different situations. The field of management draws considerably from applied psychology to learn how individuals interact with each other in various workplace settings.

For example, in the United States, restaurant employees and bartenders often receive the majority of their compensation from tips. This encourages faster customer service, friendlier engagement with customers, and the desire to provide repeat customers with preferred treatment. This norm is not always the case in many European countries where employees are paid through a fixed hourly rate. The different compensation systems has implications for how employees interact with customers, and we can accurately predict differences based on research in applied psychology. In addition, we can draw from applied psychology to assess how restaurants use visuals to encourage purchase of menu items, purposely choose to omit pricing of dishes to encourage patrons to order more expensive items, and suggest legitimacy by noting "signature" dishes and cocktails.[15] Such dynamics can be explained with principles of behavior reinforcement and other elements of applied psychology such as research on persuasion and decision biases that have been studied for decades. Such knowledge can be powerful for landing a job as well.[16] Consequently, a considerable portion of management essentially covers the applied psychology found in workplace settings.

For example, recent research suggests that biases in funding female entrepreneurs (who only receive 2% of venture financing despite owning 35% of all businesses) may stem from the different interactions commonly encountered by men versus women in the venture funding process. While men tend to be asked questions associated with "winning" funding, women are often pitched questions that focus more on the possibility of failure and stress the avoidance of "losing."[17] Concepts such as decision biases and individual differences also make up an important portion of the material you will learn studying management.

Leadership

Leadership is defined as the social and informal sources of influence individuals use to inspire the actions of others. Leadership involves actions taken to mobilize others to work toward a common goal. Leadership also includes an understanding of when, where, and how to use more formal sources of authority and power, such as position or ownership. Increasingly, we live in a world where good *management* requires good *leaders* and *leadership*. More than ever before, competition among employers and countries for the best and brightest—coupled with increased labor mobility and the nature of global competition—puts pressure on firms to invest in present and future leadership capabilities.

leadership

The act of influencing others toward a goal.

General Electric (GE) exemplifies a corporation with an excellent reputation for developing leaders. In contrast to many companies, GE has generally filled the CEO position with individuals who have been developed through their experience with the company. Their addition of Larry Culp as CEO in 2018 marked the first time GE had ever filled the top position in the company with an outside candidate.[18] Whereas GE has been around for more than 125 years, another winning firm in terms of leadership—Google—has only been around since 1998. Both firms emphasize leadership in terms of being exceptional at developing people. Google's founders, Sergey Brin and Larry Page, built a company around the idea that work should be challenging and the challenge should be fun.[19] Google's culture is relatively unique in corporate America, and Google espouses the practice of putting employees first when it comes to daily life in all its offices. There is an emphasis on team achievements and pride in individual accomplishments that contribute to the company's overall success. Ideas are traded, tested, and put into practice quickly. Observers and employees note that meetings that would take hours elsewhere are frequently little more than a conversation in line for lunch and few walls separate those who write the code from those who write the checks. This highly communicative environment fosters productivity and camaraderie fueled by the realization that millions of people rely on Google results. Leadership at Google amounts to a deep belief that if you give the proper tools to a group of people who like to make a difference, they will.[20]

Entrepreneurship

Reese Witherspoon epitomizes the entrepreneurial spirit and was named one of *Fast Company* magazine's most creative people in 2018 based on her creation of production company Hello Sunshine that places women's voices at the forefront of films.

Source: Featureflash Photo Agency/Shutterstock.com

Entrepreneurship is defined as the recognition of opportunities (needs, wants, problems, and challenges) and the use or creation of resources to implement innovative ideas for new, thoughtfully-planned ventures. An **entrepreneur** is a person who engages in the process of entrepreneurship. Entrepreneurship is best understood as a process because it often involves more than simply coming up with a good idea—someone also has to convert that idea into action. As an example of both, Google's leaders suggest that its point of distinction "is anticipating needs not yet articulated by our global audience, then meeting them with products and services that set new standards. This constant dissatisfaction with the way things are is ultimately the driving force behind the world's best search engine."[21]

Entrepreneurs and their entrepreneurial activities are the catalysts for much value creation. They identify and create new markets, as well as foster change in existing ones. However, such value creation first requires an opportunity. Indeed, the opportunity-driven nature of entrepreneurship is critical. Opportunities are typically characterized as problems in search of solutions, and the best opportunities are big problems in search of big solutions. In other words, bigger problems will often mean there will be a bigger market for the product or service that the entrepreneur creates. The problem-solving, opportunity-seeking nature of entrepreneurship is a fundamental building block for effective principles of management.

Strategy

Strategy refers to the creation of an organization's long-term purpose, articulated in clear goals and objectives that can be incorporated into a coherent plan of action. An organization has a *good* or even *great* strategy when this plan takes advantage of unique resources and capabilities that results in a firm that can perform well for years or even decades. **Strategy** refers to the central, integrated, externally-oriented concept of how an organization will achieve its objectives.[22] **Strategic management** is the body of knowledge that answers questions surrounding how firms differ, and how those differences impact firm performance over time.

Strategic management is important to all organizations because when correctly formulated and communicated, strategy provides leaders and employees with a clear set of guidelines for their daily actions. An effective strategy helps managers and individuals answer difficult choices such as: What do I do today? What should my organization be doing? What should it stop doing? One example of a culture-changing successful strategic decision is found in the case of Netflix. Threatened by the cable and streaming success of HBO and physical distribution and cost of Redbox, Netflix decided to engage in a major strategic change to create their own original content. Their gamble paid off with hits such as *House of Cards, Daredevil, Orange is the New Black, Stranger Things*, and *Unbreakable Kimmy Schmidt*. Netflix also features a number of shows that explicitly incorporate strategic management challenges, such as the hit *Gentefied* that shows a family taqueria as they plot to navigate the waters of gentrification in Los Angeles.[23]

So far, their decision to engage in a strategy of developing creative content rather than continuing to simply rely on distribution of existing movie and television offerings represents a major strategic change in direction that has paid off for Netflix and their subscribers.[24]

entrepreneurship

The recognition of opportunities (needs, wants, problems, and challenges) and the use or creation of resources to implement innovative ideas for new, thoughtfully planned ventures.

entrepreneur

A person who engages in the process of entrepreneurship.

strategy

The central, integrated, externally-oriented concept of how an organization will achieve its objectives.

strategic management

Examines how actions and events involving top executives, firms, and industries influence a firm's success or failure.

Binge much? The idea of Netflix streaming content instead of mailing out DVDs seemed pretty strange just a few years ago but skeptics have chilled as the success of their strategic move to focus on new and streaming content such as *Gentefied* continued to inspire bold entrepreneurial actions.

Source: Shutterstock.com

Synchronizing Psychology, Leadership, Entrepreneurship, and Strategy

Psychology, leadership, entrepreneurship, and strategy are the inspiration for important, valuable, and useful principles of management that relate to each other in meaningful ways. In terms of principles of management, you can think of leadership, entrepreneurship, and strategic management as answering questions about "who," "what," and "how." Psychology helps us understand how individuals think, behave, and interact with others. Leadership helps us understand who helps lead the organization forward using the critical characteristics of good leadership. Entrepreneurial firms and entrepreneurs in general are fanatical about identifying opportunities and solving problems—for any organization, entrepreneurship answers big questions about "what" an organization's purpose might be. Strategic management aims to make sure "what" decisions are made with the goal of impacting the firm's overall performance long-term.

Key Takeaway

The principles of management are drawn from four specific areas—psychology, leadership, entrepreneurship, and strategic management. Psychology helps us understand individual behavior. Leadership helps us understand who leads the organization forward and what the critical characteristics of good leadership might be. Entrepreneurs are fanatical about identifying opportunities and solving problems—for any organization, entrepreneurship answers big questions about "what" an organization's purpose might be. Strategic management aims to make sure that the right choices are made—specifically, that a good strategy is in place—to exploit those big opportunities.

Discussion Questions

1. What psychology concepts you may have learned in other classes seem most likely to help understand behavior in the workplace?
2. How do you define leadership, and who would you identify as a great leader? How much does your personal experience help shape your responses to this question?
3. Have you ever had an idea for a new product or service? If so, did you pursue it? Why or why not?
4. Now that you have read this section, how is the idea of strategy similar to or different from the idea you held before this course?
5. Address the following alone or in a group. What roles do leadership, entrepreneurship, and strategy play in good principles of management? Can you be an effective organization by employing strong leadership, entrepreneurship, or strategy? Explain your answer.

1.3 Planning, Organizing, Leading, and Controlling

Learning Objectives

1. Know the dimensions of the planning-organizing-leading-controlling (P-O-L-C) framework.
2. Understand the importance of each P-O-L-C dimension.

Four major functions at the heart of management are planning, organizing, leading, and controlling (the P-O-L-C framework). The four functions are highly integrated when carried out in the day-to-day realities of running an organization. Although these functions may not all be part of the day-to-day actions of actual managers on any given day,[25] the P-O-L-C categorization of management functions continues to serve as an effective framework for classifying the activities managers engage in as they attempt to achieve organizational goals.[26]

Music Rap-Up: Planning, Organizing, Leading, Controlling

Twinprov perform their original rap song written to accompany this book on the topic of management functions of P-O-L-C.

View in the online reader

Planning

Planning is the function of management that involves setting objectives and determining a course of action for achieving those objectives. Planning requires that managers be aware of environmental conditions facing their organization and forecast future conditions. It also requires that managers be effective decision makers.

Planning is a process consisting of several steps. The process begins with **environmental scanning**, where planners must be aware of the critical contingencies and trends facing their organizations in terms of economic conditions, their competitors, and their customers. Planners must then attempt to forecast future conditions. These forecasts form the basis for planning.

Planners must establish objectives, which are statements of tangible actions that need to be achieved, and a timeline for their completion. Planners must then identify alternative courses of action after evaluating the various alternatives, planners must make decisions about the best courses of action for achieving objectives. They then formulate necessary steps and ensure effective implementation of plans. Finally, planners must constantly evaluate the success of their plans and take corrective action when necessary.

There are many different types of plans and planning.

environmental scanning

The act of analyzing the critical external contingencies facing an organization in terms of economic conditions, competitors, and customers.

The emergence of Millennials as the largest segment of the United States workforce has led to an obsession to market to Millennials for organizations and a focus on work-life balance by many Millennial employees.

Source: Shutterstock.com

FIGURE 1.4 The P-O-L-C Framework

The P-O-L-C framework has been a popular structure since the first principles of management books were written less than a century ago. However, the four functions can be seen as critical management elements in antiquity. Here, we explain how elements of P-O-L-C were utilized to manage the Roman Empire for nearly a thousand years.

Planning involves setting objectives and determining a course of action for achieving those objectives. Hallmarks of planning in the Roman Empire included impressive architectural feats like bridges, roads, aqueducts, baths, and other structures that multitudes of people visit to this day. The city grid used in modern-day city planning was popularized in Roman colonies.

Organizing is the management function that involves developing an organizational structure and allocating human resources to ensure the completion of objectives, often through the design of individual jobs within the organization. Organization in the Roman Empire is best illustrated through their military. The Roman military was composed of legions of about five thousand soldiers; these were then organized into smaller units (e.g., cohorts of about six centuries or a hundred men).

Leading involves social and informal sources of influence used to inspire others to take action utilizing knowledge of personalities, values, attitudes, and emotions. Leadership in the Roman Republic was headed by two consuls elected annually and advised by a senate. This system of checks and balances is often emulated in both governments and corporations today.

Controlling involves ensuring that managerial actions do not deviate from standards by creating processes and procedures that ensure consistent behavior. The establishment of Roman Law allowed for the peaceful control of citizens, conquered lands, and property rights in a manner that kept peace more efficiently than previous global powers.

Source: http://en.wikipedia.org/wiki/File:Maccari-Cicero.jpg (Roman senate picture); all other images © Shutterstock.

strategic planning

The process of analyzing competitive opportunities and threats, as well as the strengths and weaknesses of the organization, and then determining how to position the organization to compete effectively in its environment.

Strategic planning involves analyzing competitive opportunities and threats, as well as the strengths and weaknesses of the organization, and then determining how to position the organization to compete effectively in its environment. Strategic planning has a long time frame, often three years or more. Strategic planning generally includes the entire organization and includes formulation of objectives. Strategic planning is often based on the organization's mission, which is its fundamental reason for existence. An organization's top management most often conducts strategic planning. For example, the LEGO company (LEGO is an abbreviation derived from two Danish words "leg" and "godt" and means "play well") made a decision in 1958 that impacts their company today. In that year, they committed to their current plastic brick size so that bricks in 1958 can be combined with generations of bricks from the last 60 years. This represented a significant change from early products such as wooden bricks and a wooden toy duck that was once a signature product.

Tactical planning refers to intermediate-range (one to three years) planning that is designed to develop relatively concrete and specific means to implement the strategic plan. Middle-level managers often engage in tactical planning.

tactical planning

Intermediate-range planning that is designed to develop relatively concrete and specific means to implement the strategic plan.

Operational planning generally assumes the existence of organization-wide or subunit goals and objectives and specifies ways to achieve them. Operational planning is short-range (less than a year) planning that is designed to develop specific action steps that support the strategic and tactical plans.

For the LEGO company, strategic planning can be found in their commitment to make their bricks and mini-figures interchangeable regardless of theme in a particular set. Tactical planning can be found in their commitment to create agreements to produce sets featuring characters from *Star Wars*, *Harry Potter*, and their own original LEGO movies. Operational planning is found in the decision to sell to specific distributors such as Target and specialty toy stores.

For LEGO, strategic planning is found in their commitment to the interchangeable nature of their bricks and mini-figures allowing customers to combine classic sets with updates such as their Friends line introduced in 2012.

Source: Ekaterina_Minaeva/Shutterstock.com

Organizing

Organizing is the function of management that involves developing an organizational structure and allocating human resources to ensure the accomplishment of objectives. The structure of the organization is the framework within which effort is coordinated. The structure is usually represented by an organization chart, which provides a graphic representation of the chain of command within an organization. Decisions made about the structure of an organization are generally referred to as organizational design decisions.

operational planning

Assumes the existence of goals and objectives and specifies ways to achieve them.

Organizing also involves the design of individual jobs within the organization. Decisions must be made about the duties and responsibilities of individual jobs, as well as the manner in which the duties should be carried out. Decisions made about the nature of jobs within the organization are generally called "job design" decisions.

Organizing at the organizational level involves deciding how best to departmentalize, or cluster, jobs into departments to effectively coordinate efforts. There are many different ways to departmentalize, including organizing by function, product, geography, or customer. Many larger organizations use multiple methods of departmentalization.

Organizing at the level of a particular job involves how best to design individual jobs to most effectively use human resources. Traditionally, **job design** was based on principles of division of labor and specialization, which assumed that the more narrow the job content, the more proficient the individual performing the job could become. However, experience has shown that it is possible for jobs to become too narrow and specialized. For example, a recent list of most repetitive jobs found frozen pea tester (the individual who checks the temperature of frozen peas on a production line) to be among the most repetitive jobs. Close behind was the task of threading strings for bookmarks.[27] Another list highlighted costume character entertainer and night security guard.[28] When job fatigue results from such processes, negative outcomes are often the result, including decreased job satisfaction and organizational commitment, increased absenteeism, turnover, and accidents. But the news is not all bad; a recent study found that boredom can lead to creativity and increased individual productivity.[29]

job design

The process of putting together various elements to form a job, bearing in mind organizational and individual worker requirements.

These aren't the jobs you're looking for! Although it may be a blast at Halloween, a recent study found costume character entertainer to top the most boring jobs in the world list.

Source: Mauro Rodrigues/ Shutterstock.com

Leading

Leading involves the social and informal sources of influence that individuals use to inspire action taken by others. If managers are effective leaders, their subordinates will be enthusiastic about exerting effort to attain organizational objectives.

Behavioral sciences, such as psychology and sociology, have made many contributions to understanding this function of management. Personality research and studies of job attitudes provide important information as to how managers can most effectively lead subordinates. For example, this research tells us that to become effective at leading, managers must first understand their subordinates' personalities, values, attitudes, and emotions.

Studies of motivation and motivation theory provide important information about the ways in which workers can be energized to put forth productive efforts. Studies of communication provide direction as to how managers can effectively and persuasively communicate. Studies of leadership and leadership style provide information regarding questions, such as, "What makes a manager a good leader?" and "In what situations are certain leadership styles most appropriate and effective?"

Controlling

The old adage "measure twice and cut once" refers to the importance of quality control. Quality control ensures that the organization delivers on its promises.

Source: Shutterstock.com

Controlling involves ensuring that performance does not deviate from standards. Controlling consists of three steps, which include (1) establishing performance standards, (2) comparing actual performance against standards, and (3) taking corrective action when necessary. Performance standards are often stated in monetary terms such as revenue, costs, or profits, but may also be stated in other terms, such as units produced, number of defective products, or levels of quality or customer service.

The measurement of performance can be achieved in several ways, depending on the performance standards, including financial statements, sales reports, production results, customer satisfaction, and formal performance appraisals. Managers at all levels engage in the managerial function of controlling to some degree.

The managerial function of controlling should not be confused with control in the behavioral or manipulative sense. This function does not imply that managers should attempt to control or to manipulate the personalities, values, attitudes, or emotions of their subordinates. Instead, this function of management concerns the manager's role in taking necessary actions to ensure that the work-related activities of subordinates are consistent with and contributing toward the accomplishment of organizational and departmental objectives.

Effective controlling requires the existence of plans, since planning provides the necessary performance standards or objectives. Controlling also requires a clear understanding of where responsibility for deviations from standards lies. Two traditional control techniques are budget and performance audits. An audit involves an examination and verification of records and supporting documents. A budget audit provides information about where the organization is with respect to what was planned or budgeted for, whereas a performance audit might try to determine whether the figures reported are a reflection of actual performance. Although controlling is often thought of in terms of financial criteria, managers must also control production and operations processes, procedures for delivery of services, compliance with company policies, and many other activities within the organization.

The management functions of planning, organizing, leading, and controlling are widely considered to be the best means of describing the manager's job, as well as the best way to classify accumulated knowledge about the study of management. Although there have been tremendous changes in the environment faced by managers and the tools used by managers to perform their roles, managers still perform these essential functions.

Key Takeaway

The principles of management include four critical functions: planning, organizing, leading, and controlling. This P-O-L-C framework provides useful guidance for common managerial roles.

Discussion Questions

1. What are the management functions that comprise the P-O-L-C framework?
2. Imagine that you are redesigning an organization to maximize its cost effectiveness. Which of the four P-O-L-C aspects would you most focus on and why?
3. Imagine you are hoping to create a highly creative organization to invent new products and processes. In this scenario, how would you emphasize each of the P-O-L-C aspects to best ensure you were creating an environment where ideas could thrive?

1.4 Economic, Social, and Environmental Performance

Learning Objectives

1. Define economic, social, and environmental performance.
2. Understand how economic performance is related to social and environmental performance.

A stakeholder approach to management focuses on the desire to satisfy multiple, often competing, constituents who have a claim on an organization's actions and outcomes. Economic performance is a very important outcome to a firm's **stakeholders**, such as investors or owners, because this performance eventually provides them with a return on their investment. Other stakeholders, like the firm's employees and society at large, are also deemed to benefit from such performance. Increasingly, noneconomic accomplishments, such as reducing waste and pollution, are also viewed as critical performance targets that managers must meet to satisfy stakeholders. The notion of the triple bottom line refers to the measurement of business performance along social, environmental, *and* economic dimensions. We discuss economic, social, and environmental performance in the following section and conclude it with a brief discussion of the interdependence of economic performance with other forms of performance.

stakeholders

Individuals and organizations who are actively involved in the organization or whose interests may be positively or negatively affected as a result of what the organization does.

The triple bottom line emphasizes the three Ps: people (social concerns), planet (environmental concerns), and profits (economic concerns). Companies like Patagonia show their commitment to such practices by working to become certified Benefit Corporations also known as B Corps.

Source: LMWH/Shutterstock.com

The iconic Snoop Dogg's assertion that he keeps his "mind on his money and his money on his mind" epitomizes a focus on economic performance.

Source: Jaguar PS/Shutterstock.com

Economic Performance

Traditionally, economic performance of a firm is a function of its success in producing benefits for its owners, accomplished through the efficient use of resources to produce some form of profit. Simply put, an organization makes a profit when its revenues (money it receives from sales) are more than its costs in a given period of time, such as three months, six months, or a year. Profits accrue to firms because customers are willing to pay a certain price for a product or service, as opposed to a competitor's product or service of a higher or lower price. If customers are only willing to make purchases based on price, then a firm, at least in the face of competition, will only be able to generate profit if it keeps its costs under control.

Social and Environmental Performance

Corporate social responsibility (CSR) is a concept whereby organizations consider the interests of society by taking responsibility for the impact of their activities on customers, suppliers, employees, shareholders, communities, and the environment in all aspects of their operations. This obligation is seen to extend beyond the statutory obligation to comply with legislation and sees organizations voluntarily taking further steps to improve the quality of life for employees and their families, as well as for the local community and society at large. Such actions result in the corporate social performance of an organization.

Integrating Economic, Social, and Environmental Performance

Interest in integrating economic, social, and environmental performance has never been higher as evidenced by the World Economic Forum's 2020 theme, "Stakeholders for a Cohesive and Sustainable World."[30] Still, managing a firm's actions to achieve a triple bottom line in a way that actually builds up all three facets of performance—economic, social, and environmental—is challenging. Advocates of CSR argue that achieving success in each type of performance is possible, and consideration of all stakeholders should be the way all firms are evaluated. Increasingly, evidence is mounting that attention to a triple bottom line is more than being "responsible"; instead, it's just good business. Critics argue that CSR detracts from the fundamental economic role of businesses; still, others argue that it is an attempt to preempt the role of government as a watchdog over powerful multinational corporations.

A review of nearly 170 research studies on the relationship between CSR and firm performance reported that there appeared to be no negative shareholder effects of such practices. In fact, these reports showed that there was a small positive relationship between CSR and shareholder returns.[31] Similarly, companies that pay good wages and offer good benefits to attract and retain high-caliber employees "are not just being socially responsible; they are merely practicing good management."[32]

Warby Parker exemplifies a venture based on social goals by donating a pair of glasses for every pair purchased.

Source: Shutterstock.com

The financial benefits of social or environmental CSR initiatives vary by context. For example, environment-friendly strategies are much more complicated in the consumer products and services market. Cosmetics retailer The Body Shop and StarKist Seafood Company (a strategic business unit of Heinz Food) both undertook environmental strategies, but only the former succeeded. The Body Shop goes to great lengths to ensure that its business is ecologically sustainable.[33] It actively campaigns against human rights abuses and for animal and environmental protection and is one of the most respected firms in the world, despite its small size. Consumers pay premium prices for products from The Body Shop, likely because they believe that it simply costs more to provide goods and services that are environmentally friendly. The Body Shop has been very successful with this strategy.

StarKist, too, adopted a CSR approach when it decided to purchase and exclusively sell dolphin-safe tuna. At the time, biologists thought that the dolphin population decline was a result of the thousands killed in the course of tuna harvests. However, consumers were unwilling to pay higher prices for StarKist's environmental product attributes. Moreover, since tuna were bought from commercial fishermen, this particular practice afforded the firm no protection against imitation by competitors. Finally, in terms of credibility, the members of the tuna industry had launched numerous unsuccessful campaigns in the past touting their interest in the environment, particularly the world's oceans. Thus consumers did not perceive StarKist's efforts as sincerely "green."

Whole Foods is a company that has recently received mixed media attention with regard to their CSR and other organizational practices. Noted for their use of natural and organic products, Whole Foods has been recently highlighted as one of the most socially responsible companies in the United States.[34] Despite their enviable reputation, sales slowed recently amidst allegations from the New York City Department of Consumer Affairs that Whole Foods overcharged customers by listing incorrect weights on some prepackaged food items.[35] Only time will tell how consumers ultimately value the efforts of Whole Foods despite conflicting media reports.

Key Takeaway

Organizational performance can be viewed along three dimensions—financial, social, and environmental—collectively referred to as the triple bottom line, where the latter two dimensions are included in the definition of CSR. While there remains debate about whether organizations should consider environmental and social impacts when making business decisions, there is increasing pressure to include such CSR activities in what constitutes good principles of management. This pressure is based on arguments that range from CSR helps attract and retain the best and brightest employees, to showing that the firm is being responsive to market demands, to observations about how some environmental and social needs represent great entrepreneurial business opportunities in and of themselves.

Discussion Questions

1. Why is financial performance important for organizations?
2. What are some examples of financial performance metrics?
3. What dimensions of performance beyond financial are included in the triple bottom line?
4. How does CSR relate to the triple bottom line?
5. Describe the pros and cons of the triple bottom line approach.

1.5 Performance of Individuals and Groups

Learning Objectives

1. Understand the key dimensions of individual-level performance.
2. Understand the key dimensions of group-level performance.
3. Know why individual- and group-level performance goals need to be compatible.

Managers are concerned with organization-level outcomes such as economic, social, or environmental performance, innovation, or the ability to change and adapt. Most organizations involve the management of more than one person. Consequently, understanding concepts of individual and group performance are important to effective management in most firms. We highlight key aspects of individual and group performance below.

Individual-Level Performance

in-role performance

The things that you have to do as part of your job and its job description.

organizational citizenship behaviors (OCBs)

Voluntary behaviors employees perform to help others and benefit the organization.

Individual-level performance relates to tasks individuals perform in their job (referred to as **in-role performance**), and those things that add value but are not part of a formal job description. These "extras" are called extra-role performance, or **organizational citizenship behaviors (OCBs)**. Generally, in-role performance relates to productivity and quality dimensions associated with certain standards that you must meet to do your job. In contrast, OCBs can be understood as individual behaviors that are beneficial to the organization and are discretionary, but not directly or explicitly recognized by the formal reward system.[36] Here, we outline a number of examples commonly cited as OCBs.

Altruism is a helping behavior that refers to voluntary actions that help others with work problems such as instructing new hires how to use equipment or helping coworkers catch up with work backlogs.[37] Not wasting time (the average American worker wastes 6 hours watching March Madness at work yearly) is an example of altruism as an OCB.

Interpersonal helping is a helping behavior that focuses on assisting coworkers in their jobs when such support is needed.

Courtesy is a helping behavior that includes gestures that facilitate the prevention of problems such as touching base with someone before committing to actions that will affect them or providing advance notice to someone in regards to scheduling.

Peacemaking is a helping behavior that refers to actions that help prevent, resolve, or mitigate unconstructive interpersonal conflict.

Cheerleading is a helping behavior that refers to the use of encouraging and reinforcing words and gestures with coworkers.

Sportsmanship is a citizen-like posture of tolerating the inevitable inconveniences and impositions of work without complaining or grievance.

Organizational loyalty refers to identification with and allegiance to the organization as a whole, transcending the parochial interests of individuals, work groups, and departments.

Representative behaviors include defending the organization against threats, contributing to its good reputation, and cooperating with others to serve the interests of the whole.

Organizational compliance (or *obedience)* refers to an orientation toward organizational structure, job descriptions, and personnel policies that recognizes and accepts the necessity and desirability of a rational structure of rules and regulations. Obedience may be demonstrated by a respect for rules and instructions, punctuality in attendance and task completion, and stewardship of organizational resources.

Individual initiative (or *conscientiousness)* involves a pattern of going beyond minimally required levels of attendance, punctuality, housekeeping, conserving resources, and related matters of internal maintenance.

Civic virtue involves responsible, constructive involvement in the political process of the organization, including not just expressing opinions, but reading one's mail, attending meetings, and keeping abreast of larger issues involving the organization.

Self-development includes all the steps that workers take to voluntarily improve their knowledge, skills, and abilities so they are better able to contribute to their organizations. Examples include seeking out and taking advantage of advanced training courses, keeping abreast of the latest developments in one's field, or even learning a new set of skills to expand the range of one's contributions to an organization.

OCB advocates suggest we should make everyday Common Courtesy Day in our hearts.

Source: Shutterstock.com

The need to train individuals to work in groups has resulted in the near universal adoption of group projects in most business schools.

Source: Shutterstock.com

Group-Level Performance

A **group** is a collection of individuals. Group-level performance focuses on both the outcomes and process of collections of individuals, or groups. In some cases, individuals might be expected to work on their own agendas in the context of a group. Groups might also consist of project-related groups, such as a product group or an entire store or branch of a company. The performance of a group consists of the inputs of the group minus any process loss that results in the final output. Examples of group performance outcomes include the quality of a product and the ramp-up time to production or the sales for a given month.

group

A collection of individuals who interact with each other such that one person's actions have an impact on other members.

Steve Carell stars as Mark Baum in the movie *The Big Short* outlining the factors that led to the bursting of the United States housing bubble and subsequent financial crisis of 2007–2008. The movie focused on how a team of opportunistic investors was able to work together to predict and profit from the market collapse.

Source: JStone/Shutterstock.com

team

A cohesive coalition of people working together to achieve mutual goals.

What is the difference between a *group* and a *team*? A collection of people is not a team, though they may learn to function in that way. A **team** is a cohesive coalition of people working together to achieve the team agenda (i.e., teamwork). Being on a team is not equal to total subordination of personal agendas, but it does require a commitment to the vision and involves each individual directly accomplishing the team's objective. Teams differ from other types of groups in that members are focused on a joint goal or product, such as a presentation, completing in-class exercises, discussing a topic, writing a report, or creating a new design or prototype. Moreover, teams also tend to be defined by their relatively smaller size. For example, according to one definition, "A team is a *small* number of people with complementary skills who are committed to a common purpose, performance goals, and approach for which they are mutually accountable."[38]

The purpose of assembling a team is to accomplish bigger goals that would not be possible for the individual working alone or the simple sum of many individuals' independent work. Teamwork is also needed in cases where multiple skills are needed or where buy-in is required from certain key stakeholders. Teams can, but do not always, provide improved performance. Working together to further the team agenda seems to increase mutual cooperation between what are often competing factions. The aim and purpose of a team is to perform, to get results, and to achieve victory in the workplace and marketplace. The very best managers are those who can gather together a group of individuals and mold them into an effective team.

Compatibility of Individual and Group Performance

Managers need to understand the compatibility of individual and group performance, typically with respect to goals and incentives. What does this mean? Looking at goals first, there should be compatibility between individual and group goals. For example, do the individuals' goals contribute to the achievement of the group goal or are they contradictory? Incentives also need to be aligned between individuals and groups. A disconnect between these is most likely when individuals are rewarded for action that is not consistent with the goal. For example, the contracts of many professional athletes have been criticized for rewarding individual statistics (such as individual scoring) instead of group goals such as team wins. Finally, firms need to be careful to match their goals with their reward structures. For example, if the organization's goal is to increase group performance but the firm's performance appraisal process rewards individual employee productivity, then the firm is unlikely to create a strong team culture.

Key Takeaway

Individual and group performance are important components of organizational performance. Principles of management incorporate two key facets of individual performance: in-role performance and OCB (or extra-role performance). Group performance is a function of how well individuals achieve a combination of individual and group goals. A team is a type of group that is relatively small with members who are willing and able to subordinate individual goals and objectives to those of the larger group.

Discussion Questions

1. What is in-role performance? In your opinion, what can managers do to increase in-role performance of employees?

2. If extra-role performance is not directly recognized by reward systems, what motivates employees to display these behaviors?
3. Can you think of any situations in which in-role and extra-role performance may not be beneficial for the work group or the organization? Provide examples.
4. What differentiates a team from a group? Is this distinction an important one?
5. Consider the definitions of different types of citizenship behaviors. Who are the targets or beneficiaries of these behaviors? Do you feel that behaviors with different beneficiaries may have different causes? Why or why not?

1.6 Managing Preferred Learning Styles

Learning Objectives

1. Know your preferred learning style.
2. Know how to match your preferred style to the circumstances.
3. Use the gauge-discover-reflect framework.
4. Learn about journaling as a tool.

Principles of management courses typically combine knowledge about skills and the development and application of those skills. For these reasons, it is helpful to develop a strategy for learning about and developing management skills. The first part of this strategy should be based on your own dispositions, or preferences, toward learning. The second part of this section will offer some specific frameworks and tools to help you be more effective.

Assess Your Preferred Learning Style

In order to best maximize your learning in this course as well as other learning situations, it is important to understand different learning styles. Some people prefer to learn by seeing information. For example, if you notice that you retain more information by reading and seeing diagrams and flow charts, you may be inclined to learning as a *visual learner*. If you primarily like to learn by listening to others, such as in lectures, conversations, and videos, you may be inclined toward being an *auditory learner*. Finally, if you have a preference for actually doing things and learning from trial and error, you may be inclined toward being a *kinesthetic learner*. If you are unaware of or curious about your primary learning style, take a moment to diagnose your style at the following website. And, keep in mind that you are able to learn in a variety of ways regardless of your preferred style and that multiple approaches can reinforce learning.

What Is Your Preferred Learning Style?

Take the following online preferred learning style quiz to find out what type of learning preference you may have: https://vark-learn.com/the-vark-questionnaire/.

FIGURE 1.5 Tips for Learning to Learn

The learning style of individuals has numerous implications for how to best manage the learning experience. We provide learning recommendations for each style here. For various reasons, using flash cards seems to help with all three learning styles. For a person who prefers to learn via auditory means, saying the answers aloud when using flash cards helps to solidify concepts. For a visual learner, seeing the answers written down on the flash card can be helpful. And for the kinesthetic learner, the act of creating and organizing cards helps the concepts stick.

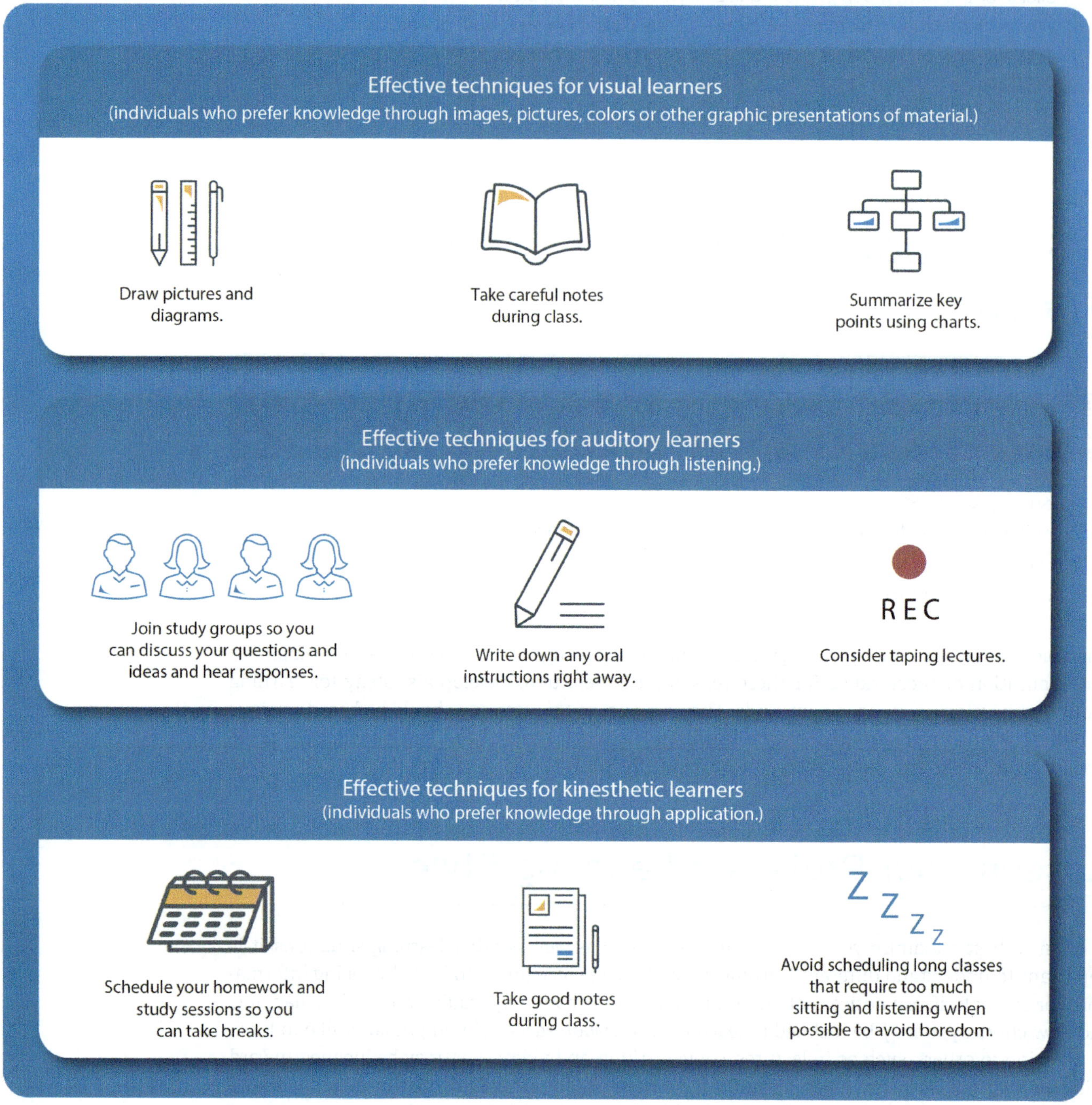

Gauge-Discover-Reflect

Individuals can maximize the value of learning about learning styles by embracing the gauge-discover-reflect process. You have already begun to apply this process by gauging your learning style. The three essential components are (1) *gauge*—take stock of your knowledge and capabilities about a topic; (2) *discover*—learn enough about a topic so that you can set specific development goals that you can apply and practice, and later gauge again your progress toward your set goals; and (3) *reflect*—step back and look at the ways you have achieved your goals, take the opportunity to set new ones, and chronicle this experience and thought process in a daily journal.

Journaling

Research suggests that one way to document personal learning and achievement regarding goals is to chronicle progress in some form of a journal.[39]

There are also various exercises that you can partake in through journaling. These allow you to challenge yourself and think more creatively and deeply. An effective journal entry should be written with clear images and feelings. You should aim to include your reactions along with the facts or events related to your developmental goals. The experience of certain experiments may not necessarily be what you thought it would be, and this is what is important to capture. You are bound to feel turmoil in various moments, and these feelings are excellent fodder for journaling. Journaling allows you to vent and understand emotions. These types of entries can be effective at giving yourself a more rounded perspective on past events.

Perhaps not surprisingly, iconic artist Frida Kahlo added colorful illustrations to chronicle her emotions and thoughts in her journaling efforts.

Source: ararat.art/Shutterstock.com

In addition to the goals you are evaluating, there are numerous possibilities for writing opportunities in a journal. You can reflect on the day, the week, or even the year. You can reflect on events that you have been a part of or people you have met. Look for conclusions that you may have made or any conflicts that you faced. Most important, write about how you felt. This will allow you to examine your own emotional responses. You may find that you need to make a personal action or response to those conflicts. The conclusions that you make from your journal entries are the ingredients for self-growth. Facing those conflicts may also change your life for the better, as you are able to grow as a person.

Taking time to review what you have written can also be valuable. Think about each journal entry you have made and what it means. This is the true aspect of self-growth through journaling. It is easy to recognize changes in yourself through your journaling. You may find that you had a disturbing idea one day, but the next your attitude was much better. You may also find that your attitude grows and improves day by day. This is what makes journaling a true self-growth tool.

Journaling is inexpensive, but effective journaling requires time and commitment. The time factor itself can be small, only about 10 minutes a day or maybe 30 minutes a week, depending on how you would like to summarize your life. You do, however, have to be motivated to write on a regular basis. Even if you do not have a lot of time to write, you will still be able to enjoy the large amount of personal growth that is available through journaling. Perhaps this suggests that your first goal may be to set aside time for journaling.

Key Takeaway

Different individuals approach the learning process in unique ways. Understanding these differences can help you with your objectives related to principles of management. Beyond this general understanding of your own learning style, you also have an opportunity to put together your own survival kit for this course. Your kit will have answers and resources based on the gauge-discover-reflect framework.

Discussion Questions

1. What is your preferred learning style?
2. Were you surprised by your preferred learning style?
3. What target learning issue could you use to experiment with the gauge-discover-reflect framework?

1.7 Case in Point: The Power of the People at Cayuga Collection

Andrea Bonilla, Co-founder and Vice President, Cayuga Collection

Source: Photographed in Costa Rica by Mike Dell. Used by permission from Cayuga Collection.

The Cayuga Collection is an excellent example of how an organization can exert power and influence to positively impact its employees, customers, and the community at large. While the name *Cayuga* comes from Cayuga Lake in Ithaca, New York where its two founders went to school at Cornell University, *The Cayuga Way* means "travel done differently" and also "travel done inclusively." Founded in 1999 by Hans Pfister and Andrea Bonilla, the Cayuga Collection offers luxury vacation properties while supporting sustainable practices. Since that time, the company has opened up multiple new markets and has grown to include over 400 staff members across three countries, including Costa Rica, Nicaragua, and Panama. They specialize in properties with no more than 50 rooms, focus on the luxury segment of the market, and have a strong commitment to sustainability, evidenced by the 1,500+ acres of rainforest that they protect. What is the key to the company's success? According to the founders, it's not simply an innovative approach to sustainable luxury vacations. More importantly, it's "all about the people."

The Cayuga Collection is a pioneer in the area of eco-tourism, largely due to their ingenious solutions grounded in the power of people who know the area best—the locals who live there and make up the community. When they began, they focused more on the efficient use of resources and conserving the natural environment. However, as the tourism industry shifted toward sustainability, the Cayuga Collection began to realize that, without "buy in" from staff and the local communities where their properties reside, their sustainability efforts were not going to be effective. From design solutions, building and infrastructure, to the day-to-day operations, the Cayuga Collection leads and learns from the people around them. They are continually asking, "How can we make this even better?" and have learned that good ideas come from within. In fact, they created the Cayuga Innovation Contest to tap into the collective knowledge of their 400+ staff members and to date have come up with 65 actionable innovative ideas to help blend luxury and sustainability. It is clear that the team of passionate men and women dedicated to *The Cayuga Way* have greatly contributed to the success of the company.

Due to their innovation and success, the Cayuga Collection has garnered worldwide acclaim. Their hotels have seen famous guests such as Nobel prize winners, CEOs, politicians, and celebrities like Charlize Theron. In 2010 they won the *World Saver Award* from Condé Nast *Traveler* and *Travel + Leisure*'s Global Vision Award in the *Environmental Leadership* category. They were also honored with the 2017 National Geographic World Legacy Award in the category of *Earth Changers,* recognizing their cutting-edge leadership in environmentally friendly business practices and green technology. In 2018, The World Travel & Tourism Council awarded Cayuga the Tourism for Tomorrow Award in the *People* category.

By creating authentic and truly meaningful experiences for their guests, the Cayuga Collection persuades people to think differently about what "luxury" means. As co-founder and Vice President Andrea Bonilla says, "It's about creating awareness. When guests come to our properties, for example, our staff needs to be able to show them that the luxury they are receiving there is not about things. It's about people. Connecting with the land, learning new ways to connect with the environment around you, and connecting with each other creates a unique vision and everyone wants to work towards the same goal."

Beyond empowering their employees and persuading their guests to think differently about eco-tourism, the Cayuga Collection seeks to positively influence the local communities and surrounding ecosystems. For example, they buy local, toiletries come in refillable glass containers and include products produced in Costa Rica, and they've banned all single-use plastics from their properties. They've also created smart solutions for irrigating their verdant hotel grounds. Finally, they run programs to help local schools and communities.

Part of the power of the Cayuga approach is one of persuading people to think differently than they normally do about what luxury means. Cayuga also attempts to get people to think differently about what eco-tourism means since their properties are all located in remote destinations that mainly require flights to reach them.

By buying local, employing local, and establishing programs that benefit local communities and ecosystems, the Cayuga Collection has built a successful enterprise. More importantly, however, they have demonstrated how power and influence can be used for good.[40]

Multimedia Extension—The Cayuga Way: Our Sustainable Philosophy

View in the online reader

Case Discussion Questions

1. The Cayuga Collection places great value on feedback and insight from employees. What unique perspective can employees provide that might not necessarily be available from an outside party?
2. The Cayuga Collection has won numerous awards while also attracting high-profile guests. What are some other metrics that could be used to quantify this organization's success?
3. The Cayuga Collection has become successful by simultaneously prioritizing people, profit, and the planet, also known as the "triple bottom line" approach. In your opinion, what are some of the barriers organizations may face when attempting to adopt this approach?
4. If you were the CEO of the Cayuga Collection, would you, in any way, try to redefine what it means to do business "The Cayuga Way"? If so, please describe the changes you would make.
5. The Cayuga Collection focuses on the luxury segment of the market. Do you think their model could be implemented in non-luxury vacation markets? Please explain.

Endnotes

1. Retrieved from https://www.forbes.com/sites/lizryan/2018/02/11/ten-skills-every-manager-needs-but-90-of-them-lack/#1a47a4316149.
2. Retrieved from http://www.businessinsider.com/best-resume-soft-skills-employers-look-for-jobs-2018-4.
3. Retrieved from http://blogs.wsj.com/briefly/2015/09/03/5-tips-for-procrastinating-less/.
4. Retrieved from https://www.burning-glass.com/the-biggest-human-capital-management-challenge-closing-the-management-skills-gap/.
5. Griffin, M., Learmonth, M & Piper, N. 2018. Organizational Readiness: Culturally Mediated Learning Through Disney Animation. *Academy of Management Learning & Education, 17* (1), 4–23.
6. We draw this definition from a biography of Mary Parker Follett (1868–1933) written by Graham, P. (1995). *Mary Parker Follett: Prophet of Management*. Boston: Harvard Business School Press. Follett was an American social worker, consultant, and author of books on democracy, human relations, and management. She worked as a management and political theorist, introducing such phrases as "conflict resolution," "authority and power," and "the task of leadership."
7. The fundamental notion of principles of management was developed by French management theorist Henri Fayol (1841–1925). He is credited with the original planning-organizing-leading-controlling framework (P-O-L-C), which, while undergoing very important changes in content, remains the dominant management framework in the world. See Fayol, H. (1916). *General and Industrial Management*. Paris: Institute of Electrical and Electronics Engineering.
8. Ghoshal, S. & Bartlett, C. (1996). *The Individualized Corporation: A Fundamentally New Approach to Management*. New York: Collins Business.
9. Bishop, Todd. "Exclusive: Satya Nadella Reveals Microsoft's New Mission Statement, Sees 'tough Choices' Ahead." *Geek Wire*. June 25, 2015. Accessed from http://www.geekwire.com/2015/exclusive-satya-nadella-reveals-microsofts-new-mission-statement-sees-more-tough-choices-ahead/.
10. Bishop, Todd. "Exclusive: Satya Nadella Reveals Microsoft's New Mission Statement, Sees 'tough Choices' Ahead." *Geek Wire*. June 25, 2015. Accessed July 18, 2018. http://www.geekwire.com/2015/exclusive-satya-nadella-reveals-microsofts-new-mission-statement-sees-more-tough-choices-ahead/.
11. Retrieved from https://ftw.usatoday.com/2020/03/hgtv-shows-ranked-fixer-upper-home-town-house-hunters.
12. Mintzberg, H. (1973). *The Nature of Managerial Work*. New York: Harper & Row.
13. Retrieved from https://www.fastcompany.com/40572040/reese-witherspoon-most-creative-people-2018?utm_source=postup&utm_medium=email&utm_campaign=Fast Company Daily&position=1&partner=newsletter&campaign_date=05312018.
14. Retrieved from http://www.nytimes.com/2015/09/24/business/international/volkswagen-chief-martin-winterkorn-resigns-amid-emissions-scandal.html.
15. Retrieved from https://www.salon.com/2017/12/12/restaurants-use-menu-psychology-to-make-you-spend-more-money_partner/.
16. Retrieved from https://www.thebalancecareers.com/how-to-use-psychology-to-help-you-get-hired-2061312.
17. Retrieved from https://www.scientificamerican.com/article/why-female-entrepreneurs-have-a-harder-time-raising-venture-capital1/.
18. Retrieved from https://www.bloomberg.com/news/articles/2018-10-02/ge-taps-first-outside-ceo-to-speed-flannery-s-glacial-revamp.
19. Retrieved from http://www.google.com/intl/en/corporate/tenthings.html.
20. Bock, L. (2015). *Work rules!: Insights from inside Google that will transform how you live and lead*. New York: Twelve Books.
21. Retrieved from http://www.google.com/intl/en/corporate/tenthings.html.
22. Hambrick, D., & Fredrickson, J. (2001). Are you sure you have a strategy? *Academy of Management Executive, 15*(4), 2.
23. Retrieved from https://www.americamagazine.org/arts-culture/2020/06/11/netflixs-gentefied-best-american-tv-show-about-gentrification.
24. Laporte, Nicole. "Netflix: The Red Menace." *Fast Company*. January 7, 2014. Retrieved from http://www.fastcompany.com/3024158/netflix-the-red-menace.
25. Mintzberg, H. (1973). *The Nature of Managerial Work*. New York: Harper & Row; Lamond, D. (2004). A matter of style: Reconciling Henri and Henry. *Management Decision, 42*(2), 330–356.
26. Lamond, D. (2004). A matter of style: Reconciling Henri and Henry. *Management Decision, 42*(2), 330–356.
27. Retrieved from https://www.coburgbanks.co.uk/blog/friday-funnies/the-40-most-boring-jobs/.
28. Retrieved from https://content.wisestep.com/boring-jobs-world/.
29. Park, G., Lim, B.C., &Oh, H. (2019). Why Being Bored Might Not Be a Bad Thing after All. *Academy of Management Discoveries 5* (1), 78–92.
30. Retrieved from https://www.brookings.edu/blog/future-development/2020/01/21/stakeholder-capitalism-arrives-at-davos/.
31. Margolis, J., & Elfenbein, H. H. (2008). Doing well by doing good? Don't count on it. *Harvard Business Review, 86*, 1–2.
32. Reich, R. (2007). *Supercapitalism: The transformation of business, democracy, and everyday life*. New York: Knopf.
33. Retrieved from http://www.bodyshop.com.
34. Retrieved from http://www.fastcoexist.com/3044744/americans-think-toms-and-whole-foods-are-the-most-socially-responsible-companies-sort-of.
35. Retrieved from http://fortune.com/2015/07/29/whole-foods-sales-over-charging/.
36. Organ, D. W. (1988). *Organizational citizenship behavior: The good soldier syndrome*. Lexington, MA: Lexington Books.
37. Harvey, J., Bolino, M.C., & Kelemen, T.K. 2018. Organizational citizenship behavior in the 21st Century: How Might going the extra mile look different at the start of the new millennium? *Research in Personnel and Human Resources Management*, Volume 36, 51–110. Emerald Publishing Limited
38. Katzenbach, J. R., & Smith, D. K. (1993). *The wisdom of teams: Creating the high-performance organization*. Boston: Harvard Business School Press.
39. Bromley, K. (1993). *Journaling: Engagements in reading, writing, and thinking*. New York: Scholastic.
40. Case written by Talya Bauer and Berrin Erdogan to accompany Bauer, T. N., & Erdogan, B. (2021). *Organizational Behavior: Bridging Science and Practice (4.0)*. Boston, MA: FlatWorld. Partially based on ideas and information contained in Martin, M. (2019). Women share how to lead with purpose at Skift Travel Forum. *Forbes*. https://www.forbes.com/sites/michellemartin/2019/10/07/women-share-how-to-lead-with-purpose-at-skift-travel-forum/#11c7c7a49122; Sustainability leaders project. https://sustainability-leaders.com/hans-pfister-interview/?fbclid=IwAR2u0_N53y1WmelFWnL-clzr0auJeuMfX2zMb1FCkHB3R-u3h51TZ6ecz33U; Should we all stop flying on vacation? https://www.cayugacollection.com/should-we-all-stop-flying-on-vacation/; Cayuga Collection. (2019). A little ingenuity goes a long way. Retrieved from https://www.cayugacollection.com/sustainability/; Zueras, D. (2020). Andrea Bonilla, la tica que apuesta al ecoturismo de lujo con Cayuga Collection. E&N. Retrieved from https://www.estrategiaynegocios.net/centroamericaymundo/1351891-330/andrea-bonilla-la-tica-que-apuesta-al-ecoturismo-de-lujo-con-cayuga.

CHAPTER 2
History, Trends, Globalization, and Ethics

For every English-speaking college graduate in the United States, there are approximately three English-speaking college graduates in India each year.

Source: Shutterstock.com

Chapter Learning Objectives

Reading this chapter will help you accomplish the following:

1. Learn key figures and concepts in management history.
2. Know the context for contemporary principles of management.
3. Understand key global trends.
4. See how globalization is affecting management principles and practices.
5. Appreciate the importance of value-based leadership (ethics) in management.

The planning-organizing-leading-controlling (P-O-L-C) framework is summarized in Table 2.1. One of the key challenges in management is navigating the tension between "classic" management principles that are enduring while taking care to continually monitor an ever-changing world. Each facet of the P-O-L-C framework must be constantly monitored in order to be successful in a turbulent and changing environment. Consequently, managers must be aware of key trends that impact workforce practices. For example, a trend such as the increased percentage of Millennials in the workforce (they now make up the largest generation by percentage) has considerable implications for individuals and the organizations where they work.[1] Meanwhile, members of Generation Z (individuals born after 1996) are on track to be the most diverse generation both ethnically and racially, as well as the most educated generation to date.[2] This chapter explores a number of classic management concepts from management history, and also begins to explore a number of current trends with the potential to impact the future of management. Knowledge of both classic and current realities is important to succeed when managing in today's world.

TABLE 2.1 The P-O-L-C Framework

Planning	Organizing	Leading	Controlling
1. Vision & Mission	1. Organization Design	1. Leadership	1. Systems/Processes
2. Strategizing	2. Culture	2. Decision Making	2. Strategic Human Resources
3. Goals & Objectives	3. Social Networks	3. Communications	
		4. Groups/Teams	
		5. Motivation	

Wise leaders realize the critical task of acting as a leader. These tasks involve setting the tone to manage *what* gets done but also providing guidance for *how* it gets done. To begin this chapter and provide context for current management ideas we examine management practices throughout history.

2.1 Management History

Learning Objectives

1. Explain the early motivation for the development of principles of management.
2. Know what problems these principles solved.
3. Recognize the limitations of these early views of management.

Early management principles were born of necessity. Examples ranged from the need to establish and implement early governments to the desire to accomplish tasks such as the building of the pyramids that involved managing large labor forces. Classic books on military strategy such as Sun Tzu's *The Art of War* continue to serve as sources of inspiration for "battles" in the marketplace.

Chinese military strategist Sun Tzu provided maxims for military strategy that continue to inspire organizational strategists today.

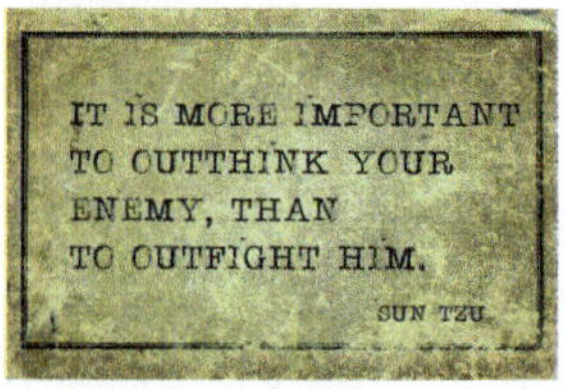

Source: Shutterstock.com

FIGURE 2.1 Management History Timeline

The practice of management has existed throughout the ages. Here, we illustrate several key events in the timeline of management.

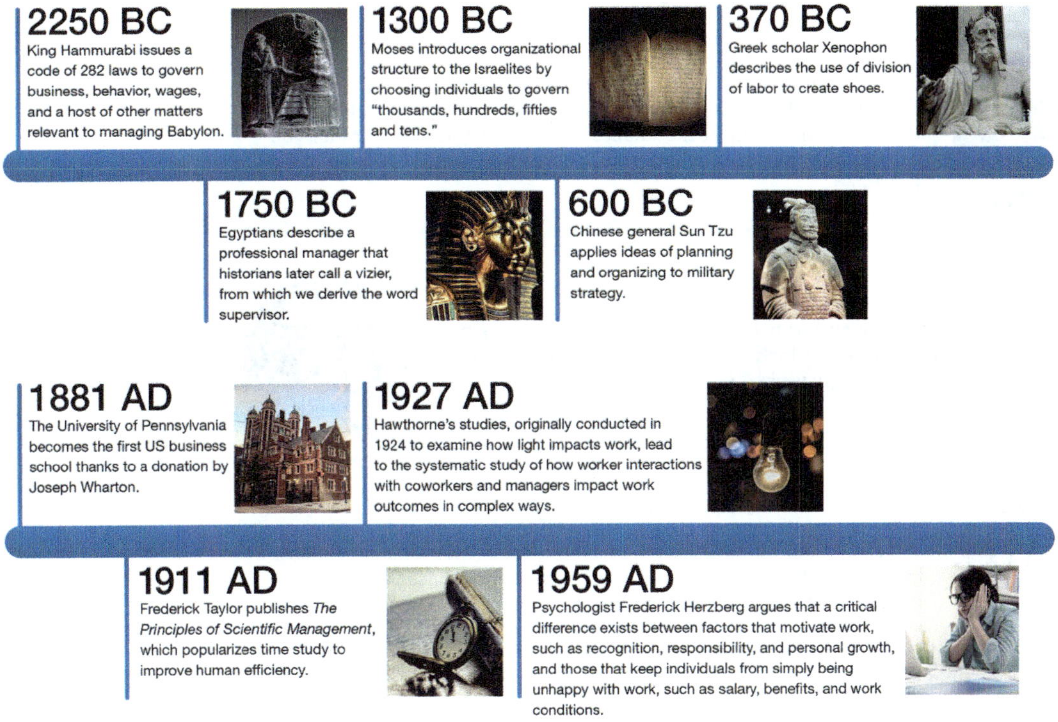

Source: Shutterstock.com, Xian Shanxi Province China _ Shutterstock.com, Jaroslav Moravcik _ Shutterstock.com

Early Management Principles

Although examples of effective management practices have existed for centuries, one of the most influential sets of modern principles was developed by **Henri Fayol**, a French mining engineer. In 1888, Fayol became director of a mining company. The company was not performing well at the time Fayol became manager, but he was able to return the company to profitability. When he retired, Fayol chronicled his actions to save the company. He helped develop an "administrative science" and formulated principles that he thought all organizations should follow. Many of his ideas are considered classic principles today.

Henri Fayol

Fayol was one of the most influential contributors to modern concepts of management, having proposed that there are five primary functions of management: (1) planning, (2) organizing, (3) commanding, (4) coordinating, and (5) controlling.

FIGURE 2.2 Fayol's 14 Principles of (Restaurant) Management

French mining engineer Henri Fayol developed 14 key principles of management in the early 1900s that continue to influence management practices today. Here, we apply Fayol's principles to issues found in restaurant management.

1. Specialization/division of labor. By specializing in a limited set of activities, workers become more efficient and increase their output. Unless you are dining at the smallest of mom-and-pop restaurants, you will generally find the tasks of cooking food and waiting tables separated.

2. Authority/responsibility. Managers must have the authority to issue commands; however, with authority comes the responsibilty to ensure that work gets done. Not surprisingly, many restaurant managers are less than forgiving when employees come in a few minutes late.

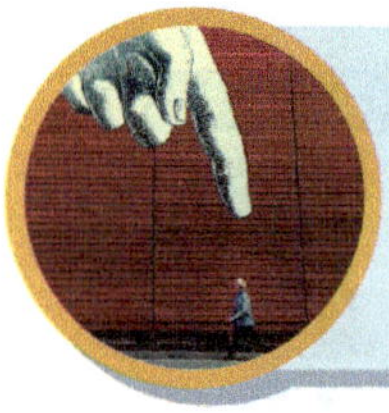

3. Discipline. Workers must obey orders if the business is to run smoothly. Good discipline is the result of effective leadership. Workers must understand the rules and management should use penalties judiciously if workers violate the rules. Employees who miss too many shifts or display other behaviors in conflict with company policy may find themselves looking for other job opportunities.

4. Unity of command. An employee should receive orders only from one boss to avoid conflicting instructions. This leads some restaurants to designate a single manager on duty, or shift manager, to make it clear who is in charge.

5. Unity of direction. Each unit or group has only one boss and follows one plan so that work is coordinated efficiently. This principle can be challenging in restaurants as different managers may emphasize different preferred workplace behaviors.

6. Subordination of individual interest. The interests of one person should never take precedence over what is best for the company as a whole. Although many employees may prefer to have weekends off, schedules are rotated to keep a full staff when restaurants are at their busiest.

7. Remuneration. Workers must be paid fairly for their services. While some claim the word "tips" is an acronym for "to insure proper service," this is unfortunately not related to the true origin of the word.

8. Centralization. Centralization refers to whether decisions are centralized—made by management—or decentralized—made by employees. Fayol believed that whether a company should centralize or decentralize its decision making depended on the company's situation and the quality of its workers. In most restaurants, decision making is fairly centralized, although some employees are empowered to offer a free meal to unsatisfied customers.

9. Line of authority. The line of authority moves from top management down to the lowest ranks. This hierarchy is necessary for unity of command, but communication can also occur laterally if the bosses are kept aware of it. The line should not be overextended or have too many levels. In restaurants, employees from busboy to cook to waiter can go directly to the manager on duty if workplace problems arise.

10. Order. Orderliness refers to the environment and materials as well as policies and rules. People and materials should be in the right place at the right time.

11. Equity. Fairness, dignity, and respect should pervade the organization. Bosses must treat employees well, with a "combination of kindliness and justice." Treating employees with the same respect shown to customers is an important, although sometimes overlooked, policy that restaurant managers should embrace.

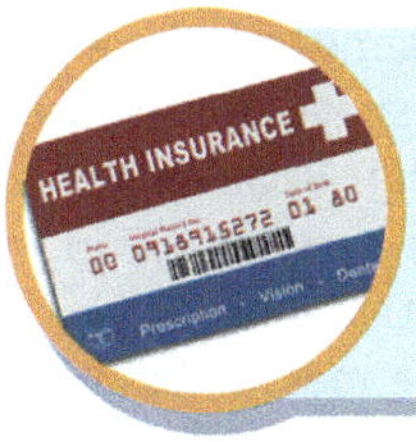

12. Stability of tenure. Organizations do best when tenure is high and turnover is low. People need time to learn their jobs and stability promotes loyalty. High employee turnover is inefficient. Rewarding excellent performance and engaging in fun events can help keep employees in the high-turnover restaurant industry. Offering benefits such as health insurance is one excellent way to keep employees in industries that face high turnover.

13. Initiative. Allowing everyone in the organization the right to create plans and carry them out will make employees more enthusiastic and will encourage them to work harder. Although restaurant employees, in general, have little discretion over daily operations, a suggestion box is always a positive symbol that an organization is open to new ideas.

14. Esprit de corps. Harmony and team spirit across the organization builds morale and unity. Look no further than the company softball team to see an example where workers could volunteer their free time based on the unity built at work.

Source: Fayol, H. (1914). *Administration industrielle et generale.* Photos: Shutterstock.com

Time and Motion

Frederick Winslow Taylor

Developer of scientific management, which deals with the efficient organization of production in the context of a competitive enterprise that has to control its production costs.

Applying scientific management principles to daily use, Frank Gilbreth found he could button his vest four seconds faster if he started from the bottom rather than the top.

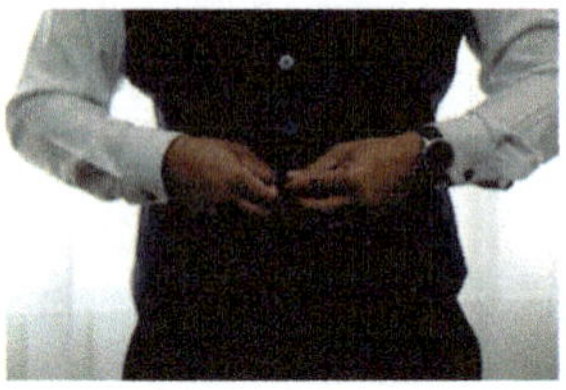

Source: Shutterstock.com

Lillian Gilbreth's work on the *Psychology of Management* led her to become one of the world's first management consultants. Lillian also invented the foot-pedal trashcan found in homes and dorms across the globe today.

Source: Smithsonian Institution from United States—Lillian Moller Gilbreth (1878–1972)

Frank Gilbreth and Lillian Moller Gilbreth

Associates of Taylor also interested in standardization of work to improve productivity.

In the United States, the work of **Frederick Winslow Taylor**—a contemporary of Fayol's—led him to be known as the "father" of scientific management. Taylor formalized the principles he developed in his 1911 book, *The Principles of Scientific Management*. Taylor described how productivity could be greatly improved by applying scientific principles to management; for this reason, scientific management is sometimes referred to as Taylorism.

Taylor is most famous for his "time studies," in which he used a stopwatch to measure how long it took a worker to perform a task, such as shoveling coal or moving heavy loads. He then experimented with different ways to perform tasks to save time. Sometimes the improvement came from better tools. For example, Taylor devised the "science of shoveling," in which he conducted time studies to determine how much weight a worker could lift with a shovel without tiring. He determined that 21 pounds was the optimal weight.[3] But since the employer expected each worker to bring his own shovel, and there were different materials to be shoveled on the job, it was hard to ensure that 21-pound optimum. So, Taylor provided workers with the optimal shovel for each density of materials, like coal, dirt, snow, and so on. With these optimal shovels, workers became three or four times more productive, and they were rewarded with pay increases.

Husband-and-wife team **Frank Gilbreth and Lillian Moller Gilbreth** were associates of Taylor that were also interested in standardization of work to improve productivity.[4] They improved on Taylor's time studies, devising "motion studies," by photographing the individual movements of each worker (they attached lights to workers' hands and photographed their motions at slow speeds). The Gilbreths carefully analyzed key motions and removed unnecessary ones. These motion studies were preceded by timing each task, so the studies were called "time and motion studies."

Applying time and motion studies to bricklaying, for example, the Gilbreths devised a way for workers to lay bricks that eliminated wasted motion and raised their productivity from 1,000 bricks per day to 2,700 bricks per day. Frank Gilbreth applied the same technique to personal tasks such as devising, "the best way to get dressed in the morning." He suggested the best way to button a vest, for example, was from bottom up rather than top down. Why? Because then a man could straighten his tie in the same motion, rather than having to raise his hands back up from the bottom of the waistcoat. Frank even studied efficiencies of throwing motions through recording baseball games, and his work was later used to teach military troops the most effective ways to throw a hand grenade!

Did time and motion studies lead to the development of the film industry? You bet! In fact, a famous bet by Leland Stanford (founder of Stanford University) arose surrounding the question of does a horse "fly" in the sense of having all legs in the air while galloping. He hired Eadweard Muybridge to settle this bet and you may have seen the famous horse photos developed by Muybridge's forerunner of moving pictures shown below. (By the way, the answer is yes to the question of horses having all hooves off the ground while galloping).[5]

Muybridge's early work led to later developments in motion pictures and settled the bet that horses can indeed fly.

Source: Shutterstock.com

Music Rap-Up: Time and Motion

Twinprov perform a rap discussing advancements in management history throughout the ages.

View in the online reader

Limitations of the Early Views

Fayol, Taylor, and the Gilbreths all addressed productivity improvements and examined how to run an organization smoothly. But those views generally presumed that managers were overseeing manual labor tasks. As work began to require less manual labor and more knowledge work, some of the principles they had developed became less effective. At the same time, some argued that the principles of Taylorism tended to dehumanize workers. The writer Upton Sinclair, one of Taylor's vocal critics, raised awareness of deplorable working conditions in the meatpacking industry in his 1906 book, *The Jungle*. Sinclair pointed out the relatively small increase in pay (61%) that workers received compared with their increased productivity (362%). Frederick Taylor answered Sinclair's criticism, saying that workers should not get the full benefit because it was management that devised and taught the workers to produce more. But Taylor's own words compared workers to beasts of burden. He argued that the average worker is "not an extraordinary man difficult to find; he is merely a man more or less the type of an ox, heavy both mentally and physically."[6]

When work is primarily manual, there is considerable benefit to observing workers performing a task, and much can be gained by study with the goal of devising the most efficient motions and tools to perform that task. While researchers continue to examine companies such as McDonald's and Starbucks to study ways their services can be delivered with greater speed and efficiency, managers cannot see inside the head of a software developer to devise the fastest way to write code, as effective software programming depends on knowledge possessed by the engineer rather than simply typing speed. Nonetheless, Taylor remains a key inspiration as a source of managerial efficiencies and, even in the digital age, individuals continue to be faced by the opportunities and challenges spawned by scientific management.

A service-based economy requires interactions between employees and customers. Employees have to be able to improvise, and they must be motivated to serve the customer in a friendly manner. Therefore, new management theories were developed to address the new world of management and overcome the shortcomings of previous approaches.

Early views of management were heavily oriented toward efficiency at the expense of attention to the manager-as-leader. That is, a manager basically acts as a foreman that directs resources to complete predetermined goals or projects. For example, a manager may engage in hiring, training, and scheduling employees to accomplish work in the most efficient and cost-effective manner possible. A manager is considered a failure if he or she is not able to complete the project or goals with efficiency or when the cost becomes too high. However, a leader within a company develops individuals to complete predetermined goals and projects. A leader develops relationships with his or her employees by building communication, by evoking images of success, and by eliciting loyalty. Thus, later views of management evoke notions of leaders and leadership in discussing the challenges and opportunities for modern managers.

The deplorable factory conditions chronicled in Upton Sinclair's *The Jungle* challenged ideas of scientific management and led to the advent of the FDA.

Source: Everett Historical/ Shutterstock.com

Frederick Taylor's work on scientific management in the early 1900s continues to influence management thought today.

Source: By Grap - Gaugler, Eduard (Hrsg.): Taylor, Frederick Winslow: The principles of scientific management; Vademecum zu dem Klassiker der Wissenschaftlichen Betriebsführung. Düsseldorf: Verlag Wirtschaft und Finanzen, 1996., Public Domain, https://commons.wikimedia.org/w/index.php?curid=8682965.

"Modern" Management Ideas

The work of Peter F. Drucker was influential in the dissemination of modern management thought to practicing managers. **Peter Drucker** was the first scholar to write about how to manage knowledge workers, with his earliest work appearing in 1969. Drucker's work was inspired by Frederick Taylor and other pioneers of management thought, and Drucker moved the field forward by addressing topics like the management of professionals, the discipline of entrepreneurship and innovation, and the study of how individuals make decisions. Drucker's work was so influential that in 2005 *BusinessWeek* celebrated Drucker as "the man who invented management."[7]

Peter Drucker's writings and work with GE, Coca-Cola, IBM, and other corporations led him to become one of the leading management gurus in the last century.

Source: TPYXA_ILLUSTRATION/ Shutterstock.com

Peter Drucker

A prolific management guru and the first scholar to write about how to manage knowledge workers.

In 1982, another management advancement appeared when Tom Peters and Robert Waterman wrote *In Search of Excellence*, which became an international best seller and ushered in a business revolution by changing the way managers viewed their relationships with employees and customers. On the basis of the authors' research focusing on 43 of America's most successful companies in six major industries, the book introduced nine principles of management that are embodied in excellent organizations:[8]

1. *Managing Ambiguity and Paradox*

   The ability of managers to hold two opposing ideas in mind at the same time and still be able to function effectively.
2. *A Bias for Action*

   A culture of impatience with lethargy and inertia that otherwise leaves organizations unresponsive.
3. *Close to the Customer*

   Staying close to the customer to understand and anticipate customer needs and wants.
4. *Autonomy and Entrepreneurship*

   Actions that foster innovation and nurture customer and product champions.
5. *Productivity through People*

   Treating rank-and-file employees as a source of quality.
6. *Hands-On, Value-Driven*

   A management philosophy that guides everyday practice and shows management's commitment.
7. *Stick to the Knitting*

   Stay with what you do well and the businesses you know best.
8. *Simple Form, Lean Staff*

   The best companies have very minimal, lean headquarters staff.
9. *Simultaneous Loose-Tight Properties*

   Autonomy in shop-floor activities plus centralized values.

A 2018 survey by *Fast Company* magazine placed St. Jude Children's Research Hospital at the top of brands who most inspire with their mission.

Source: Shutterstock.com

Warren Bennis

Pioneered a new theory of leadership that addressed the need for leaders to have vision and to communicate that vision.

Following up, Peters wrote a *Passion for Excellence*, which placed further emphasis on leadership, innovation, and valuing people. His book *Thriving on Chaos*, published the day of the biggest stock market crash of the time ("Black Monday," October 19, 1987), addressed the uncertainty of the times; and *Liberation Management*, published in 1992, laid out 45 prescriptions for how to lead companies in a rapidly-changing world. The book called for empowering people by involving everyone in decision making and eliminating bureaucratic rules and humiliating conditions. Peters urged organizational leaders to celebrate and recognize employees for their contributions. His advice to leaders was to "master paradox" (i.e., develop a level of comfort with complexity and ambiguity) and establish direction for the company by developing an inspiring vision and leading by example.

Beginning in the 1970s, **Warren Bennis** pioneered a new theory of leadership that addressed the need for leaders to have vision and to communicate that vision. More than just a manager, an effective leader was defined as someone with the ability to influence and motivate others not only to perform work tasks, but also to support the organization's values and meet the organization's goals.

Key Takeaway

Early management theorists developed principles for managing organizations that suited the times. A century ago, few workers were highly educated; most work was manual, tasks were repetitive, and rates of change were slow. Hierarchy brought unity and control, and principles of management in which managers defined tasks and coordinated workers to move in a unified direction made sense. As the economy moved from manufacturing to services, the need for engaging workers' minds and hearts became more important. Drucker, Peters, and Waterman presented ideas on how managers could achieve excellence in a continually changing business environment, while Bennis encouraged managers to become inspiring leaders who empowered people.

Discussion Questions

1. What goals seem to dominate early management principles? Why do you think this is the case?
2. Do you see any commonalities between Fayol's principles of management from 1911 and those of Tom Peters in the 1990s? What do you think accounts for this?
3. Are there any jobs today for which time and motion studies would make sense? Would any other skills need to be taught as well?
4. How would you put some of the ideas of the 1990s into practice?
5. What aspects of P-O-L-C would be most likely to change based on what you have learned in this section?

2.2 Contemporary Principles of Management

Learning Objectives

1. Recognize organizations as social movements.
2. Understand the benefits of social networking.
3. Learn the concept of learning organizations.
4. Understand the value of virtual organizations.

Corporations as Social Movements

Traditionally, corporations have been conceptualized as organizations with clear boundaries, formal procedures, and well-defined authority structures. In contrast, social movements are seen as more spontaneous and fluid. The term **social movement** refers to a type of group action that is focused on specific political or social issues; examples include the civil rights movement, the feminist movement, the Occupy Wall Street movement of 2011, the Women's March of 2017, and the #MeToo movement.[9] More recently, Black Lives Matter has become a global movement with financial and other support from individuals such as Taylor Swift and Seth Rogan and organizations such as Netflix, Disney, and the NFL.[10] Leaders of social movements depend on charisma rather than authority to motivate participants to action. Contemporary management theory is showing that the lines between the two are blurring—corporations are becoming more like social movements, and social movements are taking on more permanence. Just as companies are outsourcing specific jobs, so social movements can contract out tasks like lobbying and fundraising.

In 2020 Black Lives Matter become a global movement in the wake of the death of George Floyd.

Source: Ira Bostic/Shutterstock.com

Corporations are increasingly using their products to reflect the changes in society associated with social movements.[11] For example, Puma recently launched a campaign to celebrate Tommie Smith and John Carlos who raised their fists with a Black Power salute to protest racial injustice at the 1968 Olympics upon winning the gold and silver medals in the 200-meter sprint.[12] Thus, more and more leading businesses are harnessing the mechanics of social movements to improve how they will manage their businesses in the future.

social movement

A type of group action that is focused on specific political or social issues.

Social Networking

Social networking refers to systems that allow members of a specific site to learn about other members' skills, talents, knowledge, or preferences. A global example of social networking is found in LinkedIn's expansion to China—an effort that initially doubled the number of users in China from four to eight million between 2014 and 2015.[13] As of 2020, the number of LinkedIn users in China topped forty-eight million.[14]

social networking

Systems that allow members of a specific site to learn about other members' skills, talents, knowledge, or preferences.

Social networks involve groups of individuals who share a common interest or passion. Social settings websites such as OkCupid, Match.com, Bumble, and Tinder have resulted in numerous budding new relationships and profits in the billions.[15] In the corporate world, a social network is made up of individuals who share an employer and, potentially, other interests as well.

Today, social networks are starting points for corporate innovation—potentially limitless arrangements of individuals inspired by opportunities, affinities, or tasks. People feel better and work better when they belong to a group of people like themselves.[16] This new attitude toward social networks in the workplace has been fueled by the growth of social networking sites such as Facebook, Instagram, and Meetup.

Groundbreaking social media pioneer Facebook was started by then-college student Mark Zuckerberg in 2004 as a way of connecting a social network—specifically, university students. Since then, Facebook has changed the way organizations connect as well. Most companies maintain a presence on Facebook that allows consumers to chime in about their passions (or lack of them) for corporate offerings, news, and products while also using other social media such as Instagram, Snapchat, and others to also keep followers engaged.

With roughly 100 million users, Instagram is following in the footsteps of parent company Facebook in continuing to grow their social network.

Source: Jirapong Manustrong/ Shutterstock.com

As Zuckerberg once told the *Wall Street Journal*, "We just want to share information more efficiently."[17] And, in the information age, that's what social networks do best. At the same time, individuals looking to share their most recent latte picture should be wary. In recent years, a continuing number of threats to cyber security have plagued organizations. Perhaps most publicized was social media innovator Facebook, whose lack of security led to over fourteen million users' posts being made public for days.[18] In addition to concerns over security, social media stress disorder can now be clinically diagnosed for those who feel compelled to engage in various social media outlets.[19]

Learning Organizations

learning organization

An organization skilled at creating, acquiring, and transferring knowledge, and at modifying its behavior to reflect new knowledge and insights.

A **learning organization** is "an organization skilled at creating, acquiring, and transferring knowledge, and at modifying its behavior to reflect new knowledge and insights."[20] The following are the five building blocks of learning organizations:

1. *Systematic problem solving*. The company must have a consistent method for solving problems, using data and statistical tools rather than assumptions.
2. *Experimentation*. Experiments are a way to test ideas in small steps. Experiments let companies hunt for and test new knowledge, such as new ways of recycling waste or of structuring an incentive program.
3. *Learning from past experience*. It's essential for companies to review projects and products to learn what worked and what didn't. Boeing, for example, systematically gathered hundreds of "lessons learned" from previous airplane models, such as the 737 and 747, which it applied to the 757s and 767s, making those the most successful, error-free launches in Boeing's history.
4. *Learning from others*. Recognizing that good ideas come from anywhere, not just inside the company, learning organizations network with other companies in a continual search for good ideas to adapt and adopt.
5. *Transferring knowledge*. Sharing knowledge quickly throughout the organization is the way to make everyone a smart, contributing member.

Virtual Organizations

A **virtual organization** is one where employees work remotely—sometimes within the same city, but more often across a country and across national borders. Even before the COVID-19 pandemic, more than 26 million Americans (16% of the workforce) engaged in remote work.[21] The company relies on computer and telecommunications technologies instead of physical presence for communication between employees. E-mail, collaboration software, wikis, Web meetings (e.g., like Webex or GoToMeeting), phone, and instant messaging are used extensively to keep everyone in touch. Virtual companies present special leadership challenges because it is essential for leaders to keep people informed of what they are supposed to be doing and what other parts of the organization are doing. Communication in a common area is preferable to one-on-one communication because it keeps everyone updated and promotes learning across the organization.

Research has found positive benefits of telecommuting such as increased job satisfaction, increased performance, and less work stress.

Source: Shutterstock.com

The Value of Wikis

Wikis provide companies with a number of benefits:[22]

- Wikis pool the talent of experts as well as everyone from across the company and beyond it—in all time zones and geographic locations.
- Input from unanticipated people brings fresh ideas and unexpected connections.
- Wikis let people contribute to a project any time, giving them flexibility in managing their time.
- It's easy to see the evolution of an idea, and new people can get up to speed quickly by seeing the history of the project.
- Co-creation of solutions eliminates the need to "sell" those solutions to get buy-in.
- Done correctly, wikis can cut the need for e-mail by 75% and the need for meetings by 50%.

With more and more companies outsourcing work to other countries, managers are turning to tools like wikis to structure project work globally. A **wiki** is a way for many people to collaborate and contribute to an online document or discussion (see "The Value of Wikis"). The document remains available for people to access anytime. The most famous example is Wikipedia. A "wikified" organization puts information into everyone's hands and empowers workers directly. Google is well known as a company that empowers employees to share information freely within the organization, but it also has strong deterrents, such as financial and legal consequences, to sharing information outside of the organization. People who are passionate about an idea can tap into the network to make the idea happen. Customers, too, can rally around an issue and contribute their opinions. Many companies that are not solely virtual use the principles of a virtual organization as a way to structure the work of globally distributed teams. Verifone, one of the largest providers of electronic payment systems worldwide, has development teams working on software projects around the world. In what the company calls a "relay race," developers in Dallas working on a rush project send unfinished work at quitting time to another development center in Laupahoehoe, Hawaii. When the sun sets there, the project is handed off to programmers in Bangalore, India, for further work, and by morning, it's back in Dallas, 16 hours closer to completion.

virtual organization

Organizations with members who are geographically apart and who usually work via telecommunication technology while appearing to others to be a single, unified organization with a real physical location.

wiki

An Internet-based method for many people to collaborate and contribute to a document or discussion.

Wikis such as Wikipedia pool knowledge from numerous experts globally to collect and disseminate knowledge.

Source: monticello/Shutterstock.com

Virtual organizations also pose management challenges. In practical terms, if everyone is empowered to be a decision maker but various people disagree, how can decisions be made? If all workers can work at the times they choose, how can management be sure that workers are doing their work—as opposed to reading websites for fun, shopping, or networking with friends—and that they are taking appropriate breaks from work to avoid burnout? There are also challenges related to the virtual environment's dependence on computers and Web security.

Key Takeaway

In today's fast-changing world, organizations are becoming more like social movements, with more fluid boundaries and more participation in leadership across all levels. Social networks within corporations let employees connect with one another and access the people who have the skills, knowledge, or connections to get the job done. Continuous learning is important for individuals and organizations as a whole to transfer knowledge and try out new ideas as the pace of change increases. Virtual organizations can speed up project completion time, but they pose new challenges for managers on how to manage remote workers. Communications technologies let employees work from anywhere—around the corner or around the world—and require special attention to managing communication.

Discussion Questions

1. What commonalities do you see between organizations and social movements?
2. How could you use a social network to help with a specific task, such as helping new employees adjust to the organization?
3. Do intraorganizational social networks inspire employees or do they create more problems than they are worth? Please explain your position.
4. How can social networks help managers plan, organize, lead, and control?
5. What are the potential advantages and potential disadvantages of a virtual organization?
6. What aspects of P-O-L-C would be most likely to change based on what you have learned in this section?

2.3 Trends

Learning Objectives

1. Explain key trends that impact the changing nature of work.
2. Describe the implications of these trends for individuals and organizations.

Wise individuals and managers keep a careful eye on trends to help navigate an ever-changing global environment in effort to place themselves in positions to take advantage of societal changes. Here we examine ten major trends that track important ways in which the world is changing.

Summary of Key Trends

Rise of Millennials

In 2015, the Millennial generation (roughly defined as individuals born between 1981 and 1996)[23] officially became the largest generation represented in the workforce.[24] The rise of Millennials in prime working years has implications for the success of businesses in a number of industries. For example, Millennial dollars have been associated with increased spending on independent retailers that produce in smaller quantities with the goal of providing a more individualized experience with higher quality materials.[25] One particular example of this phenomena that has received widespread news coverage is the rise of the craft brewing industry.[26] While there were fewer than 100 U.S. breweries in the late 1970s, a 2020 report shows the number now exceeds 8,000.[27] The rise of Millennials may also serve to promote change in a number of other industries. For example, while Millennials enjoy travel at more than twice the rate of individuals in previous generations, they are more likely to value the unique experience of an Airbnb or boutique hotel rather than large chains such as Marriott, Hilton, and Hyatt.[28] The desire for more craft experiences by Millennials and others is also likely to lead to the decline of certain ways of doing business that fail to engage the craft aesthetic or desire to meet shopping needs in a more experiential manner than traditional retail experiences. While tiny homes have been embraced by Millennials, some designers believe this trend (coupled with concerns emanating from the Coronavirus pandemic) might create growing demand for tiny offices in the future.[29]

Might the frenzy for tiny homes expand to tiny offices in the future? Only time will tell.

Source: Lea Rae/Shutterstock.com

Increasing Concern for the Environment

An analysis by the National Oceanic and Atmospheric Administration (NOAA) suggests that there have been more catastrophic weather events in recent years than ten and twenty years ago.[30] Increased debate surrounds the growing threat of global warming, with its potential to lead to failing crops, rising sea levels, shortages of drinking water, and increasing death tolls from disease outbreaks such as malaria and dengue fever. Currently, 191 nations have signed the Kyoto Protocol on climate change and pledged to begin the long process of reducing greenhouse gas emissions. According to McKinsey's Global Survey of Business Executives, executives across the world believe that business plays a wider role in society and has responsibility to address issues such as environmental concerns beyond just following the letter of the law to minimize pollution.[31] Costa Rica has set a goal to become completely carbon neutral by 2021. Currently, 99% of their electrical energy comes from renewable sources. In addition to countries, more and more companies now watch the "triple bottom line." Companies realize they have to take bold steps to minimize their carbon footprint, create environmentally friendly products, and manage the company for more than just the next quarter's profits. Companies are also realizing that they may increase their revenues and profitability by committing to environmental programs. For example, U.S.-based banana producer Chiquita forged a partnership with the Rainforest Alliance, and they worked together to find creative ways for satisfying both environmental and business needs, resulting in increased productivity and reduced costs.[32]

Storms such as Hurricane Irma in 2017 provide a strong example for why many are increasingly concerned with environmental changes.

Source: Shutterstock.com

Greater Personalization and Customization

Companies like New York–based Finding Ferdinand, with their focus on custom cosmetics, epitomize the growing trend toward customization in the marketplace.

Source: Shutterstock.com

Consumers are demanding more say in products and services. One size no longer fits all, and that means tailoring products and services to meet specific customer preferences. As companies sell their products globally, tailoring has to meet vastly different needs, cultural sensitivities, and income levels. Customization impacts industries ranging from insurance to automobiles and technology—ensuring a number of additional management opportunities globally.[33]

Faster Pace of Innovation

New models, new products, and new variations—companies are speeding new products to market in response to customer demands. David Glazer, engineering director at Google, explained how his company adapts to this fast pace: "Google has a high tolerance for chaos and ambiguity. When we started OpenSocial [a universal platform for social-network applications], we didn't know what the outcome was going to be." So Google started running a bunch of experiments. "We set an operational tempo: when in doubt, do something," Glazer said. "If you have two paths and you're not sure which is right, take the fastest path."[34] The pace of innovation can be seen in other industries such as esports given that 70% of individuals between the age of 16 and 64 enjoy some form of gaming.[35]

Increasing Disparity between Income Classes

The World Economic Forum has noted the deepening income disparity between the poor and wealthy as a top-ten trend impacting all nations globally.[36] In the United States alone, the share of national income owned by the top 1% of the population has doubled since 1980 to reach nearly 20% of the nation's wealth. While this wealth allows for increasing customization of goods and services for individuals that can afford such luxuries, it also has the potential to disenfranchise those that do not hold such wealth.

Increased Social Media Connectivity

The increasing prevalence of social media has individuals of all ages engaging in an increasing series of online interactions.

Source: Shutterstock.com

We can now use the internet to connect with people as never before. By 2016, more than 3 billion people were online, and that number continues to increase each year as the developing world catches up with the developed world on internet usage.[37] Through over 644 million websites, we can access information, words, sounds, pictures, and video with an ease previously unimaginable as 69% of people on earth are covered by relatively fast broadband service; 94% of Americans enjoy such access.[38]

Rise in Global Instability

A recent global market report by McKinsey highlights concerns surrounding global instability.[39] While we can now tap into more global suppliers and global talent than ever possible, political challenges and economic instability also cause concern for managers. The global problems we face will require people to work together to solve them. Ideas need to be shaped and implemented. Moving ideas around the world is a lot less costly and generates less greenhouse gases than moving people and products around the world. Organizations and social movements alike are using social networking to help people find others with the skills and talents to solve pressing problems.

Yemen was ranked #1 on the Fragile State Index ranking countries with ineffective governments.

Source: Shutterstock.com

Increased Mobility

We can now reach employees, suppliers, and customers wherever they are. Over 8 billion mobile phone subscriptions exist around the world.[40] And, like internet use, mobile phone adoption continues to grow. The penetration of mobile phones is changing the way we do business because people are more connected and able to share more information. Two-way, real-time dialogue and collaboration are available to people anytime, anywhere. The low cost of phones, compared with computers, puts them in the hands of more people around the world, and the increasing sophistication of software and services for the phone expands its use in business settings. Phones are not just a voice communication device—they can send text as well as be a connective device to send data. The fastest mobile phone growth is in developing countries, bringing connectivity to the remotest regions. India has over one billion mobile phone users and is adding millions of new users every year.[41] Fishermen off the coast of southern India can now call around to prospective buyers of their catch before they go ashore, which is increasing their profits by 8% while actually lowering the overall price consumers have to pay for fish by 4%.[42] In South Africa, 85% of small businesses rely solely on mobile phones.

Rise of the Creative Class

With blogs, Etsy, Flickr, Instagram, Pinterest, and YouTube, anyone can post their creative efforts. And with open source and wikis, anyone can contribute ideas and insights. We have ubiquitous opportunities for creativity that are nurturing a new creative class. The demand for workers and ability for workers to work from anywhere may lead to an "e-lance economy." Workers may become free agents, working temporarily on one project and then moving to another when that project is done. Mobile connectivity means these new workers can live anywhere in the world and can work from anywhere in their community. For managers, this means managing workers who might be in a cubicle in Columbus, Ohio, an apartment in Amsterdam, or an internet café in Bangalore.

Want a personalized birthday greeting from Kermit the frog or a customized mike drop to start your next presentation? Platforms such as Fiverr offer creative services starting for, you guessed it . . . $5.

Source: Funstock/Shutterstock.com

Increasing Collaboration

Aggregation sites such as Reddit demonstrate the power of collaboration in social media.

Source: Gil C/Shutterstock.com

The power of collaboration allows more people together to solve more problems more quickly. To design new products quickly—and make sure they meet consumer needs—companies are now looking beyond their four walls for innovation. Google, for example, identifies itself as an organization that believes in open, decentralized innovation. "Google can't do everything. And we shouldn't," said Andy Rubin, senior director of Mobile Platforms. "That's why we formed the Open Handset Alliance with more than 34 partners."[43] While the handset alliance is about open cellphones (i.e., phones that aren't tied to any particular phone company and can be programmed by users just like Apple "apps"), collaboration means much more than communications. People can collaborate, building coalitions, projects, and products.[44] Groups self-organize on the web. For example, the MIT-based Vehicle Design Summit is virtual, so students from around the world can participate.

Key Takeaways

Today's world faces many challenges, from the need to protect the natural environment to the rapid pace of innovation and change. The rise of millennials impacts small and big retailers alike. Technological connectivity is bringing the world closer together and enabling people to work from anywhere. Demand for talent and low-cost workers gives rise to outsourcing and employees working remotely, whether from home or from remote different countries. At the same time, information is now available to more and more people. This drives demand for personalization. It increases complexity but at the same time gives us the collaborative tools needed to solve tough problems.

Discussion Questions

1. How do you manage innovation if ideas can come from anywhere, including people who aren't your direct employees—or aren't even part of the company?
2. If, according to some trends, you can work anytime and anywhere, how do you decide when to work? When do you stop working?
3. What advantages do you see from an increasingly global workforce?
4. How could the rise of the millennials impact conventional retail sales?
5. Which of the ten trends presented here depend on technology?
6. What aspects of P-O-L-C would be most likely to change based on what you have learned in this section?

2.4 Globalization and Principles of Management

Learning Objectives

1. Explain why global trends might influence management principles.
2. Describe the GLOBE project and why it is relevant to management.
3. Understand how cultural dimensions affect business and management decisions.

Globalization and Cross-Cultural Lessons

Despite the growing importance of global business, there continues to be a lack of managers trained with global leadership competencies. Communicating and working with people from different countries can be a challenge due to language issues as well as numerous different cultural norms. For example, in the United States, individuals tend to be fairly direct in business communication. In other cultures, particularly in southern Europe and Japan, the answer to a question begins with background and context—not simply the most direct answer—so that the listener will understand how the person arrived at the conclusion. Similarly, in some cultures, it is considered rude to deliver bad news or say "no" to a request—instead, the speaker would give a noncommittal answer like "we'll see" or "we'll try."

Country-by-country differences are so prevalent that a worldwide team of scholars proposed to create and validate a theory of the relationship between culture and societal, organizational, and leadership effectiveness. Called the GLOBE Project, 170 researchers working together for 10 years collected and analyzed data on cultural values and practices and leadership attributes from more than 17,000 managers in 62 societal cultures. The GLOBE report identified the following nine dimensions of culture.[45]

The "publish or perish" culture in universities where faculty are granted lifetime employment through tenure or invited to find a job elsewhere without sufficient publications after a probationary period is an example of a performance-oriented society common in the United States.

Source: Shutterstock.com

Performance Orientation

Should you reward people for performance improvement and excellence? In **performance-oriented** countries like the United States and Singapore, the answer is yes. Organizations in these countries use employee training and development to help people improve their skills and performance. In countries like Russia and Greece, however, family and background count for more than performance.

performance-oriented

Societies that reward people for performance improvement and excellence.

Uncertainty Avoidance

Individuals in countries high in uncertainty avoidance such as Switzerland seek order, consistency, and structure, such as the Swiss law that you cannot only own a single Guinea pig (because it would get lonely).

Source: Shutterstock.com

uncertainty avoidance

The extent to which members of a society attempt to cope with anxiety by minimizing uncertainty.

assertive cultures

The degree to which a society is assertive, confrontational, or aggressive in relationships with others.

You are much more likely to hear "no problem" than "no" with Indian nationals, who avoid delivering bad news.

Source: Shutterstock.com

power distance

The extent to which the less powerful members of institutions and organizations expect and accept that power is distributed unequally.

gender egalitarianism

Refers to the degree to which a society is characterized by equal opportunities and access to resources for men and women.

Uncertainty avoidance reflects the extent to which members of a society attempt to cope with anxiety by minimizing uncertainty. Should you establish rules, procedures, and social norms to help your employees deal with uncertainty? In countries where uncertainty avoidance is high, like Brazil and Switzerland, the answer is yes. People in such societies want strict rules, laws, and policies to eliminate or control the unexpected. Employees in these countries tend to seek order, consistency, and structure. Countries with low uncertainty avoidance, in contrast, are less rule-oriented. They tolerate a variety of opinions and are open to change and taking risks. Malaysia is an example of a country with low uncertainty avoidance.

Assertiveness

How assertive, confrontational, or aggressive should you be in relationships with others? In highly **assertive cultures** like the United States and Austria, competition between individuals and groups is encouraged. Managers may set up incentives that reward the best idea, even if it is contrary to established practices. People in less assertive countries, like Sweden and New Zealand, prefer harmony in relationships and emphasize loyalty and solidarity.

Power Distance

Power distance reflects the extent to which the less powerful members of institutions and organizations expect and accept that power is distributed unequally. Should you distribute decision-making power equally among the group? In high-power-distance countries like Thailand, Brazil, and France, the answer is no. People in these societies expect unequal power distribution and greater stratification, whether that stratification is economic, social, or political. People in positions of authority in these countries expect (and receive) obedience. Decision making is hierarchical with limited participation and communication. Australia, in contrast, has a power-distance rating that is much lower than the world average. The Australian view reinforces cooperative interaction across power levels and stresses equality and opportunity for everyone.

Gender Egalitarianism

Gender egalitarianism refers to the degree to which a society is characterized by equal opportunities and access to resources for men and women. Countries with low gender egalitarianism are male dominated. Men hold positions of power to a much greater extent in low-gender-egalitarianism countries like Egypt and South Korea. Companies operating in more gender-egalitarian countries such as the Nordic countries, Germany, and the Netherlands encourage tolerance for diversity of ideas and roles regardless of gender.

Institutional Collectivism

Institutional collectivism refers to the extent to which people act predominantly as a member of a lifelong group or organization. In countries with high institutional collectivism such as Sweden, a more effective motivational strategy is to reward groups rather than individuals. Countries with low institutional collectivism, such as in the United States, emphasize individual achievement and rewards. Individuals in countries low in institutional collectivism, such as the United States, are more likely to express individual values and value individual achievements.

institutional collectivism

The extent to which people act predominantly as a member of a lifelong group or organization.

Humane Orientation

Humane orientation is the extent to which a culture and society rewards people for being fair, altruistic, generous, and kind to others. In countries such as Malaysia, this practice is more prevalent and encouraged than in low-humane-orientation countries such as Germany.

humane orientation

The extent to which a culture and society rewards people for being fair, altruistic, generous, and kind to others.

Future Orientation

Will your employees favor activities that involve planning and investing in the future for long-term reward? Or do they want to see short-term results? **Future orientation** is defined as one's expectations and the degree to which one is thoughtful about the future. It is a multifaceted concept that includes planning, realism, and a sense of control. Companies in countries with high future orientation, such as China and Singapore, will have a longer-term planning horizon, and they will be more systematic about planning. Corporations in countries that are the least future-oriented, such as Argentina and Russia, will be more opportunistic and less systematic. At the same time, they'll be less risk averse.

future orientation

One's expectations and the degree to which one is thoughtful about his or her future. It is a multidimensional concept that includes such dimensions as planning, realism, and control.

Global Ventures Gone Awry

When Corning proposed a joint venture with a Mexican glass manufacturer, Vitro, the match seemed made in heaven. But just two years later, the venture was terminated. What happened? Cultural clashes eroded what could have been a lucrative partnership. To start, American managers were continually frustrated with what they perceived to be slow decision making by Mexican managers. Mexico ranks higher on the power distance dimension than the United States—company structures are hierarchical, and decisions are made only by top managers. Loyalty to these managers is a high priority in Mexico, and trying to work around them is considered taboo. Mexicans also have a less urgent approach to time. They see time as more abundant than their US counterparts. As a result, Mexicans thought that Americans wanted to move too fast on decisions, and they perceived American directness in communication as aggressive.[46]

Managing across Borders

Lines on the Map Miss the Real Story

Diversity is more than variations between countries. Sometimes critical differences appear in different regions of the same country. For example, some parts of Mexico do not use Spanish as the primary language. Walmart Mexico's Juchitan store, for example, conducts business in the local Zapotec tongue, encourages female employees to wear traditional Zapotec skirts, and does the morning company cheer in Zapotec.

Talent Abroad

Countries often vary in level of talent and the supply of managerial, skilled, and unskilled labor. Companies should not assume that emerging-market countries offer inferior labor pools. GM, for instance, found that 50% of its assembly-line workers in India have college degrees—a ratio much higher than in other countries.

Local Solutions by People Who Understand Local Needs

Nokia uses local designers to create country-specific handset models. The models designed in India for Indians are dust resistant and have a built-in flashlight. The models designed in China for the Chinese have a touch screen, stylus, and Chinese character recognition. Local designers are more likely to understand the needs of the local population than headquarters-located designers.

Source: Strategies in emerging markets conference, held by the MIT Center for Transportation and Logistics (CTL) on March 7, 2007, Cambridge, MA.

Key Takeaway

Because the business environment increasingly depends on collaboration across regional and national borders, a successful global manager needs to be culturally sensitive and have an understanding for how business is done in different cultures. In some countries, loyalty to the group is key. Other countries celebrate mavericks and rule breakers if they can get things done. Knowing how best to communicate with your coworkers and employees—whether to be direct or indirect, whether to follow strict protocol or be more casual, whom to involve in decisions—are all important considerations.

Discussion Questions

1. You've just been made a manager in Sweden, known for its institutional collectivism. What incentives and reward structures would you use to motivate your employees?
2. How might you prepare workers for an overseas assignment, helping them adjust to their new location and culture effectively?
3. Your company has 12 branches in the United States and will be opening its first branch in Brazil. Your company prides itself on its self-managed teams. Will you keep this policy in the new country? Why or why not?
4. You're a manager in Japan, and you've just discovered that a team leader under your supervision has made a mistake that will result in a quality problem. How will you handle this mistake?
5. You work in Hong Kong for a Swiss-owned firm. The Swiss are known for their high uncertainty avoidance. What differences might you expect to see from your Swiss bosses compared with your Hong Kong employees?

2.5 Developing Your Values-Based Leadership Skills

Learning Objectives

1. Describe the ethical challenges managers are likely to face.
2. Understand why ethics are relevant to principles of management.
3. Discover what decision-making framework you can use to help integrate ethics into your own principles of management.

Ethical Challenges Managers Face

Imagine a scenario where it's late at night and the office is quiet—except that you hear a nagging voice in your head. Your product is already two weeks behind schedule. You've got to get it out this week or you might lose the deal. But you've discovered a problem. To correct the problem would mean another three-week delay—and you know the client won't go for that. It's a small error—it'll probably never be discovered or become an issue. What do you do?

Managers constantly face similar issues. Ethical dilemmas can arise from a variety of areas, such as the following:

- Advertising (desire to present your product or service in the best light).
- Sourcing of raw materials (does the company buy from a supplier who may be underpaying their people or damaging the environment)?
- Privacy (should the company monitor private e-mails that employees write on company time? or the websites they visit during work hours)?
- Safety (employee and community).
- Pay scales (relation of the pay of top executives to the rest of the company).
- Product pricing policies (variable pricing, discounts).
- Communication (with stockholders, announcements of plant closings, etc.).

It's easy to think that people who behave unethically are simply bad people or have a fatal character flaw. But in reality, it is often the situation or circumstances that create the ethical pressures. A global study of business ethics, published by the American Management Association, found that the main reasons for a lapse of ethics are:

1. pressure to meet unrealistic business objectives/deadlines;
2. a desire to further one's career; and
3. a desire to protect one's livelihood.[47]

Volkswagon produced an exhausting auto scandal when it was discovered that over 10 million vehicles worldwide were equipped with software that significantly underreported the amount of emissions created by their vehicles.

Source: Djordje Novakov/ Shutterstock.com

You may have developed your own personal code of ethics, but the social environment of the organization can be a barrier to fulfilling that code if management is behaving unethically. At now-defunct Enron, former vice president Sherron Watkins pointed out accounting misdeeds surrounding the company, but failed to take action beyond sending a memo to the company's chairman. Although she was hailed as a hero and whistleblower, she did not personally disclose the issue to the public. Similarly, auditors at former accounting and consulting giant Arthur Andersen saw the questionable practices that Enron was pursuing, but when the auditors reported these facts to management, Arthur Andersen's managers pointed to the $100 million of business they were getting from the Enron account. Those managers put profits ahead of ethics. In the end, both companies were ruined, not to mention the countless employees and shareholders left shattered, with many financially bankrupt. More recently, Apple was slow to reveal a bug in their popular FaceTime app that allowed people to eavesdrop on others before answering calls.[48]

Sarbanes-Oxley Act

Government act that sought to reform corporate governance practices in large U.S. public companies.

Since 2002, when the **Sarbanes-Oxley Act** was passed, companies have been required to write a code of ethics. The act sought to reform corporate governance practices in large U.S. public companies. The purpose of the Act is to, "define a code of ethics as a codification of standards that is reasonably necessary to deter wrongdoing and to promote honest and ethical conduct," including the ethical handling of actual or apparent conflicts of interest, compliance with laws, and accountability to adhere to the code.[49] The U.S. financial crisis of late 2008 pointed out that other areas, particularly in the financial services industry, needed stiffer regulations and regulatory scrutiny as well, and those moves began to take effect in early 2009. Some companies go a step further and articulate a set of values that drives their code of conduct.

FIGURE 2.3 Sarbanes-Oxley Act of 2002 (SOX)

In the early 2000s, highly publicized fraud at Enron, WorldCom, Tyco, and other firms revealed significant issues, including conflicts of interest by auditors and securities analysts, boardroom failures, and inadequate funding of the Securities and Exchange Commission. In response, Senator Paul Sarbanes and Representatives Michael Oxley sponsored legislation that contained what former President George W. Bush called "the most far-reaching reforms of American business practices since the time of Franklin D. Roosevelt." We outline the eleven aspects of the law here.

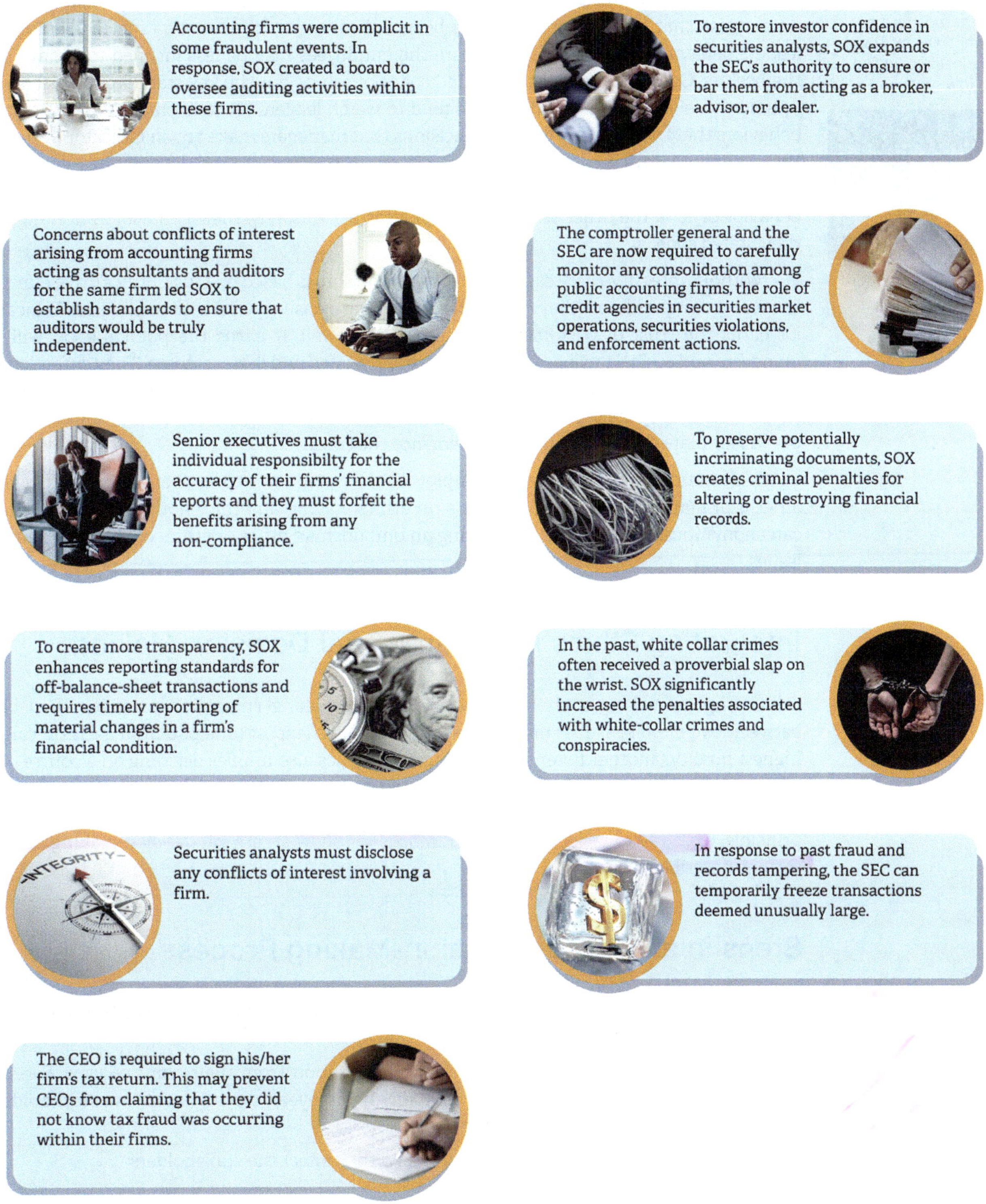

Source: Shutterstock.com

Importance of Ethics in Management

Supplemental insurance carrier Aflac has been listed as one of the world's most ethical companies by The Ethisphere Institute for five years in a row.

Source: Shutterstock.com

Ethical behavior among managers is important in organizations because leaders set the moral tone of the organization and serve as role models. Ethical leaders build trust in organizations. Thus it is no surprise that ethical leadership has been linked to employee motivation.[50] If employees see leaders behaving unethically, chances are the employees may be less inclined to behave ethically themselves. Companies may have printed codes of ethics, but the key standard is whether leaders uphold those values and standards. We tend to watch leaders for cues on appropriate actions and behaviors that the company expects. Decisions that managers make are an indicator of their ethics. If the company says it cares about the safety of employees but then does not buy enough protective gear for them, it is not behaving in line with its code. Likewise, if managers exhibit unsafe behavior or look the other way when employees act unsafely, their behavior is not aligned with their stated code.

Without integrity, there can be no trust. Leadership is based on trust. Ethics drive effectiveness because employees know they can do the right thing decisively and with confidence. Ethical behavior earns the trust of customers and suppliers as well. It earns the public's good will. Ethical managers and ethical businesses tend to be more trusted and better treated. They suffer less resentment, inefficiency, litigation, and government interference. If top management cuts corners, however, or if they make shady decisions, then no matter how good the code of ethics sounds, people will emulate the questionable behavior, not the code.

Wise managers make it clear to employees that they can expect them to conduct business in an ethical manner by offering seminars on ethics, having an ethics hotline by which employees can anonymously raise issues, and having an ombudsman office or ethics committee to investigate issues.

Integrating Ethics into Managerial Decision Making

Ethics implies making a choice between decision-making rules. For instance, when choosing between two suppliers, does management choose the cheapest (one potential decision rule) or the highest quality (another potential decision rule). Ethics also implies deciding on a course of action when no clear decision rule is available. Dilemmas occur when the choices are incompatible and when one course of action seems to better serve your self-interest but appears to violate a moral principle. One way to tackle ethical dilemmas is to follow an ethical decision-making process, like the one described below.

Steps in an Ethical Decision-Making Process

1. Assess the situation. What are individuals being asked to do? Is it illegal? Is it unethical? Who might be harmed?
2. Identify the stakeholders and consider the situation from their point of view. For example, consider the point of view of the company's employees, top management, stockholders, customers, suppliers, and community.
3. Consider the alternatives available and how they affect the stakeholders:
   - consequences;
   - duties, rights, and principles; and
   - implications for personal integrity and character.

4. How does the action make you feel about yourself? How would you feel if your actions were reported tomorrow in the *Wall Street Journal* (or your daily newspaper)? How would you explain your actions to your mother or to your child?
5. Make a decision. This might involve going to your boss or to a neutral third party (such as an ombudsman or ethics committee). Know your values and your limits. If the company does nothing to rectify the situation, do you want to continue working for the company?
6. Monitor outcomes. How did the decision work out? How did it turn out for all concerned? If you had to do it over again, what would you do differently?[51]

If you see unethical behavior in others, confronting it as early as possible is generally better. Early on, you have more of an opportunity to talk with the person in a fact-finding (rather than an accusatory) way. The discussion may prevent the situation from escalating. Keeping silent because you want to avoid offending the person may lead to much greater problems later on. As French playwright Jean-Baptiste Poquelin or Moliere wrote, "It's not only for what we do that we are held responsible, but for what we do not do."

Key Takeaway

Management involves decision making, and decisions often have an ethical component. Beyond personal ethics or a moral code, managers make decisions that reflect the company as a whole, affecting its future success and vitality. Ethics does not just mean following the law but it also involves acting in accordance with basic values.

Discussion Questions

1. What are the consequences of unethical behavior?
2. If you were writing a code of ethics for your company, what would you include?
3. In times of economic downturn, is ethical behavior a luxury or a mandate?
4. Imagine you just found out that one of your employees has lied on an expense report. He is a great employee and one of your best salespeople. How would you handle this ethical violation?
5. Nobel laureate economist Milton Friedman said that, "The social responsibility of business is to increase its profits." Do you agree with this view? Why or why not?

2.6 Case in Point: Employee Engagement in Organizational Change Toward B Corp Status

Source: Sheila Fitzgerald/Shutterstock.com

Brew Dr. Kombucha and Tea, formerly known as Townshend's Tea Company, was founded in 2006 with the vision of creating a tea culture in the United States. In 2008, the company began producing kombucha (a beverage made out of fermented sweet tea) under the brand Brew Dr. Kombucha. While both brands, which are jointly operated, are growing, sales of Brew Dr. Kombucha account for the majority of the company's business with a distribution network across the U.S., Canada, Mexico, and multiple countries in Europe. When it comes to tea, the company focuses on sustainable and fair practices. As their website notes about how they source their tea, "The world's most meticulous and well-traveled tea buyers are able to form on-the-ground relationships with the families who farm and produce our teas. Each of them specializes in a particular region, and then imports the tea directly to us. Having a trusted partner directly at the source insures that not only are our teas abundantly flavorful, but that tea producers are treated fairly for their trade."

Since its inception, Brew Dr. Kombucha and Tea has emphasized community development and environmental sustainability as core components of its business model so much so that its management embraced the opportunity to formalize these principles through "B Corp certification." B Corps are for-profit companies that are certified by the nonprofit B Lab if they meet rigorous standards of social and environmental performance, accountability, and transparency; they strive to use the power of markets to help solve social and environmental problems. Certification is recognition of a philosophy and actions taken by any organization regardless of how it is formed. It is voluntary and can be changed at any time. Over 2,000 Certified B Corps exist in 50 countries in 130 industries. Many of these companies are small- to medium-sized organizations, which is where much of the growth in this type of company has emerged. Certification is independent, third-party, and consists of an application of 170 questions covering such aspects of the business as energy efficiency and employee programs and practices. A total of 200 points is possible, but the certification does not expect that any company will ever be able to achieve a perfect score. In fact, a score of 80 points is enough to become certified. Notable companies with B Corp certification include Ben & Jerry's (the first wholly owned subsidiary to become certified) and Kickstarter. Natura, a Brazilian cosmetics company, became the first publicly traded Certified B Corp in 2014. Beyond those companies that formally apply for certification, over 40,000 organizations use the free self-assessment tool available at http://bimpactassessment.net to help them benchmark their social and environmental impact.

Upon initially completing the impact assessment in early 2017, Brew Dr. Kombucha and Tea was just shy of meeting the performance requirement set forth by B Lab to become certified. The responsibilities associated with completing the first assessment had fallen on two members of the management team. To ensure broader organizational buy-in, as well as accuracy in completing the assessment, Brew Dr. Kombucha and Tea convened a team of nearly 30 employees to conduct a comprehensive review of the impact assessment in late 2017. This self-selected group of employees was organized into subcommittees focused on the four B Corp impact areas: governance, workers, community, and environment. Employees were assigned a question or questions from their respective impact areas to review in greater detail. They were then tasked with providing recommendations around operational changes that would lead to an improved impact assessment score.

The number of employees who volunteered to assist with this project and the enthusiasm with which they approached the project was a testament to Brew Dr. Kombucha and Tea's culture of transparency and participation. Each employee who volunteered was passionate about building upon the values they had come to appreciate in their organization and reinforcing them by formalizing previously informal processes and procedures. For example, in developing an Environmentally Sustainable Purchasing Policy, a member of the environment subcommittee sought to set a standard of sustainable procurement of goods and demonstrate the company's commitment to environmental, economic, and social stewardship by providing employees with clear and consistent instructions on how to consider and purchase supplies and services. Previously, employees had been encouraged to purchase sustainable alternatives when given the option, but no policy had been created to ensure this was the norm. Thus the pursuit of B Corp certification provided a unique opportunity to embed some of these behaviors into the DNA of the company to ensure continued alignment with founding values as the company grows.

Brew Dr. Kombucha and Tea provides one example of organizational change inspired by a desire to formally adhere to principles of sustainability and social good. The changes were made even more meaningful by the inclusion of its employees in the assessment and implementation processes. Moreover, the employees tasked with driving this organizational change were motivated by the potential to establish a framework under which the company could grow ethically and responsibly for generations of employees to come.[52]

Multimedia Extension—B Corporation Founders Video

View in the online reader

Case Discussion Questions

1. If you were a Brew Dr. employee, would you have volunteered to assist with the B Corp assessment? Why or why not?
2. What are some pros and cons of including employees in organizational change management?
3. Can you think of some ways the pursuit of B Corp certification might lead to organizational change, even for a company that already embodies sustainability and social good?
4. Imagine that you are a manager at a young and rapidly growing company like Brew Dr., and you are interested in acquiring a B Corp certification for your firm. How would you go about

implementing any necessary change? What steps would you follow before, during, and after the change?

5. How do you think the pursuit of B Corp certification might impact an organization's bottom line? Please explain.

Endnotes

1. Retrieved from http://fortune.com/2015/06/23/know-your-millennial-co-workers/; Retrieved from http://www.pewresearch.org/fact-tank/2018/04/11/millennials-largest-generation-us-labor-force/.
2. Retrieved from https://www.pewsocialtrends.org/essay/on-the-cusp-of-adulthood-and-facing-an-uncertain-future-what-we-know-about-gen-z-so-far/.
3. Retrieved from http://mentalfloss.com/article/63341/frederick-winslow-taylor-patron-saint-shovel.
4. Retrieved from http://en.wikipedia.org/wiki/Cheaper_by_the_Dozen. *Cheaper by the Dozen* was made into a 1950 motion picture starring Clifton Webb and Myrna Loy as Frank and Lillian Gilbreth.
5. Retrieved from https://www.diyphotography.net/horse-bet-inspired-birth-cinematography/.
6. Sinclair, U. (1911, June). A criticism. *American Magazine*, 243–244; Taylor, F. W. (June 1911). An answer to the criticism. *American Magazine*, 243–244. Retrieved from http://stevens.cdmhost.com/cdm4/document.phpCISO-ROOT=/p4100coll1&CISOPTR=244&REC=14&CISOSHOW=242.
7. Retrieved from https://www.drucker.institute/perspective/about-peter-drucker/.
8. Peters, T. J., & Waterman, R. H. (1982). *In Search of Excellence*. New York: Knopf.
9. Retrieved from http://www.theatlantic.com/politics/archive/2015/06/the-triumph-of-occupy-wall-street/395408/.
10. Retrieved from https://www.cnn.com/2020/07/26/us/black-lives-matter-explainer-trnd/index.html.
11. Retrieved from https://www.imd.org/research-knowledge/articles/hitch-ing-a-ride-on-social-or-political-movements-can-help-firms-profit/.
12. Retrieved from https://en.wikipedia.org/wiki/Tommie_Smith.
13. Retrieved from http://www.pcworld.com/article/2881012/linkedins-china-bet-starts-paying-off-with-increase-in-users.html.
14. Retrieved from https://www.businessofapps.com/data/linkedin-statistics/.
15. Retrieved from http://www.wsj.com/articles/the-dating-business-love-on-the-rocks-1433980637.
16. Rummler, L. (2007, July). Corporate social networking updates definition of women's groups. Retrieved from http://www.talentmgt.com/newsletters/recruitment_perspectives/2007/July/380/index.php.
17. Vara, V. (2007, May 21). Facebook opens its pages as a way to fuel growth. *Wall Street Journal*. Retrieved from http://online.wsj.com/public/article/SB117971397890009177-wjdKPmjAqS_9ZZb-wiRp_CoSqvwQ_20070620.html.
18. Retrieved from https://www.wired.com/story/facebook-bug-14-million-users-posts-public/.
19. Retrieved from https://www.psychologytoday.com/us/blog/your-online-secrets/201710/do-you-have-social-media-disorder.
20. Garvin, D. (1993, July–August). Building a learning organization. *Harvard Business Review*, 78–91.
21. Retrieved from https://www.apa.org/monitor/2019/10/cover-remote-work#:~:text=In a 2015 research review,less work stress or exhaustion.
22. Tapscott, A., & A. D. Williams. (2006). *Wikinomics: How Mass Collaboration Changes Everything*. New York: Portfolio.
23. Retrieved from http://www.pewresearch.org/fact-tank/2018/03/01/defining-generations-where-millennials-end-and-post-millennials-begin/.
24. Retrieved from http://www.pewresearch.org/fact-tank/2015/05/11/millennials-surpass-gen-xers-as-the-largest-generation-in-u-s-labor-force/.
25. Retrieved from http://www.enterrasolutions.com/2015/07/eating-drinking-and-shopping-with-millennials.html.
26. Retrieved from http://smallbiztrends.com/2015/09/millennials-craft-beer.html.
27. Retrieved from https://www.beveragedaily.com/Article/2020/04/15/US-craft-beer-grew-4-in-2019-but-faces-difficult-2020-with-coronavirus.
28. Retrieved from http://www.fastcompany.com/3047872/innovation-agents/inside-marriotts-attempt-to-win-over-millennials.
29. Retrieved from https://www.travelandleisure.com/culture-design/tiny-offices-dutch-invertuals.
30. Retrieved from http://www.ncdc.noaa.gov/oa/climate/severeweather/extremes.html.
31. Retrieved from http://www.mckinsey.com/insights/economic_studies/economic_conditions_snapshot_june_2015_mckinsey_global_survey_results.
32. Unruh, G., & Ettenson, R. (2010, November). Winning in the green frenzy. *Harvard Business Review, 88*(11).
33. Retrieved from http://www.mindshareworld.com/uk/news/mindshare-trends-2015-mass-personalisation.
34. Retrieved from http://www.fastcompany.com/magazine/123/google.html.
35. Retrieved from https://community.connection.com/the-top-5-esports-trends-for-2020/.
36. Retrieved from http://reports.weforum.org/outlook-global-agenda-2015/top-10-trends-of-2015/1-deepening-income-inequality/.
37. Retrieved from http://www.internetworldstats.com/stats.htm.
38. Retrieved from https://www.fcc.gov/reports-research/reports/broadband-progress-reports/eighth-broadband-progress-report.
39. Retrieved from http://www.mckinsey.com/business-functions/strategy-and-corporate-finance/our-insights/five-forces-reshaping-the-global-economy-mckinsey-global-survey-results.
40. Retrieved from https://www.statista.com/statistics/262950/global-mobile-subscriptions-since-1993/#:~:text=Number of mobile subscriptions worldwide 1993-2019&text=In 2019, the number of,from 7.9 billion in 2018.
41. Retrieved from https://www.forbes.com/sites/saritharai/2016/01/06/india-just-crossed-1-billion-mobile-subscribers-milestone-and-the-excitements-just-beginning/#283643707db0.
42. Corbett, S. (2008, April 13). Can the cellphone help end global poverty? *New York Times*.
43. Retrieved from http://www.fastcompany.com/magazine/123/google.html.
44. Friedman, T. (2005). *The World Is Flat: A Brief History of the Twenty-first Century* (p. 81). New York: Farrar, Straus & Giroux.
45. Javidan, M., Dorfman, P. W., de Luque, M. S., & House R. J. (2006, February). In the eye of the beholder: Cross cultural lessons in leadership from Project GLOBE. *Academy of Management Perspectives, 20*, 67–90.
46. Brake, T. (1996). *The Global Leader* (p. 203). New York: McGraw-Hill.
47. *The Ethical Enterprise: A Global Study of Business Ethics*. (2005). New York: American Management Association.
48. Retrieved from https://www.businessinsider.com/tech-scandals-2019-wework-ipo-bezos-divorce-whatsapp-breach-epstein-2019-12#january-a-group-facetime-bug-lets-people-eavesdrop-on-other-users-1.
49. Retrieved from http://www.sec.gov/news/press/2002-150.htm.
50. Piccolo, R. F., Greenbaum, R., den Hartog, D. N., & Folger, R. (2010). The relationship between ethical leadership and core job characteristics. *Journal of Organizational Behavior, 31*, 259–278.
51. Hartman, L., and DesJardins, J. (2008). *Business Ethics: Decision-Making for Personal Integrity and Social Responsibility*. New York: McGraw-Hill.
52. Case written by Talya Bauer, Berrin Erdogan, and Rachel Mattenberger to accompany Talya Bauer and Berrin Erdogan, *Organizational Behavior: Bridging Science and Practice (4.0)*. Boston, MA: FlatWorld. Partially based on ideas and information contained in Goodman, M. (2013). Make it good officially. Entrepreneur. Retrieved from http://www.bcorporation.net/sites/default/files/Entrepreneur_Mag_Feature.pdf; Freeland, C. (2013). Capitalism, but with a little heart. *The New York Times*. Retrieved from http://www.nytimes.com/2013/07/19/us/19iht-letter19.html?_r=0; Why B Corps Matter. Retrieved from http://www.bcorporation.net/what-are-b-corps/why-b-corps-matter; B Corps. Our history. Retrieved from http://www.bcorporation.net/what-are-b-corps/the-non-profit-behind-b-corps/our-history; Honeyman, R. (2014). The B Corp Handbook: How to Use Business as a Force for Good; Brew Dr. Kombucha. (2020). Wholesale. Retrieved from https://www.brewdrkombucha.com/wholesale-kombucha/.

CHAPTER 3

Personality, Attitudes, and Work Behaviors

Tom Hanks and Julia Roberts share a million dollar smile and both regularly play characters with great charisma. Research finds that charisma is a valuable trait commonly found in both stars and CEOs.

Source: Kathy Hutchins/Shutterstock.com

Experts have shown that job satisfaction is not just a function of environmental factors (such as workplace aesthetics and design, lighting, and temperature) but is partially due to personality. Some people have a disposition to be happier in life and at work than others regardless of the specific aspects of their job or the places where they work.

Individuals who have a positive affective disposition (a tendency to experience positive moods more often than negative moods) are generally more satisfied with their jobs and more committed to their companies, while those who have a negative disposition tend to be less satisfied and less committed.[1] This is not surprising, as people who are determined to see the glass as "half full" will notice positive aspects in their work environment, while those with the opposite disposition will find more to complain about on a regular basis. In addition to affective disposition, people who have positive core self-evaluations (individuals who have high generalized self-efficacy, high self-esteem, internal locus of control, and low levels of neuroticism) tend to have more positive job attitudes.[2] Either these people are more successful in finding jobs and companies that will make them happy and build better relationships at work, which would increase their satisfaction and commitment, or they simply see their environment as more positive. Whichever is the case, it seems that personality is related to work attitudes. But personalities are not set in stone, and individuals can change their educational credentials, move jobs, engage in self-improvement, exercise, and engage in a host of other activities that impact changes in personality over time.[3] This chapter explores key research relevant to understanding personality, attitudes, and work behaviors.

Chapter Learning Objectives

Reading this chapter will help you accomplish the following:

1. Understand the roles of personality and values in determining work behaviors.
2. Explain the process of perception and how it affects work behaviors.
3. Identify the major work attitudes that affect work behaviors.
4. Define the concept of person–organization fit and how it affects work behaviors.
5. List the key set of behaviors that matter for organizational performance.
6. Be able to develop your positive attitude skills.

TABLE 3.1 The P-O-L-C Framework

Planning	Organizing	Leading	Controlling
1. Vision & Mission	1. Organization Design	1. Leadership	1. Systems/Processes
2. Strategizing	2. Culture	2. Decision Making	2. Strategic Human Resources
3. Goals & Objectives	3. Social Networks	3. Communications	
		4. Groups/Teams	
		5. Motivation	

All individuals are unique and we each bring a number of different personality traits, values, and attitudes to the organizations where we works. Stable as well as changing personality traits affect how individuals behave and perform. Moreover, companies hire people with the expectation that they have certain knowledge, skills, abilities, personalities, and values. Employees' personalities, attitudes, and work behaviors affect how managers approach each of the planning-organizing-leading-controlling (P-O-L-C) framework dimensions. Here are just a few examples:

- Individuals that are more extroverted and authoritarian are more likely to emerge as leaders.[4]
- Celebrity CEO Richard Branson notes personality as one of the top qualities he looks for in candidates because it can't be taught.[5]
- Employee preferences for job design and enrichment (two aspects of organizing) may be a function of individuals' personalities and values.
- Leading effectively requires an understanding of employees' personalities, values, and attitudes.
- Absenteeism and turnover can challenge a manager's ability to control costs and performance (at the group and individual levels).

Therefore, it is important for managers to understand an individual's personality and other characteristics that matter for employee and manager behaviors.

Pledge to be friendly? Research finds a link between extroversion and emergence as a leader.

Source: Shutterstock.com

3.1 Personality and Values

Learning Objectives

1. Identify the major personality traits that are relevant to organizational behavior.
2. Explain the potential pitfalls of personality testing.
3. Describe the relationship between personality and work behaviors.
4. Understand the concept of values.
5. Describe the link between values and work behaviors.

Personality

personality

The relatively stable feelings, thoughts, and behavioral patterns a person has.

Personality encompasses a person's relatively stable feelings, thoughts, and behavioral patterns. Each of us has a unique personality that differentiates us from others, and understanding someone's personality gives us clues about how that person is likely to act and feel in a variety of situations. To manage effectively, it is helpful to understand the personalities of different employees. This knowledge is also valuable to provide insights into which types of jobs individuals with certain personalities are more likely to find success and fulfillment.

When scholars discuss personality characteristics as being "stable," this does not mean that an individual's personality exhibits no degree of change.[6] You probably remember how you have changed and evolved as a result of your own life experiences, attention you received in early childhood, the style of parenting you were exposed to, successes and failures you had in high school, and other life events. In fact, personality changes over long periods of time. For example, we tend to become more socially dominant, more conscientious (organized and dependable), and more emotionally stable between the ages of 20 and 40, whereas openness to new experiences tends to decline as we age.[7] Even though we treat personality as relatively stable over short periods of time, changes occur. Moreover, even in childhood, our personality shapes who we are and has lasting consequences for us. For example, studies show that part of our career success and job satisfaction later in life can be explained by our childhood personality.[8]

Is our behavior in organizations dependent on personality? Yes and no. While we will discuss the effects of personality for employee behavior, most of the relationships we describe are modest. For example, having a sociable and outgoing personality may encourage people to seek friends and prefer social situations. This does not mean that their personality will immediately affect their work behavior. At work, we often have a specific job to do and a particular role to perform. Therefore, our behavior may be more strongly affected by what is expected of us, as opposed to how we want to behave. When people have a lot of freedom at work, their personality will become a stronger influence over their behavior.[9]

Music Rap-Up: The Big Five Personality Traits

Twinprov perform rap on Big Five personality traits.

View in the online reader

Big Five Personality Traits

How many personality traits exist? In the English language alone, more than 15,000 words describing personality have been identified. When researchers analyzed the traits describing personality characteristics, they realized that many different words might be used to describe a single dimension of personality. When these words were grouped, five dimensions emerged that explain much of the variation in our personalities.[10] The "Big Five" dimensions of Openness, Conscientiousness, Extraversion, Agreeableness, and Neuroticism can be remembered using the acronym OCEAN. Everyone has some degree of each of these traits; it is the unique configuration of how high a person rates on some traits and how low on others that produces the individual quality we call personality. Keep in mind these five are not necessarily the only traits that exist. There are other, specific traits that represent dimensions not captured by the Big Five. Still, understanding the main five traits gives us a good start for describing personality.

FIGURE 3.1 The Big Five Personality Traits

Researchers have discovered that five key traits explain much of the variation in individual personalities. We outline each of these traits here.

Openness is the degree to which a person is curious, original, intellectual, creative, and open to new ideas.

Conscientiousness refers to the degree to which a person is organized, systematic, punctual, achievement-oriented, and dependable.

Extraversion is the degree to which a person is outgoing, talkative, and sociable.

Agreeableness is the degree to which a person is affable, tolerant, sensitive, trusting, kind, and earnest.

Neuroticisim refers to the degree to which a person is anxious, irritable, and temperamental.

Source: Shutterstock.com

Openness is the degree to which a person is curious, original, intellectual, creative, and open to new ideas. People high in openness seem to thrive in situations that require being flexible and learning new things. For example, in a study tracking individuals from childhood to the age of 64, childhood openness showed indirect effects on upward social mobility because these individuals were more likely to acquire higher levels of education.[11] As employees, they have an advantage when they enter into a new organization. Their open-mindedness leads them to seek a lot of information and feedback about how they are doing and to build relationships, which leads to quicker adjustment to the new job.[12] Open people are highly adaptable to change, and teams that experience unforeseen changes in their tasks do well if they are populated with people high in openness.[13] Compared with people low in openness, they are also more likely to start their own business.[14] One downside of openness is that absorption in creative pursuits has been shown to result in less time spent with spouses at home, which could lead to higher work-life conflict.[15]

openness

The degree to which a person is curious, original, intellectual, creative, and open to new ideas.

conscientiousness

The degree to which a person is organized, systematic, punctual, achievement-oriented, and dependable.

Conscientiousness refers to the degree to which a person is organized, systematic, punctual, achievement-oriented, and dependable. Conscientiousness is the one personality trait that uniformly predicts how high a person's performance will be across a variety of occupations and jobs. Conscientiousness has advantages on and off the job. For example, conscientiousness measured during childhood predicts likelihood of unemployment in adulthood (with high conscientiousness predicting low unemployment).[16] Not surprisingly, conscientiousness is the trait most desired by recruiters, and highly conscientious applicants tend to succeed in interviews.[17] Once they are hired, conscientious employees tend to perform well and have higher levels of motivation, lower levels of turnover, lower levels of absenteeism, and higher levels of safety performance at work.[18] In other words, conscientious employees are highly desirable to businesses. In return, companies tend to reward those who have this trait, treating them in more fair and considerate ways.[19] Finally, conscientiousness is a particularly valuable trait for entrepreneurs. Highly conscientious people are more likely to start their own business compared with those who are not, and their firms have longer survival rates and better performance.[20] This trait is not without a downside, however. When they experience failure, such as in the form of unemployment, the well-being of conscientious people is much more negatively affected.[21]

extraversion

The degree to which a person is outgoing, talkative, sociable, and enjoys being in social situations.

Extraversion is the degree to which a person is outgoing, talkative, sociable, and enjoys socializing. Interacting with others and being social energizes extraverts, whereas similar levels of stimulation and interactions may be viewed as draining to someone who is an introvert. Extraverts tend to be assertive, interpersonally dominant, seek sensation, enthusiastic, and are more likely to experience positive emotions as well. The overall evidence based on a large meta analysis suggest that the extraversion provides motivational, emotional, and interpersonal advantages to individuals at work, and most of its advantages are due to their higher enthusiasm, positive emotions, assertiveness, and dominance, whereas their sociability actually has fewer benefits, and sensation seeking is a downside.[22]

A bucket list is an effective way to plan and organize potential new experiences.

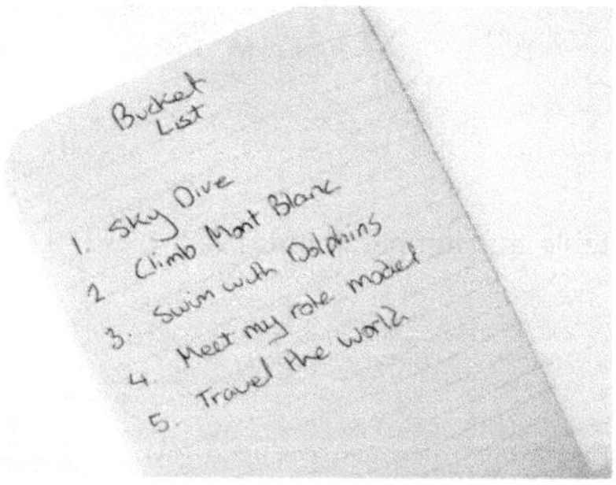

Source: Shutterstock.com

One of the established findings is that extraverts tend to be effective in jobs involving sales. For example, when obligated to show "service with a smile," they are more effective and convincing, which results in earning more tips from customers, whereas similar behaviors seem to backfire for introverts and result in less tips![23] Moreover, they tend to be effective as managers and they demonstrate inspirational leadership behaviors.[24] Extraverts do well in social situations, and, as a result, they tend to be effective in job interviews. Part of this success comes from preparation, as they are likely to reach out to their social network in order to prepare for the interview.[25] Extraverts have an easier time than introverts when adjusting to a new job. Adjusting to a new job requires seeking out information and feedback early on, which extraverts are generally more comfortable with.[26] Interestingly, extraverts are also found to be happier at work, which may be because of the relationships they build with the people around them and their easier adjustment to a new job.[27] However, they do not necessarily perform well in all jobs; jobs depriving them of social interaction may be a poor fit. Moreover, they are not necessarily model employees. For example, they tend to have higher levels of absenteeism at work, potentially because they may miss work to spend time with or attend to the needs of friends.[28]

Agreeableness is the degree to which a person is affable, tolerant, sensitive, trusting, kind, and warm. Individuals who are high in agreeableness are likable and get along with others. Not surprisingly, agreeable people help others at work consistently; this personality trait is consistently related to prosocial behaviors, or showing generosity, cooperation, and support for others.[29] They are also better able to cope with stressors such as family interference with work.[30] This may reflect their ability to show empathy and to give people the benefit of the doubt. Agreeable individuals may be a valuable addition to their teams and may be effective leaders because they create a positive environment when they are in leadership positions. In fact, they are regarded as highly ethical leaders by their subordinates.[31] At the other end of the spectrum, people low in agreeableness are less likely to show these positive behaviors. Moreover, people who are disagreeable are shown to quit their jobs unexpectedly, perhaps in response to a conflict with a boss or a peer.[32] Does research on agreeableness suggest that we should only look for agreeable people when hiring? You might expect some jobs to require a low level of agreeableness. When hiring a lawyer, would you prefer a person quick to compromise or someone who can stand up to an opponent? People high in agreeableness may also be too trusting and submissive, sacrificing their own well-being for others. A study of teaching effectiveness found that agreeableness was negatively related to a host of teaching outcomes.[33] Research shows that agreeable individuals tend to have lower levels of financial credit ratings, which may be a result of making promises they are not able to keep or possibly cosigning loans for friends and family and then getting into financial trouble.[34] Because they avoid conflict, they may miss opportunities for initiating constructive change or get into difficulties while attempting to please others. Research also suggests that even though all five of the big five personality traits are correlated with organizational commitment, agreeableness has the strongest relationship.[35]

Rumored to have cut off a portion of his ear, Vincent Van Gogh, one of the world's most famous—and most neurotic—artists, did not see success during his lifetime. As someone rumored to have only sold one painting in his career, his experience follows research showing the relationship between chronic job insecurity and slight increases in neuroticism.

Source: Everett - Art/Shutterstock.com

agreeableness

The degree to which a person is nice, tolerant, sensitive, trusting, kind, and warm.

Neuroticism refers to the degree to which a person is anxious, irritable, temperamental, and moody. It is perhaps the only Big Five dimension where scoring high is undesirable. People very high in neuroticism experience a number of problems at work. Neuroticism has a high degree of overlap with perfectionistic tendencies, such as being overly concerned about making mistakes and doubting one's actions.[36] Most of their problems are due to difficulties in handling stress. Neurotic employees experience lower levels of satisfaction with their lives, indicating their habitual levels of unhappiness.[37] Research has shown that they are more prone to experience stressors such as work-life conflict, more negatively affected by stressors such as autocratic leadership, and have less healthy ways of coping with their daily stress, such as in the form of increasing their daily intake of alcohol.[38] Out of the big five traits, neuroticism is the strongest (and negative) correlate of job satisfaction.[39] This personality trait has mixed effects on job search behavior: On the one hand, neurotic individuals experience greater burnout on the job and greater financial inadequacy, motivating them to look for an alternative. On the other hand, neurotic individuals feel less confident about their ability to find a new job, discouraging them from seeking a new job.[40]

neuroticism

The degree to which a person is anxious, irritable, aggressive, temperamental, and moody.

Scholars commonly study how patterns of Big Five characteristics relate to work behaviors. For example, chronic job insecurity over several years has been found to predict small increases in neuroticism and decreases in agreeableness and conscientiousness.[41] In addition, scholars have found that CEOs viewed as more conscientious are seen as less risky in general but more likely to effectively translate risk assessment into success for their firms; in contrast, CEOs seen as higher in extroversion and neuroticism struggle translating risk into shareholder returns.[42]

Activity Link

Evaluate Yourself on the Big Five Personality Traits

See how you score on these factors: http://www.outofservice.com/bigfive.

Other Personality Dimensions

In addition to the Big Five personality dimensions, researchers have proposed various other traits relevant to understanding personality. These include self-monitoring, proactive personality, self-esteem, and self-efficacy.

self-monitoring

The extent to which a person is capable of altering one's actions and appearance in social situations.

Self-monitoring refers to the extent to which a person is capable of altering his or her actions and appearance in social situations. People who are self-monitors are social chameleons who understand what the situation demands and act accordingly, while low social monitors tend to act the way they feel.[43] High self-monitors are sensitive to the types of behaviors the social environment expects from them. Their greater ability to modify their behavior according to the demands of the situation and to manage their impressions effectively is a great advantage for them.[44] In general, they tend to be more successful in their careers. They are more likely to get cross-company promotions, and even when they stay with one company, they are more likely to advance.[45] Self-monitors also become the "go to" person in their company and they enjoy central positions in social networks.[46] They are rated as higher performers and emerge as leaders.[47] While they are effective in influencing other people and get things done by managing their impressions, this personality trait has some challenges that need to be addressed. First, when evaluating the performance of other employees, they tend to be less accurate. It seems that while trying to manage their impressions, they may avoid giving accurate feedback to their subordinates to avoid confrontations. This tendency may create problems for them if they are managers. Second, high self-monitors tend to experience higher levels of stress, probably caused by behaving in ways that conflict with their true feelings. In situations that demand positive emotions, they may act happy although they are not feeling happy, which puts an emotional burden on them. Finally, high self-monitors tend to be less committed to their companies. They may see their jobs as a stepping-stone for greater things, which may prevent them from forming strong attachments and loyalty to their current employer.[48]

proactive personality

A person's inclination to fix what is wrong, change things, and use initiative to solve problems.

Proactive personality refers to a person's inclination to fix what is perceived as wrong, change the status quo, and use initiative to solve problems. Instead of waiting to be told what to do, proactive people take action to initiate meaningful change and remove the obstacles they face along the way. In general, having a proactive personality has a number of advantages for these people. For example, they tend to be more successful in their job searches.[49] Proactive employees are also more successful over the course of their careers because they use initiative and acquire greater understanding of the politics within the company.[50] Proactive people are valuable assets to their companies because they may have higher levels of performance.[51] They adjust to their new jobs quickly because they understand the political environment better, make friends more quickly, and are more responsive to feedback they receive.[52] Proactive people are eager to learn and engage in many developmental activities to improve their skills.[53] Despite all their potential, under some circumstances a proactive personality may be a liability for an individual or an organization. Individuals who are proactive but who are perceived as too pushy, try to change things other people are not willing to let go, or use their initiative to make decisions that do not serve a company's best interests. Research shows that a proactive person's success depends on his or her understanding of the company's core values, their ability and skills to perform the job, and their ability to assess situational demands correctly.[54]

self-esteem

The degree to which a person has overall positive feelings about oneself.

Self-esteem is the degree to which a person has overall positive feelings about oneself. People with high self-esteem view themselves in a positive light, are confident, and respect themselves. On the other hand, people with low self-esteem experience high levels of self-doubt and question their self-worth. High self-esteem is related to higher levels of satisfaction with one's job, higher levels of performance on the job, and higher levels of creativity at work.[55] People with low self-esteem are attracted to situations where they will be relatively invisible, such as large companies.[56] Managing employees with low self-esteem may be challenging at times because negative feedback given with the intention of improving performance may be viewed as a negative judgment on their worth as an employee. Individuals with low self-esteem are sensitive to social feedback, and they interpret ambiguous situation as definitive signals of social exclusion, which in turn leads to negative self-evaluations.[57] Therefore, effectively managing employees with relatively low self-esteem requires tact and providing lots of positive feedback when discussing performance incidents.

Self-efficacy is a belief that one can perform a specific task successfully. Research shows that the belief that we can do something is a good predictor of whether we can actually do it. Self-efficacy is different from other personality traits in that it is job specific. You may have high self-efficacy in being successful academically, but low self-efficacy in relation to your ability to fix your car. At the same time, people have a certain level of generalized self-efficacy, and they have the belief that whatever task or hobby they tackle, they are likely to be successful in it.

self-efficacy

A belief that one can perform a specific task successfully.

Research shows that self-efficacy at work is related to job performance.[58] This relationship is probably a result of people with high self-efficacy setting higher goals for themselves and being more committed to these goals, whereas people with low self-efficacy tend to procrastinate.[59] Managerial self-efficacy is a good predictor of whether the manager seeks input from employees as mangers with low self-efficacy will be more defensive of themselves, and less likely to want to hear about how they can manage more effectively.[60]

Is there a way of increasing employees' self-efficacy? Hiring people who are capable of performing their tasks and training people to increase their self-efficacy may be effective. Some people may also respond well to verbal encouragement. By showing that you believe they can be successful and effectively playing the role of a cheerleader, you may be able to increase self-efficacy. Giving people opportunities to test their skills so that they can see what they are capable of doing (or empowering them) is also a good way of increasing self-efficacy.[61]

Personality Testing in Employee Selection

Personality is a potentially important predictor of work behavior. In job interviews, companies try to assess a candidate's personality and the potential for a good match. Unfortunately, research has shown that most interviewers are not particularly good at detecting the one trait that best predicts performance—conscientiousness.[62] One method some companies use to detect the people who are potentially good job candidates is personality testing. Several companies now conduct pre-employment personality tests.[63] Companies using them believe that these tests improve the effectiveness of their selection and reduce turnover. For example, Overnight Transportation in Atlanta found that using such tests reduced their on-the-job delinquency rates by 50%–100%.[64]

Organizations using personality tests should ensure that the questions they ask are not being used to discriminate based on sex, race, age, disability, or other legally protected characteristics.

Source: Shutterstock.com

Experts have not yet reached an agreement regarding the best way to select employees, and the topic is highly controversial. Some experts cite data indicating that personality tests predict performance, while others note important criteria such as job satisfaction. Some journalists have gone as far as comparing personality testing to astrology.[65] A key consideration in this debate is that differences in how individuals complete the test influence its validity. Imagine filling out a personality test in class. Assume you fill it out as honestly as you can. Then, if your instructor correlates your personality scores with your class performance, we could say that the correlation is meaningful. In employee selection, one complicating factor is that people filling out the survey in a hiring context do not have a strong incentive to be honest. In fact, they have a greater incentive to guess what the job requires and answer the questions to match what they think the company is looking for. As a result, the rankings of the candidates who take the test may be affected by their ability to fake desired qualities. Some experts believe that this is a serious problem. In fact, it is estimated that 20%–50% of all job applicants give fake responses in personality tests.[66] Others point out that even with **faking**, the tests remain valid because the scores are still related to job performance.[67] It is even possible that the ability to fake is related to a personality trait that increases success at work, such as self-monitoring. This issue raises potential questions regarding whether personality tests are the most effective way of measuring candidate personality.

faking

The practice of answering questions in a way one thinks the company is looking for.

The Wonderlic Cognitive Ability Test is used by the National Football League when evaluating the learning aptitude of new players entering the draft such as 2020 #1 pick Joe Burrow.

Source: lev radin/Shutterstock.com

Scores are not only distorted for other reasons beyond the fact that some candidates can fake their answers better than others. For example, using a survey assumes that individuals understand their own personalities, but this may not be the case. How supervisors, coworkers, and customers see our personality may matter more than how we see ourselves. Therefore, using self-report measures may not be the best way of measuring someone's personality, whereas asking our former colleagues or supervisors may reveal more accurate answers. In fact, observers are surprisingly accurate in assessing our personality. In one study, evaluators were able to accurately assess the personality of others simply by looking at and rating their Facebook pages.[68] In addition, individuals may be tempted to give aspirational answers to surveys. If you are asked whether you are honest, you may think, "Yes, I always have the intention to be honest." While this answer relates to how you value honesty, it may say nothing about your actual level of honesty in any given situation.

Another problem with personality tests is the uncertain relationship between performance and personality. Research has shown that personality is not a particularly strong predictor of how a person will perform at work. According to one estimate, personality at best explains about 10%–15% of variation in job performance. Our performance at work depends on many factors, and personality does not seem to be the key factor for performance. In fact, cognitive ability (overall mental intelligence) is a more powerful predictor of job performance and instead of personality tests, cognitive ability tests may do a better job of predicting who will be good performers. Personality is a better predictor of job satisfaction and other attitudes, but screening people out based on the assumption that they may be unhappy at work is a challenging argument to make in an employee selection context.

Organizations that decide to use personality tests for selection should be aware of their limitations. Relying only on personality tests for selection of an employee is a bad idea, but if they are used together with other tests, such as tests of cognitive abilities, better decisions may be made. The company should ensure that the test fits the job and actually predicts performance. This is called validating the test. Before giving the test to applicants, the company could give it to existing employees to find out the traits that are most important for success in this particular company and job. Then, in the selection context, the company can pay particular attention to those traits.

The company should also make sure that the test does not discriminate against people on the basis of sex, race, age, disabilities, and other legally protected characteristics. Although personality testing has become a business exceeding $500 million dollars, controversy surrounding the use of such tests is also on the rise.[69] Rent-a-Center experienced legal difficulties when the test they used was found to violate the Americans with Disabilities Act (ADA). The company used the Minnesota Multiphasic Personality Inventory for selection purposes, but this test was developed to diagnose severe mental illnesses; it included items such as "I see things or people around me others do not see." In effect, the test served the purpose of a clinical evaluation and was discriminating against people with mental illnesses, which is a protected category under ADA.[70]

Values

Values refers to people's stable life goals, reflecting what is most important to them. Values are established throughout one's life as a result of accumulating life experiences, and tend to be relatively stable.[71] The values that are important to people tend to affect the types of decisions they make, how they perceive their environment, and their actual behaviors. Moreover, people are more likely to accept a job offer when the company possesses the values people care about.[72] Value attainment is one reason people stay in a company, and when an organization does not help them attain their values, they are likely to decide to leave if they are dissatisfied with the job itself.[73]

Dove's longstanding commitment to improving self-esteem is one key reason they are a top brand trusted by Gen Z—a generation known to anchor their purchasing in ethical considerations.

Source: Bborriss.67/Shutterstock.com

What are the values people care about? As with personality dimensions, researchers have developed several frameworks, or typologies, of values. One particularly useful framework includes 10 values outlined in Figure 3.2.[74]

Values of a generation also change and evolve in response to the historical context that the generation grows up in. It is important to keep in mind that generational differences, where they exist, are modest, and are not strong enough to justify treating different age groups differently in the workplace. At the same time, research identified some differences in the values of different generations. For example, Generation Xers (those born between 1965 and 1979) are thought to be more individualistic and are interested in working toward organizational goals so long as they coincide with their personal goals. This group, compared to the Baby Boomers (those born between 1946 and 1964), is also less likely to see work as central to their life and more likely to desire a quick promotion.[75] Millennials (those born between 1980 and 2000) value leisure more, report less work centrality than boomers, and value work-life balance.[76] Generation Z is thought to be heavily driven by the search for truth and able to put personal differences aside in efforts to mobilize toward social issues and causes tied to their beliefs.[77] It should be noted that despite important generational tendencies, the cut-offs between generations tend to be fuzzy, and the trends tend to be gradual.[78]

The values a person holds may affect their employment. For example, someone who has an orientation toward strong stimulation may pursue extreme sports and select an occupation that involves fast action and high risk, such as fire fighter, police officer, or emergency medical doctor. Someone who has a drive for achievement may more readily act as an entrepreneur. Moreover, whether individuals will be satisfied at a given job may depend on whether the job provides a way to satisfy their dominant values. Therefore, understanding employees at work requires understanding the value orientations of employees.

FIGURE 3.2 Valuing Your Career Choices

Values refers to the stable life goals held by individuals. The values individuals hold dear have implications for the types of industries and jobs individuals find interesting. Here, we pair values included in the Schwartz (1992) Value Inventory with examples of jobs that reflect those values.

Achievement

The desire for personal success. Careers in sales often focus on this value by offering commissions to align individuals with organizational outcomes.

Benevolence

The desire to protect the well-being of people who are close to the person. Allstate Insurance's pledge that "you're in good hands" demonstrates the role of benevolence common to many insurance agencies.

Conformity

Being motivated through self-discipline and obedience to the will of others. Careers in the military might be a good fit for individuals who hold such values in high regard.

Hedonism

The desire for pleasure in life. The gaming industry has been referred to as a "sin" industry due to its ties with what many consider hedonistic activities. Such a perspective has been embraced by the Las Vegas Convention and Visitors Authority marketing slogan, "What happens in Vegas, stays in Vegas."

Power

The desire for control over others, attaining authority and prestige. The 2006 comedic drama *The Devil Wears Prada* illustrates the role of power within the fashion industry.

Security

Valuing safety and stability. Firefighters and police officers undergo extensive training to help them achieve goals of protecting and serving others.

Self-direction

The desire to be free and independent. Many academics are drawn to a career in research because of the ability to independently pursue their intellectual curiosity on any number of topics with relatively little outside influence.

Stimulation

The desire for a stimulating and exciting life. Careers in big-game hunting, adventure travel, and deep-sea diving exemplify jobs that embrace the need for stimulation.

Tradition

Acceptance of social customs and traditional ideas in society. Individuals valuing traditional ideas might enjoy working in event planning.

Universalism

The desire to protect the well-being of all people with a care for social justice. Groups that promote human rights, such as Amnesty International, demonstrate a potential career choice for individuals who value universalism.

Source: Shutterstock.com, Piotr Swat Shutterstock.com

Key Takeaway

Personality traits and values are two dimensions in which individuals differ. Personality is the unique, relatively stable pattern of feelings, thoughts, and behaviors that each individual displays. Big Five personality dimensions (Openness, Conscientiousness, Extraversion, Agreeableness, and Neuroticism) are important traits; others that are particularly relevant for work behavior include self-efficacy, self-esteem, social monitoring, and proactive personality. While personality is a stronger influence over job attitudes, its relationship to job performance is weaker. Some companies use personality testing to screen out candidates. Companies using personality tests are advised to validate their tests and use them to supplement other techniques with greater validity, such as tests of cognitive ability. Companies must also ensure that a test does not discriminate against any protected group. Values express a person's life goals; they are similar to personality traits in that they are relatively stable over time. In the workplace, a person is more likely to accept a job that provides opportunities for value attainment. People are also more likely to remain in a job or career that satisfies their values.

Discussion Questions

1. Think about the personality traits covered in this section. Can you think of jobs or occupations that seem particularly suited to each trait? Which traits would be universally desirable across all jobs?
2. What are the unique challenges of managing employees who have low self-efficacy and self-esteem? How would you deal with this situation?
3. What are some methods that companies can use to assess employee personality?
4. Have you ever held a job where your personality did not match the demands of the job? How did you react to this situation? How were your attitudes and behaviors affected?
5. Identify ways in which the Big Five (of the manager and/or the employees) may affect how you as a manager would carry out the Leadership function.

3.2 Perception

Learning Objectives

1. Understand the influence of biases in the process of perception.
2. Describe how we perceive visual objects and how these tendencies may affect our behavior.
3. Describe the biases inherent in our perceptions of other people.

perception

The process with which individuals detect and interpret environmental stimuli.

Our behavior is not only a function of our personality, values, and preferences, but also a function of specific situations. We interpret our environment, formulate responses, and act accordingly. **Perception** may be defined as the process with which individuals detect and interpret environmental stimuli. What makes human perception so interesting is that we do not solely respond to the stimuli in our environment. We go beyond the information that is present in our environment and pay selective attention to some aspects, and ignore other elements that may be immediately apparent to other people. Our perception of the environment is not entirely rational. For example, have you ever noticed that while glancing at a news website, information that is interesting or important to you seems to jump out of the page and catches your eye? If you are a sports fan, while scrolling down the pages you may immediately see a news item describing the latest success of your team. If you were recently turned down for a loan, an item of financial news may jump out at you. Therefore, what we see in the environment is a function of what we value, our needs, our fears, and our emotions.[79] In fact, what we see in the environment may be objectively, flat-out wrong because of our personality, values, or emotions. For example, one experiment showed that when people who were afraid of spiders were shown spiders, they inaccurately thought that the spider was moving toward them.[80] In this section, we will describe some common tendencies we engage in when perceiving objects or other people, and the consequences of such perceptions.

Visual Perception

Our visual perception goes beyond the physical information available to us; this phenomenon is commonly referred to as an "optical illusion." Artists and designers of everything from apparel to cars to home interiors make use of optical illusions to enhance the look of the product. Managers rely on their visual perception to form opinions about people and objects around them and to make sense of data presented in graphical form. Therefore, understanding how our visual perception may be biased is important.

For example, we extrapolate from the information available to us and may see things that are not actually there. Similarly, when we look at objects that are partially blocked, we see the whole.[81]

FIGURE 3.3
Danish psychologist Edgar Rubin created this famous image, which can be perceived as a vase form or two faces.

Source: Shutterstock.com

Look at Figure 3.3. What do you see? Most people look at this figure and see two faces *or* a goblet, depending on which color they focus on. Our visual perception is often biased because we do not perceive objects in isolation. A good example of this is shown in Figure 3.4. To most people, the circle on the left appears bigger, but this is because it is surrounded by smaller circles. The contrast between the focal object and the objects surrounding it may make an object bigger or smaller to our eye.

The 2015 viral meme "the dress" demonstrates differences in perception in viewers who see the dress as blue and black versus gold and white.

Source: Shutterstock.com

How do these tendencies influence behavior in organizations? You may have realized that the fact that our visual perception is faulty may make witness testimony faulty and biased. How do we know whether the employee you judge to be hardworking, fast, and neat really possess those qualities? Is it really true, or are we comparing this person to other people in the immediate environment? Or let's say that you do not like one of your peers and you think that this person is constantly on social media during work hours. Are you sure? Have you really seen this person surf unrelated websites, or is it possible that you assumed this every time you saw them scrolling on their phone? Our biased visual perception may lead to inaccurate inferences about the people around us.

Video Link

View more illusions here: http://www.squidoo.com/artistic-illusions.

FIGURE 3.4 Optical Illusion

Although our perceptions may suggest otherwise, the two circles in the middle of the six outer circles are the same size.

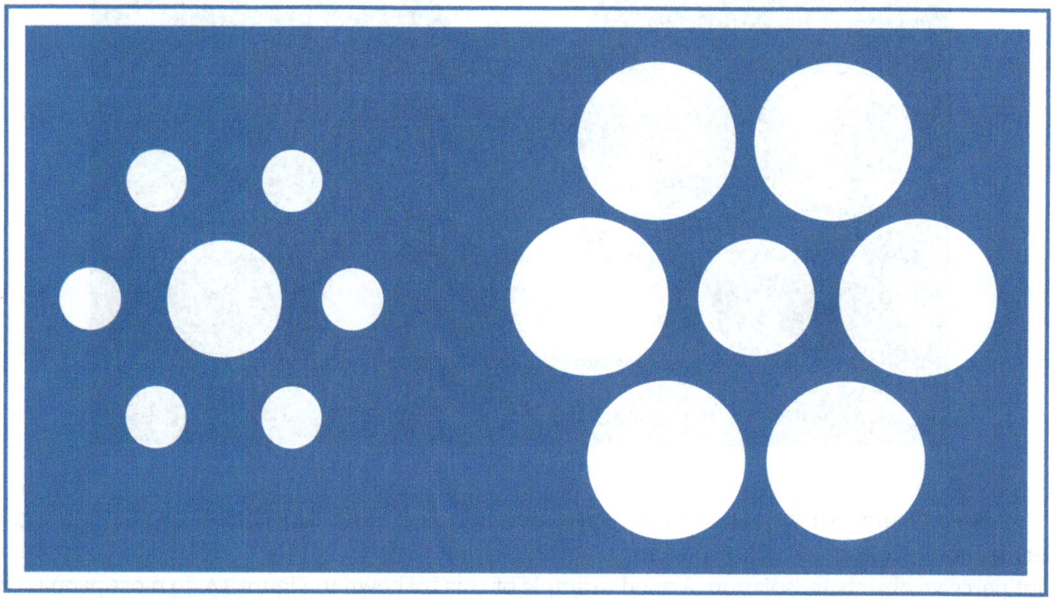

Self-Perception

Human beings are prone to errors and biases when perceiving themselves. The types of bias people have depend on their personality. Many people suffer from **self-enhancement bias**, in which individuals tend to overestimate performance and capabilities and see themselves in a more positive light than others see them. At the same time, other people have the opposing extreme, which may be labeled as **self-effacement bias** (or modesty bias). This is the tendency to underestimate performance and capabilities and see events in a way that portrays them in a more negative light. Individuals with low self-esteem are more prone to making this error. These tendencies have real consequences for behavior in organizations. For example, people who suffer from extreme levels of self-enhancement tendencies may not understand why they are not getting promoted or rewarded, while those who have a tendency to self-efface may project low confidence and take more blame for their failures than necessary. One recent study found that investors are less likely to invest in a company when they observe CEO "humblebrags" about their firm's positive performance.[82]

When human beings perceive themselves, they are also subject to the **false consensus error**. Simply put, such individuals overestimate how similar they are to other people.[83] An example of this error is when individuals assume that whatever quirks they have are shared by a larger number of people than in reality. People who take office supplies home, tell white lies to their boss or colleagues, or take credit for other people's work to get ahead may genuinely feel that these behaviors are more common than they are in reality. The problem for behavior in organizations is that, when people believe that a behavior is common and normal, they may repeat the behavior more freely. Under some circumstances, this may lead to a high level of unethical or even illegal behaviors.

In regard to accurate self-perception, research finds individuals using dating apps do better when they have a stranger select their profile picture.

Source: Shutterstock.com

self-enhancement bias

The tendency to overestimate our performance and capabilities and to see ourselves in a more positive light than others see us.

self-effacement bias

The tendency to underestimate our performance and capabilities, and see events in a way that puts us in a more negative light.

false consensus error

How we as human beings overestimate how similar we are to other people.

Social Perception

How we perceive others in our environment is also shaped by our biases. Moreover, how we perceive others will shape our behavior, which, in turn, will shape the behavior of the person we are interacting with.

One of the factors biasing our perception is **stereotypes**. Stereotypes are generalizations based on group characteristics. For example, believing that women are more cooperative than men, or that men are more assertive than women are stereotypes. Stereotypes may be positive, negative, or neutral. Human beings have a natural tendency to categorize the information around them to make sense of their environment. What makes stereotypes potentially discriminatory and a perceptual bias is the tendency to generalize from a group to a particular individual. If the belief that men are more assertive than women leads to choosing a man over an equally (or potentially more) qualified female candidate for a position, the decision will be biased, illegal, and unfair.

Stereotypes often create a situation called **self-fulfilling prophecy**. This cycle occurs when people automatically behave as if an established stereotype is accurate, which leads to reactive behavior from the other party that confirms the stereotype.[84] If you have a stereotype such as "Texans are friendly," you are more likely to be friendly toward a Texan. Because you are treating the other person nicely, the response you get may also be better, which confirms your original belief that Texans are friendly. Of course, the opposite is also true. Suppose you believe that "young employees are slackers." You are less likely to give a young employee high levels of responsibility or interesting and challenging assignments. The result may be that the employee reporting to you may become increasingly bored at work and then withhold effort, confirming your suspicions that young people are slackers.

stereotypes

Generalizations based on a group characteristic.

self-fulfilling prophecy

When an established stereotype causes one to behave in a certain way, which leads the other party to behave in a way that makes the stereotype come true.

selective perception

When we pay selective attention to parts of the environment while ignoring other parts.

Stereotypes persist because of a process called selective perception. **Selective perception** simply means that we pay selective attention to parts of the environment while ignoring other parts. When we observe our environment, we see what we want to see and ignore information that may seem out of place. Here is an interesting example of how selective perception leads our perception to be shaped by the context: As part of a social experiment, the *Washington Post* newspaper arranged for Joshua Bell, the internationally acclaimed violin virtuoso, to perform in a corner of the Metro station in Washington, D.C. The violin he was playing was worth $3.5 million, and tickets for Bell's concerts usually cost around $100. During his 45-minute rush-hour performance, only one person recognized him, only a few realized that they were hearing extraordinary music, and he made only $32 in tips. When you see someone playing at the metro station, would you expect them to be extraordinary?[85]

A job interview is one situation where impressions formed during the first few minutes may have lasting consequences for your relationship with future colleagues. Previous research showing that a firm handshake with three or four up-and-down pumps is key to making a positive impression is likely to be challenged in the wake of social distancing norms.

Source: Shutterstock.com

Our background, expectations, and beliefs will shape which events we notice and which events we ignore. For example, the functional background of executives affects the changes they perceive in their environment.[86] Executives with a background in sales and marketing see the changes in the demand for their product, while executives with a background in information technology may more readily perceive the changes in the technology the company is using. Selective perception may perpetuate stereotypes, because we are less likely to notice events that go against our beliefs. A person who believes that men drive better than women may be more likely to notice women driving poorly than men driving equally poorly. As a result, a stereotype is maintained because information to the contrary may not reach our brain.

Let's say we noticed information that goes against our beliefs. What then? Unfortunately, this is no guarantee that we will modify our beliefs and prejudices. First, when we see examples that go against our stereotypes, we tend to come up with subcategories. For example, people who believe that women are more cooperative see an assertive female as a "career woman." Therefore, the example to the contrary does not violate the stereotype and is explained as an exception to the rule.[87] Second, we may simply discount the information. In one study, people who were either in favor of or opposed to the death penalty were shown two studies, one showing purported benefits from the death penalty and the other discounting any benefits. People rejected the study that went against their belief as methodologically inferior and actually reinforced the belief in their original position even more.[88] In other words, trying to debunk people's beliefs or previously established opinions with data may not necessarily help.

Your LinkedIn profile provides a critical first impression to would-be employers.

Source: Roman Pyshchyk/Shutterstock.com

One other perceptual tendency that may affect work behavior is **first impressions**. The first impressions we form about people tend to have a lasting impact. People have a tendency to use irrelevant information such as baby-faceness, similarity to familiar faces, fitness, or youthfulness to arrive at impressions relating to the person's competence, warmth, or power.[89] First impressions, once formed, are surprisingly resilient to contrary information. The reason is that, once we form first impressions, they become independent of the evidence that created them. It is possible to reverse first impressions by providing information that results in a complete reinterpretation of initial information, but this is not always easy and feasible.[90] Being aware of this tendency and consciously opening your mind to new information may protect you against some of the downsides of this bias. Also, it would be to your advantage to pay careful attention to the first impressions you create, particularly during job interviews.

first impressions

Initial thoughts and perceptions we form about people that tend to be stable and resilient to contrary information.

As a manager, you can protect yourself against this tendency by creating awareness and making a conscious effort to open your mind to new information. It would also be to your advantage to pay careful attention to the first impressions you create, particularly during job interviews or other key social situations.

Key Takeaway

Perception is how we make sense of our environment in response to environmental stimuli. While perceiving our surroundings, we go beyond the objective information available to us and our perception is affected by our values, needs, and emotions. There are many biases that affect human perception of objects, self, and others. When perceiving the physical environment, we fill in the gaps and extrapolate from the available information. When perceiving others, stereotypes influence our behavior. Stereotypes may lead to self-fulfilling prophecies. Stereotypes are perpetuated because of our tendency to pay selective attention to aspects of the environment and ignore information inconsistent with our beliefs. Understanding the perception process gives us clues to understanding human behavior.

Discussion Questions

1. What are some of the typical errors that we experience when we observe physical objects?
2. What are the problems of false consensus error? How can managers deal with this tendency?
3. Describe a situation where perception biases have or could affect any of the P-O-L-C facets. Use an example you have experienced or observed, or, if you do not have such an example, create a hypothetical situation. How do we manage the fact that human beings develop stereotypes? Is there such a thing as a good stereotype? How would you prevent stereotypes from creating unfairness in management decisions?
4. Describe a self-fulfilling prophecy you have experienced or observed in action. Was the prophecy favorable or unfavorable? If unfavorable, how could the parties have chosen different behaviors to produce a more positive outcome?

3.3 Work Attitudes

Learning Objectives

1. Define "work attitudes."
2. Describe the relationship between attitudes and behaviors.
3. Define and differentiate between job satisfaction, organizational commitment, and job engagement.
4. List the factors related to work attitudes.
5. Describe the consequences of work attitudes.
6. Identify the ways in which companies can track work attitudes in the workplace.

attitude

Our opinions, beliefs, and feelings about aspects of our environment.

job satisfaction

The feelings people have toward their jobs.

organizational commitment

The emotional attachment people have toward the company they work for.

job engagement

Investment of one's mental, emotional, and physical energies at work.

Our behavior at work often depends on how we feel about being there. Therefore, making sense of how people behave depends on understanding their work attitudes. An **attitude** refers to our opinions, beliefs, and feelings about aspects of our environment. We have attitudes toward the food we eat, people we interact with, courses we take, and various other things. At work, two particular job attitudes have the greatest potential to influence how we behave. These are job satisfaction and organizational commitment. **Job satisfaction** refers to the feelings people have toward their job. If the number of studies conducted on job satisfaction is an indicator, job satisfaction is probably the most important job attitude. Institutions such as Gallup Inc. or the Society for Human Resource Management (SHRM) periodically conduct studies of job satisfaction to track how satisfied employees are at work. A 2018 SHRM study revealed that 89% of respondents were at least somewhat satisfied with their jobs.[91] More recently, a 2020 CNBC and SurveyMonkey survey actually found an uptick in employee happiness after the COVID-19 pandemic despite widespread anxiety.[92] **Organizational commitment** is the emotional attachment people have toward the company they work for. There is a high degree of overlap between job satisfaction and organizational commitment, because things that make us happy with our job often make us more committed to the company as well. Finally, job engagement is a more recently developed motivational concept that is similar to a work attitude. **Job engagement** refers to the investment of one's mental, emotional, and physical energies at work. Engagement reflects employees' enthusiasm, involvement, and satisfaction with their work, and it has implications for workplace behavior.[93] Given that job engagement has similar predictors and outcomes, and organizations track job engagement in a way similar to how the other two are tracked, we focus on these three concepts in our discussion of work attitudes.

The connection between work attitudes and behaviors depends on the attitude in question. Your attitudes toward your colleagues may influence whether you actually help them on a project, but they may not be a good predictor of whether you will quit your job. Second, attitudes are more strongly related to intentions to behave in a certain way, rather than actual behaviors. When you are dissatisfied with your job, you may have the intention to leave. Whether you will actually leave is a different story. Your leaving will depend on many factors, such as availability of alternative jobs, your employability in a different company, and sacrifices you have to make while changing jobs. In other words, while attitudes give us hints about how a person might behave, it is important to note that behavior is also strongly influenced by situational constraints.

What Causes Positive Work Attitudes?

What makes you satisfied with your job, develop commitment to your company, and feel engaged at work? Research shows that people pay attention to several aspects of their work environment, including how they are treated, the relationships they form with colleagues and managers, and the actual work they perform. In addition, what people value at any given time may be a function of the economic circumstances and the job market. For example, during an economic recession, job security is likely to become a more salient influence over job attitudes. In this section, we summarize the factors that show consistent relations with job satisfaction and organizational commitment.

FIGURE 3.5 Factors Contributing to Job Attitudes

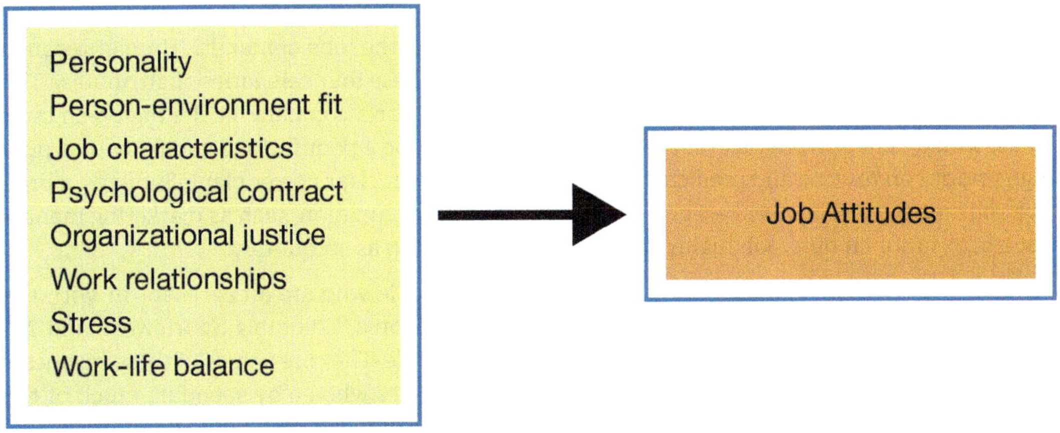

Personality

Can assessing the work environment fully explain how satisfied we are on the job? Interestingly, some experts have shown that job satisfaction is not purely environmental and is partially due to our personality. Some people have a disposition to be happy in life and at work regardless of environmental factors.

It seems that people who have a positive affective disposition (those who have a tendency to experience positive moods more often than negative moods) tend to be more satisfied with their jobs and more committed to their companies, while those who have a negative disposition tend to be less satisfied and less committed.[94] This is not surprising, as people who are determined to see the glass as "half full" will notice the good things in their work environment, while those with the opposite character will find more things to complain about. In addition to our affective disposition, people who have positive core self-evaluations (individuals who have high generalized self-efficacy, high self-esteem, internal locus of control, and low levels of neuroticism) tend to have more positive job attitudes.[95] Research also suggests that even though all five of the big five personality traits are correlated with organizational commitment, agreeableness has the strongest relationship.[96] Either these people are more successful in finding jobs and companies that will make them happy and build better relationships at work, which would increase their satisfaction and commitment, or they simply see their environment as more positive—whichever is the case, it seems that personality is related to work attitudes.

Person–Environment Fit

The fit between what we bring to our work environment and environmental demands influences both our behavior and our work attitudes. Therefore, person–job fit and person–organization fit are positively related to job satisfaction and commitment. When the abilities of individuals match those of the job's demands and the company's values, individuals tend to be more satisfied with the job and more committed to the company.[97]

person-organization fit

The degree to which a person's values, personality, goals, and other characteristics match those of the organization.

person-job fit

The degree to which a person's skill, knowledge, abilities, and other characteristics match the job's demands.

The importance of person–job fit is critical when recruiting for dangerous jobs such as those found in fire fighting.

Source: Shutterstock.com

When companies hire employees, they are interested in assessing at least two types of fit. **Person-organization fit** refers to the degree to which a person's personality, values, goals, and other characteristics match those of the organization. **Person-job fit** is the degree to which a person's knowledge, skills, abilities, and other characteristics match the job's demands. (Human resources professionals often use the abbreviation KSAO to refer to these four categories of attributes.) Thus, someone who is proactive and creative may be a great fit for a company in the high-tech sector, which would benefit from risk-taking individuals, but may be a poor fit for a company that puts a high priority on routine and predictable behavior, such as a nuclear power plant. Similarly, a proactive and creative person may be a great fit for a field-based occupation, such as marketing manager, but a poor fit for an office job highly dependent on rules, such as accountant.

Some companies are in a great position to attract people who are an excellent fit with their organization. For example, lifestyle retailers such as Patagonia, Columbia Sportswear, and Nike draw people who are attracted to an active, outdoorsy lifestyle. The core values of these businesses, such as preserving the environment, appeal to job candidates who enjoy spending much of their time in nature. To someone who enjoys surfing, being a product tester for surfing gear may be highly appealing. Thus, it is no surprise that when people fit into their organization, they tend to be more satisfied with their jobs, more committed to their companies, and more influential, and they remain at their companies longer.[98]

Job Characteristics

Employees tend to be more satisfied and committed in jobs that involve certain characteristics. The ability to use a variety of skills, feel empowered at work, receive feedback on the job, and perform a significant task, are some job characteristics related to satisfaction and commitment. However, the presence of these factors is not important for everyone. Some people have a high need for growth; these employees tend to be more satisfied when their jobs help them build new skills and improve existing knowledge, skills, and abilities.[99]

Organizational Justice and the Psychological Contract

Organizational fairness plays a large role in our satisfaction level. People pay attention to the fairness of company policies and procedures, fair and kind treatment from supervisors, and equity of their pay and other rewards they receive from the company.[100] Organizational justice can be classified into three categories: (1) procedural (fairness in the way policies and processes are carried out), (2) distributive (fairness in the allocation of resources or compensation and benefits), and (3) interactional (fairness in the degree to which people are treated with dignity and respect).

psychological contract

The unspoken, informal understanding that an employee will contribute certain things to the organization and will receive certain things in return.

The **psychological contract** is the unspoken, informal understanding that an employee will contribute certain things to the organization (e.g., work ability and a willing attitude) and will receive certain things in return (e.g., reasonable pay and benefits). Under the psychological contract, an employee may believe that if he or she works hard and receives favorable performance evaluations, he or she will receive an annual bonus, periodic raises and promotions, and will not be laid off. Since the "downsizing" trend of the past twenty years, many commentators have declared that the psychological contract is violated more often than not.

Relationships at Work

Relationships employees establish with coworkers, managers, and the organization are key influences over job attitudes. The people we interact with, their degree of compassion, our level of social acceptance in our work group, and whether we are treated with respect are all important factors surrounding our happiness at work. Research also shows that our relationship with our manager, how considerate the manager is, and whether we build a trust-based relationship with our manager are critically important to our job attitudes.[101] Other people serve a number of key functions for employees. Coworkers and managers may affect employee job attitudes by providing task assistance, career support, emotional support, friendship, helping with personal growth, and providing opportunities for individuals to assist and mentor others. Finally, **perceived organizational support**, or the degree to which employees feel that the organization cares about their well being, values them, and fulfills their needs is an important influence over job attitudes.[102]

perceived organizational support

The degree to which employees feel that the organization cares about their well being, values them, and fulfills their needs.

Stress

Not surprisingly, the amount of stress present in our job is related to our satisfaction and commitment. For example, experiencing role ambiguity (vagueness in relation to what our responsibilities are), role conflict (facing contradictory demands at work), organizational politics, and worrying about the security of our job are all stressors that make people dissatisfied. Among new employees, stress caused by uncertainty (regarding relationships or one's ability to perform well) is particularly relevant to job attitudes. On the other hand, not all stress is bad. Some stressors actually make us happier. For example, working under time pressure and having a high degree of responsibility are stressful, but they can also be perceived as challenges and tend to be related to high levels of satisfaction.[103]

Work-Life Balance

In the 1950s, work was all-consuming. Employees went to work, worked long hours, and the rest of the family accepted that work came first. As society changed, the concept of always putting work first became outdated. In modern times, more employees expect to lead balanced lives, pursue hobbies, travel, and spend more time with their family while at the same time continuing to succeed at work. The notion of work-family conflict is one cause of job dissatisfaction. This conflict can be particularly strong for women because of the time necessary for pregnancy and giving birth, as well as uneven distribution of childcare and housework, but men struggle with it as well. When work life interferes with family life, we are more stressed and unhappy with our jobs. Research shows that family-supportive workplace policies and supervisory family support are related to more positive job attitudes. For example, Cisco Systems offers paid parental leave, on-site childcare arrangements, and a flexible work environment, resulting in a family-supportive environment for employees.[104]

Assessing Work Attitudes in the Workplace

attitude surveys

Surveys that measure employee attitudes at work.

pulse surveys

Short surveys given to employees very frequently.

Given that work attitudes provide valuable clues about who will leave or stay with an organization, why some individuals will perform better, and which employees will be more engaged, tracking satisfaction and commitment levels is valuable for companies. If there are company-wide issues that make employees unhappy and disengaged, these need to be resolved. There are at least three systematic ways in which companies can track work attitudes, namely, attitude surveys, exit interviews, and sentiment analysis. Companies such as Facebook, PwC, Google, and others routinely give **attitude surveys**, to employees to track their work attitudes over time. Surveys give employees a chance to voice their concerns, and they can be powerful tools to make changes in the organization.[105] Companies can get more out of these surveys if responses are held confidential. Moreover, the success of these surveys depends on the credibility of management in the eyes of employees. If management periodically collects these surveys but no action comes out of them, employees may adopt a more cynical attitude and start ignoring these surveys, hampering the success of future efforts. A recent variation of attitude surveys is **pulse surveys**, which are very short surveys given to employees frequently (such as every week or every month). These surveys allow businesses to track job attitudes over time and gain an assessment of changes in attitudes.

exit interview

A meeting with the departing employee.

An **exit interview** involves a meeting with the departing employee. This meeting is often conducted by a member of the human resource management department. The departing employee's manager is the worst person to conduct the interview, because managers are often one of the primary reasons an employee is leaving in the first place. If conducted well, this meeting may reveal what makes employees dissatisfied at work and give management clues about areas for improvement. Experts recommend that having these interviews conducted by a second level manager (the manager's manager) may have advantages as it may lead to changes. Making these interviews mandatory for at least some groups of employees (such as high potential employees), conducting the meeting halfway between departure announcement and actual departure, conducting the meeting face to face or over the phone, following a semi-structured approach, and being a good listener during the interview are among other recommendations for these interviews.[106]

sentiment analysis

Automatic identification and coding of positive and negative sentiments in a text.

Finally, **sentiment analysis** is the automatic identification and coding of positive and negative sentiments in a text. This technique is often used in marketing to analyze customer emotions toward a company's product, but recently found its way to talent management. A company may analyze employees' internal blog posts, open ended questions in attitude surveys, emails, or comments left in internal discussion boards to identify attitudes toward particular subjects. For example, during COVID-19 pandemic, IBM organized online Ask me Anything sessions with the company's Chief Medical Officer. Employees were invited to ask questions and add written comments. These comments were later anonymized and fed into IBM's sentiment analytics tool Watson Tone Analyzer to get a sense of employee attitudes and reactions.[107]

Key Takeaway

Work attitudes are the feelings we have toward different aspects of the work environment. Job satisfaction and organizational commitment are two key attitudes that are the most relevant to important outcomes. Attitudes create an intention to behave in a certain way and may predict actual behavior under certain conditions. People develop positive work attitudes as a result of their personality, fit with their environment, stress levels they experience, relationships they develop, perceived fairness of their pay, company policies, interpersonal treatment, whether their psychological contract is violated, and the presence of policies addressing work-life conflict. When people have more positive work attitudes, they may have the inclination to perform better, display citizenship behaviors, and be absent less often and for shorter periods of time, and they are less likely to quit their jobs within a short period of time. When workplace attitudes are more positive, companies benefit in the form of higher safety and better customer service, as well as higher company performance.

Discussion Questions

1. What is the difference between job satisfaction and organizational commitment? How do the two concepts relate to one another?
2. Do you think making employees happier at work is a good way of motivating people? When would high satisfaction not be related to high performance?
3. In your opinion, what are the three most important factors that make people dissatisfied with their job? What are the three most important factors relating to organizational commitment?
4. How important is pay in making people attached to a company and making employees satisfied?
5. Do you think younger and older people are similar in what makes them happier at work and committed to their companies? Do you think there are male–female differences? Explain your answers.

3.4 Work Behaviors

Learning Objectives

1. Define job performance, organizational citizenship, absenteeism, and turnover.
2. Explain factors associated with each type of work behavior.

One of the important goals of the field of management is to understand why people behave the way they do. We focus on five key work behaviors: job performance, organizational citizenship behaviors, counterproductive work behaviors, absenteeism, and turnover. The first two behaviors are desirable ones, whereas the other three are generally regarded as undesirable. While these five are not the only organizational behaviors managers are interested in, understanding these behaviors and the major influences over each type of behavior will provide valuable knowledge about key workplace behaviors. We summarize the major research findings about the causes of each type of behavior in Table 3.2.

TABLE 3.2 Summary of Factors That Have the Strongest Influence Over Work Behaviors

Job Performance	Citizenship	Counterproductive Work Behaviors	Absenteeism	Turnover
General mental abilities	How we are treated at work	Personality	Health problems	Poor performance
How we are treated at work	Personality	Negative job attitudes	Work/life balance issues	Positive work attitudes (–)
Stress (–)	Positive work attitudes	How we are treated at work	Positive work attitudes (–)	Stress
Positive work attitudes	Age of the employee		Age of the employee (–)	Personality
Personality				Age and tenure of the employee (–)

Note: Negative relationships are indicated with (–)

Job Performance

job performance

Also known as in-role performance, the degree to which an employee successfully fulfills the factors included in the job description.

Job performance, or in-role performance, refers to the degree to which an employee successfully fulfills the duties outlined in their job description. For each job, the content of job performance may differ. Measures of job performance include quality and quantity of work performed by the employee, the accuracy and speed with which the job is performed, and the overall effectiveness of the person on the job.

In many companies, job performance determines whether a person is promoted, rewarded with pay raises, given additional responsibilities, or fired from the job. Therefore, most employers observe and track job performance. This is accomplished by tracking data on topics such as the number of sales the employee closes, the number of clients the employee visits, the number of defects found in the employee's output, or the number of customer complaints or compliments received about the person's work. In some jobs, objective performance data may not be available, and instead supervisor, coworker, customer, and subordinate assessments of the quality and quantity of work performed by the person become the indicators of job performance. Job performance is one of the main outcomes studied in organizational behavior and is an important variable managers must assess when they are engaged in the controlling role.

What Are the Major Predictors of Job Performance?

general mental ability

Our reasoning abilities, verbal and numerical skills, analytical skills, or overall intelligence level.

Under which conditions do people perform well, and what are the characteristics of high performers? The most powerful influence over our job performance is our **general mental ability**, also known as cognitive ability or intelligence, and often abbreviated as "g." General mental ability can be divided into several components—reasoning abilities, verbal and numerical skills, and analytical skills—and it seems to be important across different situations. It seems that "g" starts influencing us early in our school days because it is strongly correlated with measures of academic success even in childhood.[108] In adult life, "g" is also correlated with different measures of job performance.[109] It seems that the influence of "g" on performance is important across different settings, but there is also variation. In jobs with high complexity, it is much more critical to have high general mental abilities. Examples of such jobs are manager, sales representative, engineer, and professions such as law and medicine. In jobs such as police officer and clerical worker, the importance of "g" for high performance is still important but weaker.

Perceptions of organizational justice and *interpersonal relationships* are factors determining performance level. When employees feel they are being fairly treated by the company, when management is supportive and rewards high performance, and when individuals trust the people they work with, performance is better. The primary reason seems to be that when individuals believe they are treated well, they want to reciprocate. Therefore individuals treat the company well by performing their jobs more effectively.

The *stress* experienced on the job also determines performance level. When individuals are stressed, mental energies are drained. Instead of focusing on the task at hand, individuals become preoccupied with dealing with the stressor. Because attention and energies are diverted to dealing with stress, performance suffers. Having role ambiguity and experiencing conflicting role demands are related to lower performance.[110] Further, a recent survey found that financial stress impacts 48% of workers in the U.S.[111] When people are in debt or are worrying about their mortgage payments or college payments of their kids, their performance will suffer. The resulting loss of productivity in the workplace costs American businesses approximately $500 billion each year.[112]

Work attitudes, particularly job satisfaction and job engagement, are also correlates of job performance.[113] Many studies have been devoted to understanding whether happy employees are more productive. Some studies show weak correlations between satisfaction and performance while others show higher correlations.[114] The correlation between commitment and performance tends to be even weaker.[115]

Finally, job performance has a modest relationship with *personality traits*. Among the personality traits that are most strongly correlated with job performance are conscientiousness, emotional intelligence, and proactive personality. Research has shown that personality is a stronger predictor of job performance in "weak situations," where there are not too many restrictions and employees have a great deal of freedom in structuring their work.[116] Further, studies indicate that when self-reported personality measures are used, the results tend to be weaker than when observer measures of personality are used. This is probably not surprising, given that self-reported personality measures may not reflect the reality as it is experienced by one's coworkers and subordinates, which may be more relevant to how the employee is assessed by others at work.[117]

The fact that general mental ability influences job performance may come as no surprise to singer John Legend, who boasts an IQ of 135 to go along with his Emmy, Grammy, Oscar, and Tony.

Source: Jaguar PS / Shutterstock.com

Organizational Citizenship Behaviors

While *job performance* refers to the performance of duties listed in one's job description, organizational citizenship behaviors involve performing behaviors that are more discretionary. **Organizational citizenship behaviors (OCB)** are voluntary behaviors employees perform to help others and benefit the organization. Helping a new coworker understand how things work in the company and volunteering to organize the company picnic are some examples of citizenship behaviors. These behaviors contribute to the smooth operation of business. Interestingly, while citizenship behaviors help others, under some conditions such as when employees feel unsupported, demonstrating greater levels of citizenship may lead to citizenship fatigue, or feelings of being tired and worn out as a result of being a good citizen.[118]

organizational citizenship behaviors (OCB)

Voluntary behaviors employees perform to help others and benefit the organization.

What are the major predictors of citizenship behaviors? Unlike job performance, citizenship behaviors do not depend on one's general mental abilities. Job performance, to a large extent, depends on general mental abilities. When you add the education, skills, knowledge, and abilities that are needed to perform well, the role of motivation on performance becomes more limited. As a result, just because someone is motivated will not mean that the person will perform well. For citizenship behaviors, in contrast, the motivation-behavior link is clearer.

Perhaps the most important factor explaining citizenship behaviors is *organizational justice* and *interpersonal relationships*. When individuals have a good relationship with their managers; are supported, treated fairly, and attached to peers; and trust the people at work, they are more likely to engage in citizenship behaviors. In a high-quality relationship, individuals feel the obligation to reciprocate and go the extra mile to help out coworkers. Further, the trajectory of how people are treated matters too. One study has shown that employees reciprocated fair treatment with higher citizenship behaviors when the current level of fairness they were experiencing was higher than what they experienced in the past, as opposed to when it was lower than what they experienced in the past.[119]

Personality is yet another explanation for why individuals perform citizenship behaviors. Personality is a modest predictor of actual job performance but a much better predictor of citizenship. People who are conscientious and agreeable tend to perform citizenship behaviors more often than others.[120]

Job attitudes are also moderately related to citizenship behaviors. People who are happier at work, those who are more committed to their companies, and those who have overall positive attitudes toward their work situation tend to perform citizenship behaviors more often than others. When people are unhappy, they tend to be disengaged from their jobs and rarely go beyond the minimum that is expected of them.[121]

Interestingly, age seems to be related to the frequency with which we demonstrate citizenship behaviors. People who are older are better citizens. It is possible that with age we gain more experiences to share. It becomes easier to help others because we have more accumulated company and life experiences to draw from.[122]

Counterproductive Work Behaviors

counterproductive work behaviors (CWB)

Intentional employee behaviors that harm the organization.

Counterproductive work behaviors (CWB) is an umbrella term describing the different ways in which employees harm their organizations. CWBs are intentional, so honest mistakes are not considered to be CWBs. Some examples of CWBs include abusing others (gossiping, spreading rumors, harassment, insulting, and embarrassing others), production deviance (intentionally performing at a low level, such as by ignoring instructions or by slowing down and reducing performance), theft (intentionally stealing money or things), sabotage (intentionally damaging equipment and the physical environment), and withdrawal behaviors (taking long breaks, being tardy, or skipping work altogether indicating that the person is physically and mentally somewhere else during work hours).[123] Absenteeism may be considered a CWB, but it may also have legitimate reasons such as poor health. Therefore, we will discuss absenteeism separately in the next section.

As you can see, CWBs are harmful behaviors and if left unchecked, they have the potential to seriously harm the organization. However, they are also hard to act on, because management is not always in a position to observe and notice these behaviors. In fact, research has shown that employees admit to performing more of these behaviors than what observers such as supervisors and coworkers report.[124]

Why do employees display CWBs? Research has shown that employee personality is a powerful influence. For example, negative affectivity, or experiencing negative emotions very frequently is a strong correlate of these behaviors, whereas positive affectivity shows the opposite relationship. Further, employees who have higher levels of conscientiousness are less likely to display these behaviors. Aside from personality traits, findings from a meta analysis showed that job attitudes (job satisfaction and organizational commitment), and to a lesser extent, organizational justice perceptions were predictors of CWBs. When employees are content with their jobs and organizations, and when they feel that they are treated in a fair manner, with dignity and respect, they are less likely to display these behaviors.[125]

Absenteeism

Absenteeism refers to unscheduled absences from work. Such absences are costly to companies because of their unpredictable nature. When an employee has an unscheduled absence from work, companies struggle to find replacement workers at the last minute. This may involve hiring contingent workers, having other employees work overtime, or scrambling to cover for an absent coworker. According to the Bureau of Labor Statistics, nearly 3% of an employer's workforce will be absent every day.[126] A SHRM/Kronos study estimated that absenteeism costs employers 21%–22% of total payroll.[127] While absenteeism is a problem organizations need to deal with, they need to be careful not to encourage **presenteeism**, or showing up to work when they are sick. Creating a strong attendance culture to combat absenteeism may create the opposite problem of presenteeism, resulting in slower recovery for the employee, and contagion of illnesses.[128]

absenteeism

Unscheduled absences from work.

presenteeism

Showing up to work despite being sick.

What causes absenteeism? Some absenteeism is related to health reasons. For example, reasons such as lower back pain, migraines, accidents on or off the job, or acute stress are important reasons for absenteeism.[129] Health-related absenteeism is costly, but it would be unreasonable and unfair to institute organizational policies penalizing such absences. When an employee has a contagious illness, showing up at work will infect coworkers and will not be productive. Indeed, companies are finding that programs aimed at keeping workers healthy are effective in dealing with this type of absenteeism. Companies using wellness programs, educating employees about proper nutrition, helping them exercise, and rewarding them for healthy habits, have reported reduced absenteeism. In fact, a transportation authority in Austin, Texas, notes that the return on investment of their wellness program focusing on weight loss and nutrition is $2.50 for every dollar spent.[130]

Work-life balance is another common reason for absences. Staying home to care for a sick child or relative, attending the wedding of a friend or relative, or skipping work to study for an exam are all common reasons for unscheduled absences. Companies may deal with these by giving employees more flexibility in work hours. If employees can manage their own time, they are less likely to be absent. Organizations such as Lahey Clinic Foundation Inc. in Burlington, MA, find that instead of separating sick leave and paid time off, merging them is effective in dealing with unscheduled absences. When a company has "sick leave" but no other leave for social and family obligations, employees may fake being sick and use their "sick leave." Instead, having a single paid time off policy would allow workers to balance work and life, and allow companies to avoid unscheduled absences. Some companies such as IBM Corporation got rid of sick leave altogether and instead allow employees to take as much time as they need, as long as their work gets done.[131]

Citizens of Denmark are often cited as the happiest in the world based on their incorporation of hygge (the Danish word meaning well-being)—a combination of attitudes, behaviors, and aesthetics encouraging work-life balance. You can get a glimpse of this concept by dimming your lights, putting on some comfy socks and snuggling up with a good book.

Source: Shutterstock.com

Sometimes, absenteeism is a form of work withdrawal and a step followed by turnover. In other words, *poor work attitudes* lead to absenteeism. When employees are dissatisfied with their work, have low organizational commitment, or perceive that they are treated unfairly, they are likely to be absent more often. In this case, management may deal with absenteeism by investigating the causes of dissatisfaction and dealing with them directly.

Research does not reveal a consistent link between personality and absenteeism, but there is one demographic criterion that predicts absenteeism—age. Interestingly, and against some stereotypes that increased age would bring more health problems, research shows that age is negatively related to both frequency and duration of absenteeism. That is, younger workers are the ones more likely to be absent. Because of reasons that include higher loyalty to their company and a stronger work ethic, older employees are less likely be absent from work.[132]

Turnover

turnover

Employee departure from an organization.

Turnover refers to an employee's leaving an organization. Turnover may be voluntary or involuntary. Voluntary turnover refers to departure initiated by the employee, whereas involuntary turnover is initiated by the organization, which includes termination and layoffs. High turnover has potentially harmful consequences for the organization, particularly for customer service, quality and service performance, and workplace safety.[133] When employees leave, their jobs still need to be performed by someone, so companies spend time recruiting, hiring, and training new employees, all the while suffering from lower productivity. Yet, not all turnover is bad. Turnover is particularly a problem when high-performing employees leave, while a poor performer's turnover may actually give the company a chance to improve productivity and morale.

Why do employees leave? An employee's *performance* level is an important reason. People who perform poorly are actually more likely to leave. These people may be fired, may be encouraged to quit, or may quit because of their fear of being fired. If a company has pay-for-performance systems, poor performers will find that they are not earning much due to their substandard performance. This pay discrepancy gives poor performers an extra incentive to leave. On the other hand, instituting a pay-for-performance system does not mean that high performers will always stay with the company. Note that high performers may find it easier to find alternative jobs, so when they are unhappy, they can afford to leave their jobs voluntarily.[134]

Jobs in retail are historically among the highest in turnover.

Source: Shutterstock.com

Work attitudes are often the primary culprit in why people leave. When workers are unhappy at work, and when they are not attached to their companies, they are more likely to leave. Loving the things they do, being happy with the opportunities for advancement within the company, and being happy about pay are all aspects of work attitudes relating to turnover. Of course, the link between work attitudes and turnover is not direct. When employees are unhappy, they might have the intention to leave and may start looking for a job, but their ability to actually leave will depend on many factors such as their employability and the condition of the job market. Events that erode employee engagement may increase turnover rate in a company. For example, one study showed that downsizing of a company's workforce by 1% was followed by a 31% increase in voluntary turnover the next year.[135]

People are more likely to quit their jobs if they experience *stress* at work as well. Stressors such as role conflict and role ambiguity drain energy and motivate people to seek alternatives. For example, call center employees experience a great deal of stress because of poor treatment from customers, long work hours, and constant monitoring of their every action. Companies such as EchoStar realize that one method that is effective in retaining their best employees is to give them opportunities to move to higher-responsibility jobs elsewhere in the company. When a stressful job is a step toward a more desirable job, employees seem to stick around longer.[136]

There are also individual differences in the reasons people leave or stay with organizations. For example, *personality* is a factor in the decision to quit one's job. People who are conscientious, agreeable, and emotionally stable are less likely to quit their jobs. Many explanations are possible. People with these personality traits may perform better at work, which leads to lower turnover. Or they may have better relations with coworkers and managers, which is a factor in their retention. Whatever the reason, it seems that some people are likely to stay longer at any given job regardless of the circumstances.[137]

Whether individuals leave a job or stay also depends on *age* and *how long they have been at an organization*. It seems that younger employees are more likely to leave. This is not surprising because people who are younger often have fewer responsibilities such as supporting a household or having dependents. As a result, they can quit a job they dislike much more easily. They may also have higher expectations and thus be more easily disappointed when a job proves to be less rewarding than they had imagined. Similarly, people who have been with a company for a short period of time can quit more easily. For example, Sprint Corporation found that many of their new hires were quitting within 45 days of their hiring dates. When they investigated, they found that newly hired employees were experiencing a lot of stress from avoidable problems such as unclear job descriptions or problems with hooking up their computers. Sprint was able to solve the turnover problem by paying special attention to orienting new hires. New employees experience a lot of stress at work, and there is usually not much keeping them in the company, such as established bonds to a manager or colleagues. New employees may even have ongoing job interviews with other companies when they start working. This, too, gives them the flexibility to leave more easily.

job embeddedness

A condition when employees have strong links to other people and their communities, have high fit with their jobs and organizations, and when leaving their job would entail many sacrifices.

In addition to examining why employees leave, researchers also examined why people stay in an organization. There are factors at work that prevent employees from leaving. Sometimes it is hard or undesirable for people to leave, because they have strong ties to the place. This idea is represented by the concept of **job embeddedness**. Individuals have high job embeddedness when they have strong links to other people and their communities, have high fit with their jobs and organizations, and when leaving their job would entail many sacrifices (such as valuable benefits, giving up well-liked colleagues, or having to give up the prestige of working in a well-known company). Having high job embeddedness reduces the likelihood of turnover, and serves as a buffer for the factors that would ordinarily push individuals to leave their jobs.[138] For example, one study showed that organizational corporate social responsibility was positively related to pride in working where, which was related to higher levels of job embeddedness, and therefore lower probability of leaving the organization.[139]

Key Takeaway

Employees demonstrate a wide variety of positive and negative behaviors at work. Among these, five are critically important and have been extensively studied in the management literature. Job performance is the degree of success with which one accomplishes the tasks listed in one's job description. A person's abilities, particularly general mental ability, are the main predictor of job performance in many occupations. How we are treated at work, the level of stress experienced at work, work attitudes, and, to a lesser extent, our personalities are also factors related to one's job performance. Citizenship behaviors are tasks helpful to the organization that go above and beyond one's job description. Performance of citizenship behaviors are less a function of our abilities and more of motivation. How individuals are treated at work, personality, work attitudes, and age, are the main predictors of citizenship. Among negative behaviors employees demonstrate, counterproductive work behaviors, absenteeism, and turnover are critically important. Counterproductive behaviors are often a function of personality traits, job attitudes, and unfair treatment. Health problems and work-life balance issues contribute to absenteeism. Poor work attitudes are also related to absenteeism, and younger employees are more likely to be absent from work. Turnover is higher among low performers, people who have negative work attitudes, and those who experience a great deal of stress. Personality and being younger are personal predictors of turnover.

Discussion Questions

1. What is the difference between performance and organizational citizenship behaviors? As a manager, how would you improve someone's performance? How would you increase citizenship behaviors?
2. Are citizenship behaviors always beneficial to the company? Can you think of any citizenship behaviors employees may perform with the intention of helping a company that may have negative consequences overall?
3. Have you ever observed counterproductive behaviors at work or school? Why did they happen? How could they have been prevented?
4. What are the major causes of absenteeism at work? How can companies minimize the level of absenteeism that takes place?
5. In some companies, managers are rewarded for minimizing the turnover within their department or branch. A part of their bonus is directly tied to keeping the level of turnover below a minimum. What do you think about the potential effectiveness of these programs? Do you see any downsides to such programs?

3.5 Developing Your Positive Attitude Skills

Learning Objectives

1. Learn to be happier at work.
2. Leverage your attitudes for optimum work performance.

Have you ever wondered how you could be happier at work and how greater work satisfaction could improve your overall effectiveness? Here are some ideas that may help you achieve a great sense of peace for yourself as well as when you are working with a negative coworker.

Research shows that acting positive at work can actually help you become happier over time, as emotions can be influenced by actions.

Source: Shutterstock.com

- *Leverage your Big Five traits.* Your personality is a big part of your happiness. Which of the Big Five positive traits represent strengths? Be aware of them and look for opportunities to express them at work. Are you high on Neuroticism? If so, work to overcome this challenge. If you choose to find the negative side of everything, you will.
- *Find a job and company that fit you well.* Good fit with the job and company are important to your happiness. This starts with knowing yourself, your chosen career, and the particular job in question: What do you want from the job? What do you enjoy doing?
- *Get accurate information about the job and the company.* Ask detailed questions about what life is like in this company. Do your research. Read about the company; use your social network to understand the company's culture.
- *Develop good relationships at work.* Make friends. Try to get a mentor if your company does not have a formal mentoring program. Approach a person you admire and attempt to build a relationship with this person. An experienced mentor can be a great help in navigating life at a company. Your social network can help you weather the bad days and provide you with emotional and instrumental support during your time at a company as well as afterward.
- Pay is important, but *job characteristics matter more to your job satisfaction.* So avoid sacrificing key job elements for a little more money. When choosing a job, look at the level of challenge and the potential of the job to make you feel engaged.
- *Be proactive in managing organizational life.* If the job is stressful, cope with it by effective time management and development of a good social network, as well as being proactive in getting to the source of stress. Do not be afraid to ask for direction if you need more guidance.
- *Know when to leave.* If the job makes you unhappy over an extended period of time and there is little hope of solving the problems, it may be time to look elsewhere.

Key Takeaway

Promoting a positive work attitude will increase your overall effectiveness as a manager. You can increase your own happiness at work by knowing yourself as a person, by ensuring that you work at a job and company where you fit in, and by building effective work relationships with your manager, coworkers, and subordinates. Concentrating on the motivating potential of the job when choosing a job and solving the problems you encounter in a proactive manner may be helpful as well.

Discussion Questions

1. Do you believe that your own happiness at work is in your hands? What have you done in the past to increase your own satisfaction with work?
2. Consider the most negative person you work or interact with. Why do you think they focus more on the negative side of life?
3. On the basis of what you have read in this chapter, can you think of ways in which you can improve your effectiveness in dealing with negative coworkers?

3.6 Case in Point: Zoom Video Communications Delivering Happiness

Source: Tada Images/Shutterstock.com

Employees working around the world increasingly connect to each other through video conferencing technology; this trend dramatically accelerated due to the COVID-19 pandemic and the resulting increase in the number of employees working from home. Remote meetings may be conducted over a variety of different platforms, including Teams (owned by Microsoft), Hangout Meet (by Google), or Webex (by Cisco). Among these platforms owned by the giants of technology industry, the San Jose, California based Zoom emerged as a rare company that was able to take on these mature platforms by building a loyal following among thousands of business customers. Anyone can use Zoom for free, but to access more options, organizations can purchase corporate subscriptions. And many do, with the company boasting approximately 265,400 corporate customers each with over 10 employees as of this writing.

Today, Zoom is regarded as one of the most valuable cloud-based companies in the world, and it belongs to a rare group of companies that were actually profitable when they went public in March 2019. Interestingly, the company attributes its success to "delivering happiness." In fact, the S-1 statement (a document filed with the Securities and Exchange commission when the company went public) uses the word "happiness" over 50 times. Compare this to the S-1 statement of Uber, where it was not mentioned at all. Zoom views happiness of customers and happiness of people as the core elements of their corporate culture and the key to their success and future operations.

The search for happiness is a key part of the company's origin story. The company founder and CEO Eric Yuan, who immigrated to the USA when he was 27 and found a job as a software developer at the video conferencing company WebEx, rose through the ranks and became the VP of engineering. He was making a salary in the "upper six figures." But he was not happy.

Since he left his high paying job to develop his own videoconferencing software in 2011, he has been asked many times about the risk he was taking. His answer is this: "The purpose of life is to pursue happiness, and I was not happy. Then, what's the risk?"

By all metrics, Zoom is delivering happiness to customers and employees. Zoom is highly popular among its customers, because the products are user friendly and the company is innovative and responsive to customer needs and concerns. In fact, Zoom has a Net Promoter Score (a common metric to measure customer loyalty to the firm) of 70, similar to that of Apple, which is 73. At the beginning of 2020, the company had over 2,500 employees, with plans to hire upwards of 500 more people while expanding to new locations. Zoom also had a turnover rate of 3% in 2019, which is exceptionally low in the software industry. The company provides generous benefits and perks that are typical of technology companies. More importantly, employees feel appreciated and empowered at work, and believe that they have a voice in the company. A "happiness crew" of around 100 volunteers from different units of the business make sure that they host digital meet ups to connect the company's employees scattered across eight countries. The company was ranked the #2 best company to work for by Glassdoor in 2019, and #1 in happiest employees by Comparably. According to CEO Yuan, the company does not focus on revenue goals. Instead, he believes that focusing on customer and employee happiness will lead to increased growth.[140]

Multimedia Extension—Culture of Caring

View in the online reader

Case Discussion Questions

1. Review websites such as Glassdoor and Comparably to see what employees like and dislike about working at Zoom. Would you like to work in a company such as this?
2. Zoom uses "happiness" as part of their brand as an employer. What advantages and downsides do you see to this brand?
3. What is the connection between employee attitudes, customer satisfaction, and revenue growth as described in this case? How generalizable is this relationship to other industries and companies?
4. Zoom had an IPO in 2019, which made it a public company. How do you expect that this may affect their corporate culture over time?
5. The case mentions many factors that could affect employee happiness, such as happiness crews and generous perks. Which elements mentioned in the case do you believe are the most critical to employee happiness?

Endnotes

1. Connolly, J. J., & Viswesvaran, C. (2000). The role of affectivity in job satisfaction: A meta-analysis. *Personality and Individual Differences, 29,* 265–281; Thoresen, C. J., Kaplan, S. A., Barsky, A. P., de Chermont, K., & Warren, C. R. (2003). The affective underpinnings of job perceptions and attitudes: A meta-analytic review and integration. *Psychological Bulletin, 129,* 914–945.
2. Judge, T. A., Weiss, H. M., Kammeyer-Mueller, J. D., Hulin, C. L. (2017). Job attitudes, job satisfaction, and job affect: A century of continuity and of change. *Journal of Applied Psychology, 102,* 356–374.
3. Tasselli, S., Kilduff, M., & Landis, B. (2018). Personality Change: Implications for Organizational Behavior. *Academy of Management Annals*, 12, 467–493.
4. Ensari, N., Riggio, R.E., Christian, J., & Carslaw, G. (2011). Who emerges as a leader? Metaanalyses of individual differences as predictors of leadership emergence. *Personality and Individual Differences, 51*, 532–536.
5. Retrieved from https://www.inc.com/justin-bariso/hiring-for-personality-vs-hiring-for-skills-the-dueling-doctrines-of-richard-bra.html.
6. Retrieved from http://www.wsj.com/articles/SB10001424052702304279904579515702293041712.
7. Roberts, B. W., Walton, K. E., & Viechtbauer, W. (2006). Patterns of mean-level change in personality traits across the life course: A meta-analysis of longitudinal studies. *Psychological Bulletin, 132*, 1–25.
8. Judge, T. A., & Higgins, C. A. (1999). The big five personality traits, general mental ability, and career success across the life span. *Personnel Psychology, 52*, 621–652.
9. Barrick, M. R., & Mount, M. K. (1993). Autonomy as a moderator of the relationships between the big five personality dimensions and job performance. *Journal of Applied Psychology, 78*, 111–118.
10. Goldberg, L. R. (1990). An alternative "description of personality": The big-five factor structure. *Journal of Personality & Social Psychology, 59*, 1216–1229.
11. Staff, R. T., Hogan, M. J., & Whalley, L. J. (2017). Childhood intelligence and personality traits neuroticism and openness contributes to social mobility: A study in the Aberdeen 1936 Birth Cohort. *Personality and Individual Differences, 114*, 206–212.
12. Wanberg, C. R., & Kammeyer-Mueller, J. D. (2000). Predictors and outcomes of proactivity in the socialization process. *Journal of Applied Psychology, 85*, 373–385.
13. LePine, J. A. (2003). Team adaptation and postchange performance: Effects of team composition in terms of members' cognitive ability and personality. *Journal of Applied Psychology*, 88, 27–39.
14. Zhao, H., & Seibert, S. E. (2006). The big five personality dimensions and entrepreneurial status: A meta-analytic review. *Journal of Applied Psychology, 91*, 259–271.
15. Harrison, S., & Wagner, D. (2016). Spilling outside the box: The effects of individuals' creative behaviors at work on time spent with their spouses at home. *Academy of Management Journal*, 59, 841–859.
16. Egan, M., Daly, M., Delaney, L., Boyce, C. J., & Wood, A. M. (2017). Adolescent conscientiousness predicts lower lifetime unemployment. *Journal of Applied Psychology, 102*, 700–709.
17. Tay, C., Ang, S., & Van Dyne, L. (2006). Personality, biographical characteristics, and job interview success: A longitudinal study of the mediating effects of interviewing self-efficacy and the moderating effects of internal locus of control. *Journal of Applied Psychology, 91*, 446–454.
18. Judge, T. A., & Ilies, R. (2002). Relationship of personality to performance motivation: A meta-analytic review. *Journal of Applied Psychology, 87*, 797–807; Judge, T. A., Zimmerman, R. D. (2008). Understanding the impact of personality traits on individuals' turnover decisions: A meta-analytic path model. *Personnel Psychology, 61*, 309–348.
19. Huang, J. L., Cropanzano, R., Li, A., Shao, P., & Zhang, X. A. (2017). Employee conscientiousness, agreeableness, and supervisor justice rule compliance: A three-study investigation. *Journal of Applied Psychology*, 102, 1564–1589.
20. Zhao, H., & Seibert, S. E. (2006). The big five personality dimensions and entrepreneurial status: A meta-analytic review. *Journal of Applied Psychology, 91*, 259–271; Zhao, H., Seibert, S. E., Lumpkin, G. T. (2010). The relationship of personality to entrepreneurial intentions and performance: A meta-analytic review. *Journal of Management, 36*, 381–404.
21. Harrison, S., & Wagner, D. (2016). Spilling outside the box: The effects of individuals' creative behaviors at work on time spent with their spouses at home. *Academy of Management Journal, 59*, 841–859.
22. Wilmot, M. P., Wanberg, C. R., Kammeyer-Mueller, J. D., & Ones, D. S. (2019). Extraversion advantages at work: A quantitative review and synthesis of the meta-analytic evidence. *Journal of Applied Psychology*, 104, 1447–1470.
23. Chi, N. W., Grandey, A. A., Diamond, J. A., & Krimmel, K. R. (2011). Want a tip? Service performance as a function of emotion regulation and extraversion. *Journal of Applied Psychology, 96*, 1337–1346; Vinchur, A. J., Schippmann, J. S., Switzer, F. S., & Roth, P. L. (1998). A meta-analytic review of predictors of job performance for salespeople. *Journal of Applied Psychology, 83*, 586–597.
24. Bauer, T. N., Erdogan, B., Liden, R. C., & Wayne, S. J. (2006). A longitudinal study of the moderating role of extraversion: Leader-member exchange, performance, and turnover during new executive development. *Journal of Applied Psychology, 91*, 298–310; Bono, J. E., & Judge, T. A. (2004). Personality and transformational and transactional leadership: A meta-analysis. *Journal of Applied Psychology, 89*, 901–910.
25. Tay, C., Ang, S., & Van Dyne, L. (2006). Personality, biographical characteristics, and job interview success: A longitudinal study of the mediating effects of interviewing self-efficacy and the moderating effects of internal locus of control. *Journal of Applied Psychology, 91*, 446–454.
26. Wanberg, C. R., & Kammeyer-Mueller, J. D. (2000). Predictors and outcomes of proactivity in the socialization process. *Journal of Applied Psychology, 85*, 373–385.
27. Judge, T. A. Heller, D., & Mount, M. K. (2002). Five-factor model of personality and job satisfaction: A meta-analysis. *Journal of Applied Psychology, 87*, 530–541.
28. Judge, T. A., Martocchio, J. J., & Thoresen, C. J. (1997). Five-factor model of personality and employee absence. *Journal of Applied Psychology, 82*, 745–755.
29. Thielmann, I., Spadaro, G., & Balliet, G. (2020). Personality and prosocial behavior: A theoretical framework and meta-analysis. *Psychological Bulletin*, 146, 30–90.
30. Anand, S., Vidyarthi, P., Singh, S., & Ryu, S. (2015). Family interference and employee dissatisfaction: Do agreeable employees better cope with stress? *Human Relations*, 68, 691–708.
31. Walumbwa, F. O., & Schaubroeck, J. (2009). Leader personality traits and employee voice behavior: Mediating roles of ethical leadership and work group psychological safety. *Journal of Applied Psychology, 94*, 1275–1286.
32. Zimmerman, R. D. (2008). Understanding the impact of personality traits on individuals' turnover decisions: A meta-analytic path model. *Personnel Psychology, 61*, 309–348.
33. Kell, H.J. 2019. Do Teachers' Personality Traits Predict Their Performance? A Comprehensive Review of the Empirical Literature From 1990 to 2018. ETS Research Report Series. Retrieved from https://files.eric.ed.gov/fulltext/EJ1238349.pdf.
34. Bernerth, J. B., Taylor, S. G., Walker, H. J., & Whitman, D. S. (2012). An empirical investigation of dispositional antecedents and performance-related outcomes of credit scores. *Journal of Applied Psychology, 97*, 469–478.
35. Choi, D., Oh, I.S., & Colbert, A.E., (2015). Understanding organizational commitment: A meta-analytic examination of the roles of the five-factor model of personality and culture. *Journal of Applied Psychology*, 100, 1542–1567.
36. Smith, M. M. et al. (2019). Perfectionism and the five-factor model of personality: A meta-analytic review. *Personality and Social Psychology Review*, 23, 367–390.
37. Hart, P. M. (1999). Predicting employee life satisfaction: A coherent model of personality, work, and nonwork experiences, and domain satisfactions. *Journal of Applied Psychology*, 84, 564–584.
38. Allen, T. D., Johnson, R. C., Saboe, K. N., Cho, E., Dumani, S., & Evans, S. (2012). Dispositional variables and work–family conflict: A meta-analysis. *Journal of Vocational Behavior*, 80, 17–26; De Hoogh, A. H. B., & Den Hartog, D. N. (2009). Neuroticism and locus of control as moderators of the relationships of charismatic and autocratic leadership with burnout. *Journal of Applied Psychology*, 94, 1058–1067; Liu, S., Wang, M., Zhan, Y., & Shi, J. (2009). Daily stress and alcohol use: Testing the cross level moderation effects of neuroticism and job involvement. *Personnel Psychology*, 62, 575–597.
39. Judge, T. A., Heller, D., & Mount, M. K. (2002). Five-factor model of personality and job satisfaction: A meta-analysis. *Journal of Applied Psychology*, 87, 530–541.
40. Zimmerman, R. D., Boswell, W. R., Shipp, A. J., Dunford, B. B., & Boudreau, J. W. (2012). Explaining the pathways between approach-avoidance personality traits and employees' job search behavior. *Journal of Management*, 38, 1450–1475.
41. Wu, C.-H., Wang, Y., Parker, S. K., & Griffin, M. A. (2020). Effects of chronic job insecurity on Big Five personality change. *Journal of Applied Psychology*. Advance online publication. http://dx.doi.org/10.1037/apl0000488.
42. Harrison, J.S., Thurgood, G.R., Boivie, S. & Pfarrer, M.D. 2020. Perception Is Reality: How CEOs' Observed Personality Influences Market Perceptions of Firm Risk and Shareholder Returns. *Academy of Management Journal*, 63, 1166–1195.
43. Kudret, S., Erdogan, B., & Bauer, T. N. (2019). Self-monitoring personality trait at work: An integrative narrative review and future research directions. *Journal of Organizational Behavior*, 40, 193–208.
44. Turnley, W. H., & Bolino, M. C. (2001). Achieving desired images while avoiding undesired images: Exploring the role of self-monitoring in impression management. *Journal of Applied Psychology*, 86, 351–360.

45. Day, D. V., & Schleicher, D. J. Self-monitoring at work: A motive-based perspective. *Journal of Personality, 74*, 685–714; Kilduff, M., & Day, D. V. (1994). Do chameleons get ahead? The effects of self-monitoring on managerial careers. *Academy of Management Journal*, 37, 1047–1060.
46. Fang, R., Landis, B., Zhang, Z., Anderson, M. H., Shaw, J. D., & Kilduff, M. (2015). Integrating personality and social networks: A meta-analysis of personality, network position, and work outcomes in organizations. *Organization Science*, 26, 1243–1260.
47. Day, D. V., Schleicher, D. J., Unckless, A. L., & Hiller, N. J. (2002). Self-monitoring personality at work: A meta-analytic investigation of construct validity. *Journal of Applied Psychology*, 87, 390–401; Sasovova, Z., Mehra, A., Borgatti, S. P., & Schippers, M. C. (2010). Network churn: The effects of self-monitoring personality on brokerage dynamics. *Administrative Science Quarterly*, 55, 639–670.
48. Day, D. V., Schleicher, D. J., Unckless, A. L., & Hiller, N. J. (2002). Self-monitoring personality at work: A meta-analytic investigation of construct validity. *Journal of Applied Psychology*, 87, 390–401.
49. Brown, D. J., Cober, R. T., Kane, K., Levy, P. E., & Shalhoop, J. (2006). Proactive personality and the successful job search: A field investigation with college graduates. *Journal of Applied Psychology*, 91, 717–726.
50. Seibert, S. E. (1999). Proactive personality and career success. *Journal of Applied Psychology, 84*, 416–427.
51. Crant, M. J. (1995). The proactive personality scale and objective job performance among real estate agents. *Journal of Applied Psychology, 80*, 532–537.
52. Kammeyer-Mueller, J. D., & Wanberg, C. R. (2003). Unwrapping the organizational entry process: Disentangling multiple antecedents and their pathways to adjustment. *Journal of Applied Psychology, 88*, 779–794; Li, N., Harris, B., Boswell, W. R., & Xie, Z. (2011). The role of organizational insiders' developmental feedback and proactive personality on newcomers' performance: An interactionist perspective. *Journal of Applied Psychology, 96*, 1317–1327.
53. Major, D. A., Turner, J. E., & Fletcher, T. D. (2006). Linking proactive personality and the Big Five to motivation to learn and development activity. *Journal of Applied Psychology*, 91, 927–935.
54. Chan, D. (2006). Interactive effects of situational judgment effectiveness and proactive personality on work perceptions and work outcomes. *Journal of Applied Psychology, 91*, 475–481; Erdogan, B., & Bauer, T. N. (2005). Enhancing career benefits of employee proactive personality: The role of fit with jobs and organizations. *Personnel Psychology, 58*, 859–891.
55. Judge, T. A., & Bono, J. E. (2001). Relationship of core self-evaluations traits—self esteem, generalized self efficacy, locus of control, and emotional stability—with job satisfaction and job performance: A meta-analysis. *Journal of Applied Psychology, 86*, 80–92; Keller, R. T. (2012). Predicting the performance and innovativeness of scientists and engineers. *Journal of Applied Psychology, 97*, 225–233.
56. Turban, D. B., & Keon, T. L. (1993). Organizational attractiveness: An interactionist perspective. *Journal of Applied Psychology, 78*, 184–193.
57. Zilioli, S., Slatcher, R. B., Chi, P., Li, X., Zhao, J., & Zhao, G. (2016). Childhood adversity, self-esteem, and diurnal cortisol profiles across the life span. *Psychological Science*, 27, 1249–1265.
58. Bauer, T. N., Bodner, T., Erdogan, B., Truxillo, D. M., & Tucker, J. S. (2007). Newcomer adjustment during organizational socialization: A meta-analytic review of antecedents, outcomes, and methods. *Journal of Applied Psychology, 92*, 707–721.
59. Phillips, J. M., & Gully, S. M. (1997). Role of goal orientation, ability, need for achievement, and locus of control in the self-efficacy and goal-setting process. *Journal of Applied Psychology, 82*, 792–802; Steel, P. (2007). The nature of procrastination: A meta-analytic and theoretical review of quintessential self-regulatory failure. *Psychological Bulletin, 133*, 65–94.
60. Fast, N. J., Burris, E. R., & Bartel, C. A. (2014). Managing to stay in the dark: Managerial self-efficacy, ego defensiveness, and the aversion to employee voice. *Academy of Management Journal*, 57, 1013–1034.
61. Ahearne, M., Mathieu, J., & Rapp, A. (2005). To empower or not to empower your sales force? An empirical examination of the influence of leadership empowerment behavior on customer satisfaction and performance. *Journal of Applied Psychology*, 90, 945–955.
62. Barrick, M. R., Patton, G. K., & Haugland, S. N. (2000). Accuracy of interviewer judgments of job applicant personality traits. *Personnel Psychology, 53*, 925–951.
63. Retrieved from http://www.wsj.com/articles/a-personality-test-could-stand-in-the-way-of-your-next-job-1429065001.
64. Gale, S. F. (2002, April). Three companies cut turnover with tests. *Workforce, 81*(4), 66–69.
65. Retrieved from https://www.nytimes.com/2019/09/17/style/personality-tests-office.html.
66. Morgeson, F. P., Campion, M. A., Dipboye, R. L., Hollenbeck, J. R., Murphy, K., & Schmitt, N. (2007). Reconsidering the use of personality tests in personnel selection contexts. *Personnel Psychology*, 60, 683–729; Morgeson, F. P., Campion, M. A., Dipboye, R. L., Hollenbeck, J. R., Murphy, K., & Schmitt, N. (2007). Are we getting fooled again? Coming to terms with limitations in the use of personality tests for personnel selection. *Personnel Psychology*, 60; van Hooft, E. A. J., & Born, M. P. (2012). Intentional response distortion on personality tests: Using eye-tracking to understand response processes when faking. *Journal of Applied Psychology*, 97, 301–316.
67. Ones, D. S., Dilchert, S., Viswesvaran, C., & Judge, T. A. (2007). In support of personality assessment in organizational settings. *Personnel Psychology*, 60, 995–1027; Tett, R. P., & Christiansen, N. D. (2007). Personality tests at the crossroads: A response to Morgeson, Campion, Dipboye, Hollenbeck, Murphy, and Schmitt (2007). *Personnel Psychology*, 60, 967–993.
68. Kluemper, D. H., & Rosen, P. A. (2009). Future employment selection methods: Evaluating social networking Web sites. *Journal of Managerial Psychology, 24*, 567–580; Mount, M. K., Barrick, M. R., & Strauss, J. P. (1994). Validity of observer ratings of the big five personality factors. *Journal of Applied Psychology, 79*, 272–280.
69. Retrieved from http://www.wsj.com/articles/are-workplace-personality-tests-fair-1412044257.
70. Heller, M. (2005, September). Court ruling that employer's integrity test violated ADA could open door to litigation. *Workforce Management, 84*(9), 74–77.
71. Lusk, E. J., & Oliver, B. L. (1974). Research notes. American manager's personal value systems-revisited. *Academy of Management Journal, 17*, 549–554; Rokeach, M. (1973). *The nature of human values*. New York: Free Press.
72. Judge, T. A., & Bretz, R. D. (1992). Effects of work values on job choice decisions. *Journal of Applied Psychology, 77*, 261–271; Ravlin, E. C., & Meglino, B. M. (1987). Effect of values on perception and decision making: A study of alternative work values measures. *Journal of Applied Psychology, 72*, 666–673.
73. George, J. M., & Jones, G. R. (1996). The experience of work and turnover intentions: Interactive effects of value attainment, job satisfaction, and positive mood. *Journal of Applied Psychology, 81*, 318–325.
74. Schwartz, S. H. (1992). Universals in the content and structure of values: Theoretical advances and empirical tests in 20 countries. In M. Zanna (Ed.), *Advances in experimental social psychology* (pp. 1–65). San Diego, CA: Academic Press.
75. Smola, K. W., & Sutton, C. D. (2002). Generational differences: Revisiting generational work values for the new millennium. *Journal of Organizational Behavior*, 23, 363–382.
76. Twenge, J. M., Campbell, S. M., Hoffman, B. J., & Lance, C. E. (2010). Generational differences in work values: Leisure and extrinsic values increasing, social and intrinsic values decreasing. *Journal of Management*, 36, 1117–1142.
77. Retrieved from https://www.mckinsey.com/industries/consumer-packaged-goods/our-insights/true-gen-generation-z-and-its-implications-for-companies#.
78. Campbell, S. M., Twenge, J. M., & Campbell, W. K. (2017). Fuzzy but useful constructs: Making sense of the differences between generations. *Work, Aging, and Retirement*, 3, 130–139.
79. Higgins, E. T., & Bargh, J. A. (1987). Social cognition and social perception. *Annual Review of Psychology*, 38, 369–425; Keltner, D., Ellsworth, P. C., & Edwards, K. (1993). Beyond simple pessimism: Effects of sadness and anger on social perception. *Journal of Personality and Social Psychology*, 64, 740–752.
80. Riskind, J. H., Moore, R., & Bowley, L. (1995). The looming of spiders: The fearful perceptual distortion of movement and menace. *Behaviour Research and Therapy*, 33, 171.
81. Kellman, P. J., & Shipley, T. F. (1991). A theory of visual interpolation in object perception. *Cognitive Psychology, 23*, 141–221.
82. Grant, S.M., Hodge, F.D., & Sinha, R.K. How disclosure medium How disclosure medium affects investor reactions to CEO bragging, modesty, and humblebragging. *Accounting, Organizations, and Society*. Volumes 68–69, 118–134.
83. Fields, J. M., & Schuman, H. (1976). Public beliefs about the beliefs of the public. *The Public Opinion Quarterly, 40*(4), 427–448; Ross, L., Greene, D., & House, P. (1977). The "false consensus effect": An egocentric bias in social perception and attribution processes. *Journal of Experimental Social Psychology, 13*, 279–301.
84. Snyder, M., Tanke, E. D., & Berscheid, E. (1977). Social perception and interpersonal behavior: On the self-fulfilling nature of social stereotypes. *Journal of Personality and Social Psychology, 35*, 656–666.
85. Weingarten, G. (2007, April 8). Pearls before breakfast. *Washington Post*. Retrieved from http://www.washingtonpost.com/wp-dyn/content/article/2007/04/04/AR2007040401721.html.
86. Waller, M. J., Huber, G. P., & Glick, W. H. (1995). Functional background as a determinant of executives' selective perception. *Academy of Management Journal*, 38, 943–974.
87. Higgins, E. T., & Bargh, J. A. (1987). Social cognition and social perception. *Annual Review of Psychology, 38*, 369–425.
88. Lord, C. G., Ross, L., & Lepper, M. R. (1979). Biased assimilation and attitude polarization: The effects of prior theories on subsequently considered evidence. *Journal of Personality and Social Psychology*, 37, 2098–2109.
89. Zebrowitz, L. A. (2017). First impressions from faces. *Current Directions in Psychological Science*, 26, 237–242.
90. Mann, T. J., & Ferguson, M. J. (2015). Can we undo our first impressions?: The role of reinterpretation in reversing implicit evaluations. *Journal of Personality and Social Psychology*, 108, 823–849.

91. Society for Human Resource Management (2017). 2017 Employee job satisfaction and engagement: The doors of opportunity are open. Retrieved from https://www.shrm.org/hr-today/trends-and-forecasting/research-and-surveys/pages/2017-job-satisfaction-and-engagement-doors-of-opportunity-are-open.aspx.

92. Retrieved from https://www.cnbc.com/2020/05/18/cnbc-and-survey-monkey-release-latest-workforce-survey.html.

93. Rich, B. L., LePine, J. A., Crawford, E. R. (2010). Job engagement: Antecedents and effects on job performance. *Academy of Management Journal, 53,* 617–635.

94. Connolly, J. J., & Viswesvaran, C. (2000). The role of affectivity in job satisfaction: A meta-analysis. *Personality and Individual Differences, 29,* 265–281; Thoresen, C. J., Kaplan, S. A., Barsky, A. P., de Chermont, K., & Warren, C. R. (2003). The affective underpinnings of job perceptions and attitudes: A meta-analytic review and integration. *Psychological Bulletin, 129,* 914–945.

95. Judge, T. A., Weiss, H. M., Kammeyer-Mueller, J. D., Hulin, C. L. (2017). Job attitudes, job satisfaction, and job affect: A century of continuity and of change. *Journal of Applied Psychology, 102,* 356–374.

96. Choi, D., Oh, I. S., & Colbert, A. E. Choi, D., Oh, I.-S., & Colbert, A. E. (2015). Understanding organizational commitment: A meta-analytic examination of the roles of the five-factor model of personality and culture. *Journal of Applied Psychology, 100,* 1542–1567.

97. Kristof-Brown, A. L., Zimmerman, R. D., & Johnson, E. C. (2005). Consequences of individuals' fit at work: A meta-analysis of person-job, person-organization, person-group, and person-supervisor fit. *Personnel Psychology, 58,* 281–342; Verquer, M. L., Beehr, T. A., & Wagner, S. H. (2003). A meta-analysis of relations between person-organization fit and work attitudes. *Journal of Vocational Behavior, 63,* 473–489.

98. Anderson, C., Spataro, S. E., & Flynn, F. J. (2008). Personality and organizational culture as determinants of influence. *Journal of Applied Psychology, 93,* 702–710; Cable, D. M., & DeRue, D. S. (2002). The convergent and discriminant validity of subjective fit perceptions. *Journal of Applied Psychology, 87,* 875–884; Kristof-Brown, A. L., Zimmerman, R. D., & Johnson, E. C. (2005). Consequences of individuals' fit at work: A meta-analysis of person-job, person-organization, person-group, and person-supervisor fit. *Personnel Psychology, 58,* 281–342; O'Reilly, C. A., Chatman, J., & Caldwell, D. F. (1991). People and organizational culture: A profile comparison approach to assessing person-organization fit. *Academy of Management Journal, 34,* 487–516; Saks, A. M., & Ashforth, B. E. (2002). Is job search related to employment quality? It all depends on the fit. *Journal of Applied Psychology, 87,* 646–654.

99. Mathieu, J. E., & Zajac, D. M. (1990). A review and meta-analysis of the antecedents, correlates, and consequences of organizational commitment. *Psychological Bulletin, 108,* 171–194; Seibert, S. E., Wang, G., & Courtwright, S. H. (2011). Antecedents and consequences of psychological and team empowerment in organizations: A meta-analytic review. *Journal of Applied Psychology, 96,* 981–1003.

100. Cohen-Charash, Y., & Spector, P. E. (2001). The role of justice in organizations: A meta-analysis. *Organizational Behavior and Human Decision Processes, 86,* 278–321; Colquitt, J. A., Conlon, D. E., Wesson, M. J., Porter, C. O. L. H., & Ng, K. Y. (2001). Justice at the millennium: A meta-analytic review of 25 years of organizational justice research. *Journal of Applied Psychology, 86,* 425–445.

101. Bauer, T. N., Bodner, T., Erdogan, B., Truxillo, D. M., & Tucker, J. S. (2007). Newcomer adjustment during organizational socialization: A meta-analytic review of antecedents, outcomes, and methods. *Journal of Applied Psychology*, 92, 707–721; Dulebohn, J. H., Bommer, W. H., Liden, R. C., Brouer, R. L., & Ferris, G. R. (2012). A meta-analysis of antecedents and consequences of leader-member exchange: Integrating the past with an eye toward the future. *Journal of Management*, 38, 1715–1759. Gerstner, C. R., & Day, D. V. (1997). Meta-analytic review of leader-member exchange theory: Correlates and construct issues. *Journal of Applied Psychology*, 82(6), 827–844; Mathieu, J. E., & Zajac, D. M. (1990). A review and meta-analysis of the antecedents, correlates, and consequences of organizational commitment. *Psychological Bulletin*, 108, 171–194.

102. Colbert, A. E., Bono, J. E., & Purvanova, R. K. (2016). Flourishing via workplace relationships: Moving beyond instrumental support. *Academy of Management Journal*, 59, 1199–1223; Rhoades, L., & Eisenberger, R. (2002). Perceived organizational support: A review of the literature. *Journal of Applied Psychology*, 87, 698–714.

103. Ellis, A. M., Bauer, T. N., Mansfield, L. R., Erdogan, B., Truxillo, D. M., & Simon, L. S. (2015). Navigating uncharted waters: Newcomer socialization through the lens of stress theory. *Journal of Management*, 41, 203–235; Kinicki, A. J., McKee-Ryan, F. M., Schriesheim, C. A., & Carson, K. P. (2002). Assessing the construct validity of the job descriptive index: A review and meta-analysis. *Journal of Applied Psychology*, 87, 14–32; Podsakoff, N. P., LePine, J. A., & LePine, M. A. (2007). Differential challenge stressor-hindrance stressor relationships with job attitudes, turnover intentions, turnover, and withdrawal behavior: A meta-analysis. *Journal of Applied Psychology*, 92, 438–454.

104. Bagger, J., & Li, A. (2014). How does supervisory family support influence employees' attitudes and behaviors? A social exchange perspective. *Journal of Management*, 40, 1123–1150; Ernst Kossek, E., & Ozeki, C. (1998). Work-family conflict, policies, and the job-life satisfaction relationship: A review and directions for organizational behavior-human resources research. *Journal of Applied Psychology*, 83, 139–149; Cortina, H. (May 11, 2018). Here's how six companies take the lead supporting working mothers. Retrieved from https://www.forbes.com/sites/justcapital/2018/05/11/heres-how-six-companies-take-the-lead-supporting-working-mothers/#520a1e753327; Wayne, J. H., Casper, W. J., Matthews, R. A., & Allen, T. D. (2013). Family-supportive organization perceptions and organizational commitment: The mediating role of work-family conflict and enrichment and partner attitudes. *Journal of Applied Psychology*, 98, 606–622.

105. Judd, S., O'Rourke, E., & Grant, A. (March 14, 2018). Employee surveys are still one of the best ways to measure engagement. *Harvard Business Review*.

106. Spain, E. & Groysberg, B. (April, 2016). Making exit interviews count. *Harvard Business Review*, 94 (4).

107. Bubb, D., & Daly, J. (Summer, 2020). Creating whole-company resilience through emotional health and well-being. *People & Strategy, 43* (3), 18–23.

108. Kuncel, N. R., Hezlett, S. A., & Ones, D. S. (2004). Academic performance, career potential, creativity, and job performance: Can one construct predict them all? *Journal of Personality and Social Psychology, 86,* 148–161.

109. Kuncel, N. R., Hezlett, S. A., & Ones, D. S. (2004). Academic performance, career potential, creativity, and job performance: Can one construct predict them all? *Journal of Personality and Social Psychology, 86,* 148–161; Lang, J. W. B., Kersting, M., Hülsheger, U. R., & Lang, J. (2010). General mental ability, narrower cognitive abilities, and job performance: The perspective of the nested-factors model of cognitive abilities. *Personnel Psychology, 63,* 595–640.

110. Gilboa, S., Shirom, A., Fried, Y., & Cooper, C. (2008). A meta-analysis of work demand stressors and job performance: Examining main and moderating effects. *Personnel Psychology, 61,* 227–271.

111. Retrieved from https://www.stress.org/42-worrying-workplace-stress-statistics.

112. Macklin, D. (2019, August 15). Business losing $500 billion due to employees' financial stress. Retrieved from https://www.hrtechnologist.com/articles/compensation-benefits/businesses-losing-500-billion-due-to-employees-financial-stress-2/.

113. Christian, M. S., Garza, A. S., Slaughter, J. E. (2011). Work engagement: A quantitative review and test of its relations with task and contextual performance. *Personnel Psychology, 64,* 89-136; Judge, T. A., Thoresen, C. J., Bono, J. E., & Patton, G. T. (2001). The job satisfaction–job performance relationship: A qualitative and quantitative review. *Journal of Applied Psychology*, 127, 376–407; Riketta, M. (2008). The causal relation between job attitudes and performance: A meta-analysis of panel studies. *Journal of Applied Psychology*, 93, 472–481.

114. Iaffaldano, M. T., & Muchinsky, P. M. (1985). Job satisfaction and job performance: A meta-analysis. *Psychological Bulletin, 97,* 251–273; Judge, T. A., Thoresen, C. J., Bono, J. E., & Patton, G. T. (2001). The job satisfaction–job performance relationship: A qualitative and quantitative review. *Journal of Applied Psychology, 127,* 376–407; Riketta, M. (2008). The causal relation between job attitudes and performance: A meta-analysis of panel studies. *Journal of Applied Psychology, 93,* 472–481.

115. Mathieu, J. E., & Zajac, D. M. (1990). A review and meta-analysis of the antecedents, correlates, and consequences of organizational commitment. *Psychological Bulletin, 108,* 171–194; Riketta, M. (2002). Attitudinal organizational commitment and job performance: A meta-analysis. *Journal of Organizational Behavior, 23,* 257–266; Wright, T. A., & Bonnett, D. G. (2002). The moderating effects of employee tenure on the relation between organizational commitment and job performance: A meta-analysis. *Journal of Applied Psychology, 87,* 1183–1190.

116. Judge, T. A., & Zapata, C. P. (2015). The person-situation debate revisited: Effect of situation strength and trait activation on the validity of the big five personality traits in predicting job performance. *Academy of Management Journal*, 58, 1149–1179.

117. O'Boyle, E. H., Humphrey, R. H., Pollack, J. M., Hawver, T. H., & Story, P. A. (2011). The relation between emotional intelligence and job performance: A meta-analysis. *Journal of Organizational Behavior, 32,* 788–818; Oh, I.S., Wang, G., & Mount, M. K. (2011). Validity of observer ratings of the five-factor model of personality traits: A meta-analysis. *Journal of Applied Psychology, 96,* 762–773. Shaffer, J. A., & Postlethwaite, B. E. (2012). A matter of context: A meta-analytic investigation of the relative validity of contextualized and noncontextualized personality measures. *Personnel Psychology, 65,* 445–494; Thomas, J. P., Whitman, D. S., & Viswesvaran, C. (2010). Employee proactivity in organizations: A comparative meta-analysis of emergent proactive constructs. *Journal of Occupational and Organizational Psychology, 83,* 275–300.

118. Bolino, M. C., Hsiung, H.-H., Harvey, J., & LePine, J. A. (2015). "Well, I'm tired of tryin'!" Organizational citizenship behavior and citizenship fatigue. *Journal of Applied Psychology, 100,* 56–74.

119. Colquitt, J. A., Conlon, D. E., Wesson, M. J., Porter, C. O. L. H., & Ng, K. Y. (2001). Justice at the millenium: A meta-analytic review of 25 years of organizational justice research. *Journal of Applied Psychology, 86*, 425–445; Ilies, R., Nahrgang, J. D., & Morgeson, F. P. (2007). Leader-member exchange and citizenship behaviors: A meta-analysis. *Journal of Applied Psychology, 92*, 269–277; Rubenstein, A. L., Allen, D. G., & Bosco, F. A. (2019). What's past (and present) Is prologue: Interactions between justice levels and trajectories predicting behavioral reciprocity. *Journal of Management, 45*, 1569–1594.
120. Chiaburu, D. S., Oh, I.S., Berry, C. M., Li, N., & Gardner, R. G. (2011). The five-factor model of personality traits and organizational citizenship behaviors: A meta-analysis. *Journal of Applied Psychology, 96*, 1140–1166; Ilies, R., Fulmer, I. S., Spitzmuller, M., & Johnson, M. D. (2009). Personality and citizenship behavior: The mediating role of job satisfaction. *Journal of Applied Psychology, 94*, 945–959.
121. Dalal, R. S. (2005). A meta-analysis of the relationship between organizational citizenship behavior and counterproductive work behavior. *Journal of Applied Psychology, 90*, 1241–1255; Fassina, N. E., Jones, D. A., & Uggerslev, K. L. (2008). Relationship clean-up time: Using meta-analysis and path analysis to clarify relationships among job satisfaction, perceived fairness, and citizenship behaviors. *Journal of Management, 34*, 161–188; Hoffman, B. J., Blair, C. A., Meriac, J. P., & Woehr, D. J. (2007). Expanding the criterion domain? A quantitative review of the OCB literature. *Journal of Applied Psychology, 92*, 555–566; Lepine, J. A., Erez, A., & Johnson, D. E. (2002). The nature and dimensionality of organizational citizenship behavior: A critical review and meta-analysis. *Journal of Applied Psychology, 87*, 52–65.
122. Ng, T. W. H., & Feldman, D. C. (2008). The relationship of age to ten dimensions of job performance. *Journal of Applied Psychology, 93*, 392–423.
123. Spector, P. E., Fox, S., Penney, L. M., Bruursema, K., Goh, A., & Kessler, S. (2006). The dimensionality of counterproductivity: Are all counterproductive behaviors created equal? *Journal of Vocational Behavior, 68*, 446–460.
124. Berry, C. M., Carpenter, N. C., & Barratt, C. L. (2012). Do other-reports of counterproductive work behavior provide an incremental contribution over self-reports? A meta-analytic comparison. *Journal of Applied Psychology, 97*, 613–636.
125. Dalal, R. S. (2005). A Meta-analysis of the relationship between organizational citizenship behavior and counterproductive work behavior. *Journal of Applied Psychology, 90*, 1241–1255.
126. U.S. Bureau of Labor Statistics. (2020). Labor force statistics from the current population study. Retrieved from https://www.bls.gov/cps/cpsaat47.htm#cps_eeann_abs_ft_occu_ind.f.1.
127. SHRM (February 17, 2016). Managing employee attendance. Retrieved from https://www.shrm.org/resourcesandtools/tools-and-samples/toolkits/pages/managingemployeeattendance.aspx.
128. Ruhle, S. A., & Süß, S. (2020). Presenteeism and absenteeism at work—an Analysis of archetypes of sickness attendance cultures. *Journal of Business and Psychology, 35*, 241–255.
129. Farrell, D., & Stamm, C. L. (1988). Meta-analysis of the correlates of employee absence. *Human Relations, 41*, 211–227; Martocchio, J. J., Harrison, D. A., & Berkson, H. (2000). Connections between lower back pain, interventions, and absence from work: A time-based meta-analysis. *Personnel Psychology, 53*, 595–624.
130. Blackburn, G. L. (December, 2009) The ROI on weight loss at work. *Harvard Business Review*, p. 30; Parks, K. M., & Steelman, L. A. (2008). Organizational wellness programs: A meta-analysis. *Journal of Occupational and Organizational Psychology, 13*, 58–68.
131. Cole, C. L. (2002, September). Sick of absenteeism? Get rid of sick days. *Workforce, 81*(9), 56–61; Conlin, M. (2007, November 12). Shirking working: The war on hooky. *Business Week, 4058*, 72–75.
132. Martocchio, J. J. (1989). Age-related differences in employee absenteeism: A meta-analysis. *Psychology and Aging, 4*, 409–414; Ng, T. W. H., & Feldman, D. C. (2008). The relationship of age to ten dimensions of job performance. *Journal of Applied Psychology, 93*, 392–423.
133. Hancock, J. I., Allen, D. G., Bosco, F. A., McDaniel, K. R., & Pierce, C. A. (2013). Meta-analytic review of employee turnover as a predictor of firm performance. *Journal of Management, 39*, 573–603.
134. Williams, C. R., & Livingstone, L. P. (1994). Another look at the relationship between performance and voluntary turnover. *Academy of Management Journal, 37*, 269–298.
135. Griffeth, R. W., Hom, P. W., & Gaertner, S. (2000). A meta-analysis of antecedents and correlates of employee turnover: Update, moderator tests, and research implications for the next millennium. *Journal of Management, 26*, 463–488; Sucher, S. J., & Gupta, S. (May/June 2018). Layoffs that don't break your company. *Harvard Business Review, 96* (3).
136. Badal, J. (2006, July 24). "Career path" programs help retain workers. *Wall Street Journal*, B1; Griffeth, R. W., Hom, P. W., & Gaertner, S. (2000). A meta-analysis of antecedents and correlates of employee turnover: Update, moderator tests, and research implications for the next millennium. *Journal of Management, 26*, 463–488; Podsakoff, N. P., LePine, J. A., & LePine, M. A. (2007). Differential challenge stressor-hindrance stressor relationships with job attitudes, turnover intentions, turnover, and withdrawal behavior: A meta-analysis. *Journal of Applied Psychology, 92*, 438–454.
137. Salgado, J. F. (2002). The big five personality dimensions and counterproductive behaviors. *International Journal of Selection and Assessment, 10*, 117–125; Zimmerman, R. D. (2008). Understanding the impact of personality traits on individuals' turnover decisions: A meta-analytic path model. *Personnel Psychology, 61*, 309–348.
138. Lee, T. W., Burch, T. C., & Mitchell, T. R. (2014). The story of why we stay: A review of job embeddedness. *Annual Review of Organizational Psychology and Organizational Behavior, 1*, 199–216.
139. Ng, T. W. H., Yam, K. C., & Aguinis, H. (2019). Employee perceptions of corporate social responsibility: Effects on pride, embeddedness, and turnover. *Personnel Psychology, 72*, 107–137.
140. Case written by Berrin Erdogan and Talya Bauer to accompany T. N. Bauer & B. Erdogan (2021). *Organizational Behavior: Bridging Science and Practice (4.0)*. Boston, MA: FlatWorld. Partially based on ideas and information contained in Davies, N. (October 11, 2019). "Happiness crews" and "culture committees" are making isolated workers feel less lonely. Retrieved from https://www.forbes.com/sites/nigeldavies/2019/10/11/happiness-crews-and-culture-committees-are-making-isolated-workers-feel-less-lonely/#5aca7061927b; Huddleston, T. (August 21, 2019). Zoom's founder left a 6-figure job because he wasn't happy - and following his heart made him a billionaire. https://www.cnbc.com/2019/08/21/zoom-founder-left-job-because-he-wasnt-happy-became-billionaire.html; Morgan, B. (October 8, 2019). The top customer experiences? Look at the great place to work list. Retrieved from https://www.forbes.com/sites/blakemorgan/2019/10/08/the-top-customer-experiences-look-at-the-great-place-to-work-list/#6f3b7373552e; Quast, J. (October 24, 2019). Can Zoom make you... Happy? Retrieved from https://www.fool.com/investing/2019/10/24/can-zoom-make-youhappy.aspx; Taulli, T. (October 19, 2019). How Zoom created an $18 billion juggernaut. Retrieved from https://www.forbes.com/sites/tomtaulli/2019/10/19/how-zoom-created-an-18-billion-juggernaut/#e6aaa8a1cfa1; O'Grady, P. (2020, May 14). Fast-growing Zoom to hire hundreds in new Phoenix and Pittsburgh R&D centers. Silicon Valley Business Journal. Retrieved from https://www.bizjournals.com/sanjose/news/2020/05/14/zoom-growth-phoenix-pittsburgh-zm.html; Zoom Video Communications, Inc. (2020, June 2). Zoom reports first quarter results for fiscal year 2021 [Press release]. Retrieved from http://www.globenewswire.com/news-release/2020/06/02/2042560/0/en/Zoom-Reports-First-Quarter-Results-for-Fiscal-Year-2021.html.

CHAPTER 4
Developing Mission, Vision, and Values

Mattel Inc.'s vision of "creating the future of play" is evidenced in the constantly evolving designs found in their popular brands such as Barbie, American Girl, and Hot Wheels.

Source: Sean P. Aune/Shutterstock.com

Chapter Learning Objectives

Reading this chapter will help you accomplish the following:

1. Understand the roles of mission, vision, and values, in the planning process.
2. Understand how mission and vision fit into the planning-organizing-leading-controlling (P-O-L-C) framework.
3. See how creativity and passion are related to vision.
4. Incorporate stakeholder interests into mission and vision.
5. Develop statements that articulate organizational mission and vision.
6. Apply mission, vision, and values to your personal goals and professional career.

For organizationals, a key part of planning is captured in verbal and written statements of an organization's mission and vision. With a mission and vision, firms craft a strategy for achieving their general purpose and afterward establishing benchmarks for judging progress and success through clear goals and objectives. TED's simple but significant mission, "Spread Ideas," provides a clear and powerful message about their organization and goals.[1] Mission and vision communicate the organization's values and purpose, and the best mission and vision statements have an emotional component that serves to incite employees and delight customers.

TABLE 4.1 The P-O-L-C Framework

Planning	Organizing	Leading	Controlling
1. Vision & Mission	1. Organization Design	1. Leadership	1. Systems/Processes
2. Strategizing	2. Culture	2. Decision Making	2. Strategic Human Resources
3. Goals & Objectives	3. Social Networks	3. Communications	
		4. Groups/Teams	
		5. Motivation	

4.1 The Roles of Mission, Vision, and Values

Learning Objectives

1. Define mission and vision.
2. Appreciate how values are important for mission and vision.
3. Understand the roles of vision, mission, and values in the P-O-L-C framework.

Mission, Vision, and Values

values statement

A written statement that reaffirms or states outright the organization's values that might not be evident in the mission or vision statements.

A casual tour of business or organization websites expose you to the range of forms that mission and vision statements can take. For example, Lyft notes, "Our mission is to reconnect people through transportation and bring communities together."[2] Mission statements answer the questions of "Who are we?" and "What does our organization value?" Vision statements typically take the form of relatively brief, future-oriented statements—vision statements answer the question "Where is this organization going?" Increasingly, organizations also add a **values statement** that either reaffirms or states outright the organization's values that might not be evident in the mission or vision statements.

Mission and vision both relate to an organization's purpose and are typically communicated in written form. Mission statements answer questions about who the firm is and what they are doing. Oftentimes mission statements incorporate the firm's values as well. An example is found in the outdoor clothing company Patagonia, whose mission states, "To build the best product, cause no unnecessary harm, use business to inspire and implement solutions to the environmental crisis."[3] Consulting firm Bain and Company reports that 63% of the more than 1,000 firms surveyed globally reported using mission and values statements as a management tool.[4] Moreover, firms with a clearly communicated, widely understood, and collectively shared mission and vision have been shown to perform better than those without them, with the caveat that they related to effectiveness only when strategy, goals, and objectives were aligned with vision and mission.[5]

Disney inspires with their mission that encompasses both theme parks and other entertainment outlets. "The mission of The Walt Disney Company is to entertain, inform and inspire people around the globe through the power of unparalleled storytelling, reflecting the iconic brands, creative minds and innovative technologies that make ours the world's premier entertainment company."

Source: AFM Visuals/Shutterstock.com

Music Rap-Up: My Company

Twinprov perform a rap on mission, vision, and values.

View in the online reader

A **mission statement** communicates the organization's reason for being, and how it plans to serve its key stakeholders. Customers, employees, and investors are the stakeholders most often emphasized, but other stakeholders like government or communities (i.e., in the form of social or environmental impact) may also be discussed. Mission statements sometimes include a summation of the firm's values. **Values** are the beliefs of an individual or group, and in the case of organizational values, the values of the organization where members are emotionally invested.

A **vision statement**, in contrast to a mission statement, is a future-oriented declaration of the organization's purpose and aspirations. While the mission statement outlines the organization's current "purpose for being," the vision statement outlines, "based on that purpose, this is what we may one day become." A firm's strategy should flow directly from their vision, since the strategy is intended to achieve the vision and satisfy the organization's mission. Typically, vision statements are relatively brief, as in the case of Starbucks vision statement, which reads: "Establish Starbucks as the premier purveyor of the finest coffee in the world while maintaining our uncompromising principles as we grow."[6] Similarly, Walmart's tag-line version of its vision statement is "Save money. Live better."[7] A more lengthy visionary statement is found in Amazon.com, which states, "Our vision is to be earth's most customer centric company; to build a place where people can come to find and discover anything they might want to buy online."[8]

mission statement

A statement of purpose, describing who the company is and what it does.

values

Shared principles, standards, and goals.

vision statement

A future-oriented declaration of the organization's purpose and aspirations.

FIGURE 4.1 Mission Statements

While a vision describes what an organization desires to become in the future, an organization's mission is grounded in the past and present. A mission outlines the reasons for the organization's existence and explains what role it plays in society. A well-written mission statement captures the organization's identity and helps to answer the fundamental question of "Who are we?" As a practical matter, a mission statement explains to key stakeholders why they should support the organization. The following examples illustrate the connections between organizations and the needs of their stakeholders.

Harley Davidson

We ride with our customers and apply this deep connection in every market we serve to create superior value for all of our stakeholders.

Internal Revenue Service

Provide America's taxpayers top-quality service by helping them understand and meet their tax responsibilities and enforce the law with integrity and fairness to all.

Starbucks

To inspire and nurture the human spirit—one person, one cup and one neighborhood at a time.

The Estée Lauder Company

Bringing the best to everyone we touch and being the best in everything we do.

Limited Brands

Limited Brands is committed to building a family of the world's best fashion brands offering captivating customer service experiences that drive long-term loyalty and deliver sustained growth for our shareholders.

Fender Musical Instruments

We will exceed the expectations of music enthusiasts worldwide and create a community for individual expression by focusing on our people, products, and business excellence.

Source: Shutterstock.com, Nick Fox_Shutterstock.com, Andrew Armagov_Shutterstock.com, Sorbis_Shutterstock.com, gowithstock_Shutterstock.com, JHVEPhoto_Shutterstock.com, Paul Brady Photography_Shutterstock.com

FIGURE 4.2 Vision Statements
An organization's vision describes what the organization hopes to become in the future. Visions highlight the values and aspirations that lie at the heart of the organization. Although vision statements have the potential to inspire employees, customers, and other stakeholders, vision statements are relatively rare and good visions are even rarer. Some of the visions being pursued by businesses are offered here.

Alcoa

To be the best company in the world—in the eyes of our customers, shareholders, communities and people.

Avon

To be the company that best understands and satisfies the product, service, and self-fullfillment needs of women—globally.

Chevron

To be the global energy company most admired for its people, partnership, and performance.

Google

To provide access to the world's information in one click.

Kraft Heinz

To help end hunger worldwide.

Procter and Gamble

Be, and be recognized as, the best consumer products and services company in the world.

Source: Shutterstock.com, achinthamb _ Shutterstock.com

The Role of Mission and Vision

Mission and vision statements play three critical roles: (1) communicate the purpose of the organization to stakeholders, (2) inform strategy development, and (3) develop the measurable goals and objectives by which to gauge the success of the organization's strategy.

First, mission and vision provide a vehicle for communicating an organization's purpose and values to all key stakeholders. Stakeholders are those key parties who have some influence over the organization or stake in its future, such as employees, customers, investors, suppliers, and institutions such as governments. Typically, mission and vision statements are widely circulated and discussed often so that their meaning is widely understood, shared, and internalized. Research finds that meaningful vision statements are more likely to lead to more engaged employees.[9] The better employees understand an organization's purpose, through its mission and vision, the better able they will be to understand the strategy and its implementation.

Second, mission and vision create a target for strategy development. That is, one criterion of a good strategy is how well it helps the firm achieve its mission and vision. The best vision statements create a tension and restlessness with regard to the status quo—that is, they should foster a spirit of continuous innovation and improvement. London Business School professors Gary Hamel and C. K. Prahalad describe this tense relationship between vision and strategy as stretch and ambition. Indeed, a study of such able competitors as CNN, British Airways, and Sony found that these firms displaced competitors with stronger reputations and deeper pockets through their ambition to stretch their organizations in more innovative ways.[10]

Third, mission and vision provide a high-level guide, and the strategy provides a specific guide, to the goals and objectives showing success or failure of the strategy and satisfaction of the larger set of objectives stated in the mission. Such objectives include profitability goals, metrics on customer and employee satisfaction, and social and environmental responsibility measures.

Founded by Anita Roddick, the mission of The Body Shop explicitly includes a broad understanding of stakeholders by providing a commitment "to the well-being of our fellow humans and the preservation of the planet."

Source: Ashraf Photography/ Shutterstock.com

Space X provides an example of a company that embraces the ambitious vision of colonizing Mars.

Source: Shutterstock.com

Key Takeaway

Mission and vision relate to an organization's purpose and aspirations, and are typically communicated in brief written statements. A mission statement communicates the organization's reason for being and how it serves its key stakeholders. The vision statement is a narrower, future-oriented declaration of the organization's purpose and aspirations. Together, mission and vision guide strategy development, help communicate the organization's purpose to stakeholders, and inform the goals and objectives set to determine whether the strategy is on track.

Discussion Questions

1. Do you feel it is important for organizations to have mission statements? Why or why not?
2. Is a vision statement as important as, or less important than, a mission statement? Explain your answer.
3. How are values important to the content of mission and vision statements?
4. What happens if an organization's mission and vision statements do not seem sincere? How might this affect an organization?
5. How do mission and vision relate to a firm's strategy?
6. In what ways are mission and vision important for organizational goals and objectives?

4.2 Mission and Vision in the P-O-L-C Framework

Learning Objectives

1. Understand the role of mission and vision in *organizing*.
2. Understand the role of mission and vision in *leading*.
3. Understand the role of mission and vision in *controlling*.

Mission and vision play a prominent role in the planning dimension of the P-O-L-C framework. Mission and vision are also related to the organizing, leading, and controlling aspects as well. In this section, we describe each of these relationships.

Mission, Vision, and Organizing

Organizing is the function of management that involves developing an organizational structure and allocating human resources to ensure the accomplishment of objectives. The organizing facet of the P-O-L-C framework typically includes subjects such as organization design, staffing, and organizational culture. The alignment between the mission and vision has implications for various organizing activities. For instance, **organizational design** is a formal, guided process for integrating the people, information, and technology of an organization. It is used to match the form of the organization as closely as possible to the purpose(s) the organization seeks to achieve. Through the design process, organizations act to improve the probability that the collective efforts of members will be successful.

To organize, managers must connect people with each other as well as with information and technology in meaningful and purposeful ways to allow the success of such key human resources. Organization structure defines the formal relationships among people and specifies both their roles and their responsibilities. Administrative systems govern the organization through guidelines, procedures, and policies. Each part of the organization should support (or at least, not conflict with) each of the others, and together they must support the organization's purpose, as reflected in its mission and vision.

organizing

The function of management that involves developing an organizational structure and allocating human resources to ensure the accomplishment of objectives.

organizational design

A formal, guided process for integrating the people, information, and technology of an organization.

Disney's creative ability to incorporate new divisions into their structure and put a new spin on classic concepts is on full view with the new Disney+ show The Mandalorian perhaps best known for introducing a breakout character often referred to as 'baby yoda.'

Source: DANIEL CONSTANTE/Shutterstock.com

For example, in 2006, Disney acquired Pixar, a firm renowned for its creative process in animated films. Disney summarizes the Pixar strategy like this: "Pixar's [strategy] is to combine proprietary technology and world-class creative talent to develop computer-animated feature films with memorable characters and heartwarming stories that appeal to audiences of all ages."[11] Disney has helped Pixar achieve this strategy through an important combination of structural design choices. First, Pixar is an independent division of Disney and is empowered to make independent choices in all aspects of idea development. Second, Pixar gives its "creatives"—its artists, writers, and designers—great leeway over decision making. Third, Pixar protects its creatives' ability to share work in progress, up and down the hierarchy, with the aim of making it even better. As a result, innovations gained through new projects can be shared with later projects, while sharing knowledge about potential pitfalls at the same time.[12] Such acquisitions can pose challenges when different companies have their own unique cultures, but evidence seems to suggest that Disney has a strength in navigating this difficult process. For example, Disney eventually acquired Lucasfilm; this acquisition allowed for the integration of the Star Wars empire into the Disney family with new movies directed by J.J. Abrams as well as cartoons such as *Star Wars: Rebels* shown on the Disney network geared at a younger audience as well as the Disney+ hit *The Mandalorian*.[13] Impressively, Disney was able to recoup their $4 billion investment only six years after purchase.[14] Further integration by Disney will appear in its parks as well as Star Wars theme parks to further leverage the added value of the acquisition.[15]

organizational culture

A system of shared assumptions, values, and beliefs showing people what is appropriate and inappropriate behavior.

Organizational culture is the workplace environment formulated from the interaction of the employees in the workplace. Organizational culture is defined by all the life experiences, strengths, weaknesses, education, upbringing, and other attributes of the employees. While executive leaders play a large role in defining organizational culture by their actions and leadership, all employees contribute to the organizational culture.

Achieving alignment between mission and vision and organizational culture can be very beneficial to firms, but one potential downside is that organizational culture is also difficult to change. Consequently, a firm's ability to change the organization's culture to support those new directions may be difficult, or, at least, slow to achieve.

For instance, nearly two decades ago, Procter & Gamble (P&G) sought to change a fundamental part of its vision in a way that asked the organization to source more of its innovations from external partners. Historically, P&G had invested heavily in research and development and internal sources of innovation—so much so that "not invented here" (known informally as NIH) was the dominant cultural mindset.[16] NIH describes a culture that avoids using products, research, or know-how that originated anywhere other than inside the organization. It is normally used in a negative sense. As a sociological phenomenon, the "not invented here" syndrome is manifested as an unwillingness to adopt an idea or product because it originates from another culture. P&G has been able to combat this NIH bias by adopting a five-year stretch goal that at least 50% of their initiatives will include an external collaboration and moving to a hybrid research and development (R&D) structure that balances local focus and headquarters oversight.[17] P&G was gradually able to change its culture toward one that is more open to external contributions, and therefore in much better alignment with its current mission and vision.

Mission, Vision, and Leading

Leading involves influencing others toward the attainment of organizational objectives. Leading and leadership are nearly synonymous with the notions of mission and vision. A very purposeful person is often described as being "on a mission." And the success of many top leaders and entrepreneurs flows from their personal mission. Oprah Winfrey, for example, holds a personal mission, "To be a teacher. And to be known for inspiring my students to be more than they thought they could be."[18] Such a belief has led to successes in journalism, acting, television, network, and magazine development. Similarly, individuals are often viewed as leaders because they are visionary in their actions. For instance, when Walt Disney suggested building a theme park in a Florida swamp back in the early 1960s, few other people saw the development as a world-changing opportunity.

leading

Involves influencing others toward the attainment of organizational objectives.

Any task—whether launching the Oprah Winfrey Network or advancing the Disney empire—is much more difficult if attempted alone. Therefore, the more that a mission or vision challenges the status quo—and recognizing that good vision statements always need to create some dissonance with the status quo—the greater will be the organization's need of "change leaders"—individuals who will help diffuse the revolutionary philosophy even while the leader (i.e., the founder or CEO) is not present. Without real change leaders, a revolutionary vision would remain a mere idea of the visionary CEO—they are the ones who make the implementation of the transformation real.

Steve Demos' company Silk is a realization of his mission to replace cow's milk with a soy alternative.

Source: Sheila Fitzgerald/ Shutterstock.com

In many cases, we can associate revolutionary companies with the organization's visionary leaders—for instance, Apple and Steve Jobs, Dell and Michael Dell, or Google and the team of Sergey Brin and Larry Page. In all three of these organizations, the leaders focused on creating an organization with a noble mission that enabled the employees and management team not only to achieve the strategic breakthrough but also to realize their personal dreams in the process.

Vision That Pervades the Organization

A broader definition of visionary leadership suggests that, if many or most of an organization's employees understand and identify with the mission and vision, efficiency will increase because the organization's members will be making decisions fully aligned with the organization's goals. Efficiency is achieved with limited hands-on supervision because the mission and vision serve as a form of cruise control. To make frontline responsibility effective, leadership must learn to trust workers and give them sufficient opportunities to develop quality decision-making skills.

Mission and vision are also relevant to leadership well beyond the impact of one or several top executives. Even beyond existing employees, various stakeholders—customers, suppliers, prospective new employees—are visiting organizations' websites to read their mission and vision statements. In the process, they are trying to understand what kind of organization they are reading about and what the organization's values and ethics are. Ultimately, they are seeking to determine whether the organization and what it stands for are a good fit for them.

Mission, Vision, and Controlling

controlling

Ensuring that performance does not deviate from standards. Controlling consists of three steps, which include (1) establishing performance standards, (2) comparing actual performance against standards, and (3) taking corrective action when necessary.

Controlling involves ensuring that performance does not deviate from standards. Controlling consists of three steps: (1) establishing performance standards, (2) comparing actual performance against standards, and (3) taking corrective action when necessary. Mission and vision are relevant to all three steps.

Actual versus Desired Performance

The goals and objectives that flow from an organization's mission and vision provide a basis for assessing actual versus desired performance. In many ways, such goals and objectives provide feedback that helps managers assess the degree to which the organization is succeeding and provide insights into areas where corrective action may be needed. This is one reason goals and objectives should ideally be specific and measurable.

Corrective Action

Just as mission and vision should lead to specific and measurable goals and objectives and thus provide a basis for comparing actual and desired performance, corrective action should also be prompted in cases where performance falls short of performance objectives. Because mission and vision are often general, high-level statements rarely spell out what specific actions firms should take when performance is below expectations.

strategic human resources management (SHRM)

Management strategy that reflects the aim of tying the organization's human capital, its people, into the mission and vision.

Strategic human resources management (SHRM) reflects the aim of integrating the organization's human capital—its people—into the mission and vision. Human resources management alignment should integrate decisions about people with decisions about the results an organization is trying to obtain. Research indicates that organizations that successfully align human resources management with mission and vision accomplishment do so by integrating SHRM into the planning process, emphasizing human resources activities that support mission goals, and building strong human resources/management capabilities and relationships.[19]

Key Takeaway

In addition to being a key part of the planning process, mission and vision also play key roles in the organizing, leading, and controlling functions of management. While mission and vision start the planning function, they are best realized when accounted for across all four functions of management—P-O-L-C. In planning, mission and vision help to generate specific goals and objectives and to develop the strategy for achieving them. Mission and vision guide choices about organizing, too, from structure to organizational culture. The cultural dimension is one reason mission and vision are most effective when they pervade the leadership of the entire organization, rather than being just the focus of senior management. Finally, mission and vision are tied to the three key steps of controlling: (1) establishing performance standards, (2) comparing actual performance against standards, and (3) taking corrective action when necessary. Since people make the place, ultimately strategic human resources management must bring these pieces together.

Discussion Questions

1. How might mission and vision influence organizational design?
2. How might mission and vision influence leadership practices?
3. Why might a specific replacement CEO candidate be a good or poor choice for a firm with an existing mission and vision?
4. Which aspects of controlling do mission and vision influence?
5. What performance standards might reinforce a firm's mission and vision?

4.3 Creativity and Passion

Learning Objectives

1. Understand how creativity relates to vision.
2. Develop creativity tools.
3. Understand how passion relates to vision.

Creativity and passion are particularly relevant to the creation of valuable mission and vision statements. A simple definition of **creativity** is the generation of new ideas. While creativity is often conceptualized as largely an artistic attribute, creativity in business is critical to innovation and progress. Indeed, one IBM study of over 1,500 CEOs from 60 countries listed creativity as one of the key skills for business survival.[20] **Passion** in business refers to an intense, driving, or overmastering feeling or conviction. Passion is also associated with intense emotion compelling action. We highlight the relationship between creativity, passion, and vision in this section because organizational visions are intended to create uneasiness with the status quo and help inform and motivate key stakeholders to move the organization forward. Consequently, a vision statement should reflect and communicate something that is relatively novel and unique, and such novelty and uniqueness are the products of creativity and passion.

The creative passion of James Dyson led him to develop the dual cyclone vacuum cleaner, which bears his name.

Source: Keith Homan/ Shutterstock.com

creativity

The generation of new ideas.

passion

An intense, driving, or overmastering feeling or conviction. Passion is also associated with intense emotion compelling action.

Creativity and Vision

DeGraf and Lawrence developed a well-known framework consisting of four types of creativity.[21] They argued that creativity "types" could be clustered based on some combination of individual tendencies toward either flexibility or control and internal or external orientation. For the manager, their typology is especially useful as it suggests ways to manage creativity based on hiring creative individuals with particular creative skill sets. As summarized in the figure, their research suggests that there are four types of creativity: (1) investment (external orientation with high control), (2) imagination (external orientation with flexibility emphasis), (3) improvement (internal orientation with high control), and (4) incubation (internal orientation with flexibility emphasis).

The first type of creativity, *investment*, is associated with speed to market. It is also a form of creativity fostered by the desire to be highly competitive. Examples of this type of creativity are often found in the crowdfunding environment, where companies seek initial funding for first-to-market initiatives such as the development of the Hendo Hoverboard on Kickstarter.[22]

The second type of creativity, *imagination*, is characterized by new ideas and breakthroughs: Apple's stylish design of Macintosh computers and then game-changing breakthroughs with its iPad, iPhone, and Apple Watch are examples of this type of creativity. Oftentimes this type of creativity is associated with a single individual such as Apple's former CEO Steve Jobs. With Jobs' passing, many see Apple at a critical juncture in their attempts to continue to innovate without their historic leader at the helm.[23]

Produced by creative icon Yoshiaki Koizumi (noted Japanese video game designer, director, and producer), the Nintento Switch is considered one of the top ten most innovative products of the last decade.

Source: Wachiwit/Shutterstock.com

Where big ideas come from the imagination quadrant, *improvement* is a type of creativity that involves making an existing idea better. A great example of this is McDonald's Ray Kroc, who joined McDonald's as a franchise agent and then built it into the worldwide corporation it is today, utilizing the founding McDonald brothers' original idea of creating quality and cooking standards for preparing tasty burgers and fries. While there were many other burger restaurants around at the time (the 1950s), Kroc's unique process-oriented approach gave McDonald's a big advantage. The fourth type of creativity is referred to as *incubation*. Incubation is a very deliberate approach that concerns a vision of sustainability—that is, leaving a legacy. This type of creativity is more complex because it involves teamwork, empowerment, and collective action. In their chapter on problem solving, David Whetten and Kim Cameron provide Gandhi as an example of incubation creativity.

While there is no "best" creativity type, each possibility may have some contradictory or conflicting characteristics. For example, imagination and improvement emphasize different approaches to creativity. The size of the new idea, for instance, is typically much bigger with imagination (i.e., revolutionary solutions) than with improvement (i.e., incremental solutions). Investment and incubation also are very different—investment is relatively fast, and the other relatively slow (i.e., incubation emphasizes deliberation and development). Recent research even notes that daydreaming or otherwise "zoning out" at work while dealing with tricky problems can lead to meaningful breakthroughs in creativity.[24]

Creativity Tools

In this section, we introduce two creativity tools: SCAMPER and the Nominal Group Technique. These tools provide resources to develop new ideas either to craft a vision for a new company or to revise an existing mission and vision. The SCAMPER concept can be applied either individually or in groups; Nominal Group Technique is designed to bolster creativity in groups.

These tools help manage two divergent forms of thinking necessary for creativity—programmed thinking and lateral thinking. **Programmed thinking**, often called left-brained thinking, relies on logical or structured ways of creating a new product or service. In terms of mission and vision, this means a logical and deliberate process is used to develop the vision statement. **Lateral thinking** is a term coined by Edward DeBono in his book *The Use of Lateral Thinking* (1967), and it refers to changing patterns and perceptions; it is about ideas that may not be obtainable by using only traditional, step-by-step, programmed logic.[25] Lateral thinking is associated with a more creative approach to thinking and idea generation.

programmed thinking

Thinking that relies on logical or structured ways of creating a new product or service (often called left-brained thinking).

lateral thinking

A thinking process that is about changing patterns and perceptions (often called right-brained thinking).

Each type of approach—programmed versus lateral—has its strength. Logical and disciplined programmed thinking is enormously effective in making products and services better. It can, however, only go so far before all practical improvements have been carried out. Lateral thinking can generate completely new concepts and ideas and brilliant improvements to existing systems. In the wrong place, however, it can be impractical or unnecessarily disruptive.

SCAMPER

Developed by Bob Eberle, **SCAMPER** is a checklist tool that helps individuals think of changes that can be made to an existing marketplace to create a new product, a new service, or both.[26] These changes can be conceptualized either as direct suggestions or as starting points for lateral thinking. Such changes could potentially inspire a new vision statement. It may be some combination of these SCAMPER changes that lead to highly innovative solutions. For instance, the entertainment company Cirque du Soleil has modeled its shows on the traditional circus. However, it has adapted aspects of theater and opera, eliminated animals, and reduced the number of rings from three to one. As a result, it offers a highly stylized (and much more expensive!) version of what, nostalgically, we call a circus today.

Was Cirque du Soleil created using the SCAMPER technique? The world may never know.

Source: Ververidis Vasilis/ Shutterstock.com

SCAMPER

SCAMPER is a checklist tool that helps you to think of changes you can make to an existing marketplace to create a new one: a new product, a new service, or both.

FIGURE 4.3 The SCAMPER Framework

This list illustrates examples of how creativity can be fostered using the SCAMPER framework.

Substitute. What other ingredients, materials, times, or places can be used to create value?

Vegetarians can now enjoy soy versions of bacon cheeseburgers, once considered the sole domain of meat eaters, without any guilt.

Combine. How can products, services, or other elements be combined to create new arrangements?

Based on the two top interests of its founder, Sweets and Spurs is a boutique in Norman, Oklahoma, that caters to locals by selling cupcakes and cowboy boots.

Adapt. How can goods or services be altered to meet new needs?

E.L. James, best-selling British author of Fifty Shades of Grey, originally developed the book's ideas as online episodes of fan fiction based on the popular Twilight books and movies. James later removed the vampires and reworked and extended the plots of these episodes into a new trilogy—now the fastest-selling paperbacks of all time.

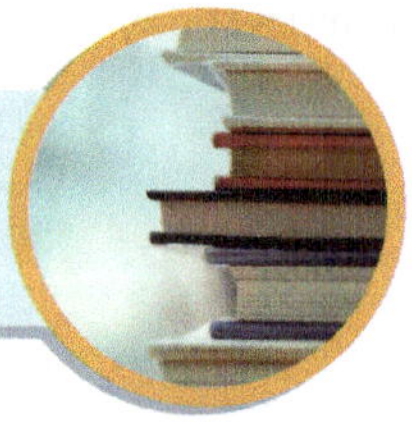

Modify. How can products be magnified, minimized, or otherwise given a different shape?

Perhaps even less likely to melt in your mouth than in your hands, M&Ms have found a new life in their miniature cousins.

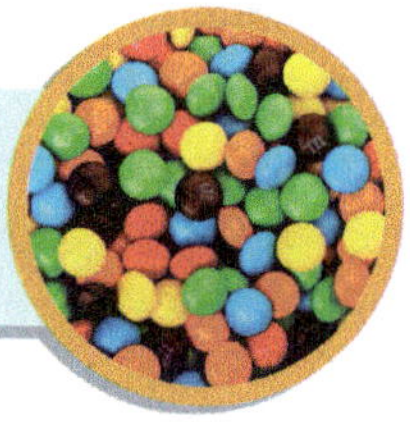

Put to other uses. How can products created for one use be repurposed for another use?

Artists have recently found value in Lego blocks, originally developed for children, as a creative medium.

Eliminate. What can be omitted, deleted, or understated to add value?

Although it lacked apps, the ability to play music, and YouTube access, the cordless phone was an impressive innovation when it first hit the market in the 1980s.

Rearrange. Can other layouts, sequences, or patterns create value for organizations?

The idea of paying first and eating second was likely seen as ridiculous before McDonald's served billions in this manner.

Source: Shutterstock.com, aperture sound_Shutterstock.com, Lewis Tse Pul Lung_Shutterstock.com, Vytdautas Kielaitis_Shutterstock.com

Nominal Group Technique

The **Nominal Group Technique (NGT)** is a method of facilitating a group of people to produce a large number of ideas in a relatively short time period.[27] In addition to using NGT to develop a mission and vision statement, it can be useful:

- to generate numerous creative ideas,
- to ensure everyone is heard,
- when there is concern that some people may not be vocal,
- to build consensus, and
- when there is controversy or conflict.

Nominal Group Technique (NGT)

A method of facilitating a group of people to produce a large number of ideas in a relatively short time period.

As shown in "NGT Preparation and Supplies," preparation and supplies are modest. The technique encourages contributions from everyone by allowing for equal participation among group members. A question is posed to the group. Individually and silently, each participant writes down his or her ideas. In round-robin fashion, each member supplies an idea until all ideas are shared. Generally, 6 to 10 people participate. "Nominal" means that the participants form a group in name only. For most of the session, they do not interact as they would in other group processes.

NGT Preparation and Supplies

Formulate your discussion question. Ensure that the wording prevents misunderstanding and is objective. Supplies needed include the following:

- Flip chart for each table
- Masking tape
- 3 × 5 cards for each participant
- Work tables
- Felt pens

The group is divided into small work groups, each with a leader. A flip chart and markers are needed at each table. Position the flip chart so that all can see the ideas. The remaining simple procedures are summarized in "NGT Procedure."

NGT PROCEDURE

1. Introduction: Briefly welcome participants, clarify the purpose of the group exercise, and explain the procedure to be followed and how results are to be used.
2. Present questions: Only present the question that is written on the chart and clarify as needed.
3. Silent generation of ideas: Each participant silently thinks of and writes down as many ideas as possible on a 3 x 5 card. Allow this for 5 to 10 minutes.
4. Record ideas: In turn, each participant reads aloud one idea, and it is recorded on the flip chart for all to see.
5. Continue until all ideas are recorded.
6. Discourage discussion, not even questions for clarification.
7. Encourage "hitchhiking," or expanding on another's statement. Ideas do not have to be from the participant's written list.
8. Participants may pass a turn and then add an idea at a subsequent turn.
9. Discourage combining ideas from individuals unless they are exactly the same.

10. Group discussion: After all ideas are recorded, give the person who suggested the idea the opportunity to explain it further.
11. Duplicates may be combined.
12. Wording may be changed if the originator agrees.
13. Delete ideas only by unanimous agreement.
14. Restrict the discussion to clarify meaning. Do not discuss the value or merit of ideas.

Passion and Vision

Passion refers to intense, driving, or overmastering feeling or conviction. Passion is also associated with intense emotion-compelling action. Passion is relevant to vision in at least two ways: (1) Passion about an idea as inspiration of the vision and vision statement and (2) shared passion among organizational members about the importance of the vision.

Passion About the Vision

Passion can help the entire business thrive.[28] While there is little academic research on the relationship between passion and vision, studies suggest that fostering engagement, a concept related to passion, in employees has a significant effect on the corporate bottom line. Gallup, for instance, has been on the forefront of measuring the effect of what it calls employee engagement. Employee engagement is a concept that is generally viewed as managing discretionary effort; that is, when employees have choices, they will act in a way that furthers their organization's interests. Engaged employees are dedicated, passionate, and absorbed in their work.[29] The consulting firm BlessingWhite offers this description of engagement and its value (and clear relationship with passion): "Engaged employees are not just committed. They are not just passionate or proud. They have a line-of-sight on their own future and on the organization's mission and goals. They are 'enthused' and 'in gear' using their talents and discretionary effort to make a difference in their employer's quest for sustainable business success."[30]

Engaged employees are those who are performing at the top of their abilities and happy about it. According to statistics that Gallup has drawn from 300,000 companies in its database, 75%–80% of employees are either "disengaged" or "actively disengaged."[31] Disengagement from a strategic human resource perspective is an enormous waste of potential. Consider Gallup's estimation of the impact if 100% of an organization's employees were fully engaged:

- Customers would be 70% more loyal.
- Turnover would drop by 70%.
- Profits would jump by 40%.

Job satisfaction studies in the United States routinely show job satisfaction ratings of 50%–60%. But one recent study by Harris Interactive of nearly 8,000 American workers went a step further.[32] What did the researchers find?

- Only 20% feel very passionate about their jobs.
- Fewer than 15% agree that they feel strongly energized by their work.
- Only 31% (strongly or moderately) believe that their employer inspires the best in them.

Consciously creating an environment where passion is both encouraged and actively developed can yield an enormous competitive advantage. That environment starts at the top through the development and active communication of mission and vision. Consistency in passion is important as research has found that differences in passion among new venture team member can result in worse business plan quality, team dynamics, and ability to raise funds.[33]

Key Takeaway

Creativity relates to the power or ability to create, and passion is intense emotion compelling action. Creativity is important if the desired mission and vision are to be novel and entrepreneurial; passion is important both from the standpoint of adding energy to the mission and vision and to key stakeholders following the mission and vision.

Discussion Questions

1. Think about a time when you have been especially creative. What factors do you think helped contribute to your creativity?
2. Why is creativity relevant to vision and vision statements?
3. What are some useful creativity tools?
4. What is passion, and how is passion relevant to vision and vision statements?
5. What is the relationship between passion and engagement?

4.4 Stakeholders

Learning Objectives

1. Learn about stakeholders and their importance.
2. Understand stakeholder analysis.
3. Learn how to map stakeholders and their level of participation.

Stakeholders and Stakeholder Analysis

Stakeholders are individuals or groups who have an interest in an organization's goods and services. A number of factors impact the degree to which various stakeholders may influence an organization. Influence reflects a stakeholder's relative power over an organization's actions; importance indicates the degree to which the organization cannot be considered successful if a stakeholder's needs, expectations, and issues are not addressed.

The American Federation of Labor and Congress of Industrial Organizations (AFL–CIO) is a powerful stakeholder as a federation of unions that represented over 12.5 million workers in 2021.

Source: Mark Van Scyoc/ Shutterstock.com

One key stakeholder group comprises the CEO and the members of the top-management team. Top managers, who often have considerable ownership in a company, are important because they serve to either originate or help implement a firm's mission and vision.

Stakeholder evaluation of quantitative and qualitative performance outcomes may help in determining if management is effective in their accomplishing a firm's mission and vision. Quantitative outcomes include stock price, total sales, and net profits, while qualitative outcomes include customer service and employee satisfaction. Naturally, different stakeholders may place more emphasis on some outcomes than other stakeholders, who often have different priorities.

Stakeholders, Mission, and Vision

"Stakeholders for a Cohesive and Sustainable World" was the 2020 theme for the World Economic Forum where over 3,000 global leaders convened to explore "stakeholder capitalism."

Source: Drop of Light/ Shutterstock.com

stakeholder analysis

The range of techniques or tools used to identify and to understand the needs and expectations of major interests inside and outside the organization environment.

Stakeholder analysis refers to the range of techniques or tools used to identify and understand the needs and expectations of major interests inside and outside the organization environment. Managers perform stakeholder analysis to gain a better understanding of the range and variety of groups and individuals who have a vested interest in the organization and its performance. Managers thus develop mission and vision statements to clarify the organization's larger purpose and to meet or exceed the needs of its key stakeholders.

Stakeholder analysis may also enable managers to identify other parties that might derail otherwise well-formulated strategies, such as local, state, national, or foreign governmental bodies. Stakeholder analysis also enables organizations to better formulate, implement, and monitor their strategies. Consequently, stakeholder analysis is a critical factor in the ultimate implementation of a strategy.

Identifying Stakeholders

The first step in stakeholder analysis is identifying major stakeholder groups. The groups of stakeholders who will, either directly or indirectly, be affected by or have an effect on a firm's strategy and its execution can run the gamut from employees, to customers, to competitors, to the government. Some organizations find value in identifying stakeholders and plotting them on a chart, similar to that shown in Figure 4.4.

FIGURE 4.4 Stakeholder Mapping

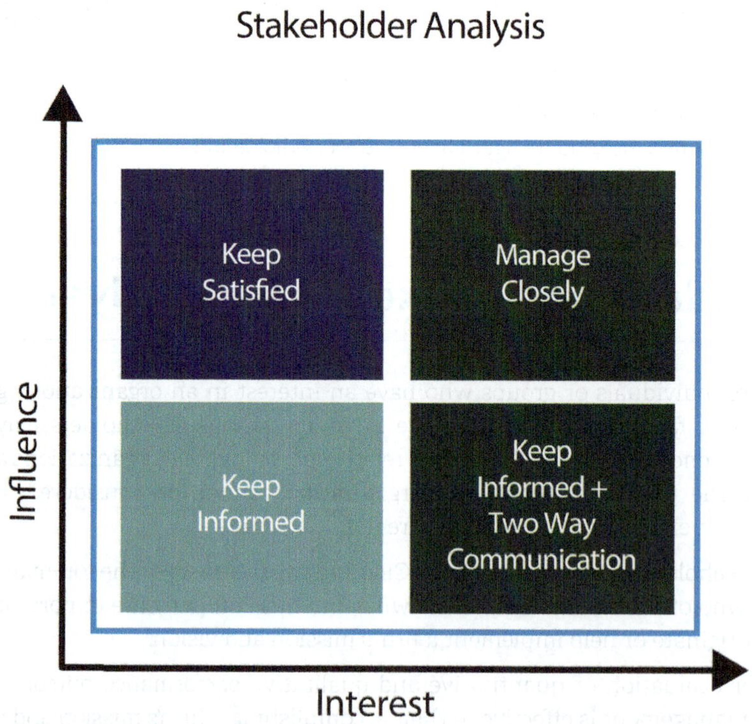

Stakeholders can be individuals or groups—communities, social or political organizations, and anyone with a claim on the organization's actions and outcomes. Groups can be broken down demographically, geographically, by level and branch of government, or according to other relevant criteria. A map of stakeholders should include such diverse groups as governmental bodies, community-based organizations, social and political action groups, trade unions and guilds, and even interested media. National and regional governments and international regulatory bodies often serve as key stakeholders for global firms or those whose strategy calls for greater international presence. Internally, key stakeholders include shareholders, business units, employees, and managers.

Steps in Identifying Stakeholders

Identifying all relevant stakeholders can be a daunting task. A list of stakeholders that is too long may reduce the effectiveness of this important tool by overwhelming decision makers with too much information. Here, we illustrate three key steps in stakeholder analysis with the goal of identifying a manageable number of the most critical stakeholders.

Step 1: Determining Influences on Mission, Vision, and Strategy Formulation. One way to analyze the importance and roles of the individuals who compose a stakeholder group is to identify the individuals and groups who should be consulted when developing or implementing a firm's strategy. These are *organizational stakeholders*, and they include all types of employees, ranging from top managers to frontline workers. *Capital-market stakeholders* are groups that affect the availability or cost of capital, that is, sources of money that fund the firm, and they include shareholders, venture capitalists, banks, and other financial intermediaries. *Product-market stakeholders* include parties with whom the firm shares its industry, including suppliers and customers. Social stakeholders consist broadly of external groups and organizations that may be affected by or exercise influence over firm strategy and performance, such as unions, governments, and activist groups.

The next two steps in the stakeholder identification process involve determining how various stakeholders are affected by the firm's strategic decisions and the degree of power that various stakeholders wield over the firm's ability to choose a course of action.

Step 2: Determining the Effects of Key Decisions on the Stakeholder. Step two in stakeholder analysis is to determine the nature of the effect of the firm's strategic decisions on the list of relevant stakeholders. Not all stakeholders are affected equally by strategic decisions. Some effects may be rather mild, and any positive or negative effects may be secondary and of minimal impact. At the other end of the spectrum, some stakeholders bear the brunt of firm decisions, good or bad.

In performing step two, determine the stakeholders who are most important based on how the firm's strategy affects the stakeholders. Managers must then determine which of the groups or individuals still on their list have direct or indirect material claims on firm performance or which are potentially adversely affected. For instance, shareholders are affected by firm strategies directly because their wealth either increases or decreases in correspondence with the firm's actions and stock performance. Other parties have economic interests in the firm as well, such as parties the firm interacts with in the marketplace, including suppliers and customers. The effects on other parties may be much more indirect. For instance, governments have an economic interest in firms doing well because they act as valuable sources of tax revenue. However, in cities that are well diversified with many employers, a single firm has minimal economic impact on what the government collects. Alternatively, in other areas, individual firms represent a significant contribution to local employment and tax revenue. In those situations, the effect of the firm's actions on the government would be much greater.

Step 3: Determining Stakeholders' Power and Influence over Decisions. The third step of a stakeholder analysis is to determine the degree to which a stakeholder group can exercise power and influence over the decisions the firm makes. Does the group have direct control over what is decided, veto power over decisions, nuisance influence, or no influence? Recognize that although the degree to which a stakeholder is affected by firm decisions is sometimes highly correlated with their power and influence over the decision, this is often not the case. For instance, in some companies, frontline employees may be directly affected by firm decisions but have no say in what those decisions are. Power can take the form of formal voting power (boards of directors and owners), economic power (suppliers, financial institutions, and unions), or political power (dissident stockholders, political action groups, and governmental bodies). Sometimes parties that exercise significant power over firm decisions do not register as having a significant stake in the firm. In recent years, for example, Walmart has encountered significant resistance in some communities by well-organized groups who oppose the entry of the megaretailer. Walmart executives now anticipate whether a vocal and politically powerful community group will oppose its new stores or aim to reduce their size, which decreases Walmart's per store profitability. Indeed, in many markets, such groups have been effective at blocking new stores, reducing their size, or changing building specifications. For example, the mayor of Beech Grove, Indiana has worked to have Walmart declared a public nuisance due to the cost of local police resources involved in response to events at a local Walmart.[34]

Identifying stakeholder groups and differentiating them based on how they are affected by firm decisions and the power they have to influence decisions may prompt additional questions:

- Are there any vulnerable points in either the firm's strategy or its potential implementation based on the impact of overlooked stakeholders?
- Which groups are mobilized and active in promoting their interests?
- Which groups will benefit from successful execution of the firm's strategy and which may be adversely affected?
- Where are various groups located? Who belongs to them? Who represents them?

Key Takeaway

This section introduced stakeholders, their roles, and how to assess their roles in the development of the organization's mission and vision. While any person or group with a stake in the organization is a stakeholder, managers are most concerned with those stakeholders who have the most influence on, or will be most influenced by, the organization. On the basis of your assessment of stakeholders, managers can be proactive in involving them in the P-O-L-C stages.

Discussion Questions

1. What are stakeholders, and why are they relevant to mission and vision?
2. Are stakeholders equally relevant to all parts of P-O-L-C, or only mission and vision?
3. What is stakeholder analysis? What are the three identification steps?
4. How does stakeholder analysis help in crafting a mission and vision statement?
5. Which important stakeholders might managers intentionally exclude from a mission or vision statement?
6. What are the risks of not conducting stakeholder analysis as an input to the formulation of mission and vision?

4.5 Developing Your Personal Mission and Vision

Learning Objectives

1. Determine what mission and vision mean for individuals.
2. Understand guidelines for developing a personal mission and vision.

Mission and vision are concepts that can be applied to individuals, personally, beyond their broader relevance to the P-O-L-C framework. Personal mission and vision provide some explanations for why individuals choose one career or set of goals over others. Thinking about and articulating mission and vision statements with regard to life plans and goals can help provide individuals with a compass that effectively directs personal objectives.

Individual Mission and Vision

The development of a personal mission and vision may be uncommon in a world where many individuals exert considerable time looking ahead to their next activity rather than reflecting on long-term career prospects. Instead, some career experts recommend that individuals should consider computing "career math" that begins by taking the age 62 (a common retirement age) and subtracting your current age.[35] This number reveals one potential number of future years of employment from a long-term perspective. Advocates of this approach suggest that individuals can then decide where they want to end up and ponder what steps could lead to the final career path and other desired outcomes. In that way, life plans and your career goals fit into an intelligent plan where individuals navigate their future from a long-term perspective.

Elon Musk embraces the personal mission statement, "If something is important enough you should try, even if the probable outcome is failure."

Source: lookus/Shutterstock.com

Guidelines

The first step in planning a career is establishing a long-term goal. Where do you want to end up, ultimately? Considerable tradeoffs in lifestyle choice exists when comparing a CEO or top executive of a large, publicly-traded company to the possibilities of working in a small firm.

BHAG

Ford Motor Company's goals of democratizing the automobile is a commonly cited example of a BHAG.

Source: overcrew/Shutterstock.com

BHAG

A big, hairy, audacious goal.

In some cases, career management can be propelled by the establishment of "stretch" goals. Jim Collins, author of *Good to Great*, describes a **BHAG**: a big, hairy, audacious goal.

There are five guiding criteria for good BHAGs that complement career goals.

1. They should be set with understanding, not bravado.
2. They should complement (a) what you are deeply passionate about (including your core values and purpose), (b) what drives your economic logic, and (c) what differentiates you (what you can be the best in the world at).
3. They should have a long timeframe—10 to 30 years.
4. They should be clear, compelling, and easy to grasp.
5. They should reflect your core values and core purpose.

Values

A well-crafted personal mission and vision should be informed by personal values, or a "Guiding Philosophy"—a set of core values and principles. Examples of core values include qualities such as diligence, creativity, or impact.[36]

Schedule

One challenging aspect of implementing a long-term goal is the establishment of more intermediate-term goals. If someone wanted to be president, what jobs should they take first and when should they aspire to begin such jobs? How does location and training play a role in the achievement of personal goals? What political connections are needed? An orderly plan for obtaining the connections and training needed and acquiring needed steppingstone jobs is necessary to put one in a position to reach more long-term aspirations.

The establishment of short-term goals should fit clearly into a coherent plan for a longer entire career. A job should be selected not only for its salary or for its opportunities for advancement but for its chances to provide training and connections to reach long-term goals. The job that is superficially attractive to you because it has a high salary, offers the opportunity for immediate advancement, or is located in a desirable place may be a mistake from a long-term career perspective in some cases. Following thoughtful steps can help identify core mission statement and values.

Step 1: Identify Past Successes. Spend some time identifying four or five examples where you have had personal success in recent years. These successes could be at work, in your community, or at home. Try to identify whether there is a common theme—or themes—to these examples. Write them down.

Step 2: Identify Core Values. Develop a list of attributes that you believe identify who you are and what your priorities are. The list can be as long as you need. Once your list is complete, see whether you can narrow your values to five or six most important values. Finally, see whether you can choose the one value that is most important to you. We've added "Generating Ideas for Your Mission and Vision" to help jog your memory and brainstorm about what you do well and really like to do.

Step 3: Make a list of the ways you could make a difference. In an ideal situation, think about how you could contribute best to

- the world in general,
- your family,

- your employer or future employers,
- your friends, and
- your community.

Generating Ideas for Your Mission and Vision

A useful mission and vision statement should include two pieces: what you wish to accomplish and contribute and who you want to be, the character strengths and qualities you wish to develop. Those pieces of information are not always obvious and may require time and reflection to articulate in meaningful ways. Try these tools for generating valuable information about yourself.

Part 1

1. Describe your ideal day. This is not about being practical. It is designed to include as many sides of you and your enthusiasms as possible: creative, competent, artistic, introverted, extraverted, athletic, playful, nurturing, contemplative, and so on.
2. Imagine yourself 132 years old and surrounded by your descendants or the descendants of your friends. You are in a warm and relaxed atmosphere (such as around a fireplace). What would you say to them about what is important in life? This exercise is designed to access the values and principles that guide your life.
3. Imagine that it is your 70th birthday (or another milestone in your life). You have been asked to write a press release about your achievements. Consider what you would want your family, friends, coworkers in your profession and in your community to say about you. What difference would you like to have made in their lives? How do you want to be remembered?

Part 2

Review your notes for these three exercises. With those responses in mind, reflect on questions 1, 2, and 3 above. Then write a rough draft (a page of any length) of your mission statement. Remember that it should describe what you want to do and who you want to be. This is not a job description. Carry it with you, post copies in visible places at home and work, and revise and evaluate. Be patient with yourself. The process is as important as the outcome. After a few weeks, write another draft. Ask yourself whether your statement was based on proven principles that you believe in, if you feel direction, motivation, and inspiration when you read it. Over time, reviewing and evaluating will keep you abreast of your own development.

Step 4: Identify Goals. Spend some time thinking about your priorities in life and the goals you have for yourself. Make a list of your personal goals, perhaps in the short term (up to three years) and the long term (beyond three years).

Step 5: Write Mission and Vision Statements. On the basis of the first four steps and a better understanding of yourself, begin writing your personal mission and vision statements.

Here are some final thoughts: A personal mission and vision statement is, of course, personal. But if you want to see whether you have been honest in developing your personal mission and vision statement, we suggest sharing the results of this process with one or more people who are close to you. Ask for their feedback. Finally, remember that mission and vision statements are not meant to be written once and blasted into stone. You should set aside some time annually to review your career, job, goals, and mission and vision statements—and make adjustments as necessary.

Key Takeaway

Mission and vision can be applied in terms of personal circumstances relevant to career management. Just as you might do in developing an organization's vision statement, you were encouraged to think of personal goals as a starting point. You also learned some ideas for developing a personal vision statement.

Discussion Questions

1. How does a personal mission and vision statement differ from one created for an organization?
2. What time period should a personal mission and vision statement cover?
3. What type of goals should you start thinking about in creating a personal mission and vision?
4. How are personal strengths and weaknesses relevant to mission and vision?
5. What stakeholders seem relevant to personal mission and vision?

4.6 Case in Point: Motivated Employees at Patagonia

Source: Sundry Photography/Shutterstock.com

Patagonia was founded in 1973 by Yvon Chouinard, a passionate outdoorsman who wanted to design clothing and gear inspired by his love of the outdoors. Since then, the company has grown to over 2,000 employees and several hundred million dollars in annual revenue. Patagonia specializes in durable, high-end gear for surfers, climbers, skiers, and runners. It is a privately held benefit corporation, which means its board is not accountable to public shareholders.

According to Chouinard, Patagonia intentionally hires people who are highly self-motivated to enable the company to encourage employee autonomy and maintain a relatively flat structure. The founder says, "I hate the idea of managing people. I don't like people telling me what to do, so I can't stand to tell other people what to do." He even wrote a book called *Let My People Go Surfing,* which provides an overview of the company's unique history and philosophy, which is now used for employee onboarding purposes.

According to Patagonia's Chief Human Resources Officer, Dean Carter, "There's just no reference for reporting relationships or traditional hierarchies. As a matter of fact, we like breaking them because, often, the best ideas aren't from the manager; they're from the person whose hands are dirty doing the real work." The company embraces the philosophy that the manager should be more of a mentor than a boss. To drive home this point, the company did away with the traditional annual performance ratings so employees don't feel like their managers are constantly judging them.

Patagonia is also known for providing exceptional benefits and perks, including a subsidized café, onsite childcare for employees (introduced in 1981—well before most companies), and flexible scheduling. The company provides childcare as a service to its employees but also treats it as an opportunity to groom future leaders by encouraging socialization and instilling confidence at a young age. As for the flexible work policy, according to Carter, people are allowed to take whatever time they need as long as they are getting their work done. He says, "People are encouraged to live the lives they want and do what they need to do, whether that's horseback riding, surfing, or seeing their kids play. If we're hiring independent people who care about the environment and the outdoors, we certainly can't have a culture that doesn't allow them to do those things." This value is also reflected in the company's policy discouraging lunchtime meetings so employees can practice yoga or go running. Patagonia even promised to keep employees on the payroll during coronavirus-related store closures in 2020, further highlighting the value the organization places on its employees.

The company is able to support this level of autonomy and flexibility by hiring strategically. They take their time to find the right candidate for each position, prioritizing characteristics like independence, passion, and ambition. Then they provide new hires with an immersive orientation and onboarding process, with significant access to senior leadership.

Patagonia's nontraditional approach to employee engagement and company culture seems to be paying off. Employee turnover is very low at 4%, and 100% of women who have taken maternity leave from the company have returned to work. The company is also in a strong financial position. According to Carter, "We're experiencing double-digit growth, despite our desire to control growth, at a time when most retailers and wholesalers are reeling, and even though 1% of our top-line sales are going to the environment."[37]

Multimedia Extension—Patagonia Supports Paid Leave

View in the online reader

Case Discussion Questions

1. What are some of the things that make Patagonia a unique workplace? Do you think these contribute to employee motivation?
2. Would you like to work for a company that gave you as much autonomy as Patagonia gives its employees? Why or why not?
3. Do you think Patagonia's company culture contributes to a positive work/life balance for its employees? How might this relate to motivation?
4. Do you think Patagonia has enjoyed so much success due to its unique company culture, or despite it? Explain.
5. Of all the employee perks that Patagonia offers, which ones would be the most motivating for you? Why?

Endnotes

1. Retrieved from https://www.fond.co/blog/best-mission-statements/.
2. Retrieved from https://www.simplemarketingnow.com/blog/flooring-the-consumer/bid/168520/what-great-brands-do-with-mission-statements-8-examples#airbnb.
3. Retrieved from http://www.patagonia.com/us/patagonia.go?assetid=2047.
4. Rigby, D., & Bilodeau, B. (2011). Management tools & trends 2011. Retrieved from http://www.bain.com/Images/BAIN_BRIEF_Management_Tools.pdf.
5. Bart, C. K., Bontis, N., & Taggar, S. (2001). A model of the impact of mission statements on firm performance. *Management Decision, 39*(1), 19–35.
6. Retrieved from http://www.starbucks.com/aboutus.
7. Retrieved from http://www.walmart.com.
8. Retrieved from http://www.forbes.com/sites/patrickhull/2012/12/19/be-visionary-think-big/.
9. Retrieved from https://www.forbes.com/sites/joefolkman/2014/04/22/8-ways-to-ensure-your-vision-is-valued/#143e78704524.
10. Hamel, G., & Prahalad, C. K. (1993, March–April). Strategy as stretch and leverage. *Harvard Business Review*, 75–84.
11. Retrieved from http://www.pixar.com/companyinfo/about_us/overview.htm.
12. Catmull, E. (2008, September). How Pixar fosters collective creativity. *Harvard Business Review*, 1–11.
13. Retrieved from http://www.bloomberg.com/bw/articles/2013-03-07/how-disney-bought-lucasfilm-and-its-plans-for-star-wars.
14. Retrieved from https://www.theverge.com/2020/9/15/21378084/mandalorian-season-2-trailer-baby-yoda-premiere-date-october.
15. Retrieved from http://www.cnbc.com/2015/08/15/star-wars-themed-land-at-planned-at-disney-parks.html.
16. Lafley, A. G., & Charan, R. (2008). *The game changer*. Upper Saddle River, NJ: Crown Books.
17. Brown, B. (2010, November/December). Why innovation matters. *Research Technology Management, 53*, 18–23.
18. Retrieved from http://www.fastcompany.com/3026791/dialed/personal-mission-statements-of-5-famous-ceos-and-why-you-should-write-one-too#2.
19. Gerhart, B. A., & Rynes, S. L. (2003). *Compensation:Compensation: Theory, evidence, and strategic implications*. Thousand Oaks, CA: Sage.
20. Retrieved from http://www.theguardian.com/media-network/media-network-blog/2014/jan/17/3-myths-creativity-in-business.
21. DeGraf, J., & Lawrence, K. A. (2002). *Creativity at Work: Developing the Right Practices to Make It Happen*. San Francisco: Jossey-Bass.
22. Retrieved from https://www.kickstarter.com/projects/142464853/hendo-hoverboards-worlds-first-real-hoverboard.
23. Retrieved from http://www.npr.org/sections/thetwo-way/2014/12/02/368037131/apple-s-success-continues-under-tim-cook-but-steve-jobs-still-looms-large.
24. Baer, M., Dane, E., & Madrid, H. (2020). Zoning out or breaking through? Linking daydreaming to creativity in the workplace. *Academy of Management Journal,* https://doi.org/10.5465/amj.2017.1283
25. De Bono, E. (1992). *Serious creativity*. New York: Harper Business; Osborn, A. (1953). *Applied imagination*. New York: Scribner's.
26. Eberle, R. (1997). *Scamper: Creative games and activities for imagination development*. New York: Prufrock Press.
27. This section is reproduced with permission of the University of Wisconsin Extension Program. A circulation version can be found at http://www.uwex.edu/ces/pdande/resources/pdf/Tipsheet3.pdf. Additional information on NGT can be gained by reading the following: Delbecq, A., Van de Ven, A., & Gustafson, D. (1975). *Group techniques for program planning: A guide to nominal group and Delphi processes*. Glenview, IL: Scott, Foresman; Tague, N. (1995). *The quality toolbox*. Milwaukee, WI: ASQC Quality Press; Witkin, B., & Altschuld, J. (1995). *Planning and conducting needs assessment: A practical guide*. Thousand Oaks, CA: Sage.
28. Retrieved from http://www.virgin.com/entrepreneur/richard-branson-the-importance-of-passion-in-business.
29. Crawford, E. R., LePine, J. A., & Rich, B. L. (2010). Linking job demands and resources to employee engagement and burnout: A theoretical extension and meta-analytic test. *Journal of Applied Psychology, 95*, 834–848.
30. BlessingWhite. (2008, April). 2008 employee engagement report. Retrieved from http://www.blessingwhite.com/eee__report.asp.
31. Retrieved from http://gmj.gallup.com/content/24880/Gallup-Study-Engaged-Employees-Inspire-Company.aspx.
32. Retrieved from http://www.agewave.com/media_files/rough.html.
33. Mol, E., Cardon, M., & Khapova, S.N. (2020). When Entrepreneurial Passion Backfires. *Harvard Business Review*. Retrieved from https://hbr.org/2020/02/when-entrepreneurial-passion-backfires.
34. Retrieved from http://www.foxbusiness.com/industries/2015/08/17/indiana-mayor-deems-local-walmart-public-nuisance/.
35. Retrieved from http://www.fastcocreate.com/3027499/career-rocket-fuel-whether-youre-a-millennial-or-eyeing-retirement-heres-what-you-really-nee.
36. Retrieved from http://www.inc.com/kevin-daum/define-your-personal-core-values-5-steps.html.
37. Case written by Rachel Mattenberger, Talya Bauer, and Berrin Erdogan to accompany Bauer, T.N. & Erdogan, B. (2021). *Organizational Behavior: Bridging Science and Practice (4.0)*. Boston, MA: FlatWorld. Partially based on ideas and information contained in Welch, L. (2013). The way I work: Yvon Chouinard, Patagonia. https://www.inc.com/magazine/201303/liz-welch/the-way-i-work-yvon-chouinard-patagonia.html; Margolin, K. (2017). How Patagonia's unique leadership structure enabled them to thrive. https://www.virgin.com/entrepreneur/how-patagonias-unique-leadership-structure-enabled-them-thrive.; Yakowicz, W. (2020, March 16). At billionaire-owned Patagonia outdoor clothing chain, employees to be paid despite store closures amid coronavirus. Forbes. Retrieved from https://www.forbes.com/sites/willyakowicz/2020/03/16/at-billionaire-owned-patagonia-outdoor-clothing-chain-employees-to-be-paid-despite-store-closures-amid-coronavirus/#2441d487edd0; Rock, D. (2020, January 9). The NLI interview: Patagonia's Dean Carter on how to treat employees like people. Forbes. Retrieved from https://www.forbes.com/sites/davidrock/2020/01/09/the-nli-interview-patagonias-dean-carter-on-how-to-treat-employees-like-people/#38e395c3188c.

CHAPTER 5
Strategic Management

Apple's strategy has enabled the company to capture the hearts and minds of music lovers worldwide through consistent innovations such as Apple Music and AirPods.

Source: Shutterstock.com

Chapter Learning Objectives

Reading this chapter will help you accomplish the following:

1. See how strategy fits in the planning-organizing-leading-controlling (P-O-L-C) framework.
2. Better understand how strategies emerge.
3. Understand strategy as trade-offs, discipline, and focus.
4. Conduct internal analysis to develop strategy.
5. Conduct external analysis to develop strategy.
6. Formulate organizational and personal strategy with the strategy diamond.

Strategic management relates to choices managers make to achieve specific goals and objectives that fulfill a firm's mission and vision in a quest to attain long-term organizational performance. Strategy is a central part of the planning function in P-O-L-C. Wise managers make choices that provide organizations with some measure of uniqueness that allows them to outperform competitors. The central position of strategy is summarized in Table 5.1. This chapter focuses on elements of strategy formulation and some of the key internal and external analyses that support the development of superior strategies. We also highlight how the concept of strategy can be applied to individuals personally and professionally.

TABLE 5.1 The P-O-L-C Framework

Planning	Organizing	Leading	Controlling
1. Vision & Mission	1. Organization Design	1. Leadership	1. Systems/Processes
2. Strategizing	2. Culture	2. Decision Making	2. Strategic Human Resources
3. Goals & Objectives	3. Social Networks	3. Communications	
		4. Groups/Teams	
		5. Motivation	

5.1 Strategic Management in the P-O-L-C Framework

Learning Objectives

1. Define strategic management.
2. Understand how strategic management fits in the P-O-L-C framework.
3. Understand the value of SWOT analysis.
4. Understand the concept of PESTEL analysis.

What Is Strategic Management?

strategy formulation

Synonymous with business planning and strategic planning. The set of processes involved in creating or determining the strategies of the organization; it focuses on the content of strategies.

strategy implementation

The methods by which strategies are operationalized or executed within the organization; it focuses on the processes through which strategies are achieved.

Strategic management reflects the firm's actions to achieve its mission and vision as seen by its achievement of specific goals and objectives. Stated differently, "strategic management examines how actions and events involving top executives (such as Apple's Tim Cook), firms (Apple), and industries (the tablet market) influence a firm's success or failure."[1] The strategic management process involves understanding a firm's strategy, scanning the external and internal environments for changes, formulating strategy, and finally, implementing strategy.[2] Others have described strategy as the pattern of resource allocation choices and organizational arrangements that result from managerial decision making.[3] Planning and **strategy formulation**, sometimes called *business planning* or *strategic planning*, have much in common, since formulation helps determine what the firm should do. **Strategy implementation** tells managers how they should go about putting the desired strategy into action. The concept of strategy is relevant to all types of organizations, from large, public corporations, to not-for-profit organizations, religious organizations, and political parties.

Strategic Management in the P-O-L-C Framework

Figure 5.1 summarizes where strategy formulation and implementation fit in the planning and other components of P-O-L-C. Strategic management is historically associated with the concept of business planning, and the idea of planning remains relevant today. For example, the desire to craft excellent business plans is still a key area of concern for managers and entrepreneurs.[4]

FIGURE 5.1 Strategic Management in P-O-L-C

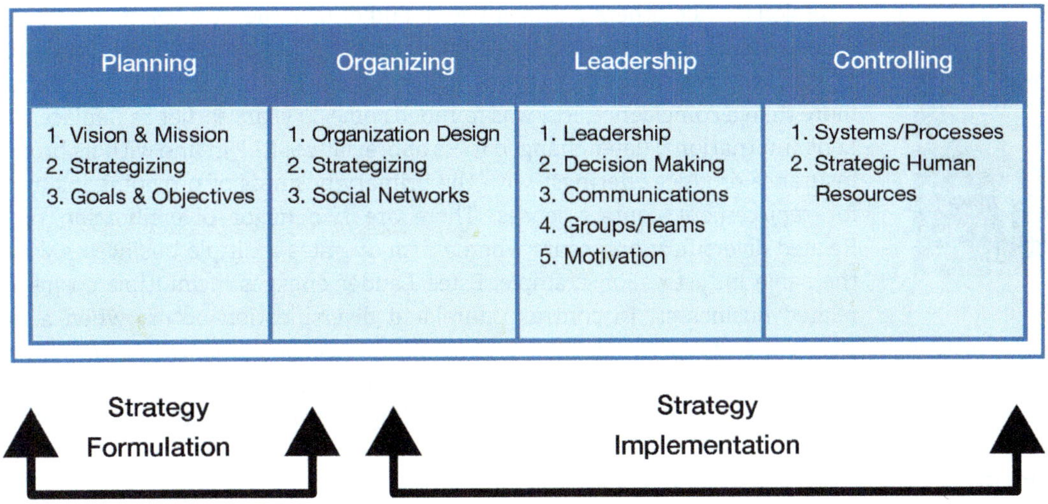

Planning begins with vision and mission and concludes with setting more specific goals and objectives. A specific strategy captures and communicates how vision and mission will be achieved and the goals and objectives that will be measured to assure that the organization is on the right path to achieving their vision and mission.

There are two aspects of strategic management for most organizations. The first, **corporate strategy**, answers strategy questions related to "What business or businesses should we be in?" and "How does our business X help us compete in business Y?" Corporate strategy considers an organization to be a portfolio of businesses, resources, capabilities, or activities. For example, McDonald's is well known for their golden arches, associated exclusively with their restaurants worldwide. McDonald's also had a majority stake in Mexican food restaurant Chipotle for several years as well.[5] McDonald's corporate strategy helped its managers evaluate and answer questions about whether it made sense for McDonald's set of businesses to include different restaurants such as McDonald's and Chipotle. While other food-service companies have multiple outlets—YUM! Brands, for example, owns Taco Bell, Pizza Hut, and KFC—McDonald's determined that one brand (McDonald's) was a better strategy for it in the future and sold Chipotle in 2006. Figure 5.2 provides a graphic guide to this kind of planning.

corporate strategy

The set of strategic alternatives that an organization chooses from as it manages its operations simultaneously across several industries and several markets.

The logic behind corporate strategy involves the concepts of synergy and diversification. **Synergy** exists when the interaction of two or more activities, such as those in a business, create a combined effect greater than the sum of their individual effects. For example, synergy arises when each of the YUM! Brands' food outlets performs better because they have common ownership and can share valuable inputs into their businesses. The idea is that the combination of certain businesses is stronger than they would be individually because they either do things more cheaply or of higher quality as a result of their coordination under a common owner.

synergy

The interaction of two or more activities, creating a combined effect greater than the sum of their individual efforts.

Synergy is evident in YUM! Brands' practice of sharing a physical location between two of their restaurant concepts like the combination of Taco Bell and Pizza Hut pictured here.

Source: Idealphotographer/Shutterstock.com

diversification

The number of different businesses that an organization is engaged in and the extent to which these businesses are related to one another.

Diversification exists when an organization participates in multiple businesses that are in some way distinct from each other, as Taco Bell is from Pizza Hut, for instance. Just as with a portfolio of stock, the purpose of diversification is to spread out risk and opportunities over a larger set of businesses. Some may be high growth, some slow growth or declining; some may perform worse during recessions, while others perform better. Sometimes the businesses can be very different, such as when fashion sunglass maker Maui Jim diversified into property and casualty insurance through its merger with RLI Corporation.[6] Perhaps more than a coincidence, RLI was founded some 60 years earlier as Replacement Lens International (later changed to its abbreviation, RLI, in line with its broader insurance product offerings), with the primary business of providing insurance for replacement contact lenses. There are two major diversification types. Related diversification occurs when a firm operates multiple businesses within the same industry. For example, Estée Lauder engages in multiple cosmetics-related businesses. In contrast, unrelated diversification occurs when a firm engages in businesses in different industries that lack similarities between each other. Warren Buffett's company, Berkshire Hathaway, engages in various businesses with little similarities to each other, such as GEICO, Fruit of the Loom, Justin Brands, Burlington Northern, and See's Candies.

FIGURE 5.2 Corporate and Business Strategy

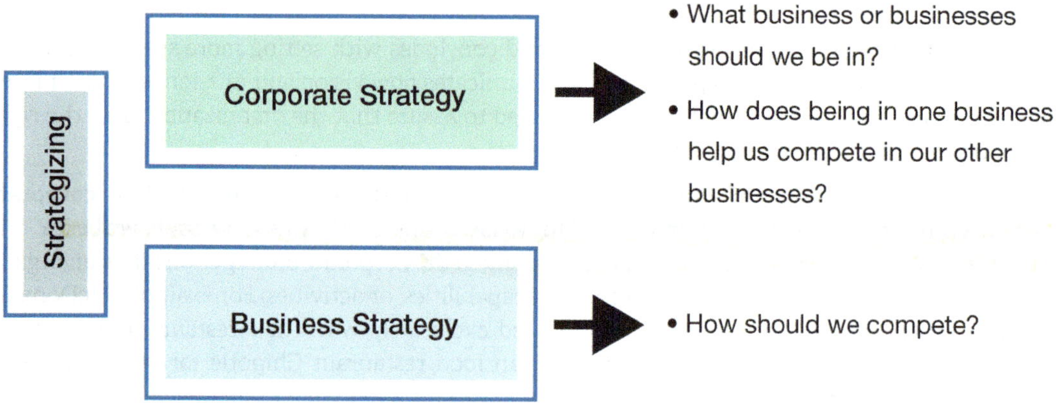

Installation of a food locker following Amazon's acquisition of Whole Foods in 2017 provides an example of corporate diversification leading to synergy.

Source: Sundry Photography/Shutterstock.com

business strategy

The set of strategic alternatives that an organization chooses from as it conducts business in a particular industry or market.

Whereas corporate strategy looks at an organization as a portfolio, **business strategy** focuses on how a given business needs to compete to be effective. All organizations need strategies to survive and thrive. A neighborhood church, for instance, may want to serve existing members, build new membership, and, at the same time, raise surplus monies to help with outreach activities that fulfill their mission. Its strategy would answer questions surrounding the accomplishment of these key objectives. In a for-profit company such as McDonald's, business strategy would help keep existing customers, grow its business by moving into new markets and taking customers from competitors like Taco Bell and Burger King, and do all this at a profit level demanded by the stock market as a publicly traded corporation.

FIGURE 5.3 The Sweet Fragrance of Success: The Brands That "Make Up" the Lauder Empire

Estée Lauder was a pioneer in the cosmetics industry. Estée Lauder summarized her zest for business by noting, "I have never worked a day in my life without selling. If I believe in something, I sell it hard." The company that bears her name has used related diversification and other growth strategies to create over two dozen brands of cosmetics, perfume, skin care, and hair care products. Here we illustrate some of the products that make up the Lauder empire.

Smashbox, acquired in 2010, is the cosmetics line of a premier photo studio founded by the great grandsons of Hollywood cosmetics legend Max Factor.

M*A*C (Makeup Art Cosmetics) products were originally designed for professional makeup artists but are now available to consumers worldwide.

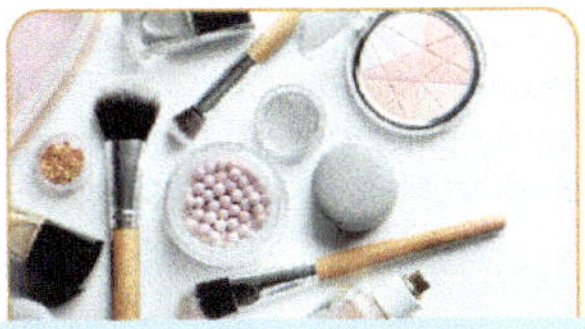

Prescriptives offers customizable cosmetics that provide an exact match to the customer's skin tone.

The Lauder empire includes a number of license agreements such as with Donna Karan's **DKNY** Be Delicious perfume.

Clinique was the first high-end allergy-tested, dermatologist-created cosmetics brand.

Bobbi Brown (namesake of the celebrated makeup artist) focuses on teaching women to be their own makeup artists.

Estée Lauder's **Sensuous** is one of the perfumes marketed under the Lauder name.

Bumble and bumble provides salon-quality shampoo, conditioner and other hair care products.

Jo Malone is a British lifestyle brand known for its unique fragrance portfolio.

Aveda's line of high-end botanical spa products was acquired in 1997.

Source: Shutterstock.com, OKcamera_Shutterstock.com, Keith Homan_Shutterstock.com, Sorbis_Shutterstock.com, TungCheung_Shutterstock.com, Oleg GawriloFF_Shutterstock.com, BestStockFoto_Shutterstock.com

SWOT Analysis

SWOT analysis

An assessment of strengths, weaknesses, opportunities, and threats.

SWOT analysis, which stands for strengths, weaknesses, opportunities, and threats, is a tool to help organizations understand internal strengths and weaknesses and external opportunities of the environment. An assessment of strengths and weaknesses occurs as a part of organizational analysis; that is, it is an audit of the company's internal workings, which are relatively easier to control than outside factors. Examining opportunities and threats is a part of environmental analysis—the company must look outside of the organization to assess opportunities and threats over which it has lesser control.

SWOT asks four basic questions about a company and its environment: (1) What can we do? (2) What do we want to do? (3) What might we do? and (4) What do others expect us to do?

FIGURE 5.4 SWOT

Chess master Bruce Pandolfini has noted the similarities between business and chess. In both arenas, you must understand your own abilities as well as your flaws. You must also know your opponents, try to anticipate their moves, and deal with considerable uncertainty. A very popular management tool that incorporates the idea of understanding the elements internal and external to the firm is SWOT (strengths, weaknesses, opportunities, and threats) analysis. Strengths and weaknesses are assessed by examining the firm, while opportunities and threats refer to external events and trends. These ideas can be applied to individuals too. Here we offer examples of SWOT analysis for organizations and for individuals who are seeking employment.

Strengths

Organizational Example – Having high levels of cash flow gives firms discretion to purchase new equipment if they wish to.

Individual Example – Strong technical and language skills, as well as previous work experience, can help individuals rise above the competition.

Weaknesses

Organizational Example – Dubious leadership and CEO scandals have plagued some corporations in recent years.

Individual Example – Poor communication skills keep many job seekers from being hired into sales and supervisory positions.

Opportunities

Organizational Example – The high cost of gasoline creates opportunities for substitute products based on alternative energy sources.

Individual Example – The U.S. economy is increasingly services based, suggesting that individuals can enjoy more opportunities in service firms.

Threats

Organizational Example – Concerns about worldwide pollution are a threat to petroleum-based products.

Individual Example – A tight job market poses challenges to new graduates.

Source: Shutterstock.com

Strengths and Weaknesses

A good starting point for strategizing is an assessment of what an organization does well and where it could benefit from improvements. In general, good strategies take advantage of *strengths* and minimize the disadvantages posed by any *weaknesses*. TOMS Shoes, for example, is known for its trendy footwear that helps others by donating a pair of shoes to a person in need for every pair of shoes sold. A weakness of TOMS Shoes is that its strategy can be easily duplicated. For example, Sketchers has launched BOBS Shoes with a similar style and mission to that of TOMS.[7] As is evidenced by the competitive dynamics of these two shoemakers, the hardest thing for an organization to do is to develop its competitive advantage into a **sustainable competitive advantage** where the organization's strengths cannot be easily duplicated or imitated by other firms nor made redundant or less valuable by changes in the external environment. For example, LEGO regularly engages in licensing agreements to update their catalogue with unique brick sets following popular movie series such as Star Wars, Harry Potter, and the LEGO movies. Meanwhile, LEGO also engages in litigation to protect their copyrights when others infringe on their unique works such as their successful case against a Chinese firm producing "copycat" LEGO sets.[8]

Lego effectively leverages the unique strength of their well known minifigures to create custom sets such as their Central Perk set from the classic sitcom *Friends*.

Source: Ekaterina_Minaeva/Shutterstock.com

sustainable competitive advantage

A competitive advantage that will exist after all attempts at strategic imitation have ceased.

Opportunities and Threats

Understanding the external environment is also critical to understanding strategic management. *Opportunities* assesses factors external to the business that could enable a business to exist and/or prosper. In SWOT analysis, opportunities refer to dynamics or trends that are opportunities for the entire industry rather than the company being analyzed. For example, an aging population could lead to opportunities in numerous industries that cater to that demographic. In the shoe industry, a desire to purchase shoes made in the United States has led to great success for firms with strategies aligned with this opportunity. *Threats* includes factors beyond the firm's control that could place the strategy, or the business, at risk. Like opportunities, these are considered external because managers typically have no control over them, but may benefit from having plans to respond to these opportunities or threats. For example, the Coronavirus pandemic was a particularly impactful threat to the service organizations.[9] A threat in the shoe industry could occur if the increased costs of raw materials diminish the profitability of all shoe makers.

Growth in the shoe industry continues to be a good example of an industry opportunity for an American made product given the number of successful competitors in the U.S.

Source: Jane Rix/Shutterstock.com

Music Rap-Up: It's SWOT It Is

Twinprov perform a rap on SWOT analysis.

View in the online reader

Internal Analysis Tools

Internal analysis tools help identify an organization's strengths and weaknesses. Two tools for internal analysis are the *value chain* and *VRIO* tools. The value chain dissects the organization and then identifies areas of unique strength or weakness. Sometimes these parts take the form of functions, like marketing or manufacturing. For instance, Disney excels at developing and profiting from its branded products, such as *Frozen* or *Pirates of the Caribbean*. This is a marketing function, as well as a design function.

Value chain functions are also called *capabilities*. VRIO—which stands for Value, Rarity, Imitability, and Organization—is a framework that suggests that a capability, or a *resource*, such as a patent or a desirable location, is likely to yield a competitive advantage to an organization when it can be shown that it is valuable, rare, difficult to imitate, and supported by the organization. Where the value chain might suggest internal areas of strength, VRIO helps predict whether those strengths will give it a competitive advantage. For example, while other movie studios can copy Disney's strategy by marketing their films, they are unlikely to successfully imitate the iconic status Disney has developed over years of marketing commitment and through association with their well-known theme parks.

External Analysis Tools

PESTEL

Stands for the political, economic, social, technological, environmental, and legal dimensions of an organization's external environment.

Two primary tools to examine the external environment are *PESTEL* and *industry analysis*. **PESTEL** is an acronym that stands for Political, Economic, Social, Technological, Environmental, and Legal environments. The PESTEL framework directs managers to collect information about, and analyze, each environmental dimension to identify the broad range of threats and opportunities facing the organization. Industry analysis, in contrast, maps out the different relationships that the organization might have with suppliers, customers, and competitors. Whereas PESTEL provides managers with a good sense of the broader macro-environment, industry analysis provides information about the organization's competitive environment and the key industry-level factors that seem to influence performance.

FIGURE 5.5 PESTEL

Examining the general environment involves gaining an understanding of key factors and trends in broader society. PESTEL analysis is a popular framework for organizing these factors and trends and isolating how they influence industries and the firms within them. Here we describe each of the six dimensions associated with PESTEL analysis: political, economic, social, technological, environmental, and legal.

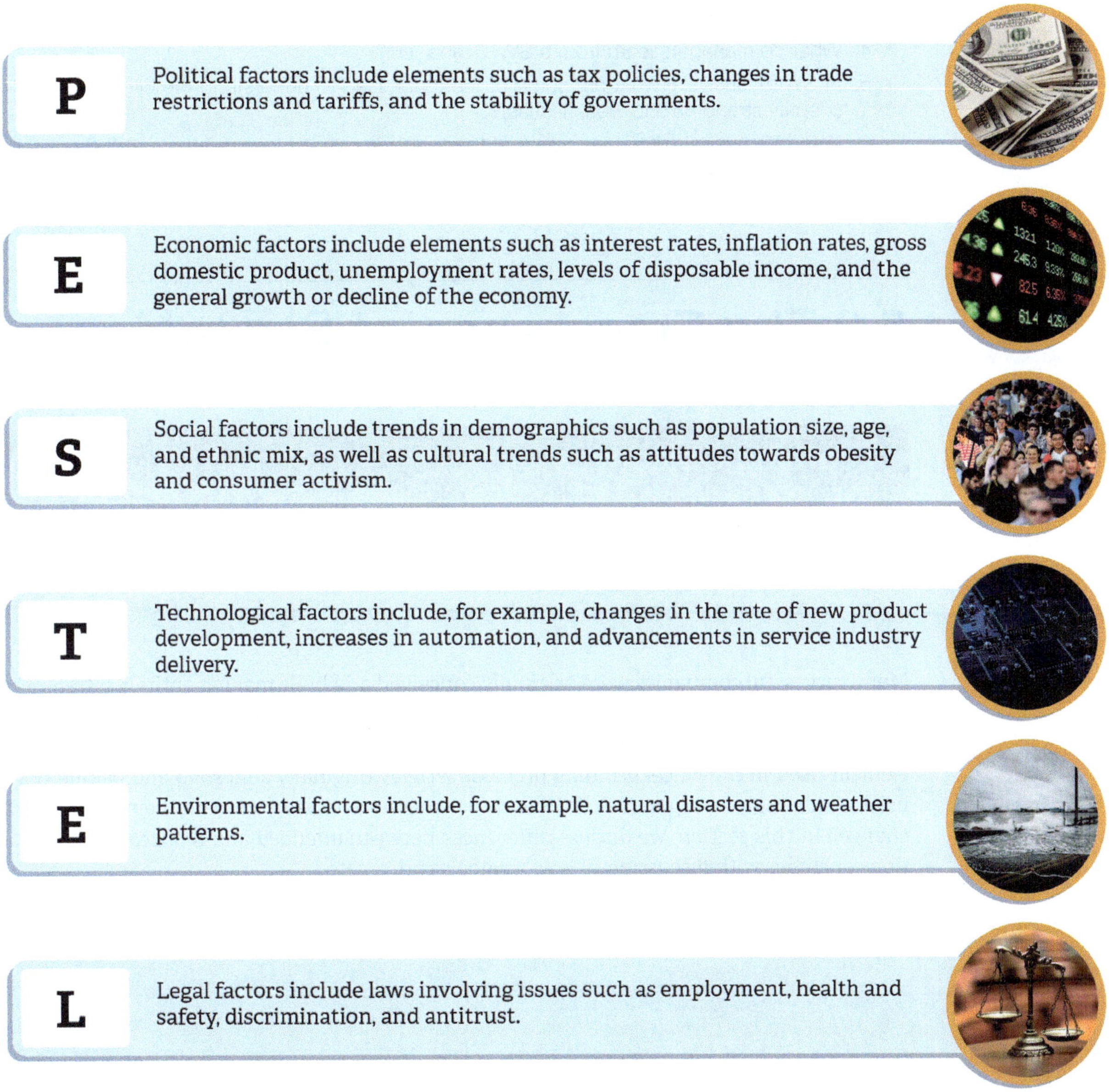

Source: Shutterstock.com, Anton Gvozdikov Shutterstock.com

Key Takeaway

Strategy formulation is an essential component of planning because it enables the organization to progress from vision and mission to goals and objectives. In terms of the P-O-L-C framework, strategy formulation is the P (planning) and strategy implementation is realized by O-L-C. Corporate strategy helps to answer questions about which businesses to compete in, while business strategy helps to answer questions about how to compete. The best strategies are based on a thorough SWOT analysis—that is, a strategy that capitalizes on an organization's strengths and weaknesses while considering the opportunities and threats of their environment.

Discussion Questions

1. What is the difference between strategy formulation and strategy implementation?
2. What is the difference between business strategy and corporate strategy?
3. What are some of the forms of diversification, and what do they mean?
4. What do managers learn from a SWOT analysis?
5. In SWOT analysis, what are some of the tools used to understand the internal environment (identify strengths and weaknesses)?
6. In SWOT analysis, what are some of the tools used to understand the external environment (identify opportunities and threats)?

5.2 The Emergence of Strategies

Learning Objectives

1. Understand the difference between intended and realized strategy.
2. Understand how strategy is formulated.
3. Understand the need for a balance between strategic design and emergence.

Many successful companies were originally conceived and built making entirely different products than we know them for today. For example, 3M (makers of Scotch tape and Post-it Notes) was originally launched when the Minnesota Mining and Manufacturing Company sold corundum (an element used in the wheel grinding process); Wrigley originally sold soap and baking powder and used gum simply as a gimmick.[10] How do business strategies come into being and why do they change? In this section, we discuss differences between *intended* and *realized* strategies. The section concludes with discussion of how strategies are created.

FIGURE 5.6 Strategic Planning and Learning: Intended, Emergent, and Realized Strategies

Strategic planning, usually in the form of a business plan, is a key aspect of creating a new venture. Many well-known firms, however, owe their success to their ability to adapt rather than to their original plan. Most firms begin by pursuing their plans (also known as intended strategy), but unexpected opportunities that arise over time can lead firms in much different directions than could have ever been anticipated (emergent strategy). Ultimately, the intended and emergent strategies each contribute to a firm's realized strategy. In the cases below, the original intended strategy can barely be detected within today's strategy.

	Intended Strategy	Emergent Strategy	Realized Strategy
	David McConnell aspired to be a writer. When his books were not selling, he decided to give out perfume as a gimmick.	The perfumes McConnell gave out with his books were popular, inspiring the foundation of the California Perfume Company.	The company changed its name to Avon in 1939, and its direct marketing system remained popular for decades. Avon is now available online and in retail outlets worldwide.
	When Scott and Don Rasmussen were fired from the New England Whalers, they envisioned a cable television network that focused on sports events in the state of Connecticut.	As the network became successful, ESPN branched out beyond the local softball games and demolition derbies that were first broadcast.	ESPN is now billed as the worldwide leader in sports, owning several ESPN affiliates as well as production of ESPN magazine, ESPN radio, and broadcasting for ABC.
	In 1977, a cash-strapped advertiser gave a radio station managed by Lowell Paxson 112 electric can openers to pay off an overdue bill. The can openers were offered over the air for $9.95 and quickly sold out.	An idea emerged. Soon the radio station featured a regular show called "Suncoast Bargaineers." In 1982, Paxson and a partner launched the Home Shopping Club on local cable television in Florida.	Today the Home Shopping Network has evolved into a retail powerhouse. The company sells tens of thousands of products on television channels in several countries and over the internet.

Source: Shutterstock.com

Intended and Realized Strategies

The best-laid plans of mice and men often go awry. —Robert Burns, "To a Mouse," 1785

As one example of an emergent strategy, Tiffany & Co. originally began as a stationary company.

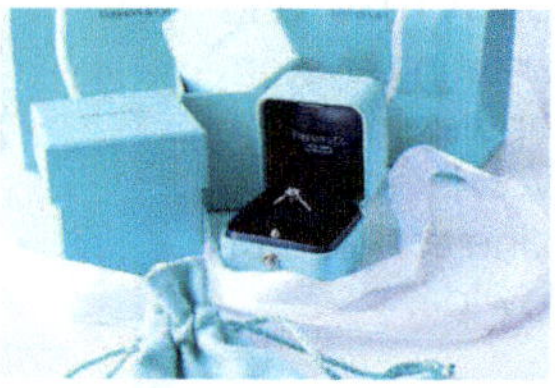

Source: graceliuphotos/Shutterstock.com

intended strategy

The strategy conceived by managers and the impetus for initial attempts at strategy implementation.

realized strategy

The actual strategy that is implemented and comes to fruition as a consequence of implementation and other internal and external factors.

emergent strategy

A pattern of action that develops over time in an organization in the absence of vision, mission, and goals, or despite missions and goals, or in addition to what was conceived in the intended and deliberate strategies.

deliberate

A plan of action flowing from the intended strategy, that an organization chooses and implements to support its vision, mission, and goals.

The quote from Scottish poet Robert Burns is applicable to how strategies are often developed over time. While some strategies are the outcome of a rational, predictable, analytical planning process, a fine plan does not guarantee a successful outcome. A number of factors can result from a strategic plan. In some cases, the plan may simply be poorly constructed. In others, competitors may be able to undermine the advantages of the plan. In addition, a plan could make sense conceptually but fail due to poor execution.

How organizations create strategies has emerged as an area of intense debate within the field of strategic management. Henry Mintzberg and his colleagues at McGill University distinguish intended, deliberate, realized, and emergent strategies.[11] **Intended strategy** is strategy as conceived by the top management team. Here, rationality is limited and the intended strategy is the result of a process of negotiation, bargaining, and compromise, involving many individuals and groups within the organization. However, **realized strategy**—the actual strategy that is implemented—is only partly related to that which was intended. Mintzberg suggests only 10%–30% of intended strategies actually become a reality.

The primary determinant of realized strategy is what Mintzberg terms **emergent strategy**—the decisions that emerge from the complex processes in which individual managers interpret the intended strategy and adapt to changing external circumstances.[12] Thus, the realized strategy is a consequence of **deliberate** and emerging factors. Analysis of Honda's successful entry into the U.S. motorcycle market has provided a battleground for the debate between those who view strategy making as primarily a rational, analytical process of deliberate planning and those that envisage strategy as emerging from a complex process of organizational decision making.[13]

FIGURE 5.7 Intended, Deliberate, Realized, and Emergent Strategies

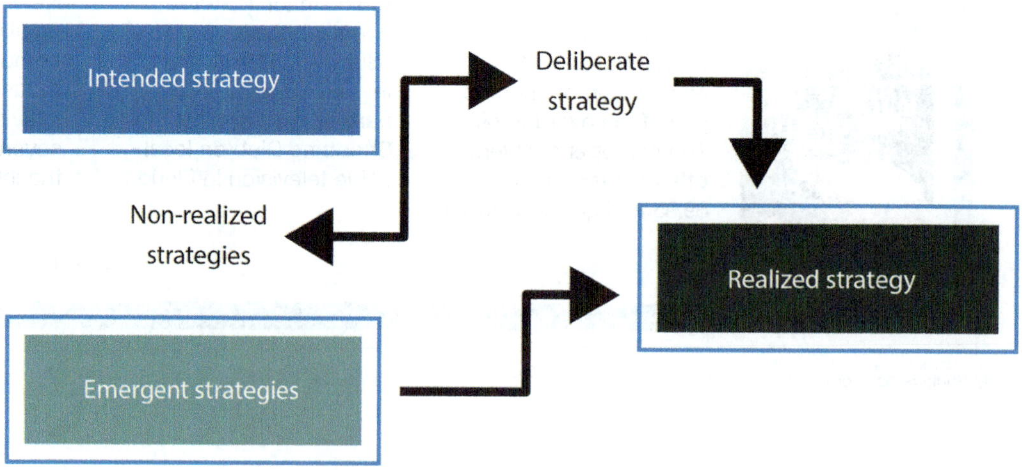

What's the Best Way to Develop a Strategy?

Mintzberg's advocacy of strategy creation as an iterative process involving experimentation and feedback is not necessarily an argument against the rational, systematic design of strategy. The critical issues are, first, determining the balance of design and emergence and, second, how to guide the process of emergence. The strategic planning systems of most companies involves a combination of design and emergence. Thus, headquarters sets guidelines in the form of vision and mission statements, business principles, performance targets, and capital expenditure budgets. However, within the strategic plans that are decided, divisional and business unit managers have considerable freedom to adjust, adapt, and experiment.

Key Takeaway

Strategy development is a process. Most organizations use planning to create intended strategies that they hope to follow. Managers must exercise flexibility in their strategies, as changes in an organization's situation may give rise to new opportunities and challenges. Organizations often respond by using emergent strategies. The realized strategies ultimately embraced by organizations are a product of both intended and realized strategies.

Discussion Questions

1. What is an intended strategy?
2. What is a realized strategy?
3. Why is it important to understand the difference between intended and realized strategies?
4. Why is there not a perfect match-up between realized and intended strategies?
5. What might interfere with the realization of an intended strategy?

5.3 Understanding Generic Business-Level Strategies

Learning Objectives

1. Understand generic business-level strategies.
2. Understand strategy as trade-offs between cost and differentiation.
3. Understand the role of focus in business-level strategies.

A strategy provides a company with focus. Strategy is ultimately about choice—what the organization does and does not do. The word "decide" is derived from a word whose meaning literally references cutting off, and an effective strategic decision involves cutting off at least some potential actions from a sea of possibilities.[14] While vision and mission provide a good sense of direction for the organization, they are not meant to serve as, or take the place of, an actual strategy. Strategy is about choices leading to trade-offs that make the firm distinctive in the eyes of stakeholders.

In this section, we explain strategic focus—that is, how trade-offs are reconciled—as well as two frameworks for thinking about what such focus might entail.

What Is Strategic Focus?

strategic focus

When an organization is clear about its mission and vision and has a coherent, well-articulated strategy for achieving those.

While there are different schools of thought about how strategies are derived, researchers generally agree that **strategic focus** is a common characteristic across successful organizations. Strategic focus occurs when an organization is very clear about its mission and vision and has a coherent, well-articulated strategy for achieving those strategic elements. When a once-profitable firm encounters performance problems, it is not uncommon to hear business analysts say that the firm's managers have lost focus on the customers or markets where they were once highly successful. For instance, Dell Computer's strategy is highly focused around the efficient sale and manufacture of computers and computer peripheral devices. However, during the mid-2000s, Dell started branching out into other products such as digital cameras, DVD players, and flat-screen televisions. As a result, it lost focus on its core sales and manufacturing business, and its performance lagged. In 2013, Dell was involved in a leveraged buyout (LBO), where the once publicly-traded company became a private firm.[15] More recently, Dell has focused on becoming the world's largest privately held integrated technology company by purchasing data storage company EMC in 2015 for a deal approximating $67 billion.[16] Dell's history of branching out into different avenues, however, continues to this day as they recently started collaborating with actress, entrepreneur, and activist Nikki Reed (Rosalie Hale from the *Twilight* series) to create a line of jewelry from recycled gold found in motherboards.[17] Only time will tell if their focus (or lack thereof) will help or hurt Dell in the future. Meanwhile, they regularly appear on lists such as *Fast Company*'s most innovative companies of 2019.[18]

Strategy as Trade-Offs

Stitch Fix's curation and online delivery of outfits allows for a focus on customers who may dislike shopping but love unboxing.

Source: Shutterstock.com

Three of the most widely read books on competitive analysis in the 1980s were Michael Porter's *Competitive Strategy*, *Competitive Advantage*, and *Competitive Advantage of Nations*.[19] In his various books, Porter developed generic business-level strategies that, he argues, can be used independently or in combination to create a defendable position and to outperform competitors, whether they are within an industry or across nations. The strategies involve (1) overall cost leadership, (2) differentiation, and (3) focus on a particular market niche (leading to either focused cost leadership or focused differentiation).

Cost Leadership, Differentiation, and Scope

These strategies are termed *generic* because they can be applied to any size or form of business. These strategies involve trade-offs because Porter argues that a firm must choose to embrace one strategy or risk not having a strategy at all. **Overall lower cost or cost leadership** refers to the strategy where a firm's competitive advantage is based on the bet that it can develop, manufacture, and distribute products more efficiently than competitors. **Differentiation strategy** refers to the strategy where competitive advantage is based on superior products or service. Superiority arises from factors other than low cost, such as customer service, product quality, or unique style. For example, in the retail industry, Walmart pursues a cost-leadership strategy by offering low-cost goods to a broad base of customers, while Nordstrom follows a differentiation strategy offering high-end goods paired with superior customer service.

Porter suggests that another factor affecting a company's competitive position is its competitive scope. Competitive scope defines the breadth of a company's target market. A company can have a broad (mass market) competitive scope or a narrow (niche market) competitive scope. A firm following the **focus strategy** concentrates on meeting the specialized needs of its customers. One approach to focusing is to service either industrial buyers or consumers, but not both. As another example, Stitch Fix focuses on selling personal style to a niche audience by allowing for a focus on customers who either dislike or do not have the time to shop for clothes.[20]

Firms using a narrow focus strategy can also tailor advertising and promotional efforts to a particular market niche. Many automobile dealers advertise that they are the largest volume dealer for a specific geographic area (demonstrating a geographic focus). Other car dealers advertise that they have the highest customer satisfaction scores within their defined market or the most awards for their service department (demonstrating a differentiated focus).

By positioning in either broad scope or narrow scope and a low-cost strategy or differentiation strategy, an organization will fall into one of the following generic competitive strategies: cost leadership, focused cost leadership, differentiation, and focused differentiation.

overall lower cost or cost leadership

A strategy in which an organization attempts to gain a competitive advantage by reducing its costs below the costs of competing firms.

differentiation strategy

A strategy in which an organization seeks to distinguish itself from competitors through the perceived quality of its products or services.

focus strategy

A strategy in which an organization concentrates on a specific regional market, product line, or group of buyers in combination with its pursuit of either an overall cost leadership or differentiation strategy.

FIGURE 5.8 Business-Level Strategies

Firms compete in two general dimensions: The source of competitive advantage (cost or uniqueness) and the scope of operations (broad or narrow). Four possible generic business-level strategies emerge from these decisions. An example of each generic business-level strategy from the retail industry is illustrated here.

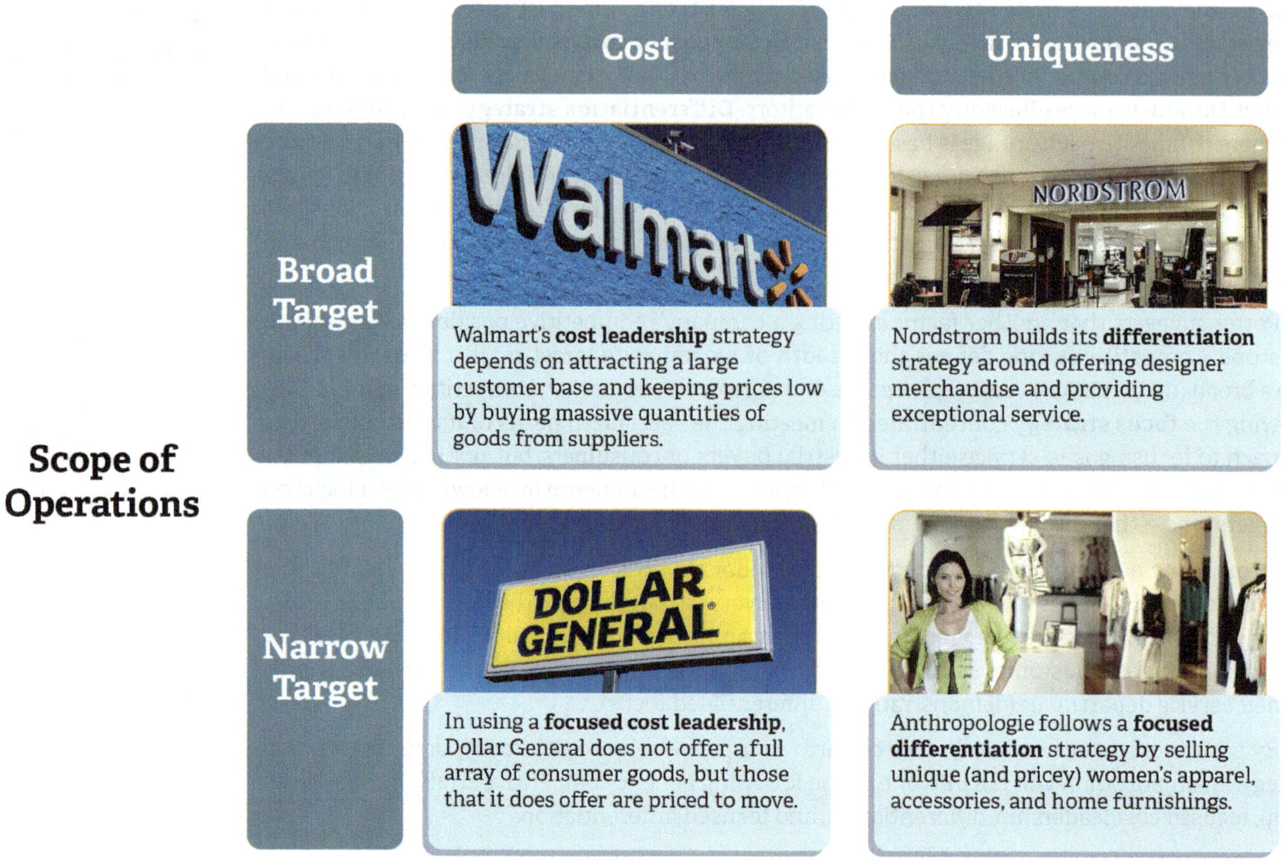

Source: Shutterstock.com, Jonathan Weiss_Shutterstock.com, Ken Wolter_Shutterstock.com

Cost Leadership/Low Cost

Cost leadership is a low-cost, broad-based market strategy. Firms pursuing this type of strategy must be particularly efficient in engineering tasks, production operations, and physical distribution. Because these firms focus on a large market, they must also be able to minimize costs in marketing and research and development (R&D). A low-cost leader can gain significant market share enabling it to procure a more powerful position relative to both suppliers and competitors. This strategy is particularly effective for organizations in industries where there is limited possibility of product differentiation and where buyers are very price sensitive. For example, Southwest Airlines has been successful implementing a low-cost strategy due to their use of more fuel-efficient planes, reliance on point-to-point routes (versus a hub strategy of many competitors), and use of secondary airports that are less likely to face congestion compared to larger airports.[21]

Overall cost leadership is not without potential problems. Two or more firms competing for cost leadership may engage in price wars that drive profits to very low levels. Ideally, a firm using a cost-leader strategy will develop an advantage that others cannot easily copy. Cost leaders also must maintain their investment in state-of-the-art equipment or face the possible entry of more cost-effective competitors. Major changes in technology may drastically change production processes so that previous investments in production technology are no longer advantageous. Finally, firms may become so concerned with maintaining low costs that they overlook needed changes in production or marketing.

The cost-leadership strategy may be more difficult in a dynamic environment because some of the expenses that firms may seek to minimize are research and development costs or marketing research costs—expenses the firm may need to incur to remain competitive.

Focused Low Cost

A cost-focus strategy is a low-cost, narrowly focused market strategy. Firms employing this strategy may focus on a particular buyer segment or a particular geographic segment and must locate a niche market that wants or needs an efficient product and is willing to forgo extras to pay a lower price for the product. A company's costs can be reduced by providing little or no service, providing a low-cost method of distribution, or producing a no-frills product.

Differentiation

A differentiation strategy involves marketing a unique product to a broad-based market. Because this type of strategy involves a unique product, consumers may be willing to pay a higher price for a product they perceive as different. The product difference may be based on product design, method of distribution, or any aspect of the product that is valued by a broad group of consumers. A company choosing this strategy must develop and maintain a product perceived as different enough from the competitors' products to warrant the price difference. An example is found in the Wunder Unders, Fast and Free tights, and other premier products sold by apparel manufacturer Lululemon—a brand described by industry experts as exhibiting radical differentiation.[22]

College sophomores and soccer moms alike recognize the differentiated image associated with Lululemon and their products.

Source: Jeff Bukowski/Shutterstock.com

Focused Differentiation

A differentiation-focus strategy is the marketing of a differentiated product to a narrow market, often involving a unique product and a unique market. This strategy is viable for a company that can convince consumers that its narrow focus allows it to provide better goods and services than its competitors.

NBA legend and successful entrepreneur Shaquille O'Neal owns over 100 Five Guys franchises.

Source: Krista Kennell/Shutterstock.com

Differentiation does not allow a firm to ignore costs; it makes a firm's products less susceptible to cost pressures from competitors because customers see the product as unique and are willing to pay extra to have the product with the desirable features. Differentiation can be achieved through real product features or through advertising that causes the customer to perceive that the product is unique. An example is found in British sportswear manufacturer Barbour, whose sporting jacket is commonly seen donned by models at Coachella and was perhaps most prominently featured by James Bond in the movie *Skyfall*.[23] To protect their differentiated brand from those that would seek to offer imitation merchandise, Barbour offers counterfeit education on their website with a feature that allows potential customers to enter websites where their clothing is sold to ensure authenticity.[24]

Differentiation may lead to customer brand loyalty, resulting in customers being less sensitive to changes in price. Differentiation may also lead to higher profit margins. Since customers see the product as different from competing products, customers are willing to pay a premium for these features. As long as the firm can increase the selling price by more than the marginal cost of adding the features, the profit margin is increased. Firms must be able to charge more for their differentiated product than it costs them to make it distinct, or else they may be better off making generic, undifferentiated products. Firms must remain sensitive to cost differences. They must carefully monitor the incremental costs of differentiating their product and make certain the difference is reflected in the price.

Averaging fewer than 4,000 sales a year for over a decade Rolls Royce serves as the epitome of focused differentiation.

Source: AmorSt-Photographer/ Shutterstock.com

Firms pursuing a differentiation strategy are vulnerable to different competitive threats than firms pursuing a cost-leader strategy. Customers may sacrifice features, service, or image for cost savings. Price-sensitive customers may be willing to forgo desirable features in favor of a less costly alternative. This can be seen in the growth in popularity of store brands and private labels. Often, the same firms that produce name-brand products also produce the private-label products. The two products may be physically identical, but stores are able to sell the private-label products for a lower price because very little money was put into advertising to differentiate the private-label product.

Imitation may also reduce the perceived differences between products when competitors copy product features. Thus, for firms to be able to recover the cost of marketing research or R&D, they may need to add a product feature that is not easily copied by a competitor. A final risk for firms pursuing a differentiation strategy is changing consumer tastes. The feature that customers like and find attractive about a product this year may not make the product popular next year. Changes in customer tastes are especially obvious in the fashion industry, where consumer tastes change with the seasons and fads can make certain clothes extremely popular for short time periods.

Straddling Positions or Stuck in the Middle?

Can forms of competitive advantage be combined? That is, can a firm straddle strategies so that it is simultaneously the low-cost leader and a differentiator? A number of companies seek to balance elements of cost and differentiation. For example, there has been a recent boom in the popularity of food trucks that specialize in a range of culinary options ranging from a gourmet PB&J to specialty chicken and wings to a focus on traditional Hawaiian cuisine without luau prices.[25] This approach conflicts with Porter's historic assertion that a successful strategy requires a firm to stake out a market position aggressively and that different strategies involve distinctly different approaches to competing and operating the business. Some research suggests that straddling strategies is a recipe for below-average profitability compared to the industry. Porter also argues that straddling strategies is an indication that the firm's managers have not made necessary choices about the business and its strategy. A straddling strategy may be especially dangerous for narrow-scope firms that have been successful in the past, but then start neglecting their focus.

An organization pursuing a differentiation strategy seeks competitive advantage by offering products or services that are unique from those offered by rivals, either through design, brand image, technology, features, or customer service. Alternatively, an organization pursuing a cost-leadership strategy attempts to gain competitive advantage based on being the overall low-cost provider of a product or service. To be "all things to all people" can mean becoming "stuck in the middle" with no distinct competitive advantage. The difference between being "stuck in the middle" and successfully pursuing combination strategies merits discussion. Although Porter describes the dangers of not being successful in either cost control or differentiation, some firms have been able to succeed using combination strategies.

The sustained popularity of food trucks provide a common example of businesses that can integrate elements of both differentiation and low cost.

Source: Michael Gordon/Shutterstock.com

Research suggests that, in some cases, it is possible to be a cost leader while maintaining a differentiated product. Southwest Airlines has combined cost-cutting measures with differentiation. The company has been able to reduce costs by not assigning seating and by eliminating meals on its planes. It has also been able to promote in its advertising that its fares are so low that checked bags fly free, in contrast to the fees that competitors such as American and United charge for checked luggage. Southwest's consistent low-fare strategy has attracted a significant number of passengers, allowing the airline to succeed.

Some industry environments may actually call for combination strategies. Trends suggest that executives operating in highly complex environments, such as healthcare, do not have the luxury of choosing exclusively one strategy over another. The hospital industry may represent such an environment, as hospitals must compete on a variety of fronts. Combination strategies are both feasible and necessary to compete successfully. For instance, reimbursement to diagnosis-related groups, and the continual lowering of reimbursement ceilings have forced hospitals to compete on the basis of cost. At the same time, many of them jockey for position with differentiation based on such features as technology and birthing rooms. Thus, many hospitals may need to adopt some form of hybrid strategy to compete successfully.[26]

Key Takeaway

Strategic focus seems to be a common element in strategies across successful firms. Two prevalent views of strategy where focus is a key component are strategy as trade-offs and strategy as discipline. Michael Porter identifies three elements of strategy: (1) cost leadership, (2) differentiation, or (3) a focus of cost leadership or differentiation on a particular market niche. Firms can straddle these strategies, but such firms face the risk of being 'stuck in the middle' without a particular strategic focus.

Discussion Questions

1. What is strategic focus and why is it important?
2. What are Porter's generic strategies?
3. Can a firm simultaneously pursue a low-cost and a differentiation strategy?

5.4 Developing Strategy Through Internal Analysis

Learning Objectives

1. Learn the value of internal analysis.
2. Understand resources, capabilities, and core competencies.
3. Learn how to evaluate resources, capabilities, and core competencies using VRIO analysis.

In this section, we focus on aspects of business analysis internal to a particular organization. The primary purpose for internal analysis is to understand the unique resources, capabilities, and core competencies of organizations that differentiate them from other organizations and potentially enable them to outperform their competitors over time.

Internal Analysis

Seth Godin's (2003) book *Purple Cow: Transform Your Business by Being Remarkable* focuses on the idea of highlighting a firm's uniqueness to create competitive advantage.

Source: Shutterstock.com

core competencies

A particular bundle of resources and capabilities that provides unique competitive advantages to a firm.

By exploiting internal resources and capabilities and meeting the demanding standards of global competition, firms create value for customers.[27] Value is measured by a product's performance characteristics and by its attributes for which customers are willing to pay.[28] Those particular bundles of resources and capabilities that provide unique advantages to the firm are considered **core competencies.**[29] Core competencies are resources and capabilities that serve as a source of a firm's competitive advantage over rivals. Core competencies distinguish a company competitively from rivals and emerge over time through an organizational process of accumulating and learning how to deploy different resources and capabilities. Core competencies are "crown jewels of a company," the activities the company performs especially well compared with competitors that add unique value to its goods or services over a long period of time.[30] For example, Apple computer regularly provides new products that excite customers based on their core competency in innovation.[31]

Sometimes consistency and predictability provide value to customers, such as the type of value Walgreens drugstores provides. As a *Fortune* magazine writer noted, "Do you realize that from 1975 to 2000, Walgreens beat Intel? It beat Intel nearly two to one, GE almost five to one. It also beat 3M, Coke, Boeing, and Motorola during that time."[32] Walgreens was able to do this by using its core competencies to offer value desired by its target customer group. Instead of responding to the trends of the day, "During the internet scare of 1998 and 1999, when slogans of 'Change or Die!' were all but graffitied on the subway, Walgreens obstinately stuck to its corporate credo of 'Crawl, walk, run.' Its refusal to act until it thoroughly understood the implications of e-commerce was deeply unfashionable, but . . . Walgreens is the epitome of the inner-directed company."[33] Thus Walgreens creates value by focusing on the unique capabilities it has built, nurtured, and continues to improve across time. Even as recently as late 2017, Walgreens boasted strong earnings when other pharmacy concepts were struggling.[34]

Resources and Capabilities

Resources

Broad in scope, *resources* cover a spectrum of individual, social, and organizational assets.[35] Typically, any given resource alone does not yield a competitive advantage.[36] Instead, core competencies that yield a competitive advantage are often created through the *unique bundling of several resources.*[37] For example, Amazon.com has combined service and distribution resources to develop its competitive advantages. The firm started as an online bookseller, directly shipping orders to customers. It quickly grew large and established a distribution network through which it could ship "millions of different items to millions of different customers." In 2018, Amazon expanded their bundle when they launched Amazon Prime Wardrobe, allowing customers to try on their clothing offerings before they buy.[38] Compared with Amazon's use of combined resources, traditional bricks-and-mortar companies find it harder to establish an effective online presence. These difficulties led many retailers to develop partnerships with Amazon. Retailers such as Eddie Bauer and Foot Locker now sell merchandise on Amazon.com, and Amazon now handles the entire online presence and shipping for retailers including Britain's Marks & Spencer. Arrangements such as these are useful to the bricks-and-mortar companies because they are not accustomed to shipping so much diverse merchandise directly to individuals.

Some resources are tangible while others are intangible. *Tangible resources* are assets that can be seen and quantified. Production equipment, manufacturing plants, and formal reporting structures are examples of tangible resources. *Intangible resources* typically include assets that are rooted deeply in the firm's history and have accumulated over time. Because they are embedded in unique patterns of routines, intangible resources are relatively difficult for competitors to analyze and imitate. Knowledge, trust between managers and employees, ideas, the capacity for innovation, managerial capabilities, organizational routines (the unique ways people work together), scientific capabilities, and the firm's reputation for its goods or services, and how it interacts with people (such as employees, customers, and suppliers) are all examples of intangible resources.[39]

The Bronco name was a resource Ford was able to deploy when they relaunched the line in 2020.

Source: huang zixing/ Shutterstock.com

FIGURE 5.9 Resources and Capabilities

Resources and capabilities are the basic building blocks that organizations use to create strategies. These two building blocks are tightly linked—capabilities tend to arise from using resources over time.

Resources can be divided into two main types:

Tangible resources are resources that can be readily seen, touched, and quantified. Physical assets such as a firm's property, plant, and equipment are considered to be tangible resources, as is cash.

Intangible resources are quite difficult to see, touch, or quantify. Intangible resources include, for example, the knowledge and skills of employees, a firm's reputation, and a firm's culture. In a nod to Starbucks' outstanding reputation, the firm ranks fifth in *Fortune* magazine's 2018 list of "World's Most Admired Companies." Only Apple, Amazon, Alphabet (Google), and Berkshire Hathaway enjoy a stronger reputation.

While resources refer to what an organization *owns*, capabilities refer to what the organization can do. More specifically, capabilities refer to the firm's ability to bundle, manage, or otherwise exploit resources in a manner that provides value added and, hopefully, advantage over competitors.

A *dynamic capability* exists when a firm is skilled at continually updating its array of capabilities to keep pace with changes in its environment. Disney, for example, buys firms and divests divisions to maintain its market leadership over time while Coca-Cola has an uncanny knack for building new brands and products as the soft-drink market evolves. Not surprisingly, both of these firms rank among the top eighteen of *Fortune*'s "World's Most Admired Companies" for 2018.

Source: Shutterstock.com

Capabilities

Capabilities are the firm's capacity to deploy resources that have been purposely integrated to achieve a desired end state.[40] Capabilities emerge over time through complex interactions among tangible and intangible resources. Capabilities can be tangible, like a business process that is automated, but most of them tend to be tacit and intangible. Critical to forming competitive advantages, capabilities are often based on developing, carrying, and exchanging information and knowledge through the firm's human capital.[41] Because a knowledge base is grounded in organizational actions that may not be explicitly understood by all employees, repetition and practice increase the value of a firm's capabilities. For example, while Apple has undoubtedly been viewed as an innovative company based on delivery of market-changing new products, a key element of their success is their capability of making small, steady improvements over time.[42]

Knowledge possessed by human capital is among the most significant of an organization's capabilities and may ultimately be at the root of all competitive advantages. "A company's value derives not from things, but from knowledge, know-how, intellectual assets, competencies—all of it embedded in people."[43] Given this reality, the firm's challenge is to create an environment that allows people to fit their individual pieces of knowledge together so that, collectively, employees possess as much organizational knowledge as possible.[44]

To help firms develop an environment in which knowledge is widely spread across all employees, some organizations have created the new upper-level managerial position of chief learning officer (CLO). Establishing a CLO position highlights a firm's belief that "future success will depend on competencies that traditionally have not been actively managed or measured—including creativity and the speed with which new ideas are learned and shared."[45] In general, the firm should manage knowledge in ways that will support its efforts to create value for customers.[46]

FIGURE 5.10 The Value Chain

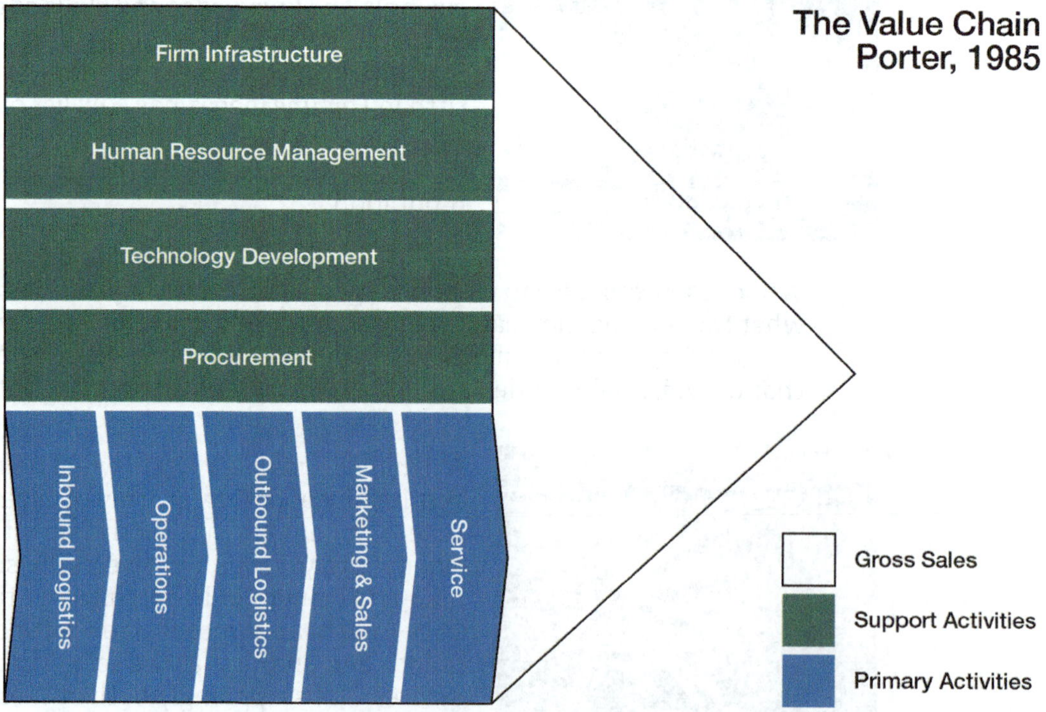

Source: Adapted from Porter, M. (1985). *Competitive Advantage*. New York: Free Press. Exhibit is creative commons licensed at http://en.wikipedia.org/wiki/Image:ValueChain.PNG.

Capabilities are often developed in specific functional areas (such as manufacturing, R&D, and marketing) or in a part of a functional area (for example, advertising). The **value chain**, popularized by Michael Porter's book, *Competitive Advantage*, is a useful tool for taking stock of organizational capabilities. The value chain framework outlines key activities that highlight the value-added capabilities that differentiate some firms from others. In the value chain, some of the activities are deemed to be primary, in the sense that these activities add direct value to the creation of goods and services. In Figure 5.11, primary activities are logistics (inbound and outbound), marketing, and service. Support activities support the creation of goods and services and include how the firm is organized (infrastructure), human resources, technology, and procurement. Products pass through all activities of the chain in order, and at each activity, the product has the potential to gain value. A firm is effective to the extent that the chain of activities gives the products more added value than the value chain configurations of competitors. An example is found in Voodoo Doughnut in Portland, Oregon. While many local donut makers serve standard offerings, Voodoo Doughnut sells unique offerings such as a Bacon Maple Bar, The Loop (featuring Fruit Loops Cereal), their Dirt donut (featuring Oreo cookies), and the Marshall Mathers (featuring M&Ms).[47] Such unique donuts represent value-added in the value chain element of operations, and their popularity has subsequently led Voodoo to be able to develop value-added in marketing. For example, they have partnered with Rogue brewery to create a Bacon Maple Ale beer based on their popular donut.[48]

Birchbox's monthly cosmetics delivery service provides an example of a company where outbound logistics is a key value added function.

Source: urbanbuzz/Shutterstock.com

value chain

The primary and support activities that an organization uses to create value in the form of products or services.

FIGURE 5.11 Adding Value within a Value Chain

Doughnut shops buy commodity products (such as flour and grease) and transform them into delectable treats. Consumers are willing to pay much more for doughnuts than they would for flour and grease. Below we illustrate how primary and support activities in the value chain can add value for doughnut shops.

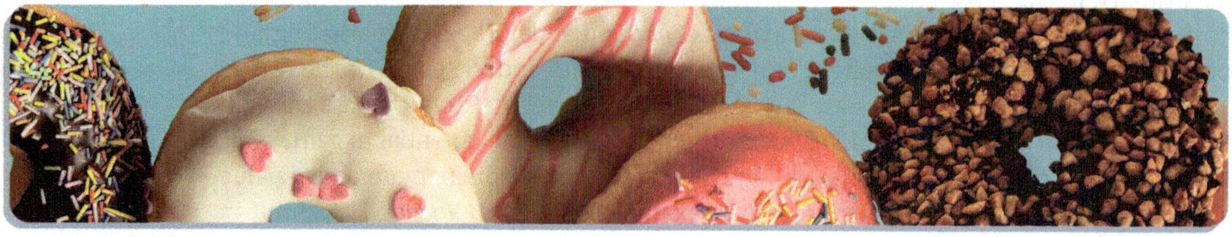

Primary activities involve the creation and distribution of goods and services.

A healthy doughnut? Not really, but the **inbound logistics** of organic ingredients from a local farmer's market makes the Donut Plant in New York City unique.

Operations at the Coffee an' Donut Shop in Westport, Connecticut, rely on a secret doughnut recipe. Former President Clinton had the doughnuts shipped to the White House regularly.

Voodoo Doughnut in Portland, Oregon uses a van as part of its **outbound logistics**. The van takes their unique offerings, such as a bacon-maple doughnut, far beyond their store.

Marketing and sales for Randy's Donuts in Inglewood, California, is aided by an attention-grabbing building.

What is a "dirty snowball"? Helping customers understand their unique menu is an important **service** offered by the Voodoo Doughnut staff.

Support activities are important supplementary aids to primary activities.

As an example of **firm infrastructure**, the explosive growth of Tim Hortons under Ron Joyce's leadership led Canada to have the highest per-capita consumption of doughnuts in the world.

A key **human resource management** issue for all doughnut shops is ensuring that a friendly face greets each customer.

The conveyor belt used by Krispy Kreme is a **technology** that creates efficiency and a visual enticement for potential customers.

Large chains such as Dunkin' Donuts enjoy low prices in their **procurement** process because they buy supplies in bulk.

Source: Shutterstock.com

VRIO Analysis

Given that almost anything a firm possesses can be considered a resource or capability, how can managers attempt to narrow down the ones that are core competencies, and explain why firm performance differs? To lead to a sustainable competitive advantage, a resource or capability should be valuable, rare, inimitable (including nonsubstitutable), and organized to take advantage of the value added. This VRIO framework is the foundation for internal analysis.[49] **VRIO** is an acronym for *valuable, rare, inimitable*, and *organization*.

VRIO

Stands for valuable, rare, inimitable, and organization.

If you ask managers why their firms do well while others do poorly, a common answer is likely to be "our people." What is it about people that is especially valuable? Why do competitors employ dissimilar people? Can competitors hire excellent employees away? Or is there something special about the organization that brings out the best in people? These kinds of questions get to the heart of why some resources help firms more than others.

TABLE 5.2 VRIO and Relative Firm Performance

Valuable?	Rare?	Difficult to Imitate?	Supported by Organization?	Competitive Implications	Performance
No	—	—	Yes	Competitive Disadvantage	**Below Normal**
Yes	No	—	Yes	Competitive Parity	**Normal**
Yes	Yes	No	Yes	Temporary Competitive Advantage	**Above Normal**
Yes	Yes	Yes	Yes	Sustained Competitive Advantage	**Above Normal**

The ability to identify whether an organization has VRIO resources will also likely explain their competitive position. In Table 5.2 a firm's performance relative to industry peers is likely to vary according to the level to which resources, capabilities, and, ultimately, core competencies satisfy VRIO criteria. The four criteria are explored next.

Valuable

A resource or capability is said to be valuable if it allows the firm to exploit opportunities or negate threats in the environment. Union Pacific's extensive network of rail-line property and equipment in the Gulf Coast of the United States is valuable because it allows the company to provide a cost-effective way to transport chemicals. Because the Gulf Coast is the gateway for the majority of chemical production in the United States, the rail network allows the firm to exploit a market opportunity. If a resource does not allow a firm to minimize threats or exploit opportunities, it does not enhance the competitive position of the firm. In fact, some scholars suggest that owning resources that do not meet the VRIO test of value actually puts the firm at a competitive disadvantage.[50]

Rare

A resource is rare simply if it is not widely possessed by other competitors. Of the criteria, this is probably the easiest to judge. For example, Coke's brand name is valuable but most of Coke's competitors (Pepsi, 7Up) also have widely recognized brand names. Of course, Coke's brand may be the most recognized, but that makes it more valuable rather than more rare.

Because they provide an exclusive right to produce a specific product, patents (such as the drone patented by Amazon) can be considered rare resources.

Source: Shutterstock.com

A firm that possesses valuable resources that are not rare is not in a position of advantage relative to competitors. Rather, valuable resources that are commonly held by many competitors simply allow firms to be on par with competitors. However, when a firm maintains possession of valuable resources that are also rare in the industry, they are in a position of competitive advantage over other firms that do not possess the resource. Sports enthusiasts have applied this logic to argue why professional sports teams should be reluctant to draft running backs early in the draft since valuable talent is generally available in later rounds.[51] While quarterbacks are often considered riskier selections, they are also considered to possess a potential level of payoff that is both more valuable as well as more rare.

How rare do the resources need to be for a firm to have a competitive advantage? If only one firm possesses the resource, it has significant advantage over all other competitors. For instance, Monsanto had such an advantage for many years because they owned the patent to aspartame, the chemical compound in NutraSweet; they had a valuable and extremely rare resource. Because during the lifetime of the patent they were the only firm that could sell aspartame, they had an advantage in the artificial-sweetener market. However, meeting the condition of rarity does not always require exclusive ownership. When only a few firms possess the resource, they will have an advantage over the remaining competitors. For instance, Toyota and Honda both have the capabilities to build cars of high quality at relatively low cost.[52] Their products regularly beat rival firms' products in both short-term and long-term quality ratings.[53] Thus, the criterion of rarity requires that the resource not be widely possessed in the industry. It also suggests that the more exclusive a firm's access to a particularly valuable resource, the greater the benefit. For example, in an industry where layoffs have been common over the years, Southwest Airlines is rare in their ability to have an exceptional organizational culture where a spirit of encouraging fun while serving others thrives.[54]

Inimitable

An inimitable (the opposite of *imitable*) resource is difficult to imitate or to create ready substitutes for. A resource is inimitable and nonsubstitutable if it is difficult for another firm to acquire or to substitute something else in its place. A valuable and rare resource or capability will grant a competitive advantage as long as other firms do not gain subsequent possession of the resource or a close substitute. If a resource is valuable and rare and responsible for a market leader's competitive advantage, it is likely that competitors lacking the resource or capability will do all that they can to obtain the resource or capability themselves. The concept of imitation includes any form of *acquiring* the lacking resource or *substituting* a similar resource that provides equivalent benefits. The criterion important to be addressed is whether competitors face a *cost disadvantage* in acquiring or substituting the resource that is lacking. For example, Netflix's strategy of creating exclusive content makes it more difficult for other cable or streaming services to copy their portfolio of offerings.[55]

RC Cola has developed many firsts in the soft drink industry such as the first diet cola, first caffeine-free cola, and first pop-top cola. Unfortunately, their innovations were not inimitable by their larger rivals.

Source: emka74/Shutterstock.com

Organized

The fourth and final VRIO criterion that determines whether a resource or capability is the source of competitive advantage recognizes that mere possession or control is necessary but not sufficient to gain an advantage. The firm must likewise have the *organizational* capability to exploit the resources. The question of organization is broad and encompasses many facets of a firm but essentially means that the firm is able to capture any value that the resource or capability might generate. Organization, essentially the same form as that taken in the P-O-L-C framework, spans such firm characteristics as control systems, reporting relationships, compensation policies, and management interface with both customers and value-adding functions in the firm. Although listed as the last criterion in the VRIO tool, the question of organization is a necessary condition to be satisfied if a firm is to reap the benefits of any of the three preceding conditions. Thus, a valuable but widely-held resource only leads to competitive parity for a firm if they also possess the capabilities to exploit the resource. Likewise, a firm that possesses a valuable and rare resource will not gain a competitive advantage unless it can actually put that resource to effective use.

Key Takeaway

Internal analysis begins with the identification of resources and capabilities. Resources can be tangible and intangible; capabilities may have such characteristics as well. VRIO analysis is a way to distinguish resources and capabilities from core competencies. Specifically, VRIO analysis should show you the importance of value, rarity, inimitability, and organization as building blocks of competitive advantage.

Discussion Questions

1. What is the objective of internal analysis?
2. What is the difference between a resource and a capability?
3. What is the difference between a tangible and an intangible resource or capability?
4. What is a core competency?
5. What framework helps you identify those resources, capabilities, or core competencies that provide competitive advantage?
6. Why might competitive advantage for a firm be fleeting?

5.5 Developing Strategy Through External Analysis

Learning Objectives

1. Understand the basics of general environment analysis.
2. Learn the value of Porter's Five Forces industry analysis.
3. Understand the differences between competitors and substitutes using the Porter's Five Forces industry analysis framework.

In this section, we highlight the basic aspects of external analysis useful for strategy formulation that are useful in the determinants of a firm's opportunities and threats. Specifically, we focus on several aspects of external analysis.

The General Environment

When appraising the external environment of the organization, managers often start with its general environment. The general environment is composed of trends and dimensions in the broader society that influence firms and industries.[56] As mentioned in our discussion of SWOT analysis, an assessment of the general environment examines the six segments that compose the acronym PESTEL (political, economic, social, technical or technological, environmental, and legal).

Firms cannot directly control the general environment's segments and elements. Accordingly, successful companies gather the information required to understand each segment and its implications for the selection and implementation of the appropriate strategies. For example, in 2015 Millennials (defined as individuals between the ages of 18 and 34 in 2015) became the largest group in the U.S. workforce.[57] This trend of an increasing number of Millennial workers has implications for the kinds of businesses that will succeed in the future, as Millennials have often been associated with a lower propensity for risk coupled with a higher desire for unique "craft" experiences and products. Meanwhile Generation Z is known to base purchasing decisions on brands they believe in (while avoiding brands that they feel compromise their values).[58]

Although the degree of impact varies, general environmental segments affect all industries and its firms. The challenge to the firm is to evaluate those elements in each segment that are of the greatest importance. Resulting from these efforts should be a recognition of environmental opportunities and threats. An understanding of the general environment provides insights into potential industries that may grow or decline in the future. In the next section we present a framework for analyzing industries that provides more in-depth insights into the potential of a particular industry environment.

Porter's Five-Forces Analysis of Market Structure

FIGURE 5.12 Porter's Five Forces

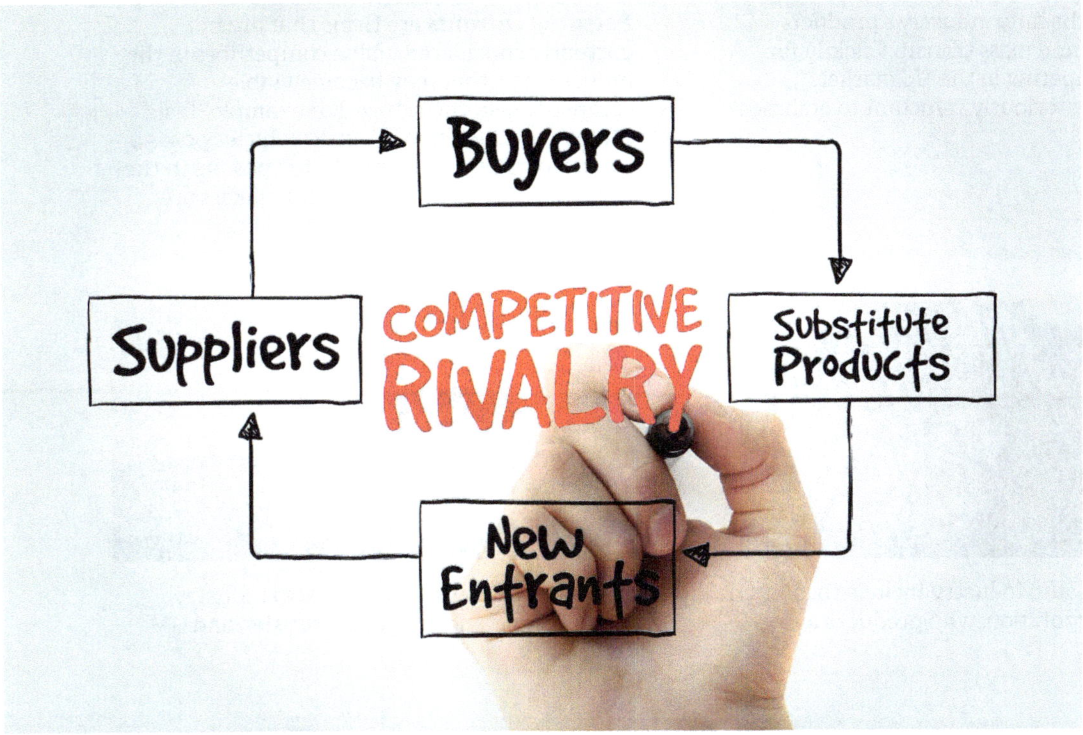

Source: Shutterstock.com

One of the most well-known frameworks used to analyze industries is Michael Porter's five forces. Porter's model attempts to analyze the attractiveness of an industry by considering five forces within a market that impact industry profitability. According to Porter, the likelihood of firms making profits in a given industry depends on five factors: (1) barriers to entry and the threat of potential new entrants, (2) buyer power, (3) supplier power, (4) threat from substitutes, and (5) rivalry among industry competitors.[59]

FIGURE 5.13 Industry Analysis

Understanding the dynamics that shape how much profit potential exists within an industry is key to knowing how likely a particular firm is to succeed within the industry. There are five key forces that determine the profitability of a particular industry.

Substitutes for the auto industry's products include bicycles and mass transit. Luckily for automakers competing in the US market, Americans are notoriously reluctant to embrace these substitutes.

Potential entrants are firms that are not currently considered viable competitors in the industry but that may become viable competitors in the future. For example, Tesla Motors' production of electric vehicles poses a threat to displace the traditional powers in the auto industry, and Chinese auto makers are rumored to be eyeing the US market.

Suppliers to the auto industry include firms such as Lear Corporation, who produces auto interior systems.

Industry competitors in the auto industry include firms such as Ford, Chrysler, and GM.

Buyers are those firms that buy directly from the industry such as automobile dealerships. Automakers also have to pay careful attention to end users, of course, such as individual drivers and rental car agencies.

Source: Shutterstock.com, Ayman alakgras_Shutterstock.com

Compared with the general environment, the industry environment has a more direct effect on the firm's strategic competitiveness and above-average returns. Porter's five-forces model of competition expands the arena for competitive analysis compared to previous efforts to examine competition. Historically, when studying the competitive environment, firms concentrated on companies with which they competed directly. However, firms must search more broadly to identify current and potential competitors by identifying potential customers, as well as the firms serving them. Understanding industries is particularly important because, in recent years, industry boundaries have become blurred. For example, telecommunications companies now compete with broadcasters, software manufacturers provide personal financial services, airlines sell mutual funds, and automakers sell insurance and provide financing.[60]

The five-forces model recognizes that suppliers can become a firm's competitors (by integrating forward), as can buyers (by integrating backward). For example, in the late 1990s Pepsi entered into the restaurant market by purchasing Pizza Hut, Taco Bell, and KFC.[61] While they eventually sold off these restaurants, the acquisition showed the power to enter into a different industry and the majority of restaurants in these chains continue to serve Pepsi products.

Another way to think about industry profit potential is that these five sets of stakeholders are competing for profits in the given industry. For instance, if a supplier to an industry is powerful, they can charge higher prices. If the industry members are not able to pass those higher costs onto their buyers in the form of higher prices, then the industry members make less profit. For example, if jewelry stores are dependent on a large company like De Beers for diamonds, then De Beers actually is extracting more relative value from the industry than are the industry members (i.e., the retail jewelry business).

New Entrants

The likelihood of new entry is a function of the extent to which barriers to entry exist. Evidence suggests that companies often find it difficult to identify new competitors.[62] Identifying potential new entrants to an industry is important because they can threaten the market share of existing competitors. For example, in 1983 only 49 breweries existed in the United States; today, that number exceeds 8,000 due to the number of craft brewers and the low barriers to entry in this industry.[63] Subsequently, market share has greatly diminished for large brewers that once completely dominated the industry. One reason new entrants pose such a threat is that they bring additional production capacity. Unless the demand for a good or service is increasing, additional capacity holds consumers' costs down, resulting in less revenue and lower returns for competing firms. Often, new entrants have a keen interest in gaining a large market share. As a result, new competitors may force existing firms to be more effective and efficient and to learn how to compete in new dimensions (for example, using an internet-based distribution channel).

Microbreweries have flourished in the U.S. thanks partly to the low barriers for new entrants.

Source: Shutterstock.com

The more difficult it is for other firms to enter a market, the more likely it is that existing firms can make relatively high profits. The likelihood that firms will enter an industry is a function of two factors: barriers to entry and the retaliation expected from current industry participants. Entry barriers make it difficult for new firms to enter an industry and often place them at a competitive disadvantage even when they are able to enter. As such, high entry barriers increase the returns for existing firms in the industry.[64]

Buyer Power

The stronger the power of buyers in an industry, the more likely it is that they will be able to force down prices and reduce the profits of firms that provide the product. Firms seek to maximize the return on their invested capital. Alternatively, buyers (often but not always final customers of an industry or firm) want to buy products at the lowest possible price—the point at which the industry earns the lowest acceptable rate of return on its invested capital. To reduce their costs, buyers bargain for higher-quality, greater levels of service, and lower prices. These outcomes are achieved by encouraging competitive battles among the industry's firms. Buyer power is typically low when the buyer is the ultimate consumer, but when the buyer refers to larger corporations (especially in industries where few firms exist) buyer power can be significant.

Supplier Power

The stronger the power of suppliers in an industry, the more difficult it is for firms within that sector to make a profit, because suppliers can determine the terms and conditions on which business is conducted. Increasing prices and reducing the quality of its products are potential means used by suppliers to exert power over firms competing within an industry. If a firm is unable to recover cost increases by its suppliers through its pricing structure, its profitability is reduced by its suppliers' actions. For example, the airline industry is influenced significantly by oil as a key supply to fuel planes.

Substitutes

A great substitute for soda—iced coffee is the most commonly purchased drink of Gen Z and 65% hit up a convenience store at least once a month for their drink of choice.

Source: Shutterstock.com

This power of substitutes refers to the ease with which buyers can switch to another product in a *different* industry that accomplished the same goals as the industry's goods and services, such as using aluminum cans rather than glass or plastic bottles to package a beverage. The ease of switching depends on what costs would be involved (e.g., while it may be easy to sell Coke or Pepsi in bottles or cans, transferring all your data to a new database system and retraining staff could be expensive) and how similar customers perceive the alternatives to be. Substitute products are goods or services from outside a given industry that perform similar or the same functions as a product that the industry produces. For example, as sugar substitutes, NutraSweet and Stevia place an upper limit on sugar manufacturers' prices to the degree that individuals, consumers, and manufacturers believe such sweeteners and sugar perform the same function. Other product substitutes include e-mail delivery of documents instead of overnight deliveries, plastic containers rather than glass jars, and coffee substituted for soft drinks.[65]

In general, product substitutes present a strong threat to a firm when customers face few, if any, switching costs and when the substitute product's price is lower or its quality and performance capabilities are equal to or greater than those of the competing product. Differentiating a product along dimensions that customers value (such as price, quality, service after the sale, and location) reduces a substitute's attractiveness.

Rivalry

Rivalry in the Five-Forces framework refers to the degree of competition between existing firms. The higher the degree of rivalry, the more difficult it is for existing firms to generate high profits. The most prominent factors that experience shows affect the intensity of firms' rivalries are: (1) numerous competitors, (2) slow industry growth, (3) high fixed costs, (4) lack of differentiation, (5) high strategic stakes, and (6) high exit barriers.

Numerous or Equally Balanced Competitors

Intense rivalries are common in industries with many competitors. With multiple competitors, it is common for a few firms to believe that they can act without eliciting a response. However, evidence suggests that other firms generally are aware of competitors' actions, often choosing to respond to them. At the other extreme, industries with only a few firms of equivalent size and power also tend to have strong rivalries. The large and often similar-sized resource bases of these firms permit vigorous actions and responses. For example, the constant competition between Coca-Cola and Pepsi has led this rivalry to be dubbed the "Cola Wars."[66]

Slow Industry Growth

When a market is growing, firms try to use resources effectively to serve an expanding customer base. Growing markets reduce the pressure to take customers from competitors. However, rivalry in nongrowth or slow-growth markets becomes more intense as firms battle to increase their market shares by attracting their competitors' customers.

Typically, battles to protect market shares are fierce. The instability in the market that results from these competitive engagements reduces profitability for firms throughout the industry, as is demonstrated by the commercial aircraft industry. The market for large aircraft is expected to decline or grow only slightly over the next few years. To expand market share, Boeing and Airbus compete aggressively in terms of the introduction of new products and product and service differentiation.

High Fixed Costs or High Storage Costs

When fixed costs account for a large part of total costs, companies try to maximize the use of their productive capacity. Doing so allows the firm to spread costs across a larger volume of output. However, when many firms attempt to maximize their productive capacity, excess capacity is created on an industry-wide basis. To then reduce inventories, individual companies typically cut the price of their product and offer rebates and other special discounts to customers. These practices, however, often intensify competition. The pattern of excess capacity at the industry level followed by intense rivalry at the firm level is observed frequently in industries with high storage costs. Perishable products, for example, lose their value rapidly with the passage of time. As their inventories grow, producers of perishable goods often use pricing strategies to sell products quickly.

Lack of Differentiation or Low Switching Costs

When buyers find a differentiated product that satisfies their needs, they frequently purchase the product loyally over time. Industries with many companies that have successfully differentiated their products have less rivalry, resulting in lower competition for individual firms.[67] However, when buyers view products as commodities (as products with few differentiated features or capabilities), rivalry intensifies. In these instances, buyers' purchasing decisions are based primarily on price and, to a lesser degree, on service.

The effect of switching costs is identical to that described for differentiated products. The lower the buyers' switching costs, the easier it is for competitors to attract buyers through pricing and service offerings. High switching costs, however, at least partially insulate the firm from rivals' efforts to attract customers. Interestingly, the switching costs—such as pilot and mechanic training—are high in aircraft purchases; yet, the rivalry between Boeing and Airbus remains intense because the stakes for both are extremely high.

High Strategic Stakes

Competitive rivalry is likely to be high when it is important for several of the competitors to perform well in the market. For example, although it is diversified and is a market leader in other businesses, Samsung has targeted market leadership in the consumer electronics market. This market is quite important to Sony and other major competitors such as Hitachi, Matsushita, NEC, and Mitsubishi. Thus, we can expect substantial rivalry in this market over the next few years.

High strategic stakes can also exist in terms of geographic locations. For example, Japanese automobile manufacturers committed to a significant presence in the U.S. marketplace. A key reason for this is that the United States is the world's single largest market for auto manufacturers' products. Because of the stakes involved in this country for Japanese and U.S. manufacturers, rivalry among firms in the U.S. and global automobile industry is highly intense. While close proximity tends to promote greater rivalry, physically proximate competition has potentially positive benefits as well. For example, when competitors are located near one another, it is easier for suppliers to serve them and they can develop economies of scale that lead to lower production costs. Additionally, communications with key industry stakeholders such as suppliers are facilitated and more efficient when they are close to the firm.[68]

High Exit Barriers

It's a tough road to climb for firms hoping to leave the auto industry where exit barriers are notoriously high.

Source: Pan_photo/Shutterstock.com

Sometimes companies continue competing in an industry even though the returns on their invested capital are low or negative. Firms making this choice likely face high exit barriers, which include economic, strategic, and emotional factors, causing companies to remain in an industry when the profitability of doing so is questionable.

Attractiveness and Profitability

Using Porter's analysis, firms are likely to generate higher profits if:

- the industry is difficult to enter,
- there is limited rivalry,
- buyers are relatively weak,
- suppliers are relatively weak,
- there are few substitutes.

Profits are likely to be low if:

- the industry is easy to enter,
- there is a high degree of rivalry between firms within the industry,
- buyers are strong,
- suppliers are strong,
- it is easy to switch to alternatives.

Effective industry analyses are products of careful study and interpretation of data and information from multiple sources. A wealth of industry-specific data is available to be analyzed. Because of globalization, international markets and rivalries must be included in the firm's analyses. In fact, research shows that in some industries, international variables are more important than domestic ones as determinants of strategic competitiveness. Furthermore, because of the development of global markets, a country's borders no longer restrict industry structures. In fact, movement into international markets enhances the chances of success for new ventures as well as more established firms.[69]

Following a study of the five forces of competition, the firm can develop the insights required to determine an industry's attractiveness in terms of its potential to earn adequate or superior returns on its invested capital. In general, the stronger competitive forces are, the lower the profit potential for an industry's firms. An unattractive industry has low entry barriers, suppliers and buyers with strong bargaining positions, strong competitive threats from product substitutes, and intense rivalry among competitors. These industry characteristics make it very difficult for firms to achieve strategic competitiveness and earn above-average returns. Alternatively, an attractive industry has high entry barriers, suppliers and buyers with little bargaining power, few competitive threats from product substitutes, and relatively moderate rivalry.[70]

Key Takeaway

External environment analysis is a key input into strategy formulation. PESTEL is an external environment analysis framework that helps guide your prospecting in the political, economic, social, technological, environmental, and legal spheres of an organization's external environment. Porter's five forces provides a deeper look at industry analysis considering (1) barriers to entry and new entry threats, (2) buyer power, (3) supplier power, (4) threat from substitutes, and (5) rivalry, as key external environmental forces in developing strategy.

Discussion Questions

1. What are the six dimensions of the environment that are of broad concern when you conduct a PESTEL analysis?
2. Which of the PESTEL dimensions do you believe to be most important, and why?
3. What are the five forces referred to in the Porter framework?
4. Is there a dimension of industry structure that Porter's model appears to omit?

5.6 Formulating Organizational and Personal Strategy with the Strategy Diamond

Learning Objectives

1. Learn about the strategy diamond.
2. See how you can add staging, pacing, and vehicles to the strategy.
3. Use the diamond to formulate your personal strategy.

This section introduces the strategy diamond, a tool that helps managers understand how clearly and completely they have crafted a strategy. The diamond relates to both business and corporate strategy, and provides a checklist of what elements an effective strategy should cover. The section concludes by applying the strategy diamond to help develop a personal strategy.

The Strategy Diamond

strategy diamond

A framework comprising five facets for understanding the content of a strategy; the facets are arenas, differentiators, vehicles, staging and pacing, and economic logic.

The **strategy diamond** was developed by strategy researchers Don Hambrick and Jim Fredrickson as a framework for checking and communicating a strategy; their classic article asks the question, "Are you sure you have a strategy?"[71] In critiquing the field of strategic management, these researchers noted that "after more than 30 years of hard thinking about strategy, consultants and scholars have provided executives with an abundance of frameworks for analyzing strategic situations. . . . Missing, however, has been any guidance as to what the product of these tools should be—or what actually constitutes a strategy."[72]

Their critiques and analysis concluded that effective strategies necessarily have five parts. The figure summarizes the parts of their diamond model, its facets, and some examples of the different ways to consider each facet. The diamond model consists of an integrated set of choices. In this section we discuss each facet.

FIGURE 5.14 The Strategy Diamond

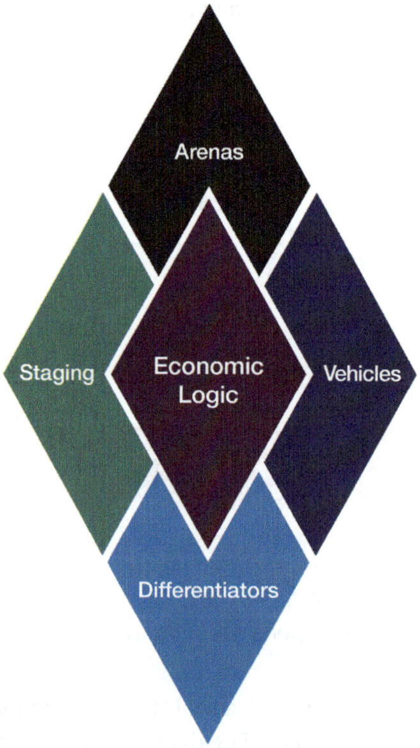

Source: Adapted from Hambrick, D. C., & Fredrickson, J. W. (2001). Are you sure you have a strategy? *Academy of Management Executive, 19* (4), 51–62.

ARENAS: Where will we be active (and with how much emphasis)?

- Which product categories?
- Which channels?
- Which market segments?
- Which geographic areas?
- Which core technologies?
- Which value-creation stages?

VEHICLES: How will we get there?

- Internal development?

- Joint ventures?
- Licensing/franchising?
- Alliances?
- Acquisitions?

DIFFERENTIATORS: How will we win?

- Image?
- Customization?
- Price?
- Styling?
- Product reliability?
- Speed to market?

ECONOMIC LOGIC: How will returns be obtained?

- Lowest costs through scale advantages?
- Lowest costs through scope and replication advantages?
- Premium prices due to unmatchable service?
- Premium prices due to proprietary product features?

STAGING: What will be our speed and sequence of moves?

- Speed of expansion?
- Sequence of initiatives?

Arenas, Differentiators, and Economic Logic

The first three facets of the strategy diamond—arenas, differentiators, and economic logic—are traditional in the sense that they address three longstanding hallmarks of strategizing. Specifically, strategy matches up market needs and opportunities (located in arenas) with unique features of the firm (shown by its differentiators) to yield positive performance (economic logic). While performance is typically viewed in financial terms, it can have social or environmental components as well.

Answers to strategy questions about *arenas* tell managers and employees *where* the firm will be active. For instance, Nike is headquartered in Washington County, on the outskirts of Beaverton, Oregon. Today, Nike's geographic market arenas are most major markets around the globe, but in the early 1960s, Nike's arenas were limited to Pacific Northwest track meets accessible by founder Phil Knight's car. In terms of product markets (another part of *where*), the young Nike company sold only track shoes.

Beyond geographic-market and product-market arenas, an organization can also make choices about the value-chain arenas in its strategy. To emphasize the *choice* part of this value-chain arena, Nike's competitor New Balance manufactures nearly all the athletic shoes that it sells in the United States. Thus these two sports-shoe companies compete in similar geographic- and product-market arenas but differ greatly in terms of their choice of value-chain arenas.

Differentiators include elements that are unique to the firm, such that they provide a competitive advantage in its current and future arenas. A differentiator could be something related to an organization's tangible or intangible assets. A **tangible asset** has a value and physically exists. Land, machines, equipment, automobiles, and even cash, are examples of tangible assets. For instance, the oceanfront land on California's Monterey Peninsula, where the Pebble Beach Golf Course and Resort is located, is a differentiator for it in the premium golfcourse market. An **intangible asset** is a nonphysical resource that provides gainful advantages in the marketplace. Brands, copyrights, software, logos, patents, goodwill, and other intangible factors afford name recognition for products

tangible asset

An asset that has a value and physically exists.

intangible asset

An asset that cannot be physically touched, or is not physical in nature.

and services. The Nike brand has become a valuable intangible asset because of the broad awareness and reputation for quality and high performance that it has built. Differentiators can also be found in capabilities—that is, *how* the organization does something. Walmart, for instance, is very good at keeping its costs low. Nike, in contrast, focuses on developing leading-edge, high-performance athletic performance technologies, as well as up-to-the-minute fashion in active sportswear.

The Nike "Swoosh," created by a Portland State University student for Phil Knight in 1971, provides a well-known example of an intangible asset.

Source: Coompia77/Shutterstock.com

The third facet of the strategy diamond in this traditional view is *economic logic*, which explains how the firm makes money. Economic logic tells us how profits will be generated above the firm's cost of capital (costs associated with procuring cash to operate a firm). The collapse in the late 1990s of stock market valuations for internet companies lacking in profits—or any prospect of profits—marked a return to economic reality. Profits above the firm's cost of capital are required to yield sustained or longer-term shareholder returns. While the economic logic can include environmental and social profits (benefits reaped by society), the strategy must earn enough financial profits to keep investors (owners, tax payers, governments, and so on) willing to continue to fund the organization's costs of doing business. A firm performs well (i.e., has a strong, positive economic logic) when its differentiators are well aligned with its chosen arenas.

Vehicles

The first three facets of the strategy diamond—arenas, differentiators, and economic logic—might be considered the traditional facets of strategizing in that they cover the basics: (1) external environment, (2) internal organizational characteristics, and (3) some fit between these elements has positive performance consequences. The fourth facet of the strategy diamond is called *vehicles*.

Vehicles refers to how firms pursue a new arena through internal means, through help from a new partner or some other outside source, or even through acquisition. An example is found in ubiquitous toymaker LEGO, which deftly utilizes licensing beginning with their deals bringing Star Wars characters to the LEGO universe that now includes characters from its own popular movie as well as mini figures ranging from Batman to Captain Jack Sparrow to Harry Potter.[73]

In the context of vehicles, this is where organizations determine if they plan to grow organically, acquisitively, or through a combination of both. *Organic growth* is the growth rate of a company excluding any growth from takeovers, acquisitions, or mergers. *Acquisitive growth*, in contrast, refers precisely to any growth from takeovers, acquisitions, or mergers. Augmenting either organic or acquisitive growth is growth through partnerships with other organizations. Sometimes such partnership-based growth is referred to as *co-opetition*, because an organization cooperates with others, even some competitors, in order to compete and grow.

Vehicles are considered part of the strategy because there are different skills and competencies associated with different vehicles. For instance, acquisitions fuel rapid growth, but they are challenging to negotiate and put into place. Similarly, alliances spread risk and let each partner focus on what it does best. Growing through alliances requires organizations to excel at managing relationships where firms are dependent upon each other and where no one firm has direct control. Organic growth, particularly for firms that have grown primarily through partnering or acquisition, has its own distinct challenges because the organization is on its own to put together everything needed to fuel growth.

Staging and Pacing

Staging and pacing constitute the fifth and final facet of the strategy diamond. *Staging and pacing* reflect the sequence and speed of strategic moves. This powerful facet of strategizing helps firms think about timing and next steps, instead of creating a strategy that is a static, monolithic plan. As an example, the managers of Chuy's, a chain of Austin, Texas-based Tex-Mex restaurants, wanted to grow the business outside of Austin, but at the same time, they knew it would be difficult to manage restaurants that were farther away. How should they identify cities in which to experiment with new outlets? Their creative solution was to choose cities that were connected to Austin by Southwest Airlines. Since Southwest is inexpensive and its point-to-point system means that cities are never much more than an hour apart, the Austin managers could easily and regularly visit their new ventures out of town. Because strategizing is about making choices, sequencing and speed should be key choices along with the other facets of the strategy. The staging and pacing facet also helps to reconcile the designed and emergent portions of strategy.

The Strategy Diamond and Personal Growth and Development Strategy

The strategy diamond is a useful professional and personal tool for managers. How might it benefit individuals personally? Figure 5.15 maps out how personal strategy fits in the planning aspect of P-O-L-C. Personal strategy should be guided by a personal mission and vision. Let's examine how the strategy diamond might be applied to personal growth and development objectives.

FIGURE 5.15 Planning and Your Personal Growth and Development Strategy

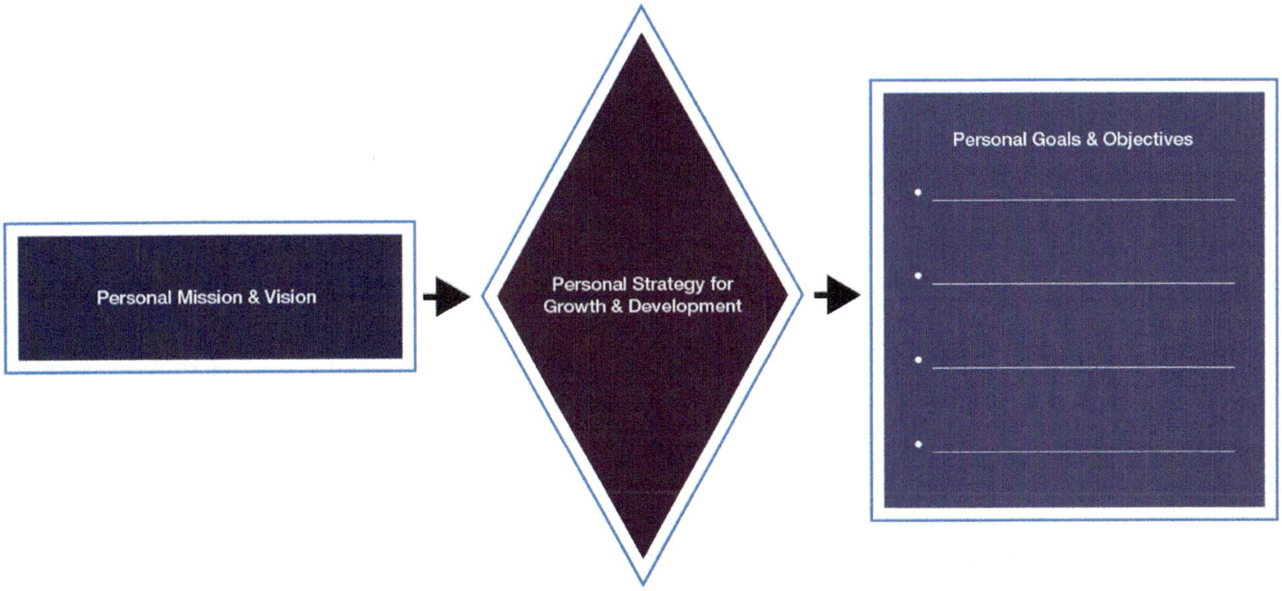

Personal Arenas and Differentiators

Arenas and differentiators will answer personal growth and development questions such as the following:

- What type of work do I want to do?
- What leisure activities do I like?
- Where do I want to live?
- What capabilities (differentiators) do I need to participate in these arenas?
- What organizations value these capabilities (differentiators)?
- What capabilities (differentiators) do I want to have and excel in?

Personal arenas can include a preferred recreational activity (surfing), a specific job, or simply a geographic location. For instance, do you want to be a store manager, an accountant, an entrepreneur, or a CEO? Or do you want to live in a certain locale? It can also be a combination of several criteria. For example, perhaps you want to be a software designer for Google and live in San Francisco.

The more specific individuals are about the arenas in their strategy, the better they will be able to plot out additional facets. Using Google as an example, personal differentiators would likely have to include the demonstration of excellence in software design and an affinity for the Google corporate culture. More broadly, the differentiator facet of personal strategy should map on to an arena's facet in a manner that clearly fits together. Such differentiators are subject to VRIO, in that when an individual's capabilities are valuable and rare, they may be more likely to economically benefit from them with employers.

Personal Vehicles

The personal vehicles facet of strategy answers questions such as the following:

- What do I need to accomplish on my own?
- What do I want to accomplish on my own?
- What do I need to accomplish with the help of others?
- Who are they?

We often think that our careers and quality of life are based on personal choices and actions alone. If that is your belief (i.e., you are a rugged individualist), then your personal growth and development strategy seems to be highly dependent on what you do but not on the contributions of others.

On some level we have to develop our own knowledge and capabilities to move forward. However, the concept of division of labor suggests that individuals and organizations typically get most things done through and with others.

The vehicles component of your personal strategy diamond should spell out how your growth and development is a function of what you do (when we talk about organizations, we refer to this as organic growth), and what you depend on others to do. The better you understand your dependence on others, the better you will likely be able to manage those relationships.

Personal Staging and Pacing

Personal staging and pacing answers questions such as the following:

- What sequence of events does my strategy require?
- What are the financial requirements and consequences of each event?
- What is my deadline for the first event?
- Is the deadline flexible? Can I manage the pacing of the achievement of each event?
- How will timing affect achievement of my personal growth and development strategy?
- Do some events provide an opportunity to reconsider or adjust my strategy?

For instance, if you want to be a manager of a retail store it is likely you might need a related college degree and experience. Your personal staging and pacing would answer questions about how you would achieve these, the financial implications of each, as well as their timing.

Personal Economic Logic

Personal economic logic answers questions such as the following:

- How does achievement of my strategy help me pay the bills?
- What dimensions of my strategy, like arenas or differentiators, is the economic logic of my strategy most dependent on?
- How sustainable is the economic logic of my strategy?

We can see this logic clearly when magazines publish lists of high-demand jobs.[74] When employees have skills that are in high demand by employers, the price of those skills, in the form of a paycheck, is usually bid up in the market. For organizations, economic logic is typically viewed in terms of financial performance. However, increasingly, firms target social and environmental performance as well—similarly, the economic logic of strategy can have implications for what individuals might do to improve social and environmental conditions. This can happen directly through volunteer hours or indirectly through financial support of valued causes.

Key Takeaway

The application of the strategy diamond involves first identifying the organization's arenas, differentiators, and economic logic. This step summarizes many of the traditional views in strategic management. The second step involves contemplating how the organization would compete or grow in existing or new arenas—considering where vehicles come into play. Finally, the sequencing and speed of strategic initiatives related to the facet of staging and pacing should be considered. Together, these five facets (i.e., arenas, differentiators, economic logic, vehicles, staging, and pacing) constitute the strategy diamond. The strategy diamond is also valuable in its application to the implementation of personal strategies.

Discussion Questions

1. What are the five facets of the Hambrick and Fredrickson strategy diamond?
2. If a firm is performing poorly financially, what might this say about the differentiators, arenas, or both?
3. Why is it important to consider vehicles as part of an organization's strategy?
4. What are some ways that you might apply staging and pacing to an organization's strategy?

5.7 Case in Point: At Costco, Strong Culture Leads to Strong Performance

Source: Michael Gordon/Shutterstock.com

Costco is a membership-based warehouse club that sells anything from electronics to groceries to furniture, with over 250,000 employees around the world. The first Costco opened in 1973 in Seattle, Washington, as a wholesale club business. Today the company operates nearly 800 warehouses in over 10 countries. Costco is known for acquiring large quantities of products at wholesale prices and passing the savings along to its customers. It is also known for being one of the top places to work, ranking #1 as America's best large employer in 2017, #1 in best company culture for large companies in 2018, and remaining in the top 5 of best large employers in 2019.

Costco's culture is founded on human connection. The company treats its employees like family and strives to always do the right thing by its customers. One Costco employee is quoted as saying, "I love the fact that while I'm at work, I don't feel like I'm working. Most of my colleagues are having fun doing what they do every day, which makes for an extremely happy work atmosphere."

Costco differentiates itself from its competitors by treating employees exceptionally well, providing generous compensation and benefits, emphasizing work-life balance, and extending ample leadership and professional development opportunities to its staff. Seventy cents of every dollar spent by Costco goes toward employee wages. Approximately 90% of Costco's employees are hourly workers, and the average wage is $23. Costco has demonstrated its intent to stay true to its ethos even in the face of criticism by Wall Street and during challenging economic times, never cutting jobs or failing to give raises. This loyalty to employees has led to a very low turnover rate: 7%, compared with others in the industry as high as 60 to 70%. In fact, over 60% of Costco employees in the US have been at Costco for more than five years.

Another thing that sets Costco apart is its opportunities for professional development. Many of the company's senior executives started as frontline staff. When the founder of the company, James Sinegal, was acting CEO, he spent about 200 days each year visiting warehouses, providing constructive feedback to managers around how to constantly be teaching employees and developing their skillsets. Costco also solicits feedback from employees at all levels of the organization around how to improve delivery of goods and services to members and improve efficiencies that reduce costs. By giving all employees a platform to share their voices, Costco sets the stage for high levels of employee pride and satisfaction.

Costco's emphasis on culture seems to have paid off for the organization. The company is the second-largest retailer in the world with more than $149 billion in sales and a brand value exceeding $17 billion. Costco's share price and membership numbers have consistently trended upward over the last 20 years, and the company continues to open new brick-and-mortar stores despite the industry trend toward e-commerce.[75]

Multimedia Extension—Doing the Right Thing When Dollars Are on the Line: Jim Sinegal

View in the online reader

Case Discussion Questions

1. What are some of the ways that Costco demonstrates a people-oriented culture?
2. Why do you think a strong company culture founded on connection, such as Costco's, is so unique in the retail industry?
3. Do you think it is important for a company like Costco to adhere to its values around employee treatment, even during difficult times? Why or why not?
4. To what extent do you think Costco's success is attributable to the way the company treats its employees? Explain.
5. How might Costco's practice of promoting from within impact employee performance and job satisfaction? Explain.

Endnotes

1. Ketchen., D.J., & Short, J.C. (2018). *Mastering Strategic Management*. (Second Edition) Boston: FlatWorld.
2. Ketchen., D.J., & Short, J.C. (2018). *Mastering Strategic Management*. (Second Edition) Boston: FlatWorld.
3. Mintzberg, H. (1978). Patterns in strategy formulation. *Management Science, 24*, 934–949.
4. Retrieved from http://www.forbes.com/sites/autumnadeigbo/2015/10/11/6-steps-to-writing-an-award-winning-business-plan/.
5. Carpenter, M. A., & Sanders, W. G. (2008). Fast food chic? The Chipotle burrito. University of Wisconsin Business Case.
6. Retrieved from http://www.secinfo.com/dRqWm.89X3.htm#34f.
7. Retrieved from http://www.fastcompany.com/1696887/toms-vs-bobs-how-skechers-shot-themselves-foot.
8. Retrieved from https://www.globaltimes.cn/content/1199653.shtml.
9. Retrieved from https://www.mckinsey.com/business-functions/operations/our-insights/coronavirus-impact-on-service-organizations-weathering-the-storm.
10. Retrieved from http://mentalfloss.com/article/22822/15-companies-originally-sold-something-else.
11. Mintzberg, H. (1987, July–August). Crafting strategy. *Harvard Business Review*, 66–75; Mintzberg, H. (1996). The entrepreneurial organization. In H. Mintzberg & J. B. Quinn (Eds.), *The strategy process* (3rd ed.). Englewood Cliffs, NJ: Prentice-Hall; Mintzberg, H., & Waters, J. A. (1985). Of strategies, deliberate and emergent. *Strategic Management Journal, 6*, 257–272.
12. See Mintzberg, H. (1978). Patterns in strategy formulation. *Management Science, 24*, 934–948; Mintzberg, H., & Waters, J. A. (1985). Of strategies, deliberate and emergent. *Strategic Management Journal, 6*, 257–272; and Mintzberg, H. (1988). *Mintzberg on management: Inside our strange world of organizations*. New York: Free Press.
13. The two views of Honda are captured in two Harvard cases: *Honda [A]*. (1989). Boston: Harvard Business School, Case 384049, and *Honda [B]*. (1989). Boston: Harvard Business School, Case 384050.
14. Retrieved from https://hbr.org/2014/01/the-big-lie-of-strategic-planning.
15. Retrieved from http://www.bloomberg.com/news/articles/2013-10-29/dell-completes-24-9-billion-leveraged-buyout.
16. Retrieved from http://www.latimes.com/business/la-fi-dell-emc-20151012-story.html.
17. Retrieved from https://blog.dell.com/en-us/dell-recycles-gold-motherboards-nikki-reed-jewelry/.
18. Retrieved from https://www.fastcompany.com/most-innovative-companies/2019/sectors/consumer-electronics.
19. Porter, M. (1985). *Competitive advantage: Creating and sustaining superior performance*. New York: Free Press; Porter, M. (1989). *Competitive advantage of nations*. New York: Free Press; Porter, M. (1980). *Competitive strategy: Techniques for analyzing industries and companies*. New York: Free Press; Porter, M. (2001, March). Strategy and the Internet. *Harvard Business Review*, 63–78; Retrospective on Michael Porter's (2002). *Competitive strategy* [Special section]. *Academy of Management Executive, 16*, 40–65.
20. Retrieved from https://hbr.org/2018/05/stitch-fixs-ceo-on-selling-personal-style-to-the-mass-market.
21. Retrieved from http://marketrealist.com/2015/07/southwests-low-cost-strategy-helps-maintain-competitive-edge/.
22. Retrieved from https://www.businessinsider.com/radical-differentiation-at-lululemon-2012-3.
23. Retrieved from http://www.gq-magazine.co.uk/style/articles/2012-11/01/james-bond-barbour-waxed-jacket-skyfall-daniel-craig.
24. Retrieved from http://www.barbour.com/counterfeit-education.

25. Ketchen, D.J., & Short, J.C. (2015). *Mastering Strategic Management*. (Second Edition) Boston: FlatWorld.
26. Walters, B. A., & Bhuian, S. (2004). Complexity absorption and performance: A structural analysis of acute-care hospitals. *Journal of Management*, *30*, 97–121.
27. McEvily, S. K., & Chakravarthy, B. (2002). The persistence of knowledge-based advantage: An empirical test for product performance and technological knowledge. *Strategic Management Journal, 23*, 285–305; Buckley, P. J., & Carter, M. J. (2000). Knowledge management in global technology markets: Applying theory to practice. *Long Range Planning, 33*(1), 55–71.
28. Pocket Strategy. (1998). *Value* (p. 165). London: The Economist Books.
29. Prahalad, C. K., & Hamel, G. (1990). The core competence of the organization. *Harvard Business Review, 90*, 79–93.
30. Hafeez, K., Zhang, Y. B., & Malak, N. (2002). Core competence for sustainable competitive advantage: A structured methodology for identifying core competence. *IEEE Transactions on Engineering Management, 49*(1), 28–35; Prahalad, C. K., & Hamel, G. (1990). The core competence of the corporation. *Harvard Business Review, 68*(3), 79–93.
31. Ward, S. (2020). What is a core competency? Retrieved from https://www.thebalancesmb.com/core-competency-in-business-2948314.
32. Useem, J. (2001, February 19). Most admired: Conquering vertical limits. *Fortune*, pp. 84–96.
33. Useem, J. (2001, February 19). Most admired: Conquering vertical limits. *Fortune*, pp. 84–96.
34. Retrieved from https://www.marketwatch.com/story/walgreens-pulls-off-solid-quarter-at-time-when-pharmacy-and-retail-are-suffering-2017-10-25.
35. Eisenhardt, K., & Martin, J. (2000). Dynamic capabilities: What are they? *Strategic Management Journal, 21*, 1105–1121; Michalisin, M. D., Kline, D. M., & Smith. R. D. (2000). Intangible strategic assets and firm performance: A multi-industry study of the resource-based view, *Journal of Business Strategies, 17*, 91–117.
36. West, G. P., & DeCastro, J. (2001). The Achilles heel of firm strategy: Resource weaknesses and distinctive inadequacies. *Journal of Management Studies, 38*, 26–45; Deeds, D. L., DeCarolis, D., & J. Coombs. (2000). Dynamic capabilities and new product development in high technology ventures: An empirical analysis of new biotechnology firms. *Journal of Business Venturing, 15*, 211–229; Chi, T. (1994). Trading in strategic resources: Necessary conditions, transaction cost problems, and choice of exchange structure. *Strategic Management Journal, 15*, 271–290.
37. Berman, S., Down, J., & Hill, C. (2002). Tacit knowledge as a source of competitive advantage in the National Basketball Association. *Academy of Management Journal, 45*, 13–31.
38. Retrieved from https://www.bustle.com/p/what-is-amazon-prime-wardrobe-the-service-lets-you-try-on-clothes-before-you-buy-theres-no-catch-9538677.
39. Feldman, M. S. (2000). Organizational routines as a source of continuous change, *Organization Science, 11*, 611–629; Knott, A. M., & McKelvey, B. (1999). Nirvana efficiency: A comparative test of residual claims and routines. *Journal of Economic Behavior & Organization, 38*, 365–383.
40. Helfat, C. E., & Raubitschek, R. S. (2000). Product sequencing: Co-evolution of knowledge, capabilities, and products. *Strategic Management Journal, 21*, 961–979.
41. Hitt, M. A., Bierman, L., Shimizu, K., & Kochhar, R. (2001) Direct and moderating effects of human capital on strategy and performance in professional service firms: A resource-based perspective. *Academy of Management Journal, 44*, 13–28; Hitt, M. A., Ireland, R. D., & Lee, H. (2000). Technological learning, knowledge management, firm growth and performance: An introductory essay. *Journal of Engineering and Technology Management, 17*, 231–246; Hoopes, D. G., & Postrel, S. (1999). Shared knowledge: "Glitches," and product development performance. *Strategic Management Journal, 20*, 837–865; Quinn, J. B. (1994). *The Intelligent Enterprise*. New York: Free Press.
42. Retrieved from http://time.com/3712678/apple-innovation/.
43. Dess, G. G., & Picken, J. C. (1999). *Beyond productivity*. New York: AMACOM.
44. Coy, P. (2002, Spring). High turnover, high risk [Special Issue]. *BusinessWeek*, p. 24.
45. Baldwin, T. T., & Danielson, C. C. (2000). Building a learning strategy at the top: Interviews with ten of America's CLOs. *Business Horizons, 43*, 5–14.
46. Kuratko, D. F., Ireland, R. D., & Hornsby, J. S. (2001). Improving firm performance through entrepreneurial actions: Acordia's corporate entrepreneurship strategy. *Academy of Management Executive, 15*, 60–71; Hansen, M. T., Nhoria, N., & Tierney, T. (1999). What's your strategy for managing knowledge? *Harvard Business Review, 77*(2), 106–116.
47. Retrieved from http://voodoodoughnut.com.
48. Retrieved from http://www.rogue.com/rogue_beer/voodoo-bacon-maple-ale/.
49. VRIO analysis is at the core of the resource-based view of the firm. Wernerfelt, B. (1984). A resource-based view of the firm. *Strategic Management Journal, 5*, 171–180; Barney, J. B. (1991). Firm resources and sustained competitive advantage. *Journal of Management, 19*, 99–120.
50. Barney, J. B. (1991). Firm resources and sustained competitive advantage. *Journal of Management, 17*, 99–120.
51. Retrieved from http://insider.espn.com/nfl/draft2012/insider/story/_/id/7606991/why-nfl-teams-draft-running-backs-early-first-round.
52. Dyer, J. H., Kale, P., & Singh, H. (2004, July–August). When to ally and when to acquire. *Harvard Business Review*, 109–115.
53. Dyer, J. H., & Hatch, N. (2004). Using Supplier Networks to Learn Faster. *Sloan Management Review, 45*(3), 57–63.
54. Retrieved from http://www.forbes.com/sites/kenmakovsky/2013/11/21/behind-the-southwest-airlines-culture/.
55. Retrieved from http://www.nytimes.com/2015/04/20/business/media/netflix-is-betting-its-future-on-exclusive-programming.html?_r=0.
56. Fahey, L. (1999). *Competitors*. New York: Wiley; Walters, B. A., & Priem, R. L. (1999). Business strategy and CEO intelligence acquisition. *Competitive Intelligence Review, 10*(2), 15–22.
57. Retrieved from http://www.pewresearch.org/fact-tank/2015/05/11/millennials-surpass-gen-xers-as-the-largest-generation-in-u-s-labor-force/.
58. Retrieved from https://www.mckinsey.com/industries/consumer-packaged-goods/our-insights/true-gen-generation-z-and-its-implications-for-companies.
59. Porter, M. E. (1980). *Competitive strategy*. New York: Free Press.
60. Hitt, M. A., Ricart I Costa, J., & Nixon, R. D. (1999). *New managerial mindsets*. New York: Wiley.
61. Retrieved from http://www.fool.com/investing/general/2014/04/19/5-things-you-probably-didnt-know-about-yum-brands.aspx.
62. Geroski, P. A. (1999). Early warning of new rivals. *Sloan Management Review, 40*(3), 107–116.
63. Retrieved from https://www.beveragedaily.com/Article/2020/04/15/US-craft-beer-grew-4-in-2019-but-faces-difficult-2020-with-coronavirus.
64. Robinson, K. C., & McDougall, P. P. (2001). Entry barriers and new venture performance: A comparison of universal and contingency approaches. *Strategic Management Journal, 22*, 659–685.
65. Retrieved from http://www.businessinsider.com/millennials-habits-different-from-baby-boomers-2018-3.
66. Retrieved July 18, 2018. http://www.cbsnews.com/news/coke-pepsi-and-the-new-front-in-the-cola-wars/
67. Deephouse, D. L. (1999). To be different, or to be the same? It's a question (and theory) of strategic balance. *Strategic Management Journal, 20*, 147–166.
68. Chung, W., & Kalnins, A. (2001). Agglomeration effects and performance: Test of the Texas lodging industry. *Strategic Management Journal, 22*, 969–988.
69. Kuemmerle, W. (2001). Home base and knowledge management in international ventures. *Journal of Business Venturing, 17*, 99–122; Lorenzoni, G., & Lipparini, A. (1999). The leveraging of interfirm relationships as a distinctive organizational capability: A longitudinal study. *Strategic Management Journal, 20*, 317–338.
70. Porter, M. E. (1980). *Competitive strategy*. New York: Free Press.
71. Hambrick, D. C., & Fredrickson, J. W. (2001). Are you sure you have a strategy? *Academy of Management Executive, 19*, 51–62.
72. Hambrick, D. C., & Fredrickson, J. W. (2001). Are you sure you have a strategy? *Academy of Management Executive, 19*, 51–62, esp. 53.
73. Retrieved from http://www.wired.com/2014/02/infoporn-legos/.
74. Retrieved from http://money.usnews.com/money/careers/slideshows/15-awesome-jobs-that-pay-more-than-90k.
75. Case written by Rachel Mattenberger, Talya Bauer, and Berrin Erdogan to accompany T. N. Bauer & B. Erdogan (2021). *Organizational Behavior: Bridging Science and Practice (4.0)*. Boston, MA: FlatWorld. Partially based on ideas and information contained in Stallard, M. (2017). Why Culture Makes Costco America's Best Employer. https://www.td.org/insights/why-culture-makes-costco-americas-best-employer; Conway, J. (2020, January 7). Number of Costco warehouses in 2019, by country. Statista. https://www.statista.com/statistics/284431/number-of-costco-warehouses-2013-by-country/; Comparably. (2018). Best company culture 2018. https://www.comparably.com/blog/best-company-culture-2018/; Valet, V. (2019, April 17). America's best large employers. Forbes. Retrieved from https://www.forbes.com/best-large-employers/#395a7284fb3e; Ryan, T. (2019). Will Costco's new $15 minimum wage hurt or benefit the chain? https://www.retailwire.com/discussion/will-costcos-new-15-minimum-wage-hurt-or-benefit-the-chain; Grotte, O. (2019). 11 Reasons Why Costco Is A Terrific Company. https://seekingalpha.com/article/4269212-11-reasons-costco-terrific-company.

CHAPTER 6

Goals and Objectives

Amazon has set an aggressive goal of enabling their readers to download "every book ever printed in any language . . . in less than 60 seconds."

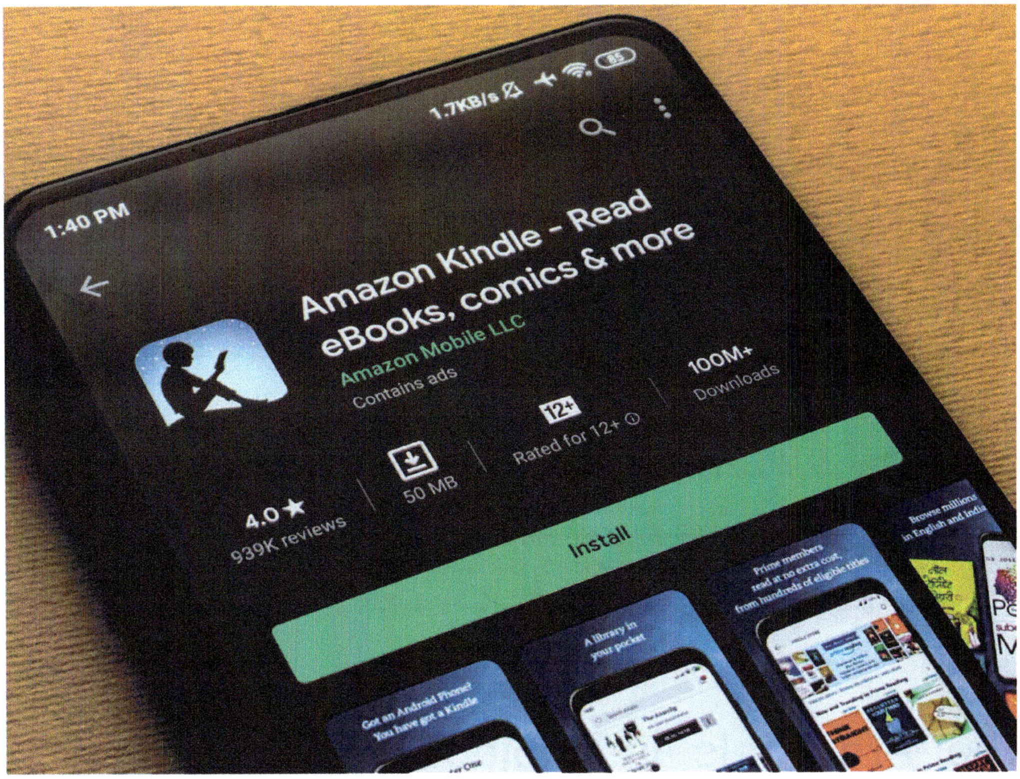

Source: sdx15/Shutterstock.com

Chapter Learning Objectives

Reading this chapter will help you accomplish the following:

1. Demonstrate an understanding of the nature of goals and objectives and their importance to effective management.
2. Explain what characterizes effective goals and objectives.
3. Understand the roles of goals and objectives in employee performance reviews.
4. See relationships among economic, social, and environmental goals and objectives.
5. Learn how to set and manage your own goals and objectives.

Goals and objectives are a critical component of management, both in terms of planning and in terms of the larger planning-organizing-leading-controlling (P-O-L-C) framework. Their role is summarized in Table 6.1. Despite their importance, goals are often neglected in managerial practice, and at times, individuals' goals are poorly aligned with the organization's strategy. This practice is problematic because one of a manager's key functions is to evaluate employee performance. Such evaluations should be based on how the achievement of individual goals and objectives contributes to functions critical to the organization's survival and success. In this chapter, we introduce the basics of creating effective goals and objectives and provide an understanding of how their usage has evolved. We also show how to develop a personalized set of goals and objectives to help achieve personal and professional aspirations.

TABLE 6.1 The P-O-L-C Framework

Planning	Organizing	Leading	Controlling
1. Vision & Mission	1. Organization Design	1. Leadership	1. Systems/Processes
2. Strategizing	2. Culture	2. Decision Making	2. Strategic Human Resources
3. Goals & Objectives	3. Social Networks	3. Communications	
		4. Groups/Teams	
		5. Motivation	

6.1 The Nature of Goals and Objectives

Learning Objectives

1. Know the difference between goals and objectives.
2. Know the relationship between goals and objectives.
3. See how goals and objectives fit in the P-O-L-C framework.

What Are Goals and Objectives?

goals

Outcome statements that define what an organization is trying to accomplish, both programmatically and organizationally.

Goals are outcome statements that define what an organization is trying to accomplish. Goals are a reflection of major actions of the organization, and provide rallying points for managers. For example, the CEO of Uber announced a goal of making their service so efficient that it is less expensive than actually owning a car.[1] Research has found the acquisition of business skills relevant to accomplishing organizational goals to be one of the most critical skills for developing effective leaders.[2] Individuals with unmet goals are more likely to engage in unethical behavior.[3] And the ability to set realistic goals is a key component in successfully attaining work-life balance (and even more valuable than having a flexible work schedule).[4]

In contrast to goals, **objectives** are very precise, time-based, measurable actions that support the completion of a goal. Objectives typically must (1) be related directly to the goal; (2) be clear, concise, and understandable; (3) be stated in terms of results; (4) begin with an action verb; (5) specify a date for accomplishment; and (6) be measurable. For example, while Uber might have a greater goal of serving as a replacement for cars, one specific objective to achieve that goal might be to "enter 20 new cities in the next six months." Without specific objectives, the general goal cannot be accomplished.

Measures are the actual metrics used to gauge performance of objectives. For instance, the *objective* of improved financial performance can be *measured* using a number of metrics, ranging from improvement in total sales, profitability, efficiencies, or stock price. Colleges and universities might measure performance by using subjective rankings, such as those found in *U.S. News & World Report*, or more objective measures, such as the percentage of faculty with doctoral degrees.[5] An old management adage says, "What gets measured, gets done." Measurement is critical to today's organizations. It is a fundamental requirement and an integral part of strategic planning and of principles of management more generally. Without measures, the accomplishment of goals and objectives is difficult to ascertain.

One application of goal-setting can be found in the "Pygmalion effect" where higher expectations of certain students can lead to higher performance.

Source: Shutterstock.com

objectives

Very precise, time-based, and measurable actions that support the completion of a goal.

measures

The actual metrics used to gauge performance of objectives.

Measurement Challenges

Organizations make three common mistakes related to measurement. First, many organizations emphasize historic financial goals and objectives, which may no longer be relevant. Second, financial outcomes are often short term in nature; consequently, focusing too much on financial measures may lead managers to overlook other key factors that might be important to the longer-term viability of the organization. For instance, *return on sales* (ROS, or net profit divided by total sales) is a commonly used measure of financial performance, and firms often set goals and objectives related to return on sales. However, an organization can increase return on sales by cutting investments in marketing and research and development (since they are costs that lessen the "return" dimension of ROS). It may be a good thing to cut such costs, but that type of cost-cutting typically hurts the organization's longer-term prospects. Decreases in marketing may reduce brand awareness, and decreases in research and development (R&D) will likely stifle new product or service development. Lastly, goals and objectives, even when they cover more than short-term financial metrics, are not often tied to strategy and ultimately to vision and mission. Instead, managers often create a laundry list of goals and objectives that lack any larger organizing logic.

Organizations such as BuzzFeed often track KPIs (Key Performance Indicators) such as the revenue per click on ads or engaging quizzes.

Source: chrisdorney/Shutterstock.com

Goals and Objectives in P-O-L-C

Goals and objectives are an essential part of planning. They also have implications for all the aspects of organizing, leading, and controlling. Broadly speaking, goals and objectives serve to:

- Gauge and report performance,
- Improve performance,
- Align effort,
- Manage accountabilities.

Goals, Objectives, and Planning

Planning typically starts with a vision and a mission. Managers then develop a strategy for realizing their vision and mission; success and progress in achieving vision and mission will be indicated by how well the underlying goals and objectives are achieved. A vision statement usually describes some broad set of goals—what the organization aspires to look like in the future. Mission statements, too, have stated goals—what the organization aspires to be for its stakeholders. For instance, Mars, Inc., the global food giant behind M&Ms, Snickers, Twix, and Skittles, sets out five mission statement goals in the areas of quality, responsibility, mutuality, efficiency, and freedom. Thus, goals are typically set for the organization as a whole and set the stage for a hierarchy of increasingly specific and narrowly-set goals and objectives.

Governor Jay Inslee proposed an aggressive goal to make the state of Washington carbon-neutral by 2045.

Source: Juli Hansen/Shutterstock.com

Unless the organization consists of only a single person, there are typically many working parts in terms of functional areas and product or service areas. Functional areas like accounting and marketing will need to have goals and objectives that, if measured and tracked, help show if and how those functions are contributing to the organization's goals and objectives. Similarly, product and service areas will likely have goals and objectives. Goals and objectives can also be set for the way that functions and product or service areas interact. For instance, are the accounting and marketing functions interacting in a way that is productive? Is marketing delivering value to product or service initiatives?

Goals, Objectives, and Organizing, Leading, and Controlling

Within the planning facet of P-O-L-C, goals and objectives tend to become more specific as you move down the levels of the organization. Similarly, the time horizon for accomplishing goals is often shorter as you move down the organization.

The way that the firm is organized can affect goals and objectives in a number of ways. For instance, a functional organizational structure, where departments are broken out by finance, marketing, operations, and so on, will likely want to track the performance of each department, but exactly what constitutes performance will probably vary from function to function.

In terms of leadership, top managers generally set goals and objectives for the entire organization. Ideally, then, lower-level managers would set or have input into the goals and objectives relevant to their respective parts of the business. For example, a CEO might believe that the company can achieve a sales growth goal of 20% per year. With this organizational goal, the marketing manager can then set specific product sales goals, as well as pricing, volume, and other objectives, throughout the year that show how marketing is on track to deliver its part of organizational sales growth. Goal setting is thus a primary function of leadership, along with holding others accountable for their respective goals and objectives. This concept of leaders embracing OKRs (Objectives and Key Results) has been adopted by a number of companies including Google, the Gates Foundation, legendary U2 star Bono, and numerous entrepreneurs.[6]

FIGURE 6.1 Goals and Objectives in Planning

Finally, goals and objectives can provide a form of control since they create a feedback opportunity regarding how well or how poorly the organization executes its strategy. Goals and objectives also are a basis for reward systems and can align interests and accountability within and across business units.

Key Takeaway

Goals are typically outcome statements, while objectives are very precise, time-based, and measurable actions that support the completion of goals. Goals and objectives are an essential element in planning and are a key reference point in many aspects of organizing, leading, and controlling. Broadly speaking, within the P-O-L-C framework, goals and objectives serve to (1) gauge and report performance, (2) improve performance, (3) align effort, and (4) manage accountabilities.

Discussion Questions

1. What is the difference between a goal and an objective?
2. Think of some specific objectives related to something you care about deeply. Now, what is the relationship between your objectives and the potential specific goals you may have?
3. What characteristics should a good objective have?
4. What four broad ways do goals and objectives fit in the P-O-L-C framework?
5. How are goals and objectives relevant to leadership?
6. In what ways do goals and objectives help managers control an organization?

6.2 Management by Objectives and the Balanced Scorecard

Learning Objectives

1. Describe the concept of management by objectives (MBO).
2. Be able to apply the Balanced Scorecard framework.
3. Understand the evolution of performance measurement systems.

management by objectives (MBO)

A systematic and organized approach that allows management to focus on achievable goals and to attain the best possible results from available resources.

Balanced Scorecard

A framework designed to translate an organization's vision and mission statements and overall business strategy into specific, quantifiable goals and objectives and to monitor the organization's performance in terms of achieving these goals.

Organizations use a variety of measurement approaches to go about setting and managing goals and objectives. In this section, we focus on two key approaches to setting goals. **Management by objectives (MBO)** is a goal-setting framework primarily used when managers and employees collaborate on setting goals. The **Balanced Scorecard** is used by top managers to make sense of multiple performance measures at the organizational level.

Management by Objectives

Management by objectives (MBO) is an approach that aims to increase organizational performance by aligning the subordinate objectives throughout the organization with the overall goals set by management. Ideally, employees get strong input to identify their objectives, timelines for completion, and so on. MBO includes ongoing tracking and feedback in the process to reach objectives.

President Kennedy's 1961 goal of sending a person to the moon by the end of the decade remains one of the most ambitious goals in human history.

Source: NASA - http://www.hq.nasa.gov/alsj/a11/AS11-40-5903HR.jpg

MBO was first outlined by Peter Drucker in 1954 in *The Practice of Management*. One of Drucker's core ideas in MBO was to create a better focus regarding where managers should spend their time and energy. According to Drucker, managers should focus on the result of work, not simply activities that occur within the work environment. Managers should delegate tasks by "negotiating a contract of objectives" with their subordinates and by refraining from dictating a detailed roadmap for implementation. MBO is about setting goals and then breaking these down into more specific objectives or key results. MBO involves (1) setting company-wide goals derived from corporate strategy, (2) determining team- and department-level goals, (3) collaboratively setting individual-level goals that are aligned with corporate strategy, (4) developing an action plan, and (5) periodically reviewing performance and revising goals.[7] A review of the literature shows that 68 out of the 70 studies conducted on this topic showed performance gains as a result of MBO implementation.[8] It also seems that top management's commitment to the process is the key to successful implementation of MBO programs.[9] Of course, MBO may not work in all contexts. For example, a study of Swedish secondary schools that instituted the program as a national policy, found that MBO had little effect on student success.[10] The classic film *Office Space* parodies a setting where MBO may not be effective. Working at the fictitious Chotchkie's, the film shows a discussion between a restaurant manager and employee where MBO is ineffectively used to set the appropriate number of whimsical buttons (flair) an employee should wear during a shift. MBO is unlikely to be effective in such cases, where a clear directive from management with little need for employee discretion is desired.

The broader principle behind MBO is to make sure that everybody within the organization has a clear understanding of the organization's goals, as well as awareness of their own roles and responsibilities in achieving objectives that will help attain those goals. The complete MBO system aims to get managers and empowered employees acting to implement and achieve their plans, which automatically achieves the organization's goals.

FIGURE 6.2 The Importance of Carefully Setting Rewards

In 1975, Steve Kerr published an article now considered a classic within the management field titled "On the Folly of Rewarding A, While Hoping for B." In it, he noted numerous examples where systems rewarded an outcome much different than what the organization hoped to achieve. Here, we illustrate several reward follies.

Health Care

In "pay-for-service" facilities, where doctors are not salaried, they may order unnecessary procedures, resulting in waste and inflated bills.

Education

While society hopes professors will aspire to become excellent teachers, many universities largely base faculty rewards on their publications and grant dollars generated.

Sports

Most coaches and professional sports owners preach the value of teamwork, yet most rewards are given for individual accomplishments.

Business

While providing honest feedback should be encouraged in organizations, giving bad news to the boss is rarely rewarded.

Source: Shutterstock.com

The Balanced Scorecard

The Balanced Scorecard is a framework designed to translate an organization's mission and vision statements and overall business strategy into specific, quantifiable goals and objectives, and to monitor the organization's performance in terms of achieving these goals. The idea of the framework is to "balance" financial targets (that can often tip the scale toward measures that might be more important for short-term performance) with measures that might help to understand long-term performance. Developed by Robert Kaplan and David Norton, the Balanced Scorecard approach to management has gained worldwide popularity since the 1996 release of their book, *The Balanced Scorecard: Translating Strategy into Action*. In 2001, the Gartner Group estimated that at least 40% of all *Fortune* 1,000 companies were using the Balanced Scorecard. More recently, the Balanced Scorecard has been advocated as an essential tool for startups, demonstrating how organizations of all sizes can benefit from this performance management tool.[11]

FIGURE 6.3 The Balanced Scorecard

Financial measures
such as return on assets and stock price—relate to effectiveness and profits.

You could ask yourself:
How can I improve my personal wealth? Measures might include cash, savings account, and retirement.

Customer measures
such as number of new or repeat customers and percentage of repeat customers—relate to customer attraction and satisfaction.

You could ask yourself:
How strong is my social network? The number of new contacts you make over time might reflect this dimension.

Internal business process measures
such as speed at serving a customer and time it takes to create a new product and get it to market—relate to organizational efficiency.

You could ask yourself:
Am I getting better at my current job? Tracking improvements in personal efficiency such as the time needed to complete a task can be helpful.

Learning and growth measures
such as the average number of new skills learned by each employee every year—relate to the future and emphasize that employee learning is often more important than formal training.

You could ask yourself:
What skills should I develop now for the future? Although the acquisition of new skills is hard to measure, the attainment of specialized licenses or earning of a graduate degree are tangible benchmarks.

Source: Shutterstock.com

One of the Balanced Scorecard's innovations is explicit attention to vision and strategy in setting goals and objectives. Stemming from the idea that assessing performance through financial returns only provides information about how well the organization did prior to the assessment, the Balanced Scorecard is a comprehensive approach that analyzes an organization's overall performance in four ways, so that future performance can be predicted and proper actions taken to create the desired future.

Balanced Scorecard Dimensions

Performance measures in the Balanced Scorecard can include both leading and lagging indicators. Leading indicators include measures that might be examined to predict poor performance of the organization in the future, such as an increase in employee turnover; whereas lagging indicators, such as a decrease in sales, reflect that performance is in decline.[12] The Balanced Scorecard focuses on four types of measures: (1) customers, (2) learning and growth, (3) internal processes, (4) and financial performance. The customer dimension looks at elements such as customer satisfaction and retention. Customer retention is often overlooked when managers consider performance metrics, but a recent study found that an increase in customer retention by 5% can result in increased profits between 25% and 95%.[13] Learning and growth explore the effectiveness of management in terms of measures of employee learning and the acquisition of employee skills that will benefit the organization in the future. The internal process dimension looks at organizational efficiency. Finally, financial performance, the most traditionally used category of performance indicators, includes assessments of measures that benefit the firm directly and immediately, such as sales.

The Balanced Scorecard in Practice

In practice, the Balanced Scorecard is more than simply a framework for thinking about goals and objectives. In its broadest scope, where the scorecard operates much like a map of the firm's vision, mission, and strategy, the Balanced Scorecard relies on four processes to bind short-term activities to long-term objectives:

1. *Translating the vision*. By relying on measurement, the scorecard forces managers to come to an agreement on the metrics they will use to translate lofty visions into everyday realities.
2. *Communicating and linking*. When a scorecard is disseminated to others in the organization, strategy becomes a tool available to everyone. As the high-level scorecard cascades down to individual business units, overarching strategic objectives and measures are translated into objectives and measures appropriate to each particular group. Thus, individual employees understand how their own productivity supports the overall strategy.
3. *Business planning*. Most companies have separate procedures (and sometimes units) for strategic planning and budgeting. The discipline of creating a Balanced Scorecard forces companies to integrate the two functions, thereby ensuring that financial budgets indeed support strategic goals. After agreeing on performance measures for the four scorecard perspectives, companies identify the most influential "drivers" of the desired outcomes and then set milestones for gauging the progress they make with these drivers.
4. *Feedback and learning*. By supplying a mechanism for strategic feedback and review, the Balanced Scorecard helps an organization foster a kind of learning often missing in companies: the ability to reflect on inferences and adjust theories about cause-and-effect relationships.

Key Takeaway

To continually understand and manage their performance, organizations track multiple goals and objectives. The management by objectives (MBO) approach is perhaps one of the earliest systematic approaches to working with goals and objectives. The Balanced Scorecard ties goals and objectives to vision, mission, and strategy by considering performance measures beyond purely financial goals and objectives.

Discussion Questions

1. Provide an example of a job where management by objectives (MBO) would be challenging to use. Defend your answer.
2. What are the advantages and disadvantages of MBO?
3. Apply the Balanced Scorecard to your college or university.
4. Provide examples of performance measures for each Balanced Scorecard dimension relevant to understanding the performance of a coffee shop.

6.3 Using Goals and Objectives in Employee Performance Evaluation

Learning Objectives

1. Understand where goals and objectives fit in employee development.
2. See how goals and objectives are part of an effective employee performance evaluation process.

Goals, Objectives, and Performance Reviews

performance evaluation

The constructive process to acknowledge an employee's performance.

A **performance evaluation** is a constructive process to acknowledge an employee's performance. Goals and objectives are critical components of effective performance evaluations because evaluation forms need to have a set of measurable goals and objectives spelled out for each area. Some of these, such as *attendance*, are more easy to describe and quantify than others, such as *knowledge*. Research suggests that individual and organizational performance increase 16% when an evaluation system based on specific goals and objectives is implemented.[14]

Role and Limitations of Performance Evaluations

One of the earliest documented examples of performance review dates to the Wei dynasty in 230 AD when an Imperial Rater utilized a nine-point scale to rate official family members. We can only guess that the evaluation was as popular then as performance reviews are today.

Source: Shutterstock.com

Most organizations conduct employee performance evaluations at least once a year, but they can occur more frequently when there is a clear rationale for doing so—for instance, at the end of a project, at the end of each month, and so on. For example, McKinsey, a leading strategy consulting firm, has managers evaluate employees at the end of every consulting engagement. So, in addition to the annual performance evaluation, consultants can receive up to 20 mini-evaluations in a year. Importantly, the timing should coincide with the needs of the organization and the development needs of the employee. In fact, the concept of performance management, or continuously assessing and developing performance with the goal of aligning individual performance with strategic objectives, is slowly replacing the idea of yearly performance assessments.[15]

Performance evaluations are critical, as they help managers feel more honest in their relationships with their subordinates and better about themselves in their supervisory roles. Subordinates are assured clear understanding of what goals and objectives are expected from them, their own personal strengths and areas for development, and a solid sense of their relationship with their supervisor. Avoiding performance issues ultimately decreases morale, decreases credibility of management, decreases the organization's overall effectiveness, and wastes more of management's time to do what is not being done properly.

It is important to recognize that performance evaluations are not without their challenges. Studies show that performance appraisal errors are extremely difficult to eliminate.[16] Training to eliminate certain types of errors often introduces other types of errors and sometimes reduces accuracy. The most common appraisal error is leniency, and managers often realize they are committing this error.

An Example of the Performance Review Process

For example, assume that the organization has determined that annual performance evaluations fit the strategic needs of the organization and the developmental needs of employees. This does not mean however, that management and employees discuss goals, objectives, and performance only once a year. In our example, the organization has opted to have a midyear information meeting and then an end-of-year performance evaluation meeting.

At some point in the year, the supervisor should hold a formal discussion with each staff member to review individual activities to date and to modify the goals and objectives that the employee is accountable for. This agreed-upon set of goals and objectives is sometimes called an employee performance plan. There should be no surprises at this meeting. The supervisor should have been actively involved in continual assessment of his or her staff through regular contact and coaching. If major concerns arise, the performance plan can be modified or the employees can receive development in areas in which they may be weak. This also is a time for the employee to provide formal feedback to the supervisor on the coaching, on the planning, and on how the process seems to be working.

At the end of the year, a final review of the activities and plans for developing the next year's objectives begins. Again, this is a chance to provide constructive and positive feedback and to address any ongoing concerns about the employee's activities and competencies. Continuing education opportunities can be identified, and for those systems linked to compensation, salary raises will be linked to the employee's performance during the year. Again, there should be no surprises to either employee or supervisor, as continual assessment and coaching should take place throughout the year. Supervisors and managers are involved in the same series of activities with their own supervisors to ensure that the entire organization is developing and focused on the same common objectives.

Performance management systems should be tailored to suit the needs of the organization and the staff. As the organization and its competitive environment change over time, the system should be changed to reflect changes to employee competencies, ranking systems, and rewards linked to the plan. For example, managers may need to show discretion during times of crisis such as the Covid-19 pandemic where employees are unable to give 100% efforts; in such cases, organizations may be wise to suspend ratings for a period of time.[17]

In times of extreme crisis such as the COVID-19 pandemic, managers should consider suspending numerical ratings when conducting remote performance reviews.

Source: Shutterstock.com

The "Your Performance Review" section below summarizes some key ideas individuals might keep in mind for their next review.

Your Performance Review

There are typically three areas to consider when reviewing performance: (1) preparation for the review, (2) what to do if the review is negative, and (3) what you should ultimately take away from the review.

Prepare for an upcoming review. Document achievements and list anything you want to discuss at the review. If you have not kept track of your achievements, you may have to spend some time figuring out what you have accomplished since your last review and, most important, how your employer has benefited, such as increased profits, grown the client roster, maintained older clients, and so on. These are easier to document when you have had clear goals and objectives.

What should you do if you get a poor review? If you feel you have received an unfair review, you should consider responding to it. You should first try to discuss the review with the person who prepared it. Heed this warning, however. Wait until you can look at the review objectively. Was the criticism you received really that off the mark or are you just offended that you were criticized in the first place? If you eventually reach the conclusion that the review was truly unjust, then set an appointment to meet with your reviewer. If there are any points that were correct, acknowledge those. Use clear examples that counteract the criticisms made. A paper trail is always helpful. Present anything you have in writing that can back you up. If you didn't leave a paper trail, remember to do this in the future.

What should you take away from a performance review? Ultimately, you should regard your review as a learning opportunity. For instance, did you have clear goals and objectives such that your performance was easy to document? You should be able to take away valuable information, whether it is about yourself or your reviewer.

Best Practices

While there is no single best way to manage performance evaluations, the collective actions across a number of high-performing firms suggests a set of best practices.

1. *Decide what you are hoping to achieve from the system.* Is it to reward the stars and to correct problems? Or is its primary function to be a tool in focusing all staff activities through better planning?
2. *Develop goals and objectives that inspire, challenge, and stretch people's capabilities.* Once goals and objectives are clearly communicated and accepted, enlist broad participation, and do not shut down ideas. Support participation and goal attainment through the reward system, such as with gainsharing or other group incentive programs.
3. *Ensure you have commitment from the top.* Planning must begin at the executive level and be filtered down through the organization to ensure that employees' plans are meaningful in the context of the organization's direction. Top managers should serve as strong role models for the performance evaluation process and attach managerial consequences to the quality of performance reviews (for instance, McKinsey partners are evaluated on how well they develop their consultants, not just the profitability of their particular practice).
4. *Ensure that all key staff are involved in the development of the performance management processes from the early phases.* Provide group orientations to the program to decrease anxiety over the implementation of a new system. It will ensure a consistent message communicated about the performance management system.
5. *If the performance management system is not linked to salary, be sure employees are aware of it.* For example, university business school professors are paid salaries based on highly competitive external labor markets, not necessarily the internal goals and objectives of the school such as high teaching evaluations, and so on. Make sure employees know the purpose of the system and what they get out of it.
6. *Provide additional training for supervisors on how to conduct the midyear and year-end performance reviews.* Ensure that supervisors are proficient at coaching staff. Training, practice, and feedback about how to avoid appraisal errors are necessary, but often insufficient, for eliminating appraisal errors. Eliminating errors may require alternative approaches to evaluation, such as calibration meetings, where managers from different departments meet and justify their ratings to each other to ensure that the ratings are consistent across departments and are defensible.
7. *Plan to modify the performance management system over time, starting with goals and objectives, to meet your organization's changing needs.* Wherever possible, study employee behaviors in addition to attitudes—the two do not always converge.

Key Takeaway

This section outlined the relationship between goals and objectives and employee performance evaluation. Performance evaluation is a tool that helps managers align individual performance with organizational goals and objectives. This tool is most effective when evaluation includes well-developed goals and objectives that are developed with the needs of both the organization and employee in mind. The section concluded with a range of best practices for the performance evaluation process, including the revision of goals and objectives when the needs of the organization change.

Discussion Questions

1. How are goals and objectives related to employee performance evaluation?
2. How often should performance evaluations be conducted?
3. What kinds of goals and objectives might be best for performance evaluation to be most effective?
4. What should be included in an employee performance plan?
5. What performance evaluation best practices appear to most directly involve goals and objectives?

6.4 Integrating Goals and Objectives with Corporate Social Responsibility

Learning Objectives

1. Understand the nature of corporate social responsibility.
2. See how corporate social responsibility can be incorporated using the Balanced Scorecard.
3. Understand that corporate social responsibility, like other goals and objectives, best helps the firm when aligned with its strategy, vision, and mission.

This section provides knowledge about the ways that goals and objectives related to social and environmental issues can enhance a firm's strategy using the Balanced Scorecard approach.

Corporate Social Responsibility

corporate social responsibility (CSR)

How companies manage the business processes to produce an overall positive impact on society.

The movement to embrace **corporate social responsibility (CSR)** has been gathering momentum for well over a decade, with 90% of the companies in the Standard & Poors Index publishing reports on sustainability in 2020.[18] A review of 82 published studies finds a positive link between corporate social performance and firm financial performance.[19] However, research examining the relationship between corporate social responsibility and company stock valuation across Asia, Europe, and the United States found significant links to stock price performance only for European firms.[20] More recently, the New York Stock Exchange found that companies able to measure the bottom-line impact of their CSR programs enhanced both their profitability and their competitive position.

CSR is about how companies manage their business processes to produce an overall positive effect on society. This growth has raised questions—how to define the concept and how to integrate it into the organization's goals and objectives. The Dow Jones Sustainability Index created a commonly accepted definition of CSR: "a business approach that creates long-term shareholder value by embracing opportunities and managing risks deriving from economic, environmental and social developments."[21] Specifically, the Dow Jones Sustainability Index looks at competence in five areas:

- *Strategy*: Integrating long-term economic, environmental, and social aspects in their business strategies while maintaining global competitiveness and brand reputation.
- *Financial*: Meeting shareholders' demands for sound financial returns, long-term economic growth, open communication, and transparent financial accounting.
- *Customer and Product*: Fostering loyalty by investing in customer relationship management, and product and service innovation that focuses on technologies and systems, which use financial, natural, and social resources in an efficient, effective, and economic manner over the long term.
- *Governance and Stakeholder*: Setting the highest standards of corporate governance and stakeholder engagement, including corporate codes of conduct and public reporting.
- *Human*: Managing human resources to maintain workforce capabilities and employee satisfaction through best-in-class organizational learning and knowledge management practices and remuneration and benefit programs.

A number of academic authors as well as global management consulting firms like McKinsey and KPMG have written about the pressures facing firms with regard to social and environmental issues. For instance, KPMG's "International Survey of Corporate Responsibility Reporting 2017" reflects the growing importance of corporate responsibility as a key indicator of nonfinancial performance, as well as a driver of financial performance.[22] In the 2017 survey, KPMG noted a significant increase in the publication of corporate responsibility reports worldwide, with 93% of the 250 largest companies worldwide reporting their corporate social responsibility. KPMG also noted that large companies not reporting corporate social responsibility activities will soon risk not being as transparent as their competitors and that smaller companies may distinguish themselves from their peers by reporting their corporate social responsibility.

Measuring Corporate Social Performance

Corporate social performance (CSP) reflects the measure of an organization's commitment to individuals, communities, and the natural environment. Although measuring a firm's social responsibility is somewhat subjective, this challenge has been addressed by Kinder, Lydenberg and Domini & Co. (KLD), a firm based in Boston that rates businesses on a number of stakeholder-related issues. KLD conducts research on publicly-traded firms for various metrics of CSP and reports such statistics to potential investors. Their database provides ratings for each firm's numerous "strengths" and "concerns" along a number of dimensions associated with corporate social performance. The results of KLD's assessment are used to develop a social investments fund and have been used extensively in academic research.[23] As recently as 2014, the Domini Social Equity Fund developed by KLD outperformed the S&P 500 index.[24]

corporate social performance (CSP)

How companies reflect their commitment to individuals, communities, and the natural environment.

FIGURE 6.4 Measuring Corporate Social Performance

Corporate social performance is defined as the degree to which a firm's actions honor ethical values that respect individuals, communities, and the natural environment. Determining whether a firm is socially responsible is somewhat subjective, but one popular approach has been developed by KLD Research & Analytics. Their work tracks "strengths" and "concerns" for hundreds of firms over time. KLD's finding are used by investors to screen socially-responsible firms and by scholars who are interested in explaining corporate social performance. We illustrate the six key dimensions tracked by KLD here.

Community strengths include engagement in charitable giving, while involvement in tax controversies exemplifies a community concern.

Product quality/safety strengths include actions such as the establishment of a well-developed quality program, while concerns arise if a firm receives fines related to product quality and/or safety.

A no-layoff policy is a strength in regard to **employee relations**, while poor union relations are a concern.

Environmental strengths include engaging in recycling, while concerns arise when penalties for air or water violations are documented.

Diversity strengths include progressive programs for the employment of the disabled, whereas fines or civil penalties that result from an affirmative action constitute a concern.

Corporate governance strengths include equitable levels of compensation for top management and board members, while concerns are raised if controversies related to accounting, transparency, or political accountability are discovered.

Source: Shutterstock.com

Key Takeaway

This section explored the challenges and opportunities of incorporating social and environmental goals and objectives into the P-O-L-C process. Many organizations refer to social and environmental activities as corporate social responsibility (CSR), and measures of such activities are considered corporate social performance (CSP).

Discussion Questions

1. What does corporate social responsibility mean?
2. Why might it be challenging for organizations to effectively set and achieve social and environmental goals and objectives, in addition to their operating goals and objectives?
3. Why might an organization pay greater attention to adding social and environmental goals and objectives today than 10 years ago?
4. How does a Balanced Scorecard help managers develop social and environmental goals and objectives?
5. In what ways does achievement of CSR goals and objectives strategically differentiate an organization?

6.5 Your Personal Balanced Scorecard

Learning Objectives

1. Develop personal applications of the Balanced Scorecard concept.
2. Learn how your vision and mission can be linked to your goals and objectives.
3. Understand how to develop SMART goals and objectives.

One of the more powerful tools in a manager's toolkit is the Balanced Scorecard, a model that groups goals, objectives, and metrics into the areas of finance, customer, internal business process, and learning and growth. The scorecard is effective because it helps managers link vision, mission, and strategy to the goals and objectives that employees strive to achieve. The scorecard concept can also be applied to personal and professional objectives.[25] Someone who does this regularly is Denise Sullivan Morrison, the President and CEO of Campbell Soup Company from 2011 to 2018. She has publicly stated, "I believe that when you have goals you declare them, and I believe in setting long-term goals and working to achieve them. I always had a long-term plan for my career and I was willing to do many different positions along the way to develop the skills to not only get the job, but to be great at the job."[26]

From an Organizational Scorecard to a Personal One

The Balanced Scorecard can be translated into an individual scorecard that helps in the achievement of personal and professional goals and objectives. An organization's scorecard starts with vision and mission, followed by goals (financial, internal business processes, customer, and learning and growth), which have corresponding objectives, metrics, and tactical activities.

Personal Mission, Vision, and Strategy

As with an organization's mission and vision, your personal mission and vision reflect who you are and where you want to go. Mission reflects your values and philosophy of life. Vision captures what you want to achieve. Which values and principles guide your way? What are your most deeply cherished aspirations? What do you want to achieve? How do you distinguish yourself in society and among your peers and family? If you were to read your biography in 20 years, what would you want it to say about you?

Personal Goals and Key Roles

Individuals should seek to manage their personal goals with the same level of detail firms use to set organizational goals.

Source: Shutterstock.com

Goals and roles are set out with respect to the areas of finance, individual strengths, and learning and growth. Finance, for instance, captures your needs and aspirations about money, as well as the financial obligations that you might have as a result of your role of caring for a parent, sibling, or child. Much like businesses that focus too much on short-term financial targets, one of the biggest mistakes in personal finance is spending too much during high-income years (focusing on short-term comforts) rather than saving for long-term security in retirement.[27] Generating contacts as well as maintaining current friendships and cultivating new ones represents a personal application of the customer dimension of the Balanced Scorecard. Becoming more efficient at managing your time represents a key internal business process goal for individuals. In recent years, a number of tools have surfaced to help individuals better learn how they value their time at the specific dollar level.[28] Such tools can be used to decide which tasks individuals might undertake in their spare time, and which tasks might be better suited to pay for or cajole others to perform. Finally, learning and growth refer to your skills, abilities, and aims with regard to personal and professional learning and growth. How can you learn and remain successful in the future? What type of skills and learning are required for future aspired roles?

Using SMART Criteria

SMART

A goal that is specific, measurable, aggressive yet attainable, realistic, and time-bound.

For personal objectives and performance measures to be most effective, wise managers rely on **SMART** criteria. These characteristics—specific, measurable, aggressive yet achievable, realistic, and time-bound—yield the acronym SMART.[29] Here is how to tell if your objectives, measures, and targets are SMART.

FIGURE 6.5 Creating SMART Goals

While missions and visions provide an overall sense of the organization's direction, goals are narrower aims that should provide clear and tangible guidance to employees. The most effective goals are those that are SMART (specific, measurable, aggressive, realistic, and time-bound.) SMART goals help provide clarity, transparency, and accountability. As detailed below, one SMART goal is Coca-Cola's aim to, by 2020, improve their water efficiency by 25%, compared with a 2010 baseline.

Specific
Coca-Cola implemented an ongoing strategy in 2010 to improve its water efficiency by a specific amount. It achieved 15% annual savings by 2018 and aims to save a total of 25% annually comparing 2010 to 2020. In contrast, goals such as "do your best" are vague, making it difficult to decide if a goal is actually reached.

Measurable
Water efficiency can be calculated, so Coca-Cola is to track its progress relative to its 25% target. If progress is slow, more resources can be devoted to achieving the goal.

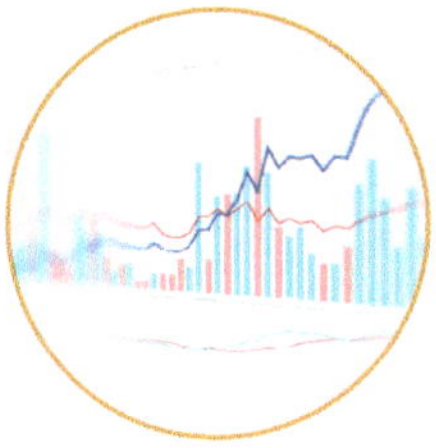

Aggressive
A series of research studies have established that performance is strongest when goals are challenging but attainable. Reaching a 25% improvement will require aggressive work by Coca-Cola, but the goal can be reached.

Realistic
If Coca-Cola's water efficiency goal was 95% improvement, Coca-Cola's employees would probably react with surprise. Reaching a goal must be feasible in order for employees to embrace it. Unrealistic goals make most people give up. And basing goals on impossible cliches, such as "give 110%" creates confusion.

Time-bound
Coca-Cola is seeking to achieve its 25% improvement by 2020. Some universities, such as Texas Tech University, provide incentives, including preferred scheduling for students who sign contracts agreeing to graduate on a four-year schedule. Deadlines such as these are motivating and they create accountability.

Source: Shutterstock.com, ferdyboy_Shutterstock.com, IrinaK_Shutterstock.com

Music Rap-Up: Get SMART

Twinprov perform a rap on SMART goal setting.

View in the online reader

Specific

A specific objective has a much greater chance of being accomplished than a general one. To set a specific objective, you must answer the six "W" questions:

- *Who*: Who is involved?
- *What*: What do I want to accomplish?
- *Where*: Identify a location.
- *When*: Establish a time frame.
- *Which*: Identify requirements and constraints.
- *Why*: Specific reasons, purposes, or benefits of accomplishing the objective.

For example, pursuing the popular goal of finishing a half-marathon has led this run to become one of the most popular events in the United States.[30] A specific objective would involve running three miles every weekend and increasing the distance by 10% each weekend until the 13.1 miles that constitutes a half-marathon was in reach. Fortunately, for many goals such as this one, individuals can rely on the experience of others who have created very specific schedules to help facilitate such long-term goals in a reasonable time frame.[31] A personal goal would be, "Get in shape." But a specific objective would say, "Get into good enough shape that six months from now I can hike to the summit of a 14,000-foot mountain and back in one day. To do so, by next Monday, I will join a health club within five miles of home and work out for at least 45 minutes, three days a week, for three months, then reassess my progress."[32]

Measurable

Establish concrete criteria for measuring progress toward the attainment of each objective you set. When you measure your progress, you stay on track, reach your target dates, and experience the exhilaration of achievement that spurs you on to continued effort required to reach your objective.

To determine whether your objective is measurable, ask questions such as: How much? How many? How will I know when it is accomplished? If you cannot track progress in regular intervals on an Excel spreadsheet in a meaningful way, it's quite possible that you need to reconsider the degree to which you are truly accessing a measurable goal.

Aggressive Yet Achievable

When you identify objectives that are most important to you, you begin to figure out ways you can make them come true. You develop the attitudes, abilities, skills, and financial capacity to reach them. You begin seeing previously overlooked opportunities to bring yourself closer to the achievement of your goals and objectives.

You can attain almost any objective you set, when you plan your steps wisely and establish a time frame that allows you to carry out those steps. Goals that may have seemed far away and out of reach eventually move closer and become attainable, because you grow and expand to match them through the achievement of nearer-term objectives. When you list your objectives, you build your self-image. You see yourself as worthy of these goals and objectives and develop the traits and personality that allow you to possess them.

Realistic

To be realistic, a goal should represent an objective toward which you are both willing and able to work. An objective can be both high and realistic; you are the only one who can decide just how high your objective should be. But be sure that every objective represents substantial progress. A high objective is frequently easier to reach than a low one because a low objective exerts low motivational force. Some of the hardest jobs you ever accomplished may seem easier because they were a labor of love.

Your objective is probably realistic if you truly believe that it can be accomplished. Additional ways to know whether your objective is realistic is to determine whether you have accomplished anything similar in the past, or ask yourself what conditions would have to exist to accomplish this objective. You might decide whether an objective to run a half-marathon is realistic based on the number of people your age and with similar ability that have been able to do it in recent years.

While an endless number of fad diets exist, a more reasonable weight loss goal for most individuals involves losing a pound a week based on a series of wise daily choices.

Source: Shutterstock.com

Time-Bound

An objective should be grounded within a time frame. With no time frame tied to it, there's no sense of urgency. If you want to lose 10 pounds, when do you want to lose it by? "Someday" won't work. But if you anchor it within a time frame, "by May 1," then you've set your unconscious mind into motion to begin working on the objective. SMART goals can also be used to help balance work and life; for example, you might commit to leaving work (a specific action) by 6 p.m. at least three days a week (a specific time period that is realistic and measurable).[33]

FIGURE 6.6 Be SMART: Vision, Mission, Goals, and You

Many of the principles for effective organizational vision, mission, and goals apply to individuals too. Here are some ideas that might help you think differently about your own aspirations and how you are working to reach them.

VISION

Young children often have grandiose visions, such as "I want to be the President of the United States." Now that you are in college, what do you aspire to become? Is your education setting the stage for you to reach this vision?

MISSION

Is your mission in life simply to accumulate as much wealth as you can? Or do you place value on your role in a family and as a member of society?

MEASURABLE

Quantifying your goals allows you to track your accomplishments over time and can help reduce stress. For example, meeting a goal of "write a page every day" might prevent panic the night before an important project is due.

AGGRESSIVE

Creating aggressive educational goals (e.g., maintain a 3.5 GPA) is likely to lead to higher performance than minimal goals (e.g., pass all my classes).

TIME-BOUND

Time management is a challenge in today's world. If you tend to procrastinate, setting interim deadlines for yourself might help you to stay on schedule.

REALISTIC

To better understand your prospects in the job market, consider researching what kinds of jobs are common for your major and experience level.

SPECIFIC

Do you create explicit rather than vague goals for yourself? This can help you to target your energy toward what is important.

Source: Shutterstock.com

Key Takeaway

The purpose of this section was to help translate the Balanced Scorecard to help break down the steps and issues to meeting personal and professional goals. In many cases, knowledge of SMART goals can be extremely beneficial in this process.

Discussion Questions

1. What can you achieve by applying the concept of a Balanced Scorecard to your personal goals?
2. How similar or different does the scorecard seem to function at an individual level as opposed to an organizational level?
3. What are key characteristics of effective objectives?
4. Why should personal objectives and measures of performance be specific?
5. What are some of the activities you can undertake to implement your scorecard?

6.6 Case in Point: Performance with a Purpose at PepsiCo.

Source: monticello/Shutterstock.com

Pepsi is a world-renowned food and beverage brand, and its manufacturer PepsiCo owns other well-known beverages such as Mountain Dew, Tropicana, and 7Up, as well as snacks such as Lay's chips, Doritos, and Quaker. As any company, its future success depends on satisfying all stakeholders. Given the size of PepsiCo and the reach of its products, the stakeholders include every one of us. For example, the high salt, fat, and sugar content of some of PepsiCo offerings may jeopardize health of customers, including children. Many PepsiCo products come in disposable plastic packages that end up in landfills and oceans. The production of PepsiCo products demands huge amounts of energy, and increases greenhouse gases contributing to climate change. The beverage production requires large amounts of water, often in areas where water is a scarce and precious resource, and when PepsiCo uses it up, there is less available for everyone else.

Anticipating that how PepsiCo reacts to these challenges would be the key to its future success, former CEO Indra Nooyi, along with key leaders in the business, set a strategy they termed Performance with Purpose (PwP) over a decade ago. Consisting of sustainability goals around financial returns, healthier products, limiting the environmental impact of the company, and supporting employees, the company aimed to make all its major decisions in the following decades with this strategy in mind. The next CEO, Ramon Laguarta, who took the helm in 2018 continues to adhere to this strategy, calling it "winning with purpose."

After defining and communicating the basics of PwP and setting company level targets for different metrics (such as "the company will reduce its absolute greenhouse gas emissions across its global value chain by 20% by 2030 against a 2015 baseline") the company set PwP-related goals for senior executives, country heads, and middle-level managers. These metrics were used in performance reviews and tied to incentives. Further, the company tied resource allocations to its sustainability impact. Any time there was a major investment under consideration, the champion of the proposal would need to explain how the project would contribute to PWP goals and objectives.

PwP had numerous, high impact and highly visible outcomes that were good for the company and for the stakeholders. For example, the company was able to reduce the fat, sugar, and salt content of many of its products and acquired healthy products to add to its line-up. PwP also drove behaviors that would be unthinkable without such a strategy. For example, a desire to produce Cheetos from whole grains and the lack of availability of machines that could be used for this purpose led the company to develop the production machinery that could handle whole grains in their own R&D center. PwP led to pulling the plug on an energy product that had the potential to be profitable but would mean selling a product, which contained high amounts of caffeine, that could be marketed to kids. It also led to its Mexican operations working with the Mexican government to support the farming of sunflowers to replace unhealthy palm oils. In 2020, the company announced plans to use 100% renewable electricity in its US operations, which represents almost 50% of its global operations. The company is moving toward renewable plastics in some products, and aluminum in others. The company supports recycling programs and beach clean up efforts, partnering with Ocean Conservancy to tackle plastic pollution in oceans.[34]

Multimedia Extension—PepsiCo Chairman and CEO Indra Nooyi: Our Sustainability Journey

View in the online reader

Case Discussion Questions

1. How do you think PwP motivates employees at PepsiCo?
2. Explain the role of goals as a motivational tool. Are there mechanisms outside of goals and incentives that would make PwP motivate employees?
3. How is PwP different from greenwashing? Do you believe that it is a marketing tool, or a fundamental shift in how the business operates?
4. How would PwP be transferred to other industries? Would it be easier or more difficult to achieve it in a smaller company?
5. Would this be the type of company you would be interested in working for? Why or why not?

Endnotes

1. Retrieved from http://www.businessinsider.com/ubers-plans-to-be-cheaper-than-owning-a-car-2015-2.
2. Kalargyrou, V., Pescosolido, A., & Kalargiros, E. A. (2012). Leadership skills in management education. *Academy of Educational Leadership Journal, 16*, 39–63.
3. Schweitzer, M.E., Ordóñez, L., & Douma, B. (2004). Goal setting as a motivator of unethical behavior. *Academy of Management Journal 47* (3), 422–432.
4. Schweitzer, M.E., Ordóñez, L., & Douma, B. (2004). Goal setting as a motivator of unethical behavior. *Academy of Management Journal 47* (3), 422–432.
5. Palmer, T. B., & Short, J. C. (2008). Mission statements in U.S. colleges of business: An empirical examination of their content with linkages to configurations and performance. *Academy of Management Learning and Education, 7*, 454–470.
6. Retrieved from http://fortune.com/2018/04/16/john-doerr-okrs/.
7. Greenwood, R. G. (1981). Management by objectives: As developed by Peter Drucker, assisted by Harold Smiddy. *Academy of Management Review, 6*, 225–230; Muczyk, J. P., & Reimann, B. C. (1989). MBO as a complement to effective leadership. *Academy of Management Executive, 3*, 131–138; Reif, W. E., & Bassford, G. (1975). What MBO really is: Results require a complete program. *Business Horizons, 16*, 23–30.
8. Rodgers, R., & Hunter, J. E. (1991). Impact of management by objectives on organizational productivity. *Journal of Applied Psychology, 76*, 322–336.
9. Rodgers, R., Hunter, J. E., & Rogers, D. L. (1993). Influence of top management commitment on management program success. *Journal of Applied Psychology, 78*, 151–155.
10. Lindberg, E., & Wilson, T. L. (2011). Management by objectives: The Swedish experience in upper secondary schools. *Journal of Educational Administration, 49*(1), 62–75.
11. Retrieved from http://www.entrepreneur.com/article/243092.
12. Denton, D. K. (2006, March). Measuring relevant things. *Performance Improvement, 45*(3).
13. Retrieved from http://www.forbes.com/sites/jerryjao/2015/01/21/customer-retention-is-king-retention-marketing-provides-greater-roi/.
14. Rynes, S., Brown, K., & Colbert, A. (2002). Seven common misconceptions about human resource practices: Research findings versus practitioner beliefs. *Academy of Management Executive, 16*(3), 92–102.
15. Aguinis, H., Joo, H., & Gottfredson, R. K. (2011). Why we hate performance management—And why we should love it. *Business Horizons, 54*, 503–507.
16. Rynes, S., Brown, K., & Colbert, A. (2002). Seven common misconceptions about human resource practices: Research findings versus practitioner beliefs. *Academy of Management Executive, 16*(3), 92–102.
17. Knight, R. (2020). How to Do Performance Reviews—Remotely. *Harvard Business Review*. Retrieved from https://hbr.org/2020/06/how-to-do-performance-reviews-remotely.
18. Retrieved September 17, 2020 from https://www.3blmedia.com/News/90-SP-500-Index-Companies-Publish-Sustainability-Reports-2019-GA-Announces-its-Latest-Annual#:~:text=In the just-completed 2020,were publishing a sustainability report.
19. Allouche, J., & Laroche, P. (2005). A meta-analytic investigation of the relationship between corporate social and financial performance. *Revue de Gestion des Ressources Humaines, 57*, 18–41.
20. Hill, R. P., Ainscough, T., Shank, T., & Manullang, D. (2007). Corporate social responsibility and socially responsible investing: A global perspective. *Journal of Business Ethics, 70*(2), 165–174.
21. Retrieved July 18, 2018. http://www.sustainability-indexes.com/sustainability-assessment/corporate-sustainability.jsp.
22. Retrieved from https://assets.kpmg.com/content/dam/kpmg/xx/pdf/2017/10/kpmg-survey-of-corporate-responsibility-reporting-2017.pdf.
23. Cho, S., Lee, C., & Park, C. K. (2012, June). Measuring corporate social responsibility: Certified public accountant. *The CPA Journal, 82*(6), 54–60.
24. Retrieved from https://www.domini.com/about-domini.
25. Retrieved from https://www.forbes.com/sites/christinawallace/2016/12/24/the-personal-balanced-scorecard/#371789e45a65.
26. Deitsch, R. (2012, September). Soup-er woman: Spelling out Campbell's success strategy. *The Costco Connection*.
27. Retrieved from http://www.forbes.com/sites/advisor/2014/05/07/biggest-retirement-planning-mistakes/.
28. Retrieved from http://lifehacker.com/find-out-how-much-your-time-is-really-worth-with-this-c-1538740426.
29. Drucker, P. (1954). *The Practice of management*. New York: HarperCollins. Drucker coined the usage of the acronym for SMART objectives while discussing objective-based management.
30. Retrieved from http://www.wsj.com/articles/the-half-marathon-achieves-its-personal-best-1413825711.
31. Retrieved from http://www.halhigdon.com/training/51131/Half-Marathon-Novice-1-Training-Program.
32. We thank Elsa Peterson, our developmental editor, for providing this example based on one of her friend's personal experiences. Another real-life comparable example is shown here: Manochio, M. (2008, September 30). Retrieved from http://www.dailyrecord.com/apps/pbcs.dll/article?AID=/20080930/COMMUNITIES12/809300311.
33. Joelle, J. (2011, December). Make your SMART goals WISE goals. *Agency Sales, 41*(11), 36.
34. Case written by Berrin Erdogan and Talya Bauer to accompany Bauer, T. N. & Erdogan, B. (2021). *Organizational Behavior: Bridging Science and Practice (4.0)*. Boston, MA: FlatWorld. Partially based on ideas and information contained in Beverage Industry Staff (February 2020). PepsiCo seeks to achieve 100 percent renewable electricity for US plants. *Beverage Industry, 8;* Jacobsen, J. (December, 2019). The best packages of 2019. Beverage Industry, 34–35; Karnani, A., McFerran, B., & Mukhopadhyay, A. (Summer 2014). Leanwashing: A hidden factor in the obesity crisis. *California Management Review, 56*, 5–30; Nooyi, I. K., & Govindarajan, V. (March-April 2020). Becoming a better corporate citizen: How PepsiCo moved toward a healthier future. *Harvard Business Review*, 94–103; Szczepanski, M. (6/14/2018). PepsiCo's recycle rally program challenges schools to reduce waste, increase recycling. Waste360; Waste Staff (1/31/2020). Waste reduction initiatives ahead of super bowl LIV.

CHAPTER 7

Organizational Structure and Change

How organizations are structured has important implications for the performance of firms and the individuals within organizations.

Source: Shutterstock.com

Chapter Learning Objectives

Reading this chapter will help you accomplish the following:

1. Define organizational structure and its basic elements.
2. Describe matrix, boundaryless, and learning organizations.
3. Describe why and how organizations change.
4. Understand reasons why people resist change, and strategies for planning and executing change effectively.
5. Build your own organizational design skills.

TABLE 7.1 The P-O-L-C Framework

Planning	Organizing	Leading	Controlling
1. Vision & Mission	1. Organization Design	1. Leadership	1. Systems/Processes
2. Strategizing	2. Culture	2. Decision Making	2. Strategic Human Resources
3. Goals & Objectives	3. Social Networks	3. Communications	
		4. Groups/Teams	
		5. Motivation	

Organizational design is one of the three tasks that fall into the organizing function in the planning-organizing-leading-controlling (P-O-L-C) framework. The organization's structure can have a powerful influence on employee actions and their job satisfaction. This chapter provides details on the types of structures used in organizations and their implications for individual and firm performance.

7.1 Organizational Structure

Learning Objectives

1. Explain the roles of formalization, centralization, levels in a hierarchy, and departmentalization in employee attitudes and behaviors.
2. Describe how the elements of organizational structure create mechanistic and organic structures.
3. Understand the advantages and disadvantages of mechanistic and organic structures for organizations.

organizational structure

How individual and team work within an organization are coordinated.

Organizational structure refers to how work is coordinated between individuals and teams within an organization. To achieve organizational goals and objectives, individual work needs to be coordinated and managed. Structure is a valuable tool in achieving coordination by specifying reporting relationships (who reports to whom), describing formal communication channels, and explaining how separate actions of individuals are linked together. Organizations can function within a number of different structures, each possessing distinct advantages and disadvantages. Famed British Prime Minister Winston Churchill once quipped, "Democracy is the worst form of government, except for all those other forms that have been tried from time to time." His point is that all structures face issues of communication and coordination when seeking to organize individuals to meet goals. Some scholars have argued that the increasing interest and popularity of zombie shows such as *The Walking Dead*, *World War Z*, and *Zombieland* serve as a powerful metaphor for individuals trapped in organizations where they are powerless and hopeless.[1] Consequently, there are considerable implications between individual work preferences and the type of organizational structure where different individuals will either flourish or struggle. Although any structure that is not properly managed will have challenges, certain organizational structures are better equipped for particular environments and tasks.

Music Rap-Up: Use the Workforce

Twinprov perform a rap applying elements of organizational structure in the Star Wars universe.

View in the online reader

Moses dividing the Israelites into groups of "thousands, hundreds, fifties, and tens" illustrates an early example of division of labor. That he received this advice from his father-in-law shows the timeless value of family wisdom.

Source: Shutterstock.com

Building Blocks of Structure

We review four aspect of structure that have been frequently studied in the literature: centralization, formalization, hierarchical levels, and departmentalization. We view these four elements as the building blocks, or elements, making up a company's structure. Then we will examine how these building blocks come together to form two different configurations of structures.

Centralization

Centralization is the degree to which decision-making authority is concentrated at higher levels in an organization. In centralized companies, many important decisions are made at higher levels of the hierarchy, whereas in decentralized companies, decisions are made and problems are solved at lower levels of the organization by employees who are closer to the problem in question. Potential advantages of centralized structures include greater vision focus with faster execution, and reduced conflict with greater control and accountability.[2]

centralization

The degree to which decision-making authority is concentrated at higher levels in an organization.

Based on the critical need to have orders followed rather than questioned, the military is likely to always be best served by a centralized organizational structure.

Source: Shutterstock.com

As an employee, where would you feel more comfortable and productive? If your answer is "decentralized," you are not alone. Decentralized companies give more authority to lower-level employees, resulting in a sense of empowerment. Centralized organizations tend to have a more negative emotional tone, resulting in employee exhaustion, whereas decentralized organizations develop a more positive emotional climate.[3] Decentralization is also good for creativity, bringing out the best in employees who have an eagerness to learn new things.[4] Job candidates are more likely to be attracted to decentralized organizations. Because centralized organizations assign decision-making responsibility to higher-level managers, they place greater demands on the judgment capabilities of CEOs and other high-level managers. Despite many perceived disadvantages, centralization may lead to more efficient operations, particularly if the company is operating in a stable environment.[5]

Companies often choose centralization to increase efficiency. For example, during the 2020 COVID-19 pandemic, Birla Carbon, the maker of carbon additives, restructured to centralize its operations. Prior to the restructuring, the company consisted of regional operations that largely acted independently in five different geographies. To achieve greater coordination and consistency across its sixteen factories, the company created a Chief Manufacturing Officer position in Asia, and another one for Americas, Europe, and Africa.[6] Further, organizations can suffer from extreme decentralization. For example, Wells Fargo believes that the misconduct scandal the organization lived through where employees and managers opened up accounts for their customers without their knowledge may have been at least partly due to decentralization, which gave too much autonomy to retail banking units and prevented oversight. Following the scandal, the bank began a centralization initiative.[7]

Organizations may consider centralizing some of their operations, while maintaining decentralization in other units. For example, centralizing purchasing allows organizations to negotiate better deals with suppliers. Pernod Ricard SA, the parent company of the Whiskey brands Jameson, Glenlivet, and Chivas Regal, found that allowing each brand to purchase its own casks for aging, storage, and shipping was too expensive, and decided to combine purchasing in a central base in Kentucky, in the United States, even though the brands operate in Canada, Ireland, and Scotland. While centralizing purchasing may make sense, companies may retain decentralization in customer-facing units to ensure that decisions are responsive to customer needs.[8]

Organizations can suffer from extreme decentralization. For example, some analysts believe that the Federal Bureau of Investigation (FBI) experiences some problems because all its structure and systems are based on the assumption that crime needs to be investigated *after* it happens. Over time, this assumption led to a situation where, instead of following an overarching strategy, each FBI unit is completely decentralized and field agents determine how investigations should be pursued. It has been argued that due to the change in the nature of crimes, the FBI needs to gather accurate intelligence *before* a crime is committed; this requires more centralized decision making and strategy development.[9] Figure 7.1 illustrates the U.S. government's organizational chart. The difficulties faced in coordinating among different branches of government, departments, and thousands of employees highlight the challenges of creating effective organizational structures, in which some elements are centralized and others are decentralized.

FIGURE 7.1 U.S. Government Organizational Structure
The US government's organizational structure is complex yet fairly simple to understand.

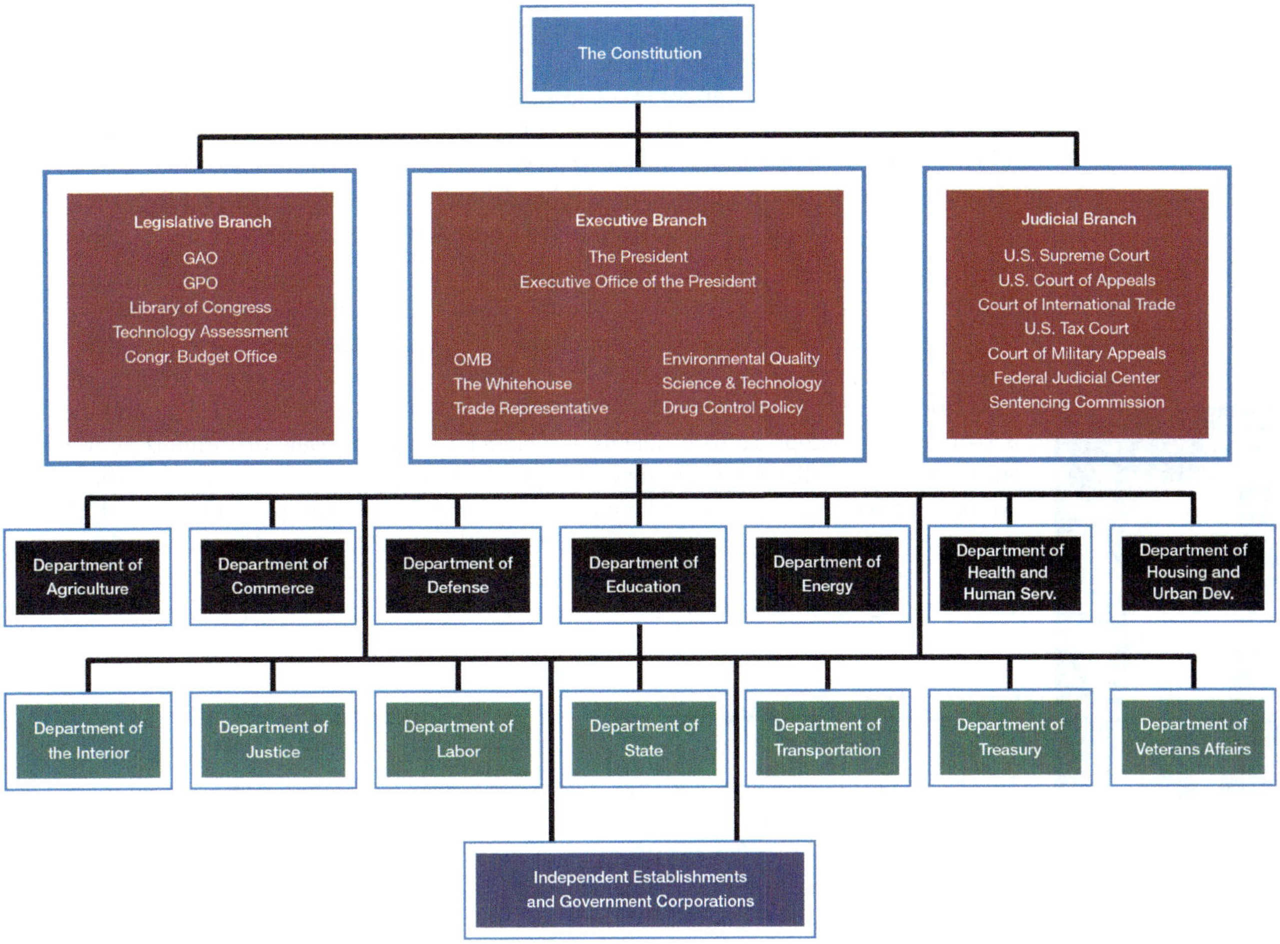

Formalization

formalization

The extent to which policies, procedures, job descriptions, and rules are written and explicitly articulated.

Formalization is the extent to which an organization's policies, procedures, job descriptions, and rules are written and explicitly articulated. Formalized structures are those in which there are many written rules and regulations. These structures control employee behavior using written rules, so that employees have little autonomy to decide on a case-by-case basis. Formalization makes employee behavior more predictable. Whenever a problem at work arises, employees know to turn to a handbook or a procedure guideline. Therefore, employees respond to problems in a similar way across the organization, which leads to consistency of behavior.

While formalization reduces ambiguity and provides direction to employees, it is not without disadvantages. A high degree of formalization may actually lead to reduced innovativeness because employees are used to behaving in a certain manner. In fact, strategic decision making in such organizations often occurs only when there is a crisis. A formalized structure is associated with reduced motivation and job satisfaction as well as a slower pace of decision making.[10] The service industry is particularly susceptible to problems associated with high levels of formalization. Sometimes employees who are listening to a customer's problems may need to take action, but the answer may not be specified in any procedural guideline or rulebook. For example, while a handful of airlines such as Southwest do a good job of empowering their employees to handle complaints, in many airlines, lower-level employees have limited power to resolve a customer problem and are constrained by stringent rules that outline a limited number of acceptable responses.

Peter Gibbons lamented the formalized policy of filling out time-consuming, yet unimportant, "TPS reports" in the 1999 film *Office Space*.

Source: By Ian Smith, CC BY-SA 2.0, https://commons.wikimedia.org/w/index.php?curid=12761301

Hierarchical Levels

tall structures

Organizations with several layers of management between frontline employees and the top level.

flat structures

Organizations with few layers, often with large numbers of employees reporting to a single manager.

Another important element of a company's structure is the number of levels it has in its hierarchy. In general, **tall structures** have several layers of management between frontline employees and top management, while **flat structures** consist of few layers. In tall structures, the number of employees reporting to each manager tends to be smaller, resulting in greater opportunities for managers to supervise and monitor employee activities. In contrast, flat structures involve a wider span of control. In such a structure, managers will be relatively unable to provide close supervision, leading to greater levels of freedom of action for each employee.

Research indicates that flat structures provide greater need satisfaction for employees, and greater levels of self-actualization.[11] At the same time, there may be some challenges associated with flat structures. Research shows that when managers supervise a large number of employees (which is more likely to happen in flat structures), employees experience greater levels of role ambiguity—the confusion that results from being unsure of what is expected of a worker on the job.[12] This is especially a disadvantage for employees who need closer guidance from managers. Moreover, in a flat structure, advancement opportunities will be more limited because there are fewer management layers. Finally, while employees report that flat structures are better at satisfying their higher-order needs such as self-actualization, they also report that tall structures are better at satisfying security needs of employees.[13] Because tall structures are typical in large and well-established companies, it is possible that when working in such organizations employees feel a greater sense of job security.

Companies such as IKEA, the Swedish furniture manufacturer and retailer, are successfully using flat structures within stores to build an employee attitude of job involvement and ownership.

Source: serdar_basak/ Shutterstock.com

The big advantage of flat structures is delegation of authority to lower levels and empowering line employees, given that managers will not be in a position to closely supervise their work. An organizational structure that takes a flat structure to the extreme is **holacracy**, or a structure where employees work in self-managing teams without having a formal manager. Employees in these companies coordinate their own work, and choose their own projects to work on. Examples of these companies include Valve (Seattle based gaming software development company), W.L. Gore (a manufacturing company famous for creating Gore-Tex fabric, with more than 10,500 employees) and Morning Star (the tomato producer with roughly 350 year-round workers and 2,000 seasonal employees), among others.[14] Anecdotally, many companies that experimented with not having a manager ended up abandoned this structure in favor of a more traditional one, including Zappos and Medium.

holacracy

A structure where employees work in self managing teams without having a formal manager.

Departmentalization

Organizational structures differ in terms of departmentalization, which are broadly categorized as either functional or divisional.

Organizations using **functional structures** group jobs based on similarity in functions. Such structures may have departments such as marketing, manufacturing, finance, accounting, human resources, and information technology. In these structures, each person serves a specialized role and handles large volumes of transactions. For example, in a functional structure, an employee in the marketing department may serve as an event planner, planning promotional events for all the products of the company.

functional structures

Structures in which jobs are grouped based on similarity in functions.

FIGURE 7.2 Functional Structure

Functional structures rely on a division of labor, whereby groups of people handle activities related to a specific function of the overall business. We illustrate functional structures in action within two types of organizations that commonly use them.

Grocery Store Functions

Grocery stockers often work at night to make sure shelves stay full during the day.

Pharmacists' specialized training allows them to command pay that can exceed $50 an hour.

Bakers wake up early to give shoppers their daily bread.

The creation of produce, deli, and butcher departments provides an efficient way to divide a grocery store physically as well as functionally.

Bagging groceries requires a friendly personality as well as knowing that eggs should not go on the bottom.

Folks that work checkout aisles should be trusted to handle cash.

Spa Functions

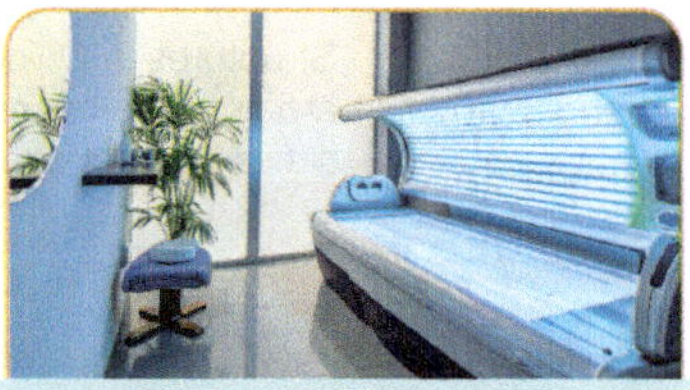

Compared to other spa functions, little training is required of a tanning bed operator—although the ability to tell time may help.

Many can buy a shotgun or parent a child without any training, but every state requires a license in order to cut hair.

Some spa employees manicure fingernails, a practice that is over four thousand years old. Many also provide pedicures, a service whose popularity has nearly doubled in the past decade.

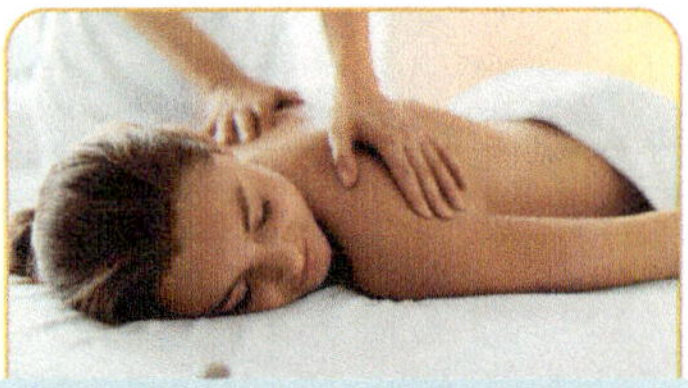

The license required of massage therapists in many states ensures that customers get the best of care.

Cucumber masks are usually applied by a skin care specialist who has taken a professional training program.

Source: Shutterstock.com

In organizations using **divisional structures**, departments represent the unique products, services, customers, or geographic locations the company is serving. Consequently, each unique product or service the company is producing will have its own department. Within each department, functions such as marketing, manufacturing, and other roles are often replicated. In these structures, employees may act more like generalists as opposed to specialists. Instead of performing specialized tasks, employees are often in charge of performing many different tasks in the service of the product. For example, a marketing employee in a company with a divisional structure may be in charge of planning promotions, coordinating relations with advertising agencies, and planning and conducting marketing research, all for the particular product line handled by his or her division.

divisional structures

When departments represent the unique products, services, customers, or geographic locations the company is serving.

In practice, many organizations are structured according to a mixture of functional and divisional forms. For example, if the company has multiple product lines, departmentalizing by product may increase innovativeness and reduce response times. Each of these departments may have dedicated marketing, manufacturing, and customer service employees serving the specific product; yet, the company may also find that centralizing some operations and retaining the functional structure makes sense and is more cost effective for roles such as human resources management and information technology. The same organization may also create geographic departments if it is serving different countries.

Each type of departmentalization has its advantages. Functional structures tend to be effective when an organization does not have a large number of products and services requiring special attention. When a company has a diverse product line, each product will have unique demands, deeming divisional (or product-specific) structures more useful for promptly addressing customer demands and anticipating market changes. Functional structures are more effective in stable environments that are slower to change. In contrast, organizations using product divisions are more agile and can perform better in turbulent environments. The type of employee who will succeed under each structure is also different. Research shows that when employees work in product divisions in turbulent environments, because activities are diverse and complex, their performance depends on their general mental abilities.[15]

German sociologist and political economist Max Weber was one of the earliest scholars to study organizations. He coined the term "bureaucracy." Bureau is the German word for office.

Source: Natata/Shutterstock.com

FIGURE 7.3 An Example of a Pharmaceutical Company with Functional Departments

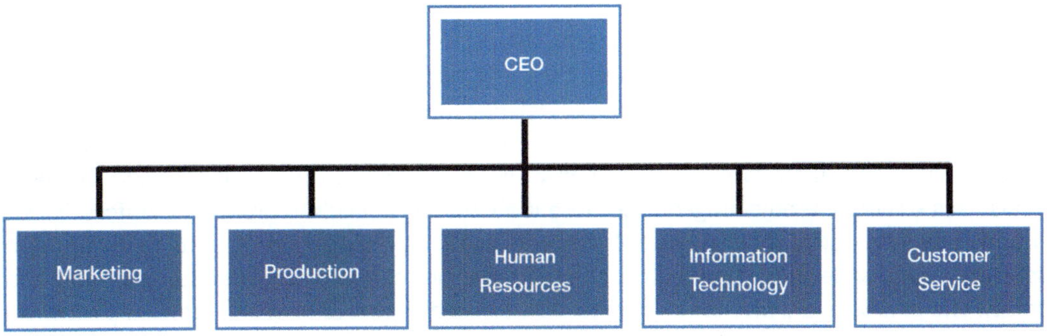

FIGURE 7.4 An Example of a Pharmaceutical Company with Product Departments

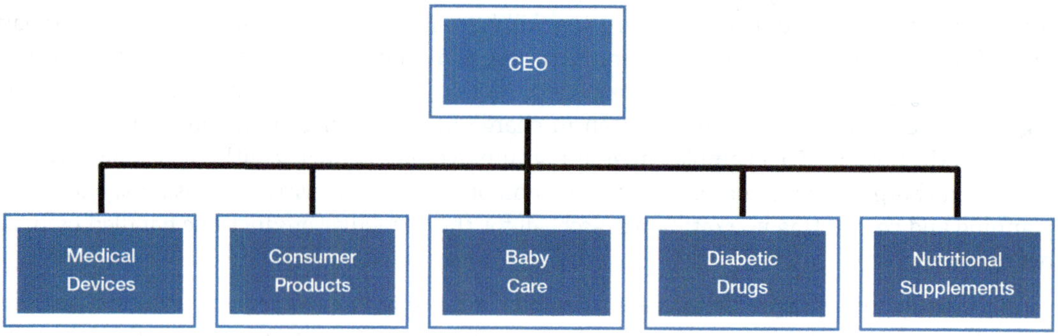

Two Configurations: Mechanistic and Organic Structures

The different elements making up organizational structures in the form of formalization, centralization, number of levels in the hierarchy, and departmentalization often coexist. One popular classification of these elements distinguishes between organizations with "mechanistic" structures and organizations with "organic" structures.

mechanistic structures

Those structures that resemble a bureaucracy and are highly formalized and centralized.

Mechanistic structures are those that resemble a bureaucracy. These structures are highly formalized and centralized. Communication tends to follow formal channels and employees are given specific job descriptions delineating their roles and responsibilities. Mechanistic organizations are often rigid and resist change, deterring innovativeness and making quick action challenging. These forms have the downside of inhibiting entrepreneurial action and discouraging the use of individual initiative on the part of employees. Mechanistic structures tend to limit individual autonomy and self-determination, which will likely lead to lower levels of intrinsic motivation on the job.[16]

Despite these downsides, however, mechanistic structures have advantages when the environment is more stable. The main advantage of a mechanistic structure is its efficiency. Therefore, in organizations that are trying to maximize efficiency and minimize costs, mechanistic structures provide advantages. For example, McDonald's has a famously bureaucratic structure where employee jobs are highly formalized, with clear lines of communication and specific job descriptions. This structure is advantageous because it allows McDonald's to produce a uniform product around the world at minimum cost. Moreover, mechanistic structures tend to be advantageous for new ventures. New businesses often suffer from a lack of structure, role ambiguity, and uncertainty. The presence of a mechanistic structure has been shown to be related to firm performance in new ventures.[17]

organic structures

Those structures that are flexible and decentralized with low levels of formalization where communication lines are more fluid and flexible.

In contrast to mechanistic structures, **organic structures** are flexible and decentralized, with low levels of formalization. In organizations with an organic structure, communication lines are more fluid and flexible. Employee job descriptions are broader and employees are asked to perform duties based on the specific needs of the organization at the time as well as their own expertise levels. Organic structures tend to be related to higher levels of job satisfaction on the part of employees. These structures are conducive to entrepreneurial behavior and innovativeness.[18] An example of a company that has an organic structure is the diversified technology company 3M. The company is strongly committed to decentralization. At 3M, there are close to 100 profit centers, with each division acting like a small company. Each division manager acts autonomously and is accountable for their actions. As operations within each division get too big and a product created by a division becomes profitable, the operation is spun off to create a separate business unit. This is done to protect the agility of the company and the small-company atmosphere.[19] One way 3M maintains their organic environment for innovation is through their policy of "15% time," where employees can spend 15% of their time on projects that are not formally sponsored by the company currently.[20]

Key Takeaway

The degree to which a company is centralized and formalized, the number of levels in the company hierarchy, and the type of departmentalization the company uses are key elements of a company's structure. These elements of structure affect the degree to which the company is effective and innovative, and such structures impact employee attitudes and behaviors at work. These elements lead to the creation of mechanistic and organic structures. Mechanistic structures are rigid and bureaucratic and help companies achieve efficiency while organic structures are decentralized, flexible, and aid companies in achieving innovativeness.

Discussion Questions

1. What are the advantages and disadvantages of decentralization?
2. All else being equal, would you prefer to work in a tall or flat organization? Why?
3. What are the advantages and disadvantages of departmentalization by product?
4. What are the key differences between mechanistic and organic structures?

7.2 Contemporary Forms of Organizational Structures

Learning Objectives

1. Learn about a matrix structure and the challenges of working in this structure.
2. Define boundaryless organizations.
3. Define learning organizations, and understand potential steps organizations can take to become learning organizations.

For centuries, technological advancements that impacted business developed slowly. Over 100 years passed between the invention of the first reliable steam engine and the first practical internal combustion engine. During these early days of advancement, communication would often go hand in hand with transportation. Instead of delivering mail hundreds of miles by horse, messages could be transported more quickly by train and then later by plane. Beginning in the 1900s, the tides of change began to rise much more quickly. From the telegraph to the telephone to the computer to the internet, each advancement brought about a need for an organization's structure to adapt and change. While earlier organizations often involved the work of individuals (such as masons or blacksmiths) or small family businesses (such as taverns and inns), the Industrial Revolution created the need to manage thousands of employees on a regular basis.

Business today is a global endeavor involving many economies and cultures. Industries that were not in existence a century ago (such as those related to high technology) demand flexibility by organizations in ways never before seen. The diverse and complex nature of the current business environment has led to the emergence of several types of organizational structures. Beginning in the 1970s, management experts began to propose organizational designs that they believed were better adapted to the needs of the emerging business environment. Each structure has unique qualities to help businesses handle their particular environment, but these advantages come at the cost of trade-offs with the benefits of more traditional organizational structures.

Matrix Organizations

matrix organizations

Organizations that cross a traditional functional structure with a product structure. Specifically, employees reporting to department managers are also pooled together to form project or product teams.

Matrix organizations have a design that combines a traditional functional structure with a product structure. Specifically, employees reporting to department managers are pooled together to form project or product teams. As a result, each person reports to a department manager as well as a project or product manager. In a matrix structure, product managers have control and say over product-related matters, while department managers have authority over matters related to company policy. Matrix structures are created in response to giving particular attention to specific products or projects. Using the matrix structure as opposed to product departments may increase communication and cooperation among departments because project managers will need to coordinate their actions with those of department managers. In fact, research shows that matrix structure increases the frequency of informal and formal communication within the organization.[21] Matrix structures also have the benefit of providing quick responses to technical problems and customer demands. The existence of a project manager keeps the focus on the product or service provided.

Despite these potential benefits, matrix structures are not without costs. In a matrix, each employee reports to two or more managers. In the movie *Office Space*, the matrix structure is parodied at the fictitious software firm Initech, where Peter Gibbons claims to have eight bosses. Although exaggerated in the film, this situation is ripe for conflict in matrix structures. Because multiple managers are in charge of guiding the behaviors of each employee, there may be power struggles and conflict among managers. As managers are more interdependent compared to a traditional or product-based structure, they will need to spend more effort coordinating their work. From the employee's perspective, there is potential for interpersonal conflict with team members as well as with leaders. The presence of multiple leaders may create role ambiguity or, worse, role conflict—being given instructions or objectives that cannot all be met because they are mutually exclusive. The necessity to work with a team consisting of employees with different functional backgrounds increases the potential for task conflict at work.[22] Solving these problems requires a great level of patience and proactivity on the part of the employee.

FIGURE 7.5 Software Company Organizational Chart

An example of a matrix structure at a software development company. Business analysts, developers, and testers each report to a functional department manager and to a project manager simultaneously.

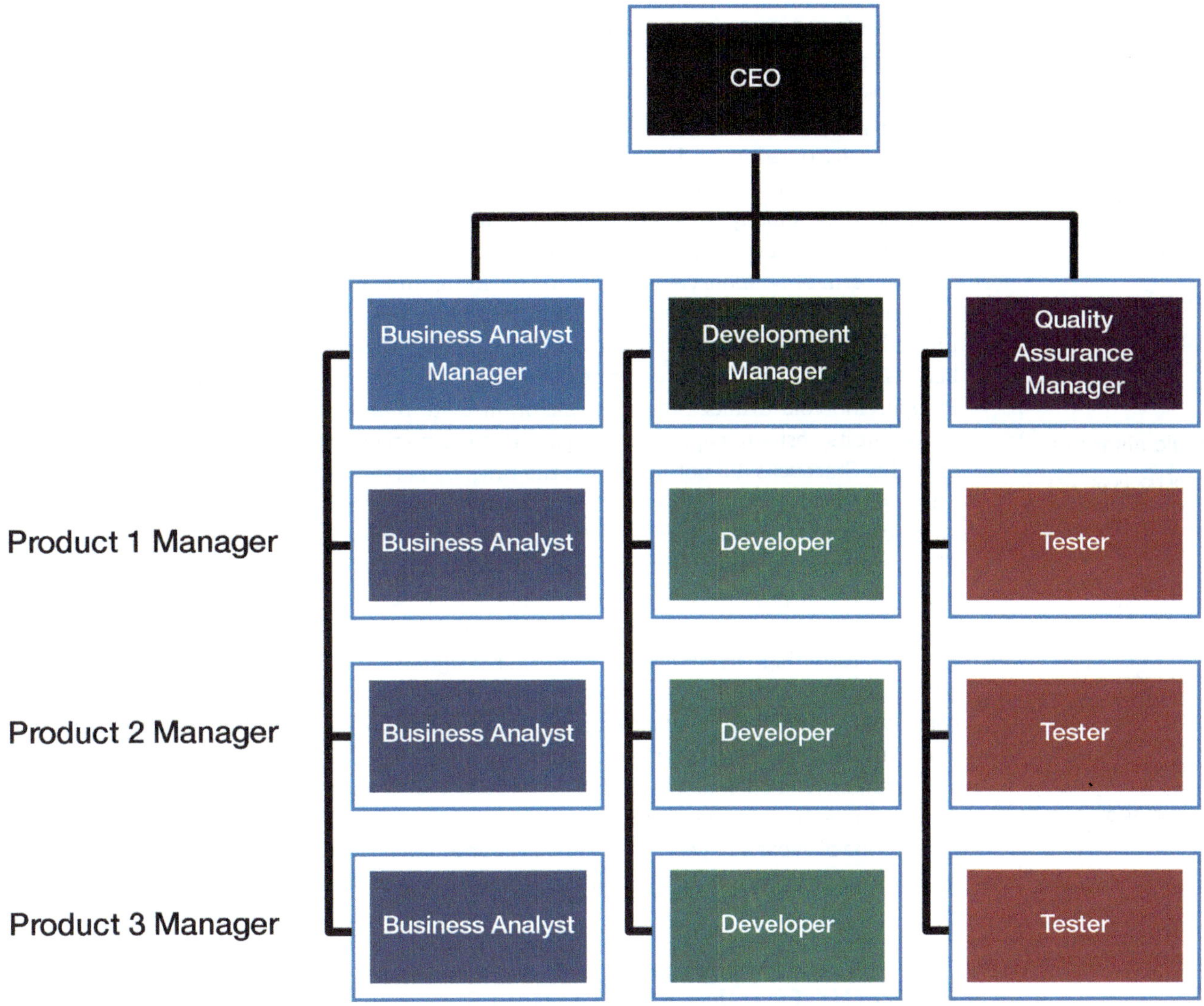

The matrix structure is used in many information technology companies engaged in software development. Sportswear manufacturer Nike is another company that uses the matrix organization successfully. New product introduction is a task shared by regional managers and product managers. While product managers are in charge of deciding how to launch a product, regional managers are allowed to make modifications based on the region.[23]

Boundaryless Organizations

boundaryless organization

An organization that eliminates traditional barriers between departments as well as barriers between the organization and the external environment.

modular organization

An organization where all the nonessential functions are outsourced.

strategic alliances

A form of boundaryless design where two or more companies find an area of collaboration and combine their efforts to create a partnership that is beneficial for all parties.

fully remote

Organizing work with the assumption that employees will work from anywhere, without being tied to a physical office.

Boundaryless organization is a term coined by Jack Welch during his tenure as CEO of GE and refers to an organization that eliminates traditional barriers between departments as well as barriers between the organization and the external environment.[24] Many different types of boundaryless organizations exist. One form is the **modular organization**, in which all nonessential functions are outsourced. The idea behind this format is to retain only the value-generating and strategic functions in-house, while the rest of the operations are outsourced to many suppliers. An example of a company with this approach is Toyota. By managing relationships with hundreds of suppliers, Toyota achieves efficiency and quality in its operations. **Strategic alliances** constitute another form of boundaryless design. In this form, similar to a joint venture, two or more companies find an area of collaboration and combine their efforts to create a partnership that is beneficial for both parties. In the process, the traditional boundaries between two competitors may be broken. As an example, Starbucks formed a highly successful partnership with PepsiCo to market its Frappuccino cold drinks. Starbucks has immediate brand-name recognition in this cold coffee drink, but its desire to capture shelf space in supermarkets required marketing savvy and experience that Starbucks did not possess at the time. By partnering with PepsiCo, Starbucks gained an important head start in the marketing and distribution of this product. Finally, organizations may embrace different levels of remote organizing. **Fully remote** organizations such as Automattic and GitLab organize work with the assumption that employees will work from anywhere, without being tied to a physical office. These companies assume that work will always be performed remotely. Fully remote companies put systems in place to enable fully remote work, hire employees without restricting themselves to particular geographies, and oftentimes may not even have a physical office. This is different from remote friendly organizations that allow partial work to be completed remotely, while assuming that the primary workplace is still the office. COVID-19 pandemic made remote work increasingly common across different industries around the world, and organizations such as the user based question and answer platform Quora that were previously remote friendly are taking steps toward becoming fully remote organizations. Similarly, Fujitsu, one of Japan's largest employers, announced that they would cut office space by 50% in the next three years, and ask its 80,000 office workers to work from home.[25]

Learning Organizations

A learning organization is one whose design actively seeks to acquire knowledge and change behavior as a result of the newly acquired knowledge. In learning organizations, experimenting, learning new things, and reflecting on new knowledge are the norms. At the same time, there are many procedures and systems in place that facilitate learning at all organization levels.

In learning organizations, experimentation and testing potentially better operational methods are encouraged. This is true not only in response to environmental threats but also as a way of identifying future opportunities. At IBM, learning is encouraged by taking highly successful business managers and putting them in charge of emerging business opportunities (EBOs). IBM is a company that has no difficulty coming up with new ideas, as evidenced by the number of patents it holds. Yet commercializing these ideas has been a problem in the past because of an emphasis on short-term results. To change this situation, the company began experimenting with the idea of setting up a structure where failure is tolerated and risk taking is encouraged, resulting in a big step toward becoming a learning organization.[26]

Learning organizations are also good at learning from experience—either their own or a competitor's. Some companies choose to conduct formal retrospective meetings to analyze the challenges encountered and areas for improvement. To learn from others, these companies vigorously study competitors, market leaders in different industries, clients, and customers. By benchmarking against industry best practices, companies can find new ways of improving their own operations. Learning organizations are also good at studying customer habits to generate ideas. For example, Xerox uses anthropologists to understand and gain insights into how customers are actually using their office products.[27] By using these techniques, learning organizations facilitate innovation and make it easier to achieve organizational change.

As the world's largest employee owned company, Publix provides an excellent example of a learning organization where collaboration and communication are valued.

Source: Ken Schulze/ Shutterstock.com

Key Takeaway

The changing environment of organizations creates the need for newer forms of organizing. Matrix structures are a cross between functional and product-based divisional structures. They facilitate information flow and reduce response time to customers but have challenges because each employee reports to multiple managers. Boundaryless organizations blur the boundaries between departments or the boundaries between the focal organization and others in the environment. Learning organizations institutionalize experimentation and benchmarking.

Discussion Questions

1. Have you ever reported to more than one manager? What were the challenges of such a situation? As a manager, what could you do to help your subordinates who have other bosses?
2. What are the advantages and disadvantages of being employed by a boundaryless organization?
3. What can organizations do to institutionalize organizational learning? What practices and policies would aid in knowledge acquisition and retention?

7.3 Organizational Change

Learning Objectives

1. Identify external forces that create change for organizations.
2. Understand how organizations respond to changes in the external environment.
3. Understand why individuals often resist change.

Why Do Organizations Change?

organizational change

The movement of an organization from one state of affairs to another.

Winston Churchill once argued, "To improve is to change; to be perfect is to change often." Despite this advice, both individuals and organizations often struggle with change. **Organizational change** is the movement of an organization from one state of affairs to another. Organizational change can take many forms. It may involve a change in a company's structure, strategy, policies, procedures, technology, or culture. The change may be planned years in advance or may be forced upon an organization because of a shift in the environment, such as a stock market drop or dramatic changes in technology. Organizational change can be radical and alter the way an organization operates, or it may be incremental and slowly change the way things are done. In any case, regardless of the type, change involves letting go of the old ways in which work is done and adjusting to the new ways. Therefore, fundamentally, it is a process that involves effective people management.

Managers carrying out any of the P-O-L-C functions often find themselves faced with the need to manage organizational change effectively. Oftentimes, the planning process reveals the need for a new or improved strategy, which is then reflected in changes to tactical and operational plans. Creating a new organizational design (the organizing function) or altering the existing design entails changes that may affect a single employee or the entire organization, depending on the scope of the changes. Effective decision making, a Leadership task, takes into account the change-management implications of decisions, planning for the need to manage the implementation of decisions. Finally, any updates to controlling systems and processes will potentially involve changes to employees' assigned tasks and performance assessments, which will require astute change management skills to implement. In short, change management is an important leadership skill that spans the entire range of P-O-L-C functions.

Workforce Demographics

Organizational change is often a response to changes in the environment. For example, both in the United States and Europe, the age of the workforce is on the rise.[28] What does this mean for companies? Organizations may realize that as the workforce gets older the types of benefits they prefer may change. Work arrangements such as flexible work hours and job sharing may become more popular as employees remain in the workforce even after retirement. As the workforce rapidly ages, it also becomes possible that employees who are unhappy with their current work situation will choose to retire, resulting in a sudden loss of valuable knowledge and expertise on the part of organizations. Therefore, organizations will have to devise strategies to retain these employees and plan for their retirement. The COVID-19 pandemic introduced unique challenges to the management of older workers. The pandemic has more adverse health implications for older individuals, resulting in higher levels of unemployment and retirements among older workers, and greater possibility of discrimination in hiring among those who choose to or need to remain in the workforce.[29]

Technology

Sometimes change is motivated by rapid developments in technology. Moore's law (a prediction by Gordon Moore, cofounder of Intel Corporation) dictates that the overall complexity of computer circuits will double every eighteen months with no increase in cost.[30] Such change is motivating corporations to rapidly change their technology. Sometimes technology produces such profound developments that companies struggle to adapt. One of the challenges retailers face due to advances in technology as of this writing is the concept of "showrooming." Online stores such as Amazon often offer better prices on the same merchandise compared to traditional brick and mortar shops. However, traditional retailers such as the bookseller Barnes and Noble and Best Buy make it easier to touch, feel, browse, and ultimately make a purchasing decision. Traditional retailers are finding that many customers stop by the store, try out the product, check prices online using their smart phones, and then purchase the item online rather than within the store. Retailers are struggling to survive while dealing with this concern, while others such as Toys R Us are closing their doors, finding themselves unable to compete.[31] Customers seem to still find value in seeing the product in person before buying it, explaining why they still come to the stores, but the situation does not seem sustainable, forcing the industry to seek solutions.

Globalization

Globalization can be either a threat or an opportunity for organizations, depending on their ability to adapt to relevant changes. Because of differences in national economies and standards of living from one country to another, organizations in developed countries are finding that it is often cheaper to produce goods and deliver services in developing countries. This has led many companies to offshore their manufacturing operations to countries such as China and Mexico. In the 1990s, knowledge work was thought to be safe from outsourcing, but in the 21st century we are also seeing many service operations moved to places with cheaper wages. For example, many companies have outsourced software development to India, with Indian companies such as Wipro and Infosys emerging as global giants. Given these changes, understanding how to manage a global workforce is a necessity. Today, companies are less concerned solely with a definitive choice of whether to offshore; instead, most companies face complicated global trade-offs between developing or making parts of their production process themselves instead of purchasing them from potentially less expensive global suppliers.[32]

Generational Events

A review of world history would suggest that there are some unexpected, catastrophic, and low probability events that affect multiple industries, change the habits of businesses, employees, and customers, and shape organizational life in the years to come. Examples of these events include September 11 attacks on twin towers in New York and Pentagon building in Washington, D.C. and the resulting effects on insurance, travel, and tourism industries and 2008 subprime mortgage crisis affecting the entire world economy. These events test the agility of businesses, and show the importance of being adaptable to sudden and long lasting changes.

The COVID-19 pandemic is one such generation defining event that took the world (except epidemiologists, Bill Gates, and the makers of the 2011 movie *Contagion*) by surprise in 2020. As of this writing, it is in the process of influencing industries ranging from education to health care, retail to tourism through the next decade. The effects of COVID-19 on customers and employees is multidimensional, and it is unclear which of these changes are temporary, and which represent the new normal. For example, the preference to complete retail transactions with limited interpersonal interactions is likely to motivate businesses to increase their online presence and invest in contactless technology. Further, companies are expected to speed up their automation of many tasks that are repetitive and dangerous. Several companies (usually those with pre-COVID financial challenges) that relied on physical presence in an indoor location such as 24 Hour Fitness and Gold's Gym, and businesses that relied on customers attending formal events, such as Brooks Brothers declared bankruptcy, whereas companies that facilitated working or staying at home such as Zoom, Amazon, and Netflix saw their businesses boom. Predicting how customer preferences will change and adapting proactively is the key to the survival of new and existing businesses. COVID-19 led to the normalization of remote work in many industries while creating unique challenges for parents who found themselves having to work while also taking care of kids at home. A survey of 681 large employers in May 2020 showed that while 7% of their employees worked remotely prior to the pandemic, they expected this figure to be three times as large after the pandemic. Companies that relied on workplace perks such as gyms and cafeterias are realizing that they will need new tools to build a positive employee experience. COVID-19 may serve as the impetus that leads companies to re-envision what they do, why they do it, and how they do it.[33]

Changes in the Market Conditions

Market changes may also create internal changes as companies struggle to adjust. For example, tobacco companies faced dramatic changes and threats to their products as the harmful effects of tobacco became well known. The market forces they face today are dramatically different from the times when they were able to take advantage of the 1920s women's liberation movement and encourage women to smoke under the slogan "torches of freedom." Similar changes are occurring in fast food and snack markets in response to the increasing health consciousness of customers, forcing businesses to consider healthier alternatives to their products and diversify their operations. For example, fast food giant McDonald's now offers apple slices as a substitute for their fries in children's Happy Meals.

How does a change in environment create change within an organization? Note that environmental change does not automatically change how business is done. Whether or not the organization changes in response to environmental challenges and threats depends on the decision makers' reactions to what is happening in the environment.

Growth

It is natural for small start-up companies to grow as they becoming successful. An example of this growth is the evolution of the Widmer Brothers Brewing Company. What started as two brothers brewing beer in their garage eventually became the thirteenth largest brewery, in terms of production, in the United States in 2019. This growth happened over time as their key product—Hefeweizen—grew in popularity. Expanding to meet an ever-growing demand, Widmer brothers merged with Redhook Brewery in 2008 to become Craft Brewers Alliance (CBA) Inc. The CBA now encompasses eight different breweries. Anheuser-Busch Companies Inc., which owned a minority stake in both Widmer and Redhook, continues to have a minority stake in the CBA.[34] So, while 50% of all new small businesses fail in their first year,[35] those that succeed have the potential to evolve into large, complex organizations over time.

Although they have weathered much change since their humble beginnings as a handmade playing card company in 1998, Nintendo's joint creation of the Pokémon company demonstrates they have not abandoned their roots.

Source: focal point/Shutterstock.com

Poor Performance

Change can also occur if the company is performing poorly and if there is a perceived threat from the environment. In fact, poorly performing companies often find it easier to change compared with successful companies because high performance can lead to overconfidence and reluctance to change. As a result, successful companies often keep doing what made them a success in the first place. When it comes to the relationship between company performance and organizational change, the saying "Nothing fails like success" may be fitting. For example, Polaroid Corporation was the top producer of instant films and cameras in 1994. The company filed for bankruptcy in less than a decade, unable to adapt to the rapid advances in the one-hour photo development and digital photography technologies. Successful companies that manage to change have special practices in place to keep the organization open to changes. As a case in point, Nokia finds that it is important to periodically change the perspective of key decision makers. For this purpose, they rotate heads of businesses to different posts to give them a fresh perspective. In addition to the success of a business, change in a company's upper level management is a motivator for change at the organization level. Research shows that long-tenured CEOs are unlikely to change their formula for success. Instead, new CEOs and new top management teams are needed to create change in a company's culture and structure.[36]

Resistance to Change

Organizational changes are often essential for a company to remain competitive. Failure to change may influence the ability of a company to survive. Yet employees do not always welcome changes in methods. According to a survey conducted by the Society for Human Resource Management (SHRM), employee resistance to change is one of the top reasons change efforts fail. Reactions to announcements concerning organizational change range from resistance to compliance to enthusiastic support of the change, with the latter being the exception rather than the norm.[37]

FIGURE 7.6 Reactions to Change
Reactions to change may take many forms.

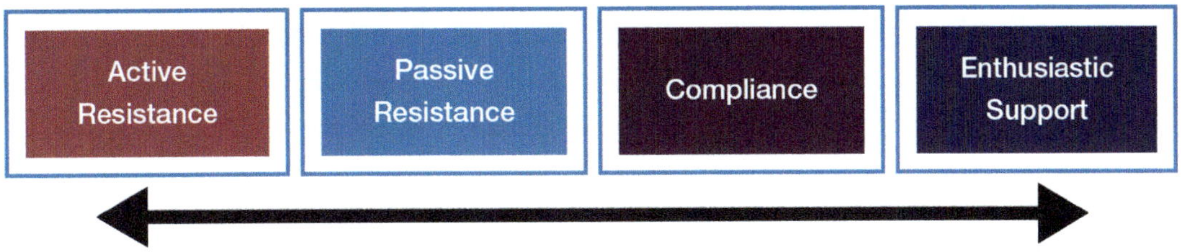

Active resistance is the most negative reaction to a proposed change attempt. Those who engage in active resistance may sabotage the change effort and be outspoken objectors to the new procedures. In contrast, **passive resistance** involves being disturbed by changes without necessarily voicing these opinions. Instead, passive resisters may dislike the change quietly, feel stressed and unhappy, and even look for a new job without necessarily bringing their concerns to the attention of decision makers. **Compliance** involves going along with proposed changes with little enthusiasm. Finally, those who show **enthusiastic support** are defenders of the new way and actually encourage others around them to give support to the change effort. Employees experience different emotions depending on their reactions: Those who display change resistance are stressed, angry and upset, whereas passive resistance is characterized by despair, helplessness, and sadness. Individuals who react to change with compliance are calm, relaxed, and content, whereas enthusiastic supporters are excited, elated, and enthusiastic.[38]

active resistance

The most negative reaction to a proposed change attempt.

passive resistance

Being disturbed by changes without necessarily voicing these opinions.

compliance

Going along with proposed changes with little enthusiasm.

enthusiastic support

Defenders of the new way and those who actually encourage others to give support to the change effort.

Any change attempt will have to overcome the resistance on the part of the people to be successful. Otherwise, the result will be loss of time and energy as well as an inability on the part of the organization to adapt to the changes in the environment and make its operations more efficient. Resistance to change also has negative consequences for the people in question. Research shows that when people react negatively to organizational change, they experience negative emotions, use sick time more often, and are more likely to voluntarily leave the company.[39] These negative effects can be present even when the proposed change clearly offers benefits and advantages over the status quo.

Figure 7.7 presents a dramatic example of how resistance to change may prevent improving the status quo. Have you ever wondered why the keyboards we use are shaped the way they are? The QWERTY keyboard, named after the first six letters in the top row, was actually engineered to slow us down. When the typewriter was first invented in the 19th century, the first prototypes of the keyboard would jam if the keys right next to each other were hit at the same time. Therefore, it was important for manufacturers to slow typists down. They achieved this by putting the most commonly used letters on the left-hand side and scattering the most frequently used letters all over the keyboard. Later, the issue of letters being stuck was resolved with the advent of modern computer keyboards. An alternative to the QWERTY keyboard developed in the 1930s by educational psychologist August Dvorak provides a much more efficient design and allows individuals to double traditional typing speeds. Yet the Dvorak keyboard never gained wide acceptance. The reasons? Large numbers of people resisted the change. Teachers and typists resisted because they would lose their specialized knowledge. Manufacturers resisted due to costs inherent in making the switch and the initial inefficiencies in the learning curve.[40] In short, the best idea does not necessarily win, and changing individual behaviors requires understanding why individuals resist change, which we address in the following section.

FIGURE 7.7 The Dvorak Keyboard

The Dvorak keyboard, shown here, is an efficient alternative to the standard keyboard design in use today. However, due to resistance from typists, teachers, manufacturers, and salespeople, a switch never occurred.

Why Do People Resist Change?

Disrupted Habits

People often resist change for the simple reason that change disrupts habits. When many individuals hop into their cars for the daily commute to work, little thought is given to driving because the activity has become routine. Individuals may even realize they have reached their destination without noticing the roads used or without conscious thoughts about body movements. Now imagine driving a truck cross-country. The loss of familiar habits and patterns would be jarring given the changes in vehicle, road conditions, purpose, and goals of driving. For this simple reason, people are sometimes surprisingly outspoken when confronted with simple changes, such as updating to a newer version of a particular software or a change in their voicemail system.

Personality

Some people are more resistant to change than others. Individuals high on the Big Five personality trait Openness to Experience will more readily accept change. Research also shows that people who have a positive self-concept are better at coping with change, probably because those who have high self-esteem may feel that whatever the changes are, they are likely to adjust to it well and be successful in the new system. People with a more positive self-concept and those who are more optimistic may also view change as an opportunity to shine as opposed to a threat that is overwhelming. Finally, risk tolerance is another predictor of how resistant someone will be to stress. For risk avoiding individuals, the possibility of a change in technology or structure may be more threatening.[41]

Feelings of Uncertainty

Change inevitably brings feelings of uncertainty. Perhaps you just found out that a class you need to graduate was cancelled. What would be your reaction? Such change is often turbulent, and it is often unclear what the consequences are going to be for each individual. The ultimate outcome may be better—or it may be worse. The feeling that the future is unclear is enough to create stress for people because it leads to a sense of lost control and requires greater attention and problem-solving effort.[42]

Fear of Failure

People also resist change when they feel that their performance may be affected under the new system. People who are experts in their jobs may be less than welcoming of the changes because they may be unsure whether their success would last under the new system. Studies show that people who feel that they can perform well under the new system are more likely to be committed to the proposed change, while those who have lower confidence in their ability to perform after changes are less committed.[43]

Personal Impact of Change

It would be too simplistic to argue that people resist all change, regardless of its form. In fact, people tend to be more welcoming of change that is favorable to them on a personal level (such as giving them more power over others or change that improves quality of life such as bigger and nicer offices). Research also shows that commitment to change is highest when proposed changes affect the work unit with a low impact on how individual jobs are performed.[44]

Prevalence of Change

Any change effort should be considered within the context of all the other changes that are introduced in a company. Does the company have a history of making short-lived changes? If the company structure went from functional to product-based to geographic to matrix within the past five years and the top management is in the process of going back to a functional structure again, a certain level of resistance is to be expected because employees are likely to be fatigued as a result of the constant changes. Moreover, the lack of a history of successful changes may cause people to feel skeptical toward the newly planned changes. Therefore, considering the history of changes in the company is important to understanding why people resist. The size of the change is also an important factor. If the company is considering a simple switch to a new computer program, the change may not be as extensive or stressful compared with a switch to an enterprise resource planning (ERP) system, which requires a significant time commitment and can fundamentally affect how business is conducted.[45]

Perceived Loss of Power

One other reason people may resist change is that change may affect their power and influence in the organization. Losing status is particularly painful for high-status individuals, disrupting their future performance.[46] Imagine that your company moved to a more team-based structure, turning supervisors into team leaders. In the old structure, supervisors were in charge of hiring and firing all those reporting to them. Under the new system, this power is given to the team. Instead of monitoring the progress the team is making toward goals, the job of a team leader is to provide support and mentoring to the team in general and ensure that the team has access to all resources to be effective. Given the loss in prestige and status in the new structure, some supervisors may resist the proposed changes even if it is better for the organization to operate around teams.

Is All Resistance Bad?

Resistance to change may be a positive force in some instances. In fact, resistance to change is a valuable feedback tool that should not be ignored. Why are people resisting the proposed changes? Do they believe that the new system will not work? If so, why not? By listening to people and incorporating their suggestions into the change effort, it is possible to make a more effective change. Some of a company's most committed employees may be the most vocal opponents of a change effort. They may fear that the organization they feel such a strong attachment to is being threatened by the planned change effort and the change will ultimately hurt the company. For example, many physicians express unhappiness with switching to maintaining electronic health records of patients. This is because these systems are often not user friendly, and prevent doctors from maintaining connections with their patients, instead forcing them to enter data while the patient is in the exam room. In this example, resistance to change is motivated by a desire to connect and serve patients better, which should provide valuable feedback to system designers.[47]

Key Takeaway

Organizations evolve in response to changes in the environment and in response to the way decision makers interpret these changes. Individuals resist change because change disrupts habits, conflicts with certain personality types, causes a fear of failure, can have potentially negative effects, can result in a potential for loss of power, and, when done too frequently, can exhaust employees.

Discussion Questions

1. Can you think of an organizational or personal change that you had to go through? Have you encountered any resistance during this change? What were the reasons?
2. How would you deal with employees who are resisting change because their habits are threatened? How would you deal with them if they are resisting because of a fear of failure?
3. Why are successful companies less likely to change? What should companies do in order to make organizational change part of their culture?

7.4 Planning and Executing Change Effectively

Learning Objectives

1. Describe Lewin's three-stage model of planned change.
2. Describe how organizations may embrace continuous change.

How do individuals and organizations plan, organize, and execute change effectively? One of the most useful frameworks surrounding the idea of organizational change is the three-stage model of planned change developed in the 1950s by psychologist Kurt Lewin.[48] This model assumes that change will encounter resistance. Therefore, executing change without prior preparation is likely to lead to failure. Instead, organizations should start with **unfreezing**, or making sure that organizational members are ready for, and receptive to, change. This is followed by **change**, or executing the planned changes. Finally, **refreezing** involves ensuring that change becomes permanent and the new habits, rules, or procedures become the norm. John Kotter, a Harvard University professor, wrote a book in 1996 titled *Leading Change* in which he discussed eight steps to changing an organization.[49] In the next section, we integrate the two models with more recent work in the area to present a road map to how organizations may want to approach change.

unfreezing

Making sure that organizational members are ready for and receptive to change.

change

Executing the planned changes.

refreezing

Ensuring that change becomes permanent and the new habits, rules, or procedures become the norm.

FIGURE 7.8 Lewin's Three-Stage Process of Change

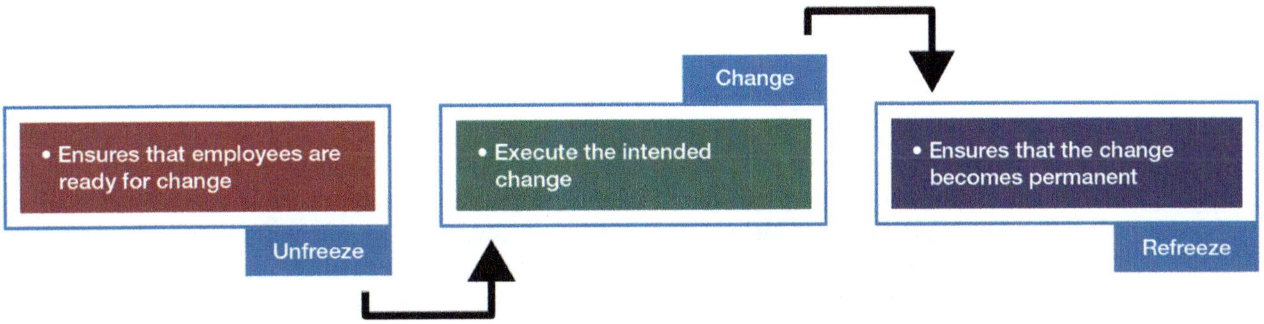

Unfreezing Before Change

Many change efforts fail because people are insufficiently prepared for change. When employees are not prepared, they are more likely to resist the change effort and less likely to effectively function under the new system. What can organizations do prior to change to prepare employees? There are a number of things that are important at this stage.

Create a Vision for Change

In successful change efforts, the leader has an overall vision for the change.[50] When this vision is exciting and paints a picture of a future that employees would be proud to be a part of, people are likely to be more committed to change. For example, Toyota is a master of *kaizen*, or continuous improvement. They also follow the philosophy of *kakushin*, or revolutionary change, as needed. Regardless of the nature of the particular change, there is an overall vision for the company that justifies and explains why change is necessary "to build the dream car of the future."[51]

Communicate a Plan for Change

Do people know what the change entails, or are they hearing about the planned changes through the grapevine or office gossip? When employees know what is going to happen, when, and why, they may conquer their discomfort with change. Research shows that those who have more information about upcoming changes are more committed to a change effort.[52] Moreover, in successful change efforts, the leader not only communicates a plan but also an overall vision for the change.[53] When this vision is exciting and paints a picture of a future that employees would be proud to be a part of, people are likely to be more committed to change.

Ensuring that top management communicates with employees about the upcoming changes also has symbolic value.[54] In any organization, many changes are done on a daily basis, with some taking root and some disappearing after a short while. When top management and the company CEO discuss the importance of the changes in meetings, employees are provided with a reason to trust that this change is a strategic initiative.

Develop a Sense of Urgency

People are more likely to accept change if they feel that there is a need for it. If employees feel their company is doing well, the perceived need for change will be smaller. Those who plan the change will need to make the case that there is an external or internal threat to the organization's competitiveness, reputation, or sometimes even its survival, and that failure to act will have dire consequences. For example, antiracism protests around the world following the killing of George Floyd by a police officer in Minnesota created a corporate urgency to review and eliminate corporate practices perpetuating racial inequality and stereotypes. Unilever stated that they would rename their top selling beauty brand "Fair & Lovely," while Johnson & Johnson would stop selling skin lightening creams, and Mars renaming their Uncle Ben's rice brands. Companies facing criticisms from their own employees as well as consumers sense an urgency to initiate organizational changes.[55]

Build a Coalition

In order to convince people that change is needed, the change leader does not necessarily have to convince every person individually. In fact, people's opinions toward change are affected by opinion leaders or those people who have a strong influence over the behaviors and attitudes of others.[56] Instead of trying to get everyone on board at the same time, it may be more useful to convince and enlist the "right people." Once these individuals agree that the proposed change is needed and will be useful, they will become helpful allies in ensuring that the rest of the organization is ready for change.[57]

Provide Support

Employees should feel that their needs are not ignored. Therefore, management may prepare employees for change by providing emotional and instrumental support. Emotional support may be in the form of frequently discussing the changes, encouraging employees to voice their concerns, and simply expressing confidence in employees' ability to perform effectively under the new system. Instrumental support may be in the form of providing a training program to employees so that they know how to function under the new system.

Allow Employees to Participate

Studies show that employees who participate in planning change efforts tend to have more positive opinions about the change. Why? They will have the opportunity to voice their concerns. They can shape the change effort so that their concerns are addressed. They will be more knowledgeable about the reasons for change, alternatives to the proposed changes, and why the chosen alternative was better than the others. Finally, they will feel a sense of ownership of the planned change and are more likely to be on board.[58] Participation may be more useful if it starts at earlier stages, preferably while the problem is still being diagnosed. For example, assume that a company suspects there are problems with manufacturing quality. One way of convincing employees that there is a problem that needs to be solved would be to ask them to take customer calls about product quality. Once employees experience the problem firsthand, they will be more motivated to solve the problem.

Executing Change

The second stage of Lewin's three-stage change model is executing change. At this stage, the organization implements the planned changes in technology, structure, culture, or procedures. The specifics of how change should be executed will depend on the type of change. However, there are three tips that may facilitate the success of a change effort.

In the 1980s, British Airways was known for its on-time departures but poor treatment of passengers, earning it the nickname "Bloody Awful." In 10 years, as a result of significant changes in its reward system and training managers to motivate and empower front-line employees, it built a service culture, now often referred to as "Bloody Awesome."

Source: Sunshine Seeds/Shutterstock.com

Continue to Provide Support

As the change is under way, employees may experience high amounts of stress. They may make mistakes more often or experience uncertainty about their new responsibilities or job descriptions. Management has an important role in helping employees cope with this stress by displaying support, patience, and continuing to provide support to employees even after the change is complete.

Create Small Wins

During a change effort, if the organization can create a history of small wins, change acceptance will be more likely.[59] If the change is large in scope and the payoff is a long-term endeavor, employees may not realize change is occurring during the transformation period. However, if people see changes, improvements, and successes along the way, they will be inspired and motivated to continue the change effort. For this reason, breaking up the proposed change into phases may be a good idea because it creates smaller targets. Small wins are also important for planners of change to make the point that their idea is on the right track. Early success gives change planners more credibility while early failures may be a setback.[60]

Eliminate Obstacles

When the change effort is in place, many obstacles may crop up along the way. There may be key people who publicly support the change effort while silently undermining the planned changes. There may be obstacles rooted in a company's structure, existing processes, or culture. It is the management's job to identify, understand, and remove these obstacles.[61] Ideally, these obstacles would have been eliminated before implementing the change, but sometimes unexpected road-blocks emerge as change is under way.

Kotter's Eight-Stage Process for Change

Harvard Business School professor John P. Kotter proposed that companies should follow eight stages when instituting change. Here is a summary of his suggested steps.

1. Create a sense of urgency when introducing the change effort
2. Build a coalition
3. Create a vision for change and make change a part of the vision
4. Communicate a plan for change
5. Eliminate obstacles to change
6. Create small wins
7. Build on change
8. Make change a part of culture

Source: Kotter, J. P. (1996). Leading change. Boston, MA: Harvard Business School Press

Refreezing

After the change is implemented, the long-term success of a change effort depends on whether change becomes part of the company's culture. In other words, the revised ways of thinking, behaving, and performing should become routine. For this reason, there are a number of things management can do.

Publicize Success

In order to make change permanent, the organization may benefit from sharing the results of the change effort with employees. What was gained from the implemented changes? How much money did the company save? How much did the company's reputation improve? What was the reduction in accidents after new procedures were put in place? Sharing concrete results with employees increases their confidence that the implemented change was a good decision.

Build on Prior Change

Once results start coming, it is important to benefit from the momentum created by these early successes by pushing for even more change. Following the philosophy of continuous improvement may be a good idea here. Instead of declaring victory early, the company is advised to make continuous improvements to how business is conducted.

Reward Change Adoption

To ensure that change becomes permanent, organizations may benefit from rewarding those who embrace the change effort (an aspect of the controlling function). The rewards do not necessarily have to be financial. The simple act of recognizing those who are giving support to the change effort in front of their peers may encourage others to get on board. When the new behaviors employees are expected to demonstrate (such as using a new computer program, filling out a new form, or simply greeting customers once they enter the store) are made part of an organization's reward system, those behaviors are more likely to be taken seriously and repeated, making the change effort successful.[62]

Embracing Continuous Change

While Lewin's three-stage model offers many useful insights into the process of implementing change, it views each organizational change as an episode with a beginning, middle, and end. In contrast with this episodic change assumption, some management experts in the 1990s began to propose that change is—or ought to be—a continuous process.

The learning organization is an example of a company embracing continuous change. By setting up a dynamic feedback loop, learning can become a regular part of daily operations. If an employee implements a new method or technology that seems to be successful, a learning organization is in a good position to adopt such ideas. By constantly being aware of how employee actions and outcomes affect others, as well as overall company productivity, the inevitable small changes throughout organizations can be rapidly absorbed and tailored for daily operations. When an organization understands that change does indeed occur constantly, it will be in a better position to make use of good changes and intervene if a change seems detrimental. Bill Gates once noted, "your most unhappy customers are your greatest source of learning."[63] It is this spirit of thirsting for organizational learning that engages some companies to encourage customer complaints to serve as springboards for areas where organizations can work toward constant improvement and change.[64]

Make Change a Part of Organizational Culture

If the change effort has been successful, change will have become a part of corporate culture. In other words, in addition to the changes in procedures, processes, or technology, the mindset of people will also have changed. If change occurs only in superficial elements, it would be misleading to declare change a success. For example, if a company institutes a wellness program emphasizing healthy habits, rewarding employees for adopting healthy choices and providing resources to maximize health, this change effort would be deemed a true success if valuing employee health and well-being also becomes a part of the organization's culture. Creating a website, and printing booklets and distributing them are all tools leading to this goal, but achieving the true goal also necessitates a change in ingrained assumptions of management and employees putting work before employee health and well-being.

Key Takeaway

Change efforts can be conceptualized as a three-step process in which employees are first prepared for change, then change is implemented, and finally, the new behavioral patterns become permanent.

Discussion Questions

1. What are the benefits of employee participation in change management?
2. Imagine that you are working at an urban university, with students having access to every building on campus except dormitories, if they live there. Now the university will move on to a system where entry into all buildings will be restricted by keycards. Further, inside each building, student access will be restricted depending on who they are, with some areas off limits to students altogether, whereas others will only allow access during business hours. Explain how you would plan and execute this change using Lewin's three-step framework.

7.5 Building Your Change Management Skills

Learning Objective

1. Identify personal guidelines for overcoming resistance to change.

Overcoming Resistance to Change

At some point in the education or career of most individuals, a situation occurs when they feel change is needed. For example, an individual might have a great idea, but others in the organization do not seem convinced or express resistance. How can individuals make change happen?

- *Listen to naysayers*. You may think that your idea is great, but listening to those who resist may give you valuable ideas about why it may not work and how to design it more effectively.
- *Is your change revolutionary*? If you are trying to dramatically change the way things are done, you will find that resistance is greater. If your proposal involves incrementally making things better, you may have better luck.
- *Involve those around you in planning the change*. Instead of providing the solutions, make them part of the solution. If they admit that there is a problem and participate in planning a way out, you would have to do less convincing when it is time to implement the change.
- *Assess your credibility*. When trying to persuade people to change their ways, it helps if you have a history of suggesting implementable changes. Otherwise, you may be ignored or met with suspicion. This means you need to establish trust and a history of keeping promises over time before you propose a major change.

- *Present data to your audience.* Be prepared to defend the technical aspects of your ideas and provide evidence that your proposal is likely to work.
- *Appeal to your audience's ideals.* Frame your proposal around the big picture. Are you going to create happier clients? Is this going to lead to a better reputation for the company? Identify the long-term goals you are hoping to accomplish that people would embrace. And keep in mind that because change often takes time, you might not always expect an immediate "yes" or "no" for your ideas.[65]
- *Understand the reasons for resistance.* Is your audience resisting because they fear change? Does the change you propose mean more work for them? Does it affect them in a negative way? Understanding the consequences of your proposal for the parties involved may help you tailor your pitch to your audience.[66]

Key Takeaway

There are several steps you can take to help you overcome resistance to change. Many of them share the common theme of respecting those who are resistant so you can understand and learn from their concerns.

Discussion Questions

1. What do you think are some key reasons why people resist change?
2. Do you think some people are more resistant to change regardless of what it is? Why do you think this is?

7.6 Case in Point: Evolving through Acquisition: The Campbell Soup Company

Source: calimedia/Shutterstock.com

In December 2017, Campbell announced that it acquired Pacific Foods which is a leading producer of organic broth, soup, and other shelf-stable food products. Campbell is reportedly looking toward the organic food category for growth to compensate for declining sales in the traditional processed food market. According to the company, it plans to focus its traditional products on older consumers, while relying on Pacific Foods to appeal to a younger demographic. Pacific Foods is expected to be a key driver of growth for Campbell as younger generations represent an increasing share of the consumer market.

Campbell expects to accelerate the growth of Pacific Foods by expanding distribution, increasing marketing support for brand building, and investing in research and development and the supply chain. As a wholly owned subsidiary of Campbell, Pacific Foods is expected to continue operation of its Oregon facilities, which employ over 500 people in the region. Shortly after the acquisition was announced, leaders at Pacific Foods decided to pursue B Corp certification.

B Corps are for-profit companies that are certified by the nonprofit B Lab if they meet rigorous standards of social and environmental performance, accountability, and transparency and which strive to use the power of markets to help solve social and environmental problems. Over 3,000 Certified B Corps exist in 71 countries in 150 industries. Many of these companies are small to medium-sized organizations, which is where much of the growth in this type of company has emerged. Notable companies with B Corp certification include Ben & Jerry's (the first wholly owned subsidiary to become certified), Patagonia, and Kickstarter. Certification is independent, third-party, and consists of an assessment of approximately 200 questions covering such aspects of the business as energy efficiency and employee programs and practices. In 2018, Pacific Foods began its B Corp assessment.[67]

Multimedia Extension—Campbell Soup CEO: Don't Be a Victim of Change

View in the online reader

Case Discussion Questions

1. How would you compare Campbell Soup and Pacific Foods? What are some key similarities and key differences between the two companies?
2. How might Pacific Foods benefit from their acquisition by Campbell?
3. In what ways might the acquisition of Pacific Foods influence the organizational structure of Campbell?
4. Why do you think Pacific Foods decided to pursue B Corp certification so soon after being acquired by Campbell Soup? Can you think of any organizational or cultural characteristics that might be preserved through this type of certification?

Endnotes

1. Retrieved from http://www.thenational.ae/business/industry-insights/the-life/the-walking-dead-what-zombies-tell-us-about-the-economy.
2. Retrieved from http://smallbusiness.chron.com/advantages-centralized-organizational-structure-21410.html.
3. Knight, A. P., Menges, J. I., & Bruch, H. (2018). Organizational affective tone: A meso perspective on the origins and effects of consistent affect in organizations. *Academy of Management Journal, 61*, 191–219.
4. Hirst, G., Van Knippenberg, D., Chen, C. H., & Sacramento, C. A. (2011). How does bureaucracy impact individual creativity? A cross-level investigation of team contextual influences on goal orientation-creativity relationships. *Academy of Management Journal, 54*, 624–641.

5. Ambrose, M. L., & Cropanzano, R. S. (2000). The effect of organizational structure on perceptions of procedural fairness. *Journal of Applied Psychology, 85*, 294–304; Miller, D., Droge, C., & Toulouse, J. (1988). Strategic process and content as mediators between organizational context and structure. *Academy of Management Journal, 31*, 544–569; Oldham, G. R., & Hackman, R. J. (1981). Relationships between organizational structure and employee reactions: Comparing alternative frameworks. *Administrative Science Quarterly, 26*, 66–83; Pierce, J. L., & Delbecq, A. L. (1977). Organization Structure, individual attitudes and innovation. *Academy of Management Review, 2*, 27–37; Schminke, M., Ambrose, M. L., & Cropanzano, R. S. (2000). The effect of organizational structure on perceptions of procedural fairness. *Journal of Applied Psychology, 85*, 294–304; Turban, D. B., & Keon, T. L. (1993). Organizational attractiveness: An interactionist perspective. *Journal of Applied Psychology*, 78, 184–193; Wally, S., & Baum, J. R. (1994). Personal and structural determinants of the pace of strategic decision making. *Academy of Management Journal, 37*, 932–956.
6. Williams, T. (July 16, 2020). Marietta to Mumbai: Birla Carbon's global restructuring to more closely link two main offices. Retrieved from https://www.globalatlanta.com/marietta-to-mumbai-birla-carbons-global-restructuring-to-more-closely-link-main-offices/.
7. Wack, K. (July 17, 2017). The new buzzword at Wells Fargo is "Centralization". *American Banker.*
8. Shumsky, T., & Trentmann, N. (October 3, 2017). Finance chiefs centralize to cut costs, make smarter decisions. https://www.wsj.com/articles/finance-chiefs-centralize-to-cut-costs-make-smarter-decisions-1507021224.
9. Brazil, J. J. (2007, April). Mission: Impossible? *Fast Company, 114*, 92–109.
10. Fredrickson, J. W. (1986). The strategic decision process and organizational structure. *Academy of Management Review, 11*, 280–297; Oldham, G. R., & Hackman, R. J. (1981). Relationships between organizational structure and employee reactions: Comparing alternative frameworks. *Administrative Science Quarterly, 26*, 66–83; Pierce, J. L., & Delbecq, A. L. (1977). Organization structure, individual attitudes, and innovation. *Academy of Management Review, 2*, 27–37; Wally, S., & Baum, R. J. (1994). Strategic decision speed and firm performance. *Strategic Management Journal, 24*, 1107–1129.
11. Ghiselli, E. E., & Johnson, D. A. (1970). Need satisfaction, managerial success, and organizational structure. *Personnel Psychology, 23*, 569–576; Porter, L. W., & Siegel, J. (2006). Relationships of tall and flat organization structures to the satisfactions of foreign managers. *Personnel Psychology, 18*, 379–392.
12. Chonko, L. B. (1982). The relationship of span of control to sales representatives' experienced role conflict and role ambiguity. *Academy of Management Journal, 25*, 452–456.
13. Porter, L. W., & Lawler, E. E. (1964). The effects of tall versus flat organization structures on managerial job satisfaction. *Personnel Psychology, 17*, 135–148.
14. Gore. (n.d.). The Gore story. Retrieved from https://www.gore.com/about/the-gore-story; Morning Star Trucking. (n.d.) Retrieved from https://www.morningstartrucking.com/join-our-team/.
15. Hollenbeck, J. R., Moon, H., Ellis, A. P. J., West, B. J., Ilgen, D. R., Sheppard, L., Wagner, J. A., III. (2002). Structural contingency theory and individual differences: Examination of external and internal person-team fit. *Journal of Applied Psychology, 87*, 599–606.
16. Burns, T., & Stalker, M. G. (1961). *The Management of innovation*. London: Tavistock; Covin, J. G., & Slevin, D. P. (1988). The influence of organizational structure. *Journal of Management Studies, 25*, 217–234; Schollhammer, H. (1982). *Internal corporate entrepreneurship*. Englewood Cliffs, NJ: Prentice-Hall; Sherman, J. D., & Smith, H. L. (1984). The influence of organizational structure on intrinsic versus extrinsic motivation. *Academy of Management Journal, 27*, 877–885; Slevin, D. P., & Covin, J. G. (1990). Juggling entrepreneurial style and organizational structure—how to get your act together. *Sloan Management Review, 31*(2), 43–53.
17. Sine, W. D., Mitsuhashi, H., & Kirsch, D. A. (2006). Revisiting Burns and Stalker: Formal structure and new venture performance in emerging economic sectors. *Academy of Management Journal, 49*, 121–132.
18. Burns, T., & Stalker, M. G. (1961). *The Management of Innovation*. London: Tavistock; Covin, J. G., & Slevin, D. P. (1988). The influence of organizational structure. *Journal of Management Studies, 25*, 217–234.
19. Adair, J. (2007). *Leadership for innovation: How to organize team creativity and harvest ideas*. London: Kogan Page.
20. Retrieved from http://www.hrmagazine.co.uk/article-details/3m-md-if-you-want-to-stand-out-create-an-environment-for-innovation.
21. Joyce, W. F. (1986). Matrix organization: A social experiment. *Academy of Management Journal, 29*, 536–561.
22. Ford, R. C., & Randolph, W. A. (1992). Cross-functional structures: A review and integration of matrix organization and project management. *Journal of Management, 18*, 267–294.
23. Anand, N., & Daft, R. L. (2007). What is the right organization design? *Organizational Dynamics, 36*(4), 329–344.
24. Ashkenas, R., Ulrich, D., Jick, T., & Kerr, S. (1995). *The Boundaryless organization: Breaking the chains of organizational structure*. San Francisco: Jossey-Bass.
25. Jamali, L. (July 10, 2020). Quora CEO Adam D'Angelo on his company's shift to 'Remote-First'. https://www.kqed.org/news/11828168/quora-ceo-adam-dangelo-on-his-companys-shift-to-remote-first; Reidy, G. (July 6, 2020). One of Japan's largest employers plans to cut office space by 50%. Retrieved from https://www.bloomberg.com/news/articles/2020-07-06/one-of-japan-s-largest-employers-plans-to-halve-its-office-space#:~:text=Fujitsu Ltd. said it will,Shift for the new normal.
26. Deutschman, A. (2005, March). Building a better skunk works. *Fast Company, 92*, 68–73.
27. Garvin, D. A. (1993, July/August). Building a learning organization. *Harvard Business Review, 71*(4), 78–91.
28. Eurofound (2017). Towards age-friendly work in Europe: A life-course perspective on work and ageing from EU Agencies. Retrieved from https://www.eurofound.europa.eu/sites/default/files/ef_publication/field_ef_document/te-02-17-364-en-n.pdf; Special Committee on Aging United States Senate (December 2017). Retrieved from https://www.aging.senate.gov/imo/media/doc/Aging Workforce Report FINAL.pdf.
29. Cheng, M. (July 14, 2020). How Covid-19 is impacting employment for older workers. Retrieved from https://qz.com/1879255/how-covid-19-is-impacting-employment-for-older-workers/.
30. Moore's Law. Retrieved from Answers.com website: http://www.answers.com/topic/moore-s-law.
31. Stebbins, S., & Sauter, M. B. (July 18, 2018). Subway, Rite Aid, Toys R Us, Teavana: Retailers closing the most stores in 2018, so far. Retrieved from https://www.usatoday.com/story/money/retail/2018/04/27/retailers-closing-most-stores-2018-so-far/557275002/.
32. Retrieved from http://www.theatlantic.com/business/archive/2013/03/why-we-can-all-stop-worrying-about-offshoring-and-outsourcing/274388/.
33. Maurer, R. (May 29, 2020). Nearly 75 percent of remote workers eager to return to the office. Retrieved from https://www.shrm.org/resourcesandtools/hr-topics/talent-acquisition/pages/nearly-75-percent-remote-workers-eager-return-to-the-office.aspx; Raymond, A. K. (July 8, 2020). All the household-name companies that have filed for bankruptcy due to coronavirus. Retrieved from https://nymag.com/intelligencer/2020/07/major-companies-filing-for-bankruptcy-due-to-coronavirus.html.
34. Craft Brew Alliance. (n.d.) Retrieved June 29, 2020, from https://craftbrew.com/about.
35. Get ready. United States Small Business Association. Retrieved from http://www.sba.gov/smallbusinessplanner/plan/getready/SERV_SBPLANNER_ISENTFORU.html.
36. Barnett, W. P., & Carroll, G. R. (1995). Modeling internal organizational change. *Annual Review of Sociology, 21*, 217–236; Boeker, W. (1997). Strategic change: The influence of managerial characteristics and organizational growth. *Academy of Management Journal, 40*, 152–170; Deutschman, A. (2005, March). Building a better skunk works. *Fast Company, 92*, 68–73.
37. Anonymous. (2007, December). Change management: The HR strategic imperative as a business partner. *HR Magazine, 52*(12); Huy, Q. N. (1999). Emotional capability, emotional intelligence, and radical change. *Academy of Management Review, 24*, 325–345.
38. Oreg, S., Bartunek, J., Lee, G., & Do, B. (2018). An affect-based model of recipients' responses to organizational change events. *Academy of Management Review*, 43, 65–86.
39. Fugate, M., Kinicki, A. J., & Prussia, G. E. (2008). Employee coping with organizational change: An examination of alternative theoretical perspectives and models. *Personnel Psychology, 61*, 1–36.
40. Diamond, J. (2005). *Guns, germs, and steel: The fates of human societies*. New York: W. W. Norton.
41. Judge, T. A., Thoresen, C. J., Pucik, V., & Welbourne, T. M. (1999). Managerial coping with organizational change. *Journal of Applied Psychology, 84*, 107–122; Wanberg, C. R., & Banas, J. T. (2000). Predictors and outcomes of openness to changes in a reorganizing workplace. *Journal of Applied Psychology, 85*, 132–142.
42. Ashford, S. J., Lee, C. L., & Bobko, P. (1989). Content, causes, and consequences of job insecurity: A theory-based measure and substantive test. *Academy of Management Journal, 32*, 803–829; Fugate, M., Kinicki, A. J., & Prussia, G. E. (2008). Employee coping with organizational change: An examination of alternative theoretical perspectives and models. *Personnel Psychology, 61*, 1–36.
43. Herold, D. M., Fedor, D. B., & Caldwell, S. (2007). Beyond change management: A multilevel investigation of contextual and personal influences on employees' commitment to change. *Journal of Applied Psychology, 92*, 942–951.
44. Fedor, D. M., Caldwell, S., & Herold, D. M. (2006). The effects of organizational changes on employee commitment: A multilevel investigation. *Personnel Psychology, 59*, 1–29.
45. Labianca, G., Gray, B., & Brass D. J. (2000). A grounded model of organizational schema change during empowerment. *Organization Science, 11*, 235–257; Rafferty, A. E., & Griffin. M. A. (2006). Perceptions of organizational change: A stress and coping perspective. *Journal of Applied Psychology, 91*, 1154–1162.
46. Marr, J. C., & Thau, S. (2014). Falling from great (and not-so-great) heights: How initial status position influences performance after status loss. *Academy of Management Journal, 57*, 223–248.

47. Cohen, R. (July 28, 2017). Doctors frustrated that electronic records steal time from patients. Retrieved from https://www.reuters.com/article/us-health-records-electronics/doctors-frustrated-that-electronic-records-steal-time-from-patients-idUSKBN1AD2GT.
48. Lewin K. (1951). *Field theory in social science*. New York: Harper & Row.
49. Kotter, J. P. (1996). Leading change. Boston, MA: Harvard Business School Press.
50. Herold, D. M., Fedor D. B., Caldwell, S., & Liu, Y. (2008). The effects of transformational and change leadership on employees' commitment to a change: A multilevel study. *Journal of Applied Psychology, 93*, 346–357.
51. Stewart, T. A., & Raman, A. P. (2007, July–August). Lessons from Toyota's long drive. *Harvard Business Review, 85*(7/8), 74–83.
52. Wanberg, C. R., & Banas, J. T. (2000). Predictors and outcomes of openness to changes in a reorganizing workplace. *Journal of Applied Psychology, 85*, 132–142.
53. Herold, D. M., Fedor D. B., Caldwell, S., & Liu, Y. (2008). The effects of transformational and change leadership on employees' commitment to a change: A multilevel study. *Journal of Applied Psychology, 93*, 346–357.
54. Armenakis, A. A., Harris, S. G., & Mossholder, K. W. (1993). Creating readiness for organizational change. *Human Relations, 46*, 681–703.
55. Chaudhuri, S. (June 25, 2020). Unilever to rename Fair & Lovely skin-lightening cream amid criticism. Retrieved from https://www.wsj.com/articles/unilever-to-rename-fair-lovely-skin-lightening-cream-amid-criticism-11593085818#:~:text=LONDONâ Unilever UL -0.79%,is more attractive than dark.
56. Burkhardt, M. E. (1994). Social interaction effects following a technological change: A longitudinal investigation. *Academy of Management Journal, 37*, 869–898; Kotter, J. P. (1995, March–April). Leading change: Why transformations fail. *Harvard Business Review, 73*(2), 59–67.
57. Armenakis, A. A., Harris, S. G., & Mossholder, K. W. (1993). Creating readiness for organizational change. *Human Relations, 46*, 681–703.
58. Wanberg, C. R., & Banas, J. T. (2000). Predictors and outcomes of openness to changes in a reorganizing workplace. *Journal of Applied Psychology, 85*, 132–142.
59. Kotter, J. P. (1996). *Leading change*. Boston: Harvard Business School Press; Reay, T., Golden-Biddle, K., & Germann, K. (2006). Legitimizing a new role: Small wins and microprocesses of change. *Academy of Management Journal, 49*, 977–998.
60. Hamel, G. (2000, July/August). Waking up IBM. *Harvard Business Review, 78*(4), 137–146.
61. Kotter, J. P. (1995, March–April). Leading change: Why transformations fail. *Harvard Business Review, 73*(2), 59–67.
62. Gale, S. F. (2003). Incentives and the art of changing behavior. *Workforce Management, 82*(11), 48–54.
63. Retrieved from http://www.forbes.com/sites/theopriestley/2015/07/07/if-you-want-organizational-change-ask-the-customer-to-complain/.
64. Retrieved from http://www.forbes.com/sites/theopriestley/2015/07/07/if-you-want-organizational-change-ask-the-customer-to-complain/.
65. Retrieved from http://www.forbes.com/sites/iese/2013/09/18/presenting-your-proposal-5-ways-to-convince-investors-to-back-your-idea/.
66. Based on: McGoon, C. (1995, March). Secrets of building influence. *Communication World, 12*(3), 16; Michelman, P. (2007, July). Overcoming resistance to change. *Harvard Management Update, 12*(7), 3–4; Stanley, T. L. (2002, January). Change: A common-sense approach. *Supervision, 63*(1), 7–10.
67. Case written by Rachel Mattenberger, Talya Bauer, and Berrin Erdogan to accompany Bauer, T. & Erdogan, B.(2021). *Organizational Behavior: Bridging Science and Practice (4.0).* Boston, MA: FlatWorld. Partially based on ideas and information contained in Campbell Completes Acquisition of Pacific Foods. https://www.campbellsoupcompany.com/newsroom/press-releases/campbell-completes-acquisition-of-pacific-foods; Watrous, M. (2017). Campbell Soup Completes Pacific Food Acquisition. https://www.foodbusinessnews.net/articles/11014-campbell-soup-completes-pacific-foods-acquisition; Shah, K. (2015). Campbell's Soup Will Nix Artificial Colors and Flavors by End of 2018. https://www.eater.com/2015/7/23/9024501/campbells-soup-artificial-colors-flavors; Cheng, A. (2018). Campbell's Signals Namesake Brand Won't Target Millenials In Latest Offensive. https://www.forbes.com/sites/andriacheng/2018/10/12/in-the-latest-salvo-against-third-point-campbells-signals-namesake-brand-wont-target-millennials/#23db52ea28c6 Impact Growth Partners. (n.d.) What is a Certified B Corp? Retrieved from https://impactgrowthpartners.com/resources; Certified B Corporation (n.d.) Certification requirements. Retrieved from https://bcorporation.net/certification/meet-the-requirements.

CHAPTER 8

Organizational Culture

3M Corporation has been able to continue their innovative culture by allowing employees to use up to 15% of their workweek to develop new innovations such as their famous Post-it Notes.

Source: Shutterstock.com

Chapter Learning Objectives

Reading this chapter will help you accomplish the following:

1. Describe what organizational culture is and why it is important for an organization.
2. Understand the dimensions that make up a company's culture.
3. Understand the creation and maintenance of organizational culture.
4. Understand the factors that create cultural change.
5. Develop personal culture management skills.

Organizations, like individuals, have their own personalities—often referred to as organizational cultures. Understanding how culture is created, communicated, and changed will help individuals understand the cultures that best suit their personalities as well as methods to become more effective managers.

TABLE 8.1 The P-O-L-C Framework

Planning	Organizing	Leading	Controlling
1. Vision & Mission	1. Organization Design	1. Leadership	1. Systems/Processes
2. Strategizing	2. Culture	2. Decision Making	2. Strategic Human Resources
3. Goals & Objectives	3. Social Networks	3. Communications	
		4. Groups/Teams	
		5. Motivation	

8.1 Understanding Organizational Culture

Learning Objectives

1. Define organizational culture.
2. Understand why organizational culture is important.
3. Understand the different levels of organizational culture.

What Is Organizational Culture?

Organizational culture refers to a system of shared assumptions, values, and beliefs that indicate appropriate and inappropriate behavior within a given organization.[1] These values have a strong influence on employee behavior as well as organizational performance.[2] The concept of organizational culture was first made popular in the 1980s when Peters and Waterman's best-selling book, *In Search of Excellence*, made the argument that company success could be attributed to an organizational culture that was decisive, customer-oriented, empowering, and people-oriented. Since then, organizational culture has become the subject of numerous research studies, books, and articles. However, organizational culture is still a relatively new concept. In contrast to a topic such as leadership, which has a history spanning several centuries, organizational culture is a young but fast-growing area within organizational behavior.

Culture is largely invisible to individuals, since many elements of an organization's culture are a function of intangible social cues rather than explicit written policies. Even though culture affects all employee behaviors, thinking, and behavioral patterns, individuals tend to become more aware of their organization's culture when they have the opportunity to compare it to other organizations. Culture is related to the organizational facet of the P-O-L-C framework. The organizing function involves creating and implementing organizational design decisions. The culture of the organization is closely linked to organizational design. If you have worked in multiple organizations, you can attest to this dynamic. Maybe the first organization you worked was a place where employees dressed formally. It was completely inappropriate to question your boss in a meeting; such behaviors would only be acceptable in private. It was important to check your email at night as well as during weekends or else you would face questions on Monday about where you were and whether you were sick. Contrast this company to a second organization where employees dress more casually. You are encouraged to raise issues and question your boss or peers, even in front of clients. What is more important is not to maintain impressions but to arrive at the best solution to any problem. It is widely known that family life is very important, so it is acceptable to leave work a bit early to go to a family event. Additionally, you are not expected to do work at night or over the weekends unless there is a deadline. These two hypothetical organizations illustrate that organizations have different cultures, and culture dictates what is right and what is acceptable behavior as well as what is wrong and unacceptable.

Confirming popular opinion that may be more prevalent in some organizational cultures over others, Gallup research confirms well-being is in fact at its lowest on Mondays.

Source: Shutterstock.com

Why Does Organizational Culture Matter?

An organization's culture may be one of its strongest assets or its biggest liability. In fact, it has been argued that organizations that have a rare and hard-to-imitate culture enjoy a competitive advantage.[3] In a survey conducted by the management consulting firm Bain & Company, worldwide business leaders identified corporate culture to be as important as corporate strategy for business success.[4] This comes as no surprise to leaders of successful businesses, who are quick to attribute their company's success to their organization's culture. Culture is also important as you assess the type of organization you wish to work in as you manage your career. Research finds that the idea of "fake it until you make it" to be a successful path that job applicants might take as they work to adapt their personalities in the hiring process to accommodate differing organizational cultures.[5]

Culture, or shared values within the organization, may be related to increased performance. Researchers find a relationship between organizational cultures and company performance with respect to success indicators such as revenue, sales volume, market share, and stock prices.[6] At the same time, it is important to have a culture that fits with the demands of the company's environment. To the extent that shared values are proper for the company in question, company performance may benefit from culture.[7] For example, if a company is in the high-tech industry, having a culture that encourages innovativeness and adaptability will support its performance. However, if a company in the same industry has a culture characterized by stability, a high respect for tradition, and a strong preference for upholding rules and procedures, the company may suffer because of its culture. In other words, just as having the "right" culture may be a competitive advantage for an organization, having the "wrong" culture may lead to performance difficulties, be responsible for organizational failure, and act as a barrier preventing the company from changing and taking risks.

In addition to having implications for organizational performance, *organizational culture is an effective control mechanism dictating employee behavior*. Culture is a more powerful way of controlling and managing employee behaviors than organizational rules and regulations. For example, when a company is trying to improve the quality of its customer service, rules may not be helpful, particularly when the problems customers present are unique. Instead, creating a culture of customer service may achieve better results by encouraging employees to think like customers, knowing that the company priorities in this case are clear—keeping the customer happy is preferable to other concerns, such as saving the cost of a refund. Therefore, the ability to understand and influence organizational culture is an important item for managers to have in their toolkit when they are carrying out the controlling and organizing functions of the P-O-L-C framework.

Levels of Organizational Culture

Organizational culture consists of some aspects that are relatively visible, as well as aspects that may lie below one's conscious awareness. Organizational culture can be thought of as consisting of three interrelated levels.[8]

At the deepest level, below our awareness, lie basic **assumptions**. These assumptions are taken for granted and reflect beliefs about human nature and reality. At the second level, **values** exist. Values are shared principles, standards, and goals. Finally, at the surface, we have **artifacts**, or visible, tangible aspects of organizational culture. For example, Facebook headquarters has machines dispensing necessities such as keyboards and power cords available at no charge, by simply swiping the company badge.[9] This is an artifact. What is the meaning behind this? It reflects values such as innovativeness (not many organizations have them at the moment), performance orientation (you should be able to do your job when the help desk is closed), and cost consciousness (the system allows IT to keep track of office supplies). The unwritten assumptions behind the values are that employees are self-motivated and would want to continue to work after hours if their keyboard malfunctions and the help desk is closed, and that they can be trusted to make decisions about their needs without someone in IT vetting the decision. In other words, understanding the organization's culture may start from observing its artifacts: the physical environment, employee interactions, company policies, reward systems, and other observable characteristics. When you are interviewing for a position, observing the physical environment, how people dress, where they relax, and how they talk to others is definitely a good start to understanding the company's culture. However, simply looking at these tangible aspects is unlikely to give a full picture of the organization. An important piece of what makes up culture exists below one's degree of awareness. The values and, at a deeper level, the assumptions that shape the organization's culture can be uncovered by observing how employees interact and the choices they make, as well as by inquiring about their beliefs and perceptions regarding what is right and appropriate behavior.

An artifact of many creative software and engineering firms is a philosophy that leads many programmers to dress more casually than in other professions.

Source: Shutterstock.com

assumptions

Beliefs about human nature and reality that are taken for granted.

values

Shared principles, standards, and goals.

artifacts

The visible and tangible elements of culture.

FIGURE 8.1 Organizational Culture Levels

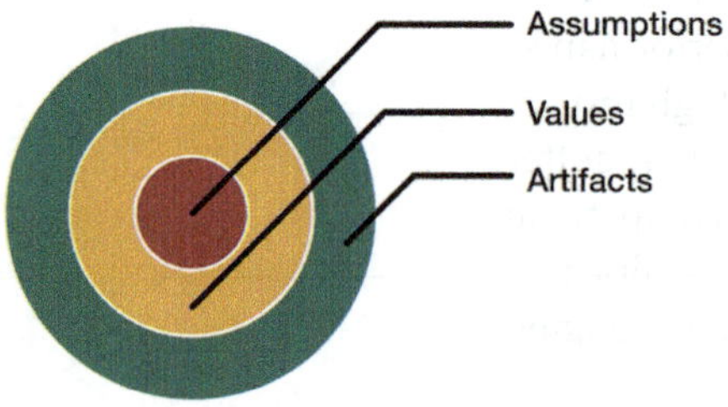

Source: Adapted from Schein, E. H. (1992). *Organizational Culture and Leadership*. San Francisco: Jossey-Bass.

Key Takeaway

Organizational culture is a system of shared assumptions, values, and beliefs that help individuals understand which behaviors are and are not appropriate within an organization. Cultures can be a source of competitive advantage for organizations. Strong organizational cultures can be an organizing as well as a controlling mechanism for organizations. Finally, organizational culture consists of three levels: assumptions that are below the surface, values, and artifacts.

Discussion Questions

1. Why do companies need culture?
2. Give an example of a company culture being a strength as well as a weakness.
3. In what ways does culture serve as a controlling mechanism?
4. If assumptions are below the surface, why do they matter?
5. Share examples of artifacts you have noticed at different organizations.

8.2 Measuring Organizational Culture

Learning Objectives

1. Understand different dimensions of organizational culture.
2. Understand the role of culture strength.
3. Explore subcultures within organizations.

Dimensions of Culture

Which values characterize an organization's culture? Even though all aspects of culture may not be immediately observable, identifying a set of values that might be used to describe an organization's culture helps us identify, measure, and manage culture more effectively. For this purpose, several researchers have proposed various culture typologies. One popular typology is the Organizational Culture Profile (OCP), where culture is represented by seven distinct values.[10]

Innovative Cultures

Twitter's propensity for rooftop meetings illustrate that the sky is the limit for their innovative culture

Source: Shutterstock.com

According to the OCP framework, companies that have **innovative cultures** are flexible and adaptable, and experiment with new ideas. These companies are characterized by a flat hierarchy in which titles and other status distinctions tend to be downplayed. For example, Snap, the maker of the one-on-one communication platform Snapchat, has been named by *Fast Company* magazine as the most innovative company in the world in 2020.[11] This is a remarkable achievement for the company that lost over 5 million users in 2018. Since then, Snap ensured that their app runs well on Android phones, allows users to utilize augmented reality (such as adding puppy ears to users' photos) and therefore leads the industry on how they use technology, and boasts an innovative structure that encourages openness in the design team, ensuring idea exchange and flow.[12]

innovative cultures

Cultures that are flexible, adaptable, and experiment with new ideas.

aggressive cultures

Cultures that value competitiveness and outperforming competitors.

Aggressive Cultures

Companies with **aggressive cultures** value competitiveness and outperforming competitors: By emphasizing this, they may fall short in the area of corporate social responsibility. For example, Wells Fargo bank's aggressive culture was reflected in the sales goals the company set, which were extremely difficult to achieve. The culture was characterized by a win-at-all-cost mentality and resulted in bending rules and in some cases breaking the law. When it was discovered that employees routinely opened up new accounts for customers without their knowledge, the resulting scandal led to the firing of 5,000 employees and resignation of the company CEO. The company settled a lawsuit for $3 billion.[13]

Outcome-Oriented Cultures

outcome-oriented cultures

Cultures that emphasize achievement, results, and action as important values.

The OCP framework describes **outcome-oriented cultures** as those that emphasize achievement, results, and action as important values. Outcome-oriented cultures hold employees as well as managers accountable for success and utilize systems that reward employee and group output. In these companies, it is more common to see rewards tied to performance indicators as opposed to seniority or loyalty. For example, Nordstrom has an outcome-oriented culture. A very large portion of an employee's pay is based on commissions. Employees are given various metrics that are directly rewarded, and they can access information about other employee's performance on these metrics to see where they stand. Top performing employees (called Pacesetters) are given special awards and merchandise discounts. The company closely monitors employee performance, rewarding stars and retraining or letting go of inadequate performers.[14] Research indicates that organizations that have a performance-oriented culture tend to outperform companies that are lacking such a culture.[15] At the same time, some outcome-oriented companies may have such a high drive for outcomes and measurable performance objectives that they may suffer negative consequences.[16]

Stable Cultures

stable cultures

Cultures that are predictable, rule oriented, and bureaucratic.

Stable cultures are predictable, rule-oriented, and bureaucratic. These organizations aim to coordinate and align individual effort for greatest levels of efficiency. When the environment is stable and certain, these cultures may help the organization be effective by providing stable and constant levels of output.[17] These cultures prevent quick action, and as a result may be a misfit to a changing and dynamic environment. Public sector institutions may be viewed as stable cultures. In another example, GM struggled with changing its bureaucratic culture while recovering from its bankruptcy in 2009. The company was characterized by slow decision making with several meetings and premeetings for key decisions, resulting in slow adoption of new technology and decision making failures such as allowing engineers to work on a Hummer sports utility vehicle long after they realized that the project would fail and being slow to respond to safety issues in some of their vehicles. One of the changes its CEO Mary Barra made was replacing the 10 page dress code with two words: "dress appropriately."[18]

People-Oriented Cultures

People-oriented cultures value fairness, supportiveness, and respect for individual rights. In these organizations, there is a greater emphasis on, and expectation of, treating people with respect and dignity.[19] One study of new employees in accounting companies found that employees, on average, stayed 14 months longer in companies with people-oriented cultures.[20] Starbucks is an example of a people-oriented culture. The company pays employees above minimum wage, offers healthcare and tuition reimbursement benefits to its part-time as well as full-time employees, and has creative perks such as weekly free coffee for all associates and the opportunity to earn a degree online. As a result of these policies, the company benefits from a turnover rate much lower than the industry average.[21]

From their social initiatives to extensive support of their own employees, Starbucks is the epitome of a people-oriented culture.

Source: Sorbis/Shutterstock.com

Team-Oriented Cultures

Companies with a **team-oriented culture** are collaborative and emphasize cooperation among employees. For example, Southwest Airlines facilitates a team-oriented culture by cross-training its employees so that they are capable of helping one another when needed. The company also emphasizes training intact work teams.[22] In Southwest's selection process, applicants who are not viewed as team players are not hired as employees.[23] In team-oriented organizations, members tend to have more positive relationships with their coworkers and particularly with their managers.[24]

people-oriented cultures

Cultures that value fairness, supportiveness, and respecting individual rights.

team-oriented cultures

Cultures that are collaborative and emphasize cooperation among employees.

detail-oriented cultures

Cultures that emphasize precision, analytical decision making, and paying attention to details.

Detail-Oriented Cultures

Organizations with **detail-oriented cultures** are characterized in the OCP framework as data-driven and emphasize precision, analytical decision making, and paying attention to details. In these companies, important decisions are made by using data, instead of personal intuition of managers. E-commerce firms such as Amazon and Alibaba are good examples of companies that use data-driven decision making a key part of their business models. The online subscription and personal shopping service Stitch Fix has built its entire business model around data-driven decision making. The company collects a wide range of data about its customers and uses stylists' judgments, algorithms, and machine learning to predict which pieces of clothing will appeal to a customer. The company sends five pieces of clothing to its customers, and the hope is that the customer will keep all of them. The company's CEO Katrina Lake notes: "Data science is not woven into our culture; it is our culture . . . Stitch Fix wouldn't exist without data science. It's that simple."[25]

FIGURE 8.2 Dimensions of Organizational Culture Profile (OCP)

Organizational culture is reflected in the different "personalities" exhibited by organizational members. Here, we illustrate how different cultures are reflected in one popular framework for examining such differences—the Organizational Culture Profile (OCP).

Culture	Example	
Innovative Cultures Companies that have innovative cultures are flexible, adaptable, and experiment with new ideas.	Snap, the maker of the one-on-one messaging platform, Snapchat, maintains user privacy, allows users to have fun through innovative features, and has a management structure allowing innovation.	
Aggressive Cultures Companies with aggressive cultures value outperforming competitors through competitive actions.	Nike has exhibited this culture in the past by embracing a mission statement that once read, "To experience the emotion of competition, winning, and crushing competitors."	
Outcome-Oriented Cultures Companies that emphasize achievement, results, and action as important values embrace an outcome-oriented culture.	The outcome oriented culture of Nordstrom involves generously rewarding employees on several performance metrics and retraining or letting go of those who do not meet the targets.	
Stable Cultures Companies that emphasize predictable, rule-oriented, and bureaucratic adherence to rules and regulations exhibit stable cultures.	IBM's adherence to such rule following and the relatively consistent physical appearance of its employees has led some to conjecture that their mysterious nickname "Big Blue" might be a reference to the conservative blue suits that at one point were a near uniform for their employees.	
People-Oriented Cultures Organizations that value fairness, supportiveness, and respecting individual rights are said to display a people-oriented culture.	Starbuck's policy of offering health care benefits, tuition reimbursement, and free coffee to both full and part-time employees make the coffee slinger a model of this profile.	
Team-Oriented Cultures Companies that emphasize cooperation and collaboration among employees display a team-oriented culture.	Southwest Airlines facilitates this culture by cross-training employees and carefully weeding out individuals that might not be team players during their interview process.	
Detail-Oriented Cultures Organizations that emphasize precision and attention to detail.	Detail-oriented cultures make data driven decisions, as in the case of Stitch Fix, where data analytics help the company identify clothing customers will keep.	

Source: Shutterstock.com

Service Culture

> **service culture**
> A culture that emphasizes high quality service.

Service culture is not one of the dimensions of OCP, but given the importance of the retail industry in the overall economy, having a service culture can make or break an organization. Some of the organizations we have illustrated in this section, such as Nordstrom and Southwest Airlines, are also famous for their service culture. In these organizations, employees are trained to serve the customer well, and cross-training is the norm. Employees are empowered to resolve customer problems in ways they see fit. Because employees with direct customer contact are in the best position to resolve any issues, employee empowerment is truly valued in these companies. For example, Umpqua Bank, operating in the northwestern United States, is known for its service culture. All employees are trained in all tasks to enable any employee to help customers when needed. Branch employees may come up with unique ways in which they serve customers better, such as opening their lobby for community events or keeping bowls full of water for customers' pets. The branches feature coffee for customers, internet kiosks, and withdrawn funds are given on a tray along with a piece of chocolate. The company adopts the same customer-centric philosophy in online banking as well. Customers can request a personal concierge banker to handle their needs, or sign up for the "BFF program" where they can do most of their communications through a smartphone.[26]

What differentiates companies with service culture from those without such a culture may be the desire to solve customer-related problems proactively. In other words, in these cultures employees are engaged in their jobs and personally invested in improving customer experience, such that they identify issues and come up with solutions without necessarily being told what to do. For example, a British Airways baggage handler noticed that first-class passengers were waiting a long time for their baggage, whereas stand-by passengers often received their luggage first. Noticing this tendency, a baggage handler notified his superiors about this problem, along with the suggestion to load first-class passenger luggage last.[27] This solution was successful in cutting the wait time by half. Such proactive behavior on the part of employees who share company values is likely to emerge frequently in companies with a service culture.

Safety Culture

> **safety culture**
> A culture that emphasizes safety as a strong workplace norm.

Some jobs are safety sensitive. For example, logger, aircraft pilot, fishing worker, steel worker, and roofer are among the top 10 most dangerous jobs in the United States.[28] In organizations where safety-sensitive jobs are performed, creating and maintaining a **safety culture** provides a competitive advantage, because the organization can reduce accidents, maintain high levels of morale and employee retention, and increase profitability by cutting workers' compensation insurance costs. Some companies suffer severe consequences when they are unable to develop such a culture. For example, British Petroleum experienced an explosion in their Texas City, Texas, refinery in 2005, which led to the death of 15 workers while injuring 170. A safety review panel concluded that the development of a safety culture was essential to avoid such occurrences in the future.[29] In companies that have a safety culture, there is a strong commitment to safety, starting at management level and trickling down to lower levels. Ohio-based Bendix commercial vehicle systems was named as among the safest companies in the U.S. in 2019 by EHS Today for their commitment to incorporating health and safety into all of their locations' activities.[30] The company prides itself in making safety an integral part of their culture and believes that with the right processes in place, all safety incidents can be prevented. Managers play a key role in increasing the level of safe behaviors in the workplace, because they can motivate employees day-to-day to demonstrate safe behaviors and act as safety role models. A study has shown that one way of cultivating a safety climate in an organization is through the daily communication and feedback sessions between supervisors and employees. When managers integrate feedback about safety behaviors of employees into daily conversations, along with productivity-related issues, there were changes in safety climate and safe behaviors of employees.[31]

Strength of Culture

strong culture

A culture that is shared by organizational members.

A **strong culture** is one that is shared by organizational members[32]—that is, a culture in which most employees in the organization show consensus regarding the values of the company. The stronger a company's culture, the more likely it is to affect the way employees think and behave. For example, cultural values emphasizing customer service will lead to higher-quality customer service if there is widespread agreement among employees on the importance of customer-service-related values.[33]

A strong culture may act as an asset or liability for the organization, depending on which values are shared. For example, research has shown that organizations where culture is strong and adaptability is emphasized demonstrate better financial performance in dynamic environments, as having an adaptable culture is well suited to a dynamic environment, and having consensus in cultural values serves as an advantage.[34] On the other hand, a strong outcome-oriented culture coupled with unethical behaviors and an obsession with quantitative performance indicators may be detrimental to an organization's effectiveness.

One limitation of a strong culture is the difficulty of changing established organizational behaviors. If an organization with widely shared beliefs decides to adopt a different set of values, unlearning the old values and learning the new ones will be a challenge, because employees will need to adopt new ways of thinking, behaving, and responding to critical events. For example, Europe's largest automaker Volkswagen has been struggling to change its culture since the revelation that their diesel cars were able to meet diesel emission standards in the U.S. by cheating on the tests. The company has been trying to become more transparent and create a culture that is not afraid to challenge authority. While steps were taken in the right direction, an attitude survey two years after the scandal suggested that the majority of employees saw little improvement in culture.[35]

A strong culture may also be a liability during a merger. During mergers and acquisitions, companies inevitably experience a clash of cultures, as well as a clash of structures and operating systems. Culture clash becomes more problematic if both parties have unique and strong cultures. For example, Amazon's acquisition of Whole Foods resulted in two companies with strong culture shaving to integrate their operations. Amazon prides itself for its efficiency, using data to reduce costs, and rigorous performance assessment, whereas Whole Foods values the personal touch and employee empowerment. The acquisition resulted in tension on the part of Whole Foods employees faced with reduced empowerment and increased centralization of decisions.[36]

Music Rap-Up: Where Do I Belong

Twinprov perform a rap discussing different organizational cultures.

View in the online reader

Do Organizations Have a Single Culture?

So far, the examples and profiles discussed as part of the Organizational Culture Profile may suggest that a company has a single culture that is shared throughout the organization. In reality, there might be multiple cultures within the organization. For example, people working on the sales floor may experience a different culture from that experienced by people working in the warehouse. Cultures that emerge within different departments, branches, or geographic locations are called **subcultures**. Subcultures may arise from the personal characteristics of employees and managers, as well as the different conditions under which work is performed. Within the same organization, marketing and manufacturing departments often have different cultures such that the marketing department may emphasize innovativeness, whereas the manufacturing department may have a shared emphasis on detail orientation. Research has shown that employee perceptions regarding subcultures were related to employee commitment to the organization.[37] Therefore, in addition to understanding the broader organization's values, managers will need to make an effort to understand subculture values to see their impact on workforce behavior and attitudes. Moreover, as an employee, you need to understand the type of subculture in the department where you will work in addition to understanding the company's overall culture.

subcultures

A set of values unique to a limited cross section of the organization.

Sometimes, a subculture may take the form of a **counterculture**. Defined as shared values and beliefs that are in direct opposition to the values of the broader organizational culture,[38] countercultures are often shaped around a charismatic leader. For example, within a largely bureaucratic organization, an enclave of innovativeness and risk taking may emerge within a single department. A counterculture may be tolerated by the organization as long as it is bringing in results and contributing positively to the effectiveness of the organization. However, its existence may be perceived as a threat to the broader organizational culture. In some cases, this may lead to actions that would take away the autonomy of the managers and eliminate the counterculture.

counterculture

Shared values and beliefs that are in direct opposition to the values of the broader organizational culture.

Key Takeaway

The OCP framework and other similar tools are useful in providing a way of analyzing and understanding the values inherent in an organization's culture. For example, innovative cultures are flexible, adaptable, and experiment with new ideas, while stable cultures are predictable, rule-oriented, and bureaucratic. Strong cultures can be an asset or liability for an organization but can be challenging to change. Multiple cultures may coexist in a single organization in the form of subcultures and countercultures.

Discussion Questions

1. Think about an organization you are familiar with. On the basis of the dimensions of OCP, how would you characterize its culture?
2. From the culture dimensions described, which dimension do you think would lead to higher levels of employee satisfaction and retention? Which one would be related to company performance?
3. What are pros and cons of an outcome-oriented culture?
4. When bureaucracies were first invented, they were considered quite innovative. Do you think that different cultures are more or less effective at different points in time and in different industries? Why or why not?
5. Can you imagine an effective use of subcultures within an organization?

8.3 Creating and Maintaining Organizational Culture

Learning Objectives

1. Understand how cultures are created.
2. Learn how to maintain a culture.
3. Recognize organizational culture signs.

How Are Cultures Created?

Where do cultures originate? Understanding this question is important in understanding how they can be changed. An organization's culture is shaped as the organization faces and deals with both external and internal challenges and learns how to deal with them. When the organization's way of doing business provides a successful adaptation to environmental challenges and ensures success, those values are retained. These values and ways of doing business are taught to new members as *the* way to do business.[39]

The factors that are most important in the creation of an organization's culture include founders' values, preferences, and industry demands.

FIGURE 8.3 Culture Creation and Maintenance

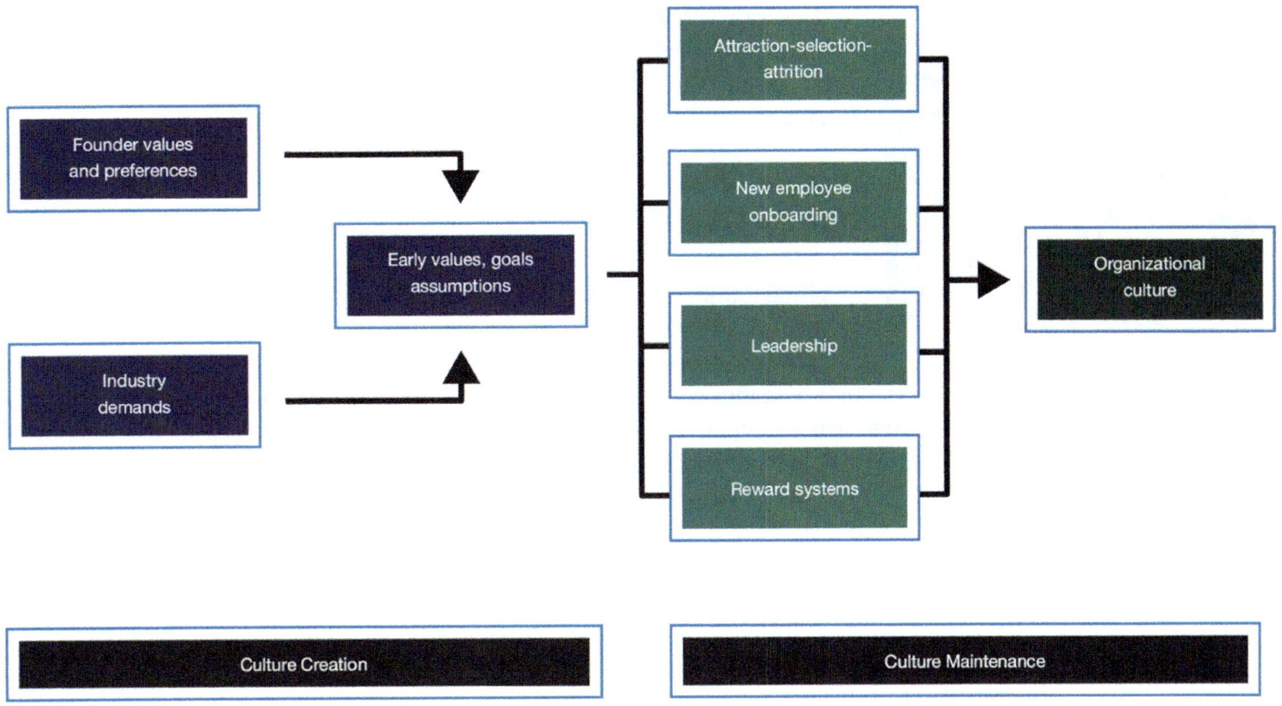

Founder Values

A company's culture, particularly during its early years, is inevitably tied to the personality, background, and values of its founder or founders, as well as their vision for the future of the organization. When entrepreneurs establish their own businesses, the way they want to do business determines the organization's rules, the structure set up in the company, and the people they hire to work with them. As a case in point, some of the existing corporate values of the ice cream company Ben & Jerry's Homemade Holdings Inc. can easily be traced to the personalities of its founders Ben Cohen and Jerry Greenfield. In 1978, the two ex-hippie high school friends opened up their first ice-cream shop in a renovated gas station in Burlington, Vermont. Their strong social convictions led them to buy only from the local farmers and devote a certain percentage of their profits to charities. The core values they instilled in their business can still be observed in the current company's devotion to social activism and sustainability, its continuous contributions to charities, use of environmentally friendly materials, and dedication to creating jobs in low-income areas. Even though the company was acquired by Unilever PLC in 2000, the social activism component remains unchanged and Unilever has expressed its commitment to traditional Ben & Jerry's values.[40] There are many other examples of founders instilling their own strongly held beliefs or personalities in the businesses they found. For example, Joseph Pratt, a history and management professor, notes, "There definitely is an Exxon way. This is John D. Rockefeller's company, this is Standard Oil of New Jersey, this is the one that is most closely shaped by Rockefeller's traditions. Their values are very clear. They are deeply embedded. They have roots in 100 years of corporate history."[41]

Ben & Jerry's managed to preserve the most unique aspects of its organizational culture despite being acquired by Unilever. The success of a merger often depends on successful harmonizing of the cultures of two distinct organizations.

Source: GagliardiPhotography/Shutterstock.com

Founder values become part of the corporate culture to the degree to which they help the company be successful. For example, the social activism of Ben & Jerry's was instilled in the company because the founders strongly believed in these issues. However, these values probably would not endure several decades later if they had not helped the company fuel its early success. In the case of Ben & Jerry's, these values helped distinguish their brand from larger corporate brands and attracted a loyal customer base. Thus, by providing a competitive advantage, these values were retained as part of the corporate culture and were taught to new members as the right way to do business.

Industry Demands

While founders undoubtedly exert a powerful influence over corporate cultures, the industry characteristics also play a role. Companies within the same industry can sometimes have widely differing cultures. At the same time, the industry characteristics and demands often act as a powerful force to create similarities among organizational cultures. For example, despite some differences, many companies in the insurance and banking industries are stable and rule-oriented, many companies in the high-tech industry have innovative cultures, and those in the nonprofit sector may be people-oriented. If the industry is one with a large number of regulatory requirements—for example, aviation, banking, healthcare, and high-reliability (such as nuclear power) industries—then we might expect the presence of a large number of rules and regulations, a bureaucratic company structure, and a stable culture. The industry influence over culture is also important to acknowledge because this shows that it may not be possible to imitate the culture of a company in a different industry, even though it may seem admirable to outsiders.

How Are Cultures Maintained?

As a company matures, its cultural values are refined and strengthened. The early values of a company's culture exert influence over its future values. Organizational culture determines what types of people are hired by an organization and what types of people are left out. Moreover, once new employees are hired, the company assimilates new employees and teaches them the way things are done in the organization. We call these processes *attraction-selection-attrition* and *onboarding* processes. We will also examine the role of *leaders* and *reward systems* in shaping and maintaining an organization's culture.

Attraction-Selection-Attrition

Organizational culture is maintained through a process known as attraction-selection-attrition (ASA). First, applicants are *attracted* to organizations they perceive they will fit into as successful employees. In other words, different job applicants will find different cultures to be attractive. Someone who has a competitive nature may feel comfortable in and may prefer to work in a company where interpersonal competition is the norm. Others may prefer to work in a team-oriented workplace. Research shows that employees with different personality traits find different cultures attractive. For example, out of the Big Five personality traits, employees who demonstrate neurotic personalities were less likely to be attracted to innovative cultures, whereas those who had openness to experience were more likely to be attracted to innovative cultures.[42]

Of course this process is imperfect, and value similarity is only one reason a candidate might be attracted to a company. There may be other, more powerful attractions such as good benefits. For example, candidates who are potential misfits may still be attracted to Apple because of the prestige associated with being an Apple employee. At this point in the process, the second component of the ASA framework prevents them from getting in: Selection. Just as candidates are looking for places where they will fit in, companies are also looking for people who will fit into their current corporate culture. Many companies are hiring people for fit with their culture, as opposed to fit with a certain job. For example, Southwest Airlines prides itself for hiring employees based on personality and attitude rather than specific job-related skills, which are learned after being hired. This is important for job applicants to know, because in addition to highlighting your job-relevant skills, you will need to discuss why your personality and values match those of the company. Companies use different techniques to weed out candidates who do not fit with corporate values. For example, at SpaceX, Elon Musk interviews all prospective hires himself, looking for specific traits that will make them a good fit, such as the ability to improvise.[43] Many retailers ensure culture fit by hiring among their customers. This way, they can make sure that job candidates are already interested in organizing their lives and understand the company's commitment to helping customers organize theirs. Companies may also use employee referrals in their recruitment process. By using their current employees as a source of future employees, companies may make sure that the newly hired employees go through a screening process to avoid potential person–culture mismatch.

Even after a company selects individuals for person–organization fit, there may be new employees who do not fit in long-term. Some candidates may be skillful in impressing recruiters and signal high levels of culture fit even though they do not necessarily share the company's values. Moreover, recruiters may suffer from perceptual biases and hire some candidates thinking that they fit with the culture even though the actual fit is low. In any event, the organization is likely to gradually eliminate candidates who do not fit in through *attrition*. Attrition refers to the natural process where candidates with poor organizational fit will leave the company. Research indicates that person–organization misfit is one of the key reasons for employee turnover.[44]

As a result of the ASA process, the company attracts, selects, and retains people who share its core values. Those people who are different in core values will be excluded from the organization either during the hiring process or later on through naturally occurring turnover. Thus, organizational culture will act as a self-defending organism where intrusive elements are kept out. Supporting the existence of such self-protective mechanisms, research shows that organizations demonstrate a certain level of homogeneity regarding personalities and values of organizational members.[45]

Hosting a scavenger hunt to dig for "fun facts" about co-workers and engaging in "lunch roulette" where employees are randomly assigned different tables to meet with new folks each week are two ideas companies use to increase engagement during the onboarding process.

Source: Shutterstock.com

New Employee Onboarding

Another way in which an organization's values, norms, and behavioral patterns are transmitted to employees is through **onboarding** (also referred to as the *organizational socialization process*).[46] Onboarding refers to the process through which new employees learn the attitudes, knowledge, skills, and behaviors required to function effectively within an organization. The immediate outcome of effective onboarding is high levels of **newcomer adjustment**, which is characterized by 1) having clarity about what is expected of them, 2) feeling confident that they can be effective in their role, and 3) feel socially accepted by their peers. This understanding and confidence in turn translates into more effective new employees who perform better and have higher job satisfaction, stronger organizational commitment, and longer tenure within the company.[47]

There are many factors that play a role in the successful adjustment of new employees. New employees bring key experiences and resources with them as the start new jobs which may help them adjust.[48] New employees can engage in several activities to help increase their own chances of success at a new organization. Organizations also engage in different activities, such as implementing orientation programs or matching new employees with mentors, which may facilitate onboarding.[49]

onboarding

The process through which new employees learn the attitudes, knowledge, skills, and behaviors required to function effectively within an organization.

newcomer adjustment

Refers to feelings of high levels of role clarity, confidence, and social acceptance.

What Can Employees Do During Onboarding?

New employees who are proactive, seek feedback, and build strong relationships tend to be more successful than those who do not.[50] For example, *feedback seeking* helps new employees. Especially on a first job, a new employee can make mistakes or gaffes and may find it hard to understand and interpret the ambiguous reactions of coworkers. New hires may not know whether they are performing up to standards, whether it was a good idea to mention a company mistake in front of a client, or why other employees are asking if they were sick over the weekend because of not responding to work-related emails. By actively seeking feedback, new employees may find out sooner rather than later any behaviors that need to be changed and gain a better understanding of whether their behavior fits with the company culture and expectations. Several studies show the benefits of feedback seeking for new employee adjustment.

Relationship building or *networking* (a facet of the organizing function) is another important behavior new employees may demonstrate. Particularly when a company does not have a systematic approach to onboarding, it becomes more important for new employees to facilitate their own onboarding by actively building relationships. According to one estimate, 35% of managers who start a new job fail and either voluntarily leave or are fired within 18 months. Of these, over 60% report being unable to form effective relationships with colleagues as the primary reason for this failure.[51] New employees may take an active role in building relations by seeking opportunities to have a conversation with their new colleagues, arranging lunches or coffee with them, participating in company functions, and making the effort to build a relationship with their new supervisor.[52]

How Can Organizations Help During Onboarding?

Many organizations, including Microsoft, UPS, and Bank of America, take a more structured and systematic approach to new employee onboarding, while others follow a "sink or swim" approach where new employees struggle to figure out what is expected of them and what the norms are.

A **formal orientation program** indoctrinates new employees to the company culture, and introduces them to their new jobs and colleagues. An orientation program has a role in making new employees feel welcome in addition to imparting information that may help them be successful in their new jobs. Many large organizations have formal orientation programs consisting of lectures, videotapes, and written material, while some may follow more informal approaches. According to one estimate, most orientations last anywhere from one to five days, and some companies are currently switching to a computer-based orientation. Ritz Carlton Hotel Company uses a very systematic approach to employee orientation and views orientation as the key to retention. In the two-day classroom orientation, employees spend time with management, dine in the hotel's finest restaurant, and witness the attention to customer service detail firsthand. During these two days, they are introduced to the company's intensive service standards, team orientation, and its own language. Later, on their twenty-first day, they are tested on the company's service standards and are certified.[53]

formal orientation program

A program used to indoctrinate new employees to the company culture, as well as introducing them to their new jobs and colleagues.

What Can Organizational Insiders Do During Onboarding?

One of the most important ways in which organizations can help new employees adjust to a company and a new job is through *organizational insiders*—namely, supervisors, coworkers, and mentors. Something as simple as pairing the new employee with someone else so that they have someone they can ask questions to or someone who will make sure that they will not need to have lunch alone will go a long way in facilitating adjustment. The New York-based ticketing platform SeatGeek has a buddy program where each newcomer is paired with someone outside their team who will nudge them to attend a social event.[54]

Research shows that leaders have a key influence over onboarding and the information and support they provide determines how quickly employees learn about the companies' politics and culture. Coworker influence determines the degree to which employees adjust to their teams. **Mentors** can be crucial to helping new employees adjust by teaching them the ropes of their jobs and how the company really operates. A mentor is a trusted person who provides an employee with advice and support regarding career-related matters. Although a mentor can be any employee or manager who has insights that are valuable to the new employee, mentors tend to be relatively more experienced than their protégés. Mentoring can occur naturally between two interested individuals or organizations can facilitate this process by having formal mentoring programs. These programs may successfully bring together mentors and protégés who would not come together otherwise.

mentor

A trusted person who provides an employee with advice and support regarding career-related matters.

Research indicates that the existence of these programs does not guarantee their success, and there are certain program characteristics that may make these programs more effective. For example, when mentors and protégés feel that they had input in the mentor-protégé matching process, they tend to be more satisfied with the arrangement. Moreover, when mentors receive training beforehand, the outcomes of the program tend to be more positive.[55] Because mentors may help new employees interpret and understand the company's culture, organizations may benefit from selecting mentors who personify the company's values. Thus, organizations may need to design these programs carefully to increase their chance of success.

One of the most famous mentor-protégé relationships in history is that of Socrates and his equally famous student, Plato.

Source: Public Domain, https://commons.wikimedia.org/w/index.php?curid=1777942

Leadership

Leaders are instrumental in creating and changing an organization's culture. There is a direct correspondence between the leader's style and an organization's culture. For example, when leaders motivate employees through inspiration, corporate culture tends to be more supportive and people-oriented. When leaders motivate by making rewards contingent on performance, the corporate culture tends to be more performance-oriented and competitive.[56] In these and many other ways, what leaders do directly influences the cultures of their organizations. This is a key point for managers to consider as they carry out their leading P-O-L-C function.

Part of the leader's influence over culture is through role modeling. Many studies have suggested that leader behavior, the consistency between organizational policy and leader actions, and leader role modeling determine the degree to which the organization's culture emphasizes ethics.[57] The leader's own behaviors will signal to individuals what is acceptable behavior and what is unacceptable. In an organization in which high-level managers make the effort to involve others in decision making and seek opinions of others, a team-oriented culture is more likely to evolve. By acting as role models, leaders send signals to the organization about the norms and values that are expected to guide the actions of its members.

Leaders also shape culture by their reactions to the actions of others around them. For example, do they praise a job well done or do they praise a favored employee regardless of what was accomplished? How do they react when someone admits to making an honest mistake? What are their priorities? In meetings, what types of questions do they ask? Do they want to know what caused accidents so that they can be prevented, or do they seem more concerned about how much money was lost because of an accident? Do they seem outraged when an employee is disrespectful to a coworker, or does their reaction depend on whether they like the perpetrator? Through the behaviors they encourage and actions they tolerate, leaders shape and maintain an organization's culture. More directly, how they support or undermine a new employee may ultimately affect how well they perform and how long the employee stays with the organization.[58]

Reward Systems

Finally, the company culture is shaped by the type of reward systems used in the organization and the kinds of behaviors and outcomes it chooses to reward and punish. One relevant element of the reward system is *whether the organization rewards behaviors or results*. Some companies have reward systems that emphasize intangible elements of performance as well as more easily observable metrics. In these companies, supervisors and peers may evaluate an employee's performance by assessing the person's behaviors as well as the results. In such companies, we may expect a culture that is relatively people- or team-oriented, and employees act as part of a family.[59] On the other hand, in companies that purely reward goal achievement, there is a focus on measuring only the results without much regard to the process. In these companies, we might observe outcome-oriented and competitive cultures. Another categorization of reward systems might be whether the organization uses rankings or ratings. In a company where the reward system pits members against one another, where employees are ranked against each other and the lower performers receive long-term or short-term punishments, it would be hard to develop a culture of people orientation and may lead to a competitive culture. On the other hand, evaluation systems that reward employee behavior by comparing them to absolute standards as opposed to comparing employees to each other may pave the way to a team-oriented culture. Whether the organization rewards performance or seniority would also make a difference in culture. When promotions are based on seniority, it would be difficult to establish a culture of outcome orientation. Finally, the types of behaviors that are rewarded or ignored set the tone for the culture. Service-oriented cultures reward, recognize, and publicize exceptional service on the part of their employees. In safety cultures, safety metrics are emphasized and the organization is proud of its low accident ratings. What behaviors are rewarded, which ones are punished, and which are ignored will determine how a company's culture evolves.

Visible Elements of Organizational Culture

What makes a culture visible to outsiders? We emphasized earlier that culture influences the way members of the organization think, behave, and interact with one another. Thus, one way of finding out about a company's culture is by observing employees or interviewing them. At the same time, culture manifests itself in some visible aspects of the organization's environment. In this section, we discuss five ways in which culture manifests itself to observers and employees. These elements are often unique and distinguish one company from others in the same industry.

FIGURE 8.4 Visual Elements of Culture

Definition	Example
Mission statements provide tangible declarations of purpose, describing who the company is and what it does. The lack of incentives for doctors helps physicians at the Mayo Clinic execute their organization's mission statement of "the needs of the patient come first."	
Rituals are repetitive activities within an organization that have symbolic meaning. To show camaraderie with his employees, Sam Adams founder Jim Koch volunteers each year to sit in a dunking booth full of stale beer.	
Rules and policies determine acceptable and unacceptable behavior within an organization. Starbucks' policy of giving each employee a free pound of coffee a week encourages a culture where customers and employees alike enjoy a caffeinated beverage.	
Physical layout—such as a company's building and layout of employee offices and other workspaces—communicates important messages about acompany's culture. LEGO, for example, utilizes a number of project rooms to inspire employees to continually innovate and create.	
Stories and language provide another way to identify an organization's culture. The story of Apple's humble beginnings, with Steve Jobs and Steve Wozniak creating their first personal computer inside Jobs's garage in Los Altos, California, epitomizes the open, creative culture of innovation and experimentation that continues at Apple today.	

Source: Shutterstock.com

Mission Statement

As discussed earlier in Chapter 4, a mission statement is a statement of purpose, describing who the company is and what it does. Many companies have mission statements, but they do not always reflect the company's values and its purpose. An effective mission statement is well known by employees, is transmitted to all employees starting from their first day at work, and influences employee behavior.

Not all mission statements are effective, because some are written by public relations specialists and can be found in a company's website, but it does not affect how employees act or behave. In fact, some mission statements reflect who the company wants to be as opposed to who they actually are. If the mission statement does not affect employee behavior on a day-to-day basis, it has little usefulness as a tool for understanding the company's culture. An oft-cited example of a mission statement that had little impact on how a company operates belongs to Enron. Their missions and values statement began, "As a partner in the communities in which we operate, Enron believes it has a responsibility to conduct itself according to certain basic principles." Their values statement included now-ironic declarations as "We do not tolerate abusive or disrespectful treatment. Ruthlessness, callousness and arrogance don't belong here."[60]

A mission statement that is taken seriously and widely communicated may provide insights into the corporate culture. For example, the Mayo Clinic's mission statement is "The needs of the patient come first." This mission statement evolved from the founders who are quoted as saying, "The best interest of the patient is the only interest to be considered." Mayo Clinics have a corporate culture that puts patients first. No incentives are given to physicians based on the number of patients they see. Because doctors are salaried, they have no interest in retaining a patient for themselves and they refer the patient to other doctors when needed.[61] Walmart Stores Inc. may be another example of a company that lives its mission statement, and therefore its mission statement may give hints about its culture: "Saving people money so they can live better."[62] In fact, their culture emphasizes thrift and cost control in everything they do. For example, even though most CEOs of large companies in the United States have lavish salaries and showy offices, Walmart's CEO and other high-level corporate officers work out of modest offices in the company's headquarters.

Rituals

Rituals are important at Mary Kay Cosmetics, where pink Cadillacs are given to top performers at large annual events.

Source: RG-vc/Shutterstock.com

rituals

Repetitive activities within an organization that have symbolic meaning.

Rituals refers to repetitive activities within an organization that have symbolic meaning.[63] Usually rituals have their roots in the history of a company's culture. They create camaraderie and a sense of belonging among employees. They also serve to teach employees corporate values and create identification with the organization. For example, at the cosmetics firm Mary Kay Inc., employees attend ceremonies recognizing their top salespeople with an award of a new car—traditionally a pink Cadillac. These ceremonies are conducted in large auditoriums where participants wear elaborate evening gowns and sing company songs that create emotions and excitement. During this ritual, employees feel a connection to the company culture and its values such as self-determination, willpower, and enthusiasm.[64] Another example of rituals is the Walmart cheer. This is a tradition Sam Walton started after visiting a manufacturing facility in South Korea. President and CEO Doug McMillan notes that the cheer is about "getting our blood flowing and choosing not to take ourselves too seriously."[65] Online prescription glasses company Warby Parker fosters a positive company culture by insisting that everyone keeps break areas clean, holding creative events and programs to promote a sense of community, and randomly sending employees to lunch with one another.[66]

Rules and Policies

Another way in which an observer may find out about a company's culture is to examine its rules and policies. Companies create rules to determine acceptable and unacceptable behavior and, thus, the rules that exist in a company will signal the type of values it has. Policies about issues such as decision making, human resources, and employee privacy reveal what the company values and emphasizes. For example, the Detroit based financial services firm Quicken Loans has a rule that states all customer calls and emails need to be answered within the same day, regardless of what time they arrive.[67] The presence of this rule is a manifestation of their competitive and customer oriented culture. The presence or absence of policies on sensitive issues such as "English-only" rules, bullying or unfair treatment of others, workplace surveillance, open-door policies, sexual harassment, workplace romances, and corporate social responsibility all provide pieces of the puzzle that make up a company's culture. This highlights how interrelated the P-O-L-C functions are in practice. Through rules and policies, the controlling function affects the organization's culture, a facet of organizing.

Physical Layout

A company's building, including the layout of employee offices, common areas, and other workspaces communicate important messages about a company's culture. For example, visitors walking into the Nike campus in Beaverton, Oregon, can witness firsthand some of the distinguishing characteristics of the company's culture. The campus is set on 74 acres and boasts an artificial lake, walking trails, soccer fields, and cutting-edge fitness centers. The campus functions as a symbol of Nike's values such as energy, physical fitness, an emphasis on quality, and a competitive orientation. In addition, at Nike headquarters wearing competitors' brands (such as Adidas) is frowned upon. This sends a strong signal that loyalty is expected. The company's devotion to athletes and their winning spirit are manifested in campus buildings named after famous athletes, photos of athletes hanging on the walls, and their statues dotting the campus.[68]

Winston Churchill, Prime Minister of the United Kingdom from 1940 to 1945, who didn't have a degree in architecture or in organizational behavior is quoted as saying, "We shape our buildings, and afterwards our buildings shape us." The layout of the office space is also a strong indicator of a company's culture. A company that has a layout where high-level managers interact with employees (such as Zappos where the CEO sits in a cubicle) indicate a culture of team orientation and egalitarianism, whereas a company where high-level managers have their own floor may indicate a higher level of hierarchy. Microsoft employees tend to have offices with walls and a door, because the culture emphasizes solitude, concentration, and privacy.[69] The degree to which playfulness, humor, and fun are part of a company's culture may be indicated in the office environment. For example, entertainment website The Chive boasts headquarters in Austin, Texas, that includes an indoor slide, hot tub, and second-story bar.[70]

Google promotes a creative and fun atmosphere by enhancing their buildings with a vast array of visual stimuli, such as this dinosaur sculpture of "Stan" who resides at the Googleplex.

Source: JHVEPhoto/Shutterstock.com

Stories

Perhaps the most colorful and effective way in which organizations communicate their culture to new employees and organizational members is through the skillful use of stories. A story can highlight a critical event an organization faced and the organization's response to it, or a heroic effort of a single employee illustrating the company's values. The stories usually engage employees emotionally and generate employee identification with the company or the heroes of the tale. One study using experiments on newly hired workers in a technology firm showed that using stories featuring how low-level employees upholding the company's expressed values was more effective than using similar stories featuring high-level employees in transmitting organizational values, whereas stories around high-level employees violating company values were related to poor attitudes among newcomers.[71] Stories shared with new employees communicate the company's history, its values and priorities, and serve the purpose of creating a bond between the new employee and the organization. For example, Arthur Fry, a scientist at 3M, was using slips of paper to mark the pages of hymns in his church choir, but they kept falling off. He remembered a superweak adhesive that had been invented in 3M's labs, and he coated the markers with this adhesive. Thus, Post-it Notes were born. However, marketing surveys showed that interest in such a product was weak and the distributors were not convinced that it had a market. Instead of giving up, Fry distributed samples of the small yellow sticky notes to administrative assistants throughout his company. Once they tried them, people loved them and asked for more. Word spread and this led to the ultimate success of the product. This story effectively describes the core values of a 3M employee—being innovative by finding unexpected uses for objects, persevering, and being proactive in the face of negative feedback.[72]

Key Takeaway

Organizational cultures are created by a variety of factors, including founders' values and preferences, industry demands, and early values, goals, and assumptions. Culture is maintained through attraction-selection-attrition, new employee onboarding, leadership, and organizational reward systems. Signs of a company's culture include the organization's mission statement, stories, physical layout, rules and policies, and rituals.

Discussion Questions

1. Do you think it is a good idea for companies to emphasize person–organization fit when hiring new employees? What advantages and disadvantages do you see when hiring people who fit with company values?
2. What is the influence of company founders on company culture? Can you think of an example based on your personal knowledge?
3. What are the methods companies use to aid with employee onboarding? What is the importance of onboarding for organizations?
4. What type of a company do you feel you would be a good fit for you? What type of a culture would be a misfit for you? In your past work experience, were there any moments when you felt that you did not fit with the organization? Why?
5. How do you think the COVID-19 pandemic will influence the physical layout of office spaces in the future? How could these changes influence organizational culture? Similarly, how do you think a move toward more remote work affect organizational culture?

8.4 Creating Culture Change

Learning Objective

1. Explain why culture change may be necessary.
2. Understand the process of culture change.

How Do Cultures Change?

Culture is part of a company's DNA and is resistant to change efforts. Many organizations may not even realize that their current culture constitutes a barrier against organizational productivity and performance. Changing company culture may be the key to the company turnaround when there is a mismatch between an organization's values and the demands of its environment.

Certain conditions may help with culture change. For example, if an organization is experiencing failure in the short run or is under threat of bankruptcy or an imminent loss of market share, it would be easier to convince managers and employees that culture change is necessary. A company can use such downturns to generate employee commitment to the change effort. However, if the organization has been successful in the past, and if employees do not perceive an urgency necessitating culture change, the change effort will be more challenging. Sometimes the external environment may force an organization to undergo culture change. Mergers and acquisitions are another example of an event that changes a company's culture. In fact, the ability of the two merging companies to harmonize their corporate cultures is often what makes or breaks a merger effort. For example, the merger of Daimler-Benz and Chrysler, two giants in the automotive industry, ended with dissolution in 2007. Looking back, analysts term the merger "the culture clash that was heard around the world." The merger was seen as a merger of equals, and yet integrating two companies with distinct cultures was a challenge that did not find a successful resolution.[73] Achieving culture change is challenging, and there are many companies that ultimately fail in this mission.

Research and case studies of companies that successfully changed their culture indicates that the following six steps increase the chances of success.[74]

FIGURE 8.5 Six Steps to Culture Change

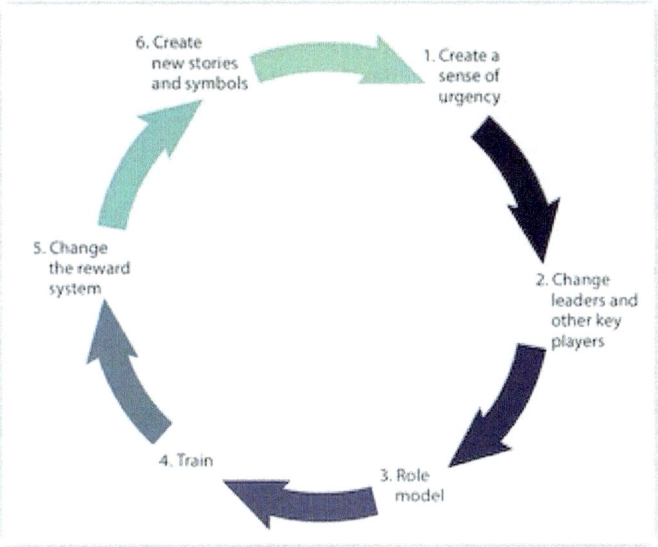

Creating a Sense of Urgency

In order for the change effort to be successful, it is important to communicate the need for change to employees. One way of doing this is to create a sense of urgency on the part of employees, explaining to them why changing the fundamental way in which business is done is so important. In successful culture change efforts, leaders communicate with employees and present a case for culture change as the essential element that will lead the company to eventual success. In other occasions, the sense of urgency is created due due to a crisis the organization faces. As a case in point, the crashes of two 737 Max airplanes revealed a serious problem in the organizational culture of Boeing and industry insiders observe that the company consistently put short term thinking and ambitious production schedules ahead of safety and long term stakeholder value. Those who could have voiced objections did not feel psychologically safe to do so. If Boeing is to survive, it will have to use the current crisis as an impetus to examine the dysfunctional aspects of its organizational culture.[75]

Changing Leaders and Other Key Players

A leader's vision is an important factor that influences how things are done in an organization. Thus, culture change often follows changes at the highest levels of the organization. Moreover, in order to implement the change effort quickly and efficiently, a company may find it helpful to remove managers and other powerful employees who are acting as a barrier to change. Because of political reasons, self interest, or habits, managers may create powerful resistance to change efforts. In such cases, replacing these positions with employees and managers giving visible support to the change effort may increase the likelihood that the change effort succeeds. For example, when the ride-sharing company Uber found itself facing multiple scandals and realized that a culture change was needed, it ousted its co-founder CEO Travis Kalanick. Uber had developed a cut-throat culture under his leadership, and top management was modeling these behaviors, such as rewarding executives who harass journalists. The new CEO, Dara Khosrowshahi, worked to instill a new set of values: build globally, live locally, celebrate differences, and doing the right thing.[76]

Role Modeling

Satya Nadella, CEO of Microsoft, was instrumental in stopping the infighting and restoring its innovative culture.

Source: drserg/Shutterstock.com

Role modeling is the process by which employees modify their own beliefs and behaviors to reflect those of the leader.[77] CEOs can model the behaviors that are expected of employees to change the culture. The ultimate goal is that these behaviors will trickle down to lower-level employees. For example, the CEO of Microsoft, Satya Nadella, transformed Microsoft culture to be more learning oriented, inclusive, and collaborative. This process was not without missteps. Just eight months after he became CEO, at a major industry event where the audience was predominantly female, he argued that women need to trust the system rather than ask for raises. The statement gathered severe backlash inside and outside the company. Instead of being defensive, he issued an apology the next day. In addition to owning up to his misstep, he used this event as an opportunity to explore his own biases, and initiated a conversation within the company around diversity, inclusion, and unconscious biases. His reaction to his own mistake modeled an openness to admitting one's mistakes and learning from them.[78]

Training

Well-crafted training programs may be instrumental in bringing about culture change by teaching employees the new norms and behavioral styles. For example, when auto repairer Midas felt the need to change its culture to be more committed to customers, they developed a program to train employees to be more familiar with customer emotions and connect better with them. Customer reports have been overwhelmingly positive in stores that underwent this training.[79]

Changing the Reward System

The criteria with which employees are rewarded and punished have a powerful role in determining the cultural values of an organization. Switching from a commission-based incentive structure to a straight salary system may be instrumental in bringing about customer focus among sales employees. Moreover, by rewarding and promoting employees who embrace the company's new values and promoting these employees, organizations can make sure that changes in culture have a lasting effect. If the company wants to develop a team-oriented culture where employees collaborate with one another, then using individual-based incentives may backfire. Instead, distributing bonuses to intact teams might be more successful in bringing about culture change.

Creating New Symbols and Stories

Finally, the success of the culture change effort may be increased by developing new rituals, symbols, and stories. During culture change, executives' actions carry symbolic meaning. Symbolic actions show executives' commitment to change, and if they resonate with people, they cause emotional reactions on the part of employees. During times of change, employees engage in a process of sensemaking, trying to interpret the actions of management and predict how long lasting such actions will be. Symbols are useful during this process and help enlist employee support.[80] Prior to its merger with United Airlines, Continental Airlines was a company that successfully changed its culture in the 1990s to be less bureaucratic and more team-oriented. One of the first things management did to show employees that they really meant to abolish many of the company's detailed procedures and create a culture of empowerment was to burn the heavy 800-page company policy manual in their parking lot. The new manual that replaced the old one was only 80 pages. This action symbolized the upcoming changes in the culture and served as a powerful story that circulated among employees. Another early action was redecorating waiting areas and repainting all their planes, again symbolizing the new order of things.[81] By replacing the old symbols and stories, the new symbols and stories will help enable the culture change and ensure that the new values are communicated.

Key Takeaway

Organizations need to change their culture to respond to changing conditions in the environment, to remain competitive, and to avoid complacency or stagnation. Culture change often begins by the creation of a sense of urgency. Next, a change of leaders and other key players may enact change and serve as effective role models of new behavior. Training can also be targeted toward fostering these new behaviors. Reward systems are changed within the organization. Finally, the organization creates new stories and symbols. Successful culture change requires managers that are proficient at all of the P-O-L-C functions. Creating and communicating a vision is part of planning; leadership and role modeling are part of leading; designing effective reward systems is part of controlling; all of which combine to influence culture, a facet of organizing.

Discussion Questions

1. Can new employees change a company's culture? If so, how?
2. Are there any conditions under which change is not possible? If so, what would such conditions be?
3. Have you ever observed a change process at an organization you were involved with? If so, what actions worked well and what actions failed?
4. What recommendations would you have for someone considering a major change of culture within their own organization?

8.5 Developing Your Personal Skills: Learning to Fit In

Learning Objectives

1. Understand what individuals can proactively do to understand a new organizational environment.
2. Learn effective guidelines for proactive onboarding.

Before You Join

How do you find out about a company's culture before you join? Several tips will allow you to more accurately gauge the culture of a company you are interviewing with.

First, *do your research*. Talking to friends and family members who are familiar with the company, doing an online search for news articles about the company, browsing the company's website, and reading websites such as Glassdoor.com, where current and former employees share their experiences, may be a good start.

Second, *observe the physical environment*. Do people work in cubicles or in offices? What is the dress code? What is the building structure? Do employees look happy, tired, or stressed? The answers to these questions are all pieces of the puzzle.

Third, *read between the lines*. For example, the absence of a lengthy employee handbook or detailed procedures might mean that the company is more flexible and less bureaucratic.

Fourth, *reflect on how you are treated*. The recruitment process is your first connection to the company. Were you treated with respect? Do they maintain contact with you or are you being ignored for long stretches at a time?

Fifth, *ask questions*. What happened to the previous incumbent of this job? What does it take to be successful in this firm? What would their ideal job candidate look like? The answers to these questions will reveal a lot about the way they do business.

Finally, *listen to your gut*. Your feelings about the place in general, and your future manager and coworkers in particular, are important signs that you should not ignore.[82]

Key Takeaway

There are a number of ways to learn about an organization's culture before you formally accept a job. Take the time to consider whether the culture you are observing truly seems like the right fit for you. Once you join a new organization, several strategies exist to maximize onboarding success.

Discussion Questions

1. What clues does your college or school give about its culture?
2. What are four things you could do today to learn more about an organization you are interested in?
3. Imagine that your good friend is starting a new job next week. What recommendations would you give your friend to help him or her do a great job onboarding into the organization?

8.6 Case in Point: The Power of Heart at Southwest Airlines

Source: OpturaDesign/Shutterstock.com

Southwest Airlines was founded in 1967 with the intention of challenging the status quo in the airline industry. The company emphasized simplicity by serving smaller airports, operating only one type of aircraft, issuing first-come-first-served boarding positions rather than seat assignments, and flying point-to-point rather than through hubs. The airline also modeled its maintenance crews after Indie 500 pit crews to expedite aircraft turnaround time. The company has enjoyed tremendous success, with 47 consecutive years of profitability. This streak was challenged by the drop in air travel in 2020 driven by travel restrictions, additional cleaning expenses, and keeping middle seats unoccupied in response to the global pandemic of COVID-19. Normally, Southwest Airlines employs over 60,000 people and serves over 130 million customers annually.

The mission of Southwest Airlines is dedication to the highest quality of customer service delivered with a sense of warmth, friendliness, individual pride, and company spirit. Southwest makes it clear that it values employees above all else. One of the airline's founders is known to have said, "The business of business is people." Southwest has a strong set of values that help define its company culture. Employees are encouraged to "Live the Southwest way" with "Warrior Spirit, Servant's Heart, and Fun-LUVing attitude" (the company's stock symbol is LUV), and to "Work the Southwest way" by emphasizing "Safety and Reliability, Friendly Customer Service, and Low Costs."

The philosophy of Southwest Airlines is that happy employees will lead to happy customers, which will translate to financial success and happy shareholders. The company embodies this emphasis on employee satisfaction in many ways. It has a department of Culture Services whose mission is to retain focus on the company's values, it recognizes and celebrates leaders at every level of the organization, it includes employees in decisions by empowering them to participate and own decisions that will impact them (such as designing new uniforms), and it offers ample opportunities for customers and coworkers to acknowledge exceptional staff. Other employee perks include substantial profit sharing, donations to employee-chosen non-profits, dinners with company executives, tuition reimbursement, professional development opportunities, and a fun and quirky work environment that supports individual expression.

When it comes to power, these positive organizational features make it easier for those within the organization to rely on referent power (liking and respecting someone), expert power as the organization listens to employees, and reward power as the organization shares its success with employees.

This investment in employee happiness has clearly paid off. Southwest Airlines enjoys an exceptionally low voluntary turnover of 4%, 85% of its employees say they're proud to work for the company, and the airline has the lowest number of customer complaints in the industry. Of course, the pandemic of COVID-19 has shaken up airlines and it is unclear which will survive the dramatic downturn in domestic and international travel which began in May 2020. The 9,000 corporate headquarters employees are primarily working from home with reports being as high as 98% through 2020. Southwest CEO, Gary Kelly, remains optimistic that Southwest will survive.[83]

Multimedia Extension—Southwest Airlines Employees Share the Spirit

View in the online reader

Case Discussion Questions

1. What is unique about Southwest Airlines, either operationally or from an organizational behavior standpoint? Do you think culture influences operations, and vice versa?
2. How does employee happiness relate to organizational success? Do you think Southwest's prioritization of its employees sets it apart in the industry?
3. What role do you think power and influence play among employees at Southwest?
4. Do you think that an organization like Southwest Airlines has more or fewer politics throughout it compared to a more hierarchical organization? Please be prepared to defend your answer.
5. Would you want to work for a company like Southwest? If so, what about the company most appeals to you?

Endnotes

1. Chatman, J. A., & Eunyoung Cha, S. (2003). Leading by leveraging culture. *California Management Review, 45*, 19–34; Kerr, J., & Slocum, J. W. (2005). Managing corporate culture through reward systems. *Academy of Management Executive, 19*, 130–138.
2. Retrieved from https://hbr.org/2015/11/how-company-culture-shapes-employee-motivation.
3. Barney, J. B. (1986). Organizational culture: Can it be a source of sustained competitive advantage? *Academy of Management Review, 11*, 656–665.
4. Why culture can mean life or death for your organization. (2007, September). *HR Focus, 84*, 9.
5. Roulin, N., & Krings, F. (2020). Faking to fit in: Applicants' response strategies to match organizational culture. Journal of Applied Psychology, 105(2), 130–145. https://doi.org/10.1037/apl0000431.
6. Kotter, J. P., & Heskett, J. L. (1992). *Corporate culture and performance*. New York: Free Press; Marcoulides, G. A., & Heck, R. H. (1993, May). Organizational culture and performance: Proposing and testing a model. *Organizational Science, 4*, 209–225.
7. Arogyaswamy, B., & Byles, C. H. (1987). Organizational culture: Internal and external fits. *Journal of Management, 13*, 647–658.
8. Schein, E. H. (1992). *Organizational culture and leadership*. San Francisco: Jossey-Bass.
9. Lev-Ram, M. (July 6, 2011). Facebook's vending machines: A Coke or a keyboard? Retrieved from http://fortune.com/2011/07/06/facebooks-vending-machines-a-coke-or-a-keyboard/.
10. Chatman, J. A., & Jehn, K. A. (1991). Assessing the relationship between industry characteristics and organizational culture: How different can you be? *Academy of Management Journal, 37*, 522–553; O'Reilly, C. A., III, Chatman, J. A., & Caldwell, D. F. (1991). People and organizational culture: A profile comparison approach to assessing person-organization fit. *Academy of Management Journal, 34*, 487–516.
11. Retrieved from https://www.fastcompany.com/most-innovative-companies/2020.
12. Wilson, M. (March 10, 2020). Snap is the world's most innovative company of 2020. Retrieved from https://www.fastcompany.com/90457684/ snap-most-innovative-companies-2020.
13. Retrieved from https://www.nytimes.com/2020/02/21/business/wells-fargo-settlement.html#:~:text=Wells Fargo has agreed to,Justice Department announced on Friday.
14. Kopelman, R. E., Chiou, A. Y., Lipani, L. J., & Zhu, Z. (September/October 2012). Interpreting the success of Zappos.com, Four Seasons, and Nordstrom: Customer centricity is but one-third of the job. *Global Business and Organizational Excellence*.
15. Nohria, N., Joyce, W., & Roberson, B. (2003, July). What really works. *Harvard Business Review, 81*, 42–52.
16. Probst, G., & Raisch, S. (2005). Organizational crisis: The logic of failure. *Academy of Management Executive, 19*, 90–105.
17. Westrum, R. (2004, August). Increasing the number of guards at nuclear power plants. *Risk Analysis: An International Journal, 24*, 959–961.
18. Fessler, L. (April 3, 2018). GM's dress code is only two words. Retrieved from https://work.qz.com/1242801/gms-dress-code-is-only-two-words/; Terlep, S (06/15/2011). GM's Latest Change Agent Tackles Designs, Red Tape. *The Wall Street Journal. 257* (138), p. B1; Welch, D. (6/29/2009). A salvage plan at GM. *BusinessWeek*, issue 4137.
19. Erdogan, B., Liden, R. C., & Kraimer, M. L. (2006). Justice and leader-member exchange: The moderating role of organizational culture. *Academy of Management Journal, 49*, 395–406.
20. Sheridan, J. (1992). Organizational culture and employee retention. *Academy of Management Journal, 35*, 1036–1056.

21. Retrieved from http://www.fool.com/investing/general/2015/05/18/the-business-reason-these-worker-perks-are-on-star.aspx.
22. Bolino, M. C., & Turnley, W. H. (2003). Going the extra mile: Cultivating and managing employee citizenship behavior. *Academy of Management Executive, 17*, 60–71.
23. Miles, S. J., & Mangold, G. (2005). Positioning Southwest Airlines through employee branding. *Business Horizons, 48*, 535–545.
24. Erdogan, B., Liden, R. C., & Kraimer, M. L. (2006). Justice and leader-member exchange: The moderating role of organizational culture. *Academy of Management Journal, 49*, 395–406.
25. Lake, K. (May/June 2018). Stitch Fix's CEO on selling personal style to the mass market. *Harvard Business Review, 96* (3); Steinmetz, K. (May 3, 2018). Stitch Fix has one of Silicon Valley's few female CEOs. But the company stands out for more than that. Retrieved from http://time.com/5264160/stitch-fix-has-one-of-silicon-valleys-fewfemale- ceos/.
26. Alix, L. (April 17, 2018). Umpqua names Tory Nixon as its first chief banking officer. *American Banker, 183* (73).
27. Ford, R. C., & Heaton, C. P. (2001). Lessons from hospitality that can serve anyone. *Organizational Dynamics*, *30*, 30–47.
28. Smith, J. (8/22/2013). America's 10 deadliest jobs. Retrieved from http://www.forbes.com/sites/jacquelynsmith/2013/08/22/americas-10-deadliest-jobs-2/.
29. Hofmann, M. A. (2007, January 22). BP slammed for poor leadership on safety. *Business Insurance*, *41*, 3–26.
30. Retrieved from https://www.ehstoday.com/americas-safest-companies-awards/article/21920452/americas-safest-companies-2019
31. Zohar, D., & Polachek, T. (2014). Discourse-based intervention for modifying supervisory communication as leverage for safety climate and performance improvement: A randomized field study. *Journal of Applied Psychology, 99*, 113–124.
32. Arogyaswamy, B., & Byles, C. M. (1987). Organizational culture: Internal and external fits. *Journal of Management, 13*, 647–658; Chatman, J. A., & Eunyoung Cha, S. (2003). Leading by leveraging culture. *California Management Review, 45*, 20–34.
33. Schneider, B., Salvaggio, A., & Subirats, M. (2002). Climate strength: A new direction for climate research. *Journal of Applied Psychology, 87*, 220–229.
34. Chatman, J. A., Caldwell, D. F., O'Reilly, C. A., & Doerr, B. (2014). Parsing organizational culture: How the norm for adaptability influences the relationship between culture consensus and financial performance in high technology firms. *Journal of Organizational Behavior, 35*, 785–808.
35. Cremer, A. (May 22, 2017). CEO says changing VW culture proving tougher than expected. Retrieved from https://www.reuters.com/article/us-volkswagen-emissions-culture/ceo-says-changing-vw-culture-proving-tougher- than-expected-idUSKBN18I2V3; Garlitos, K. (February 19, 2018). Corporate culture improvement deemed necessary after Dieselgate scandal. Retrieved on May 22, 2018 from https://www.topspeed.com/cars/ car-news/volkswagen-staff-still-not-seeing-any-culture-changes-withinthe- company-ar179938.html.
36. Anonymous (May 21, 2018). Amazon vs. Whole Foods: When cultures collide. Retrieved from https://www.forbes.com/sites/ hbsworkingknowledge/2018/05/21/httpshbswk-hbs-eduitemamazon-vswhole- foods-when-cultures-collide/#4a75f8943cf6.
37. Lok, P., Westwood, R., & Crawford, J. (2005). Perceptions of organisational subculture and their significance for organisational commitment. *Applied Psychology: An International Review, 54*, 490–514.
38. Kerr, J., & Slocum, J. W., Jr. (2005). Managing corporate culture through reward systems. *Academy of Management Executive, 19*, 130–138.
39. Schein, E. H. (1992). *Organizational culture and leadership*. San Francisco: Jossey-Bass.
40. Kiger, P. J. (April, 2005). Corporate crunch. Workforce Management, 84, 32–38; Rubis, L., Fox, A., Pomeroy, A., Leonard, B., Shea, T. F., Moss, D., Kraft, G., & Overman, S. (2005). 50 for history. *HR Magazine, 50* (13): 10–24; Smalley, S. (2007, December 3). Ben & Jerry's bitter crunch. *Newsweek*, 150, 50.
41. Mouawad, J. (2008, November 16). Exxon doesn't plan on ditching oil. International Herald Tribune. Retrieved November 16, 2008, from http://www.iht.com/articles/2008/11/16/business/16exxon.php.
42. Judge, T. A., & Cable, D. M. (1997). Applicant personality, organizational culture, and organization attraction. *Personnel Psychology, 50*, 359–394.
43. Orton-Jones, C. (May 17, 2018). Hire like Elon Musk . . . And 14 other ways to attract future leaders. Retrieved on from https://www.managers.org.uk/insights/news/2018/may/hire-like-elon-musk-and-14-other-ways-to-attract-future-leaders.
44. Kristof-Brown, A. L., Zimmerman, R. D., & Johnson, E. C. (2005). Consequences of individuals' fit at work: a meta-analysis of person–job, person–organization, person–group, and person–supervisor fit. *Personnel Psychology, 58*, 281–342; O'Reilly, C. A., III, Chatman, J. A., & Caldwell, D. F. (1991). People and organizational culture: A profile comparison approach to assessing person-organization fit. *Academy of Management Journal, 34*, 487–516.
45. Giberson, T. R., Resick, C. J., & Dickson, M. W. (2005). Embedding leader characteristics: An examination of homogeneity of personality and values in organizations. *Journal of Applied Psychology, 90*, 1002–1010.
46. Bauer, T. N., & Erdogan, B. (2010). Organizational socialization: The effective onboarding of new employees. In S. Zedeck, H. Aguinis, W. Cascio, M. Gelfand, K. Leong, S. Parker, & J. Zhou (Eds.), *APA Handbook of industrial and organizational psychology* (Vol. 3, pp. 51–64). Washington, DC: American Psychological Association.
47. Bauer, T. N., Bodner, T., Erdogan, B., Truxillo, D. M., & Tucker, J. S. (2007). Newcomer adjustment during organizational socialization: A meta-analytic review of antecedents, outcomes, and methods. *Journal of Applied Psychology, 92*, 707–721.
48. Bauer, T. N., Erdogan, B., Caughlin, D., Ellis, A. M., & Kurkoski, J. (in press). Jumpstarting the socialization experience: The longitudinal role of day one newcomer resources at organizational entry and subsequent adjustment. *Journal of Management.*
49. Klein, H. J., Polin, B., & Leigh Sutton, K. (2015). Specific onboarding practices for the socialization of new employees. *International Journal of Selection and Assessment, 23*, 263–283; Song, Y., Liu, Y., Shi, J., & Wang, M. (2017). Use of proactive socialization tactics and socialization outcomes: A latent growth modeling approach to understanding newcomer socialization process. *Academy of Management Discoveries, 3*, 42–63.
50. Bauer, T. N., & Green, S. G. (1998). Testing the combined effects of newcomer information seeking and manager behavior on socialization. *Journal of Applied Psychology, 83*, 72–83; Kammeyer-Mueller, J. D., & Wanberg, C. R. (2003). Unwrapping the organizational entry process: Disentangling multiple antecedents and their pathways to adjustment. *Journal of Applied Psychology, 88*, 779–794; Wanberg, C. R., & Kammeyer-Mueller, J. D. (2000). Predictors and outcomes of proactivity in the socialization process. *Journal of Applied Psychology, 85*, 373–385.
51. Fisher, A. (2005, March 7). Starting a new job? Don't blow it. *Fortune, 151*, 48.
52. Kim, T., Cable, D. M., & Kim, S. (2005). Socialization tactics, employee proactivity, and person-organization fit. *Journal of Applied Psychology, 90*, 232–241.
53. Durett, J. (2006, March 1). Technology opens the door to success at Ritz-Carlton. Retrieved from http://www.managesmarter.com/msg/search/article_display.jsp?vnu_content_id=100215774; Elswick, J. (2000, February). Puttin' on the Ritz: Hotel chain touts training to benefit its recruiting and retention. *Employee Benefit News, 14*, 9; The Ritz-Carlton Company: How it became a "legend" in service. (2001, January–February). *Corporate University Review, 9*, 16.
54. Schomer, S. (May 2018). Inside SeatGeek. *Inc*, 46 (4).
55. Allen, T. D., Eby, L. T., & Lentz, E. (2006). Mentorship behaviors and mentorship quality associated with formal mentoring programs: Closing the gap between research and practice. *Journal of Applied Psychology, 91*, 567–578.
56. Sarros, J. C., Gray, J., & Densten, I. L. (2002). Leadership and its impact on organizational culture. *International Journal of Business Studies, 10*, 1–26.
57. Driscoll, K., & McKee, M. (2007). Restorying a culture of ethical and spiritual values: A role for leader storytelling. *Journal of Business Ethics, 73*, 205–217.
58. Kammeyer-Mueller, J., Wanberg, C., Rubenstein, A., & Song, Z. (2013). Support, undermining, and newcomer socialization: Fitting in during the first 90 days. *Academy of Management Journal*, *56*, 1104–1124; Schaubroeck, J. M., Peng, A. C., & Hannah, S. T. (2013). *Academy of Management Journal, 56*, 1148–1168.
59. Kerr, J., & Slocum, J. W., Jr. (2005). Managing corporate culture through reward systems. *Academy of Management Executive, 19*, 130–138.
60. Kunen, J. S. (2002, January 19). Enron's vision (and values) thing. *The New York Times*, p. 19.
61. Jarnagin, C., & Slocum, J. W., Jr. (2007). Creating corporate cultures through mythopoetic leadership. *Organizational Dynamics, 36*, 288–302.
62. Wal-Mart Stores Inc. (2008). Investor frequently asked questions. Retrieved from http://walmartstores.com/Investors/7614.aspx.
63. Anand, N. (2005). *Blackwell encyclopedic dictionary of management*. Cambridge: Wiley.
64. Jarnagin, C., & Slocum, J. W., Jr. (2007). Creating corporate cultures through mythopoetic leadership. *Organizational Dynamics, 36*, 288–302.
65. McMillon, D. (December 6, 2017). We're updating our legal name to reflect how customers want to shop - Here's why. Retrieved on May 22, 2018 from https://blog.walmart.com/business/20171206/were-updating-our-legal-name-to-reflect-how-customers-want-to-shop-heres-why.
66. Patel, S. (2015). 10 examples of companies with fantastic cultures. *Entrepreneur*. Retrieved from entrepreneur.com/article/249174.
67. Taylor, B. (December 3, 2019). To build a strong culture, create rules that are unique to your company. Retrieved from https://hbr.org/2019/12/to-build-a-strong-culture-create-rules-that-are-unique-to-your-company.
68. Capowski, G. S. (1993, June). Designing a corporate identity. *Management Review, 82*, 37–41; Collins, J., & Porras, J. I. (1996). Building your company's vision. *Harvard Business Review, 74*, 65–77; Labich, K., & Carvell, T. (1995, September 18). Nike vs. Reebok. *Fortune, 132*, 90–114; Mitchell, C. (2002). Selling the brand inside. *Harvard Business Review, 80*, 99–105.
69. McGregor, J. (April 18, 2014). 9 things you didn't know about the office cubicle. Retrieved from https://www.washingtonpost.com/news/on-leadership/wp/2014/04/18/9-things-you-didnt-know-about-the-office-cubicle/?noredirect=on&utm_term=.79ad981429bc.

70. Retrieved July 18, 2018. http://www.bloomberg.com/bw/articles/2013-10-17/the-chives-founders-john-and-leo-resig-master-millennial-marketing
71. Martin, S. R. (2016). Stories about values and valuable stories: A field experiment of the power of narratives to shape newcomers' actions. *Academy of Management Journal, 59*, 1707–1724.
72. Higgins, J. M., & McAllester, C. (2002). Want innovation? Then use cultural artifacts that support it. *Organizational Dynamics, 31*, 74–84.
73. Johnson, R. (May 7, 2018). The culture clash heard around the world. *Automotive News, 92* (6828).
74. Schein, E. H. (1990). Organizational culture. *American Psychologist, 45*, 109–119.
75. Catchpole, D. (February 2020). Boeing's long descent. *Fortune, 181* (2).
76. Dunn, K. (Winter, 2020). Leadership skills: Inclusion and empathy. *Workforce, 99* (1).
77. Kark, R., & Van Dijk, D. (2007). Motivation to lead, motivation to follow: The role of the self-regulatory focus in leadership processes. *Academy of Management Review*, *32*, 500–528.
78. McKracken, H. (October, 2017). Microsoft rewrites the code. *Fast Company,* issue 219.
79. BST to guide culture change effort at NASA. (2004, June). *Professional Safety, 49*, 16; J. B. (2001, June). The Midas touch. *Training, 38*, 26.
80. Hambrick, D. C., & Lovelace, J. B. (2018). The role of executive symbolism in advancing new strategic themes in organizations: A social influence perspective.
81. Higgins, J., & McAllester, C. (2004). If you want strategic change, don't forget to change your cultural artifacts. *Journal of Change Management, 4*, 63–73.
82. Adapted from ideas in Daniel, L., & Brandon, C. (2006). Finding the right job fit. *HR Magazine, 51*, 62–67; Sacks, D. (2005). Cracking your next company's culture. *Fast Company, 99*, 85–87.
83. Case written by Rachel Mattenberger, Talya Bauer, and Berrin Erdogan to accompany Bauer, T. N. & Erdogan, B. (2021). *Organizational Behavior: Bridging Science and Practice (4.0).* Boston, MA: FlatWorld. Partially based on ideas and information contained in Hoopfer, E. (2020). Southwest Airlines CEO discusses 47-year profitability streak, HQ employees working from home and more. *Houston Business Journal.* https://www.bizjournals.com/houston/news/2020/08/15/southwest-47-years-profitable-work-from-home.html; Robertson, K. (2018). Southwest Airlines reveals 5 culture lessons. https://www.humansynergistics.com/blog/culture-university/details/culture-university/2018/05/29/southwest-airlines-reveals-5-culture-lessons; Weber, J. (2017). 17 Ways Southwest created a great company culture. https://www.glassdoor.com/employers/blog/17-ways-southwest-created-great-company-culture; Martin, E. (2015). A major airline says there's something it values more than its customers, and there's a good reason why. https://www.businessinsider.com/southwest-airlines-puts-employees-first-2015-7; and the company website: https://www.southwest.com; Southwest Airlines. (2020). Company overview. Retrieved from http://investors.southwest.com/our-company/company-overview.

CHAPTER 9

Leading People and Organizations

Mask up for Dr. Anthony Fauci who came in at number 5 on the 2020 edition of *Fortune's* annual list of World's Greatest Leaders.

Source: https://pendect.com/people/Anthony_S._Fauci

Chapter Learning Objectives

Reading this chapter will help you accomplish the following:

1. Define leadership and identify traits of effective leaders.
2. Describe behaviors that effective leaders demonstrate.
3. Specify the contexts in which various leadership styles are effective.
4. Explain the concepts of transformational, transactional, charismatic, servant, and authentic leadership.
5. Develop your own leadership skills.

TABLE 9.1 The P-O-L-C Framework

Planning	Organizing	Leading	Controlling
1. Vision & Mission	1. Organization Design	1. Leadership	1. Systems/Processes
2. Strategizing	2. Culture	2. Decision Making	2. Strategic Human Resources
3. Goals & Objectives	3. Social Networks	3. Communications	
		4. Groups/Teams	
		5. Motivation	

Leadership, by definition, is a key part of the P-O-L-C framework. Leadership may be defined as the act of influencing others to work toward a goal. Leaders exist at all levels of an organization. Some leaders hold a position of authority and may use the power that comes from their position to influence others; they are called **formal leaders**. In contrast, **informal leaders** influence without a formal position of authority within the organization. Rather, they demonstrate leadership by influencing others through personal forms of power. True leaders inspire others to willingly adopt the leader's goal as their own goal. Indeed, one of the key reasons many universities stress leadership skills in the college application process is due to the view that leaders are more likely to create meaningful and enduring differences in the world.[1]

Abraham Lincoln is frequently ranked in surveys as the greatest U.S. president for his leadership during the American Civil War and famous speeches he gave during his political career.

Source: Shutterstock.com

formal leaders

Those who hold a position of authority and may utilize the power that comes from their position, as well as their personal power to influence others.

informal leaders

Those without a formal position of authority within the organization but demonstrate leadership by influencing those around them through personal forms of power.

What makes leaders effective? What distinguishes people who are perceived as leaders from those who are not perceived as leaders? More importantly, how do we train future leaders and improve their leadership abilities? These are important questions that have attracted scholarly attention in the past several decades. In this chapter, we will review the history of leadership studies and summarize the major findings relating to these important questions. Around the world, leaders are at least partly responsible for their team's or company's success and failure. Company chief executive officers (CEOs) of major companies are routinely paid millions of dollars with the assumption that they hold their company's future in their hands as effective leaders. In politics, education, sports, and both for-profit and nonprofit sectors, the value of leadership over the behaviors of individuals and organizations is rarely questioned. When individuals and organizations fail, managers and CEOs are often viewed as responsible. Some people criticize the assumption that leadership always matters and call this belief "the romance of leadership." However, research evidence pointing to the importance of leaders for organizational success is accumulating.[2]

9.1 Who Is Considered a Leader? Trait Approaches to Leadership

Learning Objectives

1. Learn the position of trait approaches in the history of leadership studies.
2. Explain the traits that are associated with leadership.
3. Discuss the limitations of trait approaches to leadership.

The earliest approach to the study of leadership sought to identify a set a traits that distinguished leaders from nonleaders. What were the personality characteristics and the physical and psychological attributes of people who are viewed as leaders? Because of the problems in measurement of personality traits at the time, different studies used different measures. By 1940, researchers concluded that the search for leadership-defining traits was generally a futile effort. In recent years, though, after advances in personality literature such as the development of the Big Five personality framework, researchers have had more success in identifying traits that predict leadership.[3] For example, charismatic leadership, which is among the contemporary approaches to leadership, may be viewed as an example of a trait approach.

The traits that show relatively strong relations with leadership are as follows:[4]

FIGURE 9.1 Traits Associated with Leadership

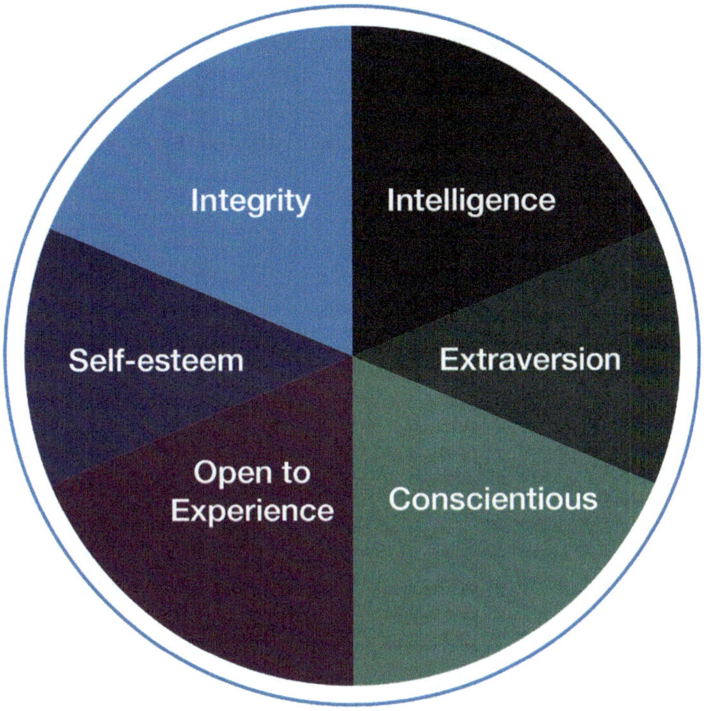

Intelligence

General mental ability, which psychologists refer to as "g" and is synonymous with "IQ" in everyday language, has been related to a person's emerging as a leader within a group. Specifically, people who have high mental abilities are more likely to be viewed as leaders in their environment.[5] We should caution, though, that intelligence is a positive but modest predictor of leadership, and when actual intelligence is measured with paper-and-pencil tests, its relationship to leadership is a bit weaker compared to when intelligence is defined as the perceived intelligence of a leader.[6] Further, intelligence seems to suffer from "too much of a good thing" syndrome: One study in a sample of middle level managers has shown that the beneficial effects of IQ were curvilinear and peaked at an IQ of around 120. The study concluded that having a leader somewhat smarter than followers is a good thing, whereas a wider gap may not be desirable.[7]

New Zealand Prime Minister Jacinda Ardern gained praise for her emotionally intelligent management of COVID-19 crisis. Her clear and consistent messaging and frequent displays of empathy resulted in high levels of trust.

Source: Shutterstock.com

In addition to having a relatively high IQ, effective leaders tend to have high emotional intelligence (EQ). People with high EQ demonstrate a high level of self awareness, motivation, empathy, and social skills. The psychologist who coined the term *emotional intelligence*, Daniel Goleman, argues that IQ is a threshold quality—it matters for entry- to high-level management jobs, but once you get there, it no longer helps leaders, because most leaders already have a high IQ. According to Goleman, what differentiates effective leaders from ineffective leaders becomes their ability to control their own emotions and understand other people's emotions, their internal motivation, and their social skills.[8]

Big Five Personality Traits

Psychologists have proposed various systems for categorizing the characteristics that make up an individual's unique personality; one of the most widely accepted is the "Big Five" model, which rates an individual according to Openness to experience, Conscientiousness, Extraversion, Agreeableness, and Neuroticism (recalling the first letters of the Big Five—OCEAN—can be a useful way to remember them). Several of the Big Five personality traits have been related to leadership emergence (whether someone is viewed as a leader by others) and effectiveness. Further, these personality traits also predict a person's motivation to lead, or their desire to attain a leadership role.[9]

TABLE 9.2 Big Five Personality Traits

Trait	Description
Openness	Being curious, original, intellectual, creative, and open to new ideas
Conscientiousness	Being organized, systematic, punctual, achievement-oriented and dependable
Extraversion	Being outgoing, talkative, sociable, and enjoying social situations
Agreebleness	Being affable, tolerant, sensitive, trusting, kind, and warm
Neuroticism	Being anxious, irritable, temperamental, and moody

Ryan Coogler's leadership is on full display through directing, producing, and screenwriting films such as *Creed* and *Black Panther*.

Source: DFree/Shutterstock.com

For example, extraversion is related to leadership. *Extraverts* are sociable, assertive, and energetic. They enjoy interacting with others in their environment and demonstrate self-confidence. Because they are both dominant and sociable in their environment, they emerge as leaders in a wide variety of situations. Out of all personality traits, extraversion has the strongest relationship to both leader emergence and leader effectiveness. This is not to say that all effective leaders are extraverts, but you are more likely to find extraverts in leadership positions. An example of an introverted leader is Jim Buckmaster, CEO of Craigslist. Known as an introvert, he admits to not having meetings because he simply does not like them.[10]

Research shows another personality trait related to leadership is *conscientiousness*. Conscientious individuals are organized, take initiative, and demonstrate persistence in their endeavors. Conscientious people are more likely to emerge as leaders and be effective as leaders. Research shows that the average level of conscientiousness among a firm's top management team is related to organizational performance over time. Finally, people who have openness to experience—those who demonstrate originality, creativity, and are open to trying new things—tend to emerge as leaders and also be quite effective. The role of agreeableness is less clear for leadership: Agreeable people who are modest, good natured, and avoid conflict are less likely to be perceived as leaders as they may be perceived as naïve or submissive.[11] At the same time, research evidence suggests that group performance and satisfaction with leader are higher for leaders who are agreeable.

Self-Esteem

Self-esteem is not one of the Big Five personality traits, but it is an important aspect of one's personality. The degree to which people are at peace with themselves and have an overall positive assessment of their self-worth and capabilities seems to be relevant to whether they will be viewed as a leader. Leaders with high self-esteem support their subordinates more, and when punishment needs to be administered, they punish more effectively.[12] It is possible that those with high self-esteem have greater levels of self-confidence and this affects their image in the eyes of their followers. Self-esteem may also explain the relationship between some physical attributes and emerging as a leader. For example, research shows a strong relationship between height and being viewed as a leader (as well as one's career success over life). This relationship emerged for both men and women. It is proposed that self-esteem may be the key to the connection of height with leadership, because people who are taller are also found to have higher self-esteem and therefore may project greater levels of charisma as well as confidence to their followers. In fact, research shows that when it comes to height, it is rewarded. One study found that each inch above average was related to $789 more per year in salary for leaders.[13]

Most U.S. presidents have been of higher-than-average height, a fact that may not have impressed the notoriously short Napoleon Bonaparte.

Source: Shutterstock.com

Integrity

Research also shows that people who are effective as leaders tend to have a moral compass and demonstrate honesty and integrity.[14] Leaders whose integrity is questioned lose their trustworthiness, and they hurt their company's business along the way. Warren Buffet, Chairman and CEO of Berkshire Hathaway, shared the following at a commencement speech: "We look for three things when we hire people. We look for intelligence, we look for initiative or energy, and we look for integrity. And if they don't have the latter, the first two will kill you."[15]

Despite problems in trait approaches, these findings can still be useful to managers and companies. For example, knowing about leader traits helps organizations select the right people for positions of responsibility. The key to benefiting from the findings of trait researchers is to be aware that not all traits are equally effective in predicting leadership potential across all circumstances. Some organizational situations allow leader traits to make a greater difference.[16] For example, in small entrepreneurial organizations where leaders have a lot of leeway to determine their own behavior, the type of traits leaders have may make a difference in leadership potential. In large, bureaucratic, and rule-bound organizations such as the government and the military, a leader's traits may have less to do with how the person behaves and whether the person is a successful leader.[17] Moreover, some traits become relevant in specific circumstances. For example, bravery is likely to be a key characteristic in military leaders, but not necessarily for business leaders in their day-to-day tasks. Scholars now conclude that instead of trying to identify a few traits that distinguish leaders from non-leaders, it is important to identify the conditions under which different traits affect a leader's performance, as well as whether a person emerges as a leader.[18]

Malala Yousafzai embody's the actions of a leader known for integrity as an activist for female education who survived an attack by the Taliban in her native Pakistan. She also holds the honor of being the youngest Nobel Prize laureate.

Source: SN040288/Shutterstock.com

Key Takeaway

Many studies searched for a limited set of personal attributes, or traits, associated with leadership success. Contemporary traits consistently linked to leadership include intelligence (both mental ability and emotional intelligence), personality (extraversion, conscientiousness, openness to experience, self-esteem), and integrity. A key limitation of the trait approach is that it ignores the situation in which leadership occurs. Therefore, it is more useful to specify the conditions under which different traits are needed.

Discussion Questions

1. What traits are evident in leaders you admire? Are they consistent with the traits discussed in this chapter? If not, why are these leaders effective despite the presence of different traits?
2. Can the findings of trait approaches be used to train potential leaders? Which traits seem easier to teach? Which are more stable?
3. How can organizations identify future leaders with a given set of traits? Which methods would be useful for this purpose?
4. What other traits can you think of that would be relevant to leadership?

9.2 What Do Leaders Do? Behavioral Approaches to Leadership

Learning Objectives

1. Explain behaviors associated with effective leadership.
2. Identify the three alternative decision-making styles leaders use and the conditions under which they are more effective.
3. Discuss the limitations of behavioral approaches to leadership.

Leader Behaviors

When leadership-trait researchers became disillusioned with progress identifying specific leadership traits in the 1940s, their attention turned to studying leader behaviors. What did effective leaders actually do compared to ineffective leaders? Which behaviors helped them to be perceived as leaders? Which behaviors increased their success? In order to understand behaviors of effective leaders, researchers at Ohio State University and the University of Michigan used many different techniques, such as observing leaders in laboratory settings as well as surveying them directly in workplace settings. This research stream led to the discovery of two broad categories of behaviors—task-oriented behaviors (sometimes called *initiating structure*) and people-oriented behaviors (also called *consideration*). **Task-oriented leader behaviors** involve structuring the roles of subordinates, providing them with instructions, and behaving in ways that will increase the performance of the group. Task-oriented behaviors are directives given to employees to get things done and to ensure that organizational goals are met. **People-oriented leader behaviors** include showing concern for employee feelings and treating employees with respect. Examples of such behaviors include listening to employees and acting in a teaching role.[19] People-oriented leaders genuinely care about the well-being of their employees and they demonstrate their concern by their actions and decisions. At the time, researchers thought that these two categories of behaviors were the keys to solving the puzzle of understanding leadership.[20] However, research did not support the argument that demonstrating both of these behaviors would necessarily make leaders effective.[21]

When we look at the overall findings regarding these leader behaviors, it seems that both types of behaviors, in the aggregate, are beneficial to organizations, but for different purposes. For example, when leaders demonstrate people-oriented behaviors, employees tend to be more satisfied and react more positively. However, when leaders are task-oriented, productivity tends to be higher.[22] Moreover, the situation in which these behaviors are demonstrated seems to matter. In small companies, task-oriented behaviors were found to be more effective than in large companies.[23] There is also some evidence that working under a leader with very high levels of task-oriented behaviors may cause burnout on the part of employees.[24]

Behavioral approaches to leadership showed that task-oriented and people-oriented behaviors are two key aspects of leadership. And, being able to flexibly change one's approach depending on the situation is important for leader effectiveness over time and across contexts.

Source: Shutterstock.com

task-oriented leader behaviors

Behaviors involving structuring the roles of subordinates, providing them with instructions and behaving in ways that will increase the performance of the group. (Also called *initiating structure*.)

people-oriented leader behaviors

Behaviors that include showing concern for employee feelings and treating employees with respect. (Also called *consideration*.)

Leader Decision Making

autocratic decision making

When leaders make the decision alone without necessarily involving employees in the decision-making process.

democratic decision making

When employees participate in the decision-making process.

laissez-faire decision making

When leaders leave employees alone to make the decision. The leader provides minimum guidance and involvement in the decision.

Another question behavioral researchers focused on was how leaders actually make decisions, and the influence of decision-making styles on leader effectiveness and employee reactions. Three types of decision-making styles were studied. In **autocratic decision making**, leaders make the decision alone without necessarily involving employees in the decision-making process. When leaders use **democratic decision making**, employees participate in the making of the decision. Finally, leaders using **laissez-faire decision making** leave employees alone to make the decision; the leader provides minimum guidance and involvement in the decision.

As with other lines of research on leadership, research did not identify one decision-making style as the best one. It seems that the effectiveness of the style the leader is using depends on the circumstances. A review of the literature shows that when leaders use more democratic decision-making styles, employees tend to be more satisfied, but the effects on decision quality or employee productivity are weaker. Moreover, instead of expecting to be involved in every single decision, employees seem to care more about the overall participativeness of the organizational climate.[25] Different types of employees may also expect different levels of involvement. In a study conducted in a research organization, scientists viewed democratic leadership most favorably and authoritarian leadership least favorably,[26] but employees working in large groups, where opportunities for member interaction were limited, preferred authoritarian leader decision making.[27] The key is to understand when each style works and vary one's style accordingly.

The track record of the laissez-faire decision-making style is more problematic. Research shows that this style is negatively related to employee satisfaction with leaders and leader effectiveness.[28] Laissez-faire leaders create high levels of ambiguity about job expectations on the part of employees, and employees also engage in higher levels of conflict when leaders are using the laissez-faire style.[29]

FIGURE 9.2 Leaders on Leadership

Here, we illustrate classic quotes from great leaders.

A leader is a dealer in hope.
—Napoleon Bonaparte

I suppose leadership at one time meant muscles; but today it means getting along with people.
—Mahatma Gandhi

It is better to lead from behind and to put others in front, especially when you celebrate victory when nice things occur. You take the front line when there is danger. Then people will appreciate your help.
—Nelson Mandela

Leadership is the art of getting someone else to do something you want done because he wants to do it.
—Dwight D. Eisenhower

No man is good enough to govern another man without that other's consent.
—Abraham Lincoln

Source: Quotes retrieved from http://www.brainyquote.com/quotes/quotes/m/mahatmagan150713.html (Mahatma Gandhi); http://www.brainyquote.com/quotes/quotes/n/nelsonmand393048.html (Nelson Mandela); http://www.brainyquote.com/quotes/quotes/d/dwightdei101562.html (Dwight D. Eisenhower). Photos: Shutterstock.com, Alessia Pierdomenico_Shutterstock.com, spatuletail_Shutterstock.com

Limitations of Behavioral Approaches

Behavioral approaches, similar to trait approaches, fell out of favor because they neglected the environment in which behaviors were demonstrated. The hope of the researchers was that the identified behaviors would predict leadership under all circumstances, but it may be unrealistic to expect that a given set of behaviors would work under all circumstances. What makes a high school principal effective on the job may be very different from what makes a military leader effective, which would be different from behaviors creating success in small or large business enterprises.

Key Takeaway

When researchers failed to identify a set of traits that would distinguish effective from ineffective leaders, research attention turned to the study of leader behaviors. Leaders may demonstrate task-oriented (initiating) and people-oriented (consideration) behaviors. Both seem to be related to important outcomes, with task-oriented behaviors more strongly relating to leader effectiveness and people-oriented behaviors leading to employee satisfaction. Leaders can also make decisions using authoritarian, democratic, or laissez-faire styles. While laissez-faire has certain downsides, there is no best style and the effectiveness of each style seems to vary across situations. Because of the inconsistency of results, researchers realized the importance of considering the context in which leadership occurs, which paved the way to contingency theories of leadership.

Discussion Questions

1. Give an example of a leader you admire whose behavior is primarily task-oriented, and one whose behavior is primarily people-oriented.
2. What are the limitations of authoritarian decision making? Under which conditions do you think authoritarian style would be more effective?
3. What are the limitations of democratic decision making? Under which conditions do you think democratic style would be more effective?
4. What are the limitations of laissez-faire decision making? Under which conditions do you think laissez-faire style would be more effective?
5. Examine your own leadership style. Which behaviors are you more likely to demonstrate? Which decision-making style are you more likely to use?

9.3 What Is the Role of the Context? Contingency Approaches to Leadership

Learning Objectives

1. Learn about the major situational conditions that determine the effectiveness of different leadership styles.
2. Identify the conditions under which highly task-oriented and highly people-oriented leaders can be successful, based on Fiedler's contingency theory.
3. Discuss the main ideas surrounding the path-goal theory of leadership.
4. Describe a method by which leaders can decide how democratic or authoritarian their decision making should be.

What is the best leadership style? After decades of management research, scholars have learned that more knowledge can be gained by asking, "Under which conditions are different leadership styles more effective?" After the disappointing results of trait and behavioral approaches, several scholars developed leadership theories that specifically incorporated the role of the environment. Researchers started following a contingency approach to leadership—rather than trying to identify traits or behaviors that would be effective under all conditions. Consequently, the attention moved toward specifying the situations under which different styles would be effective.

Fiedler's Contingency Theory

The earliest, and one of the most influential contingency theories, was developed by Fred Fiedler at the University of Washington.[30] According to the theory, a leader's style is measured by a scale called Least Preferred Coworker (LPC) scale. People who are filling out this survey are asked to think of a person who is their least preferred coworker. Then they rate this person in terms of how friendly, nice, and cooperative this person is. Imagine someone you do not enjoy working with. Can you describe this person in positive terms? If you can say that the person you disliked working with the most was still a nice person, you would have a high-LPC score. This suggests that you have a people-oriented personality and you can separate your liking of a person from your ability to work with that person. However, if you think that the person you hated working with was also someone you did not like on a personal level, you would have a low-LPC score. To you, being unable to work with someone would mean that you also dislike that person. In other words, you are a task-oriented person.

According to Fiedler's theory, different people can be effective in different situations. The LPC score is akin to a personality trait and is not likely to change. Instead, placing the right people in the right situation, or changing the situation, is important to increase a leader's effectiveness. The theory predicts that in "favorable" and "unfavorable" situations, a low-LPC leader—one who has feelings of dislike for coworkers who are difficult to work with—would be successful. When situational favorableness is medium, a high-LPC leader—one who is able to personally like coworkers who are difficult to work with—is more likely to succeed.

Fiedler's Contingency Theory relies heavily on ideas individuals have about their Least Preferred Coworker

Source: Shutterstock.com

How does Fiedler determine whether a situation is favorable, medium, or unfavorable? There are three conditions creating situational favorableness: (1) leader-subordinate relations, (2) position power, and (3) task structure. If the leader has a good relationship with most people, has high position power, and the task is structured, the situation is very favorable. When the leader has low-quality relations with employees, has low position power, and the task is relatively unstructured, the situation is very unfavorable.

Research partially supports the predictions of Fiedler's contingency theory.[31] Specifically, there is more support for the theory's predictions about when low-LPC leadership should be used, but there is less support for situations when high-LPC leadership should be more effective. Even though the theory was not supported in its entirety, it is a useful framework to think about when task- versus people-oriented leadership may be more effective. The theory continues to have lasting importance because of its explicit recognition of the role of context in understanding leadership effectiveness.

FIGURE 9.3 Situational Favorableness

Situational favorableness	Leader-subordinate relations	Position Power	Task Structure	Best Style
Favorable	Good	High	High	Low-LPC Leader
	Good	High	Low	
	Good	Low	High	
Medium	Good	Low	Low	High-LPC Leader
	Poor	High	High	
	Poor	High	Low	
	Poor	Low	High	
Unfavorable	Poor	Low	Low	Low-LPC Leader

Source: Based on information in Fiedler, F. (1967). *A Theory of Leadership Effectiveness*. New York: McGraw-Hill; Fiedler, F. E. (1964). A contingency model of leader effectiveness. In L. Berkowitz (Ed.), *Advances in Experimental Social Psychology* (Vol. 1, pp. 149–190). New York: Academic Press.

Situational Leadership

Another contingency approach to leadership is Kenneth Blanchard and Paul Hersey's Situational Leadership Theory (SLT), which argues that leaders must use different leadership styles depending on their followers' development level.[32] According to this model, employee readiness (defined as a combination of their competence and commitment levels) is the key factor determining the proper leadership style. This approach has been highly popular with 14 million managers across 42 countries undergoing SLT training and 70% of *Fortune* 500 companies employing its use.[33]

Ken Blanchard, a developer of the Situational Leadership Theory, is also known for his best-selling book *The One Minute Manager*, in which he asserts that effective managers provide goals, reprimands, and praises in one-minute increments.

Source: Shutterstock.com

The model summarizes the level of directive and supportive behaviors that leaders may exhibit. The model argues that to be effective, leaders must use the right style of behaviors at the right time in each employee's development. It is recognized that followers are key to a leader's success. Employees who are at the earliest stages of developing are seen as being highly committed but with low competence for the tasks. Thus, leaders should be highly directive and less supportive. As the employee becomes more competent, the leader should engage in more coaching behaviors. Supportive behaviors are recommended once the employee is at moderate to high levels of competence. And finally, delegating is the recommended approach for leaders dealing with employees who are both highly committed and highly competent. While the SLT is popular with managers, relatively easy to understand and use, and has endured for decades, research has been mixed in its support of the basic assumptions of the model.[34] Therefore, while it can be a useful way to think about matching behaviors to situations, overreliance on this model, at the exclusion of other models, is premature.

TABLE 9.3 Situational Leadership Theory

This theory is useful in that it helps leaders diagnose and match their style to follower readiness levels.

Diagnosis factors:				
Follower Readiness Level	Competence (Low)	Competence (Low)	Competence (Moderate to High)	Competence (High)
	Commitment (High)	Commitment (Low)	Commitment (Variable)	Commitment (High)
Recommended Leader Style	Directing Behavior	Coaching Behavior	Supporting Behavior	Delegating Behavior

Path-Goal Theory of Leadership

Robert House's path-goal theory of leadership is based on the expectancy theory of motivation.[35] Expectancy theory of motivation suggests that employees are motivated when they believe—or expect—that (a) their effort will lead to high performance, (b) their high performance will be rewarded, and (c) the rewards they will receive are valuable to them. According to the path-goal theory of leadership, the leader's main job is to make sure that all three of these conditions exist. Thus, leaders will create satisfied and high-performing employees by making sure that employee effort leads to performance, and their performance is rewarded. The leader removes roadblocks along the way and creates an environment that subordinates find motivational.

The theory also makes specific predictions about what type of leader behavior will be effective under which circumstances.[36] The theory identifies four leadership styles. Each of these styles can be effective, depending on the characteristics of employees (such as their ability level, preferences, locus of control, and achievement motivation) and characteristics of the work environment (such as the level of role ambiguity, the degree of stress present in the environment, and the degree to which the tasks are unpleasant).

Four Leadership Styles

path-goal theory of leadership

Theory stating that a leader's main job is to motivate employees with the beliefs that (1) their effort will lead to high performance, (2) their high performance will be rewarded, and (3) the rewards they will receive are valuable to them.

directive leaders

Those leaders who provide specific directions to their employees.

supportive leaders

Those leaders who provide emotional support to employees.

participative leaders

Those leaders who make sure that employees are involved in making important decisions.

achievement-oriented leaders

Those leaders who set goals for employees and encourage them to reach their goals.

The **Path-goal theory of leadership** identifies four styles leaders may adopt. **Directive leaders** provide specific directions to their employees. They lead employees by clarifying role expectations, setting schedules, and making sure that employees know what to do on a given workday. The theory predicts that the directive style will work well when employees are experiencing role ambiguity on the job. If people are unclear about how to go about doing their jobs, giving them specific directions will motivate them. However, if employees already have role clarity, and if they are performing boring, routine, and highly-structured jobs, giving them direction does not help. In fact, it may hurt them by creating an even more restricting atmosphere. Directive leadership is also thought to be less effective when employees have high levels of ability. When managing professional employees with high levels of expertise and job-specific knowledge, telling them what to do may create a low empowerment environment, which impairs motivation.

Supportive leaders provide emotional support to employees. They treat employees well, care about them on a personal level, and are encouraging. Supportive leadership is predicted to be effective when employees are under a lot of stress or when they are performing boring and repetitive jobs. When employees know exactly how to perform their jobs but their jobs are unpleasant, supportive leadership may also be effective.

Participative leaders make sure that employees are involved in making important decisions. Participative leadership may be more effective when employees have high levels of ability and when the decisions to be made are personally relevant to them. For employees who have a high internal locus of control, or the belief that they can control their own destinies, participative leadership gives employees a way of indirectly controlling organizational decisions, which will be appreciated.

Achievement-oriented leaders set goals for employees and encourage them to reach their goals. Their style challenges employees and focuses their attention on work-related goals. This style is likely to be effective when employees have both high levels of ability and high levels of achievement motivation.

TABLE 9.4 Predictions of the Path-Goal Theory Approach to Leadership

Situation	Appropriate Leadership Style
When employees have high role ambiguity	**Directive**
When employees have low abilities	
When employees have external locus of control	
When tasks are boring and repetitive	**Supportive**
When tasks are stressful	
When employees have high abilities	**Participative**
When the decision is relevant to employees	
When employees have high internal locus of control	
When employees have high abilities	**Achievement-oriented**
When employees have high achievement motivation	

Sources: Partially based on information presented in House, R. J. (1996). Path-goal theory of leadership: Lessons, legacy, and a reformulated theory. *Leadership Quarterly*, *7*, 323–352; House, R. J., & Mitchell, T. R. (1974). Path-goal theory of leadership. *Journal of Contemporary Business*, *3*, 81–97.

The path-goal theory of leadership has received partial but encouraging levels of support from researchers. Because the theory is highly complicated, it has not been fully and adequately tested.[37] The theory's biggest contribution may be that it highlights the importance of a leader's ability to change styles, depending on the circumstances. Unlike Fiedler's contingency theory, in which the leader's style is assumed to be fixed and only the environment can be changed, House's path-goal theory underlines the importance of varying one's style, depending on the situation.

Music Rap-Up: Situational Control

Twinprov perform a rap on Path-Goal Theory leadership styles.

View in the online reader

Vroom and Yetton's Normative Decision Model

Yale School of Management professor Victor Vroom and his colleagues Philip Yetton and Arthur Jago developed a decision-making tool to help leaders determine how much involvement they should seek when making decisions.[38] The model starts by having leaders answer several key questions and working their way through a decision tree based on their responses.

Imagine that you want to help your employees lower their stress so that you can minimize employee absenteeism. There are a number of approaches you could take to reduce employee stress, such as offering gym memberships, providing employee assistance programs, establishing a nap room, and so forth.[39] Should a manager decide how to reduce stress alone, consult with a group individually and then decide, consult with a group as a whole and decide, facilitate a group decision, or delegate the decision to a member of the group? The model asks a series of questions based on the nature of the decision that results in a recommendation surrounding the best method of decision-making for that specific scenario. Refer to the model and start with the first question. As each question is evaluated as high (H) or low (L), the corresponding path in Figure 9.4 leads to a different recommendation concerning the most effective way to make a decision.

FIGURE 9.4 Vroom and Yetton Leadership Decision Tree

Vroom and Yetton's leadership decision tree shows leaders which styles will be most effective in different situations.

	Decision Significance	Importance of Commitment	Leader Expertise	Likelihood of Commitment	Goal Alignment	Group Expertise	Team Competance	
PROBLEM STATEMENT	H	H	H	H	-	-	-	Decide
				L	H	H	H	Facilitate
							L	
						L	-	Consult (Group)
					L	-	-	
			L	H	H	H	H	Delegate
							L	
						L	-	Consult (Individually)
					L	-	-	
				L	H	H	H	Facilitate
							L	
						L	-	Consult (Group)
					L	-	-	
		L	H	-	-	-	-	Decide
			L	-	H	H	H	Facilitate
							L	
						L	-	Consult (Individually)
					L	-	-	
	L	H	-	H	-	-	-	Decide
				L	-	-	H	Delegate
							L	Facilitate
		L	-	-	-	-	-	Decide

Source: Used by permission from Victor H. Vroom.

1. *Decision significance*. The decision has high significance because the approach chosen needs to be effective at reducing employee stress for the insurance premiums to be lowered. In other words, there is a quality requirement to the decision. Follow the path through H.
2. *Importance of commitment*. What is the importance of employee cooperation to implement the decision? In our example, let's say the answer is high, because employees may simply ignore the resources if they do not like them. Follow the path through H.
3. *Leader expertise*. Does the leader have all the information needed to make a high-quality decision? In our example, imagine that leader expertise is low. You do not have information regarding what your employees need or what kinds of stress reduction resources they would prefer. Follow the path through L.
4. *Likelihood of commitment*. If the leader makes the decision alone, what is the likelihood that the employees would accept it? Let's assume that the answer is low. Based on the leader's experience with this group, they would likely ignore the decision if the leader makes it alone. Follow the path from L.
5. *Goal alignment*. Are the employee goals aligned with organizational goals? In this instance, employee and organizational goals may be aligned because you both want to ensure that employees are healthier. So let's say the alignment is high, and follow H.
6. *Group expertise*. Does the group have expertise in this decision-making area? Let's imagine that the group has expertise, because members have advanced degrees in human resource management. We'll say group expertise is high. Follow the path from H.
7. *Team competence*. What is the ability of this particular team to solve the problem? Let's imagine that this is a new team that just got together and they have little demonstrated expertise to work together effectively. We will answer this as low, or L.

Based on the answers to the questions we gave, the normative approach recommends consulting employees as a group. In other words, the leader may make the decision alone after gathering information from employees and is not advised to delegate the decision to the team or to make the decision alone.

Decision-Making Styles

- *Decide*. The leader makes the decision alone using available information.
- *Consult individually*. The leader obtains additional information from individual members before making the decision alone.
- *Consult as a group*. The leader shares the problem with the entire group and asks for their opinion. The leader makes the final decision alone.
- *Facilitate*. The leader shares information about the problem with group members collectively, and acts as a facilitator. The leader sets the parameters of the decision.
- *Delegate*. The leader lets the team make the decision.

Vroom and Yetton's normative model is somewhat complicated, but research results support the validity of the model. On average, leaders using the style recommended by the model tend to make more effective decisions compared to leaders using a style not recommended by the model.[40]

Key Takeaway

The contingency approaches to leadership describe the role the situation would play in choosing the most effective leadership style. Fiedler's contingency theory argued that task-oriented leaders would be most effective when the situation was the most and the least favorable, whereas relationship-oriented leaders would be effective when situational favorableness was moderate. Situational Leadership Theory takes the maturity level of followers into account. House's path-goal theory states that the leader's job is to ensure that employees view their effort as leading to performance and increase the belief that performance would be rewarded. For this purpose, leaders would use directive, supportive, participative, and achievement-oriented leadership styles, depending on what employees needed to feel motivated. Vroom and Yetton's normative decision model is a guide leaders can use to decide how participative they should be given decision environment characteristics.

Discussion Questions

1. Do you believe that the least preferred coworker technique is a valid method of measuring someone's leadership style? Why or why not?
2. Do you believe that leaders can vary their style to demonstrate directive, supportive, achievement-oriented and participative styles with respect to different employees? Or does each leader tend to have a personal style that he or she regularly uses toward all employees?
3. What do you see as the limitations of the Vroom-Yetton leadership decision-making approach?
4. Which of the leadership theories covered in this section do you think are most useful, and least useful, to practicing managers? Why?

9.4 Contemporary Approaches to Leadership

Learning Objectives

1. Learn about the difference between transformational and transactional leaders.
2. Find out about the relationship between charismatic leadership and how it relates to leader performance.
3. Learn how to be charismatic.
4. Describe how high-quality leader-subordinate relationships develop.
5. Define servant leadership and evaluate its potential for leadership effectiveness.
6. Define authentic leadership and evaluate its potential for leadership effectiveness.

What are the leadership theories that have the greatest contributions to offer today's business environment? In this section, we will review the most recent developments in the field of leadership.

Transformational Leadership

Transformational leadership theory is a more recent addition to the management literature, but more research has been conducted on this theory than all the contingency theories of leadership combined. The theory distinguishes between transformational and transactional leaders. **Transformational leaders** motivate employees by aligning employee goals with the leader's goals. Thus, employees working for transformational leaders start focusing on the company's well-being rather than on what is best for them as individual employees. However, **transactional leaders** ensure that employees demonstrate the correct behaviors because the leader provides resources in exchange.[41]

Transformational leaders have four tools in their possession, which they use to influence employees and create commitment to the company goals.[42] First, transformational leaders are charismatic. **Charisma** refers to behaviors leaders demonstrate that inspire confidence, commitment, and admiration toward the leader.[43] Charismatic individuals have a "magnetic" personality that is appealing to followers. Second, transformational leaders use **inspirational motivation** to develop a vision that is inspiring to others. Third, they use **intellectual stimulation** to challenge organizational norms and status quo, and encourage employees to think creatively and work harder. Finally, they use **individualized consideration**, which means that they show personal care and concern for the well-being of their followers. Examples of transformational leaders include Steve Jobs of Apple Inc.; Lee Iaccoca, who transformed Chrysler Motors LLC in the 1980s; and Jack Welch, who was the CEO of General Electric Company for twenty years. Each of these leaders is charismatic and is held responsible for the turnarounds of their companies.

transformational leaders

Those leaders who lead employees by aligning employee goals with the leader's goals.

transactional leaders

Those leaders who ensure that employees demonstrate the correct behaviors because the leader provides resources in exchange.

charisma

Behaviors leaders demonstrate that create confidence, commitment, and admiration toward the leader.

inspirational motivation

When leaders develop a vision that is inspiring to others.

intellectual stimulation

When leaders challenge organizational norms and status quo and encourage employees to think creatively and work harder.

individualized consideration

When leaders show personal care and concern for the well-being of their followers.

contingent rewards

Rewarding employees for their accomplishments.

active management by exception

Leaving employees alone but at the same time proactively predicting potential problems and preventing them from occurring.

passive management by exception

Leaving employees alone but then coming to the rescue if anything goes wrong.

trust

The belief that the other party will show integrity, fairness, and predictability in one's actions toward the other.

While transformational leaders rely on their charisma, persuasiveness, and personal appeal to change and inspire their companies, transactional leaders use three other methods. **Contingent rewards** mean rewarding employees for their accomplishments. **Active management by exception** involves leaving employees to do their jobs without interference, but at the same time proactively predicting potential problems and preventing them from occurring. **Passive management by exception** is similar in that it involves leaving employees alone, but in this method, the manager waits until something goes wrong before coming to the rescue.

Which leadership style do you think is more effective, transformational or transactional? Research shows that transformational leadership has a powerful influence over leader effectiveness as well as employee satisfaction.[44] In fact, transformational leaders increase the intrinsic motivation of their followers, increase performance and creativity of their followers, increase team performance, and create higher levels of commitment to organizational change efforts.[45] However, except for passive management by exception, transactional leadership styles are also effective, and they also have positive influences over leader performance as well as employee attitudes.[46] To maximize their effectiveness, leaders are encouraged to demonstrate both transformational and transactional styles. They should also monitor themselves to avoid demonstrating passive management by exception or leaving employees to their own devices until problems arise.

Why is transformational leadership more effective? The key factor may be **trust**. Trust is the belief that the leader will show integrity, fairness, and predictability in his or her dealings with others. Research shows that when leaders demonstrate transformational leadership behaviors, followers are more likely to trust the leader. The tendency to trust in transactional leaders is substantially lower. Because transformational leaders express greater levels of concern for people's well-being, and appeal to people's values, followers are more likely to believe that the leader has a trustworthy character.[47]

Mustafa Kemal Ataturk, the founder of the Turkish Republic and its first president, is known as a charismatic leader. He is widely admired and respected in Turkey and around the world. His picture appears in all schools, state buildings, denominations of Turkish lira, and in many people's homes in Turkey today.

Source: istanbulphotos/ Shutterstock.com

Is transformational leadership genetic? Some people assume that charisma is something people are born with. You either have charisma, or you don't. However, research does not support this idea. We must acknowledge that there is a connection between some personality traits and charisma. Specifically, people who have a neurotic personality tend to demonstrate lower levels of charisma, and people who are extraverted tend to have higher levels of charisma. However, personality explains only around 10% of the variance in charisma.[48] A large body of research has shown that it is possible to train people to increase their charisma and increase their transformational leadership.[49]

Even if charisma can be learned, a more fundamental question remains—is such training really needed? Charisma is only one element of transformational leadership and leaders can be effective without charisma. In fact, charisma has a dark side. For every charismatic leader whose charisma has been an asset to their firms, there are charismatic personalities who harmed their organizations or nations, such as Jeff Skilling of Enron and Elizabeth Holmes of Theranos. Leadership experts warn that when organizations are in a crisis, a board of directors or hiring manager may turn to heroes who they hope will save the organization and sometimes hire people who have no other particular qualifications outside of perceived charisma.[50]

An interesting study shows that when companies have performed well, their CEOs are perceived as charismatic, but CEO charisma has no relation to the future performance of a company.[51] So, what we view as someone's charisma may be largely because of their association with a successful company, and the success of a company depends on a large set of factors, including industry effects, the presence of an effective strategy, and historical performance. While it is true that charismatic leaders may sometimes achieve great results, the search for charismatic leaders under all circumstances may be unwarranted.

TABLE 9.5 Transformational and Transactional Leaders

Transformational Leaders		Transactional Leaders	
Charisma	Inspire commitment and confidence	**Contingent rewards**	Reward employees for accomplishments
Inspirational motivation	Develop a vision that inspires others	**Active management by exception**	Leave employees alone but proactively predict problems
Intellectual stimulation	Challenge the status quo	**Passive management by exception**	Leave employees alone and come to their rescue when things go wrong
Individualized consideration	Show support to employees		

Leader-Member Exchange (LMX) Theory

Leader-member exchange (LMX) theory proposes that the type of relationship leaders have with their followers (members of the organization) is the key to understanding how leaders influence employees. Leaders form different types of relationships with their employees. In **high-quality LMX relationships**, the leader forms a trust-based relationship with the member. The leader and member like each other, help each other when needed, and respect one another. In these relationships, the leader and the member are both ready to go above and beyond their job descriptions to promote the other's ability to succeed. For example, the success of many great NFL football teams is a function of excellent relationships between coaches and their quarterbacks.[52] In contrast, in **low-quality LMX relationships**, the leader and the member have lower levels of trust, liking, and respect toward each other. These relationships do not have to involve actively disliking each other, but the leader and member do not go beyond their formal job descriptions in their exchanges. In other words, the member does the job, the leader provides rewards and punishments, and the relationship does not involve high levels of loyalty or obligation toward each other.[53]

high-quality LMX relationships

A high-quality, trust-based relationship between a leader and a follower.

low-quality LMX relationships

A situation where the leader and the employee have lower levels of trust, liking, and respect toward each other.

FIGURE 9.5 Factors Contributing to the Development of a High-Quality Leader-Member Exchange and Its Consequences

You may have witnessed the different types of relationships managers form with their employees through your own work experiences or by observing interactions at businesses you have visited. The phenomenon where many leaders end up developing differentiated relationships with their followers is quite common. Within the same work group, they may have in-group members who are close to them and out-group members who are more distant. If you have ever been in a high-quality LMX relationship with your manager, you may attest to its advantages. Research shows that high-quality LMX members are more satisfied with their jobs, more committed to their companies, have higher levels of clarity about what is expected of them, and perform at a higher level.[54] Employees' high levels of performance may not be a surprise because employees in high LMX relations trust their leader more, have greater levels of job satisfaction, have higher levels of job motivation, and a greater sense of empowerment.[55] Because of all the help, support, and guidance they receive, those employees who have a good relationship with the manager are in a better position to perform well. Given all they receive, these employees are motivated to reciprocate to the manager, and therefore they demonstrate higher levels of citizenship behaviors such as helping the leader and coworkers.[56] Being in a high LMX relationship is also advantageous because a high-quality relationship is a buffer against many stressors, such as being a misfit in a company, having personality traits that do not match job demands, and having unmet expectations.[57] The list of benefits high LMX employees receive is long, and these employees are less likely to leave their jobs.[58]

The problem, of course, is that not all employees have a high-quality relationship, and those who are in the leader's out-group may suffer as a result. But how do you develop a high-quality relationship with your leader? It seems that this depends on many factors. Managers can help develop a high-quality and trust-based relationship by treating their employees in a fair and dignified manner.[59] They can also test to see whether the employee is trustworthy by delegating certain tasks when the employee first starts working with the manager.[60] Employees also have an active role in developing the relationship. Employees can seek feedback to improve their performance, be open to learning new things on the job, and engage in political behaviors such as flattery.[61]

Interestingly, high performance on the employee's part does not seem to be enough to develop a high-quality exchange with the leader. Instead, interpersonal factors such as personality similarity and liking are more powerful influences over how the relationship develops.[62] Finally, the relationship development occurs in a slightly different manner in different types of companies because corporate culture matters in how leaders develop these relationships. In performance-oriented cultures, how the leader distributes rewards seems to be the relevant factor, whereas in people-oriented cultures, whether the leader treats people with dignity is more important.[63]

Should you worry if you do not have a high-quality relationship with your manager? One problem in a low-quality exchange is that you may not have access to the positive work environment available to the high-quality LMX members. Second, low-LMX employees may feel that their situation is unfair. Even when their objective performance does not warrant it, those who have a good relationship with the leader tend to receive positive performance appraisals.[64] Moreover, they are more likely to be given the benefit of the doubt. For example, when high-LMX employees succeed, the manager is more likely to think that they succeeded because they put forth a lot of effort and they had high abilities, whereas for low-LMX members who perform objectively well, the manager is less likely to think so.[65] In other words, the leader may interpret the same situation differently, depending on which employee is involved and may reward low-LMX employees less even when they are performing well. In short, those with a low-quality relationship with the leader may experience a work environment that may not be very supportive or fair.

Despite its negative consequences, we cannot say that all employees want to have a high-quality relationship with the leader. Some employees may genuinely dislike the leader and may not value the rewards in the leader's possession. If the leader is not well liked in the company and is known as abusive or unethical, being close to such a person may imply guilt by association. Employees gain some of the benefits of a high-quality exchange with their manager from alternative sources, such as by having strong relationships with their team members. Finally, not all leaders are equally capable of influencing their employees by having a good relationship with their employees—it also depends on the power and influence of the leader in the company overall, and how the leader himself or herself is treated within the organization. Leaders who are more powerful will have more to share with employees who are close to them.

What LMX theory implies for leaders is that one way of influencing employees is through the types of relationships leaders form with their employees. These relationships develop naturally because of the work-related and personal interactions between the manager and the employee.

Because they occur naturally, some leaders may not be aware of the power that lies in them. These relationships have an important influence over employee attitudes and behaviors. In the worst case, they have the potential to create a negative work environment characterized by favoritism and unfairness. Therefore, managers are advised to be aware of how they build these relationships; put forth effort in cultivating these relationships consciously; be open to forming good relationships with people from all backgrounds regardless of their permanent characteristics such as sex, race, age, or disability status; and prevent these relationships from leading to an unfair work environment.

Self-Assessment: Rate Your LMX

Answer the following questions using 1 = not at all, 2 = somewhat, 3 = fully agree.

1. _____ I like my supervisor very much as a person.
2. _____ My supervisor is the kind of person one would like to have as a friend.
3. _____ My supervisor is a lot of fun to work with.
4. _____ My supervisor defends my work actions to a superior, even without complete knowledge of the issue in question.
5. _____ My supervisor would come to my defense if I were "attacked" by others.
6. _____ My supervisor would defend me to others in the organization if I made an honest mistake.
7. _____ I do work for my supervisor that goes beyond what is specified in my job description.
8. _____ I am willing to apply extra efforts, beyond those normally required, to further the interests of my work group.
9. _____ I do not mind working my hardest for my supervisor.
10. _____ I am impressed with my supervisor's knowledge of his/her job.
11. _____ I respect my supervisor's knowledge of, and competence on, the job.
12. _____ I admire my supervisor's professional skills.

Scoring:

Add your score for 1, 2, 3 = _____. This is your score on the *Liking* factor of LMX.

A score of 3 to 4 indicates a low LMX in terms of liking. A score of 5 to 6 indicates an average LMX in terms of liking. A score of 7+ indicates a high-quality LMX in terms of liking.

Add your score for 4, 5, 6 = _____. This is your score on the *Loyalty* factor of LMX.

A score of 3 to 4 indicates a low LMX in terms of loyalty. A score of 5 to 6 indicates an average LMX in terms of loyalty. A score of 7+ indicates a high-quality LMX in terms of loyalty.

Add your score for 7, 8, 9 = _____. This is your score on the *Contribution* factor of LMX.

A score of 3 to 4 indicates a low LMX in terms of contribution. A score of 5 to 6 indicates an average LMX in terms of contribution. A score of 7+ indicates a high-quality LMX in terms of contribution.

Add your score for 10, 11, 12 = _____. This is your score on the *Professional Respect* factor of LMX.

A score of 3 to 4 indicates a low LMX in terms of professional respect. A score of 5 to 6 indicates an average LMX in terms of professional respect. A score of 7+ indicates a high-quality LMX in terms of professional respect.

Source: Adapted from Liden, R. C., & Maslyn, J. M. (1998). Multidimensionality of leader-member exchange: An empirical assessment through scale development. *Journal of Management, 24*, 43–72. Used by permission of Sage Publications.

Servant Leadership

The early twenty-first century has been marked by a series of highly publicized corporate ethics scandals. As corporate ethics scandals shake investor confidence in corporations and leaders, the importance of ethical leadership and keeping long-term interests of stakeholders in mind is becoming more widely acknowledged.

Merck CEO Kenneth Frazier describes his company's value proposition as "discover and develop life-saving medicines for society."

Source: lev radin / Shutterstock.com

servant leadership

A leadership approach that defines the leader's role as serving the needs of others.

Servant leadership is a leadership approach that defines the leader's role as serving the needs of others. According to this approach, the primary mission of the leader is to develop employees and help them reach their goals. Servant leaders put their employees first, understand their personal needs and desires, empower them, and help them develop in their careers. Scholars argue that servant leaders are highly-regarded by their employees, make employees feel better about themselves, and lead to more productive employees.[66] Unlike mainstream management approaches, the overriding objective in servant leadership is not necessarily getting employees to contribute to organizational goals. Instead, servant leaders feel an obligation to their employees, customers, and the external community. Employee happiness is seen as an end in itself, and servant leaders sometimes sacrifice their own well-being to help employees succeed. In addition to a clear focus on having a moral compass, servant leaders are also interested in serving the community. In other words, their efforts to help others are not restricted to company insiders, and they are genuinely concerned about the broader community surrounding their organization.[67] Commitment to a purpose, even when it may not have an immediate payoff for the company but has clear benefits for the community is a hallmark of servant leadership. For example, the pharmaceutical company Merck's CEO Kenneth Frazier discussed his company's efforts to develop an Ebola vaccine, noting that it would have been impossible to base the decision on the robustness of the market.[68]

Even though servant leadership has some overlap with other leadership approaches, its explicit focus on ethics, community development, and self-sacrifice are distinct characteristics of this leadership style. Research shows that servant leadership has a positive effect on employee commitment, employee citizenship behaviors toward the community (such as participating in community volunteering), and job performance.[69] Leaders who follow the servant leadership approach create a climate of fairness in their departments, which results in higher levels of customer service.[70] Further, servant leaders are effective in developing teams with confidence in their capabilities, who end up performing at higher levels.[71]

Servant leadership is a tough transition for many managers who are socialized to put their own needs first, be driven by success, and tell people what to do. However, leaders who have adopted this approach attest to its effectiveness. David Wolfskehl, of Action Fast Print in New Jersey, founded his printing company when he was twenty-four. He marked the day he started asking employees what he could do for them as the beginning of his company's new culture. In the next two years, his company increased its productivity by 30%.[72]

Authentic Leadership

authentic leadership approach

Effective leaders who stay true to themselves.

Leaders have to be a lot of things to a lot of people. They operate within different structures, work with different types of people, and they have to be adaptable. At times, it may seem that a leader's smartest strategy would be to act as a social chameleon, changing his or her style whenever doing so seems advantageous. But this would lose sight of the fact that effective leaders have to stay true to themselves. The **authentic leadership approach** embraces this value—its key advice is "be yourself." Think about it: We all have different backgrounds, different life experiences, and different role models. Events over the course of our lifetime shape our values, preferences, and priorities. Instead of trying to follow societal expectations about what a leader should be like, act like, or look like, authentic leaders derive their strength from their own past experiences. Thus, one key characteristic of authentic leaders is that they are self-aware. They are introspective, understand where they are coming from, and have a thorough understanding of their own values and priorities. Second, they are not afraid to be themselves. In other words, they have high levels of personal integrity. They say what they think. They behave in a way consistent with their values—they practice what they preach. Instead of trying to imitate other great leaders, they find their style in their own personality and life experiences.[73]

One example of an authentic leader is Howard Schultz, the founder of Starbucks coffeehouses. As a child, Schultz witnessed the job-related difficulties his father experienced because of medical problems. Even though he had no idea he would have his own business one day, the desire to protect people was shaped in those years and became one of his foremost values. When he founded Starbucks, he became an industry pioneer in providing health insurance and retirement coverage to part-time as well as full-time employees.[74] Witnessing his father losing jobs because of medical problems, he became passionate about a company's need to care for its employees and beyond. In 2014, he announced a $30 million gift for U.S. troops that includes job training and research on post-traumatic stress syndrome and brain injuries.

An example of an authentic leader is Howard Schultz, the founder of Starbucks coffeehouses. Witnessing his father losing jobs because of medical problems, he became passionate about a company's need to care for its employees.

Source:
Howard Schultz by Gage Skidmore

Authentic leadership requires understanding oneself. Therefore, in addition to self-reflection, feedback from others is needed to gain a true understanding of one's behavior and effect on others. Authentic leadership is viewed as a potentially influential style because employees are more likely to trust such a leader. Moreover, working for authentic leaders is likely to lead to greater levels of satisfaction, performance, and overall well-being on the part of employees.[75]

When Leadership Goes Wrong: Abusive Leadership

In addition to investigating how to be an effective leader, scholars also investigated how not to be one. Those in positions of authority have the potential to influence employee happiness and well-being, as well as effectiveness. When they display dysfunctional behaviors, they have the ability to do harm.

Abusive leadership is defined as a sustained display of hostile verbal and nonverbal behaviors toward employees. Abusive leaders display behaviors such as giving employees the silent treatment, reminding them of their past mistakes, breaking promises, being rude, and lying to employees. Not surprisingly, employees of these leaders are more likely to quit their jobs, experience unhappiness on and off the job, and have higher levels of stress. It is estimated that abusive leaders cost organizations more than $20 billion, mostly due to lost productivity, absenteeism, and higher healthcare costs. Employees whose values are perceived to diverge from those of the manager are prime targets for abusive behaviors. There is some evidence that abusive leadership is a function of a leader's ability to regulate their emotions. For example, research has shown that leaders are more likely to engage in abusive behaviors following nights when they experience poor sleep quality.[76]

abusive leadership

A sustained display of hostile verbal and nonverbal behaviors toward employees.

Organizations should be aware that abusive leadership is contagious. In fact, new managers may model their leadership styles on abusive leaders, particularly if these abusive leaders are perceived to be competent and when the new leaders believe that ideal leaders are high in tyranny and low in interpersonal sensitivity.[77] Abusive leadership does not only hurt its targets, it is harmful for managers themselves in the form of a decline in well-being.[78] Organizations are advised to create selection and training systems and organizational cultures that prevent abusive behaviors from taking place.

Leader Humility

Google CEO Sundar Pichai is known for his humble leadership style.

Source: By World Economic Forum—An Insight, An Idea with Sundar Pichai | DAVOS 2020, CC BY 3.0, https://commons.wikimedia.org/w/index.php?curid=87519623

Popular culture and news stories often create the impression that leaders should be all-knowing and powerful. These days, there is increasing recognition that this view is misguided. Instead, humility is emerging as a behavioral style of effective leaders. Leader humility describes a leader's ability to view their own shortcomings accurately, an ability to appreciate the strengths of others, and an openness to feedback to learn and improve. Leader humility is related to many benefits for teams. For example, in teams with humble leaders, employees embrace a "shared leadership" approach to teamwork, which helps with team performance. Humble leaders are also beneficial to teams because these teams allocate tasks more effectively within the group. Finally, employees imitate humble leaders, which results in a group climate where team members demonstrate the same behaviors.[79]

At the same time, there are some boundary conditions to the effectiveness of leader humility. For example, fit with team member values matters. One study has shown that when the team has high levels of power distance, leader humility had negative effects on the team, suggesting that some teams may actually expect their leaders to be all powerful, which would diminish the usefulness of leader humility for the team.[80]

Women and Leadership

No discussion of leadership will be complete without a discussion of the role of gender. Women make up slightly more than half the U.S. population, earn around 60% of all college degrees, and represent 47% of the workforce, yet hold only 5% of the CEO positions of the Fortune 1,000 companies. The reasons for this are debated and are likely to be a combination of many factors. What does the leadership literature say about women and leadership? Are men and women different in their leadership styles or effectiveness?

Sara Blakely, founder of the underwear company Spanx, turned an initial investment of $5,000 into a fortune of over $1 billion.

Source: Gillian Zoe Segal [CC BY-SA 4.0 (https://creativecommons.org/licenses/by-sa/4.0)], from Wikimedia Commons

Here is what the meta-analytic evidence says. First, unlike what stereotypes may suggest, men are not more task oriented and women are not more relationally oriented than the opposite sex. Second, confirming stereotypes, women tend to display democratic leadership and are less likely to demonstrate autocratic leadership compared to men. There are also modest differences in transformational leadership styles, with women displaying higher levels of transformational leadership styles. At the same time, when women occupied stereotypically masculine roles, they were rated as being less effective than men. Interestingly, while women were rated as demonstrating higher performance on their jobs, they were rated lower in promotion potential. The reason for this distinction is unclear, but this finding has implications for the differential levels at which women hold leadership positions in organizations. One interesting research finding is that in a series of experiments, when women succeed in stereotypically masculine jobs, they are liked less, suggesting that there may be a penalty for successful women in some domains, which may include leadership. It seems likely that this issue will continue to be debated in the next decade.[81]

Female leaders such as Angela Merkel (Germany), Jacinda Ardern (New Zealand), and Tsai Ing-Wen (Taiwan) received praise during the COVID-19 crisis for taking the crisis seriously and taking precautions early on, and saving lives. In the U.S., a study has shown that states with female governors had fewer deaths in their states as of May 5, 2020. Further, having female leadership along with early stay at home orders was associated with fewer deaths in the state. The researchers further explored the cause of these differences by examining governors' briefings, and showed that compared to male governors, female governors expressed more empathy and confidence.[82] This study adds to the evidence base examining actual results and shows that female leaders often embrace effective leadership behaviors, leading their organizations to success.

Key Takeaway

Contemporary approaches to leadership include transformational leadership, leader-member exchange, servant leadership, and authentic leadership. The transformational leadership approach highlights the importance of leader charisma, inspirational motivation, intellectual stimulation, and individualized consideration as methods of influence. Its counterpart is the transactional leadership approach, in which the leader focuses on getting employees to achieve organizational goals. According to the leader-member exchange (LMX) approach, the unique, trust-based relationships leaders develop with employees is the key to leadership effectiveness. Recently, leadership scholars started to emphasize the importance of serving others and adopting a customer-oriented view in leadership; another recent focus is on the importance of being true to oneself as a leader. While each leadership approach focuses on a different element of leadership, effective leaders will need to change their style based on the demands of the situation, as well as using their own values and moral compass.

Discussion Questions

1. What are the characteristics of transformational leaders? Are transformational leaders more effective than transactional leaders?
2. What is charisma? What are the advantages and disadvantages of charismatic leadership? Should organizations look for charismatic leaders when selecting managers?
3. What are the differences (if any) between a leader having a high-quality exchange with employees and being friends with employees?
4. What does it mean to be a servant leader? Do you know any leaders whose style resembles servant leaders? What are the advantages of adopting such a leadership style?
5. What does it mean to be an authentic leader? How would such a style be developed?

9.5 Developing Your Leadership Skills

Learning Objectives

1. Develop your charismatic leadership skills.
2. Learn how to be a servant leader.
3. Follow a process to develop your own authentic leadership.

In this section, we provide tips to help develop charismatic, servant, and authentic leadership skills. Each of these contemporary approaches to leadership is believed to be related to employee attitudes and a healthy work environment.

Develop Your Charismatic Leadership Skills

Charismatic individuals have a "magnetic" personality that is appealing to followers. While many people assume that charisma is innate, it is possible to improve your charisma by following these suggestions:[83]

Have a vision around which people can gather. When framing requests or addressing to others, instead of emphasizing short-term goals, stress the importance of the long-term vision. When giving a message, think about the overarching purpose. What is the ultimate goal? Why should people care? What are you trying to achieve?

Tie the vision to history. In addition to stressing the ideal future, charismatic leaders bring up the history and how the shared history ties to the future.

Watch your body language. Charismatic leaders are passionate about their ideas. This involves truly believing in your own ideas. When talking to others, you may want to look confident, look individuals in the eye, and express your belief in your ideas.

Make sure that employees have confidence in themselves. You can achieve this by showing that you believe in people and trust their abilities. If they have real reason to doubt their abilities, make sure that you help them address the underlying issue, such as through training and mentoring.

Challenge the status quo. Charismatic leaders solve current problems by radically rethinking the way things are done and suggesting alternatives that are risky, novel, and unconventional.

Develop Your Servant Leadership Skills

One of the influential leadership paradigms involves leaders putting others first. This could be a challenging transition for an achievement-oriented and success-driven manager who rises to high levels. Here are some tips to achieve servant leadership.[84]

Do not ask what your employees can do for you. Think of what you can do for them. Your job as a leader is to be of service to them. How can you relieve their stress? Protect them from undue pressure? Help employees accomplish their career goals? Think about creative ways of helping ease and improve the lives of employees.

One of your key priorities should be to help employees reach their goals. This involves getting to know them personally. Learn about who they are and what their values and priorities are.

Be humble. You are not supposed to have all the answers and dictate to others. One way of achieving this humbleness may be to do volunteer work.

Be open with your employees. Ask employees questions. Give them information so that they understand what is going on in the company.

Find ways of helping the external community. Give employees opportunities to be involved in community volunteer projects or strategize about making a positive impact on the greater community.

Develop Your Authentic Leadership Skills

Authentic leaders have high levels of self-awareness and their behavior is driven by their core personal values. This leadership approach recognizes the importance of self-reflection and understanding one's life history. Address the following questions to gain a better understanding of your own core values and authentic leadership style.

Understand Your History

- *Review your life history.* What are the major events in your life? How did these events make you the person you are right now?
- *Think about your role models.* Who were your role models as you were growing up? What did you learn from your role models?

Take Stock of Who You Are Now

- *Describe your personality.* How does your personality affect your life?
- *Know your strengths and weaknesses.* What are they and how can you continue to improve yourself?

Reflect on Your Successes and Challenges

- *Keep a journal.* Research shows that journaling is an effective tool for self-reflection. Write down challenges you face and how you will surmount them; periodically review your entries to check your progress.

Make Integrity a Priority

- *Understand your core values.* What are your core values? Name three of your most important values.
- *Do an ethics check.* Are you being consistent with your core values? If not, how can you get back on track?

Understand the Power of Words

- *Words shape reality.* Keep in mind that the words you use to describe people and situations matter. For example, how might the daily reality be different if you refer to those you manage as associates or team members rather than employees or subordinates?

In view of your answers to the questions above, what kind of a leader would you be if you truly acted out your values? How would people working with you respond to such a leadership style?

Key Takeaway

Each leadership style has pros and cons. It is valuable to be able to assess them in light of your situation and your personal style. Authenticity has become recognized as being important regardless of the other leadership styles one uses. Anyone can be an authentic leader if he or she develops those skills. Understanding how to potentially develop skills associated with each style is valuable for shaping your own leadership style long-term.

Discussion Questions

1. What is the connection between leadership and ethics?
2. Do you believe that ethical leaders are more successful in organizations?
3. Have you ever had an authentic leader? What did this person do that made you consider him or her to be authentic? How effective was his or her leadership?
4. What leadership style appeals to you personally and why?

9.6 Case in Point: An Inclusive Leader Approach at Stitch Fix

Source: By Daniel G. Wells III—Own work, CC BY-SA 4.0, https://commons.wikimedia.org/w/index.php?curid=46112515

Stitch Fix is an online personal styling service that was founded in 2011 by entrepreneur Katrina Lake. Lake's vision was to disrupt the fashion retail industry by curating personalized wardrobe selections for Stitch Fix clients. In short, she sought to make personal shopping more affordable and less time-consuming using an online platform that leverages a blend of human stylists and algorithms. Starting with a modest $42 million in venture capital investment, Lake grew Stitch Fix into a company worth over a billion dollars. In 2017 Stitch Fix underwent a high-profile IPO. Lake was the youngest female founder ever to take a company public and CEO of the only female-led tech IPO of the year.

Today, Stitch Fix's vision is to transform the way people find what they love by helping customers with discovery and decision making. The company's growth is supported by strong leadership values and a sincere belief in the ability of every individual within the organization to be a leader. Stitch Fix employs people with a diverse set of skills, ranging from creative designers to merchandisers to data scientists. Company leadership prides itself on creating an accessible work environment with an approachable leadership team. The company fosters a culture that values dialogue and creative tension.

From a leadership development standpoint, Stitch Fix has established a regular 360-review process in which employees collect feedback from their peers and their leaders around how they engage with the company's "operating system." This operating system incorporates the organization's core values and leadership attributes, framed by the company's vision.

Stitch Fix invests heavily in professional development throughout the employee journey. Its new hire onboarding process is an immersive two-day process, whereby new employees are exposed to all functions of the company and their strategic pillars. Company leaders are an integral part of this training process, with employees hearing from a senior executive panel (including Katrina Lake) on their first day.

Leadership training continues throughout a Stitch Fix employee's career, regardless of his or her level within the organization. It is not limited to just managers and directors. This helps entry-level employees engage with the company in a meaningful way as potential leaders, and it holds senior leaders accountable for continuing to invest in their leadership styles. The company focuses this training around five leadership attributes: learn, develop, trust, inspire, and act. Stitch Fix hires and invests in people who are open to change and personal growth in order to support its bold vision.[85]

Multimedia Extension—She's 35—And Runs a $3 Billion Company

View in the online reader

Case Discussion Questions

1. In your opinion, how does the Stitch Fix culture of open dialogue, creative tension, and approachable leadership impact organizational innovation?
2. Why do you think Stitch Fix invests so heavily in leadership development, even for entry-level employees? What impact do you think this might have on employee engagement, morale, and retention?
3. If you were an employee, would you want to work in an environment that focused on continual learning and development? Please explain.
4. If you were a manager, would you appreciate participating in a 360-review process? How about as an individual contributor? What are some of the benefits and drawbacks of giving and receiving feedback across different levels of the organization?
5. If you were an entrepreneur with a bold vision such as Katrina Lake's, what employment leadership values might you instill early on in the founding and scaling of your company? Why would these be important to you?

Endnotes

1. Retrieved from http://www.theatlantic.com/education/archive/2014/01/why-are-american-colleges-obsessed-with-leadership/283253/.
2. Antonakis, J., & Day, D. V. (2018). Leadership: Past, present, and future. In J. Antonakis & D. V. Day (Eds.), *The nature of leadership* (p. 3–26). Sage Publications, Inc.
3. House, R. J., & Aditya, R. N. (1997). The social scientific study of leadership: Quo Vadis? *Journal of Management, 23*, 409–473.
4. Judge, T. A., Bono, J. E., Ilies, R., & Gerhardt, M. W. (2002). Personality and leadership: A qualitative and quantitative review. *Journal of Applied Psychology, 87*, 765–780.
5. House, R. J., & Aditya, R. N. (1997). The social scientific study of leadership: Quo Vadis? *Journal of Management, 23*, 409–473; Ilies, R., Gerhardt, M. W., & Huy, L. (2004). Individual differences in leadership emergence: Integrating meta-analytic findings and behavioral genetics estimates. *International Journal of Selection and Assessment, 12*, 207–219; Lord, R. G., De Vader, C. L., & Alliger, G. M. (1986). A meta-analysis of the relation between personality traits and leadership perceptions: An application of validity generalization procedures. *Journal of Applied Psychology, 71*, 402–410; Taggar, S., Hackett, R., & Saha, S. (1999). Leadership emergence in autonomous work teams: Antecedents and outcomes. *Personnel Psychology, 52*, 899–926.
6. Judge, T. A., Colbert, A. E., & Ilies, R. (2004). Intelligence and leadership: A quantitative review and test of theoretical propositions. *Journal of Applied Psychology, 89*, 542–552.
7. Antonakis, J., House, R. J., Simonton, D. K. (2017). Can super smart leaders suffer from too much of a good thing? The curvilinear effect of intelligence on perceived leadership behavior. *Journal of Applied Psychology, 102,* 1003–1021.
8. Goleman, D. (January, 2004). What makes a leader? *Harvard Business Review, 82*(1), 82–91.
9. Badura, K. L., Grijalva, E., Galvin, B. M., Owens, B. P., & Joseph, D. L. (2020). Motivation to lead: A meta-analysis and distal-proximal model of motivation and leadership. *Journal of Applied Psychology, 105*, 331–354; Judge, T. A., Bono, J. E., Ilies, R., & Gerhardt, M. W. (2002). Personality and leadership: A qualitative and quantitative review. *Journal of Applied Psychology, 87*, 765–780.
10. Buckmaster, J. (2008, May). How does he manage? Classified Web site boss. *Management Today*, 15.
11. Judge, T. A., Bono, J. E., Ilies, R., & Gerhardt, M. W. (2002). Personality and leadership: A qualitative and quantitative review. *Journal of Applied Psychology, 87*, 765–780; Toegel, G., Barsoux, J. L. (2012). How to become a better leader. *MIT Sloan Management Review, 53(3)*, 51–60.
12. Atwater, L. E., Dionne, S. D., Camobreco, J. F., Avolio, B. J., & Lau, A. (1998). Individual attributes and leadership style: Predicting the use of punishment and its effects. *Journal of Organizational Behavior, 19*, 559–576; Niebuhr, R. E., & Davis, K. R. (1984). Self-esteem: Relationship with leader behavior perceptions as moderated by the duration of the superior-subordinate dyad association, *Personality and Social Psychology Bulletin, 10*, 51–59.
13. Judge, T. A., & Cable, D. M. (2004). The effect of physical height on workplace success and income: Preliminary test of a theoretical model. *Journal of Applied Psychology, 89*, 428–441.
14. Reave, L. (2005). Spiritual values and practices related to leadership effectiveness. *Leadership Quarterly, 16*, 655–687.
15. Field, H. (May 10, 2018). 15 quotes on success from America's top CEOs. *Entrepreneur.* Retrieved from https://www.entrepreneur.com/article/313227.
16. House, R. J., & Aditya, R. N. (1997). The social scientific study of leadership: Quo Vadis? *Journal of Management, 23*, 409–473.
17. Judge, T. A., Bono, J. E., Ilies, R., & Gerhardt, M. W. (2002). Personality and leadership: A qualitative and quantitative review. *Journal of Applied Psychology, 87*, 765–780.
18. Hackman, J. R., & Wageman, R. (2007). Asking the right questions about leadership: Discussion and conclusions. *American Psychologist, 62*, 43–47.
19. Retrieved from http://www.entrepreneur.com/article/249205.
20. See House, R. J., & Aditya, R. N. (1997). The social scientific study of leadership: Quo Vadis? *Journal of Management, 23*, 409–473.
21. Nystrom, P. C. (1978). Managers and the hi-hi leader myth. *Academy of Management Journal, 21*, 325–331.
22. Judge, T. A., Piccolo, R. F., & Ilies, R. (2004). The forgotten ones? The validity of consideration and initiating structure in leadership research. *Journal of Applied Psychology, 89*, 36–51.
23. Miles, R. H., & Petty, M. M. (1977). Leader effectiveness in small bureaucracies. *Academy of Management Journal, 20*, 238–250.
24. Seltzer, J., & Numerof, R. E. (1988). Supervisory leadership and subordinate burnout. *Academy of Management Journal, 31*, 439–446.
25. Miller, K. I., & Monge, P. R. (1986). Participation, satisfaction, and productivity: A meta-analytic review. *Academy of Management Journal, 29*, 727–753.
26. Baumgartel, H. (1957). Leadership style as a variable in research administration. *Administrative Science Quarterly, 2*, 344–360.
27. Vroom, V. H., & Mann, F. C. (1960). Leader authoritarianism and employee attitudes. *Personnel Psychology, 13*, 125–140.
28. Judge, T. A., & Piccolo, R. F. (2004). Transformational and transactional leadership: A meta-analytic test of their relative validity. *Journal of Applied Psychology, 89*, 755–768.
29. Skogstad, A., Einarsen, S., Torsheim, T., Aasland, M. S., & Hetland, H. (2007). The destructiveness of laissez-faire leadership behavior. *Journal of Occupational Health Psychology, 12*, 80–92.
30. Fiedler, F. (1967). *A theory of leadership effectiveness*. New York: McGraw-Hill; Fiedler, F. E. (1964). A contingency model of leader effectiveness. In L. Berkowitz (Ed.), *Advances in experimental social psychology* (Vol. 1, pp. 149–190). New York: Academic Press.
31. Peters, L. H., Hartke, D. D., & Pohlmann, J. T. (1985). Fiedler's contingency theory of leadership: An application of the meta-analysis procedures of Schmidt and Hunter. *Psychological Buletin, 97*, 274–285; Strube, M. J., & Garcia, J. E. (1981). A meta-analytic investigation of Fiedler's contingency model of leadership effectiveness. *Psychological Buletin, 90*, 307–321; Vecchio, R. P. (1983). Assessing the validity of Fiedler's contingency model of leadership effectiveness: A closer look at Strube and Garcia. *Psychological Buletin, 93*, 404–408.
32. Hersey, P. H., Blanchard, K. H., & Johnson, D. E. (2007). *Management of Organizational Behavior: Leadership human resources.* Upper Saddle River, NJ: Prentice Hall.
33. Retrieved from http://www.situational.com/Views/SituationalLeadership/RightHereRightNow.aspx.
34. Blank, W., Green, S. G., & Weitzel, J. R. (1990). A test of the situational leadership theory. *Personnel Psychology, 43*, 579–597; Graeff, C. L. (1983). The situational leadership theory: A critical review. *Academy of Management Review, 8*, 285–291; Fernandez, C. F., & Vecchio, R. P. (2002). Situational leadership theory revisited: A test of an across-jobs perspective. *Leadership Quarterly, 8*, 67–84.
35. House, R. J. (1971). A path goal theory of leader effectiveness. *Administrative Science Quarterly, 16*(3), 321–338.
36. House, R. J. (1996). Path-goal theory of leadership: Lessons, legacy, and a reformulated theory. *Leadership Quarterly, 7*, 323–352; House, R. J., & Mitchell, T. R. (1974). Path-goal theory of leadership. *Journal of Contemporary Business, 3*, 81–97.
37. House, R. J., & Aditya, R. N. (1997). The social scientific study of leadership: Quo Vadis? *Journal of Management, 23*, 409–473; Stinson, J. E., & Johnson, T. W. (1975). The path-goal theory of leadership: A partial test and suggested refinement. *Academy of Management Journal, 18*, 242–252; Wofford, J. C., & Liska, L. Z. (1993). Path-goal theories of leadership: A meta-analysis. *Journal of Management, 19*, 857–876.
38. Vroom, V. H. (2000). Leadership and the decision making process. *Organizational Dynamics, 68*, 82–94; Vroom, V. H., & Yetton, P. W. (1973). *Leadership and decision-making*. Pittsburgh: University of Pittsburgh Press; Jago, A., & Vroom, V. H. (1980). An evaluation of two alternatives to the Vroom/Yetton Normative Model. *Academy of Management Journal, 23*, 347–355; Vroom, V. H., & Jago, A. G. (1988). *The new leadership: Managing participation in organizations*. Englewood Cliffs, NJ: Prentice Hall.
39. Retrieved from http://www.inc.com/marla-tabaka/10-cheap-ways-to-reduce-employee-stress.html.
40. Vroom, V. H., & Jago, G. (1978). On the validity of the Vroom Yetton model. *Journal of Applied Psychology, 63*, 151–162.
41. Bass, B. M. (1985). *Leadership and performance beyond expectations*. New York: Free Press; Burns, J. M. (1978). *Leadership*. New York: Harper & Row.
42. Bass, B. M. (1985). *Leadership and performance beyond expectations*. New York: Free Press; Burns, J. M. (1978). *Leadership*. New York: Harper & Row; Bycio, P., Hackett, R. D., & Allen, J. S. (1995). Further assessment of Bass's (1985) conceptualization of transactional and transformational leadership. *Journal of Applied Psychology, 80*, 468–478; Judge, T. A., & Piccolo, R. F. (2004). Transformational and transactional leadership: A meta-analytic test of their relative validity. *Journal of Applied Psychology, 89*, 755–768.
43. Shamir, B., House, R. J., & Arthur, M. B. (1993). The motivational effects of charismatic leadership: A self-concept based theory. *Organization Science, 4*, 577–594.
44. Judge, T. A., & Piccolo, R. F. (2004). Transformational and transactional leadership: A meta-analytic test of their relative validity. *Journal of Applied Psychology, 89*, 755–768.

45. Herold, D. M., Fedor, D. B., Caldwell, S., & Liu, Y. (2008). The effects of transformational and change leadership on employees' commitment to a change: A multilevel study. *Journal of Applied Psychology, 93*, 346–357; Piccolo, R. F., & Colquitt, J. A. (2006). Transformational leadership and job behaviors: The mediating role of core job characteristics. *Academy of Management Journal, 49*, 327–340; Schaubroeck, J., Lam, S. K., & Cha, S. E. (2007). Embracing transformational leadership: Team values and the impact of leader behavior on team performance. *Journal of Applied Psychology, 92*, 1020–1030; Shin, S. J., & Zhou, J. (2003). Transformational leadership, conservation, and creativity: Evidence from Korea. *Academy of Management Journal, 46*, 703–714; Wang, H., Law, K. S., Hackett, R. D., Duanxu, W., & Zhen, X. C. (2005). Leader-member exchange as a mediator of the relationship between transformational leadership and followers' performance and organizational citizenship behavior. *Academy of Management Journal, 48*, 420–432.
46. Judge, T. A., & Piccolo, R. F. (2004). Transformational and transactional leadership: A meta-analytic test of their relative validity. *Journal of Applied Psychology, 89*, 755–768.
47. Dirks, K. T., & Ferrin, D. L. (2002). Trust in leadership: Meta-analytic findings and implications for research and practice. *Journal of Applied Psychology, 87*, 611–628.
48. Bono, J. E., & Judge, T. A. (2004). Personality and transformational and transactional leadership: A meta-analysis. *Journal of Applied Psychology, 89*, 901–910.
49. Barling, J., Weber, T., & Kelloway, E. K. (1996). Effects of transformational leadership training on attitudinal and financial outcomes: A field experiment. *Journal of Applied Psychology, 81*, 827–832; Dvir, T., Eden, D., Avolio, B. J., & Shamir, B. (2002). Impact of transformational leadership on follower development and performance: A field experiment. *Academy of Management Journal, 45*, 735–744; Frese, M., Beimel, S., & Schoenborg, S. (2003). Action training for charismatic leadership: Two evaluations of studies of a commercial training module on inspirational communication of a vision. *Personnel Psychology, 56*, 671–697.
50. Khurana, R. (2002, September). The curse of the superstar CEO. *Harvard Business Review, 80*(9), 60–66.
51. Agle, B. R., Nagarajan, N. J., Sonnenfeld, J. A., & Srinivasan, D. (2006). Does CEO charisma matter? An empirical analysis of the relationships among organizational performance, environmental uncertainty, and top management team perceptions of CEO charisma. *Academy of Management Journal, 49*, 161–174.
52. Retrieved from http://www.rantsports.com/nfl/2015/01/22/top-ten-greatest-quarterbackcoach-combos-in-nfl-history/.
53. Dansereau, F., Jr., Graen, G., & Haga, W. J. (1975). A vertical dyad linkage approach to leadership within formal organizations: A longitudinal investigation of the role making process. *Organizational Behavior & Human Performance, 13*(1), 46–78; Erdogan, B., & Liden, R. C. (2002). Social exchanges in the workplace: A review of recent developments and future research directions in leader-member exchange theory. In L. L. Neider & C. A. Schriesheim (Eds.), *Leadership* (pp. 65–114). Greenwich, CT: Information Age Press; Gerstner, C. R., & Day, D. V. (1997). Meta-analytic review of leader-member exchange theory: Correlates and construct issues. *Journal of Applied Psychology, 82*, 827–844; Graen, G. B., & Uhl-Bien, M. (1995). Relationship-based approach to leadership: Development of leader-member exchange (LMX) theory over 25 years: Applying a multi-level multi-domain perspective. *Leadership Quarterly, 6*(2), 219–247; Liden, R. C., & Maslyn, J. M. (1998). Multidimensionality of leader-member exchange: An empirical assessment through scale development. *Journal of Management, 24*, 43–72.
54. Gerstner, C. R., & Day, D. V. (1997). Meta-analytic review of leader-member exchange theory: Correlates and construct issues. *Journal of Applied Psychology, 82*, 827–844; Hui, C., Law, K. S., & Chen, Z. X. (1999). A structural equation model of the effects of negative affectivity, leader-member exchange, and perceived job mobility on in-role and extra-role performance: A Chinese case. *Organizational Behavior and Human Decision Processes, 77*, 3–21; Kraimer, M. L., Wayne, S. J., & Jaworski, R. A. (2001). Sources of support and expatriate performance: The mediating role of expatriate adjustment. *Personnel Psychology, 54*, 71–99; Liden, R. C., Wayne, S. J., & Sparrowe, R. T. (2000). An examination of the mediating role of psychological empowerment on the relations between the job, interpersonal relationships, and work outcomes. *Journal of Applied Psychology, 85*, 407–416; Settoon, R. P., Bennett, N., & Liden, R. C. (1996). Social exchange in organizations: Perceived organizational support, leader-member exchange, and employee reciprocity. *Journal of Applied Psychology, 81*, 219–227; Tierney, P., Farmer, S. M., & Graen, G. B. (1999). An examination of leadership and employee creativity: The relevance of traits and relationships. *Personnel Psychology, 52*, 591–620; Wayne, S. J., Shore, L. M., & Liden. R. C. (1997). Perceived organizational support and leader-member exchange: A social exchange perspective. *Academy of Management Journal, 40*, 82–111.
55. Martin, R., Guillaume, Y., Thomas, G., Lee, A., & Epitropaki, O. (2016). Leader–member exchange (LMX) and performance: A meta-analytic review. *Personnel Psychology, 69*, 67–121.
56. Ilies, R., Nahrgang, J. D., & Morgeson, F. P. (2007). Leader-member exchange and citizenship behaviors: A meta-analysis. *Journal of Applied Psychology, 92*, 269–277.
57. Bauer, T. N., Erdogan, B., Liden, R. C., & Wayne, S. J. (2006). A longitudinal study of the moderating role of extraversion: Leader-member exchange, performance, and turnover during new executive development. *Journal of Applied Psychology, 91*, 298–310; Erdogan, B., Kraimer, M. L., & Liden, R. C. (2004). Work value congruence and intrinsic career success. *Personnel Psychology, 57*, 305–332; Major, D. A., Kozlowski, S. W., Chao, G. T., & Gardner, P. D. (1995). A longitudinal investigation of newcomer expectations, early socialization outcomes, and the moderating effects of role development factors. *Journal of Applied Psychology, 80*, 418–431.
58. Ferris, G. R. (1985). Role of leadership in the employee withdrawal process: A constructive replication. *Journal of Applied Psychology, 70*, 777–781; Graen, G. B., Liden, R. C., & Hoel, W. (1982). Role of leadership in the employee withdrawal process. *Journal of Applied Psychology, 67*, 868–872.
59. Masterson, S. S., Lewis, K., Goldman, B. M., & Taylor, M. S. (2000). Integrating justice and social exchange: The differing effects of fair procedures and treatment on work relationships. *Academy of Management Journal, 43*, 738–748.
60. Bauer, T. N., & Green, S. G. (1996). Development of a leader-member exchange: A longitudinal test. *Academy of Management Journal, 39*, 1538–1567.
61. Colella, A., & Varma, A. (2001). The impact of subordinate disability on leader-member exchange relationships. *Academy of Management Journal, 44*, 304–315; Maslyn, J. M., & Uhl-Bien, M. (2001). Leader-member exchange and its dimensions: Effects of self-effort and other's effort on relationship quality. *Journal of Applied Psychology, 86*, 697–708; Janssen, O., & Van Yperen, N. W. (2004). Employees' goal orientations, the quality of leader-member exchange, and the outcomes of job performance and job satisfaction. *Academy of Management Journal, 47*, 368–384; Wing, L., Xu, H., & Snape, E. (2007). Feedback-seeking behavior and leader-member exchange: Do supervisor-attributed motives matter? *Academy of Management Journal, 50*, 348–363.
62. Engle, E. M., & Lord, R. G. (1997). Implicit theories, self-schemas, and leader-member exchange. *Academy of Management Journal, 40*, 988–1010; Liden, R. C., Wayne, S. J., & Stilwell, D. (1993). A longitudinal study on the early development of leader-member exchanges. *Journal of Applied Psychology, 78*, 662–674; Wayne, S. J., Shore, L. M., & Liden. R. C. (1997). Perceived organizational support and leader-member exchange: A social exchange perspective. *Academy of Management Journal, 40*, 82–111.
63. Erdogan, B., Liden, R. C., & Kraimer, M. L. (2006). Justice and leader-member exchange: The moderating role of organizational culture. *Academy of Management Journal, 49*, 395–406.
64. Duarte, N. T., Goodson, J. R., & Klich, N. R. (1994). Effects of dyadic quality and duration on performance appraisal. *Academy of Management Journal, 37*, 499–521.
65. Heneman, R. L., Greenberger, D. B., & Anonyuo, C. (1989). Attributions and exchanges: The effects of interpersonal factors on the diagnosis of employee performance. *Academy of Management Journal, 32*, 466–476.
66. Retrieved from http://www.forbes.com/sites/hbsworkingknowledge/2013/05/01/why-isnt-servant-leadership-more-prevalent/.
67. Greenleaf, R. K. (1977). *Servant leadership: A journey into the nature of legitimate power and greatness* (p. 335). Mahwah, NJ: Paulist Press; Liden, R. C., Wayne, S., J., Zhao, H., & Henderson, D. (2008). Servant leadership: Development of a multidimensional measure and multi-level assessment. *Leadership Quarterly, 19*, 161–177.
68. Serafeim, G. (September/October 2020). Social impact efforts that create real value. *Harvard Business Review, 98* (5).
69. Liden, R. C., Wayne, S., J., Zhao, H., & Henderson, D. (2008). Servant leadership: Development of a multidimensional measure and multi-level assessment. *Leadership Quarterly, 19*, 161–177.
70. Liden, R. C., Wayne, S., Liao, C., & Meuser, J. (2014). Servant leadership and serving culture: Influence on individual and unit performance. *Academy of Management Journal, 57*, 1434–1542.
71. Hu, J., & Liden, R. C. (2011). Antecedents of team potency and team effectiveness: An examination of goal and process clarity and servant leadership. *Journal of Applied Psychology, 96*, 851–862.
72. Buchanan, L. (2007, May). In praise of selflessness: Why the best leaders are servants. *Inc, 29*(5), 33–35.
73. Avolio, B. J., & Gardner, W. L. (2005). Authentic leadership development: Getting to the root of positive forms of leadership. *Leadership Quarterly, 16*, 315–338; Gardner, W. L., Avolio, B. J., Luthans, F., May, D. R., & Walumbwa, F. (2005). "Can you see the real me?" A self-based model of authentic leader and follower development. *Leadership Quarterly, 16*, 343–372; George, B. (2007). Authentic leaders: They inspire and empower others. *Leadership Excellence, 24*(9), 16–17; Ilies, R., Morgeson, F. P., & Nahrgang, J. D. (2005). Authentic leadership and eudaemonic well-being: Understanding leader-follower outcomes. *Leadership Quarterly, 16*, 373–394; Sparrowe, R. T. (2005). Authentic leadership and the narrative self. *Leadership Quarterly, 16*, 419–439.
74. Shamir, B., & Eilam, G. (2005). What's your story? A life-stories approach to authentic leadership development. *Leadership Quarterly, 16*, 395–417.
75. Walumbwa, F. O., Avolio, B. J., Gardner, W. L., Wernsing, T. S., & Peterson, S. J. (2008). Authentic leadership: Development and validation of a theory-based measure. *Journal of Management, 34*, 89–126.

76. Barnes, C. M., Lucianetti, L., Bhave, D. B., & Christian, M. S. (2015). "You wouldn't like me when I'm sleepy": Leaders' sleep, daily abusive supervision, and work unit engagement. *Academy of Management Journal, 58*, 1419–1437; Tepper, B. J. (2000). Consequences of abusive supervision. *Academy of Management Journal, 43,* 178–190; Tepper, B. J. (2007). Abusive supervision in work organizations: Review, synthesis, and research agenda. *Journal of Management, 33,* 261–289.
77. Tu, M.-H., Bono, J. E., Shum, C., & LaMontagne, L. (in press). Breaking the cycle: The effects of role model performance and ideal leadership self-concepts on abusive supervision spillover. *Journal of Applied Psychology*.
78. Foulk, T. A., Lanaj, K., Tu, M. H., Erez, A., & Archambeau, L. (2018). Heavy Is the head that wears the crown: An actor-centric approach to daily psychological power, abusive leader behavior, and perceived incivility. *Academy of Management Journal, 61*, 661–684.
79. Chiu, C. Y., Owens, B. P., & Tesluk, P. E. (2016). Initiating and utilizing shared leadership in teams: The role of leader humility, team proactive personality, and team performance capability. *Journal of Applied Psychology, 101*, 1705–1720; Owens, B. P., & Hekman, D. R. (2016). How does leader humility influence team performance? Exploring the mechanisms of contagion and collective promotion focus. *Academy of Management Journal, 59*, 1088–1111; Rego, A. et al. (in press). Leader humility and team performance: Exploring the mediating mechanisms of team PsyCap and task allocation effectiveness. *Journal of Management*.
80. Hu, J., Erdogan, B., Jiang, K., Bauer, T. N., & Liu, S. (2018). Leader humility and creativity in teams: The role of advice network density and team values. *Journal of Applied Psychology, 103*, 313–323.
81. Eagly, A. H., Johannesen-Schmidt, M. C., & van Engen, M. L. (2003). Transformational, transactional, and laissez-faire leadership styles: A meta-analysis comparing women and men. *Psychological Bulletin, 129,* 569–591; Eagly, A. H., & Johnson, B. T. (1990). Gender and leadership style: A meta-analysis. *Psychological Bulletin, 108,* 233–256; Eagly, A. H., Makhijani, M. G., & Klonsky, B. G. (1992). Gender and the evaluation of leaders: A meta-analysis. *Psychological Bulletin, 111*, 3–22; Roth, P. L., Purvis, K. L., & Bobko, P. (2012). A meta-analysis of gender group differences for measures of job performance in field studies. *Journal of Management, 38,* 719–739.
82. Sergent, K., & Stajkovic, A. D. (2020). Women's leadership is associated with fewer deaths during the COVID-19 crisis: Quantitative and qualitative analyses of United States governors. *Journal of Applied Psychology, 105*, 771-783.
83. Frese, M., Beimel, S., & Schoenborg, S. (2003). Action training for charismatic leadership: Two evaluations of studies of a commercial training module on inspirational communication of a vision. *Personnel Psychology, 56*, 671–697; Shamir, B., House, R. J., & Arthur, M. B. (1993). The motivational effects of charismatic leadership: A self-concept based theory. *Organization Science, 4*, 577–594.
84. Buchanan, L. (2007, May). In praise of selflessness: Why the best leaders are servants. *Inc, 29*(5), 33–35; Douglas, M. E. (2005, March). Service to others. *Supervision, 66*(3), 6–9; Ramsey, R. D. (2005, October). The new buzz word. *Supervision, 66*(10), 3–5.
85. Case written by Rachel Mattenberger, Talya Bauer, and Berrin Erdogan to accompany Bauer, T. N. & Erdogan, B. (2021). *Organizational Behavior: Bridging Science and Practice (4.0).* Boston, MA: FlatWorld. Partially based on ideas and information contained in BOF team (2018). Why Stitch Fix is Developing a Company of Leaders. https://www.businessoffashion.com/articles/careers/why-stitch-fix-is-developing-a-company-of-leaders; Macrotrends. (2020). Stitch Fix market cap 2016-2020. Retrieved from https://www.macrotrends.net/stocks/charts/SFIX/stitch-fix/market-cap; Forbes, M. (2018). How Stitch Fix's Katrina Lake Built a $3 Billion Business. https://www.forbes.com/sites/moiraforbes/2018/08/09/katrina-lake-billion-dollar-business/amp; Thomas, L. (2020, March 10). Stitch Fix shares are taking as Wall Street fears core business could be reaching saturation point. CNBC. Retrieved from https://www.cnbc.com/2020/03/10/stitch-fix-shares-are-tanking-biz-could-be-near-saturation-point.html.

CHAPTER 10
Decision Making

Decca records distributed music by Bing Crosby, Count Basie, and the Rolling Stones—but their decision to pass on signing the British band the Beatles tops many experts' lists of worst business decisions of all time. The Beatles sold a historic 15 million records in 1964 alone and had the top five singles as well as 12 of the Billboard Hot 100 songs that same year. To date, no other artist or band has topped these accomplishments or reached over 250 million album sales like the Beatles.

Source: Lenscap Photography/Shutterstock.com

Chapter Learning Objectives

Reading this chapter will help you accomplish the following:

1. Understand the meaning of decision making.
2. Know key causes of poor decision making.
3. Compare and contrast individual and group decision making.
4. Understand how to develop your own personal decision-making skills.

TABLE 10.1 The P-O-L-C Framework

Planning	Organizing	Leading	Controlling
1. Vision & Mission	1. Organizational Design	1. Leadership	1. Systems/Processes
2. Strategizing	2. Culture	2. Decision Making	2. Strategic Human Resources
3. Goals & Objectives	3. Social Networks	3. Communications	
		4. Groups/Teams	
		5. Motivation	

Leadership effectiveness is often a reflection of the decisions that leaders make or fail to make. In this chapter, we explain both ideal and actual decision-making processes within organizations. Understanding how decisions are made, how they can be biased, and how to make decisions better, are key skills for effective individuals and managers.

10.1 Understanding Decision Making

Learning Objectives

1. Define decision making.
2. Understand different types of decisions.
3. Identify ways to enhance creativity.

Decision Making Defined

decision making

Making choices among alternative courses of action, including inaction.

Decision making refers to selecting choices among alternative courses of action—which may also include inaction. While it can be argued that management *is* decision making, a 2020 Gallup survey indicates that only 24% of managers in the United States strongly agree that well-thought-out decisions impacting organizations are made by their peers and just 14% strongly agree that their organizations make decisions at a satisfactory speed.[1] Therefore, increasing effectiveness in decision making is an important part of maximizing effectiveness at work. This chapter provides insights regarding decision making alone or in a group while avoiding common decision-making errors.

Individuals throughout organizations use the information they gather to make a wide range of decisions. These decisions may affect the lives of others and change the course of an organization. For example, the decisions made by executives and consulting firms for Enron ultimately resulted in a $60 billion loss for investors, thousands of employees without jobs, and the loss of all employee retirement funds. Sherron Watkins, a former Enron employee and now-famous whistleblower, uncovered the accounting problems and tried to enact change. Similarly, the decisions made by firms to trade in mortgage-backed securities had negative consequences for the entire U.S. economy.

Because many decisions involve an ethical component, one of the most important considerations in management is whether the decisions individuals make are ethical. Here are some basic questions to assess the ethics of a decision.[2]

- Is this decision fair?
- Will I feel better or worse about myself after I make this decision?
- Does this decision break any organizational rules?
- Does this decision break any laws?
- How would I feel if this decision was broadcast on the news?

Legendary scientist Albert Einstein was known for his tendency to incorporate a programmed decision into his dressing choices by wearing very similar outfits daily and not wearing socks.

Source: By Ferdinand Schmutzer - http://www.bhm.ch/de/news_04a.cfm?bid=4&jahr=2006, Public Domain, https://commons.wikimedia.org/w/index.php?curid=12851706

Types of Decisions

Most discussions of decision making assume that only senior executives make decisions or that only senior executives' decisions matter. This is a dangerous mistake. —Peter Drucker

To ensure consistency around the globe, such as at this St. Petersburg, Russia, location, McDonald's trains all restaurant managers (more than 275,000) at Hamburger University locations in Chicago, Tokyo, London, Sydney, Moscow, Munich, Sao Paulo, and Shanghai, where they take the equivalent of two years of college courses and learn how to make decisions. The curriculum is taught in 28 languages.

Source: forden/Shutterstock.com

programmed decisions

Choices that occur frequently enough that we develop an automated response to them.

decision rule

Automated responses used to make programmed decisions.

nonprogrammed decisions

Unique, nonroutine, and important decisions that require conscious thinking, information gathering, and careful consideration of alternatives.

strategic decisions

Decisions that are made to set the course of an organization.

tactical decisions

Decisions about how things will get done.

operational decisions

Decisions employees make each day to make the organization function.

Despite the far-reaching nature of decisions, not all decisions have major consequences or even require extensive thought. For example, individuals make simple and habitual decisions such as what to wear, what to eat, and which route to take to and from home and work. These mundane decisions usually do not take much time. Such straightforward decisions are termed **programmed decisions**; these are decisions that occur frequently enough that we develop an automated response to them. The automated response we use to make these decisions is called a **decision rule**. For example, many restaurants face customer complaints as a routine part of doing business. Because this is a recurring problem for restaurants, it may be regarded as a programmed decision. To deal with this problem, the restaurant might have a policy stating that every time they receive a valid customer complaint, the customer should receive a free dessert, which represents a decision rule.

On the other hand, unique and important decisions require conscious thinking, information gathering, and careful consideration of alternatives. These are called **nonprogrammed decisions**. For example, decisions such as how to deal with lower than expected earnings, who to appoint to an open position, or who to choose as the supplier are among the important nonprogrammed decisions facing organizations. Research indicates that nonprogrammed decisions require energy and that making such choices may deplete subsequent efforts by decision makers.[3]

Decision making can also be classified into three categories based on the level at which they occur.

1. **Strategic decisions** set the course for an organization. Changing strategic direction or introducing a new product that requires years of development would represent a strategic decision.
2. **Tactical decisions** are decisions about how things will get done. For example, issuing a coupon to increase sales would fall into this category.
3. **Operational decisions** are decisions that employees make each day to run the organization. Helping serve customer needs through routine interactions or order fulfillment would be an example of this type of decision.

In this chapter, we are going to discuss different decision-making models designed to understand and evaluate the effectiveness of nonprogrammed decisions. We will cover four decision-making approaches, including the rational decision-making model, the bounded rationality decision-making model, the intuitive decision-making model, and the creative decision-making model.

Making Rational Decisions

rational decision-making model

A decision-making model which describes the series of steps that decision makers should consider if their goal is to maximize their outcome.

The **rational decision-making model** describes a series of steps that decision makers should consider if their goal is to maximize the quality of their outcomes. This model presents formal steps with the goal of achieving an optimal result in terms of the quality of a decision.

The rational decision-making model is best applied to major decisions where the costs are high and the consequences of different decision outcomes are significant. For example, the model can be applied to the decision to purchase a new car. Step 1 involves the recognition that a new vehicle is needed. Step 2 involves selecting factors that are important, such as fuel economy, cost, and the number of passengers that the vehicle can accommodate comfortably.

Step 3 involves deciding how important each factor is in the decision outcome. For example, if price and gas mileage are key factors, they might outweigh other factors, with color or other options given medium or low importance. Step 4 requires generation of all alternatives concerning options. In step 5, information is used to evaluate each alternative against established criteria. Step 6 involves selecting the most attractive alternative. Step 7 involves executing the decision by completing the car purchase. Step 8 entails evaluating the decision; if you purchase a car and have a good experience, you are more likely to buy another car of the same model and manufacturer.

FIGURE 10.1 Steps in the Rational Decision-Making Model

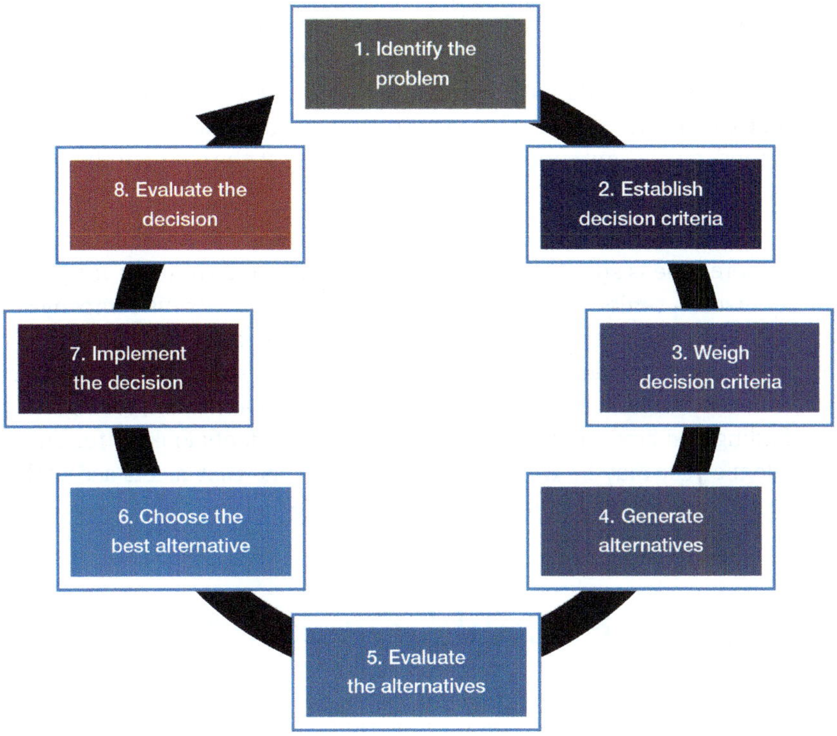

While decision makers can get off track during any of these steps, research shows that limiting the search for alternatives in the fourth step can be the most challenging and lead to failure. In fact, one researcher found that in 85% of the decisions studied, no alternatives were identified.[4] Conversely, successful managers are clear about what they want at the outset of the decision-making process, set objectives for others to respond to, carry out an unrestricted search for solutions, get key people to participate, and avoid using their power to influence the decision outcome.[5]

The rational decision-making model has important lessons for decision makers. First, when making a decision, establish **decision criteria** before beginning the search for **alternatives**. This prevents decision makers from favoring one option too much and setting criteria accordingly. For example, let's say someone started browsing for cars before setting decision criteria. They may come across a car that reflects their sense of style and form an emotional bond regarding the car. This bond might convince them that the fuel economy of the car and the innovative braking system are the most important criteria. After their purchase, they may realize that the car is too small for their friends, which limits their ability to take long trips. Setting criteria before searching for alternatives can prevent individuals from making such mistakes. Another advantage of the rational model is that it urges decision makers to generate an exhaustive set of alternatives instead of only a few. By generating a large number of alternatives covering a wide range of possibilities, individuals are likely to make a more effective decision, which does not sacrifice one criterion for the sake of another.

decision criteria

A set of parameters against which all of the potential options in decision making will be evaluated.

alternatives

Possible solutions to a problem in the decision-making process.

Despite all its benefits, the rational decision-making model involves a number of unrealistic assumptions. It assumes that people understand what decision is to be made, that they know all their available choices, that they have no perceptual biases, and that they want to make optimal decisions. Nobel Prize–winning economist Herbert Simon observed that while the rational decision-making model may be a helpful tool for working through problems, it does not represent how decisions are frequently made within organizations. In fact, Simon argued that more can be learned from studying how and when individuals deviate from the model than examining how to follow it more closely.

In most day-to-day decisions, individuals rarely sit down and complete all eight steps in the rational decision-making model. For example, the search for all possible alternatives can be time consuming and individuals are often under time pressure to make decisions. Moreover, even when access to all information is possible, it can be challenging to compare the pros and cons of each alternative and rank them according to preferences. Anyone who has recently purchased a new laptop or cellphone can attest to the challenge of sorting through the different strengths and limitations of each brand, model, and support plans and arriving at the solution that best meets their needs.

analysis paralysis

A decision-making process where more and more time is spent on gathering information and thinking about it but no decisions actually get made.

The availability of too much information and too many choices can lead to **analysis paralysis**, where more and more time is spent on gathering information and thinking about it, but no decisions actually get made. A senior executive at Hewlett-Packard admits his company suffered from this spiral of analyzing things for too long to the point where data gathering led to "not making decisions, instead of us making decisions."[6] Moreover, individuals may not always be interested in reaching an optimal decision. Home buyers may be willing and able to invest a great deal of time and energy in finding and creating their dream home, but students looking for an apartment to rent for the academic year may be willing to take the first one that meets acceptable criteria of being clean, close to campus, and within a certain price range.

Making "Good Enough" Decisions

Mattel's Magic 8 Ball may be a useful toy when making "good enough" decisions.

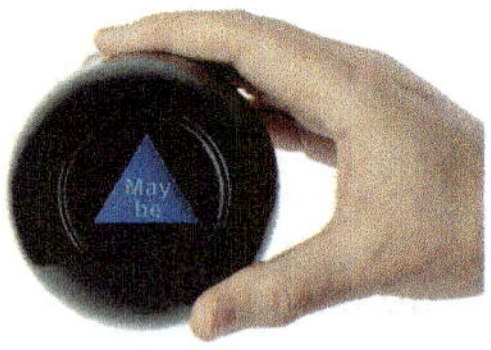

Source: Shutterstock.com

The **bounded rationality model** of decision making recognizes the limitations of decision-making processes. According to this model, individuals knowingly limit their options to a manageable set and choose the best alternative without conducting an exhaustive search for alternatives. An important part of the bounded rationality approach is the tendency to **satisfice**, which refers to accepting the first alternative that meets your minimum criteria. For example, many college graduates do not conduct a national or international search for potential job openings; instead, they focus their search on a limited geographic area and tend to accept the first offer in their chosen area, even if it may not be the ideal job situation. Satisficing is similar to rational decision making, but it differs in that rather than choosing the best choice and maximizing the potential outcome, the decision maker saves time and effort by accepting the first alternative that meets the minimum threshold. Ironically, research actually supports that taking this approach may be effective as too many choices actually lead to fewer choices being made. Research in both the lab and in the field finds that individuals are more likely to purchase a jar of gourmet jam, chocolates, or to do an optional essay assignment in class when they are offered six choices rather than twenty or more. And those with fewer choices also reported being more satisfied with their choice.[7]

bounded rationality model

A model that recognizes the limitations of decision-making processes. According to this model, individuals knowingly limit their options to a manageable set and choose the best alternative without conducting an exhaustive search for alternatives.

satisfice or satisficing

Accepting the first alternative that meets minimum criteria.

Making Intuitive Decisions

The **intuitive decision-making model** has emerged as an alternative to other decision-making processes. The model argues that in a given situation, experts making decisions scan the environment for cues to recognize patterns. This model refers to arriving at decisions without conscious reasoning.

intuitive decision-making model

Arriving at decisions without conscious reasoning. The model argues that in a given situation, experts making decisions scan the environment for cues to recognize patterns.

Managers make decisions under challenging circumstances with time pressures, constraints, a great deal of uncertainty, highly visible and high-stakes outcomes, and within changing conditions. Thus, it makes sense that they would not have the time to formally work through all the steps of the rational decision-making model. Yet when CEOs, financial analysts, and healthcare workers are asked about the critical decisions they make, seldom do they attribute success to luck. To an outside observer, it may seem like they are making guesses as to the course of action to take, but it turns out that they are systematically making decisions using a different model than was suspected earlier. Research on life-or-death decisions made by fire chiefs, pilots, and nurses finds that these experts do not choose among a list of well-thought-out alternatives. The intuitive decision-making model argues that, in a given situation, experts making decisions scan the environment for cues to recognize patterns.[8] Once a pattern is recognized, they can play a potential course of action through to its outcome based on their prior experience. Due to training, experience, and knowledge, these decision makers have an idea of how well a given solution may work. If they run through the mental model and find that the solution will not work, they alter the solution and retest it before setting it into action. If it still is not deemed a workable solution, it is discarded as an option and a new idea is tested until a workable solution is found. Once a viable course of action is identified, the decision maker puts the solution into motion. The key point is that only one choice is considered at a time. Novices are not able to make effective decisions this way because they do not have enough prior experience to draw upon.[9]

Intuitive decisions rely on scanning the environment for cues to recognize patterns and make decisions quickly.

Source: Debby Wong/ Shutterstock.com

Making Creative Decisions

In addition to the rational decision making, bounded rationality, and intuitive decision-making models, creative decision making is a vital part of being an effective decision maker. **Creativity** is the generation of new, imaginative ideas. With the flattening of organizations and intense competition among organizations, individuals and organizations are driven to be creative in decisions ranging from cutting costs to creating new ways of doing business. While creativity is the first step in the innovation process, creativity and innovation are not the same thing. Innovation begins with creative ideas, but it also involves realistic planning and follow-through.

creativity

The generation of new ideas that are original, fluent, and flexible.

The five steps to creative decision making are similar to the previous decision-making models in some keys ways. All of the models include *problem identification*, which is the step in which the need for problem solving becomes apparent. If individuals do not recognize that a problem exists, it is impossible to solve any potential dilemma. *Immersion* is the step in which the decision maker thinks about the problem consciously and gathers information. A key to success in creative decision making is having or acquiring expertise in the area being studied. Then *incubation* occurs. During incubation, the individual sets the problem aside and does not think about it for a while. At this time, the brain is actually working on the problem unconsciously. Then comes *illumination*, or the insight moment, when the solution to the problem becomes apparent to the person, usually when it is least expected. This is the "Eureka!" (meaning, "I have found it!") moment similar to what happened to the ancient Greek inventor Archimedes, who discovered how to measure the density of an object while taking a bath. Finally, the *verification and application* stage happens, when the decision maker consciously verifies the feasibility of the solution and implements the decision.

A NASA scientist describes his decision-making process leading to a creative outcome as follows—he had been trying to figure out a better way to de-ice planes to make the process faster and safer. After recognizing the problem, he had immersed himself in the literature to understand all the options, and he worked on the problem for months trying to figure out a solution. It was not until he was sitting outside a McDonald's restaurant with his grandchildren that it dawned on him. The golden arches of the "M" of the McDonald's logo inspired his solution: he would design the deicer as a series of M's![10] This represented the illumination stage. After he tested and verified his creative solution—he was done with that problem except to reflect on the outcome and process.

FIGURE 10.2 The Creative Decision-Making Process

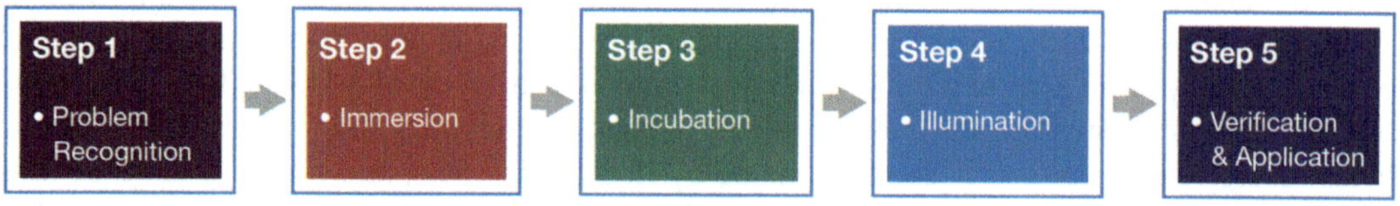

TABLE 10.2 Which Decision-Making Model Should I Use?

Decision-Making Model	Use the Model on the Left When:
Rational	Information on alternatives can be gathered and quantified.
	The decision is important.
	You are trying to maximize your outcome.
Bounded rationality	The minimum criteria are clear.
	You do not have or you are not willing to invest much time to make the decision.
	You are not trying to maximize your outcome.
Intuitive	Goals are unclear.
	There is time pressure and analysis paralysis would be costly.
	You have experience with the problem.
Creative	Solutions to the problem are not clear.
	New solutions need to be generated.
	You have time to immerse yourself in the issues.

How Do You Know If Your Decision-Making Process Is Creative?

Researchers focus on three factors to evaluate the level of creativity in the decision-making process. **Fluency** refers to the number of ideas a person is able to generate. **Flexibility** refers to how different the ideas are from one another. **Originality** refers to how unique a person's ideas are. You might say that serial entrepreneurs (those entrepreneurs who successfully start and grow different businesses) possess high levels of originality, flexibility, and fluency. Elon Musk (cofounder of PayPal and Tesla Motors) and Jack Dorsey (cofounder of Twitter and Square) are among those who developed businesses that ended up being game-changers in their industries.

FIGURE 10.3 Dimensions of Creativity

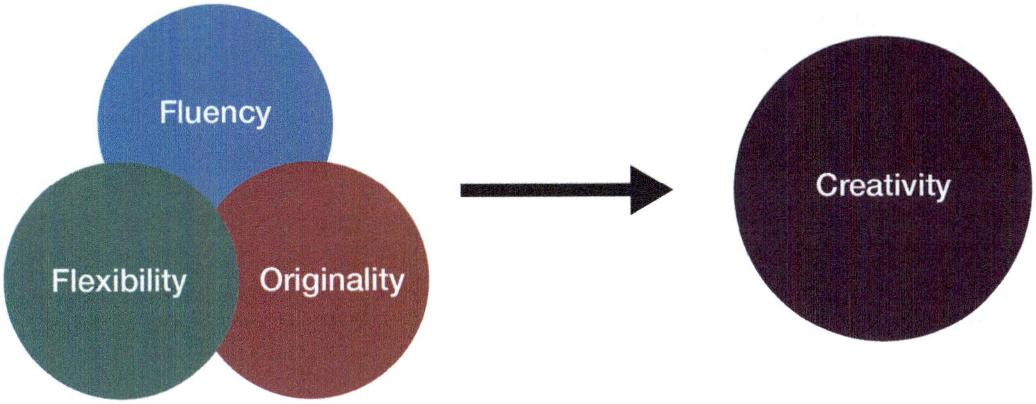

Some experts have proposed that creativity occurs as an interaction among three factors: (1) people's personality traits (openness to experience, risk taking), (2) their attributes (expertise, imagination, motivation), and (3) the context (encouragement from others, time pressure, and physical structures).[11] For example, research shows that individuals who are open to experience, less conscientious, more self-accepting, seek more feedback, and are more impulsive, tend to be more creative.[12]

There are many techniques available that enhance and improve creativity. As discussed in Chapter 4, SCAMPER is a checklist tool that helps you think of changes you can make to an existing marketplace to create a new one—a new product, a new service, or both. You can use these changes either as direct suggestions or as starting points for later thinking. This, in turn, can inspire creative ideas.

The purchase of a new home is generally considered a situation where rational decision-making should be used.

Source: Shutterstock.com

fluency

The number of ideas a person is able to generate.

flexibility

How different the ideas are from one another. If decision makers are able to generate several unique solutions to a problem, they are high on flexibility.

originality

How unique a person's ideas are.

brainstorming

A process of generating ideas that follows a set of guidelines, which includes no criticism of ideas during the process, the idea that no suggestion is too crazy, and building on other ideas (piggybacking).

idea quotas

A set number of ideas a group must reach before they are done with brainstorming.

wildstorming

A variation of brainstorming where the group focuses on ideas that are impossible and then imagines what would need to happen to make them possible.

crowdsourcing

Outsourcing a problem to a crowd.

Linus Pauling, the Nobel prize winner and referred to as one of the twenty greatest scientists of all time, said, "The best way to have a good idea is to have a lot of ideas."[13] One popular way to generate ideas is to use brainstorming. **Brainstorming** is a group process of generating ideas that follows a set of guidelines that include no criticism of ideas during the brainstorming process, the idea that no suggestion is too crazy, and building on other ideas (piggybacking). Research shows that the quantities of ideas actually leads to better idea quality in the end, so setting high **idea quotas** where the group must reach a set number of ideas before they are done is recommended to avoid process loss and to maximize the effectiveness of brainstorming. Another unique aspect of brainstorming is that the more people who are included in brainstorming, the better the decision outcome will be because the variety of backgrounds and approaches give the group more to draw from. Interestingly, research also shows that having group members brainstorm alone without interaction with each other before engaging in team brainstorming results in higher quality and quantities of ideas.[14] A variation of brainstorming is **wildstorming** where the group focuses on ideas that are impossible and then imagines what would need to happen to make them possible.[15]

A recent alternative to brainstorming is **crowdsourcing**. For some problems, gathering experts into the same room may not be feasible because the organization may not have the diversity of skills or expertise needed. Therefore, organizations are relying on the power of the masses to creatively solve business problems. Crowdsourcing is outsourcing a problem to a crowd. This process enlists the help of experts, amateurs, and those with a passion for problem solving. For example, Netflix announced in 2006 that they would pay $1 million to someone who would improve the match between their movie recommendations and customers' own ratings. The winning team improved Netflix's own recommendation algorithm by more than 10% and was awarded the cash prize in 2009. Companies are using crowdsourcing for identifying new markets and new trends, solving complex technical problems, and generating ideas for specific problems. Many individuals may work on the same problem alone and in isolation, or they may break up into small groups to collaborate.[16]

Ideas for Enhancing Organizational Creativity

Organizational creativity is vital to organizations. Here are some guidelines for enhancing organizational creativity within teams.[17]

Team Composition (Organizing/Leading)

- *Diversify your team* to give them more inputs to build on and more opportunities to create functional conflict while avoiding personal conflict.
- *Change group membership* to stimulate new ideas and new interaction patterns.
- *Leaderless teams* can allow teams freedom to create without trying to please anyone up front.

Team Process (Leading)

- *Engage in brainstorming* to generate ideas—but remember to set a high goal for the number of ideas the group should come up with, encourage wild ideas, and allow individuals to brainstorm alone before brainstorming in a group.
- *Use the nominal group technique in person or electronically* to avoid some common group process pitfalls. Consider anonymous feedback as well.
- *Use analogies* to envision problems and solutions.

Leadership (Leading)

- *Challenge teams* so that they are engaged but not overwhelmed.
- *Let people decide how to achieve goals*, rather than telling them what goals to achieve.
- *Support and celebrate creativity* even when it leads to a mistake. But set up processes to learn from mistakes as well.
- *Model* creative behavior.

Culture (Organizing)

- *Create routines* so that individuals do not spend time on routine tasks.
- *Build a physical space conducive to creativity* that is playful and humorous—this is a place where ideas can thrive.
- *Incorporate creative behavior* into the performance appraisal process.

The four different decision-making models—rational, bounded rationality, intuitive, and creative—vary in terms of how experienced or motivated a decision maker is to make a choice. Choosing the right approach will make you more effective at work and improve your ability to carry out all the P-O-L-C functions.

Key Takeaway

Decision making is choosing among alternative courses of action. There are different types of decisions, ranging from automatic, programmed decisions to more intensive nonprogrammed decisions. Structured decision-making processes include rational decision making, bounded rationality, intuitive, and creative decision making. Each of these can be useful, depending on the circumstances and the problem that needs to be solved.

Discussion Questions

1. What do you see as the main difference between a successful and an unsuccessful decision? How much does luck versus skill have to do with it? How much time needs to pass to answer the first question?
2. Research has shown that over half of the decisions made within organizations fail. Does this surprise you? Why or why not?
3. Have you used the rational decision-making model to make a decision? What was the context? How well did the model work?
4. Share an example of a decision where you used satisficing. Were you happy with the outcome? Why or why not? When would you be most likely to engage in satisficing?
5. Do you think intuition is respected as a decision-making style? Do you think it should be? Why or why not?

10.2 Faulty Decision Making

Learning Objectives

1. Understand overconfidence bias and how to avoid it.
2. Understand hindsight bias and how to avoid it.
3. Understand anchoring bias and how to avoid it.
4. Understand framing bias and how to avoid it.
5. Understand escalation of commitment and how to avoid it.

Daniel Kahneman (yet another Nobel prize winner) and Amos Tversky spent decades studying how individuals make decisions. They found that individuals are influenced by a number of biases. Understanding the nature of decision biases (also called cognitive biases) helps individuals avoid areas where their decision processes may be flawed. Below we explain the biases of anchoring and adjustment, availability bias, confirmation bias, escalation of commitment, framing bias, fundamental attribution error, hindsight bias, correlation and causality bias, overconfidence bias, and sampling bias.

Potential Challenges to Decision Making

Anchoring and Adjustment Bias

anchoring and adjustment bias

The tendency for individuals to rely too heavily on a single piece of information.

Anchoring and adjustment bias refers to the tendency for individuals to rely too heavily on arbitrary numbers, irrelevant traits or facts when making decisions. Job seekers often fall into this trap by focusing on their previous pay or a desired salary while ignoring other aspects of the job offer, such as additional benefits, their own experience, and the potential value of the working environment. Similarly, but more dramatically, lives were lost in the Great Bear Wilderness Disaster when the coroner declared all five passengers of a small plane dead within five minutes of arriving at the accident scene, which halted the search effort for potential survivors, when, in fact, the next day two survivors walked out of the forest. How could a mistake like this have been made? One theory is that decision biases played a large role in this serious error; anchoring on the fact that the plane had been consumed by flames led the coroner to call off the search for any possible survivors.[18]

Availability Bias

availability bias

A situation in which information that is more readily available is viewed as more likely to occur.

Availability bias refers to a situation in which information that is more readily available is seen as more likely to occur. For example, an illustrative study asked participants if they thought individuals were more likely to die of auto accidents or stomach cancer and, if so, by how much. Most people reported that auto accidents caused more deaths—likely because auto accidents are reported more in the news compared to stomach cancer fatalities at a rate of more than 100 to 1 while the true difference between them is actually less than 2-to-1. A less dramatic example is when you purchase a car that is white, and suddenly, you start noticing white cars all around you that you never noticed before. There aren't more white cars, but you notice them more.

Music Rap-Up: You Can't Trust Me

Twinprov perform a rap on commonly held decision biases.

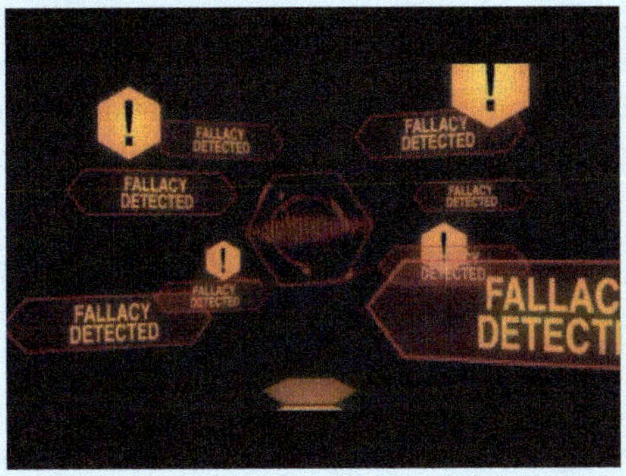

View in the online reader

Confirmation Bias

Confirmation bias occurs when a certain idea or belief is held.[19] Because we believe it, we focus and weigh information more heavily when it aligns with our beliefs and stop gathering information once we've found evidence in support of our beliefs. Finally, this bias can cause us to discount information that might serve to discredit our beliefs. Once in place, these deeply held beliefs are challenging to discount—even in the face of a great deal of opposing information.[20]

The Mandela Effect is a decision bias where individuals strongly remember something that never actually occurred such as the line, "Luke, I am your father." in *Star Wars*.

Source: Stefano Buttafoco/ Shutterstock.com

Escalation of Commitment Bias

Escalation of commitment bias occurs when individuals continue on a failing course of action after information reveals this may be a poor path to follow. It is sometimes called sunk costs fallacy because the continuation is often based on the idea that one has already invested in this course of action. For example, imagine a person purchases a used car that turns out to need another repair every few weeks. An effective way of dealing with this situation of having a "lemon car" might be to sell the car without incurring further losses, donate the car, or drive it without repairing it until it falls apart. However, many people spend hours of their time and hundreds, even thousands of dollars repairing the car in the hopes that they will justify their initial investment in buying the car.

A variety of reasons exist for escalation of commitment.[21] Research shows that two reasons are particularly important to understanding why escalation of commitment bias may occur.[22] First, decision makers do not want to admit that they were wrong and escalation of commitment is related to a desire to save face and preserve one's reputation. Second, time invested into the failing cause of action is associated with escalation of commitment. Decision makers may incorrectly believe that spending more time and energy might somehow help them recover their losses. Effective decision makers avoid escalation of commitment by distinguishing between when persistence may actually pay off versus when persistence might mean escalation of commitment.

confirmation bias

The tendency to process and analyze information in such a way that it supports one's preexisting ideas and beliefs.

escalation of commitment bias

When individuals continue on a failing course of action after information reveals this may be a poor path to follow.

Escalation of commitment is part of the game at casinos where "the house always wins" is a key component of the business model

Source: Shutterstock.com

Framing Bias

Framing bias refers to the tendency of decision makers to be influenced by the way that a situation or problem is presented. For example, when making a purchase, customers find it easier to let go of a discount as opposed to accepting a surcharge, even though they both might cost the person the same amount of money. Similarly, customers tend to prefer a statement such as "85% lean beef" as opposed to "15% fat"![23] It is important to be aware of this tendency because, depending on how a problem is presented, individuals choose an alternative that is disadvantageous simply because of how it is framed.

framing bias

The tendency of decision makers to be influenced by the way that problems are framed.

Fundamental Attribution Error

Twentieth Century Fox signing over merchandising rights to the Star Wars franchise to George Lucas for $350,000 in 1977—with its eventual value now estimated to be more than $42 billion (and counting)—seems like a big failure now. However, at the time, the deal made sense to Fox who had recently lost a lot of money due to a merchandise failure of the 1967 film, Doctor Dolittle. This is an example of hindsight bias.

Source: Willrow Hood/Shutterstock.com

fundamental attribution error

A situation in which good outcomes are attributed to personal characteristics, such as intelligence, but undesirable outcomes are attributed to external circumstances, such as weather.

Fundamental attribution error refers to a bias that exists when positive outcomes are seen as a function of personal characteristics while negative outcomes are attributed to external circumstances. In a classroom setting, a student who received a good grade in a class might be tempted to attribute this outcome to their own intelligence or exceptional work ethic. On the other hand, poor-performing students might blame course testing procedures or quality of education provided by the instructor.

Hindsight Bias

Hindsight bias occurs when individuals look backward in time where mistakes made seem obvious after they have already occurred. In other words, after a largely unpredictable event, many individuals are likely to think that they already knew an outcome was going to happen. Once we know the outcome of a situation, it is hard for us to imagine how we would have acted without such knowledge. Hindsight bias becomes a problem especially when judging someone else's decisions. For example, the term "Monday morning quarterback" has become a common phrase associated with individuals that criticize the decisions of football players in hindsight of games played the previous weekend. Therefore, it is important for decision makers to remember this bias before passing judgments on other people's actions.

hindsight bias

It occurs when a person, looking at the past, judges that a mistake that was made should have been recognized as a mistake at the time.

Judgments about Correlation and Causality Bias

How does employee satisfaction impact a firm's sales? Three elements are necessary to understand why a particular action leads to a particular outcome. These elements, which might lead to **judgments about correlation and causality bias**, include (1) correlation (Do sales increase when employees are satisfied? Do sales decrease when employees are dissatisfied?), (2) temporal order (Does an increase in employee satisfaction occur before sales increase?), and (3) ruling out other potential causes (Is something else causing increases in both satisfaction of employees and firm sales?). The first two items can be easily tracked, while the third can be difficult to isolate. Such frustration in tying actions to performance has led to one commonly quoted phrase in the business realm: "I know that half of my marketing dollars are effective, I'm just not sure which half."

judgments about correlation and causality bias

A situation in which individuals make inaccurate attributions about the causes of events.

Sampling Bias

Sampling bias occurs when individuals make generalizations from a small sample (or a single source) of information rather than through large, randomly-drawn samples that represent a wide audience. Rumors within the workplace also provide an example of the type of information that could lead to such misunderstandings. Another common example of sampling bias is using one's own personal experience and treating it like a common experience.

An example of sampling bias would be if you like mint chocolate chip ice cream you felt it meant that it was the most popular ice cream flavor (which happens to be vanilla at 27% versus 3% for chocolate chip).

Source: Shutterstock.com

sampling bias

When individuals draw broad conclusions from small sets of observations instead of more reliable sources of information derived from large, randomly-drawn samples.

Overconfidence Bias

overconfidence bias

When individuals overestimate their ability to predict future events.

Overconfidence bias occurs when individuals overestimate their ability to predict future events. Many people exhibit signs of overconfidence. For example, 82% of surveyed drivers feel they are in the top 30% of safe drivers, 86% of students at the Harvard Business School say they are better looking than their peers, and doctors consistently overestimate their ability to detect problems.[24] Much like individuals who are 100% sure they can pick the winners of this week's football games despite evidence to the contrary, these individuals are suffering from overconfidence bias. People who purchase lottery tickets as a way to make money are probably suffering from overconfidence bias—it is three times more likely for a person driving 10 miles to buy a lottery ticket to be killed in a car accident than to win the jackpot.[25]

10.3 Decision Making in Groups

Learning Objectives

1. Understand the pros and cons of individual and group decision making.
2. Learn to recognize the signs of groupthink.
3. Recognize different tools and techniques for making better decisions.

When It Comes to Decision Making, Are Two Heads Better Than One?

The answer to this question depends on several factors. Group decision making has the advantages of drawing from the experiences and perspectives of a larger number of individuals. Hence, a group may have the potential to be more creative and lead to more effective decisions. In fact, groups may also sometimes achieve results beyond what they could have done as individuals through effective delegation and division of labor and expertise. Groups may make the task more enjoyable for members. Finally, when the decision is made by a group rather than a single individual, implementation of the decision will be easier because group members will be invested in the decision. If the group is diverse, better decisions may be made because different group members may have different ideas based on their background and experiences. Research shows that for top management teams, groups that debate issues and that are diverse make decisions that are more comprehensive and better for the bottom line.[26]

social loafing

The tendency of individuals to put in less effort when working in a group context.

groupthink

The tendency to avoid critical evaluations of ideas the group favors.

Despite the necessity of utilizing groups within organizations, group decision making suffers from a number of disadvantages. For example, groups rarely outperform their best member.[27] While groups have the potential to arrive at an effective decision, they often suffer from process losses. One reason is that groups may suffer from coordination problems. Anyone who has worked with a team of individuals on a project can attest to the difficulty of coordinating members' work or even coordinating everyone's presence in a team meeting. Furthermore, groups can suffer from **social loafing**, or the tendency of some members to put forth less effort while working within a group. Groups may also suffer from **groupthink**, the tendency to avoid critical evaluation of ideas the group favors. Finally, group decision making takes a longer time compared with individual decision making, given that all members need to discuss their thoughts regarding different alternatives.

Thus, whether an individual or a group decision is preferable will depend on the specifics of the situation. For example, if there is an emergency and a decision needs to be made quickly, individual decision making might be preferred. Individual decision making may also be appropriate if the individual in question has all the information needed to make the decision and if implementation problems are not expected. On the other hand, if one person does not have all the information and skills needed to make the decision, if implementing the decision will be difficult without the involvement of those who will be affected by the decision, and if time urgency is more modest, then group decision making may be more effective.

TABLE 10.3 Advantages and Disadvantages of Different Levels of Decision Making

Individual Decision Making		Group Decision Making	
Pros	**Cons**	**Pros**	**Cons**
Typically faster than group decision making	Fewer ideas	Diversity of ideas and can piggyback on others' ideas	Takes longer
Best individual in a group usually outperforms the group	Identifying the best individual can be challenging	Greater commitment to ideas	Group dynamics such as groupthink can occur
Accountability is easier to determine	Possible to put off making decisions if left alone to do it	Interaction can be fun and serves as a teambuilding task	Social loafing—harder to identify responsibility for decisions

Groupthink

Have you ever been in a decision-making group that you felt was heading in the wrong direction, but you restrained yourself from speaking up? If so, you may have been a victim of **groupthink**. Groupthink is a tendency to avoid a critical evaluation of ideas the group favors. Irving Janis, author of a book called *Victims of Groupthink*, explained that groupthink is characterized by eight symptoms:[28]

groupthink
A tendency to avoid a critical evaluation of ideas the group favors.

1. *Illusion of invulnerability* shared by most or all of the group members that creates excessive optimism and encourages members to take extreme risks.
2. *Collective rationalizations* where members downplay negative information or warnings that might cause individuals to reconsider their assumptions.
3. *An unquestioned belief in the group's inherent morality* that may incline members to ignore ethical or moral consequences of their actions.
4. *Stereotyped views of out-groups* are seen when groups discount rivals' abilities to make effective responses.
5. *Direct pressure* on any member who expresses strong arguments against any of the group's stereotypes, illusions, or commitments.
6. *Self-censorship* when members of the group minimize their own doubts and counterarguments.
7. *Illusions of unanimity* based on self-censorship and direct pressure on the group; the lack of dissent is viewed as unanimity.
8. *The emergence of self-appointed mindguards* where one or more members protect the group from information that runs counter to the group's assumptions and course of action.

Avoiding groupthink can be a matter of life or death. In January 1986, the space shuttle *Challenger* exploded 73 seconds after liftoff, killing all seven astronauts aboard. The decision to launch *Challenger* that day, despite problems with mechanical components of the vehicle and unfavorable weather conditions, is cited as a tragic example of groupthink.

Source: NASA public domain photo at https://spaceflight.nasa.gov/gallery/images/shuttle/sts-51l/html/s85-44253.html

devil's advocate

Someone who is assigned the role of challenging and questioning the group. This person may prevent the group from premature agreement.

While research on groupthink has not confirmed all of the theory, groups do tend to suffer from symptoms of groupthink when they are large and when the group is cohesive because the members like each other.[29] The assumption is that the more frequently a group displays one or more of the eight symptoms, the worse the quality of their decisions will be. However, if your group is cohesive, it is not necessarily doomed to engage in groupthink.

Recommendations for Avoiding Groupthink

Groups Should

- Discuss the symptoms of groupthink and how to avoid them.
- Assign a rotating **devil's advocate** to every meeting. A devil's advocate is someone who is assigned the role of challenging and questioning the group, and may prevent the group from premature agreement.
- Invite experts or qualified colleagues who are not part of the core decision-making group to attend meetings, and get reactions from outsiders on a regular basis and share these with the group.
- Encourage a culture of inclusiveness where different ideas are valued.
- Debate the ethical implications of the decisions and potential solutions being considered.

Individuals Should

- Monitor their own behavior for signs of groupthink and modify behavior if needed.
- Check themselves for self-censorship.
- Carefully avoid mindguard behaviors.
- Avoid putting pressure on other group members to conform.
- Remind members of the ground rules for avoiding groupthink if they get off track.

Group Leaders Should

- Break the group into two subgroups from time to time.
- Have more than one group work on the same problem if time and resources allow it. This makes sense for highly critical decisions.
- Remain impartial and refrain from stating preferences at the outset of decisions.
- Set a tone of encouraging critical evaluations throughout deliberations.
- Create an anonymous feedback channel where all group members can contribute if desired.

Tools and Techniques for Making Better Decisions

Consensus means reaching an agreement and is a decision-making rule that groups may use when the goal is to gain support for an idea or plan of action. While consensus tends to take longer in the first place, it may make sense when support is needed to enact the plan. The process works by discussing the issues, generating a proposal, calling for consensus, and discussing any concerns. If concerns still exist, the proposal is modified to accommodate them. These steps are repeated until consensus is reached. Thus this decision-making rule is inclusive, participatory, cooperative, and democratic. Research shows that consensus can lead to better accuracy,[30] and it helps members feel greater satisfaction with decisions[31] and to have greater acceptance. However, groups take longer with this approach and groups that cannot reach consensus become frustrated.[32]

consensus

A decision-making rule that groups may use when the goal is to gain support for an idea or plan of action. The ideas are discussed and proposals are modified until a unanimous decision is reached.

The **Delphi Technique** is unique because it is a group process using written responses to a series of questionnaires instead of physically bringing individuals together to make a decision. The first questionnaire asks individuals to respond to a broad question, such as stating the problem, outlining objectives, or proposing solutions. Each subsequent questionnaire is built from the information gathered in the previous one. The process ends when the group reaches a consensus. Facilitators can decide whether to keep responses anonymous. This process is often used to generate best practices from experts. For example, Purdue University professor Michael Campion used this process when he was editor of the research journal *Personnel Psychology* and wanted to determine the qualities that distinguished a good research article. Using the Delphi Technique, he was able to gather responses from hundreds of top researchers from around the world without ever having to leave his office and distill them into a checklist of criteria that he could use to evaluate articles submitted to the journal.[33]

Delphi Technique

A group process that uses written responses to a series of questionnaires instead of physically bringing individuals together to make a decision.

Ethical champions have been found to be able to move groups to be more ethically aware, to reduce moral disengagement, and, ultimately, to engage in more ethical team decisions.[34] One effective tool for ethical champions is to create a business frame that highlights the business benefits of ethical decisions. Nurses and other health care providers face decisions all day long. Recommendations for them to behave as ethical champions include ensuring that every patient and family member is treated with compassion and respect, supporting their own personal decision making, and to help them resolve conflicts about their care.[35]

ethical champions

Refer to team members who step up to champion an ethical decision in their team.

Majority rule refers to a decision-making rule where each member of the group is given a single vote, and the option that receives the greatest number of votes is selected. This technique has remained popular, perhaps because of its simplicity, speed, ease of use, and representational fairness. Research also supports majority rule as an effective decision-making technique.[36] However, those who did not vote in favor of the decision will be less likely to support it.

majority rule

A decision-making rule where each member of the group is given a single vote and the option that receives the greatest number of votes is selected.

Nominal Group Technique (NGT), a technique we discussed in Chapter 4, was developed to help with group decision making by ensuring that all members participate fully. NGT is not a technique to be used at all meetings routinely. Rather, it is used to structure group meetings when members are grappling with problem solving or idea generation. It follows four steps.[37] First, each member of the group engages in a period of independently and silently writing down ideas. Second, the group goes in order around the room to gather all the ideas that were generated. This continues until all ideas have been shared. Third, a discussion takes place around each idea and members ask for and give clarification and make evaluative statements. Finally, individuals vote for their favorite ideas by using either ranking or rating techniques. Following the four-step NGT helps to ensure that all members participate fully and avoids group decision-making problems such as groupthink.

Nominal Group Technique (NGT)

A technique designed to help with group decision making by ensuring that all members participate fully.

group decision support systems

Interactive computer-based systems that are able to combine communication and decision technologies to help groups make better decisions.

knowledge management systems

Systems for managing knowledge in organizations, supporting creation, capture, storage, and dissemination of information.

decision trees

Diagrams where answers to yes or no questions lead decision makers to address additional questions until they reach the end of the tree.

Group decision support systems (GDSS) are interactive computer-based systems that are able to combine communication and decision technologies to help groups make better decisions. Organizations know that having effective **knowledge management systems** to share information is important and their spending reflects this reality. Research shows that a GDSS can actually improve the output of group collaborative work through higher information sharing.[38] As the popularity of these systems grows, they risk becoming counterproductive. Humans can only process so many ideas and information at one time. As virtual meetings grow larger, it is reasonable to assume that information overload can occur and good ideas will fall through the cracks, essentially recreating a problem that the GDSS was intended to solve that is to make sure every idea is heard. Another problem is the system possibly becoming too complicated. If the systems evolve to a point of uncomfortable complexity, it has recreated the problem of the bully pulpit and shyness. Those who understand the interface will control the narrative of the discussion, while those who are less savvy will only be along for the ride.[39] Lastly, many of these programs fail to take into account the factor of human psychology. These systems could make employees more reluctant to share information due to lack of control, lack of immediate feedback, the fear of online backlash.

Decision trees are diagrams in which answers to yes or no questions lead decision makers to address additional questions until they reach the end of the tree. Decision trees are helpful in avoiding errors such as framing bias.[40] Decision trees tend to be helpful in guiding the decision maker to a predetermined alternative and ensuring consistency of decision making—that is, every time certain conditions are present, the decision maker will follow one course of action as opposed to others if the decision is made using a decision tree.

Key Takeaway

There are trade-offs between making decisions alone and within a group. Groups have greater diversity of experiences and ideas than individuals, but they also have potential process losses such as groupthink. Groupthink can be avoided by recognizing the eight symptoms discussed. Finally, there are a variety of tools and techniques available for helping to make more effective decisions in groups, including the Nominal Group Technique, Delphi Technique, majority rule, consensus, GDSS, and decision trees.

Discussion Questions

1. Do you prefer to make decisions in a group or alone? What are the main reasons for your preference?
2. Have you been in a group that used the brainstorming technique? Was it an effective tool for coming up with creative ideas? Please share examples.
3. Have you been in a group that experienced groupthink? If so, how did you deal with it?
4. Which of the decision-making tools discussed in this chapter (NGT, Delphi, etc.) have you used? How effective were they?

10.4 Developing Your Personal Decision-Making Skills

Learning Objectives

1. Understand techniques to avoid making poor decisions.
2. Learn how to utilize a project premortem.

Perform a Project "Premortem" to Fix Problems Before They Happen

Doctors routinely perform postmortems to understand what went wrong with a patient who has died. The idea is for everyone to learn from the unfortunate outcome so that future patients will not meet a similar fate. In a similar vein, research suggests that the simple exercise of imagining what could go wrong with a given decision can increase the ability to identify reasons for future successes or failures by 30%.[41] A "premortem" is a way to imagine and to avoid what might go wrong before spending a cent or having to change course along the way.[42]

Gary Klein, an expert on decision making in fast-paced, uncertain, complex, and critical environments, recommends that decision makers follow this six-step premortem process to increase their chances of success.

1. A planning team comes up with an outline of a plan, such as the launching of a new product.
2. Either the existing group or a unique group is then told to imagine looking into a crystal ball and seeing that the new product failed miserably. They then write down all the reasons they can imagine that might have led to this failure.
3. Each team member shares items from their list until all the potential problems have been identified.
4. The list is reviewed for additional ideas.
5. The issues are sorted into categories in the search for themes.
6. The plan should then be revised to correct the flaws and avoid these potential problems.

The premortem technique allows groups to truly delve into "what if" scenarios. For example, in a premortem session at a *Fortune* 50 company, an executive imagined that a potential billion-dollar environmental sustainability project might fail because the CEO had retired.

Key Takeaway

There are a number of ways to learn about decision making that can help make you more effective. If the decision is important, conduct a premortem to anticipate what might go wrong. When a decision is going to involve others, be proactive in getting them to buy in before the decision is made. Individuals and groups can suffer from decision-making traps and process losses. Understanding that you can spot and avoid these traps is important in helping to make you a more effective manager.

Discussion Questions

1. How might you use the premortem technique to be more effective within groups at school or work?
2. Imagine that your good friend is starting a new job next week as a manager. What recommendations would you give your friend to be successful with decision making at work when starting out?

10.5 Case in Point: Making the Decision to Invest in Detroit

Source: Shutterstock.com

Unexpected problems often require unexpected solutions and the history of transportation is full of surprises and ingenious solutions. Back in the late 1800s, major cities were facing a huge problem. In New York City, the vast amount of waste generated by horse-drawn transportation (an estimated 3 million pounds of manure each day) was increasing at an alarming rate. In fact, it was predicted that if the problem remained unaddressed, manure would reach the third story windows of Manhattan by 1930. New York City, along with other major cities at the time, struggled to develop a remedy to this dire situation. Thankfully, an unexpected solution rendered the need for horse-drawn transportation obsolete: the invention of the automobile. By 1912, the number of cars outnumbered horses and by 1917, the city's last horse-drawn streetcar stopped running. Fast-forward to the 1950s and the automobile market was thriving, with most of the production taking place in Detroit, Michigan. Nicknamed the Motor City, Detroit's automobile sector employed upwards of 300,000 individuals at the height of its production. But by the 2000s,

Detroit's automobile industry was in severe decline. The shuttering of auto factories resulted in unemployment, record levels of defaults in housing, and an estimated 78,000 city structures were abandoned.

From those challenges emerged new industries and now Detroit is home to a new transportation industry . . . bicycles. What is so surprising about this is that the bicycle industry in the United States has been dwindling as brands such as Huffy and Trek moved the production of their bicycles to other countries. In fact, 99% of bicycles sold in the United States are not made here. However, a few bicycle companies in Detroit are experiencing unprecedented growth. Take, for example, Detroit Bikes. Founded in 2011 by Zak Pashak who invested $2.5 million into a 50,000 square foot factory, Detroit Bikes not only assembles bikes in Detroit but also manufactures as many of the parts as possible. The factory is staffed by auto industry veterans from GM and other carmakers and is capable of producing up to 150 bikes per day and assembling up to 400 bikes per day.

But, the road to success has been rocky for the company. In an interview, the founder Zak Pashak admitted that several decisions that the company made early on were mistakes. One example was that the company focused on consumers rather than on the distribution channel for selling to consumers. He also notes that his attitude was overly confident and that affected his decision making along the way. For example, when he thought that the organization was going to get a large order in San Francisco, he ramped up staffing to 50 employees. When that deal fell through, he cut back staff to only 10 full-time employees. The company produces up to 10,000 bikes per year and in 2020, began assembly of Canadian-owned Schwinn's classic Collegiate cruiser in a partnership with them.

Detroit Bikes isn't the only company vying for attention in Detroit. Shinola is a large competitor who made the decision to hand-assemble their bicycles in Detroit rather than creating most of the parts locally, as Detroit Bikes does (except for their recent partnership with Schwinn, which is assembly only). Shinola was founded in 2011 and made the decision to diversify its offerings to include watches (they produce up to 700 watches per day) and leather watch bands and other leather products. Their watches are sold in companies ranging from Walmart to Neiman Marcus. Shinola employs over 500 people. They design all their products in Detroit and then source parts globally with assembly back in Detroit as well. Their decision seems to be paying off, as their brand and diversification strategies have led to the expansion to hotels (The Shinola Hotel, a boutique hotel in Downtown Detroit, is 8 stories high) and an online publication, *The Journal*.

Even though Detroit has seen unemployment rates as high as 21%, Shinola decided to pay its employees more than minimum wage and offer generous medical benefits. As the founders say, "If we take care of our people, they'll take care of our customers and our business." This decision has paid off so far as the company continues to enter new markets with a consistent mantra of "We start with the best product we can find (or imagine) and then make the numbers work."

The stories of Detroit Bikes and Shinola demonstrate that there often are multiple ways to solve problems. While both companies saw an opportunity to invest in the economy of Detroit, they each took different paths. Only time will tell if their decision to locate in Detroit and go "all in" on the city as part of the brand will pay off for Detroit Bikes and Shinola.[43]

Multimedia Extension—Detroit Bikes Manufacturing

View in the online reader

Multimedia Extension—Take a Tour of Shinola

View in the online reader

Case Discussion Questions

1. Were you surprised by the solution to the problem of horse waste in New York City during the late 1800s? What implications do you think this case has on decision making and generating alternative solutions to problems?
2. In addition to hand-assembling their bikes, Detroit Bikes manufactures many of their own parts. Do you think the decision to manufacture their own parts will be profitable in the long run? Please explain.
3. How did the overconfidence of Zak Pashak, founder of Detroit Bikes, negatively impact the company?
4. In what way(s) are the decisions made by Shinola similar to Detroit Bikes? In what way(s) are they different?
5. Please give two examples of how Shinola decided to invest in its employees.

Endnotes

1. Musser, C., & Sundaram, D. (2020, May 13). Steps to effective decision-making in organizations. Gallup. https://www.gallup.com/workplace/310439/steps-effective-decision-making-organizations.aspx.
2. Adapted from ideas contained in Blanchard, K., & Peale, N. V. (1988). *The power of ethical management*. New York: William Morrow.
3. Vohs, K. D., Baumeister, R. F., Schmeichel, B. J., Twenge, J. M., Nelson, N. M., & Tice, D. M. (2008). Making choices impairs subsequent self-control: A limited-resource account of decision making, self-regulation, and active initiative. *Journal of Personality and Social Psychology, 94*, 883–898.
4. Nutt, P. C. (1994). Types of organizational decision processes. *Administrative Science Quarterly, 29*, 414–550.
5. Nutt, P. C. (1998). Surprising but true: Half the decisions in organizations fail. *Academy of Management Executive, 13*, 75–90.
6. Zell, D. M., Glassman, A. M., & Duron, S. A. (2007). Strategic management in turbulent times: The short and glorious history of accelerated decision making at Hewlett-Packard. *Organizational Dynamics, 36*, 93–104.
7. Iyengar, S. S., & Lepper, M. R. (2000). When choice is demotivating: Can one desire too much of a good thing? *Journal of Personality and Social Psychology, 79*, 995–1006.
8. Breen, B. (2000, August). "What's your intuition?" *Fast Company*, 290; Klein, G. (2003). *Intuition at work*. New York: Doubleday; Salas, E., & Klein, G. (2001). *Linking expertise and naturalistic decision making*. Mahwah, NJ: Lawrence Erlbaum.
9. Dane, E., Rockmann, K. W., & Pratt, M. G. (2012). When should I trust my gut? Linking domain expertise to intuitive decision-making effectiveness. *Organizational Behavior and Human Decision Processes, 119*, 187–194.
10. Interview by author Talya Bauer at Ames Research Center, Mountain View, CA, 1990.
11. Amabile, T. M. (1988). A model of creativity and innovation in organizations. In B. M. Staw & L. L. Cummings (Eds.), *Research in Organizational Behavior, 10*, 123–167. Greenwich, CT: JAI Press; Amabile, T. M., Conti, R., Coon, H., Lazenby, J., & Herron, M. (1996). Assessing the work environment for creativity. *Academy of Management Journal, 39*, 1154–1184; Ford, C. M., & Gioia, D. A. (2000). Factors influencing creativity in the domain of managerial decision making. *Journal of Management, 26*, 705–732; Tierney, P., Farmer, S. M., & Graen, G. B. (1999). An examination of leadership and employee creativity: The relevance of traits and relationships. *Personnel Psychology, 52*, 591–620; Woodman, R. W., Sawyer, J. E., & Griffin, R. W. (1993). Toward a theory of organizational creativity. *Academy of Management Review, 18*, 293–321.
12. De Stobbeleir, K. E. M., Ashford, S. J., & Buyens, D. (2011). Self-regulation of creativity at work: The role of feedback-seeking behavior in creative performance. *Academy of Management Journal, 54*, 811–831; Feist, G. J. (1998). A meta-analysis of personality in scientific and artistic creativity. *Personality and Social Psychology Review, 2*, 290–309.
13. Quote retrieved from http://www.whatquote.com/quotes/linus-pauling/250801-the-best-way-to-have.htm.
14. Girotra, K., Terwiesch, C., & Ulrich, K. T. (2010). Idea generation and the quality of the best idea. *Management Science, 56*, 591–605.
15. Scott, G., Leritz, L. E., & Mumford, M. D. (2004). The effectiveness of creativity training: A quantitative review. *Creativity Research Journal, 16*, 361–388.
16. Afuah, A., & Tucci, C. L. (2012). Crowdsourcing as a solution to distant search. *Academy of Management Review, 37*, 355–375; Lohr, S. (2009, July 19). The crowd is wise (when focused). *New York Times. Business News*.
17. Adapted from ideas in Amabile, T. M. (1998). How to kill creativity. *Harvard Business Review, 76*, 76–87; Gundry, L. K., Kickul, J. R., & Prather, C. W. (1994). Building the creative organization. *Organizational Dynamics, 22*, 22–37; Hoever, I. J., van Knippenberg, D., van Ginkel, W. P., & Barkema, H. G. (2012). Fostering team creativity: Perspective taking as key to unlocking diversity's potential. *Journal of Applied Psychology, 97*, 982–996; Keith, N., & Frese, M. (2008). Effectiveness of error management training: A meta-analysis. *Journal of Applied Psychology, 93*, 59–69; Pearsall, M. J., Ellis, A. P. J., & Evans, J. M. (2008). Unlocking the effects of gender faultlines on team creativity: Is activation the key? *Journal of Applied Psychology, 93*, 225–234; Thompson, L. (2003). Improving the creativity of organizational work groups. *Academy of Management Executive, 17*, 96–109.
18. Becker, W. S. (2007). Missed opportunities: The Great Bear Wilderness Disaster. *Organizational Dynamics, 36*, 363–376.
19. Nickerson, R. S. (1998). Confirmation bias: A ubiquitous phenomenon in many guises. *Review of General Psychology, 2*, 175–220.
20. Kappes, A., Harvey, A. H., Lohrenz, T., Montague, P. R., & Sharot, T. (2020). Confirmation bias in the utilization of others' opinion strength. *Nature Neuroscience, 23*, 130–137.
21. Moon, H. (2001). The two faces of conscientiousness: duty and achievement striving in escalation of commitment dilemmas. *Journal of Applied Psychology, 86*, 533 ; Sleesman, D. J., Conlon, D. E., McNamara, G., & Miles, J. E. (2012). Cleaning up the big muddy: A meta-analytic review of the determinants of escalation of commitment. *Academy of Management Journal, 55*, 541–562 ; Sleesman, D. J., Lennard, A. C., McNamara, G., & Conlon, D. E. (2018). Putting Escalation of Commitment in Context: A Multilevel Review and Analysis. *Academy of Management Annals, 12*, 178–207.
22. Moon, H. (2001). Looking forward and looking back: Integrating completion and sunk-cost effects within an escalation-of-commitment progress decision. *Journal of Applied Psychology, 86*, 104.
23. Li, S., Sun, Y., & Wang, Y. (2007). 50% off or buy one get one free? Frame preference as a function of consumable nature in dairy products. *Journal of Social Psychology, 147*, 413–421.
24. Tilson, W. (1999, September 20). The perils of investor overconfidence. Retrieved from http://www.fool.com/BoringPort/1999/BoringPort990920.htm.
25. Orkin, M. (1991). *Can you win? The real odds for casino gambling, sports betting and lotteries*. New York: W. H. Freeman.
26. Carpenter, M. A., Geletkanycz, M. A., & Sanders, W. M. (2004). Upper echelons research revisited: Antecedents, elements, and consequences of top management team composition. *Journal of Management, 30*, 749–778; Simons, T., Pelled, L. H., & Smith, K. A. (1999). Making use of difference: Diversity, debate, decision comprehensiveness in top management teams. *Academy of Management Journal, 42*, 662–673.
27. Miner, F. C. (1984). Group versus individual decision making: An investigation of performance measures, decision strategies, and process losses/gains. *Organizational Behavior and Human Performance, 33*, 112–124.
28. Janis, I. L. (1972). *Victims of groupthink*. New York: Houghton Mifflin.
29. Esser, J. K. (1998). Alive and well after 25 years: A review of groupthink research. *Organizational Behavior and Human Decision Processes, 73*, 116–141; Mullen, B., Anthony, T., Salas, E., & Driskell, J. E. (1994). Group cohesiveness and quality of decision making: An integration of tests of the groupthink hypothesis. *Small Group Research, 25*, 189–204.
30. Roch, S. G. (2007). Why convene rater teams: An investigation of the benefits of anticipated discussion, consensus, and rater motivation. *Organizational Behavior and Human Decision Processes, 104*, 14–29.
31. Mohammed, S., & Ringseis, E. (2001). Cognitive diversity and consensus in group decision making: The role of inputs, processes, and outcomes. *Organizational Behavior and Human Decision Processes, 85*, 310–335.
32. Peterson, R. (1999). Can you have too much of a good thing? The limits of voice for improving satisfaction with leaders. *Personality and Social Psychology, 25*, 313–324.
33. Campion, M. A. (1993). Article review checklist: A criterion checklist for reviewing research articles in applied psychology. *Personnel Psychology, 46*, 705–718.
34. Chen, A., Treviño, L. K., & Humphrey, S. E. (2020). Ethical champions, emotions, framing, and team ethical decision making. *Journal of Applied Psychology, 105*, 245–273.
35. American Nurses Association (2020). Ethics and human rights. https://www.nursingworld.org/practice-policy/nursing-excellence/ethics/.
36. Hastie, R., & Kameda, T. (2005). The robust beauty of majority rules in group decisions. *Psychological Review, 112*, 494–508.
37. Delbecq, A. L., Van de Ven, A. H., & Gustafson, D. H. (1975). *Group techniques for program planning: A guide to nominal group and Delphi processes*. Glenview, IL: Scott, Foresman.
38. Lam, S. S. K., & Schaubroeck, J. (2000). Improving group decisions by better pooling information: A comparative advantage of group decision support systems. *Journal of Applied Psychology, 85*, 565–573.
39. Nunamaker, J. F., Jr., Dennis, A. R., Valacich, J. S., Vogel, D. R., George, J. F. (1991, July). Electronic meetings to support group work. *Communications of the ACM, 34*(7), 40–61.
40. Wright, G., & Goodwin, P. (2002). Eliminating a framing bias by using simple instructions to "think harder" and respondents with managerial experience: Comment on "breaking the frame." *Strategic Management Journal, 23*, 1059–1067.
41. Mitchell, D. J., Russo, J., & Pennington, N. (1989). Back to the future: Temporal perspective in the explanation of events. *Journal of Behavioral Decision Making, 2*, 25–38.
42. Breen, B. (2000, August). What's your intuition? *Fast Company*, 290; Klein, G. (2007, September). Performing a project premortem. *Harvard Business Review*, 18–19; Klein, G. (2003). *The power of intuition: How to use your gut feelings to make better decisions at work*. New York: Random House; Pliske, R., McCloskey, M., & Klein, G. (2001). Decision skills training: Facilitating learning from experience. In E. Salas & G. Klein (Eds.), *Linking expertise and naturalistic decision making* (pp. 37–53). Mahwah, NJ: Lawrence Erlbaum.

43. Case written by Talya Bauer and Berrin Erdogan to accompany Bauer, T., & Erdogan, B. (2021). *Organizational Behavior: Bridging Science and Practice (4.0).* Boston, MA: FlatWorld. Partially based on ideas and information contained in Jones, S. (2020). Detroit Bikes brings Schwinn production back to U.S. *The Detroit News*. https://www.detroitnews.com/story/business/2020/07/15/detroit-bikes-brings-schwinn-production-back-united-states/3251266001/; Wieczner, J. (2014). Motor-less city? Bankrupt Detroit's booming bike industry. Fortune, https://fortune.com/2014/10/09/detroit-bicycle-manufacturing/; Detroit Bikes (2020). About us. https://detroitbikes.com/pages/our-story; Adams, S. (2017). At Detroit Bikes, idealism meets the reality of manufacturing in the U.S.A. *Forbes.* https://www.forbes.com/sites/forbestreptalks/2017/06/12/at-detroit-bikes-idealism-meets-the-reality-of-manufacturing-in-the-u-s-a/#26364b0336af; http://www.newyorker.com/magazine/2009/11/16/hosed; Friedman, M. (1912). Hot, flat, and crowded: Why we need a green revolution. Shinola (2020). Our Story. https://www.shinola.com/our-story; Williams, A. (2016). Shinola takes its 'Detroit cool' message on the road. *The New York Times.* https://www.nytimes.com/2016/01/07/fashion/shinola-watches-bicycles-leather-goods-expansion.html; Tullman, H. (2015). Shinola founder Tom Kaartsotis spoke with the entrepreneurs of Chicago's 1871 incubator about how he brought manufacturing back to Detroit. Inc., https://www.inc.com/howard-tullman/4-lessons-from-shinola.html; Weber, P. (2013). The rise and fall of Detroit: A timeline. The Week, https://theweek.com/articles/461968/rise-fall-detroit-timeline; Walsh, D. (2020, May 20). Michigan unemployment rate climbs to 22.7% in April, highest on record. Retrieved from https://www.crainsdetroit.com/employment/michigan-unemployment-rate-climbs-227-april-highest-record#:~:text=The unemployment rate for the,from 4.6 percent in March.

CHAPTER 11

Communication in Organizations

A sender's choice of communication channel affects the quality of what is actually understood by the receiver.

Source: Girts Ragelis/Shutterstock.com

Chapter Learning Objectives

Reading this chapter will help you accomplish the following:

1. Define communication and understand the communication process.
2. Understand and overcome barriers to effective communication.
3. Compare and contrast different types of communication.
4. Compare and contrast different communication channels.
5. Develop effective personal communication skills.

TABLE 11.1 The P-O-L-C Framework

Planning	Organizing	Leading	Controlling
1. Vision & Mission	1. Organization Design	1. Leadership	1. Systems/Processes
2. Strategizing	2. Culture	2. Decision Making	2. Strategic Human Resources
3. Goals & Objectives	3. Social Networks	3. Communications	
		4. Groups/Teams	
		5. Motivation	

11.1 Understanding Communication

Learning Objectives

1. Define communication.
2. Understand the communication process.

communication

The process by which information is exchanged between individuals through a common system of symbols, signs, or behavior.

Communication supports each of a manager's P-O-L-C functions, as the ability to effectively communicate is a necessary condition for successfully planning, organizing, leading, and controlling. Communication is vital to coordinating actions and articulating goals. Communication is defined in Webster's dictionary as "a process by which information is exchanged between individuals through a common system of symbols, signs, or behavior."[1] We know that 50%–90% of a manager's time is spent communicating,[2] and, communication ability is related to a manager's performance.[3] In most work environments, a miscommunication is an annoyance—it can interrupt workflow by causing delays and interpersonal strife. But in some work arenas, like operating rooms and airplane cockpits, communication can be a matter of life and death.

Effective communication is as important in sports as in business. Few teams have demonstrated such consistent communication and success as the U.S. Women's National Soccer Team.

Source: feelphoto/Shutterstock.com

So, just how prevalent is miscommunication in the workplace? You may not be surprised to learn that the relationship between miscommunication and negative outcomes is very strong. For example, over half of medical malpractice cases suggest some form of miscommunication between patients and healthcare providers.[4] While malpractice suits are commonly filed against doctors based on the outcome of their treatments, a study of malpractice suits found that a primary influence on whether or not a doctor is sued is the doctor's communication style. While the combination of a bad outcome and patient unhappiness can quickly lead to litigation, a warm, personal communication style leads to greater patient satisfaction. Simply put, satisfied patients are less likely to sue.[5] Further, data suggest that deficient interpersonal communication has resulted in over 1,000 fatalities in the airline industry.[6]

In business, poor communication costs money and wastes time. It has been estimated that workers spend 16% of their time in unnecessary meetings and 23% of their time reading and responding to unnecessary emails.[7] In contrast, effective communication is an asset for organizations and individuals alike. Effective communication skills, for example, are an asset for job seekers. A study of recruiters at 85 business schools ranked communication and interpersonal skills as one of the most important skills they were looking for, with 89% of the recruiters noting their importance.[8] On the flip side, good communication can help a company retain star employees. Surveys find that when employees think their organizations do a good job of keeping them informed about matters that affect them and they have ready access to the information they need to do their jobs, they are more satisfied with their employers.[9] Good communication increases a company's market value. It is understood when you foster ongoing communications internally, you will have more satisfied employees who will be better equipped to effectively communicate with your customers. Research finds that poor communications in a large company can cost the organization upwards of $62 million per year. In contrast, companies with leaders who are highly effective communicators show higher stakeholder returns compared to companies whose leaders are the least effective communicators.[10] We will explore the definition and benefits of effective communication later in this section.

The Communication Process

It is helpful to understand the communication process as it helps avoid common problems and to be more effective communicators. Communication fulfills three main functions within an organization: (1) transmitting information, (2) coordinating effort, and (3) sharing emotions and feelings. All these functions are vital to a successful organization. The coordination of effort within an organization helps people work toward the same goals. Transmitting information is vital to an organization's ability to function. Coordinating effort within the organization helps people work toward the same goals. Sharing emotions and feelings bonds teams and unites people in times of celebration and crisis. Effective communication helps people grasp issues, build rapport with coworkers, and achieve consensus. So, how can we communicate effectively? The first step is to understand the communication process.

Famed Irish writer George Bernard Shaw once quipped, "The single biggest problem in communication is the illusion that it has taken place." As the only person to ever win both a Nobel Prize and an Oscar, his advice on communication is noteworthy.

Source: Shutterstock.com

We all exchange information with others countless times a day, by phone, e-mail, text, video conference, and of course, in person. Let us take a moment to see how a typical communication works using this as a guide in Figure 11.1.

FIGURE 11.1 The Process Model of Communication

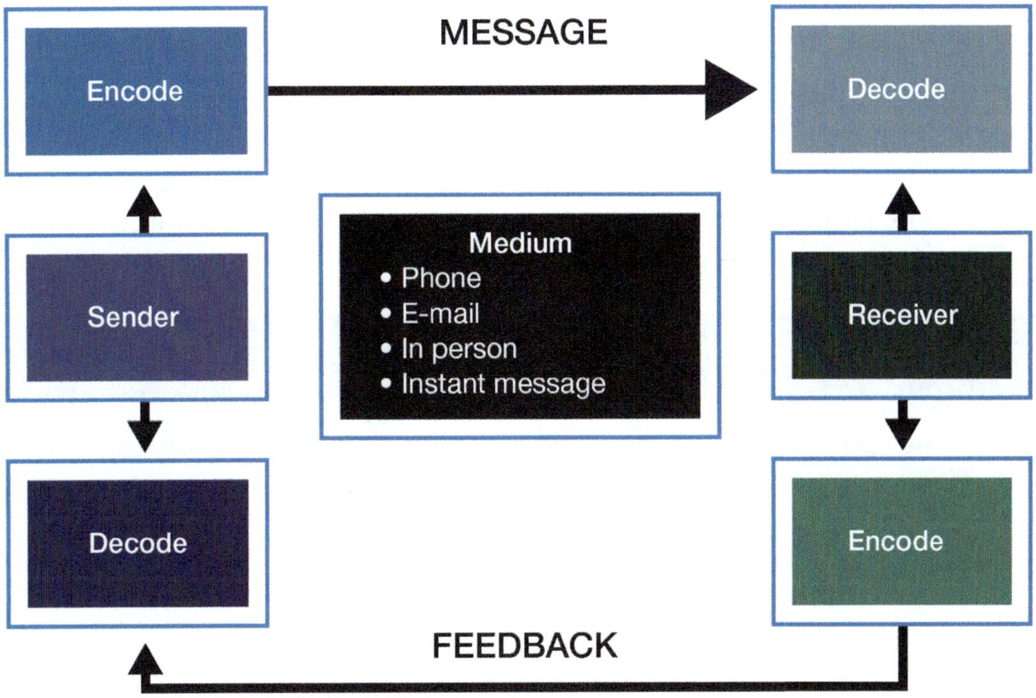

A **sender**, such as a manager, coworker, or customer, originates the message with a thought. For example, the manager's thought could be *"We need to complete this report this week. We took more time than we promised the client "*

The sender **encodes** the message, translating the idea into words. The manager may communicate this thought by saying, *"James, I can't believe we are not done with this report already. Our relationship with the client is on the line. Please make sure that this gets done."*

The **medium** of this encoded message may be spoken words, written words, or signs.

The **receiver** is the person who receives the message.

The receiver **decodes** the message by assigning meaning to the words. James may translate this message as, *"I need to stay late and finish this report tonight. I need to let my sister know that I can't attend her birthday dinner tonight."*

The meaning that the receiver assigns may not be the meaning that the sender intended, because of such factors as noise. **Noise** is anything that interferes with or distorts the message being transformed. Noise can be external in the environment (such as distractions) or it can be within the receiver. For example, the receiver may be extremely nervous and unable to pay attention to the message. In our example, James may have interpreted his deadline as being shorter than the manager intended because of his lack of experience with the manager's communication style, past conflicts about timeliness, or a desire to make a good impression. Noise can even occur within the sender: The sender may be unwilling to take the time to convey an accurate message, or the words that are chosen can be ambiguous and prone to misinterpretation. In the next scene, James may learn that he sacrificed a family get-together and his evening for a task that could have waited for a few days, which could damage his morale and his trust in the manager.

Miscommunications like these happen in the workplace every day. But how does a miscommunication happen? It helps to think of the communication process. The series of arrows pointing the way from the sender to the receiver and back again can, and often do, fall short of their target. A meta-analysis of over 9,000 teams found that it is the quality of communication that matters most for team performance, not the frequency per se.[11] So, if you have to choose whether to focus on communication frequency or quality, invest in quality communications.

sender
The person initiating a communication.

encode
The translation of ideas into words.

medium
The method used to convey a sender's message.

receiver
The person who a message is intended to reach.

decode
The process of assigning meaning to a received message.

noise
Anything that interferes with or distorts the message being transformed.

Key Takeaway

Communication is vital to organizations. Poor communication is prevalent and can have serious repercussions. Communication fulfills three functions within organizations: transmitting information, coordinating, and sharing emotions and feelings. Noise can disrupt or distort communication.

Discussion Questions

1. Where have you seen the communication process break down—at work? At school? At home?
2. Where in the communication process have you experienced the most breakdowns in communication? Why do you believe this is the case?
3. Give an example of noise during the communication process.

11.2 Communication Barriers

Learning Objectives

1. Understand the different ways that the communication process can be sidetracked.
2. Understand the role poor listening plays in communication problems.
3. Understand what active listening is.
4. Learn strategies to become a more effective listener.

Barriers to Effective Communication

Several barriers stand in the way of effective communication. These include filtering, selective perception, information overload, emotional disconnects, lack of source familiarity or credibility, workplace gossip, semantics, gender differences, differences in meaning between sender and receiver, and biased language. We explain each of these barriers in the following.

Filtering

Filtering is the distortion or withholding of information to manage a person's reactions. Some examples of filtering include a manager's keeping a division's poor sales figures from her superior, in this case, the vice president. The old saying, "Don't shoot the messenger!" illustrates the tendency of message receivers to vent their negative response to unwanted messages on the sender. A gatekeeper (the vice president's assistant, perhaps) who doesn't pass along a complete message is also filtering. Additionally, the vice president may delete the email announcing the quarter's sales figures before reading it, blocking the message before it arrives.

filtering

The distortion or withholding of information to manage a person's reactions.

Filtering prevents members of an organization from getting a complete picture of reality. To maximize the possibility of sending and receiving effective communications, it's helpful to deliver a message in multiple ways and to seek information from multiple sources. In this way, the effect of any one person's filtering the message will be diminished. Since people tend to filter bad news more often when communicating with a superior, it is also helpful to remember that subordinates in an organization may be wary of sharing bad news. One way to defuse the tendency to filter is to reward employees who clearly convey information, regardless of whether the news is good or bad.

Here are some of the criteria that individuals may use when deciding whether to filter a message or pass it on:

- *Past experience.* Was the sender rewarded or criticized for passing along news of this kind in the past?
- *Knowledge, perception of the speaker.* Has the receiver's direct superior made it clear that "no news is good news"?
- *Emotional state, involvement with the topic, level of attention.* Does the sender's fear of failure or criticism prevent him from conveying the message? Is the topic within his realm of expertise, increasing his confidence in his ability to decode it, or is he out of his comfort zone when it comes to evaluating the message's significance? Are personal concerns impacting his ability to judge the message's value?

A field study found that managers can expect, on average, to do only *three minutes* of uninterrupted work on any one task before being interrupted by an incoming e-mail, instant message, phone call, coworker, or other distraction.

Source: Shutterstock.com

selective perception

The personal filtering of what we see and hear to suit our own needs.

information overload

What occurs when the information processing demands on an individual's time to perform interactions and internal calculations exceed the supply or capacity of time available for such processing.

multitasking

Refers to performing more than one activity at the same time.

Selective Perception

Selective perception refers to filtering information to suit our own needs. This process is often unconscious. Small things can command our attention when we're visiting a new city or a new company. Over time, however, we begin to make assumptions about the way things are on the basis of our past experience. Often, much of this process is unconscious. "We simply are bombarded with too much stimuli every day to pay equal attention to everything so we pick and choose according to our own needs." Selective perception is a necessary tool that provides efficiency in a complex culture, but it can also lead to mistakes in communication. A classic study on selective perception involved participants watching a particularly violent football game between Princeton and Dartmouth. Participants rooting for a specific team counted more infractions committed by the other team. In other words, when communicating with others, we have a tendency to hear what we want to hear, or see what we want to see. Famed Irish writer George Barnard Shaw once quipped, "The single biggest problem in communication is the illusion that it has taken place." As one of only two to ever win both a Nobel Prize and an Oscar, his advice on communication is noteworthy.

Information Overload and the Illusion of Multitasking

Information overload can be defined as "occurring when the information processing demands on an individual's time to perform interactions and internal calculations exceed the supply or capacity of time available for such processing."[12] Messages reach us in countless ways every day. Some are societal—advertisements that we may hear or see in the course of our day. Others are professional—e-mails, memos, voice mails, and conversations from our colleagues. Others are personal—messages and conversations from our loved ones and friends.

Experts note that information overload is "A symptom of the high-tech age, which is too much information for one human being to absorb in an expanding world of people and technology. The sources of information overload include TV, newspapers, and magazines as well as wanted and unwanted regular mail, email, and faxes. It has been exacerbated enormously because of the formidable number of results obtained from Web search engines."[13] Other research shows that working in such a fragmented fashion has a significant negative effect on efficiency, creativity, and mental acuity.[14]

Many individuals react to being bombarded with e-mails, phone calls, text messages, and other information by what they consider to be multitasking. **Multitasking** refers to performing more than one activity at the same time. However, paying attention to multiple communications media at the same time, such as texting while listening to a colleague, may best be characterized as the "illusion of multitasking." Unlike listening to music and writing a report, which may be accomplished simultaneously, trying to communicate through multiple media usually does not result in positive outcomes, because the individual is switching attention from one task to another in quick succession. Your brain needs to constantly refocus on a different activity. As a result, the effectiveness of the communication suffers. In one study, when mobile phones were used during negotiations, negotiators achieved worse outcomes and were perceived as less trustworthy. In another study, when participants were multitasking by interacting with multiple partners over text messages and phone, their task performance suffered compared to participants who were focused on a single task. Further, while they thought that they were doing an adequate job with both their conversation partners, their partners rated them lower, presumably because they felt they were shortchanged.[15]

Emotional Disconnects

Emotional disconnects happen when the sender or the receiver is upset, whether about the subject at hand or about some unrelated incident that may have happened earlier. Effective communication requires a sender and a receiver who are open to speaking and listening to one another, despite possible differences of opinion or personality. One or both parties may have to put their emotions aside to achieve the goal of communicating clearly. A receiver who is emotionally upset tends to ignore or distort what the sender is saying. A sender who is emotionally upset may be unable to present ideas or feelings effectively.

Lack of Source Familiarity or Credibility

Lack of source familiarity or credibility can derail communications, especially when humor is involved. Sarcasm and irony are subtle and have a high potential to be misunderstood. Lack of familiarity with the source of a joke can lead to misinterpreting humor, especially in less rich information channels like email. Similarly, if the sender lacks credibility or is untrustworthy, the message will not get through. Receivers may be suspicious of the sender's motivations. ("Why am I being told this?") Likewise, if the sender has communicated erroneous information in the past, or has created false emergencies, his current message may be filtered. In other words, it is important to recognize that who communicates the message is often as important as what is being communicated. Feedback coming from a trustworthy source will have more value compared to feedback coming from someone who is not trusted.

Workplace Gossip

Workplace gossip, also known as the **grapevine**, is a lifeline for many employees seeking information about their company.[16] Researchers agree that the grapevine is an inevitable part of organizational life, with 70% of all organizational communication occurring at the grapevine level.[17] Employees trust their peers as a source of messages, but the grapevine's informal structure can be a barrier to effective communication from the managerial point of view. Its grassroots structure gives it greater credibility in the minds of employees than information delivered through official channels, even when that information is false. A study of the positive side of gossip found that the likelihood that information would be shared made individuals less likely to act in a selfish manner.[18] Some downsides of the office grapevine are that gossip offers politically-minded insiders a powerful tool for disseminating communication (and self-promoting miscommunications) within an organization. In addition, the grapevine lacks a specific sender, which can create a sense of distrust among employees concerning who is at the root of the gossip network. When the news is volatile, suspicions may arise as to the person or persons behind the message. Managers who understand the grapevine's power can use it to send and receive messages of their own. They also decrease the grapevine's power by sending official messages quickly and accurately, should big news arise.

grapevine

The informal gossip network within a given organization.

Semantics

semantics

The meanings of words and the study of meaning in communication.

jargon

The language of specialized terms used by a group of profession.

Semantics is the study of meaning in communication. Words can mean different things to different people, or they might not mean anything to other people. For example, companies often have their own acronyms and buzzwords (called business jargon) that are clear to them but impenetrable to outsiders. At IBM, GBS is focusing on BPTS, using expertise acquired from the PwC purchase (which had to be sold to avoid conflicts of interest in light of SOX) to fend off other BPO providers and inroads by the Bangalore tiger. Translation: IBM's Global Business Services (GBS) division is focusing on offering companies Business Process Transformation Services (BPTS), using the expertise it acquired from purchasing the management-consulting and technology-services arm of PricewaterhouseCoopers (PwC), which had to sell the division because of the Sarbanes-Oxley Act (SOX, enacted in response to the major accounting scandals like Enron). The added management expertise puts it above business process outsourcing (BPO) vendors that focus more on automating processes rather than transforming and improving them. Chief among these BPO competitors is Wipro, often called the "Bangalore tiger" because of its geographic origin and aggressive growth. Given the amount of messages we send and receive every day, it makes sense that humans would try to find a shortcut—a way to communicate things in code. In business, this code is known as jargon. **Jargon** is the language of specialized terms used by a group or profession. It is common shorthand among experts and if used sensibly can be a quick and efficient way of communicating. Most jargon consists of unfamiliar terms, abstract words, nonexistent words, acronyms, and abbreviations, with an occasional euphemism thrown in for good measure. Every profession, trade, and organization has its own specialized terms.[19]

There are benefits to using jargon—a quicker way to send an effective communication similar to the way text message abbreviations can send common messages in a shorter, yet understandable way. The use of jargon also communicates expertise. For example, if you are an accounting major, you will be expected to be familiar with terms such as "balance sheet," "accounts receivable," and "ROI," and asking for clarification will introduce doubts about your expertise. However, jargon can be an obstacle to effective communication, causing listeners to tune out or fostering ill feelings between partners in a conversation. When jargon rules the day, the message can get obscured. A key question to ask yourself before using jargon is, "Who is the receiver of my message?" If you are a specialist speaking to another specialist in your area, jargon may be the best way to send a message while forging a professional bond—similar to the way best friends can communicate in code. For example, an IT technician communicating with another IT technician may use jargon as a way of sharing information in a way that reinforces the pair's shared knowledge. But that same conversation should be held in Standard English, free of jargon, when communicating with staff members outside the IT group.

Gender Differences in Communication

Much has been written about men and women having different perspectives and styles and that's also true about common thinking about gender and communication. However, while there seem to be communication style differences between men and women, we need to be aware of them without exaggerating these differences. In fact, when uncovered, many of these differences are modest, and there is more overlap across genders than there are differences.[20] And yet small differences in patterns of behavior may sometimes have profound effects on how one is perceived at work, and the effectiveness of communication. So we are highlighting a few relevant research findings in this area.

There is quite a bit of research suggesting that women are less likely to be dominant or assertive in communications. For example, one study compared how much female and male senators spoke on the Senate floor. The more powerful male senators were, the more they spoke. Yet power had no effect on how much a female senator spoke. The same effect was replicated in an experiment. In both of these studies, low-power females limited the amount of time they spoke. Finally, in a follow-up experiment to these two studies, subjects reading about either a male or female CEO who speaks more than others rated the female CEO lower in competence and suitability for leadership. In other words, women may be speaking less in high-stakes communication events such as meetings because there may be a backlash against women who are perceived to speak more than others, which does not exist for men who dominate conversations.[21] Supporting these findings, it has been observed that women tend to withhold their opinions more in meetings, and what they perceive as "passion" in these conversations is often perceived as "too much emotion" by men.

Despite the existence of best-selling books such as Deborah Tannen's *You Just Don't Understand: Women and Men in Conversation*, research studies have found few differences in communication styles between men and women.

Source: Shutterstock.com

How can organizations deal with these differences? Increasing gender balance may be helpful, as will proactively ensuring that all attendees at a meeting have an opportunity to have their voices heard. Asking direct questions to the quieter members may go a long way in achieving inclusiveness.[22]

Biased Language

Biased language can offend or stereotype others on the basis of their personal or group affiliation. Words and actions that stereotype others on the basis of personal or group affiliation are examples of bias. Table 11.2 provides a list of words that have the potential to be perceived as derogatory or demeaning. The column on the right provides alternative words that can be used instead.

TABLE 11.2 Words Matter: Choose Them Thoughtfully

While the words on the left may be fine with some, using the alternatives on the right avoids any potential problems altogether.

Instead of Using These Terms	Consider Using These Instead
black attorney	attorney
businessman	business person
chairman	chair or chairperson
cleaning lady	cleaner or maintenance worker
male nurse	nurse
manpower	staff or personnel

Effective communication is clear, factual, and goal-oriented. It is also respectful. Referring to a person by one adjective (a *brain*, a *diabetic*, an *invalid*) reduces that person to that one characteristic. Language that belittles or stereotypes a person poisons the communication process. Language that insults an individual or group based on age, ethnicity, sexual preference, or political beliefs violates public and private standards of decency, ranging from civil rights to corporate regulations.

The effort to create a neutral set of terms to refer to heritage and preferences has resulted in a debate over the nature of "political correctness." Proponents of political correctness see use of language as a way to defuse the volatile nature of words that stereotyped groups and individuals in the past. Critics of political correctness see its vocabulary as stilted and needlessly cautious.

Many companies offer new employees written guides on standards of speech and conduct. These guides, augmented by common sense and courtesy, are solid starting points for effective and respectful workplace communication. Tips for appropriate workplace speech include, but are not limited, to the following:

- Replace pronouns such as *he* and *she* with more gender-neutral options such as *they* sends a signal that gender does not matter in the workplace.
- Rely on human resources-generated guidelines.
- Remember that terms that feel respectful or comfortable to you may not be comfortable or respectful to others.

Poor Listening and Active Listening

Effective listening has been identified as a key skill in many professions, including sales managers, accountants, customer service employees, contractors, and health care professionals, among others. Not listening can be costly. For example, if every Starbucks employee misheard one $10 order each day, their errors would cost the company a billion dollars annually. To teach its employees to listen, Starbucks created a code that helps employees taking orders hear the size, flavor, and use of milk or decaffeinated coffee. The person making the drink echoes the order aloud. In a different estimate, Fortune 500 companies waste $75 million in a typical year in meetings, and a big chunk of this waste is due to a lack of listening to what is being said.[23] Research shows that effective listening has a behavioral and an emotional component. Behaviors such as paraphrasing (repeating) what was heard, asking probing questions to clarify a point, and answering questions when asked are behavioral aspects of listening. Emotional aspects include showing that you care about the speaker, trying to actively understand the speaker, trying to relate to the speaker, and showing concern about what is being said and what is being left unsaid. Together, these behavioral and emotional elements of a conversation leave the speaker with a sense that he or she was heard.[24]

"The greatest compliment that was ever paid to me was when one asked me what I thought, and attended to my answer."—Henry David Thoreau

Source: Sarawut Itsaranuwut/ Shutterstock.com

active listening

Giving full attention to what other people are saying.

How can you improve your listening skills? The Roman philosopher Cicero said, "Silence is one of the great arts of conversation." How often have we been in a conversation with someone else when we are not really listening but itching to convey our portion? This behavior is known as "rehearsing." It suggests the receiver has no intention of considering the sender's message and is actually preparing to respond to an earlier point instead. Effective communication relies on another kind of listening: active listening.

Active listening can be defined as giving full attention to what other people are saying, taking time to understand the points being made, asking questions as appropriate, and not interrupting at inappropriate times.[25]Active listening creates a real-time relationship between the sender and the receiver by acknowledging the content and receipt of a message. For example, repeating and confirming a message's content offers a way to confirm that the correct content is flowing between colleagues. The process creates a bond between coworkers while increasing the flow and accuracy of messaging.

Carl Rogers, founder of the "person-centered" approach to psychology, formulated five rules for active listening:

1. Listen for message content,
2. Listen for feelings,
3. Respond to feelings,
4. Note all cues,
5. Paraphrase and restate.

Fortunately, listening is a skill that can be learned.[26] The first step is to decide that we want to listen. Casting aside distractions, such as by reducing background or internal noise, is critical. The receiver takes in the sender's message silently, without speaking. Second, throughout the conversation, show the speaker that you're listening. This can be accomplished nonverbally by nodding your head and keeping your attention focused on the speaker. You can also do it verbally, by saying things like, "Yes," "That's interesting," or other such verbal cues. As you're listening, pay attention to the sender's body language for additional cues about how they're feeling. Interestingly, silence plays a major role in active listening. During active listening, we are trying to understand what has been said, and in silence we can consider the implications. Finally, if anything is not clear, ask questions. Confirm that you've heard the message accurately, by repeating back a crucial piece like, "Great, I'll see you at 2 p.m. in my office." At the end of the conversation, a "thank you" from both parties communicates mutual respect.

In summary, active listening creates a more dynamic relationship between a receiver and a sender. It strengthens personal investment in the information being shared. It also forges healthy working relationships among colleagues by making speakers and listeners equally valued members of the communication process.

Key Takeaway

Many barriers to effective communication exist. Examples include filtering, selective perception, information overload, emotional disconnects, lack of source familiarity or credibility, workplace gossip, semantics, gender differences, differences in meaning between sender and receiver, and biased language. The receiver can enhance the probability of effective communication by engaging in active listening, which involves (1) giving one's full attention to the sender and (2) checking for understanding by repeating the essence of the message back to the sender.

Discussion Questions

1. Most individuals are poor listeners. Do you agree or disagree with this statement? Please support your position.
2. Please share an example of how differences in shared meaning have affected you.
3. Give an example of selective perception.
4. Do you use jargon in your classes? If so, do you think it helps or hampers communication? Why or why not?
5. In your experience, how is silence used in communication? How does your experience compare with the recommended use of silence in active listening?

11.3 Different Types of Communication

Learning Objectives

1. Understand different types of communication.
2. Understand how communication channels affect communication.
3. Recognize different communication directions within organizations.

Types of Communication

Communication can be categorized into three basic types: (1) verbal communication, in which you listen to a person to understand their meaning; (2) written communication, in which you read their meaning; and (3) nonverbal communication, in which you observe a person and infer meaning. Each has its own advantages and disadvantages.

Verbal Communication

Verbal communication in business may take place over the phone, in person, or via video conferencing. With verbal communication, the medium of the message is *oral*. Research shows that individuals tend to enjoy verbal communication, and it is effective in helping to build relationships at work.[27] In addition, oral communication has a special place at work, including the role of storytelling and crucial conversations.

Storytelling

storytelling

The narrative account of an event or events.

Storytelling has been shown to be an effective form of verbal communication; it serves an important organizational function by helping to construct common meanings for individuals within the organization. Stories can help clarify key values and help demonstrate cultural norms and expectations within an organization, and story frequency, strength, and tone are related to higher organizational commitment.[28] The quality of the stories entrepreneurs tell is related to their ability to secure capital for their firms.[29] More recently, storytelling with data and visuals has become a powerful medium used to persuade others toward action.

Crucial Conversations

crucial conversations

Discussions where the stakes are high, opinions vary, and emotions run strong.

While the process may be the same, high-stakes communication require more planning, reflection, and skill than normal day-to-day interactions at work. Examples of high-stakes communication events include asking for a raise or presenting a business plan to a venture capitalist. In addition to these events, there are also many times in our professional lives when we have **crucial conversations**—discussions in which not only are the stakes high but opinions vary and emotions run strong.[30] One of the most consistent recommendations from communications experts is to work toward using "and" instead of "but" as you communicate under these circumstances. In addition, be aware of your communication style and practice flexibility; it is under stressful situations that communication styles can become the most rigid. High-stakes communication requires a lot of preparation, even when it looks as if it is spontaneous. For example, if you are thinking about making a key point and go against the consensus opinion at a meeting, it would be useful to practice what you are going to say so that what you say is clear, concise, and impactful.

Written Communication

In contrast to verbal, or oral, communication, written business communications are *printed messages*. Email and text messages are easy and cheap methods of collaborating at work. There are also alternatives to email, in the form of online collaboration software. Company-level social platforms such as Yammer, Jive, and Chatter allow users to collaborate and communicate using Intranets (within the company only) via chat, instant messaging, blogs, and managing tasks in an integrated platform. Other written documents may include handbooks, procedures, policies, and websites. Written communication is often asynchronous. That is, the sender can write a message that the receiver can read at any time, unlike a conversation that is carried on in real time. A written communication can also be read by many people (such as all employees in a department or all customers). It's a "one-to-many" communication, as opposed to a one-to-one conversation. There are exceptions, of course: A voice mail is an oral message that is asynchronous. Conference calls and speeches are oral one-to-many communications, and emails can have only one recipient or many.

Normally, a verbal communication takes place in real time. Written communication, by contrast, can be constructed over a longer period of time. It also can be collaborative. Multiple people can contribute to the content on one document before that document is sent to the intended audience.

Verbal and written communications have different strengths and weaknesses. In business, the decision to communicate verbally or in written form can be a powerful one. As we'll see in the following, each style of communication has particular strengths and pitfalls. When determining whether to communicate verbally or in writing, ask yourself: Do I want to convey facts or feelings? Verbal communications are a better way to convey feelings. Written communications do a better job of conveying facts.

The use of safety checklists reduced number of complications and deaths during surgeries.

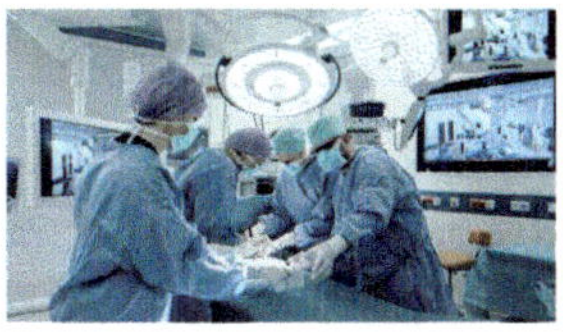

Source: Shutterstock.com

Picture a manager making a speech to a team of 20 employees. The manager is speaking at a normal pace. The employees appear interested. But how much information is being transmitted? Humans listen much faster than they speak. The average public speaker communicates at a speed of about 125 words a minute, and that pace sounds fine to the audience. (In fact, anything faster than that probably would sound strange. To put that figure in perspective, someone having an excited conversation speaks at about 150 words a minute.) Based on these numbers, we could assume that the audience has more than enough time to take in each word the speaker delivers, which actually creates a problem. The average person in the audience can hear 400 to 500 words a minute.[31] Consequently, the audience has more than enough time to hear. As a result, their minds may wander.

As you can see, oral communication is the most often used form of communication, but it is also an inherently flawed medium for conveying specific facts. Knowing this information allows individuals to make more intelligent communication choices based on the kind of information one desires to convey.

Most jobs involve some degree of writing. According to the National Commission on Writing, 67% of salaried employees in large American companies and professional state employees have some kind of writing responsibility. Half of responding companies reported that they take writing into consideration when hiring professional employees, and 91% always take writing into account when hiring.[32] Luckily, it is possible to learn to write clearly. Below are some tips on writing well.

Music Rap-Up: Don't Say A Word

Twinprov perform a rap on nonverbal communication.

View in the online reader

Nonverbal Communication

What you say is a vital part of any communication. But what you *don't say* can be even more important. Research also shows that 55% of in-person communication comes from nonverbal cues like facial expressions, body stance, and tone of voice. According to one study, only 7% of a receiver's comprehension of a message is based on the sender's actual words; 38% is based on paralanguage (the tone, pace, and volume of speech), and 55% is based on *nonverbal cues* (body language).[33]

Body language matters when we are on Zoom meetings as well. Eye contact, sitting straight, sitting back so others can see your gestures are some tips in improving your body language in video conferences.

Source: Shutterstock.com

Research shows that nonverbal cues can also affect whether you get a job offer. Judges examining videotapes of actual applicants were able to assess the social skills of job candidates with the sound turned off. They watched the rate of gesturing, time spent talking, and formality of dress to determine which candidates would be the most successful socially on the job.[34] For this reason, it is important to consider how we appear in business as well as what we say. The muscles of our faces convey our emotions. We can send a silent message without saying a word.

To be effective communicators, one's body language, appearance, and tone need to be aligned with the words one is trying to communicate. Research shows that when individuals are lying, they are more likely to blink more frequently, shift their weight, and shrug.[35] What happens when verbal and nonverbal cues are in conflict? Nonverbal communication is thought to be more spontaneous and therefore harder to fake. As a result, when in doubt, we believe in the nonverbal cues rather than what is actually being said.[36]

A different tone can change the perceived meaning of a message. See Table 11.3 for how clearly this can be true. If we only read these words, we would be left to wonder, but during a conversation, the tone conveys a great deal of information.

Don't Use That Tone With Me!

Changing your tone can dramatically change your meaning.

TABLE 11.3

Placement of the emphasis	What it means
I did not tell Chris you were late.	Someone else told Chris you were late.
I did **not** tell Chris you were late.	This did not happen.
I did not **tell** Chris you were late.	I may have implied it.
I did not tell **Chris** you were late.	But maybe I told Sharon and José.
I did not tell Chris **you** were late.	I was talking about someone else.
I did not tell Chris you **were** late.	I told him you still are late.
I did not tell Chris you were **late**.	I told him you were attending another meeting.

Source: Based on ideas in Kiely, M. (October, 1993). When "no" means "yes." *Marketing*, 7–9.

Following are a few examples of nonverbal cues that can support or detract from a sender's message including body language and a focus on eye contact, facial expressions, posture, touch, and space.

Body Language

A simple rule of thumb is that simplicity, directness, and warmth convey sincerity. And sincerity is vital for effective communication. A firm handshake, given with a warm, dry hand, is a great way to establish trust.[37] A weak, clammy handshake conveys a lack of trustworthiness. Gnawing one's lip conveys uncertainty. A direct smile conveys confidence. And, crossing one's arms is often perceived as indicating a lack of openness to ideas being presented.

Facial Expressions

The human face can produce thousands of different expressions. These expressions have been decoded by experts as corresponding to hundreds of different emotional states.[38] Our faces convey basic information to the outside world. Happiness is associated with an upturned mouth and slightly closed eyes; fear with an open mouth and wide-eyed stare. Flitting ("shifty") eyes and pursed lips convey a lack of trustworthiness. The effect of facial expressions in conversation is instantaneous. Our brains may register them as "a feeling" about someone's character.

Eye Contact

In business, the style and duration of eye contact varies greatly across cultures. In the United States, looking someone in the eye (for about a second) is considered a sign of trustworthiness. Establishing and maintaining eye contact is often the first step in building a connection with someone else. This seems to be true even in interactions with non-humans. An experimental study showed that shoppers were more likely to choose a cereal if the cartoon on the box was looking at the shopper as opposed to looking away. At the same time, uninterrupted eye contact for an extended period of time will be intimidating.

Posture

The position of our body relative to a chair or another person is another powerful silent messenger that conveys interest, aloofness, professionalism—or lack thereof. Head up, back straight (but not rigid) implies an upright character. In interview situations, experts advise mirroring an interviewer's tendency to lean in and settle back in her seat. The subtle repetition of the other person's posture conveys that we are listening and responding. And research shows that one's own body language can influence how powerful a person feels.[39]

Touch

The meaning of a simple touch differs between individuals and cultures. In Mexico, when doing business, men may find themselves being grasped on the arm by another man. To pull away is seen as rude. In Indonesia, to touch anyone on the head or touch anything with one's foot is considered highly offensive. Americans, as we have noted, place great value on a firm handshake, but one that is too strong is also a problem.

Space

Anthropologist Edward T. Hall coined the term *proxemics* to denote the different kinds of distance that occur between people. These distances vary between cultures. Standing too far away from a colleague (such as a public speaking distance of more than seven feet) or too close to a colleague (intimate distance for embracing) can thwart effective verbal communication in business. Figure 11.2 outlines the basic proxemics of everyday life and their associated meaning.[40] One of the challenging aspects of social distancing during the COVID-19 pandemic was the avoidance of coming closer than 6 feet from others—even those we are personal with. Even handshaking became discouraged during this time which in the United States is a common form of nonverbal communication in business.

FIGURE 11.2 Interpersonal Distances

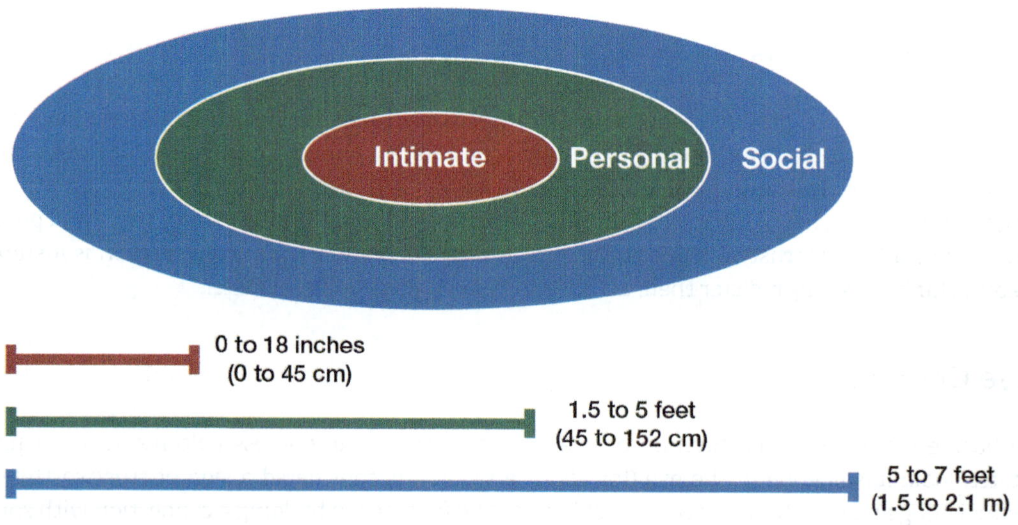

FIGURE 11.3 Cultural Risk: When in Rome

The phrase "When in Rome, do as the Romans do" is used to encourage travelers to embrace local customs. An important part of fitting in is avoiding behaviors that locals consider offensive. Here we illustrate a number of activities that would go largely unnoticed in the United States but could raise concerns in other countries.

Do you pride yourself on your punctuality? You may be wasting your time in Latin American countries, where the locals tend to be about 20 minutes behind schedule.

Many Muslim countries consider a woman's clothing to be inappropriate if it reveals anything beside the face and hands.

In many Asian and Arabian countries, showing the sole of your shoe is considered rude.

If you want to signal "Check please!" to catch the attention of your garcon in France or Belgium, remember that snapping your fingers is vulgar there.

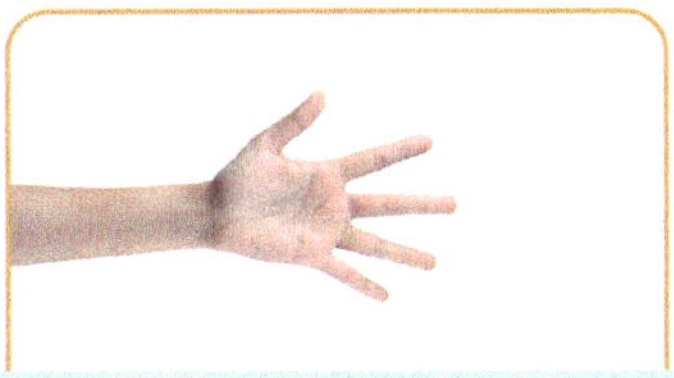

Do not eat with your left hand in India or Malaysia. That hand is associated with unclean activities reserved for the bathroom.

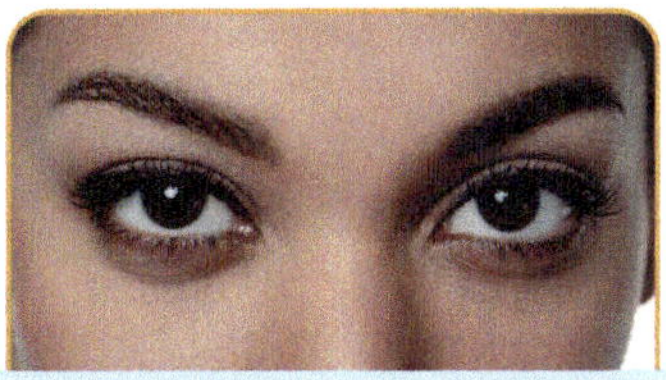

In Japan, direct eye contact is viewed as impolite.

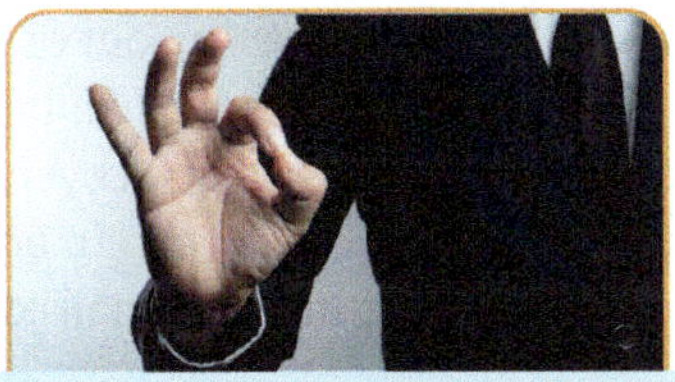

If everything is OK when you're in Brazil, avoid making this hand signal. It's the equivalent to giving someone the middle finger.

Do not clean your plate in China. Leaving food on the plate indicates the host was so generous that the meal could not be finished.

Source: Shutterstock.com

Communication Channels

The channel, or medium, used to communicate a message affects how accurately the message will be received. Channels vary in their *information richness*. Information-rich channels convey more nonverbal information. Research shows that effective managers tend to use more information-rich communication channels than less effective managers.[41] Figure 11.4 illustrates the information richness of different information channels.

The key to effective communication is to match the communication channel with the goal of the message.[42] For example, written media may be a better choice when the sender wants a record of the content, has less urgency for a response, is physically separated from the receiver, and doesn't require a lot of feedback from the receiver, or when the message is complicated and may take some time to understand. Oral communication, on the other hand, makes more sense when the sender is conveying a sensitive or emotional message, needs feedback immediately, and does not need a permanent record of the conversation. See for a summary of when to use verbal versus written communication.

Like face-to-face and telephone conversations, video conferencing has high information richness, because receivers and senders can see or hear beyond just the words that are used—they can see the sender's body language or hear the tone of their voice. Handheld devices, blogs, and written letters and memos offer medium-rich channels, because they convey words and pictures or photos. Formal written documents, such as legal documents and budget spreadsheets, convey the least richness, because the format is often rigid and standardized. As a result, the tone of the message is often lost.

Although decried by some as being too cartoony and unprofessional, Comic Sans font has been reported to be helpful for dyslexics to read.

Source: https://en.wikipedia.org/wiki/Comic_Sans#/media/File:ComicSansSpec3.svg

The growth of email has been spectacular, but it has also created challenges in managing information and an ever-increasing speed of doing business. Approximately 59% (4.54 billion people) of the world's population use the internet.[43] Internet users around the world send an estimated 306 billion emails every day, and many of those are spam or scam attempts.[44] That makes email the second most popular medium of communication worldwide, second only to voice. A 2005 study estimated that less than 1% of all written human communications even reached paper—and, of course, this percentage has gone down even further since then.[45] To combat the overuse of email, companies such as Intel have even instituted "no email Fridays" where all communication is done via other communication channels. And some companies such as Daimler, a German-based automotive company, have eliminated vacation email overload. Referred to as the "Mail on Holiday" policy, employees are able to set up out of office emails that alert the sender that they are on vacation and that the email has been deleted. It then directs them to either contact someone else who is covering their work or to contact them again when they return from vacation.[46] In addition to organizational strategies, learning to be more effective in your email communications is an important skill.

FIGURE 11.4 Information Channels and Richness

This illustrates the information richness of different information channels.

Information Channel	Example	Information Richness
Face-to-Face Conversation		↑ **High**
Video Conferencing		↑ **High**
Telephone Conversation		↑ **High**
Emails		→ **Medium**
Handheld Devices		→ **Medium**
Blogs		→ **Medium**
Written Letters and Memos		→ **Medium**
Formal Written Documents		↓ **Low**
Spreadsheets		↓ **Low**

Source: Adapted from information in Daft, R. L., & Lengel, R. H. (1984). Information richness: A new approach to managerial behavior and organizational design. In B. Staw & L. Cummings (Eds.), Research in organizational behavior (Vol. 6, pp. 191–233). Greenwich, CT: JAI Press; and Lengel, R. H., & Daft, R. L. (1988). The selection of communication media as an executive skill. Academy of Management Executive, 11, 225–232. Photos: Shutterstock.com

TABLE 11.4 Guide for When to Use Written versus Verbal Communication

Use Written Communication Under These Conditions:	Use Verbal Communication Under These Conditions:
when conveying facts is important	when conveying emotion and feelings
when the message needs to become part of a permanent file	when the message does not need to be permanent
when there is little time urgency	when there is time urgency
when you do not need immediate feedback	when you need immediate feedback
when the ideas are complicated	when the ideas are simple or can be made simple with explanations

Business E-Mail Do's and Don'ts

1. DON'T make email your default way of communication, Sometimes calling them or talking to them is more appropriate.
2. DON'T put anything in an e-mail that you don't want the world to see.
3. DON'T answer an email in anger or while feeling strong emotions. You might regret it!
4. DON'T routinely "cc" everyone all the time. Reducing inbox clutter is a great way to increase communication.
5. DON'T hit Send until you spellcheck your email.
6. DO use a subject line that summarizes your message, adjusting it as the message changes over time.
7. DO make your request in the first line of your e-mail. (And if that's all you need to say, stop there!)
8. DO end your e-mail with a brief sign-off such as, "Thank you," followed by your name and contact information.
9. DO think of a work email as a binding communication.
10. DO let others know if you've received an e-mail in error.

Source: Adapted from information in Leland, K., & Bailey, K. (2000). Customer service for dummies. New York: Wiley; Information Technology Services (1997). Top 10 email dos and top ten email don'ts. Retrieved July 1, 2008, from the University of Illinois at Chicago Medical Center Web site: http://www.uic.edu/hsc/uicmc/its/customers/email-tips.htm; Kawasaki, G. (2006, February 3). The effective emailer. Retrieved September 13, 2012, from How to Change the World website: http://blog.guykawasaki.com/2006/02/the_effective_e.html.

An important although often ignored rule when communicating emotional information is that email's lack of richness can be your loss. As we saw in Figure 11.4, email is a medium-rich channel. It can convey facts quickly. But when it comes to emotion, e-mail's flaws make it far less desirable a choice than oral communication—the 55% of nonverbal cues that make a conversation comprehensible to a listener are missing. E-mail readers do not pick up on sarcasm and other tonal aspects of writing as much as the writer believes they will.[47]

The sender may believe that certain emotional signifiers have been included in a message. But, with written words alone, those signifiers are not there. This gap between the form and content of email inspired the rise of emoticons—symbols that offer clues to the emotional side of the words in each message. Generally speaking, however, emoticons are not considered professional in business communication.

Individuals often feel uncomfortable conveying an emotionally laden message verbally, especially when the message contains unwanted news. Sending an e-mail to your staff that there will be no bonuses this year may seem easier than breaking the bad news face-to-face, but that does not mean that e-mail is an effective or appropriate way to deliver this kind of news. When the message is emotional, the sender should use verbal communication. Indeed, a good rule of thumb is that more emotionally-laden messages require more thought in the choice of channel and how they are communicated.

Direction of Communication Within Organizations

Information can move horizontally, from a sender to a receiver, or vertically, down from top management or up from the front line. Information can also move diagonally between and among levels of an organization, such as a message from a customer-service representative up to a manager in the manufacturing department, or a message from the chief financial officer sent down to all department heads.

FIGURE 11.5 Direction of Communication
Communication flows in many different directions within an organization.

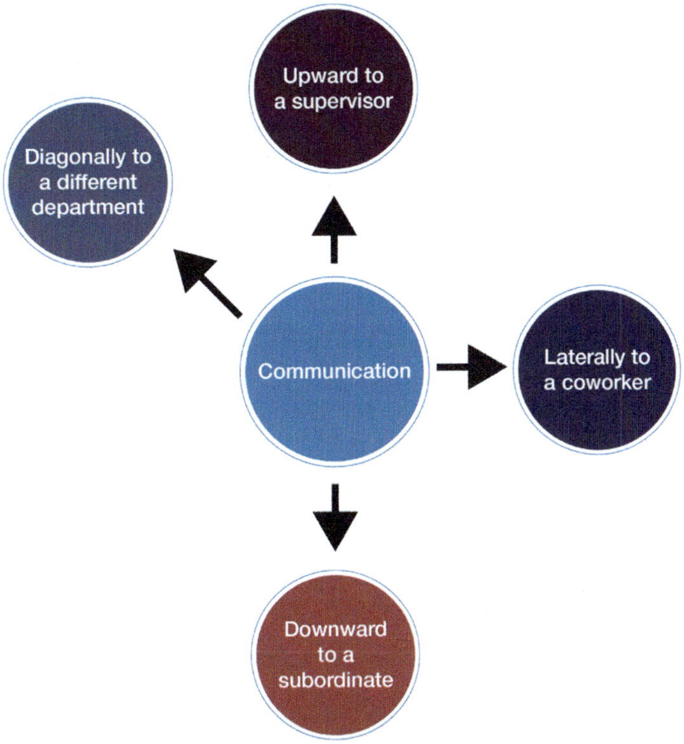

The organizational status of the sender can affect the receiver's attentiveness to the message. For example, consider the following: A senior manager sends a memo to a production supervisor. The supervisor, who has a lower status within the organization, is likely to pay close attention to the message. The same information, conveyed in the opposite direction, however, might not get the attention it deserves. The message would be filtered by the senior manager's perception of priorities and urgencies.

Requests are just one kind of communication in business. Other communications, either verbal or written, may seek, give, or exchange information. Research shows that frequent communications with one's supervisor is related to better job performance ratings and overall organizational performance.[48] Research also shows that lateral communication done between peers can influence important organizational outcomes such as turnover.[49]

External Communications

External communications deliver specific business messages to individuals outside an organization. They may announce changes in staff or strategy, earnings, and more. The goal of an external communication is to create a specific message that the receiver will understand and share with others. Examples of external communications include press releases, ads, web pages, and customer communications.

Press Releases

Public relations professionals create external communications about a client's product, services, or practices for specific receivers. These receivers, it is hoped, will share the message with others. In time, as the message is passed along, it should *appear* to be independent of the Sender, creating the illusion of an independently generated consumer trend, public opinion, and so on.

The message of a public relations effort may be *b2b* (business to business), *b2c* (business to consumer), or media related. The message can take different forms. Press releases try to convey a newsworthy message, real or manufactured. It may be constructed like a news item, inviting editors or reporters to reprint the message in part, or as a whole, with or without acknowledgment of the sender's identity. Public relations campaigns create messages over time, through contests, special events, trade shows, and media interviews in addition to press releases.

Ads

Advertising places external business messages before target receivers through media buys. A media buy is a fee that is paid to a television network, website, or magazine by an advertiser for an on-air, site, or publication ad. The fee is based on the perceived value of the audience who watches, reads, or frequents the space where the ad will appear.

Red is commonly used in fast food advertising as the color red has been found to encourage appetite.

Source: Shutterstock.com

In recent years, receivers have begun to filter advertiser's messages, a phenomenon that is perceived to be the result of the large amount of ads the average person sees each day and a growing level of consumer wariness of paid messaging. Advertisers, in turn, are trying to create alternative forms of advertising that receivers won't filter. The *advertorial* is one example of an external communication that combines the look of an article with the focused message of an ad. Product placements in videos, movies, and games are other ways that advertisers strive to reach receivers with commercial messages.

Web Pages

A web page's external communication can combine elements of public relations, advertising, and editorial content, reaching receivers on multiple levels and in multiple ways. Banner ads, blogs, and advertiser-driven "click-through" areas are just a few of the elements that allow a business to deliver a message to a receiver online. The perceived flexibility of online communications can impart a less formal (and therefore, more believable) quality to an external communication. A message relayed in a daily blog post, for example, will reach a receiver differently than if it is delivered in an annual report. The popularity and power of blogs is growing, with 54% of *Fortune* 500 companies having official blogs (up from 4% in 2005).[50] In fact, blogs have become so important to companies such as Coca-Cola, Eastman Kodak, and Marriott International Inc. that they have created official positions within their organizations titled "chief blogging officer."[51] The "real-time" quality of web communications may appeal to receivers who might filter out traditional ads and public relations messages because of their "prefab" quality. Despite a "spontaneous" feel, many online pages can be revisited many times in a single day. For this reason, clear and accurate external communications are as vital for online use as they are in traditional media.

Customer Communications

Customer communications can include social media, letters, catalogs, direct mail, e-mails, text messages, and telemarketing messages. Some receivers automatically filter bulk messages like these. Others will be receptive. The key to a successful external customer communication is to convey a business message in a personally compelling way—dramatic news, a money-saving coupon, and so forth.

Key Takeaway

Types of communication include verbal, written, and nonverbal. Different communication channels are more or less effective at transmitting different kinds of information. Some types of communication are information rich while others are medium rich. In addition, communications flow in different directions within organizations. A major internal communication channel is e-mail, which is convenient but needs to be handled carefully. External communication channels include PR/press releases, ads, web pages, and customer communications such as letters and catalogs.

Discussion Questions

1. How could you use your knowledge of communication richness to be more effective in your own communications?
2. What are the three biggest advantages and disadvantages you see regarding technology and communications?
3. Explain the difference between internal and external communications in an organization, giving examples of each.

11.4 Developing Your Personal Communication Skills

Learning Objectives

1. Learn how to improve your own listening habits.
2. Learn how to handle personal communications in a career-friendly manner.
3. Learn how to avoid communication freezers.

By being sensitive to the errors outlined in this chapter and adopting active listening skills, you may increase your communication effectiveness, increasing your ability to carry out the managerial functions of planning, organizing, leading, and controlling. The following are additional tools for helping you increase your communication effectiveness.

Ten Ways to Improve Your Listening Habits

1. **Start by stopping.** Take a moment to inhale and exhale quietly before you begin to listen. Your job as a listener is to receive information openly and accurately.
2. **Don't worry about what you'll say when the time comes.** Silence can be a beautiful thing.
3. **Join the sender's team.** When a speaker pauses, summarize what you believe they said. "What I'm hearing is that we need to focus on marketing as well as sales. Is that correct?" Be attentive to physical as well as verbal communications. "I hear you saying that we should focus on marketing. But the way you're shaking your head tells me the idea may not really appeal to you—is that right?"
4. **Don't multitask while listening.** Listening is a full-time job. It's tempting to multitask when you and the sender are in different places, but doing that is counterproductive to individuals personally and research has found multitasking to be inefficient if not altogether impossible.[52] Because the human mind can only focus on one thing at a time, lack of focus increases the chances that you'll have questions later, requiring more of the speaker's time. (And when the speaker is in the same room, multitasking signals a disinterest that is considered rude.)
5. **Try to empathize with the sender's point of view.** You don't have to agree; but can you find common ground?
6. **Confused? Ask questions.** There's nothing wrong with admitting you haven't understood the sender's point. You may even help the sender clarify the message.
7. **Establish eye contact.** Making eye contact with the speaker (if appropriate for the culture) is important.
8. **What is the goal of this communication?** Ask yourself this question at different points during the communication to keep the information flow on track. Be polite. Differences in opinion can be the starting point of consensus.
9. **It's great to be surprised.** Listen with an open mind, not just for what you *want* to hear.
10. **Pay attention to what is not said.** Does the sender's body language seem to contradict the message? If so, clarification may be in order.

Source: Adapted from information in Barrett, D. J. (2006). Leadership communication. New York: McGraw-Hill/Irwin; Improving verbal skills. Retrieved April 21, 2016, from http://www.itstime.com/aug97.htm; Ten tips: Active Listening from Communication at work. (2007, June 4). Retrieved April 21, 2016, from http://communication.atwork-network.com/2007/06/04/ten-tips-active-listening.

Professional Communications

Communication can occur without your even realizing it. Consider the following:

- *Is your e-mail name professional?* The typical convention for business e-mail contains some form of your name. While an e-mail name like "LazyGirl" or "DeathMonkey" may be fine for chatting online with your friends, they may send the wrong signal to individuals you e-mail, such as professors and prospective employers.
- *Is your outgoing voice mail greeting professional?* If not, change it. Prospective recruiters will draw certain conclusions if, upon calling you, they hear a message that screams, "Party, party, party!"

- *Do you have a "private" social networking website on Pinterest, Google+, or Facebook?* If so, consider what it says about you to employers or clients. If it is information you would not share at work, it probably shouldn't be there.
- *Googled yourself lately?* If not, you probably should. Potential employers have begun searching the web as part of background checking and you should be aware of what's out there about you. It is possible to set up automated alerts so that every time your name is mentioned on the web, you are notified.

Communication Freezers

Communication freezers put an end to effective communication by making the receiver feel judged or defensive. Typical communication stoppers include criticizing, blaming, ordering, judging, or shaming the other person. The following are some examples of things to avoid saying:[53]

Giving insincere praise is one example of a "conversation killer."

Source: Shutterstock.com

1. Telling people what to do:
   - "You must . . ."
   - "You cannot . . ."
2. Threatening with "or else" implied:
   - "You had better . . ."
   - "If you don't . . ."
3. Making suggestions or telling other people what they ought to do:
   - "You should . . ."
   - "It's your responsibility to . . ."
4. Attempting to educate the other person:
   - "Let me give you the facts."
   - "Experience tells us that . . ."
5. Judging the other person negatively:
   - "You're not thinking straight."
   - "You're wrong."
6. Giving insincere praise:
   - "You have so much potential."
   - "I know you can do better than this."
7. Psychoanalyzing the other person:
   - "You're jealous."
   - "You have problems with authority."
8. Making light of the other person's problems by generalizing:
   - "Things will get better."
   - "Behind every cloud is a silver lining."
9. Asking excessive or inappropriate questions:
   - "Why did you do that?"
   - "Who has influenced you?"
10. Making light of the problem by kidding:

- "Think about the positive side."
- "You think *you've* got problems!"

Key Takeaway

By practicing the skills associated with active listening, you can become more effective in your personal and professional relationships. Managing your online communications appropriately can also help you avoid career pitfalls. Finally, be aware of and work to avoid the types of remarks that freeze communication.

Discussion Questions

1. How can you assess if you are engaging in active listening?
2. How does it feel when someone does not seem to be listening to you?
3. Some companies have internal social networking pages where employees can mingle and share ideas and information. Do you think this practice is a good idea? Why or why not?
4. What advice would you give to someone who is going to become a first-time manager in terms of communication?

11.5 Case in Point: Communication that Transcends Cultures at IKEA

Source: NP27/Shutterstock.com

IKEA is a Swedish-founded multinational company that designs and sells furniture, appliances, and home accessories. It has been the world's largest furniture retailer since 2008. The company was founded in Sweden in 1943. It grew slowly and intentionally but over time it became an industry giant. Today IKEA has stores in over 50 countries, including China and India where other big box retailers have failed. IKEA earns billions of dollars globally in annual operating profit. It also regularly appears on *Fortune*'s coveted *Great Places to Work* and *Best Employers for New Grads* lists.

IKEA even keeps its products' Swedish names consistent across countries. The company's founder was dyslexic, so he found it easier to make sense of familiar names rather than product codes. Product names range from Swedish islands to first names to Norwegian cities. Keeping these consistent ensures product names don't get lost in translation between markets.

In 2012, IKEA hired a new head of design, Marcus Engman, who was tasked with revamping its product development and getting more creative in the process. He did so by improving communication between divisions and communicating more transparently with consumers to help them reframe their perceptions of the brand. Although Engman left IKEA in 2018 to start his own consulting agency, his efforts have left a lasting impact on the organization.

This transparency extends to the internal company culture, as well. The company's Dublin store hosts an all-hands "huddle" in the store's restaurant every morning before the store opens. This is an opportunity for management to share the previous day's sales results and delegate responsibilities for the day, and for all employees to share store news with each other.

Even IKEA's senior executives understand the value of strong communication. Michael Ward, president of IKEA Canada, has strong storytelling skills and is able to communicate a strong vision for his employees as well as for the business. He takes his senior management team's diverse opinions and synthesizes them into a strategy. In particular, he is known for looking out for team members in meetings who are quiet and appear to be deep in thought. He will ask them directly about what they are thinking to signal to them that he is interested in their perspectives, no matter how outlandish they may seem. This helps drive more productive conversations during meetings and encourages transparent communication between team members.[54]

Multimedia Extension—The IKEA Group—The Story of How We Work

View in the online reader

Case Discussion Questions

1. Does it surprise you that IKEA has been successful in so many countries? Do you think its standardized communication has contributed to its success? Why or why not?
2. How might a policy of transparency with consumers positively impact an organization? Are there any potential downsides to this approach?
3. What are some ways in which internal organizational communication might impact external marketing and vice versa? Do you see this being the case with IKEA?
4. Open and clear communication is a high priority for IKEA and feedback from employees of all levels is encouraged. How would you feel about working at an organization like this? Would you feel comfortable speaking your mind?
5. If you were a senior executive at a large multinational group, such as IKEA, what communication styles would you leverage to ensure your company's success? Explain.

Endnotes

1. *Merriam-Webster online dictionary*. (2008). Retrieved from http://www.merriam-webster.com/dictionary/communication.
2. Schnake, M. E., Dumler, M. P., Cochran, D. S., & Barnett, T. R. (1990). Effects of differences in subordinate perceptions of superiors' communication practices. *The Journal of Business Communication, 27*, 37–50.
3. Penley, L. E., Alexander, E. R., Jernigan, I. E., & Henwood, C. I. (1991). Communication abilities of managers: The relationship of performance. *Journal of Management, 17*, 57–76.
4. Hoffman, J. (2016, February 2). Malpractice risks of health care communication failures. CRICO. Retrieved from https://www.rmf.harvard.edu/Clinician-Resources/Newsletter-and-Publication/2016/SPS-The-Malpractice-Risks-of-Health-Care-Communication-Failures.
5. Communications skills cut malpractice risk—study reveals most important reason that patients decide to file malpractice suits is because of poor communication by physicians and not medical errors. (1997, October). *USA Today*.
6. Friginal, E., Mathews, E., & Roberts, J. (2019). *English in Global Aviation: Context, Research, and Pedagogy*. Bloomsbury Publishing.
7. James, G. (2019, October 8). The average worker spends 51 percent of each workday on these 3 unnecessary tasks. Inc. Retrieved from https://www.inc.com/geoffrey-james/the-average-worker-spends-51-of-each-workday-on-these-3-unnecessary-tasks.html.
8. Alsop, R. (2006, September 20). The top business schools: Recruiters' M.B.A. picks. *Wall Street Journal Online*. Retrieved from http://online.wsj.com/article/SB115860376846766495.html?mod=2_1245_1.
9. Mercer. (2003, June). What are the bottom line results of communicating? *Pay for Performance Report*, p. 1. Retrieved from http://www.mercerHR.com.
10. Grossman, D. (2011, July 16). The cost of poor communications. *Provoke*. Retrieved from https://www.provokemedia.com/latest/article/the-cost-of-poor-communications.
11. Marlow, S. L., Lacerenza, C. N., Paoletti, J., Burke, C. S., & Salas, E. (2018). Does team communication represent a one-size-fits-all approach?: A meta-analysis of team communication and performance. *Organizational Behavior and Human Decision Processes, 144*, 145–170.
12. Schick, A. G., Gordon, L. A., & Haka, S. (1990). Information overload: A temporal approach. *Accounting, Organizations, and Society, 15*, 199–220.
13. Retrieved from *PC Magazine* encyclopedia http://www.pcmag.com/encyclopedia_term/0,2542,t=information+overload&i=44950,00.asp, and reinforced by information in Dawley, D. D., & Anthony, W. P. (2003). User perceptions of e-mail at work. *Journal of Business and Technical Communication, 17*, 170–200.
14. Based on Overholt, A. (2001, February). Intel's got (too much) mail. *Fast Company*. Retrieved from http://www.fastcompany.com/online/44/intel.html and http://blogs.intel.com/it/2006/10/information_overload.php.
15. David, P., Xu, L., Srivastava, J., & Kim, J. H. (2013). Media multitasking between two conversational tasks. *Computers in Human Behavior, 29*, 1657–1663; Krisnan, A., Kurtzberg, T. R., & Naquin, C. E. (2014). The curse of the smartphone: Electronic multitasking in negotiations. *Negotiation Journal, 30*, 191–208.
16. Kurland, N. B., & Pelled, L. H. (2000). Passing the word: Toward a model of gossip and power in the workplace. *Academy of Management Review, 25*, 428–438.
17. Crampton, S. M. (1998). The informal communication network: factors influencing grapevine activity. *Public Personnel Management*, Retrieved from http://www.allbusiness.com/management/735210-1.html.
18. Beersma, B., & Van Kleef, G. (2011). How the grapevine keeps you in line: Gossip increases contributions to the group. *Social Psychological and Personality Science, 2*, 642–649.
19. Wright, N. (n.d.). Keep it jargon-free. Retrieved from the Plain Language Action and Information Network website: http://www.plainlanguage.gov/howto/wordsuggestions/jargonfree.cfm.
20. MacGeorge, E. L., Graves, A. R., Feng, B., Gillihan, S. J., & Burleson, B. R. (2004). The myth of gender cultures: Similarities outweigh differences in men's and women's provision of and responses to supportive communication. *Sex Roles, 50*, 143–175.
21. Brescoll, V. L. (2011). Who takes the floor and why: Gender, power, and volubility in organizations. Administrative *Science Quarterly, 56*, 622–641.
22. Heath, K., Flynn, J., & Holt, M. D. (June, 2014). Women, find your voice. *Harvard Business Review*.
23. Ripley, R., & Watson, K. (May, 2014). We are learning. Are you listening? *Chief Learning Officer*, 34–37.
24. Pryor, S., Malshe, A., & Paradise, K. (2013). Salesperson listening in the extended sales relationship: An exploration of cognitive, affective, and temporal dimensions. *Journal of Personal Selling and Sales Management, 33*, 185–196.
25. O*NET Resource Center, the nation's primary source of occupational information. Retrieved from http://online.onetcenter.org/skills.
26. Brownell, J. (1990). Perceptions of effective listeners: A management study. *Journal of Business Communications, 27*, 401–415.
27. Kacmar, K. M., Witt, L. A., Zivnuska, S., & Gully, S. M. (2003). The interactive effect of leader-member exchange and communication frequency on performance ratings. *Journal of Applied Psychology, 88*, 764–772.
28. McCarthy, J. F. (2008). Short stories at work: Storytelling as an indicator of organizational commitment. *Group & Organization Management, 33*, 163–193.
29. Martens, M. L., Jennings, J. E., & Devereaux, J. P. (2007). Do the stories they tell get them the money they need? The role of entrepreneurial narratives in resource acquisition. *Academy of Management Journal, 50*, 1107–1132.
30. Patterson, K., Grenny, J., McMillan, R., & Switzler, A. (2002). *Crucial conversations: Tools for talking when stakes are high*. New York: McGraw-Hill.
31. Lee, D., & Hatesohl, D. Listening: Our most used communication skill. Retrieved from the University of Missouri website: http://extension.missouri.edu/explore/comm/cm0150.htm.
32. Flink, H. (2007, March). Tell it like it is: Essential communication skills for engineers. *Industrial Engineer, 39*, 44–49.
33. Mehrabian, A. (1981). *Silent messages*. New York: Wadsworth.
34. Gifford, R., Ng, C. F., & Wilkinson, M. (1985). Nonverbal cues in the employment interview: Links between applicant qualities and interviewer judgments. *Journal of Applied Psychology, 70*, 729–736.
35. Siegman, A. W. (1985). *Multichannel integrations of nonverbal behavior*. Hillsdale, NJ: Lawrence Erlbaum.
36. Knapp, M. L., Hall, J. A., & Horgan, T. G. (2014). *Nonverbal communication in human interaction*. Boston, MA: Cengage Learning.
37. Retrieved from http://abcnews.go.com/Health/story?id=118168&page=1.
38. Ekman, P., Friesen, W. V., & Hager, J. C. The facial action coding system (FACS). Retrieved from http://face-and-emotion.com/dataface/facs/manual.
39. Carney, D. R., Cuddy, A. J. C., & Yap, A. J. (2015). Review and summary of research on the embodied effects of expansive (vs. contractive) nonverbal displays. *Psychological Science, 26*, 657–663.
40. Hall, E. T. (1966). *The hidden dimension*. New York: Doubleday.
41. Allen, D. G., & Griffeth, R. W. (1997). Vertical and lateral information processing; Fulk, J., & Boyd, B. (1991). Emerging theories of communication in organizations. *Journal of Management, 17*, 407–446; Yates, J., & Orlikowski, W. J. (1992). Genres of organizational communication: A structurational approach to studying communication and media. *Academy of Management Review, 17*, 299–326.
42. Barry, B., & Fulmer, I. S. (2004). The medium and the message: The adaptive use of communication media in dyadic influence. *Academy of Management Review, 29*, 272–292.
43. Koetsier, J. (2020, February 18). Why 2020 is a critical global tipping point for social media. *Forbes*. Retrieved from https://www.forbes.com/sites/johnkoetsier/2020/02/18/why-2020-is-a-critical-global-tipping-point-for-social-media/#64325f9a2fa5.
44. Clement, J. (2019, August 9). Number of e-mails per day worldwide 2017-2023. *Statista*. Retrieved from https://www.statista.com/statistics/456500/daily-number-of-e-mails-worldwide/.
45. http://www.sims.berkeley.edu/research/projects/how-much-info/index.htm, as cited in David K. Isom. (2005, October 19). Electronic discovery: New power, new risks. Retrieved from http://utahbar.org/barjournal2000/html/november_2003_2.html.
46. Connley, C. (2017, August 17). This company has an ingenious way to free employees from email on vacation. CNBC. Retrieved from https://www.cnbc.com/2017/08/17/one-companys-genius-way-to-free-employees-from-email-on vacation.html#:~:text=German automaker Daimler has implemented,while away from the office.
47. Kruger, J. (2005). Egocentrism over email: Can we communicate as well as we think? *Journal of Personality and Social Psychology, 89*, 925–936.
48. Snyder, R. A., & Morris, J. H. (1984). Organizational communication and performance. *Journal of Applied Psychology, 69*, 461–465; Kacmar, K. M., Witt, L. A., Zivnuska, S., & Guly, S. M. (2003). The interactive effect of leader-member exchange and communication frequency on performance ratings. *Journal of Applied Psychology, 88*, 764–772.
49. Krackhardt, D., & Porter, L. W. (1986). The snowball effect: Turnover embedded in communication networks. *Journal of Applied Psychology, 71*, 50–55.
50. Nanji, A. (2017). Social media and blog usage by *Fortune* 500 companies in 2017. Retrieved from https://www.marketingprofs.com/charts/2017/33156/social-media-and-blog-usage-by-fortune-500-companies-in-2017.
51. Chief blogging officer title catching on with corporations. (2008, May 1). *Workforce Management*. Retrieved July 18, 2018 from http://www.workforce.com/section/00/article/25/50/77.html.
52. Retrieved from http://www.inc.com/larry-kim/why-multi-tasking-is-killing-your-brain.html.
53. Adapted from information in Tramel, M., & Reynolds, H. (1981). *Executive leadership*. Englewood Cliffs, NJ: Prentice Hall; Saltman, D., & O'Dea, N. (n.d.). Conflict management workshop PowerPoint presentation. Retrieved from http://www.nswrdn.com.au/client_images/6806.PDF; Communication stoppers. Retrieved from *Mental Health Today* website: http://www.mental-health-today.com/Healing/communicationstop.htm.

54. Case written by Rachel Mattenberger, Talya Bauer, and Berrin Erdogan to accompany Bauer, T. N. & Erdogan, B. (2021). *Organizational Behavior: Bridging Science and Practice (4.0).* Boston, MA: FlatWorld. Partially based on ideas and information contained in Shoulberg, W. (2018). Why Ikea succeeds around the world while other retailers falter, https://www.forbes.com/sites/warrenshoulberg/2018/07/30/put-another-stamp-on-the-ikea-passport/#69c48ca3f7cb; Pownall, A. (2018, September 5). Marcus Engman to leave IKEA and start own consultancy. Dezeen. Retrieved from https://www.dezeen.com/2018/09/05/ikea-head-of-design-marcus-engman-leaves/; Cohen, D. (2019). How Ikea got cool: The furniture giant's rise from boring basics to hyped homegoods. https://www.esquire.com/lifestyle/a25998144/ikea-evolution-new-design-collaborations-collections; Attfield, P. (2019). CEO for a day: U of T student experiences Ikea Canada's team culture. https://www.theglobeandmail.com/business/careers/management/article-ceo-for-a-day-u-of-t-student-experiences-ikea-canadas-team-culture; Pope, C. (2019). Conor Pope's day working in Ikea: 'What the f**k are you doing in that yellow?' https://www.irishtimes.com/life-and-style/people/conor-pope-s-day-working-in-ikea-what-the-f-k-are-you-doing-in-that-yellow-1.3825927.

CHAPTER 12

Managing Groups and Teams

Ultimately defeating Thanos to complete the Endgame, the Avengers serve as one of the most powerful teams in the Marvel Universe.

Source: Anton_Ivanov/Shutterstock.com

Chapter Learning Objectives

Reading this chapter will help you accomplish the following:

1. Recognize and understand group dynamics and development.
2. Understand the difference between groups and teams.
3. Understand how to organize effective teams.
4. Recognize and address common barriers to team effectiveness.
5. Build and maintain cohesive teams.

TABLE 12.1 The P-O-L-C Framework

Planning	Organizing	Leading	Controlling
1. Vision & Mission	1. Organization Design	1. Leadership	1. Systems/Processes
2. Strategizing	2. Culture	2. Decision Making	2. Strategic Human Resources
3. Goals & Objectives	3. Social Networks	3. Communications	
		4. Groups/Teams	
		5. Motivation	

Groups and teams are found everywhere on today's landscape, and team-management skills are required within each of the planning-organizing-leading-controlling (P-O-L-C) functions. This is exemplified by the statistic that 91% of high-level managers surveyed agreed with the statement "teams are central to organizational success."[1] For instance, planning may often occur in teams, particularly in less centralized organizations or toward the higher levels of the firm. When making decisions about the structure of the firm and individual jobs, managers conducting their organizing function must determine how teams will be used within the organization. Teams and groups have implications for the controlling function because teams require different performance assessments and rewards. And, some cultures tend to prefer to work in teams more than others. Students from Africa, China, and the Middle East prefer to work in teams more than American students.[2] Finally, teams and groups are a facet of the leading function. Today's managers must be both good team members and good team leaders. Managing groups and teams is a key component of leadership.

12.1 Group Dynamics

Learning Objectives

1. Understand the difference between informal and formal groups.
2. Learn the stages of group development.
3. Understand the punctuated equilibrium model.
4. Learn how group cohesion, social loafing, and collective efficacy can affect groups.

Because many tasks in today's world have become so complex, groups and teams have become an essential component of an organization's success. Group success depends on the successful management of its members and making sure all aspects of work are fair for each member. Being able to work in a group is a key skill for managers and employees alike.

Types of Groups: Formal and Informal

group

A collection of individuals who interact with each other such that one person's actions have an impact on the others.

A **group** is a collection of individuals who interact with each other such that one person's actions have an impact on the others. In organizations, most work by necessity is done within groups. How groups function has important implications for organizational productivity. Groups where people get along, feel the desire to contribute, and are capable of coordinating their efforts may have high performance levels, whereas those characterized by extreme levels of conflict or hostility may demoralize members of the workforce.

In organizations, groups can be classified into two basic types—informal and formal. **Informal work groups** are made up of two or more individuals who are associated with one another in ways not prescribed by the formal organization. For example, a few people in the company who get together to play tennis on the weekend would be considered an informal group. A **formal work group** is made up of managers, subordinates, or both—with close associations among group members that influence the behavior of individuals in the group.

Employees at Google are encouraged to find micro-communities by joining interest groups with fellow Googlers. There are "Gleeglers" who sing together, "Snowglers" who ski together, and "Greyglers," older Google employees who share interests and support each other.

Source: Shawn Goldberg/Shutterstock.com

Stages of Group Development

Knowledge of effective groups can be better understood by learning how groups develop. American organizational psychologist Bruce Tuckman presented a now well-known model of group development in 1965 that is still widely used today. On the basis of his observations of group behavior in a variety of settings, he proposed a four-stage map of group evolution, known as the Forming-Storming-Norming-Performing Model.[3] Later he enhanced the model by adding a fifth and final stage, adjourning. The phases are illustrated in Figure 12.1. Just as an individual moves through developmental stages such as childhood, adolescence, and adulthood, so does a group, although in a much shorter period of time.

Informal work groups

Groups made up of two or more individuals who are associated with one another in ways not prescribed by the formal organization.

formal work group

A group made up of managers, subordinates, or both—with close associations among group members that influence the behavior of individuals in the group.

According to this theory, to facilitate a group successfully, the leader needs to move through various leadership styles over time. Generally, this is accomplished by first being more direct, eventually serving as a coach, and later, once the group is able to assume more power and responsibility for itself, shifting to delegator.

While research has not confirmed that this is descriptive of how groups progress, knowing and following these steps can help groups be more effective. For example, groups that do not go through the storming phase early on will often return to this stage toward the end of the group process to address unresolved issues. Another example of the validity of the group development model involves groups that take the time to get to know each other socially in the forming stage. When this socialization occurs, groups tend to handle future challenges better because the individuals have an understanding of each other's needs.

FIGURE 12.1 Stages of the Group Development Model

Forming

In the **forming** stage, the group comes together for the first time. The members may already know each other or they may be total strangers. In either case, there is a level of formality, some anxiety, and a degree of guardedness as group members are not sure how they will fit into the group or how work will be conducted. "Will I be accepted? What will my role be? Who has the power in the group?" These are some of the questions participants think about during this stage of group for-

forming

The stage in which the group comes together for the first time.

mation. Because of the large amount of uncertainty, members tend to be polite, conflict avoidant, and observant. They are trying to figure out the "rules of the game" without being too vulnerable. At this point, they may also be quite excited and optimistic about the task, perhaps experiencing a level of pride at being chosen to join a particular group.

Group members are trying to achieve several goals at this stage, although this may not necessarily be done consciously. First, they are trying to get to know one another. Often this can be accomplished by finding some common ground. Members also begin to explore group boundaries to determine what will be considered acceptable behavior. "Can I interrupt? Can I leave when I feel like it?" This trial phase may also involve testing the appointed leader or seeing whether a leader emerges from the group. At this point, group members are also discovering how the group will work in terms of what needs to be done and who will be responsible for each task. This stage is often characterized by abstract discussions about issues to be addressed by the group; those who like to get moving can become impatient with this part of the process. This phase is usually short in duration, perhaps a meeting or two. Research examining initial impressions in geographically diverse MBA groups found individuals that were geographically dissimilar but expressed positive emotions such as joy had influence early in a project but geographically dissimilar members who expressed disappointment in early stages were rated as more influential in later stages.[4]

Storming

storming

This is the phase when group members begin to explore their power and influence and they often stake out their territory by differentiating themselves from the other group members rather than seeking common ground.

Once group members feel sufficiently safe and included, they tend to enter the **storming** phase. Participants focus less on keeping their guard up as they shed social facades, becoming more authentic and more argumentative. Group members begin to explore their power and influence, and they often stake out their territory by differentiating themselves from the other group members rather than seeking common ground. Discussions can become heated as participants raise conflicting points of view and values, or disagree over how tasks should be accomplished and who should be responsible for certain tasks. It is not unusual for group members to become defensive, competitive, or jealous. Group members may take sides or begin to form cliques within the group. Questioning and resisting direction from the leader is also quite common. "Why should I have to do this? Who designed this project in the first place? Why do I have to listen to you?"

Although little seems to get accomplished at this stage, it actually serves an important purpose—group members are becoming more authentic as they express their deeper thoughts and feelings. What they are really exploring is "Can I truly be myself, have power, and be accepted?" During this chaotic stage, a great deal of creative energy that was previously buried is released and available for use, but it takes skill to move the group from Storming to Norming. In many cases, the group gets stuck in the storming phase.

Once group members discover that they can be authentic and that the group is capable of handling differences without dissolving, they are ready to enter the next stage, norming.

Norming

norming

Stage when participants find it easy to establish their own ground rules (or *norms*) and define their operating procedures and goals.

Group members often feel relief at the **norming** stage, and they are much more committed to each other and the group's goal. Feeling energized, group members are now ready to get to work. Finding themselves more cohesive and cooperative, participants find it easy to establish their own ground rules (or *norms*) and define their operating procedures and goals. The group tends to make big decisions, while subgroups or individuals handle the smaller decisions. It is hoped at this point that group members are more open and respectful toward each other and willing to ask one another for both help and feedback. They may even begin to form friendships and share more personal information. At this point, the leader should become more of a facilitator by stepping back and letting the group assume more responsibility for its goal. Since the group's energy is running high, this is an ideal time to host a social or team-building event.

Performing

Be it virtual or in person, happy hours are one common norm of high performing teams.

Source: Shutterstock.com

Galvanized by a sense of shared vision and a feeling of unity, the group is ready to move into high gear. Members are more interdependent, individuality and differences are respected, and group members feel themselves to be part of a greater entity. At the **performing** stage, participants are not only getting the work done, but they also pay greater attention to *how* they are doing it. They ask such questions as, "Do our operating procedures best support productivity and quality assurance? Do we have suitable means for addressing differences that arise so we can preempt destructive conflicts? Are we relating to and communicating with each other in ways that enhance group dynamics and help us achieve our goals? How can I further develop as a person to become more effective?" By now, the group has matured, becoming more competent, autonomous, and insightful. Group leaders can finally move into coaching roles and help members grow in skill and leadership. These leadership shifts are essential for managers enacting the Leadership function to keep in mind. In fact, a manager who leads multiple teams may find it necessary to shift leadership styles not only over time but between teams at different stages.

performing

The stage in which participants are not only getting the work done, but they also pay greater attention to *how* they are doing it.

Adjourning

Adjourning is the final stage when the group separates. Many groups or teams formed in a business context are project-oriented and therefore are temporary. Alternatively, a working group may dissolve because of an organizational restructuring. As with graduating from school or leaving home for the first time, these endings can be bittersweet, with group members feeling a combination of victory, grief, and insecurity about what is coming next. For those who like routine and bond closely with fellow group members, this transition can be particularly challenging. Group leaders and members alike should be sensitive to handling these endings respectfully and compassionately. An ideal way to close a group is to set aside time to debrief ("How did it all go? What did we learn?"), acknowledge one another, and celebrate a job well done.

adjourning

The fifth and final stage later added to the Tuckman model.

Many organizations and teams are realizing that how you adjourn may make a difference for future performance. Conducting a meeting at the end of a project or an event may turn the project into a learning opportunity. Referred to as **after-action review**, *retrospective meeting*, *debriefing meeting*, or even *post-mortem*, these meetings help members discuss what went right, what went wrong, and what could have been done differently.[5] Research shows that after-action reviews result in performance gains, higher levels of team confidence, a greater openness of communication, and have beneficial effects on team cohesiveness. The U.S. Army is an organization that utilizes after-action reviews extensively and consistently.[6]

after-action review

A meeting conducted at the end of a project or event, where team members discuss what went right, what went wrong, and what could have been done differently. Commonly used alternative names include "retrospective meeting", "debrief meeting", or post mortem.

FIGURE 12.2 Developing the Avengers

The five phases in the Stages of the Group Development Model can be seen in a number of well-known groups—both real and imagined. Here, we apply the model to the development seen in the 2012 blockbuster *The Avengers*.

Forming

The Avengers were formed when S.H.I.E.L.D. (Strategic Homeland Intervention, Enforcement, and Logistics Division) agent Phil Coulson brought together superheroes Iron Man, Thor, Captain America, Hulk, Black Widow, and Hawkeye.

Storming

Storming occurs as Avengers members begin to argue over how best to defeat their enemy, the dreaded Loki. Storming also arises as several members express concern with Dr. Bruce Banner, who can turn into the uncontrollable Hulk at a moment's notice.

Norming

When S.H.I.E.L.D.'s flying aircraft carrier, the Helicarrier, is attacked, the Avengers begin to search for norms as they fight a common enemy.

Performing

As the Avengers rally to protect New York and defeat Loki, they realize the team must work together to perform at the level necessary to defeat such a powerful foe. The Hulk plays a critical role in the defense of the city.

Adjourning

As the film ends, S.H.I.E.L.D. agent Nick Fury notes that the Avengers will return when they are again needed. The Avengers may not be ready to adjourn, as shown in one of the film's post-credit scenes, where the Avengers dine in silence at a local shawarma restaurant.

Source: Anton_Ivanov_Shutterstock.com, Olena Z_Shutterstock.com, F.jarabica_Shutterstock.com

Music Rap-Up: Rocking This Meeting

Twinprov perform a rap on stages of group development.

View in the online reader

The Punctuated-Equilibrium Model

The five-stage model assumes a linear process. According to the model, a group progresses to the performing stage, at which point it finds itself in an ongoing, smooth-sailing situation until the group dissolves. In reality, subsequent researchers, most notably Joy H. Karriker, have found that the life of a group is much more dynamic and cyclical in nature.[7] For example, a group may operate in the performing stage for several months. Then, because of a disruption, such as a competing emerging technology that changes the rules of the game or the introduction of a new CEO, the group may move back into the storming phase before returning to performing. Ideally, any regression in the linear group progression will ultimately result in a higher level of functioning. Proponents of this cyclical model draw from behavioral scientist Connie Gersick's study of **punctuated equilibrium**.[8]

punctuated equilibrium

The theory that change within groups occurs in rapid, radical spurts rather than gradually over time.

FIGURE 12.3 The Punctuated Equilibrium Model

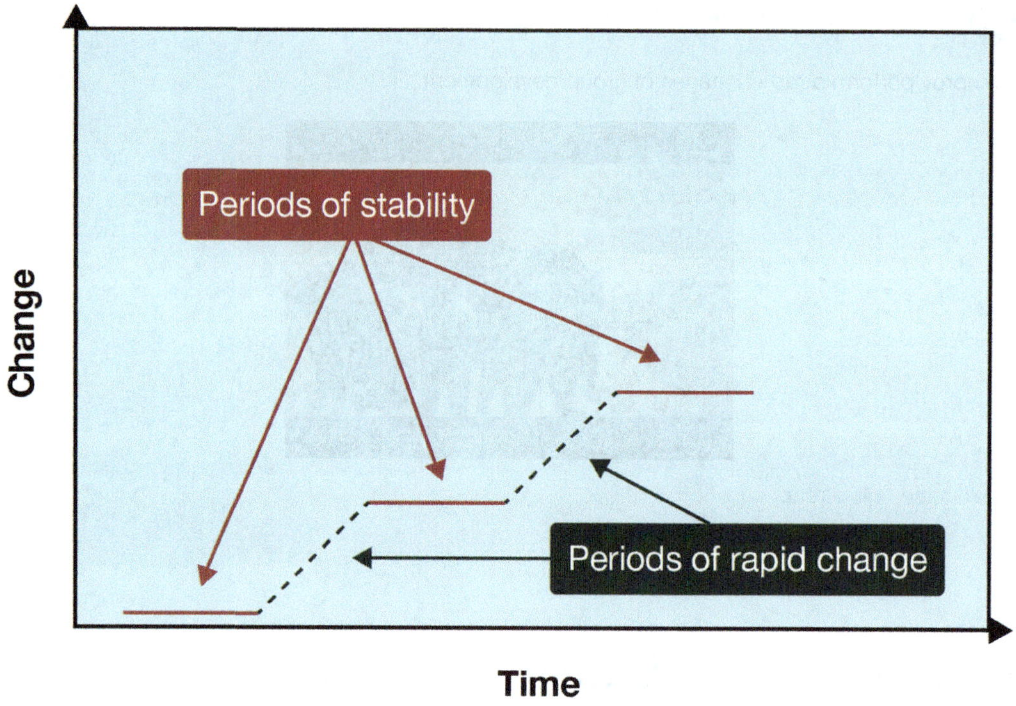

The concept of punctuated equilibrium was first proposed in 1972 by paleontologists Niles Eldredge and Stephen Jay Gould, who both believed that evolution occurred in rapid, radical spurts rather than gradually over time. Identifying numerous examples of this pattern in social behavior, Gersick found that the concept applied to organizational change. She proposed that groups remain fairly static, maintaining a certain equilibrium for long periods. Change during these periods is incremental, largely due to the resistance to change that arises when systems take root and processes become institutionalized. In this model, revolutionary change occurs in brief, punctuated bursts, generally catalyzed by a crisis or a problem that breaks through the systemic inertia and shakes up the deep organizational structures in place. At this point, the organization or group has the opportunity to learn and create new structures that are better aligned with current realities. Whether the group does this is not guaranteed. In sum, in Gersick's model, groups can repeatedly cycle through the Storming and Performing stages, with revolutionary change taking place during short transitional windows. For organizations and groups who understand that disruption, conflict, and chaos are inevitable in the life of a social system, these disruptions represent opportunities for innovation and creativity. Research supports the idea that team engagement changes over time and intensifies near deadlines.[9]

Cohesion, Social Loafing, and Collective Efficacy

cohesion

The degree of camaraderie within the group.

Cohesion can be thought of as a kind of social glue. It refers to the degree of camaraderie within the group. Cohesive groups are those in which members are attached to each other and act as one unit. The more cohesive a group, the more productive it will be, and the more rewarding the experience will be for the group's members.[10] Members of cohesive groups tend to have the following characteristics: they have a collective identity; they experience a moral bond and a desire to remain part of the group; they share a sense of purpose, working together on a meaningful task or cause; and they establish a structured pattern of communication.

The fundamental factors affecting group cohesion include the following:

- **Similarity.** The more similar group members are in terms of age, sex, education, skills, attitudes, values, and beliefs, the more likely the group will bond.
- **Stability.** The longer a group stays together, the more cohesive it becomes.
- **Size.** Smaller groups tend to have higher levels of cohesion.
- **Support.** When group members receive coaching and are encouraged to support their fellow team members, group identity strengthens.
- **Satisfaction.** Cohesion is correlated with how pleased group members are with one another's performance, behavior, and conformity to group norms.

As you might imagine, there are many benefits in creating a cohesive group. Members are generally more personally satisfied and feel greater self-confidence and self-esteem in a group where they feel they belong. For many, membership in such a group can be a buffer against stress, which can improve mental and physical well-being. Because members are invested in the group and its work, they are more likely to regularly attend and actively participate in the group, taking more responsibility for the group's functioning. In addition, members can draw on the strength of the group to persevere through challenging situations that might otherwise be too hard to tackle alone.

Does cohesion result in a higher performing team? The answer is: It depends. There are certainly conditions in which cohesion is an advantage for team effectiveness. When efficiency, or completing a task quickly and using fewer resources is the goal, cohesion is an advantage. Further, cohesion is more strongly related to performance behaviors rather than outcomes. In other words, cohesive teams do the right things, but of course doing the right things may not always have positive results due to environmental constraints.[11]

One advantage of cohesive groups is their tendency to share information and knowledge. Because they trust each other, members of cohesive groups have an advantage when it comes to sharing information, which often is a key component of innovativeness and creativity.[12]

Can a Group Have Too Much Cohesion?

Keep in mind that groups can have too much cohesion.[13] Because members can come to value belonging over all else, an internal pressure to conform may arise where some members modify their behavior to adhere to group norms. Members may become conflict avoidant, focusing on trying to please one another so as not to be ostracized. In some cases, members might censor themselves to maintain the party line. As such, the group is dominated by a superficial sense of harmony and discourages diversity of thought. Having less tolerance for deviants who threaten the group's static identity, cohesive groups will often disapprove of members who dare to disagree. Members attempting to make a change may be criticized, undermined, or even ostracized by other members, who perceive their attempts as a threat to the status quo. The painful possibility of being marginalized can keep many members in line with the majority.

The more strongly members identify with the group, the easier it is to see outsiders as inferior, or in extreme cases, as enemies. It is easy to see how this can lead to increased insularity. This form of prejudice can have a downward spiral effect. The group is not getting corrective feedback from within its own confines, and it is closing itself off from input and a cross-fertilization of ideas from the outside. In such an environment, groups can easily adopt extreme ideas that will not be challenged. Denial increases as problems are ignored and failures are blamed on external factors. With limited, often biased, information and no internal or external opposition, groups like these can make disastrous decisions.

groupthink

A group pressure phenomenon that creates a tendency to avoid a critical evaluation of ideas the group favors.

Groupthink is a group pressure phenomenon that creates a tendency to avoid a critical evaluation of ideas the group favors. Groupthink is most common in highly cohesive groups.[14]

Cohesive groups can go awry in much milder ways. For example, group members can value their social interactions so much that they have fun together but spend little time on accomplishing their assigned task. Or a group's goal may begin to diverge from the larger organization's goal and those trying to uphold the organization's goal may be criticized (for example, students may tease the class "brain" for doing well in school).

In addition, research shows that cohesion leads to acceptance of group norms.[15] Groups with high task commitment tend to do well, but imagine a group where the norms are to work as little as possible. As you might imagine, these groups get little accomplished and can actually work together against the organization's goals.

FIGURE 12.4 Group Dimensions

Groups with high cohesion and high task commitment tend to be the most effective.

	Low task commitment	High task commitment
Low group cohesion	Low performance	Performance ranges depending on a number of factors
High group cohesion	Low performance	High performance

Social Loafing

Social loafing refers to the tendency of individuals to put in less effort when working in a group context. This phenomenon, also known as the Ringelmann effect, was first noted by French agricultural engineer Max Ringelmann in 1913. In one study, he had people pull on a rope individually and in groups. He found that as the number of people pulling increased, the group's total pulling force was less than the sum of individual efforts had been when measured alone.[16]

The Ringelmann effect found that as the number of group members increases, the effort of each member decreases.

Source: Shutterstock.com

Why do people work less hard when they are working with other people? Observations show that as the size of the group grows, this effect becomes larger as well.[17] The social loafing tendency is not so much a matter of laziness as a matter of perceiving that one will receive neither one's fair share of rewards if the group is successful nor blame if the group fails. Rationales for this behavior include, "My own effort will have little effect on the outcome." "Others aren't pulling their weight, so why should I?" Or "I don't have much to contribute, and no one will notice anyway." This is a consistent effect across a great number of group tasks and across cultures.[18] Research also shows that perceptions of fairness are related to less social loafing.[19] Therefore, teams that are deemed more fair should also see less social loafing.

social loafing

The tendency of individuals to put in less effort when working in a group context.

Collective Efficacy

collective efficacy

A group's perception of its ability to successfully perform well.

Collective efficacy refers to a group's perception of its ability to successfully perform well.[20] A group with high collective efficacy is one whose members share a belief in the group's capability to pursue its agreed-upon course of action and attain its goals. Collective efficacy is influenced by a number of factors, including watching others ("that group did it and we're better than them"), verbal persuasion ("we can do this"), and how a person feels ("this is a good group"). Research shows that a group's collective efficacy is positively related to its performance.[21] In addition, this relationship is stronger when task interdependence (the degree an individual's task is linked to someone else's work) is high rather than low.[22]

Key Takeaway

Groups may be either formal or informal. Groups go through developmental stages much like individuals do. The Forming-Storming-Norming-Performing-Adjourning Model is useful in prescribing stages that groups should pay attention to as they develop. The punctuated-equilibrium model of group development argues that groups often move forward during bursts of change after long periods without change. Groups that are similar, stable, small, supportive, and satisfied tend to be more cohesive than groups that are not. Cohesion can help support group performance if the group values task completion, but too much cohesion can also be a concern for groups. Social loafing increases as groups become larger. When collective efficacy is high, groups tend to perform better.

Discussion Questions

1. How do the tactics related to group dynamics involve the managerial functions outlined by the P-O-L-C framework?
2. If you believe the punctuated-equilibrium model is true about groups, how can you use this knowledge to help your own group?
3. Think about the most cohesive group you have ever been in. How did it compare to less cohesive groups in terms of similarity, stability, size, support, and satisfaction?
4. Why do you think social loafing occurs within groups? What can be done to combat this problem?
5. Have you seen instances of collective efficacy helping or hurting a team? Explain your answer.

12.2 Understanding Team Design Characteristics

Learning Objectives

1. Understand differences between groups and teams.
2. Understand the factors leading to the rise in the use of teams.
3. Understand how tasks and roles affect teams.
4. Identify different types of teams.
5. Identify team design considerations.

Effective teams give companies a significant competitive advantage. In a high-functioning team, the sum is truly greater than the parts. Team members not only benefit from one another's diverse experiences and perspectives but also stimulate each other's creativity. For many people, working in a team can be more fun than working alone. In this section, we define a team and its difference from a group and explain different team characteristics, types of teams companies use, and how to design effective teams.

Differences Between Groups and Teams

process loss

Any aspect of group interaction that inhibits group functioning.

team

A cohesive coalition of people working together to achieve mutual goals.

Organizations consist of groups of people. What exactly is the difference between a group and a team? A group is a collection of individuals. Within an organization, groups might consist of project-related groups such as a product group or division or they can encompass an entire store or branch of a company. The performance of a group consists of the inputs of the group minus any process losses such as the quality of a product, ramp-up time to production, or the sales for a given month. **Process loss** is any aspect of group interaction that inhibits group functioning.

What is the difference between a *group* and a *team*? A collection of people is not a team, though they may learn to function in that way. A **team** is a particular type of group—a cohesive coalition of people working together to achieve mutual goals. Being on a team does not equate to a total suppression of personal agendas, but it does require a commitment to the vision and involves each individual working toward accomplishing the team's objective. Teams differ from other types of groups in that members are focused on a joint goal or product, such as a presentation, discussing a topic, writing a report, creating a new design or prototype, or winning a team competition. Moreover, teams also tend to be defined by their relatively smaller size. For instance, according to one definition, "A team is a *small* number of people with complementary skills who are committed to a common purpose, performance goals, and approach for which they are mutually accountable."[23]

The purpose of assembling a team is to accomplish larger, more complex goals than what would be possible for an individual working alone or by pooling the efforts of several individuals working independently. Teamwork is also needed in cases where multiple skills are required from several individuals. Teams can, but do not always, provide improved performance. Working together to further a team agenda seems to increase mutual cooperation between what are often competing factions. The aim and purpose of a team is to perform, get results, and achieve success in the workplace. The best managers are those who can gather together a group of individuals and mold them into an effective team.

The key properties of a true team include **collaborative action** where, along with a common goal, teams have collaborative tasks. Conversely, in a group, individuals are responsible only for their own area. They also share the rewards of strong team performance with their **compensation based on shared outcomes**. Compensation of individuals must be based primarily on a shared outcome, not individual performance. Members are also willing to **sacrifice for the common good** in which individuals give up scarce resources for the common good instead of competing for those resources. For example, soccer and basketball teams, in which the individuals actively help each other, forgo their own chance to score by passing the ball, and win or lose collectively as a team.

Teams in Organizations

The early 1990s saw a dramatic rise in the use of teams within organizations, along with dramatic results such as the Miller Brewing Company increasing productivity 30% in the plants that used self-directed teams compared with those that used the traditional organization. This same method allowed Texas Instruments in Malaysia to reduce defects from 100 parts per million to 20 parts per million. In addition, Westinghouse reduced its cycle time from 12 weeks to 2 weeks, and Harris Electronics was able to achieve an 18% reduction in costs.[24] The team method has served countless companies over the years through both quantifiable improvements and more subtle individual worker-related benefits.

Companies such as Schneider Electric, maker of Square D of circuit breakers, switched to self-directed teams and found that overtime on machines like the punch press dropped 70% under teams. Productivity increased because the setup operators were able to manipulate the work in much more effective ways than a supervisor could dictate.[25] In 2001, clothing retailer Chico's Retailer Services Inc. was looking to grow its business. The company hired Scott Edmonds as president, and two years later revenues had almost doubled from $378 million to $760 million. By 2006, revenues were $1.6 billion and Chico's had nine years of double-digit, same-store sales growth. And the company has continued to do well since he left. What did Edmonds do to get these results? He created a horizontal organization with high-performance teams that were empowered with decision-making ability and accountability for results.

The use of teams also began to increase because advances in technology have resulted in more complex systems that require contributions from multiple people across the organization. Overall, team-based organizations have more motivation and involvement, and teams can often accomplish more than individuals.[26] It is no wonder organizations are relying on teams more and more.

Teams are not a cure-all for organizations. To determine whether a team is needed, organizations should consider whether a variety of knowledge, skills, and abilities are needed, whether ideas and feedback are needed from different groups within the organization, how interdependent the tasks are, if wide cooperation is needed to get things done, and whether the organization would benefit from shared goals.[27] If the answer to these questions is "yes," then a team or teams might make sense. For example, research shows that the more team members perceive that outcomes are interdependent, the better they share information and the better they perform.[28]

Team Tasks and Roles

Teams differ in terms of the tasks they are trying to accomplish. Richard Hackman identified three major classes of tasks: (1) production tasks, (2) idea-generation tasks, and (3) problem-solving tasks.[29] **Production tasks** include actually making something, such as a building, a product, or a marketing plan. **Idea-generation tasks** deal with creative tasks, such as brainstorming a new direction or creating a new process. **Problem-solving tasks** refer to coming up with plans for actions and making decisions, both facets of managerial P-O-L-C functions (planning and leading). For example, a team may be charged with coming up with a new marketing slogan, which is an idea-generation task, while another team might be asked to manage an entire line of products, including making decisions about products to produce, managing the production of the product lines, marketing them, and staffing their division. The second team has all three types of tasks to accomplish at different points in time.

production tasks

Tasks that include actually making something such as a building, a product, or a marketing plan.

idea-generation tasks

Creative tasks such as brainstorming a new direction or creating a new process.

problem-solving tasks

Tasks involving coming up with plans for actions and making decision.

Task Interdependence

Another key to understanding how tasks are related to teams is to understand their level of task interdependence. **Task interdependence** refers to the degree that team members depend on one another to get information, support, or materials from other team members to be effective. Research shows that as the team's task requires communication, collaboration, and coordination, team performance will be highly dependent on how cohesive the team is, whereas in teams with low levels of task interdependence, cohesion does not make much difference.[30]

task interdependence

The degree that team members depend on one another to get information, support, or materials from other team members to be effective.

FIGURE 12.5 Task Interdependence

Task interdependence refers to the degree that team members depend on one another to reach the goals of the team. Interdependence varies significantly based on the type of team. Here, we illustrate the three different types of task interdependence using different team sports.

Pooled interdependence exists when team members work independently and simply combine their efforts to create the team's output. This type of interdependence is seen in football where each player often has a unique "assignment" he is responsible for during a specific play.

Reciprocal interdependence exists when individuals work together and ideas and project assignments are passed back and forth until the project is complete. This type of interdependence is seen in basketball where players must be constantly alert to receive a pass, rebound, or transition between offense and defense.

Sequential interdependence exists when one person's output becomes another person's input. This interdependence is common in baseball where the ball is fielded and then relayed from player to player until it reaches its ultimate destination (hopefully).

Source: Shutterstock.com

There are three types of task interdependence. **Pooled interdependence** exists when team members may work independently and simply combine their efforts to create the team's output. For example, when students meet to divide the sections of a research paper and one person assembles the sections together to create one paper, the team is using the pooled-interdependence model. However, they might decide that it makes more sense to start with one person writing the introduction of their research paper, then the second person reads what was written by the first person and, drawing from this section, writes about the findings within the paper. Using the findings section, the third person writes the conclusions. If one person's output becomes another person's input, the team would be experiencing **sequential interdependence**. And finally, if the student team decided that in order to create a top notch research paper they should work together on each phase of the research paper so that their best ideas would be captured at each stage, they would be undertaking **reciprocal interdependence**. Another important type of interdependence that is not specific to the task itself is **outcome interdependence**, where the rewards that an individual receives depend on the performance of others.

pooled interdependence

This exists when team members may work independently and simply combine their efforts to create the team's output.

sequential interdependence

Where one person's output becomes another person's input.

reciprocal interdependence

The point at which team members work on each task simultaneously.

outcome interdependence

A time when rewards that an individual receives depend on the performance of others.

Team Roles

The success of U.S. Airways Flight 1549 to land with no fatalities when it crashed into the Hudson River in New York City is a good example of an effective work team.[31] For example, reports show that Captain Chesley Sullenberger took over flying from copilot Jeff Skiles, who had handled the takeoff, but had less experience in the Airbus.[32] This is consistent with the research findings that effective teams divide up tasks so the best people are in the best positions.

Studies show that individuals who are more aware of team roles and the behavior required for each role perform better than individuals that do not. This fact remains true for both student-project teams as well as work teams, even after accounting for intelligence and personality.[33] Early research found that teams tend to have two categories of roles consisting of those related to the tasks at hand and those related to the team's functioning. For example, teams that only focus on production at all costs may be successful in the short run, but if they pay no attention to how team members feel about working 70 hours a week, they are likely to experience high turnover. Teams also do well when their members have different cognitive styles.[34]

Based on decades of research on teams, ten key roles have been identified.[35] Team leadership is effective when leaders are able to adapt the roles they are contributing to, or asking others to contribute to, fit what the team needs, given its stage and the tasks at hand.[36] Ineffective leaders might always engage in the same task role behaviors when what they really need to do is focus on social roles, put disagreements aside, and get back to work. While these behaviors can be effective from time to time, if the team does not modify its role behaviors as things change, they most likely will not be effective.

FIGURE 12.6 Team Roles

Teams are based on many roles being carried out as summarized by the Team Role Typology. These 10 roles include task roles (contractor, creator, contributor, completer, and critic), social roles (calibrator, communicator, and cooperator), and boundary-spanning roles (consul and coordinator).

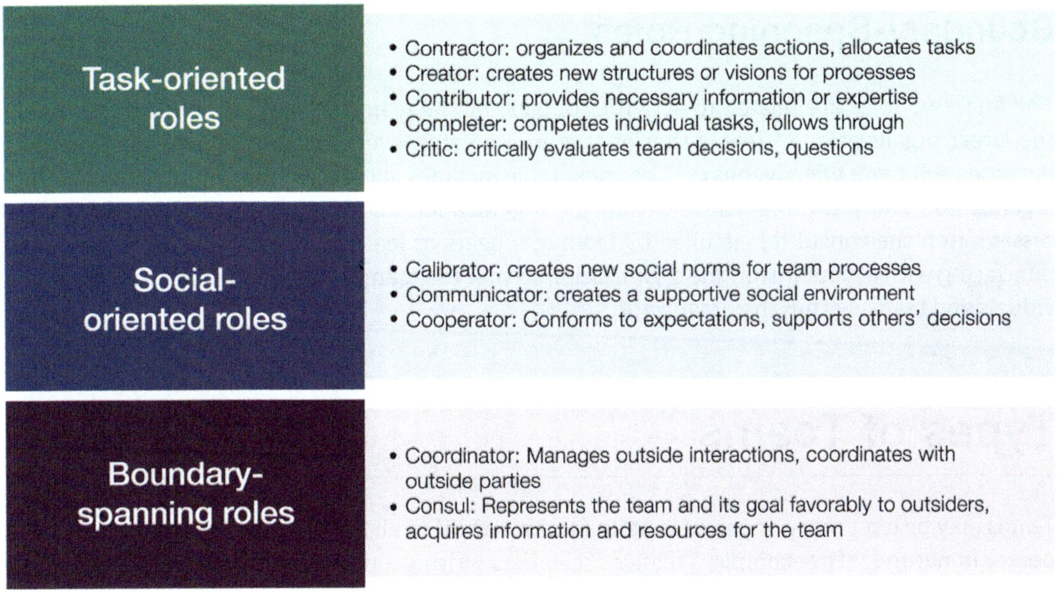

Source: Based on Mumford, T. V., Van Iddekinge, C. H., Morgeson, F. P., & Campion, M. A. (2008). The team role test: Development and validation of a team role knowledge situational judgment test. *Journal of Applied Psychology, 93*, 250–267; Mumford, T. V., Campion, M. A., & Morgeson, F. P. (2006). Situational judgments in work teams: A team role typology. In J. A. Weekley & R. E. Ployhart (Eds.), *Situational judgment tests: Theory, measurement (pp. 319–343). Mahwah, NJ: Lawrence Erlbaum.*

Task Roles

Five roles make up the task portion of the role typology. The contractor role includes behaviors that serve to organize the team's work, including creating team timelines, production schedules, and task sequencing. The creator role deals more with changes in the team's task process structure. For example, reframing the team goals and looking at the context of goals would fall under this role. The contributor role is important because it brings information and expertise to the team. This role is characterized by sharing knowledge and training those who have less expertise to strengthen the team. Research shows that teams with highly intelligent members and evenly distributed workloads are more effective than those with uneven workloads.[37] The completer role is also important, as it is often where ideas are transformed into action. Behaviors associated with this role include following up on tasks such as gathering needed background information or summarizing the team's ideas into reports. Finally, the critic role includes "devil's advocate" behaviors, which go against the assumptions being made by the team.

Social Roles

Social roles serve to keep the team operating effectively. When the social roles are filled, team members feel more cohesive and the group is less prone to suffer process losses or biases, such as social loafing, groupthink, or a lack of participation from all members. Three roles fall under the umbrella of social roles. The cooperator role includes supporting those with expertise toward the team's goals; this is a proactive role. The communicator role includes behaviors that are targeted at collaboration, such as practicing good listening skills and appropriately using humor to defuse tense situations. Having a good communicator helps the team to feel more open to sharing ideas. Finally, the calibrator role is an important one and serves to keep the team on track in terms of suggesting any needed changes to the team's process. This role includes initiating discussions about potential team problems such as power struggles or other tensions. Similarly, this role may involve settling disagreements or pointing out what is working and what is not in terms of team process.

Boundary-Spanning Roles

The final two roles are related to activities outside of the team that help to connect the team to the larger organization.[38] Teams that engage in a greater level of boundary-spanning behaviors increase their team effectiveness.[39] The consul role includes gathering information from the larger organization and informing those within the organization about team activities, goals, and successes; often the consul role is filled by team managers or leaders. The coordinator role includes interfacing with others within the organization so that the team's efforts are in line with other individuals and teams within the organization.

Types of Teams

Teams may be temporary or permanent. In fact, one-third of all teams in the United States are temporary in nature.[40] For example, a team of scientists writing a research article for publication may be temporary, virtual, and cross-functional.

Teams may be permanent or long term, but more typically, a team exists for a limited time. In fact, one-third of all teams in the United States are temporary.[41] An example of a temporary team is a **task force** that addresses a specific issue or problem until it is resolved. Other teams may be temporary or ongoing such as **product-development teams**. In addition, matrix organizations have **cross-functional teams** where individuals from different parts of the organization staff the team, which may be temporary or long-standing in nature.

task force

A temporary team that is asked to address a specific issue or problem until it is resolved.

product-development teams

A type of team that may be either temporary or ongoing.

cross-functional teams

Teams that involve individuals from different parts of the organization staff.

virtual teams

Teams in which members are not located in the same physical place.

Virtual Teams

Virtual teams are teams in which members are not located in the same physical place. They may work in different cities, states, or even different countries. Some virtual teams are formed by necessity, such as to take advantage of lower labor costs in different countries; one study found that upward of 8.4 million individuals worldwide work virtually on at least one team.[42] Some estimates suggest that between 30% and 45% of individuals work at home or as virtual employees.[43] Often, virtual teams are formed to take advantage of distributed expertise or time—the needed experts may be living in different cities. A company that sells products around the world, for example, may need technologists who can solve customer problems at any hour of the day or night. It may be difficult to find the caliber of people needed who would be willing to work at 2 a.m. on a Saturday, for example. So companies organize virtual technical support teams. BakBone Software, for instance, has a 13-member technical-support team. Each member has a degree in computer science and members are divided among offices in California, Maryland, England, and Tokyo. BakBone believes it has been able to hire stronger candidates by drawing from a diverse talent pool and hiring in different geographic regions rather than limiting hiring to one region or time zone.[44] Some companies go a step further, eliminating corporate offices altogether. Automattic, the company that provides hosting services for the blogging tool WordPress, has employees in more than 70 different countries, where employees work from their homes. The company maintains office space in San Francisco for occasional use, but most communication among team members is online.[45] During the COVID-19 pandemic, many high-profile organizations such as Facebook and Twitter are allowing employees to work from home—indefinitely in many cases.

Despite potential benefits, virtual teams present special management challenges, particularly to the controlling function. Managers often think that they have to see team members working to believe that work is being done. Because this kind of oversight is impossible in virtual team situations, it is important to devise evaluation schemes that focus on deliverables. Are team members delivering what they said they would? In self-managed teams, are team members producing the results the team decided to measure itself on?

Another special challenge of virtual teams is building **trust**. Will team members deliver results just as they would in face-to-face teams? Can members trust one another to do what they said they would do? Companies often invest in bringing a virtual team together at least once so members can get to know one another and build trust.[46] In manager-led virtual teams, managers should be held accountable for their team's results and evaluated on their ability as a team leader.

trust

The belief that the other party will show integrity, fairness, and predictability in one's actions toward the other.

Finally, communication is especially important in virtual teams, be it through e-mail, phone calls, conference calls, project management tools, and/or online meetings such as those on Microsoft Teams or Zoom that help organize work. If individuals in a virtual team are not fully engaged and tend to avoid conflict, team performance can suffer.[47] Choosing the right technological aids will help virtual teams be successful. Tools to schedule meeting times, such as Doodle, document sharing tools, such as Dropbox or Google docs, and tools that allow joint and simultaneous creation of presentations, such as Prezi, enable virtual teams to coordinate and communicate more effectively.

Top Management Teams

Top management teams are appointed by the chief executive officer (CEO) and, ideally, reflect the skills and areas that the CEO considers vital for the company. There are no formal rules about top management team design or structure. The top management team includes representatives from functional areas, such as finance, human resources, and marketing or key geographic areas, such as Europe, Asia, and North America. Depending on the company, other areas may be represented such as legal counsel or the company's chief technologist. Typical top management team member titles include chief operating officer (COO), chief financial officer (CFO), chief marketing officer (CMO), or chief technology officer (CTO). Because CEOs spend an increasing amount of time outside their companies (i.e., with suppliers, customers, regulators, and so on), the role of the COO has taken on a much higher level of internal operating responsibilities. In most American companies, the CEO also serves as chairman of the board and can have the additional title of president. Companies have top management teams to help set the company's vision and strategic direction, key tasks within the planning P-O-L-C function. Top teams make decisions on new markets, expansions, acquisitions, or divestitures. The top team is also important for its symbolic role—how the top team behaves dictates the organization's culture and priorities by allocating resources and by modeling behaviors that will likely be emulated lower down in the organization. Importantly, the top team is most effective when team composition is functionally and demographically diverse and when it can truly operate as a *team*, not just as a *group* of individual executives.[48] The board of directors is an example of one important team within corporations as well as nonprofit organizations that utilize boards as a key decision-making body.

top management teams

Teams that are appointed by the chief executive officer (CEO) and, ideally, reflect the skills and areas that the CEO considers vital for the company.

succession planning

The process of identifying future members of the top management team.

That "the people make the place" holds especially true for members of the top management team. In a study of 15 firms that demonstrated excellence, defined as sustained performance over a 15-year period, leadership researcher Jim Collins noted that those firms attended to people first and strategy second. "They got the right people on the bus, moved the wrong people off the bus, ushered the right people to the right seats—then they figured out where to drive it."[49] The best teams plan for turnover. **Succession planning** is the process of identifying future members of the top management team. Effective succession planning allows the best top teams to achieve high performance today and create a legacy of high performance for the future.

Board Roles

Source: Claudio Divizia/Shutterstock.com

William Shakespeare once wrote, "All the world's a stage, and the men and women merely players." This analogy applies well to boards of directors. When the performance of board members is impressive, the company is able to put on a dynamic show. But if a board member phones in their role, failure may soon follow. We discuss the different roles board members may play below.

- **Accountant:** Board members may, at times, approve financial objectives
- **Lawyer:** Ensuring the firm complies with applicable law is a key role.
- **Advisor:** Providing advice on strategic issues is a critical role that is overlooked by less effective boards.
- **Activists:** Boards must ensure that the rights and interests of stakeholders (especially stockholders) are represented.
- **Human Resource Manager:** Boards must monitor the CEO and engage in hiring, firing and the administration of CEO compensation.
- **Agent:** Because board members may serve in powerful positions at other companies, a well-networked board member may be able to bring new connections to the firm.

Team Leadership and Autonomy

Teams also vary in terms of how they are led. **Traditional or manager-led teams** are teams in which the manager serves as the team leader. The manager assigns work to other team members. These types of teams are the most natural to form, wherein managers have the power to hire and fire team members and are held accountable for the team's results. However, a meta-analysis of nearly 14,000 teams found that the more hierarchical that team's were, the more conflict they had and the less effective they were.[50] This doesn't mean that all teams which have a more hierarchical nature are problematic. But, it does mean that care should be taken when thinking about team leadership to ensure that everyone feels heard and that conflict is managed appropriately.

traditional or manager-led teams

Teams where the manager serves as the team leader.

FIGURE 12.7 Building a Better Team Leader at Google

Here are the top eight behaviors:

1. Be a good coach.
2. Empower your team and don't micromanage.
3. Express interest in team members' success and personal well-being.
4. Be productive and results-oriented.
5. Be a good communicator and listen to your team.
6. Help your employees with career development.
7. Have a clear vision and strategy for the team.
8. Have key technical skills so you can help advise the team.

Individuals within the People Analytics group at Google, Inc., sought to find out what key behaviors the best team leaders engaged in. They pored over the performance reviews, feedback surveys, and award nominations to statistically uncover what those considered the "best bosses" did to earn that title. This project was code-named "Project Oxygen." What they found illustrated how important it is for teams to be led by the right leaders who engage in the right behaviors.

Source: photosearch/Shutterstock.com

Self-managed teams are a newer form of team that rose in popularity with the Total Quality Movement in the 1980s. Unlike manager-led teams, these teams manage themselves and do not report directly to a supervisor. Instead, team members select their own leader, and they may even take turns in the leadership role. Self-managed teams also have the power to select new team members. As a whole, the team shares responsibility for a significant task, such as assembly of an entire car. The task is ongoing rather than temporary, such as a charity fund drive for a given year.

self-managed teams

Teams that manage themselves and do not report directly to a supervisor. Instead, team members select their own leader, and they may even take turns in the leadership role.

Organizations began to use self-managed teams as a way to reduce hierarchy, by allowing team members to complete tasks and solve problems on their own. The benefits of self-managed teams extend much further. Research has shown that employees in self-managed teams have higher job satisfaction, increased self-esteem, and higher growth on the job. The benefits to the organization include increased productivity, increased flexibility, and lower turnover. Self-managed teams can be found at all levels of the organization, and they bring particular benefits to lower-level employees by giving them a sense of ownership of their jobs that they may not otherwise have. The increased satisfaction can also reduce absenteeism, because employees do not want to let their team members down.

Typical team goals are improving quality, reducing costs, and meeting deadlines. Teams also have a "stretch" goal, which is difficult to reach but important to the business unit. Many teams have special project goals as well. Texas Instruments (TI), a company that makes semiconductors, used self-directed teams to make improvements in work processes.[51] Teams were allowed to set their own goals in conjunction with managers and other teams. TI also added an individual component to the typical team compensation system. This individual component rewarded team members for learning new skills that added to their knowledge. These "knowledge blocks" include topics such as leadership, administration, and problem solving. The team decides what additional skills people might need to help the team meet its objectives. Team members would then take classes or otherwise demonstrate their proficiency in that new skill on the job to be certified for mastering the skill. Individuals could then be evaluated based on their contribution to the team and how they are building skills to support the team.

empowered teams

Teams that have the responsibility as well as the authority to achieve their goals.

Self-managed teams are **empowered**, which means that they have the *responsibility* as well as the *authority* to achieve their goals. Team members have the power to control tasks and processes and to make decisions. Research shows that particularly in teams faced with clear and stable tasks, having an established structure within the team has been shown to be helpful. In other words, these teams would benefit from having a clear division of labor, members specialized in performing different tasks, and communication protocols, rules, and guidelines. In self-managed teams, having such a structure is helpful in increasing learning and minimizing conflict.[52] Self-managed teams may still have a leader who helps them coordinate with the larger organization.[53] For a product team composed of engineering, production, and marketing employees, empowerment means that the team can decide everything about a product's appearance, production, and cost without having to get permission or sign-off from higher management. As a result, empowered teams can more effectively meet tighter deadlines. At AT&T, for example, the model 4200 phone team cut development time in half while lowering costs and improving quality by using the empowered team approach.[54]

TABLE 12.2 Team Leadership is a Major Determinant of How Autonomous a Team Can Be

Traditionally managed teams	Self-managed teams	Self-directed team
Leader resides outside the team	The team manages itself but still has a team leader	The team makes all decisions internally about leadership and how work is done
Potential for low autonomy	Potential for low, medium, or high autonomy	Potential for high autonomy

Designing Effective Teams

Designing an effective team means making decisions about team composition (who should be on the team), team size (the optimal number of people on the team), and team diversity (should team members be of similar background, such as all engineers, or of different backgrounds). Answering these questions will depend, to a large extent, on the type of task that the team will be performing. Teams can be charged with a variety of tasks, from problem solving to generating creative and innovative ideas to managing the daily operations of a manufacturing plant.

Who Are the Best Individuals for the Team?

A key consideration when forming a team is to ensure that all the team members are qualified for the roles they will fill for the team. This process often entails understanding the knowledge, skills, and abilities (KSAs) of team members as well as the personality traits needed before starting the selection process.[55] For example, when GE decided to manufacture jet engines after 20 years of not doing so, they staffed the new factory not just with engineers but with engineers holding FAA (Federal Aviation Administration) licenses. The superior qualifications of the engineers allowed the team to effectively make key decisions with minimal oversight. When talking to potential team members, it is important to communicate the job requirements and norms of the team. To the degree that this is not possible, such as when already-existing groups are used, it is important to think of ways to train the team members as much as possible to help ensure success. In addition to task knowledge, research has shown that individuals who understand the concepts covered in this chapter and in this book, such as conflict resolution, motivation, planning, and leadership actually perform better on their jobs. This finding holds for a variety of jobs, including officers in the U.S. Air Force, employees at a pulp mill, or team members at a box manufacturing plant.[56]

How Large Should My Team Be?

Interestingly, research has shown that regardless of team size, the most active team member speaks 43% of the time. The difference is that the team member who participates the least in a three-person team is still active 23% of the time versus only 3% in a ten-person team.[57] When deciding team size, a good rule of thumb is a size of two to twenty members. The majority of teams have 10 members or less because the larger the team, the harder it is to coordinate and interact as a team. With fewer individuals, team members are more able to work through differences and agree on a common plan of action. They have a clearer understanding of others' roles and greater accountability to fulfill their roles (remember social loafing?). Some tasks, however, require larger team sizes because of the need for diverse skills or because of the complexity of the task. In those cases, the best solution is to create subteams, where one member from each subteam is a member of a larger coordinating team. The relationship between team size and performance seems to greatly depend on the level of task interdependence, with some studies finding larger teams outproducing smaller teams and other studies finding just the opposite.[58] The bottom line is that team size should be matched to the goals of the team.

The ideal size for a team depends on the task. Groups larger than 10 members tend to be harder to coordinate and often break into subteams to accomplish the work.

Source: Shutterstock.com

How Diverse Should My Team Be?

Team composition and team diversity often go hand in hand. Teams whose members have complementary skills are often more successful, because members can see each other's blind spots. One team member's strengths can compensate for another's weaknesses.[59] For example, consider the challenge that companies face when trying to forecast future sales of a given product. Workers who are educated as forecasters have the analytic skills needed for forecasting, but these workers often lack critical information about customers. Salespeople, in contrast, regularly communicate with customers, which means they're in the know about upcoming customer decisions. But salespeople often lack the analytic skills, discipline, or desire to enter this knowledge into spreadsheets and software that will help a company forecast future sales. Putting forecasters and salespeople together on a team tasked with determining the most accurate product forecast each quarter makes the best use of each member's skills and expertise.

Diversity in team composition can help teams come up with more creative and effective solutions. Research shows that teams that believe in the value of diversity performed better than teams that do not.[60] The more diverse a team is in terms of expertise, gender, age, and background, the more ability the group has to avoid the problems of groupthink.[61] For example, different educational levels for team members were related to more creativity in R&D teams and faster time to market for new products.[62] Members will be more inclined to make different kinds of mistakes, which means that they'll be able to catch and correct those mistakes. At the same time, a diversity of team members in their individual value orientations is related to conflict within the group and lower levels of cohesion. This means that teams with diversity will need to learn to manage the resulting conflict in order to reap the benefits of diversity.[63]

Key Takeaway

Groups and teams are not the same thing. Organizations have moved toward the extensive use of teams within organizations. The tasks a team is charged with accomplishing affect how they perform. Teams may have task and/or outcome interdependence. Team roles consist of task, social, and boundary-spanning roles. Different types of teams include task forces, product development teams, cross-functional teams, and top management teams. Team leadership and autonomy vary, depending on whether the team is traditionally managed, self-managed, or self-directed. Teams are most effective when they comprise members with the right skills for the tasks at hand, are not too large, and contain diversity across team members. Decisions about where and how to use teams, the leadership of teams, and the structure of teams illustrate the overlap in the organizing and leading P-O-L-C functions.

Discussion Questions

1. Think of the last team you were on. Did the task you were asked to do affect the team? Why or why not?
2. Which of the 10 work roles do you normally take in a team? How difficult or easy do you think it would be for you to take on a different role?
3. Have you ever worked on a virtual team? If so, what were the challenges and advantages of working virtually?
4. How large do you think teams should be and why?

12.3 Managing Effective Teams

Learning Objectives

1. Understand how to create team norms, roles, and expectations.
2. Identify keys to running effective team meetings.
3. Putting it all together, list the seven drivers of team success.

When it comes to the management of teams, a variety of factors relate to a team's success or failure. We have already covered the importance of team members as well as team roles and types of teams in the previous section. In the next section, we will cover several team processes related to success, including establishing team norms, agreeing upon shared team contracts, establishing psychological safety within the team, engaging in regular team performance after-action reviews, and running effective meetings.

Establishing Team Norms and Contracts

A key to successful team design is to have clear norms, roles, and expectations among team members. Problems such as social loafing or groupthink can be avoided by paying careful attention to team member differences and providing clear definitions for roles, expectancy, measurement, and rewards.

Establish Team Norms

Norms are shared expectations concerning behaviors within a group or team. Just as new employees learn to understand and share the assumptions, organizational norms, and values that are part of an organization's culture, they also must learn team norms. This understanding helps teams be more cohesive and perform better. Norms are a powerful way of ensuring coordination within a team. For example, is it acceptable to be late to meetings? How prepared are you supposed to be at the meetings? Is it acceptable to criticize someone else's work? These norms are shaped early during the life of a team and affect whether the team is productive, cohesive, and successful.

norms

Shared expectations about how things operate within a group or team.

Agree Upon Team Contracts

Scientific research, as well as experience working with thousands of teams, shows that teams that are able to articulate and agree on established ground rules, goals, and roles and develop a **team contract** around these standards are better equipped to face challenges that may arise within the team.[64] Having a team contract does not necessarily mean that the team will be successful, but it can serve as a roadmap when the team veers off course. Questions that can help to create a meaningful team contract include the following:

- **Team values and goals.** What are our shared team values? What is our team goal?
- **Team roles and leadership.** Who does what within this team? (Who takes notes at the meeting? Who sets the agenda? Who assigns tasks? Who runs the meetings?) Does the team have a formal leader? If so, what are his or her roles?
- **Team decision making.** How are minor decisions made? How are major decisions made?
- **Team communication.** Who do you contact if you cannot make a meeting? Who communicates with whom? How often will the team meet?
- **Team performance.** What constitutes good team performance? What if a team member tries hard but does not seem to be producing quality work? How will poor attendance/work quality be managed?

team contract

A contract that includes agreements on established ground rules, goals, and roles.

A team contract can help articulate expectations and serve as a roadmap for successful team interactions.

Source: Shutterstock.com

Establish Psychological Safety

Psychological safety refers to the perception that the consequences of taking interpersonal risks in workplace contexts are worth the risk.[65] This matters for individuals as well as organizations in terms of effectiveness. Research has established the critical nature of establishing psychological safety within teams as it fosters the sharing of ideas, open communication such as engaging in voice behaviors, healthy levels of risk-taking, and increased creativity.[66] Trust is also important for team performance.[67] After reviewing the literature, Amy Edmondson, an expert in the area of teams and psychological safety concluded that "Evidence from empirical studies conducted in diverse organizational and industrial contexts, across multiple countries and regions (e.g., the United States, Israel, Taiwan), supports the idea that psychological safety matters greatly for workplace effectiveness, and suggests a surprising level of generalizability of the research findings."[68] This is consistent with work done at Google where they set out to study what makes teams successful. Their project—entitled Project Aristotle—looked at 180 teams within Google and found that across all kinds of teams, it was psychological safety that separated teams that were doing OK versus those that were thriving and successful.[69]

Engage in Team Performance After-Action Reviews

A meta-analysis of over 2,000 individuals in teams showed that teams that engage in team after-action reviews (or debriefs) are 25% more effective than those that do not.[70] These findings held across teams as well as individuals and for simulated and real settings, as well as for medical and non-medical teams. One good thing about after-action reviews is that they are relatively inexpensive and do not need to take a great deal of time (the average after-action review studied was 18 minutes long). After-action reviews are commonly used in organizations such as Harley-Davidson, British Petroleum, and Motorola. To maximize their effectiveness, it is recommended to engage in debriefs that encourage active self-learning and reflection, have a developmental intent, focus on specific events or team milestones, and include reflection on multiple sources of information regarding team challenges and successes.[71] The steps to a debrief can be simple or more elaborate but four simple questions are helpful to reflect upon, as a team, after a team milestone to keep everyone on track, avoid major project derailments, and to align expectations and team efforts.

1. What did we want or expect to happen?
2. What were the actual results?
3. What went well?
4. What can we sustain or improve upon and how?

Managing Effective Teams: Workplace Meetings

Anyone who has been involved in a team knows it involves team meetings. While few individuals relish meetings, they serve an important function in terms of information sharing and decision making. They also serve an important social function and can help to build team cohesion and a task function in terms of coordination. Unfortunately, many of us have attended lengthy meetings that we later felt wasted time and where little happened that could not have been accomplished by reading an email in five minutes. To run effective meetings, it helps to think of what should happen before, during, and after meetings.[72]

How To Make Workplace Meetings More Effective

Steven Rogelberg, University of North Carolina at Charlotte

View in the online reader

Before the Meeting

Much of the effectiveness of a meeting is determined before the team gathers. There are six key strategies to ensure that the team members get the most out of their meeting.

Is a meeting needed? Leaders should do a number of things before the meeting to help make it effective. The first thing is to be sure a meeting is even needed. If the meeting is primarily informational, ask yourself whether it is imperative that the group fully understands the information and whether future decisions will be built on this information. If so, a meeting may be needed. If not, perhaps simply communicating with everyone in a written format will save valuable time. Similarly, decision-making meetings make the most sense when the problem is complex and important, there are questions of fairness to be resolved, and commitment is needed moving forward.

Decide who should be at the meeting, and only invite those. The more people who attend the meeting, the less each person will participate. So there should be a reason why each person is invited to the meeting. Consider who should absolutely be there and limit your invitation to only those individuals. Be sure to inform anyone not at the meeting of any new information, policies, or decisions that might affect them or to which they might have insights.

Decide how long the meeting should be and keep it short. The longer the meeting, the more distractions there will be, such as people checking e-mail or daydreaming. Keep them short.

Create and distribute an effective agenda. An agenda is important in helping to inform those invited about the purpose of the meeting. It also helps organize the flow of the meeting and keep the team on track. But, research shows that just having an agenda is not enough. While agendas are important tools, the most important factor for effectiveness is to focus on what happens within the meeting itself and shift the agenda accordingly.

Determine how all members can attend. Many teams include physically distributed individuals working in different locations and time zones. Being clear about how to join the meeting virtually, if that is possible, is important as is making sure that technology is in place so things will work smoothly.[73]

Send a reminder before the meeting. Reminding everyone of the purpose, time, and location of the meeting helps everyone prepare themselves. Anyone who has attended a team meeting only to find there is no reason to meet because members have not completed their agreed-upon tasks knows that, as a result, team performance or morale can be negatively affected. Follow up to make sure everyone is prepared. As a team member, inform others immediately if you will not be ready with your tasks so they can determine whether the meeting should be postponed.

During the Meeting

During the meeting, there are several things you can do to make sure the team starts and keeps on track.

Start the meeting on time. Waiting for members who are running late only punishes those who are on time and reinforces the idea that it's OK to be late. Starting the meeting promptly sends an important signal that you are respectful of everyone's time.

Although it might be tempting to wait on individuals who are running late, effective meetings begin promptly to signal respect for those who arrived on time.

Source: Shutterstock.com

Get on the same page. Jeff Bezos, CEO of Amazon, is known for starting meetings with quiet reading time where everyone reads the relevant information related to that meeting. This can be effective in making sure everyone is informed and responding to the same information. He also argues that it helps deal with time management and information overload as time is carved out to prepare for the meeting as part of the meeting. This approach may not work for everyone but it is something worth considering if folks tend to come to meetings unprepared.

Follow the meeting agenda. Veering off agenda communicates to members that it is not important. It also makes it difficult for others to keep track of where you are in the meeting and can facilitate important points not being addressed.

Manage group dynamics for full participation. There are a number of group dynamics that can limit a team's functioning. Be on the lookout for full participation and engagement from all team members as well as any potential problems such as social loafing, group conflict, or groupthink.

Summarize the meeting with action items. Be sure to clarify team member roles moving forward. If tasks are not clear, chances are role confusion will arise later. There should be clear notes from the meeting regarding who is responsible for each action item and the timeframes associated with next steps.

End the meeting on time. This is vitally important as it shows that you respect everyone's time and are organized. If another meeting is needed to follow up, schedule it later, but don't let the meeting run over.

Conducting meetings standing up has been shown to save time and keep information flowing across the team.[74]

Source: Shutterstock.com

After the Meeting

Follow up on action items. After the meeting understand critical action items. In addition, it may be necessary to follow up on the action items of others. Jack Dorsey, cofounder of Twitter and Square, manages by transparency and trust. At Square, in any meeting with more than three people, one person is required to take notes and make them available to the whole company (regardless of the topic).

Putting It All Together

Scott Tannenbaum and Eduardo Salas have studied teams in a variety of contexts from board rooms, student teams, military teams, medical teams, production teams, and astronauts. They have done a great deal of research on what seems to really make a difference when it comes to driving effective team performance. In other words, they boiled down research on this topic and found that there are seven drivers of team success.

Most of these key drivers have already been covered in this chapter as well as previous chapters but putting them all together can be useful. When considering a new or established team, ask yourself these seven questions to ensure that all the team factors are in place (see Table 12.3).

TABLE 12.3

Driver	Fundamental Question
Capability	Do we have the right people with the right mix of *knowledge, skills*, and other attributes?
Cooperation	Do members possess the right *beliefs and attitudes* about their team?
Coordination	Are team members exhibiting the necessary *teamwork behaviors* for team success?
Communication	Do team members *communicate* effectively with each other and with people outside the team?
Cognition	Do team members possess a *shared understanding* about key factors such as priorities, roles, and vision?
Coaching	Does the leader and/or team members demonstrate the necessary *leadership* behaviors?
Conditions	Is the *context* in which the team operates favorable for performing effectively (e.g., ample resources, supportive culture)?

Used with permission, Tannenbaum & Salas (2021). *Teams that Work*. Oxford University Press.

Teamwork Success Checklist

Eduardo Salas, Rice University

View in the online reader

Key Takeaway

Much like group development, team socialization takes place over the life of the team. The stages move from evaluation to commitment to role transition. Team norms are important for the team process and help to establish who is doing what for the team and how the team will function. Creating a team contract helps with this process. Keys to address in a team contract are team values and goals, team roles and leadership, team decision making, team communication expectations, and how team performance is characterized. Psychological safety is a key ingredient when it comes to effective team management. Team meetings can help a team coordinate and share information. Effective meetings include preparation, management during the meeting, and follow-up on action items generated in the meeting. Finally, there are seven drivers of team performance with associated questions which you can ask to help you put it all together.

Discussion Questions

1. Have the norms for most of the teams you have belonged to been formal or informal? How do you think that has affected these teams?
2. Have you ever been involved in creating a team contract? Explain how you think that may have influenced how the team functioned.
3. Should the person requesting a meeting always prepare a meeting agenda? Why or why not?
4. Do you think conducting team meetings standing up is a good idea? Why or why not?

12.4 Barriers to Effective Teams

Learning Objective

1. Recognize common barriers to effective teams and how to address them.

Problems can arise in any team that will hurt the team's effectiveness. Here are some common problems faced by teams and how to deal with them including challenges in knowing where to begin, dominating team members, poor member engagement and performance, lack of communication and coordination, and poorly managed team conflict.

Common Problems faced by Teams

Challenges of Knowing Where to Begin

At the start of a project, team members may be at a loss as to how to begin. Also, they may have reached the end of a task but are unable to move on to the next step or put the task to rest. Floundering often results from a lack of clear goals, so the remedy is to go back to the team's mission or plan and make sure that it is clear to everyone. Team leaders can help move the team past floundering by asking, "What is holding us up? Do we need more data? Do we need assurances or support? Does anyone feel that we've missed something important?"

Dominating Team Members

Some team members may have a dominating personality that encroaches on the participation or airtime of others. This overbearing behavior may hurt team morale or the momentum of the team. A good way to overcome this barrier is to design a team evaluation to include a "balance of participation" in meetings. Knowing that fair and equitable participation by all will affect the team's performance evaluation will help team members limit domination by one member and encourage participation from all members, even shy or reluctant ones. Team members can say, "We've heard from Mary on this issue, so let's hear from others about their ideas."

Poor Performance of Some Team Members

Research shows that teams deal with poor performers in different ways, depending on members' perceptions of the reasons for poor performance.[75] In situations in which the poor performer is perceived as lacking in ability, teams are more likely to train the member. In situations in which members perceive the individual as simply low on motivation, they are more likely to try to motivate or reject the poor performer. Keep in mind that justice is an important part of keeping individuals working hard for the team.[76] Be sure that poor performers are dealt with in a way that is deemed fair by all the team members.

Lack of Communication and Coordination

We know from research regarding team role as well as processes that effective teams have strong communication and coordination. This is critical for teams dealing with complex and important tasks. One study of 1,839 global virtual teams found that communication frequency and coordination were related to team performance.[77] Such findings also highlight the importance of engaging in regular check-ins, information sharing, and debriefs as described in this chapter. Thinking of communication as an investment in your team rather than as "wasted time" can be useful. Research showing that teams that eat meals together are more effective is inline with organizations such as Google, which has cafes and areas for employees to meet informally over coffee and meals.[78]

Poorly Managed Team Conflict

Disagreements among team members are normal and should be expected. Healthy teams raise issues and discuss differing points of view because that will ultimately help the team reach stronger, more well-reasoned decisions. Unfortunately, sometimes disagreements arise owing to personality issues or feuds that predated a team's formation. Ideally, teams should be designed to avoid bringing adversaries together on the same team.[79] If that is not possible, the next best solution is to have adversaries discuss their issues privately, so the team's progress is not disrupted. The team leader or other team members can offer to facilitate the discussion. One way to make a discussion between conflicting parties meaningful is to form a behavioral contract between the two parties. That is, if one party agrees to do X, then the other will agree to do Y.[80] Research suggests that an important factor of how teams deal with conflict is how safe that team's members feel in expressing their concerns as we read about earlier regarding team trust and perceptions of psychological safety.[81]

Key Takeaway

Barriers to effective teams include the challenges of knowing where to begin, dominating team members, poor performance of team members, and poorly managed team conflict.

Discussion Questions

1. Have you ever been involved in a team where one or more dominating team members hurt the team's performance? Share what happened and how the team dealt with this.
2. Have you ever been involved in a team where conflict erupted between team members? How was the situation handled?

12.5 Developing Your Team Skills

Learning Objective

1. Identify guidelines for developing cohesion in your team.

Steps to Creating and Maintaining a Cohesive Team

There are several steps managers can take to help build a cohesive team. For example:

- Align the group with the greater organization. Establish common objectives in which members can get involved.
- Let members have choices in setting their own goals. Include them in decision making at the organizational level.
- Define clear roles. Demonstrate how each person's contribution furthers the group goal—everyone is responsible for a special piece of the puzzle.
- Situate group members in proximity to one another. This builds familiarity.
- Give frequent praise, both to individuals and to the group, and encourage them to praise each other. This builds individual self-confidence, reaffirms positive behavior, and creates an overall positive atmosphere.
- Treat all members with dignity and respect. This demonstrates that there are no favorites and everyone is valued.
- Celebrate differences. This highlights each individual's contribution while also making diversity a norm.
- Establish common rituals. Thursday morning coffee, monthly potlucks—these reaffirm group identity and create shared experiences.

Key Takeaway

There are many things managers can do to help build a cohesive team. One key thing to remember is that too much cohesion without strong performance norms can be a problem. Many of the ways to build cohesive groups are also fun, such as celebrating successes and creating rituals.

Discussion Questions

1. Think of the most cohesive group you have ever been in. What factors made the group so close?
2. What are some challenges you see to creating a cohesive group?
3. How does team size affect cohesion?

12.6 Case in Point: Building Teams with Kindness

Daniel Lubetzky, Founder and Executive Chairman of Kind LLC

Source: https://commons.wikimedia.org/wiki/Category:Daniel_Lubetzky#/media/File:Daniel_Lubetzky_(April_14,_2015).jpg. CCL 2.0.

Kind LLC is a food company that sells products such as snack bars, granola bars, and granola. Daniel Lubetsky, an immigrant from Mexico and the son of a holocaust survivor, founded the company in 2004. When he was a child, his father recounted stories about his experiences during the holocaust. One story in particular, about a surprising act of kindness his father encountered from a German soldier, inspired Lubetsky to build a company that would encourage people to live kinder lives.

Lubetsky first founded PeaceWorks, another food company whose mission is to support peace through economic cooperation and unlikely supply chain partnerships. While traveling the world in support of PeaceWorks, Lubetsky recognized a need for healthier, tastier snacks for people on the go. Thus, he created Kind.

Kind's stated mission is to make the world a little kinder, and it aims to accomplish this by starting with its workplace culture. Kind employs approximately 500 people, endearingly referred to by Lubetsky as "team members," to acknowledge their shared contribution toward achieving the company's goals. The company's values include ownership, teamwork, transparency, caring, and developing self & others.

According to Lubetsky, Kind's culture is founded on constructive feedback. Team members are expected to communicate openly and honestly and are encouraged to provide candid feedback to one another, regardless of title or rank. This communication framework helps to create a culture of trust, loyalty, and professional development.

Lubetsky also encourages a culture of empathy, which is manifested by the company demonstrating to team members that it cares about them as people, not just as professionals. One example of this is the "KINDOs" program, which encourages team members to formally celebrate each other each month for acting in a way that aligns with the company's values. Kind leadership also does their best to avoid letting people go. In most cases, rather than team members being fired, they will have an opportunity to develop the skills necessary to thrive in their role or they will be reassigned to a role that better fits their interests or skills.

Finally, teams at Kind are expected to share ownership in accomplishing the tasks necessary to succeed. This means that everybody in the company, regardless of role or position, is expected to get their hands dirty. According to Lubetsky, who took on many different operational roles when founding the company, ". . . there's no task too small or insignificant for me—or any of us—to do."[82]

Multimedia Extension—What Makes Us Kind

View in the online reader

Case Discussion Questions

1. Kind's mission is to "make the world a little kinder, one snack at a time." How does the organization demonstrate this mission in the way it treats its employees?
2. How do you think values such as honesty, empathy, and shared ownership impact the way teams work together? What other values have you experienced that contribute to effective teamwork?
3. One key aspect of Kind's culture is constructive feedback, regardless of employee seniority. What are some of the positive outcomes of this type of culture? What are some potential difficulties?
4. In what ways do you think Daniel Lubetsky's childhood experiences might impact his current leadership style? What effect do you think this has on his teams?
5. How would you describe the nuances between the terms, "employees" and "team members?" Do you think this type of vocabulary matters to members of an organization?

Endnotes

1. Martin, A., & Bal, V. (2006). *The state of teams: CCL research report*. Greensboro, NC: Center for Creative Leadership.
2. Retrieved from http://www.bloomberg.com/bw/articles/2014-06-06/why-american-business-students-dislike-working-in-teams.
3. Tuckman, B. (1965). Developmental sequence in small groups. *Psychological Bulletin, 63*, 384–399.
4. George, E., Li, J., & Gupta, V. (2020). Geographical Dissimilarity and Team Member Influence: Do Emotions Experienced in the Initial Team Meeting Matter? *Academy of Management Journal* doi.org/10.5465/amj.2017.0744 Retrieved from https://journals.aom.org/doi/epub/10.5465/amj.2017.0744.summary.
5. Reiter-Palmon, R., Kennel, V., Allen, J. A., Jones, K. J., & Skinner, A. M. (2015). Naturalistic decision making in after-action review meetings: The implementation of and learning from post-fall huddles. *Journal of Occupational and Organizational Psychology, 88*, 322–340.
6. Villado, A. J., & Arthur, W. J. (2013). The comparative effect of subjective and objective after-action reviews on team performance on a complex task. *Journal of Applied Psychology, 98*, 514–528.
7. Karriker, J. H. (2005). Cyclical group development and interaction-based leadership emergence in autonomous teams: an integrated model. *Journal of Leadership & Organizational Studies, 11*, 54–64.
8. Gersick, C. J. G. (1991). Revolutionary change theories: A multilevel exploration of the punctuated equilibrium paradigm. *Academy of Management Review, 16*(1), 10–36.
9. Larson, N. L., McLarnon, M. J., & O'Neill, T. A. (in press). Challenging the "static" quo: Trajectories of engagement in team processes toward a deadline. *Journal of Applied Psychology*.
10. Beal, D. J., Cohen, R. R., Burke, M. J., & McLendon, C. L. (2003). Cohesion and performance in groups: A meta-analytic clarification of construct relations. *Journal of Applied Psychology, 88*, 989–1004; Evans, C. R., & Dion, K. L. (1991). Group cohesion and performance: A meta-analysis. *Small Group Research, 22*, 175–186.
11. Beal, D. J., Cohen, R. R., Burke, M. J., & McLendon, C. L. (2003). Cohesion and performance in groups: A meta-analytic clarification of construct relations. *Journal of Applied Psychology, 88*, 989–1004; Picazo, C., Gamero, N., Zornoza, A., & Peiró, J. M. (2015). Testing relations between group cohesion and satisfaction in project teams: A cross-level and cross-lagged approach. *European Journal of Work and Organizational Psychology, 24*, 297–307.
12. Guler, I., & Nerkar, A. (2012). The impact of global and local cohesion on innovation in the pharmaceutical industry. *Strategic Management Journal, 33*, 535–549.
13. Park, W. W., Kim, M. S., & Gully, S. M. (2017). Effect of Cohesion on the Curvilinear Relationship Between Team Efficacy and Performance. *Small Group Research, 48*, 455-481.
14. Janis, I. L. (1972). *Victims of groupthink*. New York: Houghton Mifflin.
15. Goodman, P. S., Ravlin, E., & Schminke, M. (1987). Understanding groups in organizations. *Research in Organizational Behavior, 9*, 121–173.
16. Karau, S. J., & Williams, K. D. (1993). Social loafing: A meta-analytic review and theoretical integration. *Journal of Personality and Social Psychology, 65*, 681–706.

17. Karau, S. J., & Williams, K. D. (1993). Social loafing: A meta-analytic review and theoretical integration. *Journal of Personality and Social Psychology, 65*, 681–706.
18. Gabrenya, W. L., Latane, B., & Wang, Y. (1983). Social loafing in cross-cultural perspective. *Journal of Cross-Cultural Perspective, 14*, 368–384; Harkins, S., & Petty, R. E. (1982). Effects of task difficulty and task uniqueness on social loafing. *Journal of Personality and Social Psychology, 43*, 1214–1229; Taylor, D. W., & Faust, W. L. (1952). Twenty questions: Efficiency of problem-solving as a function of the size of the group. *Journal of Experimental Psychology, 44*, 360–363; Ziller, R. C. (1957). Four techniques of group decision-making under uncertainty. *Journal of Applied Psychology, 41*, 384–388.
19. Price, K. H., Harrison, D. A., & Gavin, J. H. (2006). Withholding inputs in team contexts: Member composition, interaction processes, evaluation structure, and social loafing. *Journal of Applied Psychology, 91*, 1375–1384.
20. Bandura, A. (1997). *Self-efficacy: The exercise of control*. San Francisco: Jossey-Bass.
21. Gully, S. M., Incalcaterra, K. A., Joshi, A., & Beaubien, J. M. (2002). A meta-analysis of team-efficacy, potency, and performance: Interdependence and level of analysis as moderators of observed relationships. *Journal of Applied Psychology, 87*, 819–832; Porter, C. O. L. H (2005). Goal orientation: Effects on backing up behavior, performance, efficacy, and commitment in teams. *Journal of Applied Psychology, 90*, 811–818; Tasa, K., Taggar, S., & Seijts, G. H. (2007). The development of collective efficacy in teams: A multilevel and longitudinal perspective. *Journal of Applied Psychology, 92*, 17–27.
22. Barrick, M. R., Bradley, B. H., Kristof-Brown, A. L., & Colbert, A. E. (2007). The moderating role of top management team interdependence: Implications for real teams and working groups. *Academy of Management Journal, 50*, 544–557.
23. Katzenbach, J. R., & Smith, D. K. (1993). *The wisdom of teams: Creating the high-performance organization*. Boston: Harvard Business School Press.
24. Welins, R., Byham, W., & Dixon, G. (1994). *Inside Teams*. San Francisco: Jossey-Bass.
25. Moskal, B. (1988, June 20). Supervisors, begone! *Industry Week*, p. 32.
26. Cannon-Bowers, J. A., & Salas, E. (2001, February). Team effectiveness and competencies. In W. Karwowski (Ed.), *International encyclopedia of ergonomics and human factors* (1383). London: CRC Press.
27. Rees, F. (1997). *Teamwork from start to finish*. San Francisco: Jossey-Bass.
28. De Dreu, C. K. W. (2007). Cooperative outcome interdependence, task reflexivity, and team effectiveness: A motivated information processing perspective. *Journal of Applied Psychology, 92*, 628–638.
29. Hackman, J. R. (1976). Group influences on individuals. In M. D. Dunnette (Ed.), *Handbook of industrial and organizational psychology*. Chicago: Rand-McNally.
30. Gully, S. M., Devine, D. J., & Whitney, D. J. (2012). A meta-analysis of cohesion and performance: Effects of level of analysis and task interdependence. *Small Group Research, 43*, 702–725.
31. Sutton, R. (2009, January 18). Miracle on the Hudson: The group dynamics angle. *Work matters.* Retrieved from http://bobsutton.typepad.com/my_weblog/2009/01/miracle-on-the-hudson-the-group-dynamics-angle.html.
32. Caruso, D. B. (2009, January 18). 5 white-knuckled minutes aboard Flight 1549. *Yahoo! News.* Retrieved from http://news.yahoo.com/s/ap/20090118/ap_on_re_us/plane_splashdown_cockpit_drama.
33. Mumford, T. V., Van Iddekinge, C. H., Morgeson, F. P., & Campion, M. A. (2008). The team role test: Development and validation of a team role knowledge situational judgment test. *Journal of Applied Psychology, 93*, 250–267.
34. Miron-Spektor, E., Erez, M., & Naveh, E. (2011). The effect of conformist and attentive-to-detail members on team innovation: Reconciling the innovation paradox. *Academy of Management Journal, 54*, 740–760.
35. Bales, R. F. (1950). *Interaction process analysis: A method for the study of small groups*. Cambridge, MA: Addison-Wesley; Benne, K. D., & Sheats, P. (1948). Functional roles of group members. *Journal of Social Issues, 4*, 41–49; Belbin, R. M. (1993). *Management teams: Why they succeed or fail*. Oxford: Butterworth-Heinemann.
36. Kozlowski, S. W. J., Gully, S. M., McHugh, P. P., Salas, E., & Cannon-Bowers, J. A. (1996). A dynamic theory of leadership and team effectiveness: Developmental and task contingent roles. In G. Ferris (Ed.), *Research in personnel and human resource management* (Vol. 14, pp. 253–305). Greenwich, CT: JAI Press; Kozlowski, S. W. J., Gully, S. M., Salas, E., & Cannon-Bowers, J. A. (1996). Team leadership and development: Theory, principles, and guidelines for training leaders and teams. In M. M. Beyerlein, D. A. Johnson, & S. T. Beyerlein (Eds.), *Advances in interdisciplinary studies of work teams* (Vol. 3, pp. 253–291). Greenwich, CT: JAI Press.
37. Ellis, A. P. J., Hollenbeck, J. R., Ilgen, D. R., Porter, C. O. L. H., West, B. J., & Moon, H. (2003). Team learning: Collectively connecting the dots. *Journal of Applied Psychology, 88*, 821–835.
38. Anacona, D. G. (1990). Outward bound: Strategies for team survival in an organization. *Academy of Management Journal, 33*, 334–365; Anacona, D. G. (1992). Bridging the boundary: External activity and performance in organizational teams. *Administrative Science Quarterly*, *37*, 634–665; Druskat, V. U., & Wheeler, J. V. (2003). Managing from the boundary: The effective leadership of self-managing work teams. *Academy of Management Journal*, *46*, 435–457.
39. Marrone, J. A., Tesluk, P. E., & Carson, J. B. (2007). A multi-level investigation of antecedents and consequences of team member boundary-spanning behavior. *Academy of Management Journal*, *50*, 1423–1439.
40. Gordon, J. (1992). Work teams: How far have they come? *Training, 29*, 59–62.
41. Gordon, J. (1992). Work teams: How far have they come? *Training, 29*, 59–62.
42. Ahuja, M., & Galvin, J. (2003). Socialization in virtual group. *Journal of Management, 29*, 161–185.
43. Retrieved from http://www.forbes.com/sites/meghanbiro/2014/01/12/telecommuting-is-the-future-of-work/.
44. Alexander, S. (2000, November 10). Virtual teams going global. *InfoWorld*. Retrieved from http://www.infoworld.com/articles/ca/xml/00/11/13/001113cavirtual.html.
45. Silverman, R. E. (September 5, 2012). Careers: Step into the office-less company: How one tech firm manages 123 at-home employees scattered across 26 countries and 94 cities. *Wall Street Journal;* Automattic. (n.d.) Work with us. https://automattic.com/work-with-us/.
46. Kirkman, B. L., Rosen, B., Gibson, C. B., Tesluk, P. E., & McPherson, S. O. (2002). Five challenges to virtual team success: Lessons from Sabre, Inc. *Academy of Management Executive, 16*, 67–79.
47. Montoya-Weiss, M. M., Massey, A. P., & Song, M. (2001). Getting it together: Temporal coordination and conflict management in global virtual teams. *Academy of Management Journal, 44*, 1251–1262.
48. Carpenter, M. A., Geletkanycz, M. A., & Sanders, W. G. (2004). The upper echelons revisited: The antecedents, elements, and consequences of TMT composition. *Journal of Management, 30*, 749–778.
49. Collins, J. (2001, July–August). Level leadership. *Harvard Business Review*, 66–76.
50. Greer, L. L., de Jong, B. A., Schouten, M. E., & Dannals, J. E. (2018). Why and when hierarchy impacts team effectiveness: A meta-analytic integration. *Journal of Applied Psychology, 103*, 591–613.
51. Welins, R., Byham, W., & Dixon, G. (1994). *Inside teams*. San Francisco: Jossey-Bass.
52. Bundersoon, J. S., & Boumgarden, P. (2010). Structure and learning in self-managed teams: Why "bureaucratic" teams can be better learners. *Organization Science, 21*, 609–624.
53. Morgeson, F. P. (2005). The external leadership of self-managing teams: Intervening in the context of novel and disruptive events. *Journal of Applied Psychology, 90*, 497–508.
54. Parker, G. (1994). *Cross-functional teams*. San Francisco: Jossey-Bass.
55. Humphrey, S. E., Hollenbeck, J. R., Meyer, C. J., & Ilgen, D. R. (2007). Trait configurations in self-managed teams: A conceptual examination of the use of seeding for maximizing and minimizing trait variance in teams. *Journal of Applied Psychology, 92*, 885–892.
56. Hirschfeld, R. R., Jordan, M. H., Field, H. S., Giles, W. F., & Armenakis, A. A. (2006). Becoming team players: Team members' mastery of teamwork knowledge as a predictor of team task proficiency and observed teamwork effectiveness. *Journal of Applied Psychology, 91*, 467–474; Stevens, M. J., & Campion, M. A. (1999). Staffing work teams: Development and validation of a selection test for teamwork settings. *Journal of Management, 25*, 207–228.
57. McGrath, J. E. (1984). *Groups: Interaction and performance*. Englewood Cliffs, NJ: Prentice Hall; Solomon, H. (1960). *Mathematical thinking in the measurement of behavior*. Glencoe, IL: Free Press.
58. Campion, M. A., Medsker, G. J., & Higgs, A. C. (1993). Relations between work group characteristics and effectiveness: Implications for designing effective work groups. *Personnel Psychology, 46*, 823–850; Magjuka, R. J., & Baldwin, T. T. (1991). Team-based employee involvement programs: Effects of design and administration. *Personnel Psychology, 44*, 793–812; Vinokur-Kaplan, D. (1995). Treatment teams that work (and those that don't): An application of Hackman's group effectiveness model to interdisciplinary teams in psychiatric hospitals. *Journal of Applied Behavioral Science, 31*, 303–327.
59. Jackson, S. E., Joshi, A., & Erhardt, N. L. (2003). Recent research on team and organizational diversity: SWOT analysis and implications. *Journal of Management, 29,* 801–830; van Knippenberg, D., De Dreu, C. K. W., & Homan, A. C. (2004). Work group diversity and group performance: An integrative model and research agenda. *Journal of Applied Psychology, 89,* 1008–1022.
60. Homan, A. C., van Knippenberg, D., Van Kleef, G. A., & De Dreu, C. K. W. (2007). Bridging faultlines by valuing diversity: Diversity beliefs, information elaboration, and performance in diverse work groups. *Journal of Applied Psychology, 92,* 1189–1199.
61. Surowiecki, J. (2005). *The wisdom of crowds.* New York: Anchor Books.

62. Eisenhardt, K. M., & Tabrizi, B. N. (1995). Accelerating adaptive processes: Product innovation in the global computer industry. *Science Quarterly, 4,* 84–110; Shin, S. J., & Zhou, J. (2007). When is educational specialization heterogeneity related to creativity in research and development teams? Transformational leadership as a moderator. *Journal of Applied Psychology, 92,* 1709–1721.
63. Woehr, D. J., Arciniega, L. M., & Poling, T. L. (2013). Exploring the effects of value diversity on team effectiveness. *Journal of Business and Psychology, 28,* 107–121.
64. Katzenbach, J. R., & Smith, D. K. (1993). *The wisdom of teams: Creating the high-performance organization*. Boston: Harvard Business School Press; Porter, T. W., & Lilly, B. S. (1996). The effects of conflict, trust, and task commitment on project team performance. *International Journal of Conflict Management, 7*, 361–376.
65. Edmondson, A. C. (1999). Psychological safety and learning behavior in work teams. *Administrative Science Quarterly, 44*, 350–383.
66. Delizonna, L. (2017). High-performing teams need psychological safety. Here's how to create it. *Harvard Business Review.* Retrieved from https://hbr.org/2017/08/high-performing-teams-need-psychological-safety-heres-how-to-create-it; Hu, J., Erdogan, B., Jiang, K., Bauer, T. N., & Liu, S. (2018). Leader humility and team creativity: The role of team information sharing, psychological safety, and power distance. *Journal of Applied Psychology, 103*, 313; Li, A. N., Liao, H., Tangirala, S., & Firth, B. M. (2017). The content of the message matters: The differential effects of promotive and prohibitive team voice on team productivity and safety performance gains. *Journal of Applied Psychology, 102*, 1259–1270; Newman, A., Donohue, R., & Eva, N. (2017). Psychological safety: A systematic review of the literature. *Human Resource Management Review, 27*, 521–535; Spoelma, T. M., & Ellis, A. P. (2017). Fuse or fracture? Threat as a moderator of the effects of diversity faultlines in teams. *Journal of Applied Psychology, 85*, 102–111.
67. De Jong, B. A., Dirks, K. T., & Gillespie, N. (2016). Trust and team performance: A meta-analysis of main effects, moderators, and covariates. *Journal of Applied Psychology, 101*, 1134–1150.
68. Edmondson, A. C., & Lei, Z. (2014). Psychological safety: The history, renaissance, and future of an interpersonal construct. *Annual Review of Organizational Psychology and Organizational Behavior, 1*, 23–43.
69. Duhigg, C. (2016). What Google learned from its quest to build the perfect team. *The New York Times Magazine*. Retrieved from https://www.nytimes.com/2016/02/28/magazine/what-google-learned-from-its-quest-to-build-the-perfect-team.html?mtrref=duckduckgo.com&login=email.
70. Tannenbaum, S. I., & Cerasoli, C. P. (2013). Do team and individual debriefs enhance performance? A meta-analysis. *Human Factors, 55*, 231–245.
71. Darling, M., Parry, C., & Moore, J. (2005). Learning in the thick of it. *Harvard Business Review, 83*, 84–92.
72. Haynes, M. E. (1997). *Effective meeting skills*. Menlo Park, CA: Crisp.
73. White, M. (2014). The management of virtual teams and virtual meetings. *Business Information Review, 31*, 111–117.
74. See Bluedorn, A. C., Turban, D. B., & Love, M. S. (1999). The effects of stand-up and sit-down meeting formats on meeting outcomes. *Journal of Applied Psychology, 84*, 277–285. This technique is used by Johnson & Johnson, Ritz-Carlton, ThoughtWorks, Agile Software, and Corning.
75. Jackson, C. L., & LePine, J. A. (2003). Peer responses to a team's weakest link: A test and extension of LePine and Van Dyne's model. *Journal of Applied Psychology, 88*, 459–475.
76. Colquitt, J. A. (2004). Does the justice of the one interact with the justice of the many? Reactions to procedural justice in teams. *Journal of Applied Psychology, 89*, 633–646.
77. Nordbäck, E. S., & Espinosa, J. A. (2019). Effective coordination of shared leadership in global virtual teams. *Journal of Management Information Systems, 36*, 321–350.
78. Kniffin, K. M., Wansink, B., Devine, C. M., & Sobal, J. (2015). Eating together at the firehouse: How workplace commensality relates to the performance of firefighters. *Human Performance, 28*, 281–306.
79. Costa, P. L., Passos, A. M., & Bakker, A. B. (2015). Direct and contextual influence of team conflict on team resources, team work engagement, and team performance. *Negotiation and Conflict Management Research, 8*, 211–227.
80. Scholtes, P. (1988). *The team handbook*. Madison, WI: Joiner Associates.
81. Bradley, B. H., Postlewaite, B. E., Klotz, A. C., Hamdani, M. R., & Brown, K. G. (2012). Reaping the benefits of task conflict in teams: The critical role of team psychological safety climate. *Journal of Applied Psychology, 97*, 151–158.
82. Case written by Rachel Mattenberger, Talya Bauer, and Berrin Erdogan to accompany T. N. Bauer & B. Erdogan (2021). *Organizational Behavior: Bridging Science and Practice (4.0)*. Boston, MA: FlatWorld. Partially based on ideas and information contained in Au-Yeung, A. (2019, October 28). Kind, maker of snack bars, to lay off 15% of its employees by year-end. https://www.forbes.com/sites/angelauyeung/2019/10/28/kind-maker-of-snack-bar-to-lay-off-15-of-its-employees-by-year-end/#11d6981814c4; Ready, L. (2015). The amazing story behind that KIND bar you're eating. https://www.usatoday.com/story/news/2015/03/30/inspiration-nation-daniel-lubetzky-kind/70676954; Au-Yeung, A. (2019). Social Spin Doctor: Kind Bar's Daniel Lubesky Builds a $1.5 Billion Fortune on Do-Gooder Rhetoric. https://www.forbes.com/sites/angelauyeung/2019/03/05/social-spin-doctor-kind-bars-daniel-lubetzky-builds-a-15-billion-fortune-on-do-gooder-rhetoric/#2a0605b82b5f.

CHAPTER 13

Motivating Employees

Should managers use the carrot or the stick? Research has found that rewards are more effective than punishments in altering individual behavior.

Source: Shutterstock.com

Chapter Learning Objectives

Reading this chapter will help you accomplish the following:

1. Understand need-based theories of motivation.
2. Understand process-based theories of motivation.
3. Describe how fairness perceptions are determined and their consequences.
4. Learn to use performance evaluations in a motivational way.
5. Learn to apply organizational rewards in a motivational way.
6. Develop your personal motivation skills.

TABLE 13.1 The P-O-L-C Framework

Planning	Organizing	Leading	Controlling
1. Vision & Mission	1. Organization Design	1. Leadership	1. Systems/Processes
2. Strategizing	2. Culture	2. Decision Making	2. Strategic Human Resources
3. Goals & Objectives	3. Social Networks	3. Communications	
		4. Groups/Teams	
		5. Motivation	

What makes employees willing to "go the extra mile" to provide excellent service, market a company's products effectively, or achieve the goals set personally or by management? Answering questions like these is of utmost importance to understand and manage the work behavior of our peers, subordinates, and even supervisors. As with many questions involving individuals, the answers are complex and there are several theories explaining the concept of motivation. We review each of the key theories of motivation in this chapter.

13.1 Understanding Motivation

Learning Objectives

1. Understand the performance equation.
2. Explain the difference between intrinsic and extrinsic motivation.

What inspires employees to provide excellent service, market a company's products effectively, or achieve the goals set for them? Answering this question is of utmost importance if we are to understand and manage the work behavior of our peers, subordinates, and even supervisors. Put a different way, if someone is not performing well, what could be the reason?

Job performance is viewed as a function of three factors and is expressed with the following equation.[1] According to this equation, motivation, ability, and environment are the major influences over employee performance.

FIGURE 13.1 Factors of Job Performance

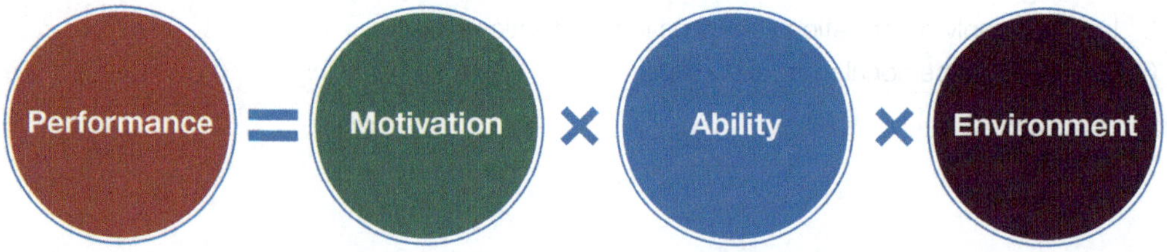

Motivation is one of the forces that lead to performance. **Motivation** is defined as the desire to achieve a goal or a certain performance level, leading to goal-directed behavior. When we refer to someone as being motivated, we mean that the person is trying hard to accomplish a certain task. Motivation is clearly important if someone is to perform well; however, it is not sufficient. **Ability**—or having the skills and knowledge required to perform the job—is also important and is sometimes the key determinant of effectiveness. Finally, **environmental** factors such as having the resources, information, and support one needs to perform well are critical to determine performance. At different times, one of these three factors may be the key to high performance. For example, for an employee sweeping the floor, motivation may be the most important factor that determines performance. In contrast, even the most motivated individual would not be able to successfully design a house without the necessary training involved in building quality homes. In the end, when we say someone is motivated is that they want to try hard and perform well. Being motivated is not the same as being a high performer and is not the sole reason why people perform well, but it is nevertheless a key influence over our performance level.

motivation

The desire to achieve a goal or a certain performance level, leading to goal-directed behavior.

ability

Having the skills and knowledge required to perform the job.

environmental

External factors that affect performance.

Intrinsic and Extrinsic Motivation

Why do you read a book, watch movies, or decide to learn to play the guitar? Or travel, go hiking, or spend time in the garden? There may be many reasons why you engage in these activities, but if your answer is because they are fun and you enjoy them, you are describing intrinsic motivation. **Intrinsic motivation** refers to pursuing an activity because it is inherently enjoyable and in the absence of apparent rewards. Other activities are driven by external rewards. For example, reading a book because you have to write a book report, or cooking a meal because someone pays you are examples of extrinsically motivated activities. **Extrinsic motivation** refers to performing an activity because it is related to desirable outcomes such as financial rewards, status, or approval from others.[2]

intrinsic motivation

Pursuing an activity because it is inherently enjoyable and in the absence of apparent rewards.

extrinsic motivation

Performing an activity because it is related to desirable outcomes such as financial rewards, status, or approval from others.

The distinction between intrinsic and extrinsic motivation is important, and has been subject to much debate. For a long time, scientific literature worked under the assumption that the presence of extrinsic rewards made a task intrinsically less motivating. There is some appeal in this idea: When we do something for money, we may enjoy it less. An example of this phenomenon would be the professional chef who refuses to make meals at home. However, recent meta analytic evidence does not support this idea. Specifically research shows that a) when individuals are intrinsically motivated, they tend to perform well, b) when there are indirect rewards for performance, performance was largely a function of intrinsic motivation, b) when there are direct rewards for performance, the importance of intrinsic motivation lessened, and rewards became a more powerful predictor of performance and d) having rewards did not reduce intrinsic motivation, and in fact increased it. Finally, intrinsic motivation mattered more for performance quality, whereas external rewards mattered more for performance quantity. These results suggest that both intrinsic and extrinsic motivation matter for understanding employee performance. Some scholars argue that instead of rewarding behaviors through extrinsic rewards, wise managers should create conditions that foester intrinsic motivation.[3] When reading the remainder of the chapter, we would encourage you to consider the effects of different motivators for extrinsic and intrinsic motivation.[4]

Key Takeaway

Job performance is a function of motivation, ability, and environment. This is important, because if the root causes of performance are misdiagnosed, we cannot hope to correct it. Employees may be motivated to perform a specific task due to intrinsic or extrinsic motivation. Both matter for performance.

Discussion Questions

1. What are the implications of assuming that a performance problem is due to lack of motivation, as opposed to lack of ability? How different would a manager's reactions to an employee lacking motivation as opposed to ability?
2. If an employee is intrinsically motivated to perform a task, is it a good idea to introduce external rewards for performance? Why or why not?

13.2 Need-Based Theories of Motivation

Learning Objectives

1. Explain how employees are motivated according to Maslow's hierarchy of needs.
2. Explain how the ERG (existence, relatedness, growth) theory addresses the limitations of Maslow's hierarchy.
3. Describe the difference among factors contributing to employee motivation and factors contributing to dissatisfaction.
4. Describe need for achievement, power, and affiliation, and how these acquired needs affect work behavior.

The earliest answer to motivation involved understanding individual needs. Specifically, early researchers thought that employees were motivated to satisfy their needs. For example, an employee who spends a considerable amount of time wandering around the office talking to people may have a social need and this behavior may be a way of satisfying that need. There are four major theories in the need-based category: Maslow's hierarchy of needs, ERG theory, Herzberg's two-factor theory, and McClelland's acquired needs theory.

Maslow's Hierarchy of Needs

Abraham Maslow is among the most prominent psychologists of the twentieth century and the hierarchy of needs, accompanied by the pyramid that represents how human needs are ranked, is an image familiar to many business students and managers. Maslow's theory is based on a simple premise: Human beings have needs that are hierarchically ranked.[5] There are some needs that are basic to all human beings, and in their absence, other needs are not considered. As we satisfy these basic needs, we start looking to satisfy higher-order needs. Once a lower-level need is satisfied, it no longer serves as a motivator.

The most basic of Maslow's needs are **physiological needs**. Physiological needs refer to the need for air, food, and water. Individuals who are hungry direct their behavior toward finding food. Once fed, the search for sustenance ceases and food no longer serves as a motivator. Once physiological needs are satisfied, people tend to become concerned about **safety**. Are they safe from danger, pain, or an uncertain future? One level up, **social needs** refer to the need to bond with other human beings, to be loved, and to form lasting attachments. Indeed, research shows that having no attachments can negatively affect health and well-being.[6] The satisfaction of social needs makes **esteem needs** more salient. Esteem needs refer to the desire to be respected by one's peers, feeling important, and being appreciated. Finally, at the highest level of the hierarchy, the need for **self-actualization** refers to "becoming all you are capable of becoming." This need manifests itself by acquiring new skills, taking on new challenges, and behaving in a way that will lead to the satisfaction of one's life goals.

Maslow's theory was not originally designed for work settings. In fact, the theory was based on his observations of individuals in clinical settings; some of the individual components of the theory found little empirical support. One criticism relates to the order in which the needs are ranked. It is possible to imagine that individuals who go hungry and are in fear of their lives might retain strong bonds to others, suggesting a different order of needs. Moreover, researchers failed to support the arguments that once a need is satisfied it no longer serves as a motivator and that only one need is dominant at a given time.[7]

Despite the lack of strong research support, Maslow's theory found obvious applications in business settings. Understanding what people need gives us clues to understanding them. The hierarchy is a systematic way of thinking about the different needs employees may have at any given point and explains different reactions they may have to similar treatment. An employee who is trying to satisfy esteem needs may feel gratified when her supervisor praises an accomplishment. However, another employee who is trying to satisfy social needs may resent being praised by upper management in front of peers if the praise sets the individual apart from the rest of the group.

How can organizations satisfy their employees' various needs? In the long run, physiological needs may be satisfied by a paycheck, but it is important to remember that pay may satisfy other needs such as safety and esteem as well. Providing generous benefits, including health insurance and company-sponsored retirement plans, as well as offering a measure of job security, will help satisfy safety needs. Social needs may be satisfied by having a friendly environment, providing a workplace conducive to collaboration and communication with others. Company picnics and other social opportunities may also be helpful if other employees are motivated by social needs, but they may cause resentment if they are not and if they have to sacrifice a Sunday afternoon for a company picnic that is not truly viewed as optional. Providing promotion opportunities at work, recognizing a person's accomplishments verbally or through more formal reward systems, and job titles that communicate to the employee that one has achieved high status within the organization are among the ways of satisfying esteem needs. Finally, self-actualization needs may be satisfied by providing development and growth opportunities on or off the job, as well as by assigning interesting and challenging work. By making the effort to satisfy the different needs each employee may have at a given time, organizations may ensure a more highly motivated workforce.

physiological needs

The need for air, food, and water.

safety

The need to be safe from danger, pain, or an uncertain future.

social needs

The need to bond with other human beings, to be loved, and to form lasting attachments with them.

esteem needs

The desire to be respected by one's peers, feeling important, and being appreciated.

self-actualization

The quality of "becoming all you are capable of becoming."

FIGURE 13.2 Maslow's Hierarchy of Needs

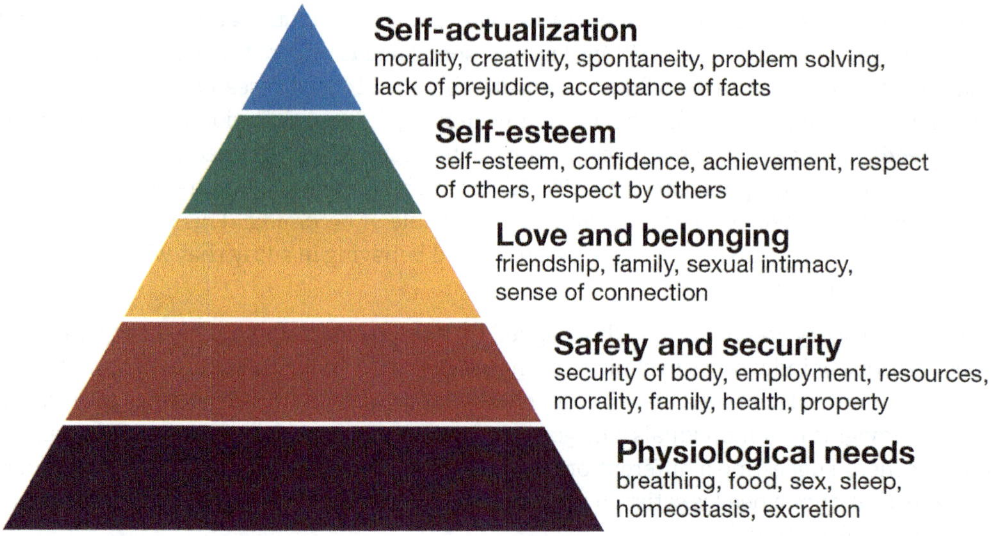

Source: Shutterstock.com

ERG Theory

existence

This need corresponds to Maslow's physiological and safety needs.

relatedness

This need corresponds to social needs.

growth

This need refers to Maslow's esteem and self-actualization.

ERG theory, developed by Clayton Alderfer is a modification of Maslow's hierarchy of needs.[8] Instead of the five needs that are hierarchically organized, Alderfer proposed that basic human needs may be grouped under three categories, namely, **Existence**, **Relatedness**, and **Growth**. Existence need corresponds to Maslow's physiological and safety needs, relatedness corresponds to social needs, and growth need refers to Maslow's esteem and self-actualization.

ERG theory's main contribution to the literature is its relaxation of Maslow's assumptions. For example, ERG theory does not rank needs in any particular order and explicitly recognizes that more than one need may operate at a given time. Moreover, the theory has a "frustration-regression" hypothesis, suggesting that individuals who are frustrated in their attempts to satisfy one need may regress to another one. For example, someone who is frustrated by the lack of growth opportunities in his job and slow progress toward career goals may regress to relatedness needs and start spending more time socializing with one's coworkers. The implication of this theory is that we need to recognize the multiple needs that may be driving an individual at a given point to understand his behavior and to motivate him.

FIGURE 13.3 ERG Theory

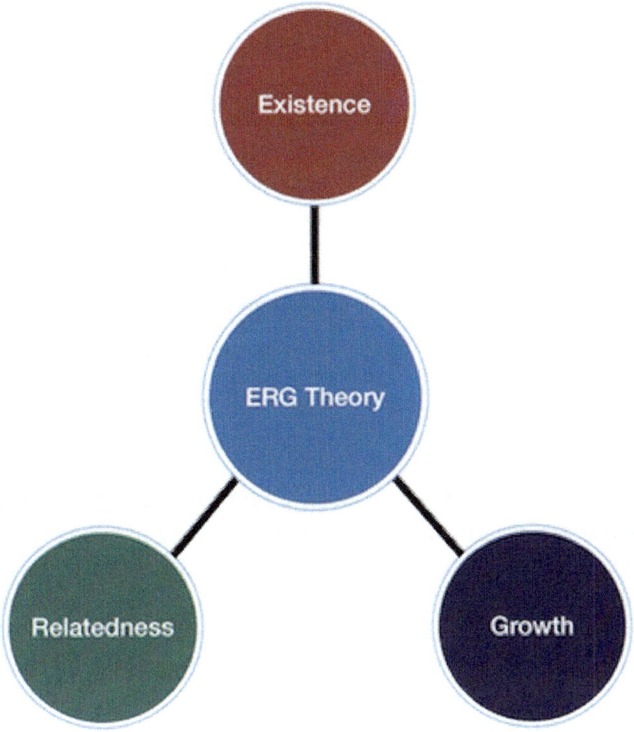

Source: Based on Alderfer, C. P. (1969). An empirical test of a new theory of human needs. *Organizational Behavior and Human Performance, 4*, 142–175.

Two-Factor Theory

Frederick Herzberg approached the question of motivation from a slightly different perspective by asking individuals what satisfies them on the job and what dissatisfies them. Herzberg came to the conclusion that aspects of the work environment that satisfy employees are very different from aspects that dissatisfy them.[9] Herzberg labeled factors causing dissatisfaction of workers as "hygiene" factors, because these factors were part of the context in which the job was performed, as opposed to the job itself. **Hygiene factors** included company policies, supervision, working conditions, salary, safety, and security on the job. For example, if you are working in an unpleasant work environment where your office is too hot in the summer and too cold in the winter, or if you are being harassed and mistreated, you would likely be miserable. However, if these problems were solved (your office temperature is just right and you are not harassed at all), would you be motivated? Most likely, you would take the situation for granted. In fact, many factors in our work environment are things that we miss when they are absent, but take for granted if they are present.

hygiene factors

The factors that include company policies, supervision, working conditions, salary, safety, and security on the job.

In Herzberg's two-factor theory hygiene factors (such as effective air conditioning) do not serve to motivate, but could keep you from being dissatisfied with your job.

Source: Shutterstock.com

motivators

The factors that are intrinsic to the job, such as achievement, recognition, interesting work, increased responsibilities, advancement, and growth opportunities.

In contrast, **motivators** are factors that are intrinsic to the job, such as achievement, recognition, interesting work, increased responsibilities, advancement, and growth opportunities. According to Herzberg's research, motivators, and not hygiene factors, are the conditions that truly motivate employees.

TABLE 13.2 The Two-Factor Theory of Motivation

Hygiene Factors	Motivators
Company policy	Achievement
Supervision and relationships	Recognition
Working conditions	Interesting work
Salary	Increased responsibility
Security	Advancement and growth

Herzberg's research, despite its intuitive appeal, has received its share of criticism.[10] One criticism relates to the primary research methodology employed when arriving at hygiene versus motivators. When people are asked why they are satisfied, they may attribute the causes of satisfaction to themselves, whereas when explaining what dissatisfies them, they may blame the situation. The classification of the factors as hygiene or motivator is not that simple either. For example, the theory views pay as a hygiene factor. However, pay often has symbolic value by showing employees that they are being recognized for their contributions as well as communicating that they are advancing within the company. Similarly, quality of supervision or relationships employees form with their supervisors may determine whether they are assigned interesting work, whether they are recognized for their potential, and whether they take on more responsibilities. Despite its limitations, the two-factor theory can be a valuable aid to managers because it points out that improving the environment in which the job is performed goes only so far in motivating employees.

Acquired Needs Theory

Among the need-based approaches to motivation, David McClelland's acquired needs theory is the one that has received the greatest amount of support. According to this theory, individuals acquire three types of needs as a result of their life experiences. These needs are need for achievement, need for affiliation, and need for power. All individuals possess a combination of these needs.

Thematic Apperception Test (TAT)

A test that assesses a person's dominant needs.

McClelland used a unique method called the **Thematic Apperception Test (TAT)** to assess the dominant need.[11] This method entails presenting research subjects with an ambiguous picture and asking them to write a story based on it. Take a look at the following picture. Who is this person? What is he doing? Why is he doing it? The story you tell about the man in the picture would then be analyzed by trained experts. The idea is that the stories the photo evokes would reflect how the mind works and what motivates the person.

The type of story you tell by looking at this picture may give away the dominant need that motivates you.

need for achievement

Having a strong need to be successful.

If the story you come up with contains themes of success, meeting deadlines, or coming up with brilliant ideas, you may be in high need for achievement. Those who have a high **need for achievement** have a strong need to be successful. As children, they may be praised for their hard work, which forms the foundations of their persistence.[12] As adults, they are preoccupied with doing things better than they did in the past. These individuals are constantly striving to improve their performance. They relentlessly focus on goals, particularly stretch goals that are challenging in nature.[13] They are particularly suited to positions such as sales, where there are explicit goals, feedback is immediately available, and their effort often leads to success. In fact, they are more attracted to organizations that are merit based and reward performance rather than seniority. They also do particularly well as entrepreneurs, scientists, and engineers.[14]

Are individuals who are high in need for achievement effective managers? Because of their success in lower level jobs where their individual contributions matter the most, those with high need for achievement are often promoted to higher level positions.[15] However, a high need for achievement has significant disadvantages in management positions. Management involves getting work done by motivating others. When a salesperson is promoted to be a sales manager, the job description changes from actively selling to recruiting, motivating, and training salespeople. Those who are high in need for achievement may view managerial activities such as coaching, communicating, and meeting with subordinates as a waste of time and may neglect these aspects of their jobs. Moreover, those high in need for achievement enjoy doing things themselves and may find it difficult to delegate any meaningful authority to their subordinates. These individuals often micromanage, expecting others to approach tasks a particular way, and may become overbearing bosses by expecting everyone to display high levels of dedication.[16]

At Hewlett-Packard, one of the most prestigious awards an employee can receive is the Golden Banana Award for technological innovation. This award began when an engineer came to his manager to report that he'd solved a challenging problem. The manager wanted to show his appreciation, looked around his desk, and found the banana he planned to eat for lunch. He handed the banana to the engineer while saying, "Well done! Congratulations!"

Source: Shutterstock.com

need for affiliation

Wanting to be liked and accepted by others.

need for power

Wanting to influence others and control their environment.

If the story you created in relation to the picture you are analyzing contains elements of making plans to be with friends or family, you may have a high need for affiliation. Individuals who have a high **need for affiliation** want to be liked and accepted by others. Wanting to be liked and accepted by others. want to be liked and accepted by others. When given a choice, they prefer to interact with others and be with friends.[17] Their emphasis on harmonious interpersonal relationships may be an advantage in jobs and occupations requiring frequent interpersonal interaction, such as a social worker or teacher. In managerial positions, a high need for affiliation may again serve as a disadvantage because these individuals tend to be overly concerned about how they are perceived by others. They may find it difficult to perform some aspects of a manager's job such as giving employees critical feedback or disciplining poor performers. Thus the work environment may be characterized by mediocrity and may even lead to high performers leaving the team.

Finally, if your story contains elements of getting work done by influencing other people or desiring to make an impact on the organization, you may have a high need for power. Those with a high **need for power** want to influence others and control their environment. A high need for power may in fact be a destructive element in relationships with colleagues if it takes the form of seeking and using power for one's own good and prestige. However, when it manifests itself in more altruistic forms such as changing the way things are done so that the work environment is more positive, or negotiating more resources for one's department, it tends to lead to positive outcomes. In fact, the need for power is viewed as an important trait for effectiveness in managerial and leadership positions.

McClelland's theory of acquired needs has important implications for motivating employees. While someone who has a high need for achievement may respond to goals, those with a high need for affiliation may be motivated to gain the approval of their peers and supervisors, whereas those who have a high need for power may value gaining influence over the supervisor or acquiring a position that has decision-making authority. And, when it comes to succeeding in managerial positions, individuals who are aware of the drawbacks of their need orientation can take steps to overcome these drawbacks.

Key Takeaway

Need-based theories describe motivated behavior as individuals' efforts to meet their needs. According to this perspective, the manager's job is to identify what people need and make the work environment a means of satisfying these needs. Maslow's hierarchy describes five categories of basic human needs, including physiological, safety, social, esteem, and self-actualization needs. These needs are hierarchically ranked, and as a lower level need is satisfied, it no longer serves as a motivator. ERG theory is a modification of Maslow's hierarchy, in which the five needs are collapsed into three categories (existence, relatedness, and growth). The theory recognizes that when employees are frustrated while attempting to satisfy higher level needs, they may regress. The two-factor theory differentiates between factors that make people dissatisfied on the job (hygiene factors) and factors that truly motivate employees (motivators). Finally, acquired-needs theory argues that individuals possess stable and dominant motives to achieve, acquire power, or affiliate with others. The type of need that is dominant will drive behavior. Each of these theories explains characteristics of a work environment that motivates employees. These theories paved the way for process-based theories that explain the mental calculations employees make to decide how to behave.

Discussion Questions

1. Many managers assume that if an employee is not performing well, the reason must be lack of motivation. What is the problem with this assumption?
2. Review Maslow's hierarchy of needs. Do you agree with the particular ranking of employee needs?
3. How can an organization satisfy employee needs that are included in Maslow's hierarchy?
4. Which motivation theory have you found to be the most useful in explaining why people behave in a certain way? Why?
5. A friend of yours demonstrates the traits of achievement motivation: This person is competitive, requires frequent and immediate feedback, and enjoys accomplishing things and doing things better than she did before. She has recently been promoted to a managerial position and seeks your advice. What would you tell her?

13.3 Process-Based Theories

Learning Objectives

1. Explain how employees evaluate the fairness of reward distributions.
2. Describe the three types of fairness that affect employee attitudes and behaviors.
3. List the three questions individuals consider when deciding whether to put forth effort at work.
4. Describe how managers can use learning and reinforcement principles to motivate employees.

In contrast to need-based theories, process-based theories view motivation as a cognitive (and potentially rational) process. Individuals analyze their environment, develop reactions and feelings, and react in certain ways. Under this category, we will review equity theory, expectancy theory, and reinforcement theory. We will also discuss the concepts of job design and goal setting as motivational strategies.

Equity Theory

Imagine you are paid $12 an hour working as an office assistant and you have held this job for six months. You are very good at what you do, coming up with creative ways to make things easier in the workplace, and you are a good colleague, willing to help others. You stay late when necessary and are flexible if asked to rearrange priorities or work hours. Now imagine that you find out your manager is hiring another employee who is going to work with you, hold the same job title, and perform the same types of tasks. This employee has more advanced computer skills, but it is unclear whether these will be used on the job. The starting pay for the new hire will be $15 an hour. How would you feel? Would you be as motivated as before, going above and beyond your duties?

referent

A person we compare ourselves to in equity theory.

If your reaction to this scenario was along the lines of "I would think it's unfair," your feelings may be explained using equity theory.[18] According to this theory, individuals are motivated by a sense of fairness in their interactions. Moreover, our sense of fairness is a result of the social comparisons we make. Specifically, we compare our inputs and outputs with someone else's inputs and outputs. We perceive fairness if we believe that the input-to-output ratio we are bringing into the situation is similar to the input/output ratio of a comparison person, or a **referent**. Perceptions of inequity create tension within us and drive us to action that will reduce perceived inequity. There is even neurological evidence that individuals react negatively to equal distribution of outcomes that disregards differences in individual contributions. In other words, our brains react in a way that shows discomfort when rewards are distributed in a way that violates equity theory.[19] This process is illustrated in Figure 13.4.

What Are Inputs and Outputs?

Equity issues are on full display in a 2020 report from payscale.com noting that women receive $0.81 for every dollar a man makes.

Source: ilkah/Shutterstock.com

Inputs are the contributions the person feels he or she is making to the environment. In the previous example, hard work, loyalty to the organization, number of months worked, level of education, training, and skills may have been relevant inputs. Outputs are the perceived rewards the person feels he or she is receiving from the situation. For the hourly wage employee in our example, the $12-an-hour pay rate was a core outcome. There may also be other, more peripheral outcomes, such as acknowledgment or preferential treatment from a manager. In the prior example, the person may reason as follows: I have been working here for six months. I am loyal, and I perform well (inputs). I am paid $12 an hour for this (outputs). The new person does not have any experience here (referent's inputs) but will be paid $15 an hour. This situation is unfair.

FIGURE 13.4 The Equity Formula

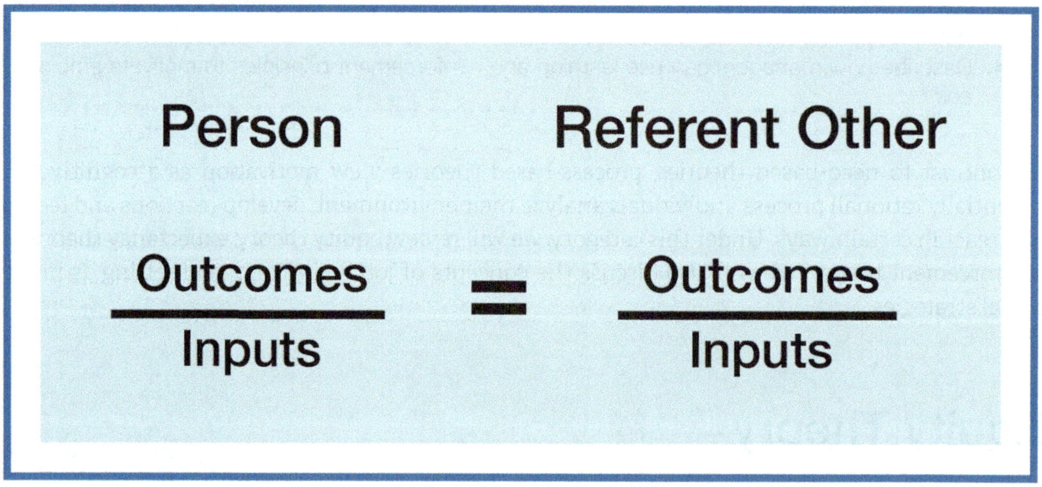

Source: Based on Adams, J. S. (1965). Inequity in social exchange. In L. Berkowitz (Ed.), *Advances in experimental social psychology* (Vol. 2, pp. 267–299). New York: Academic Press.

Because equity perceptions develop as a result of a subjective process, different people may look at exactly the same situation and perceive different levels of equity. For example, another person may look at the same scenario and decide that the situation is fair because the new hire has computer skills and the company is paying extra for these skills.

Who Is the Referent?

The referent other may be a specific person or an entire category of people. For example, some might look at want ads for entry-level clerical workers and see whether the pay offered is in the $12 per hour range; in this case, the referent other is the category of entry-level clerical workers, including office assistants, in the local area. Referents should be comparable to us—otherwise the comparison is not meaningful. It would be illogical for entry-level employees to compare themselves to the CEO of the company, given the differences in the nature of inputs and outcomes. Instead, individuals logically compare themselves to those performing similar tasks within the same organization or a different organization.

The concept of equity helps explain aggressive negotiations in professional sports, such as Cristiano Ronaldo's salary that pays more than $100 million annually, including endorsements.

Source: Oleh Dubyna/Shutterstock.com

Reactions to Unfairness

The theory outlines several potential reactions to perceived inequity, which are summarized in Table 13.3. Oftentimes, the situation may be dealt with perceptually, by *altering our perceptions of our own or referent's inputs and outputs*. For example, individuals may justify the situation by downplaying their own inputs ("I don't really work very hard on this job"), valuing the outputs more highly ("I am gaining valuable work experience, so the situation is not that bad"), distorting the other person's inputs ("He really is more competent than I am and deserves to be paid more"), or distorting the other person's outputs ("He gets $15 but will have to work with a lousy manager, so the situation is not unfair").

Another way of addressing perceived inequity is to *reduce one's own inputs or increase one's own outputs*. If individuals reduce their efforts, perceived inequity can be reduced. Indeed, research shows that people who perceive inequity tend to reduce their work performance or reduce the quality of their inputs.[20] Increasing one's outputs can be achieved through legitimate means such as negotiating a pay raise. At the same time, research shows that those feeling inequity sometimes resort to stealing to balance the scales.[21] Other options include *changing the comparison person* (for example, you may learn that others doing similar work in different organizations are paid only minimum wage) and *leaving the situation* by quitting one's job.[22] We might even consider taking legal action as a potential outcome of perceived inequity. For example, if you find out that the main reason behind a pay gap is one's sex, you may react to the situation by taking legal action, because sex discrimination in pay is illegal in the United States.

TABLE 13.3 Potential Responses to Inequity

Reaction to Inequity	Example
Distort perceptions	Changing one's thinking to believe that the referent actually is more skilled than previously thought
Increase referent's inputs	Encouraging the referent to work harder
Reduce own input	Deliberately putting forth less effort at work Reducing the quality of one's work
Increase own outcomes	Negotiating a raise for oneself or using unethical ways of increasing rewards such as stealing from the company
Change referent	Comparing oneself to someone who is worse off
Leave the situation	Quitting one's job
Seek legal action	Suing the company or filing a complaint if the unfairness in question is under legal protection

Overpayment Inequity

What would you do if you felt you were over-rewarded? In other words, how would you feel if you were the new employee in our student-worker scenario? Originally, equity theory proposed that over-rewarded individuals would experience guilt and would increase their effort to restore perceptions of equity. However, research does not provide support for this argument. Instead, it seems that individuals experience less distress as a result of being over-rewarded.[23] It is not hard to imagine that individuals find perceptual ways to deal with a situation like this, such as believing they have more skills and bring more to the situation compared to the referent person. Therefore, research does not support equity theory's predictions with respect to people who are overpaid.[24]

Individual Differences in Reactions to Inequity

Equity theory assumes that once people feel that a situation is inequitable they are motivated to react. However, does inequity disturb everyone equally? Researchers identified a personality trait that explains different reactions to inequity and named this trait **equity sensitivity**.[25] Equity sensitive individuals experience distress when they feel they are over-rewarded or under-rewarded and expect to maintain equitable relationships. At the same time, there are some individuals who are **benevolents** who give without waiting to receive much in return and **entitleds** who expect to receive a lot without giving much in return. Thus, the theory is more useful in explaining the behavior of equity-sensitive individuals, and organizations will need to pay particular attention to how these individuals view their relationships.

equity sensitivity

A personality trait that explains different reactions to inequity.

benevolents

Individuals who give without waiting to receive much in return.

entitleds

Individuals who expect to receive a lot without giving much in return.

Fairness beyond Equity: Procedural and Interactional Justice

Equity theory looks at perceived fairness as a motivator. However, the way equity theory defines fairness is limited to fairness regarding rewards. Starting in the 1970s, researchers of workplace fairness began taking a broader view of justice. Equity theory deals with outcome fairness, and therefore, it is considered to be a distributive justice theory. **Distributive justice** refers to the degree to which the outputs received from the organization are fair. Two other types of fairness have also been identified: procedural justice and interactional justice.

distributive justice

The degree to which the outcomes received from the organization are fair.

Let's assume that you found out you are getting a promotion that will include a pay raise, increased responsibilities, and prestige. If you feel you deserve to be promoted, you would perceive high distributive justice ("getting the promotion is fair"). However, if you later found out that the department manager picked you because of your family connections, how would you feel? You might still like the outcome but feel that the decision-making process was unfair since it was not performance based. This response would involve feelings of procedural injustice. **Procedural justice** refers to the degree to which fair decision-making procedures are used. Research shows that employees care about procedural justice for many organizational decisions, including layoffs, employee selection, surveillance of employees, performance appraisals, and pay decisions.[26] They tend to care about procedural justice particularly when they do not get the outcome they feel they deserve.[27] If you do not get the promotion and find out that management chose the candidate because of their connections, you may view this as adding insult to injury. When people do not get the rewards they want, they tend to hold management responsible if procedures are not fair.[28]

procedural justice

The degree to which fair decision-making procedures are used to arrive at a decision.

Research has identified many ways of achieving procedural justice. For example, giving employees *advance notice* before laying them off, firing them, or disciplining them is perceived as fairer.[29] *Allowing employees' voices into decision making* is also important.[30] When designing a performance-appraisal system or implementing reorganization, asking employees for their input may be a good idea because it increases perceptions of fairness. Even when it is not possible to have employees participate, providing *explanations* is helpful in fostering procedural justice.[31] Finally, people expect *consistency* in treatment.[32] If one person is given extra time when taking a test while another is not, individuals would perceive decision making as unfair.

The idea that "justice is blind" refers to the notion that procedural justice is applied to all who enter the U.S. legal system.

Source: Shutterstock.com

interactional justice

The degree to which people are treated with respect, kindness, and dignity in interpersonal interactions.

Now let's imagine your boss telling you that you are getting a promotion. The manager uses these exact words: "Yes, we are giving you the promotion. The job is so simple that we thought even you can handle it." Now what is your reaction? The feeling of unfairness you may now experience are explained by interactional justice. **Interactional justice** refers to the degree to which people are treated with respect, kindness, and dignity in interpersonal interactions. We expect to be treated with dignity by our peers, supervisors, and customers. When the opposite happens, we feel angry. Even when faced with negative outcomes such as a pay cut, being treated with dignity and respect serves as a buffer and can alleviate stress.[33]

Employers would benefit from paying attention to all three types of justice perceptions. In addition to being the right thing to do, justice perceptions lead to outcomes companies care about. Injustice is directly harmful to employees' psychological health and well-being and contributes to stress and depression.[34] High levels of justice created higher levels of employee commitment to organizations, are related to higher job performance, higher levels of organizational citizenship (behaviors that are not part of one's job description but help the organization in other ways, such as speaking positively about the company and helping others), and higher levels of customer satisfaction, whereas low levels of justice lead to retaliation and supporting of unionization.[35]

Expectancy Theory

Expectancy theory argues that individual motivation to put forth more or less effort is determined by a rational calculation.[36] According to this theory, individuals ask themselves three questions.

FIGURE 13.5 Summary of Expectancy Theory

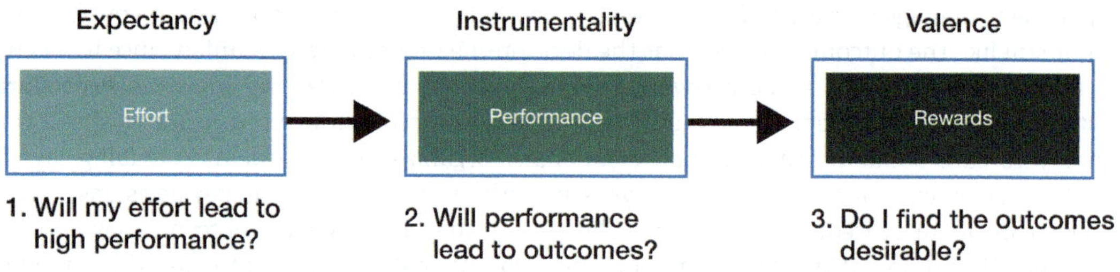

Source: Based on Porter, L. W., & Lawler, E. E. (1968). *Managerial attitudes and performance*. Homewood, IL: Irwin; Vroom, V. H. (1964). *Work and motivation*. New York: Wiley.

expectancy

The extent to which a person believes that high levels of effort will lead to outcomes of interest such as performance or success.

instrumentality

The degree to which the person believes that performance is related to secondary outcomes such as rewards.

The first question is whether the person believes that high levels of effort will lead to desired outcomes. This perception is labeled as **expectancy**. For example, do you believe that the effort you put forth in a class is related to learning worthwhile material and receiving a good grade? If you do, you are more likely to put forth effort.

The second question is the degree to which the person believes that performance is related to secondary outcomes such as rewards. This perception is labeled as **instrumentality**. For example, do you believe that passing the class is related to rewards such as getting a better job, or gaining approval from your instructor, friends, or parents? If you do, you are more likely to put forth effort.

Finally, individuals are also concerned about the value of the rewards awaiting them as a result of performance. The anticipated satisfaction that will result from an outcome is labeled as **valence**. For example, do you value getting a better job or gaining approval from your instructor, friends, or parents? If these outcomes are desirable to you, you are more likely to put forth effort.

valence

The value of the rewards awaiting the person as a result of performance.

How can managers influence these perceptions to motivate employees? In fact, managers can influence all three perceptions.[37] To influence their expectancy perceptions, managers may train their employees, or hire people who are qualified for the jobs in question. Low expectancy may also be due to employees feeling that something other than effort predicts performance, such as political behaviors on the part of employees. In this case, clearing the way to performance and creating an environment in which employees do not feel impeded will be helpful. The first step in influencing instrumentality is to connect pay and other rewards to performance using bonuses, award systems, and merit pay. Publicizing any contests or award programs is helpful in bringing rewards to the awareness of employees. It is also important to highlight that performance and not something else is being rewarded. For example, if a company has an employee-of-the-month award that is rotated among employees, employees are unlikely to believe that performance is being rewarded. In the name of being egalitarian, such a reward system may actually hamper the motivation of highest performing employees by eroding instrumentality. Finally, to influence valence, managers will need to find out what their employees value. This can be done by talking to employees, or surveying them about what rewards they find valuable.

Reinforcement Theory

Reinforcement theory is based on the work Ivan Pavlov conducted on behavioral conditioning and the later work B. F. Skinner performed on operant conditioning.[38] According to reinforcement theory, behavior is a function of its consequences. Imagine that even though no one asked you to, you stayed late and drafted a report. When the manager found out, she was ecstatic and took you out to lunch and thanked you genuinely. The consequences following your good deed were favorable, and therefore you are more likely to do similar good deeds in the future. In contrast, if your manager had said nothing about it and ignored the sacrifice you made, you would be less likely to demonstrate similar behaviors in the future, or your behavior would likely become extinct.

Despite the simplicity of reinforcement theory, how many times have you seen positive behavior ignored or, worse, negative behavior rewarded? In many organizations, this is a familiar scenario. People go above and beyond the call of duty, and yet their behaviors are ignored or criticized. People with disruptive habits may receive no punishments because the manager is afraid of the reaction the person will give when confronted. They may even receive rewards such as promotions so that the person is transferred to a different location and becomes someone else's problem. Moreover, it is common for people to be rewarded for the wrong kind of behavior. Steven Kerr labeled this phenomenon as "The folly of rewarding A while hoping for B."[39] For example, a company may make public statements about the importance of quality. Yet, they choose to reward shipments on time regardless of the number of known defects contained in the shipments. As a result, employees are more likely to ignore quality and focus on hurrying the delivery process.

TABLE 13.4 Reinforcement Methods

Positive Reinforcement	Negative Reinforcement
Positive behavior followed by positive consequences (Manager praises the employee)	Positive behavior followed by removal of negative consequences (Manager stops nagging the employee)

Punishment	Extinction
Negative behavior followed by negative consequences (Manager demotes the employee)	Negative behavior followed by removal of positive consequences (Manager ignores the behavior)

Reinforcement Interventions

McGregor's "hot stove rule" argues that punishment should be akin to touching a hot stove, where the result is severe, immediate, enforced with warning, and applied consistently and impartially.

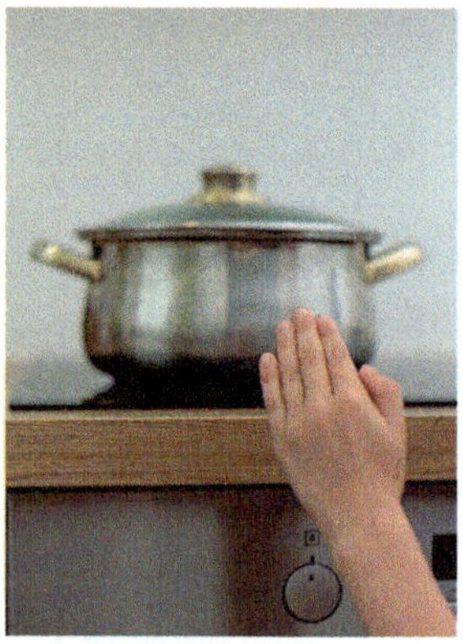

Source: Shutterstock.com

Reinforcement theory describes four interventions to modify employee behavior. Two of these are methods of increasing the frequency of desired behaviors while the remaining two are methods of reducing the frequency of undesired behaviors.

Positive reinforcement is a method of increasing the desired behavior.[40] Positive reinforcement involves making sure that behavior is met with positive consequences. Praising an employee for treating a customer respectfully is an example of positive reinforcement. If the praise immediately follows the positive behavior, the employee will see a link between behavior and positive consequences and will be motivated to repeat similar behaviors.

Negative reinforcement is also used to increase the desired behavior. Negative reinforcement involves removal of unpleasant outcomes once desired behavior is demonstrated. Nagging an employee to complete a report is an example of negative reinforcement. The negative stimulus in the environment will remain present until positive behavior is demonstrated. The problem with negative reinforcement may be that the negative stimulus may lead to unexpected behaviors and may fail to stimulate the desired behavior. For example, the person may start avoiding the manager to avoid being nagged.

Extinction is used to decrease the frequency of negative behaviors. Extinction is the removal of rewards following negative behavior. Sometimes, negative behaviors are demonstrated because they are being inadvertently rewarded. For example, it has been shown that when people are rewarded for their unethical behaviors, they tend to demonstrate higher levels of unethical behaviors.[41] Thus, when the rewards following unwanted behaviors are removed, the frequency of future negative behaviors may be reduced. If a friend is posting pictures of cute kittens on her Facebook account, liking or commenting on these pictures will make them keep coming. Completely ignoring such posts may reduce their frequency (assuming that you are interested in reducing the frequency of posts about kittens).

positive reinforcement

Reinforcement that involves making sure that behavior is met with positive consequences.

negative reinforcement

Reinforcement that involves removal of unpleasant outcomes once desired behavior is demonstrated.

extinction

The removal of rewards following negative behavior.

Punishment is another method of reducing the frequency of undesirable behaviors. Punishment involves presenting negative consequences following unwanted behaviors. Giving an employee a verbal or written warning for consistently being late to work is an example of punishment.

punishment

The presentation of negative consequences following unwanted behaviors.

Reinforcement Schedules

In addition to types of reinforcements, the timing or schedule on which reinforcement is delivered has a bearing on behavior.[42] Reinforcement is presented on a **continuous schedule** if reinforcers follow all instances of positive behavior. An example of a continuous schedule would be giving an employee a sales commission every time he or she makes a sale. **Fixed-ratio schedules** involve providing rewards every *n*th time the right behavior is demonstrated; for example, giving the employee a bonus for every 10th sale he or she makes. **Fixed-interval schedules** involve providing a reward after a specified period of time, such as giving a sales bonus once a month regardless of how many sales have been made. **Variable ratio** involves a random pattern, such as when a slot machine pays out at a casino to ensure patrons believe there is a chance the machine *might* payout with any given play.

A systematic way in which reinforcement theory principles are applied is called Organizational Behavior Modification (or **OB Mod**).[43] The model consists of five stages. The process starts with identifying the behavior that will be modified. Let's assume that we are interested in reducing absenteeism among employees. In step 2, we measure the baseline level of absenteeism. In step 3, the behavior's antecedents and consequences are determined. Why are employees absent? More important, what happens when an employee is absent? If the behavior is being unintentionally rewarded, we may expect these to reinforce absenteeism behavior. For example, suppose that absences peak each month on the days when a departmental monthly report is due, meaning that coworkers and supervisors must do extra work to prepare the report. To reduce the frequency of absenteeism, it will be necessary to think of financial or social incentives to follow positive behavior and negative consequences to follow negative behavior. In step 4, an intervention is implemented. Removing the positive consequences of negative behavior may be an effective way of dealing with the situation; for example, starting the monthly report preparation a few days earlier, or letting employees know that if they are absent when the monthly report is being prepared, their contribution to the report will be submitted as incomplete until they finish it. Punishments may be used in persistent cases. Finally, in step 5 the behavior is measured periodically and maintained.

Studies examining the effectiveness of OB Mod have been supportive of the model in general. A review of the literature found that OB Mod interventions resulted in an average of 17% improvement in performance.[44] Particularly in manufacturing settings, OB Mod was an effective way of increasing performance, although positive effects were observed in service organizations as well.

continuous schedule

A schedule in which reinforcers follow all instances of positive behavior.

fixed-ratio schedules

A schedule in which reinforcers reward every *n*th time the right behavior is demonstrated.

fixed-interval schedules

A schedule in which reinforcers reward after a specified period of time.

variable ratio

A schedule that involves providing the reinforcement on a random pattern.

OB Mod

A systematic application of reinforcement theory to modify employee behaviors in the workplace.

Slot machines (often called "one-armed bandits") are well known for their use of a variable reinforcement payout schedule.

Source: Shutterstock.com

FIGURE 13.6 Timing Is Everything: Utilizing Reinforcement Schedules

The timing (often referred to as a schedule) with which reinforcement is delivered has a bearing on the ensuing behavior. Here, we illustrate different reinforcement schedules.

Source: Shutterstock.com

Music Rap-Up: Help! I'm Under Attack

Twinprov perform a rap on reinforcement theory.

View in the online reader

Job Design

Many individuals believe that the most important motivator at work is pay. Yet, studies point to a different factor as the primary influence over worker motivation—job design. How a job is designed has a major impact on employee motivation, job satisfaction, commitment to the organization, as well as absenteeism and turnover. Job design is just one of the many organizational design decisions managers must make when engaged in the organizing function.

The question of how to properly design jobs so that employees are more productive and more satisfied has received managerial and research attention since the beginning of the 20th century.

Division of labor and specialization are common in home building with architects, plumbers, electricians, and a variety of skilled labor needed to complete different phases of new construction.

Source: Shutterstock.com

Scientific Management and Job Specialization

Perhaps the earliest attempt to design jobs was presented by Frederick Taylor in his 1911 book, *Principles of Scientific Management*. Scientific management proposed a number of ideas that have been influential in job design. One idea was to minimize waste by identifying the best method to perform the job to ensure maximum efficiency. Another one of the major advances of scientific management was **job specialization**, which entails breaking down tasks to their simplest components and assigning them to employees so that each person would perform few tasks in a repetitive manner. While this technique may be very efficient in terms of automation and standardization, from a motivational perspective, these jobs might be considered boring and repetitive and therefore associated with negative outcomes such as absenteeism.[45] Job specialization is also an ineffective way of organizing jobs in rapidly changing environments where employees close to the problem should modify their approach based on the demands of the situation.[46]

job specialization

Breaking down tasks to their simplest components and assigning them to employees so that each person would perform few tasks in a repetitive manner.

Rotation, Job Enlargement, and Enrichment

job rotation

Moving employees from job to job at regular intervals.

One of the early alternatives to job specialization was **job rotation**, which involves moving employees from job to job at regular intervals, thereby relieving the monotony and boredom typical in repetitive jobs. For example, Maids International, a company that provides cleaning services to households and businesses, uses job rotation such that maids cleaning the kitchen in one house would clean the bedroom in another house.[47] Using this technique, among others, the company was able to reduce its turnover level. In a study conducted in a supermarket, cashiers were rotated to work in different departments. As a result of the rotation, employee stress level was reduced, as measured by their blood pressure. Moreover, they reported fewer pain symptoms in their neck and shoulders.[48]

Job rotation has a number of advantages for organizations. It is an effective way for employees to acquire new skills, as the rotation involves cross-training to new tasks; this means that organizations increase the overall skill level of their employees.[49] In addition, job rotation is a means of knowledge transfer between departments. An interesting side effect of job rotation in some jobs is increased accountability and more ethical behavior. For example, loan officers tend to prepare more accurate and honest reports about their own performance when they anticipate rotation, presumably because they do not want their bad decisions to be exposed by their successor.[50] For employees, rotation is a benefit because they acquire new skills, which keeps them marketable in the long run.

Anecdotal evidence suggests that companies successfully rotate high-level employees to train their managers and increase innovativeness in the company. For example, Marriott International uses strategic movement of management trainees within a property (e.g., from banquet to sales), as well as among its 3,000 lodging properties in 70 countries, to prepare them for future assignments.[51] Dutch brewer Heineken rotates employees through a number of departments including brewing, quality assurance, packaging, and product development.[52]

job enlargement

Expanding the tasks performed by employees to add more variety.

Job enlargement refers to expanding the tasks performed by employees to add more variety. Like job rotation, job enlargement can reduce boredom and monotony as well as use human resources more effectively. When jobs are enlarged, employees view themselves as being capable of performing a broader set of tasks.[53] Job enlargement is positively related to employee satisfaction and higher-quality customer services, and it increases the chances of catching mistakes.[54] At the same time, the effects of job enlargement may depend on the *type* of enlargement. For example, exclusively giving employees simpler tasks had negative consequences on employee satisfaction with the job of catching errors, whereas giving employees more tasks that require them to be knowledgeable in different areas seemed to have more positive effects.[55]

job enrichment

A job redesign technique that allows workers more control over how they perform their own tasks.

Job enrichment is a job redesign technique that allows workers more control over how they perform their own tasks, giving them more responsibility over their jobs. As an alternative to job specialization, companies using job enrichment may experience positive outcomes such as reduced turnover, increased productivity, and reduced absences.[56] This may be because employees who have the authority and responsibility over their own work can be more efficient, eliminate unnecessary tasks, take shortcuts, and increase their own performance overall. At the same time, there is some evidence that job enrichment may sometimes cause employees to be dissatisfied.[57] The reason may be that employees who are given additional autonomy and responsibility may expect greater levels of pay or other types of compensation, and if this expectation is not met, they may feel frustrated. However, job enrichment may not be suitable for all employees.[58] Not all employees desire to have control over how they work, and if they do not have this desire, they may feel dissatisfied in an enriched job.

job crafting

Proactive changes employees make in their own job descriptions.

A recent approach to job enrichment is job crafting. **Job crafting** refers to the changes employees make to their own job description—expanding certain elements that are a better fit to their own personality or reducing the scope of the job to achieve better work-life balance—all in the service of better meeting the employees' career and life goals.[59] The idea behind job crafting is that oftentimes employees are not passive recipients of their roles and instead take an active role in shaping their own job roles and responsibilities to fit the realities of their interests, passions, and goals. Not all jobs allow job crafting, but some organizations are increasingly encouraging employees to take on an active role in the shaping of job descriptions. As an example, Deloitte employees may renegotiate their roles with management to increase or decrease the scope and visibility of the projects they take on or to increase the flexibility of their work hours.[60]

Job Characteristics Model

The **job characteristics model** is one of the most influential attempts to design jobs to increase their motivational properties.[61] Proposed in the 1970s by Hackman and Oldham, the model describes five core job dimensions, leading to three critical psychological states, which lead to work-related outcomes. In this model, shown in Figure 13.7, there are five core job dimensions.

job characteristics model

A model that describes five core job dimensions leading to three critical psychological states, which lead to work-related outcomes.

FIGURE 13.7 Job Characteristics Model

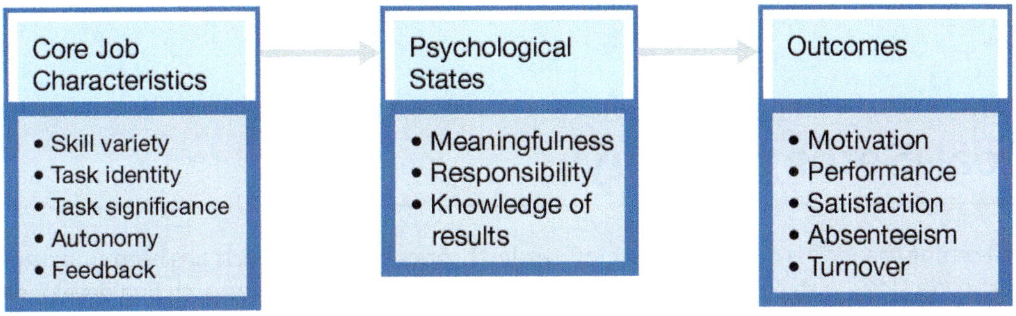

Source: Adapted from Hackman, J. R., & Oldham, G. R. (1975). Development of the job diagnostic survey. *Journal of Applied Psychology, 60*, 159–170.

Skill variety refers to the extent to which the job requires the person to use multiple high-level skills. A carwash employee whose job consists of directing cars into the automated carwash demonstrates low levels of skill variety, whereas a carwash employee who acts as a cashier, maintains carwash equipment, and manages the inventory of chemicals demonstrates higher skill variety.

skill variety

The extent to which the job requires the person to use multiple high-level skills.

Task identity refers to the degree to which the person completes a piece of work from start to finish. A Web designer who designs parts of a website will have low task identity because the work blends in with other Web designers' work, and in the end, it will be hard for the person to claim responsibility for the final output. The webmaster who designs the entire website will have higher task identity.

task identity

The degree to which the person completes an identifiable piece of work from start to finish.

Task significance refers to whether the person's job substantially affects other people's work, health, or well-being. A janitor who cleans the floors at an office building may find the job low in significance, thinking it is not an important job. However, janitors cleaning the floors at a hospital may see their role as essential in helping patients get better. When employees feel that their tasks are significant, they perform at higher levels and engage in greater levels of citizenship behaviors. Further, employees who believe their tasks are highly significant are better able to cope with the daily stressors associated with their jobs, such as their daily commute.[62]

task significance

The degree to which the person's job substantially affects other people's work, health, or well-being.

Autonomy is the degree to which a person has the freedom to decide how to perform his or her tasks. As an example, a restaurant chef working in a small restaurant who has control over the menu, concept, and pricing will have greater autonomy compared to a chef who is working in a chain restaurant who oversees the cooking process without having control over the taste of food, how it is cooked, or from where ingredients are acquired. Autonomy increases motivation at work, but it also has other benefits. Employees with autonomy can respond to workplace problems more quickly and effectively. Autonomy speeds the quality of decision making. Autonomous employees

autonomy

The degree to which the person has the freedom to decide how to perform one's tasks.

are also less likely to adopt a "this is not my job" approach to their work environment and instead be proactive (do what needs to be done without waiting to be told what to do) and creative.[63] Giving employees autonomy is also a great way to train them on the job. For example, Gucci's former CEO Robert Polet describes the autonomy he received while working at Unilever as the key to his development of leadership talents.[64] Autonomy can arise from workplace features, such as telecommuting, company structure, organizational climate, and leadership style.[65]

feedback

The degree to which the person learns how effective he or she is at work.

Feedback refers to the degree to which people learn how effective they are being at work. Feedback at work may come from other people, such as supervisors, peers, subordinates, and customers, or it may come from the job itself. A salesperson who gives presentations to potential clients, but is not informed of the clients' decisions, has low feedback at work. If this person receives notification that a sale was made based on the presentation, feedback will be high.

The relationship between feedback and job performance is more controversial. In other words, the mere presence of feedback is not sufficient for employees to feel motivated to perform better. In fact, a review of this literature shows that in about one-third of the cases, feedback was detrimental to performance.[66] In addition to whether feedback is present, the sign of the feedback (positive or negative), whether the person is ready to receive the feedback, and the manner in which feedback was given will all determine whether employees feel motivated or demotivated as a result of feedback.

Goal-Setting Theory

Goal-setting theory[67] is one of the most influential theories of motivation. It has been supported in over 1,000 studies with employees, ranging from blue-collar workers to research and development employees, and there is strong evidence that setting goals is related to performance improvements.[68] In fact, according to one estimate, goal-setting improves performance between 10% and 25% or more.[69] On the basis of evidence such as this, thousands of companies around the world are using goal-setting in some form, including companies such as Coca-Cola, PwC, Nike, Intel, and Microsoft, to name a few.

Setting SMART Goals

The mere presence of a goal does not motivate individuals. Think about New Year's resolutions that many people fail to keep. Some decided they should lose weight but then never put a concrete plan in action. Others decided that they would read more but didn't. Why did 97% of those who set New Year's resolutions fail to meet their goals?

SMART

A goal that is specific, measurable, aggressive/achievable, realistic, and timely.

Accumulating research evidence indicates that effective goals are SMART. A **SMART** goal is a goal that is **s**pecific, **m**easurable, **a**ggressive, **r**ealistic, and **t**ime-bound. Note that different sources use these acronyms slightly differently, and in some organizations A may stand for Achievable, and R may stand for Relevant (to corporate objectives). Ultimately, goals that are SMART are ones that are quantifiable, have a timeline, are relevant to corporate objectives, and are difficult so that they challenge individuals but are not so difficult that they are dismissed out of hand.

SMART (specific, measurable, achievable. realistic, timely) goals.

Source: Shutterstock.com

Specific and Measurable

Effective goals are specific and measurable. For example, "increasing sales to a region by 10%" is a specific goal, whereas deciding to "delight customers" is not specific or measurable. When goals are specific, performance tends to be higher.[70] Why? If goals are not specific and measurable, how would you know whether you have reached the goal? A wide distribution of performance levels could potentially be acceptable. For the same reason, "doing your best" is not an effective goal, because it is not measurable and does not give you a specific target.

Certain aspects of performance are easier to quantify. For example, it is relatively easy to set specific goals for productivity, sales, number of defects, or turnover rates. However, not everything that is easy to measure should be measured. Moreover, some of the most important elements of someone's performance may not be easily quantifiable (such as employee or customer satisfaction). So how do you set specific and measurable goals for these soft targets? Even though some effort will be involved, metrics such as satisfaction can and should be quantified. For example, you could design a survey for employees and customers to track satisfaction ratings from year to year.

Aggressive

This may sound counterintuitive, but effective goals are difficult, not easy. Aggressive goals are also called stretch goals. According to a Hay Group study, one factor that distinguishes companies that are ranked as "Most Admired Companies" in *Fortune* magazine is that they set more difficult goals.[71] People with difficult goals outperform those with easier goals.[72] Why? Easy goals do not provide a challenge. When goals are aggressive and require people to work harder or smarter, performance tends to be dramatically higher. One study shows that people who have a high level of self-efficacy and people who have a high need for achievement tend to set more difficult goals for themselves.[73] Finally, a series of two studies has shown that when it comes to difficult goals, who sets the goals matter. Organizationally set difficult goals were associated with heightened anxiety, whereas self-set difficult goals were related to higher levels of enthusiasm. This study points to the importance of the potential emotional reactions to difficult goals, and underlines the importance of involving employees in goal setting where possible.[74]

Realistic

While goals should be difficult, they should also be based in reality. In other words, if a goal is viewed as impossible to reach, it will not have any motivational value. In fact, setting impossible goals and then punishing people for not reaching these goals is cruel and will demotivate employees.

Time-Bound

The goal should contain a statement regarding when the proposed performance level will be reached. For example, "increasing sales to a region by 10%" is not a time-bound goal, because there is no time limit. Adding a limiter such as "by December of the current fiscal year" gives employees a sense of time urgency.

Even though it seems like a simple concept, in reality many goals that are set within organizations may not be SMART. For example, Microsoft conducted an audit of its goal setting and performance review system and found that only about 40% of the goals were specific and measurable.[75]

Why Do SMART Goals Motivate?

There are at least four reasons why goals motivate.[76] First, goals give us direction; therefore, goals should be set carefully. Giving employees goals that are not aligned with company goals will be a problem, because goals will direct employee's energy to a certain end. Second, goals energize people and tell them not to stop until they reach that point. Third, having a goal provides a challenge. When people have goals and when they reach them, they feel a sense of accomplishment. Finally, SMART goals urge people to think outside the box and rethink how they are working. If a goal is substantially difficult, merely working harder will not lead to results. Instead, you will need to rethink the way you usually work and devise a creative way of working. It has been argued that this is how designers and engineers in Japan came up with the bullet train. Having a goal that went way beyond the current speed of trains prevented engineers from making minor improvements and urged them to come up with a radically different concept.[77]

FIGURE 13.8 Why Goals Motivate

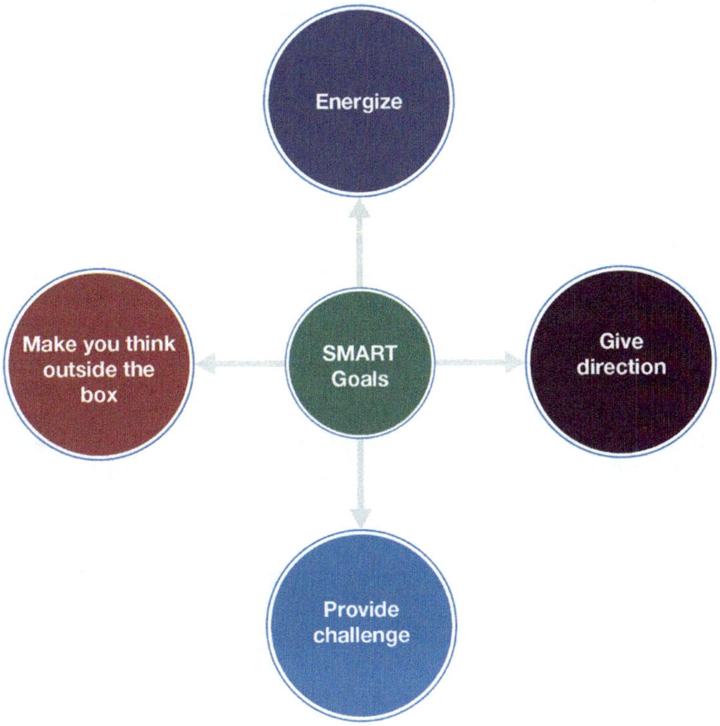

Source: Based on information contained in Latham, G. P. (2004). The motivational benefits of goal setting. *Academy of Management Executive, 18*, 126–129; Seijts, G. H., & Latham, G. P. (2005). Learning versus performance goals: When should each be used? *Academy of Management Executive, 19*, 124–131; Shaw, K. N. (2004). Changing the goal-setting process at Microsoft. *Academy of Management Executive, 18*, 139–142.

Are There Downsides to Goal-Setting?

As with any management technique, there may be some downsides to goal-setting.[78] First, setting goals for specific outcomes may hamper employee performance if employees lack skills and abilities to reach the goals. In these situations, setting goals for behaviors and for learning may be more effective than setting goals for outcomes. Second, goal-setting may motivate employees to focus on a goal and ignore the need to respond to new challenges. For example, one study found that when teams had difficult goals and when employees within the team had high levels of performance orientation, teams had difficulty adapting to unforeseen circumstances.[79] Third, goals focus employee attention on the activities that are measured, which may lead to sacrificing other important aspects of performance. When goals are set for production numbers, quality may suffer. As a result, it is important to set goals incorporating all critical aspects of performance. Finally, aggressive pursuit of goals may lead to unethical behaviors. When employees are rewarded for goal accomplishment but there are no rewards whatsoever for coming very close to reaching the goal, employees may be tempted to cheat.

No motivational theory is complete by itself, but each theory provides us with a framework we can use to analyze, interpret, and manage employee behaviors in the workplace, which are important skills managers use when conducting their leading function. In fact, motivation is important throughout the entire P-O-L-C framework because most managerial functions involve accomplishing tasks and goals through others.

Key Takeaway

Process-based theories use the mental processes of employees as the key to understanding employee motivation. According to equity theory, employees are demotivated when they view reward distribution as unfair. In addition to distributive justice, research identified two other types of fairness (procedural and interactional), which also affect worker reactions and motivation. According to expectancy theory, employees are motivated when they believe that their effort will lead to high performance (expectancy), that their performance will lead to outcomes (instrumentality), and that the outcomes following performance are desirable (valence). Reinforcement theory argues that behavior is a function of its consequences. By properly tying rewards to positive behaviors, eliminating rewards following negative behaviors, and punishing negative behaviors, leaders can increase the frequency of desired behaviors. In job design, there are five components that increase the motivating potential of a job—skill variety, task identity, task significance, autonomy, and feedback. These theories are particularly useful in designing reward systems within a company. Goal-setting theory is one of the most influential theories of motivation. To motivate employees, goals should be SMART (specific, measurable, aggressive/achievable, realistic, and timely). Setting goals and objectives is a task managers undertake when involved in the planning portion of the P-O-L-C function.

Discussion Questions

1. Your manager tells you that the best way of ensuring fairness in reward distribution is to keep your pay a secret. How would you respond to this assertion?
2. What are the distinctions among procedural, interactional, and distributive justice? List ways in which you could increase each of these justice perceptions.
3. Using an example from your own experience in school or at work, explain the concepts of expectancy, instrumentality, and valence.
4. Some practitioners and researchers consider OB Mod as unethical because it may be viewed as employee manipulation. What would be your reaction to this criticism?
5. Consider a job you held in the past. Analyze the job using the job characteristics model.
6. If a manager tells you to "sell as much as you can," is this goal likely to be effective? Why or why not?

13.4 Developing Your Personal Motivation Skills

Learning Objectives

1. Understand what you can do to give feedback through an effective performance appraisal.
2. Learn guidelines for proactively seeking feedback.

Guidelines for Giving Feedback in a Performance Appraisal Meeting

Before the meeting, ask the person to complete a self-appraisal. This is a great way of making sure that employees become active participants in the process and are heard. Complete the performance appraisal form and document your rating using several examples. Be sure that your review covers the entire time since the last review, not just recent events. Be sure that you devote sufficient time to each meeting. If you schedule too many meetings back to back, you may lose your energy in later meetings. Be sure that the physical location is conducive to a private conversation.

During the meeting, be sure to recognize effective performance through specific praise. Do not start the meeting with a criticism. Starting with positive performance instances helps establish a better mood and shows that you recognize what the employee is doing correctly. Give employees opportunities to talk. Ask them about their greatest accomplishments, as well as opportunities for improvement. Show empathy and support. Remember, your job as a manager is to help the person solve performance problems. Identify areas where you can help. Conclude by setting goals and creating an action plan for the future.

When providing performance appraisals many advocate the sandwich approach where critical feedback is provided between two pieces of praise.

Source: Shutterstock.com

After the meeting, continue to give the employee periodic and frequent feedback. Follow through on the goals that were set.[80]

Five Guidelines for Seeking Feedback

Research shows that receiving feedback is a key to performing well. If you are not receiving enough feedback on the job, make a concerted effort to seek feedback using the following guidelines.

1. Consider seeking regular feedback from your boss. This also has the added benefit of signaling to the manager that you care about your performance and want to be successful.
2. Be genuine in your desire to learn. When seeking feedback, your aim should be improving yourself as opposed to creating the impression that you are a motivated employee. If your manager thinks that you are managing impressions rather than genuinely trying to improve your performance, seeking feedback may hurt you.
3. Develop a good relationship with your manager as well as the employees you manage. This would have the benefit of giving you more feedback in the first place. It also has the upside of making it easier to ask direct questions about your own performance.
4. Consider finding trustworthy peers who can share information with you regarding your performance. Your manager is not the only helpful source of feedback.
5. Be gracious when you receive unfavorable feedback. Even though it may not feel like it at times, feedback is a tool you can use to improve your performance by using feedback constructively. Consider that the negative feedback giver probably risked your goodwill by being honest. Unless there are factual mistakes in the feedback, do not try to convince the person that the feedback is inaccurate.[81]

Key Takeaway

Providing effective feedback is a key part of a manager's job. To do so, plan the delivery of feedback before, during, and after the meeting. In addition, there are a number of ways to learn about your own performance. Take the time to seek feedback and act on it. With this information, you can maximize your success and the success of those you manage.

Discussion Questions

1. Why can discussing performance feedback with employees be so hard?
2. What barriers do you perceive in asking for feedback?
3. How would you react if one of your employees came to you for feedback?
4. Imagine that your good friend is starting a new job next week. What recommendations would you give to help your friend do a great job seeking feedback?

13.5 Case in Point: Diverse and Color Proud at Gap Inc.

TY Lim/Shutterstock.com

The San Francisco, California based Gap Inc. is a clothing giant, with over 3,500 locations in 90 countries, supported by 129,000 employees. The company owns well-known brands such as Banana Republic, Old Navy, Athleta, as well as Gap, and is a leader in casual men's, women's, and children's clothing. Gap was ranked by *Newsweek* as one of America's most responsible companies in 2020 for their commitment to doing good and giving back to their communities. Founded over 50 years ago, the company regards its prosocial values as the key to the way the business is run. Diversity and inclusion are high among these values. For example, in 2018, the company signed the "Open to All" business pledge affirming that it would treat customers, employees, and suppliers with dignity and respect, and it would provide a welcoming and safe environment to all regardless of sex, sexual orientation, national origin, race, ethnicity, religion, and disability.

Gap was named one of the world's most diverse and inclusive companies in 2018 and 2019, ranking among the top 10 in both years. For a business catering to a diverse customer base, diversity and inclusion is critical to the bottom line of the business. As a case in point, Gucci received backlash after a design resembling blackface on a sweater. Similarly, Prada came under fire when they started selling keychains that resembled racist caricatures. It is no accident that Gap seems to avoid such missteps and fiascos. In 2018, the company formed the Color Proud Council consisting of 45 employees charged with being present in all phases of a collection's creation. The council makes sure that marketing, merchandising, and hiring decisions are inclusive. One of their success stories is Banana Republic's "True Hues" collection consisting of skin colored clothing. The involvement of Color Proud Council ensured that the collection was inclusive of all skin tones, with the sales significantly beating expectations.

The company uses a number of different strategies to foster diversity and inclusion. Be One Get One (BOGO) is a mentoring program aimed at developing careers of employees. The company fosters a number of different employee resource networks, such as Asians Supporting Inclusion and Awareness (ASIA), Gap Parents, and Women in Leadership (GAPWIL). The leadership team is split evenly between men and women, but there is room to improve. For example, Michele Nyrop, Chief People Officer, noted that Banana Republic moved its creative department from New York to San Francisco, which allowed them to build their team of 200 from the ground up, resulting in greater levels of diversity in their design team. In another program aimed at diversifying entry level workers called "This Way Ahead," Gap hires young adults (those between 16–24 years old) in low income neighborhoods. Applicants are selected based on their potential as opposed to past work experience, and are provided with a job coach who will show them the way and help them get integrated into the business.[82]

Despite its highly visible efforts to create an inclusive workplace, Gap's reputation in labor relations is far from spotless and shows much need for improvement. For example, in 2007, the company admitted to having inadvertently used child labor in their subcontracted production lines produced in India. Further, in 2018, a report by Global Labor Justice revealed that female workers in their Asian factories were subject to gender-based violence and abuse, with the company agreeing to investigate the issue. These examples point to the importance of infusing domestic diversity goals and initiatives into all aspects of one's business, particularly because of the necessity to manage a global supply chain ethically.[83]

Multimedia Extension—A Culture of Equality

View in the online reader

Case Discussion Questions

1. What do you think are the stated and unstated reason's for Gap's commitment to diversity and inclusion?
2. The case described Open to All, Color Proud, mentoring, employee resource networks, and This Way Ahead as some of the specific ways in which Gap manages diversity. What are your thoughts about these practices? How resource intense are they? How useful do you believe they would be in businesses in other industries?
3. How important do you think Gap's diversity and inclusion practices are in regard to hiring and retaining its workforce?
4. In your opinion, to what extent does Gap's influence extend beyond the boundaries of the organization to impact change in the world?
5. Gap Inc. has set a high bar for proactively cultivating a culture of diversity and inclusion and yet there are instances where these goals were not universally met, particularly in their global operations. How do you reconcile the company's domestic efforts with the labor relations problems it encounters as part of its global supply chain? What is Gap's obligation to address these concerns?

Endnotes

1. Mitchell, T. R. (1982). Motivation: New directions for theory, research, and practice. *Academy of Management Review*, 7, 80–88; Porter, L. W., & Lawler, E. E. (1968). Managerial attitudes and performance. *Homewood*, IL: Dorsey Press.
2. Deci, E. L. (1972). Intrinsic motivation, extrinsic reinforcement, and inequity. *Journal of Personality and Social Psychology, 22*, 113–120.
3. Retrieved from https://www.forbes.com/sites/theyec/2020/01/03/best-practices-for-fostering-intrinsic-motivation/#4b53a8916179.
4. Cerasoli, C. P., Nicklin, J. M., & Ford, M. T. (2014). Intrinsic motivation and extrinsic incentives jointly predict performance: A 40-year meta-analysis. *Psychological Bulletin, 140*, 980–1008.
5. Maslow, A. H. (1943). A theory of human motivation. *Psychological Review, 50*, 370–396; Maslow, A. H. (1954). *Motivation and personality*. New York: Harper.
6. Baumeister, R. F., & Leary, M. R. (1995). The need to belong: Desire for interpersonal attachments as a fundamental human motivation. *Psychological Bulletin, 117*, 497–529.
7. Neher, A. (1991). Maslow's theory of motivation: A critique. *Journal of Humanistic Psychology, 31*, 89–112; Rauschenberger, J., Schmitt, N., & Hunter, J. E. (1980). A test of the need hierarchy concept by a Markov model of change in need strength. *Administrative Science Quarterly, 25*, 654–670.
8. Alderfer, C. P. (1969). An empirical test of a new theory of human needs. *Organizational Behavior and Human Performance, 4*, 142–175.
9. Herzberg, F., Mausner, B., & Snyderman, B. (1959). *The motivation to work*. New York: Wiley; Herzberg, F. (1965). The motivation to work among Finnish supervisors. *Personnel Psychology, 18*, 393–402.
10. Cummings, L. L., & Elsalmi, A. M. (1968). Empirical research on the bases and correlates of managerial motivation. *Psychological Bulletin, 70*, 127–144; House, R. J., & Wigdor, L. A. (1967). Herzberg's dual-factor theory of job satisfaction and motivation: A review·of the evidence and a criticism. *Personnel Psychology, 20*, 369–389.
11. Spangler, W. D. (1992). Validity of questionnaire and TAT measures of need for achievement: Two meta-analyses. *Psychological Bulletin, 112*, 140–154.
12. Mueller, C. M., & Dweck, C. S. (1998). Praise for intelligence can undermine children's motivation and performance. *Journal of Personality and Social Psychology, 75*, 33–52.
13. Campbell, D. J. (1982). Determinants of choice of goal difficulty level: A review of situational and personality influences. *Journal of Occupational Psychology, 55*, 79–95.
14. Harrell, A. M., & Stahl, M. J. (1981). A behavioral decision theory approach for measuring McClelland's trichotomy of needs. *Journal of Applied Psychology, 66*, 242–247; Trevis, C. S., & Certo, S. C. (2005). Spotlight on entrepreneurship. *Business Horizons, 48*, 271–274; Turban, D. B., & Keon, T. L. (1993). Organizational attractiveness: An interactionist perspective. *Journal of Applied Psychology, 78*, 184–193.
15. McClelland, D. C., & Boyatzis, R. E. (1982). Leadership motive pattern and long-term success in management. *Journal of Applied Psychology, 67*, 737–743.
16. McClelland, D. C., & Burnham, D. H. (1976). Power is the great motivator. *Harvard Business Review, 25*, 159–166.
17. Wong, M. M., & Csikszentmihalyi, M. (1991). Affiliation motivation and daily experience: Some issues on gender differences. *Journal of Personality and Social Psychology, 60*, 154–164.
18. Adams, J. S. (1965). Inequity in social exchange. In L. Berkowitz (Ed.), *Advances in experimental social psychology* (Vol. 2, pp. 267–299). New York: Academic Press.
19. Cappelen, A. W., Eichele, T., Hugdahl, K., Specht, K., Sørensen, E. Ø., & Tungodden, B. (2014). Equity theory and fair inequality: A neuroeconomic study. Proceedings of the National Academy of Sciences.
20. Carrell, M. R., & Dittrich, J. E. (1978). Equity theory: The recent literature, methodological considerations, and new directions. *Academy of Management Review, 3*, 202–210; Goodman, P. S., & Friedman, A. (1971). An examination of Adams' theory of inequity. *Administrative Science Quarterly, 16*, 271–288.
21. Greenberg, J. (1993). Stealing in the name of justice: Informational and interpersonal moderators of theft reactions to underpayment inequity. *Organizational Behavior and Human Decision Processes, 54*, 81–103.
22. Schmidt, D. R., & Marwell, G. (1972). Withdrawal and reward reallocation as responses to inequity. *Journal of Experimental Social Psychology, 8*, 207–211.
23. Austin, W., & Walster, E. (1974). Reactions to confirmations and disconfirmations of expectancies of equity and inequity. *Journal of Personality and Social Psychology, 30*, 208–216.
24. Evan, W. M., & Simmons, R. G. (1969). Organizational effects of inequitable rewards: Two experiments in status inconsistency. *IEEE Engineering Management Review, 1*, 95–108.
25. Huseman, R. C., Hatfield, J. D., & Miles, E. W. (1987). A new perspective on equity theory: The equity sensitivity construct. *Academy of Management Review, 12*, 222–234.
26. Alge, B. J. (2001). Effects of computer surveillance on perceptions of privacy and procedural justice. *Journal of Applied Psychology, 86*, 797–804; Bauer, T. N., Maertz, C. P., Jr., Dolen, M. R., & Campion, M. A. (1998). Longitudinal assessment of applicant reactions to employment testing and test outcome feedback. *Journal of Applied Psychology, 83*, 892–903; Kidwell, R. E. (1995). Pink slips without tears. *Academy of Management Executive, 9*, 69–70.
27. Brockner, J., & Wiesenfeld, B. M. (1996). An integrative framework for explaining reactions to decisions: Interactive effects of outcomes and procedures. *Psychological Bulletin, 120*, 189–208.
28. Brockner, J., Fishman, A. Y., Reb, J., Goldman, B., Spiegel, S., & Garden, C. (2007). Procedural fairness, outcome favorability, and judgments of an authority's responsibility. *Journal of Applied Psychology, 92*, 1657–1671.
29. Kidwell, R. E. (1995). Pink slips without tears. *Academy of Management Executive, 9*, 69–70.
30. Alge, B. J. (2001). Effects of computer surveillance on perceptions of privacy and procedural justice. *Journal of Applied Psychology, 86*, 797–804; Kernan, M. C., & Hanges, P. J. (2002). Survivor reactions to reorganization: Antecedents and consequences of procedural, interpersonal, and informational justice. *Journal of Applied Psychology, 87*, 916–928; Lind, E. A., Kanfer, R., & Earley, C. P. (1990). Voice, control, and procedural justice: Instrumental and noninstrumental concerns in fairness judgments. *Journal of Personality and Social Psychology, 59*, 952–959.
31. Schaubroeck, J., May, D. R., & William, B. F. (1994). Procedural justice explanations and employee reactions to economic hardship: A field experiment. *Journal of Applied Psychology, 79*, 455–460.
32. Bauer, T. N., Maertz, C. P., Jr., Dolen, M. R., & Campion, M. A. (1998). Longitudinal assessment of applicant reactions to employment testing and test outcome feedback. *Journal of Applied Psychology, 83*, 892–903.
33. Greenberg, J. (2006). Losing sleep over organizational injustice: Attenuating insomniac reactions to underpayment inequity with supervisory training in interactional justice. *Journal of Applied Psychology, 91*, 58–69.
34. Greenberg, J. (2004). Managing workplace stress by promoting organizational justice. *Organizational Dynamics, 33*, 352–365; Tepper, B. J. (2001). Health consequences of organizational injustice: tests of main and interactive effects. *Organizational Behavior and Human Decision Processes, 86*, 197–215.
35. Blader, S. L. (2007). What leads organizational members to collectivize? Injustice and identification as precursors of union certification. *Organization Science, 18*, 108–126; Colquitt, J. A., Conlon, D. E., Wesson, M. J., Porter, C. O. L. H., & Ng, K. Y. (2001). Justice at the millennium: A meta-analytic review of 25 years of organizational justice research. *Journal of Applied Psychology, 86*, 425–445; Colquitt, J. A., Rodell, J. B. (2011). Justice, trust, and trustworthiness: A longitudinal analysis integrating three theoretical perspectives. *Academy of Management Journal, 54*, 1183–1206; Rubenstein, A. L., Allen, D. G., & Bosco, F. A. (In press). What's past (and present) is prologue: Interactions between justice levels and trajectories predicting behavioral reciprocity. *Journal of Management.* Masterson, S. S. (2001). A trickle-down model of organizational justice: Relating employees' and customers' perceptions of and reactions to fairness. *Journal of Applied Psychology, 86*, 594–604.
36. Porter, L. W., & Lawler, E. E. (1968). *Managerial attitudes and performance*. Homewood, IL: Irwin; Vroom, V. H. (1964). *Work and motivation*. New York: Wiley.
37. Cook, C. W. (1980). Guidelines for managing motivation. *Business Horizons, 23*, 61–69.
38. Skinner, B. F. (1953). *Science and human behavior*. New York: Free Press.
39. Kerr, S. (1995). On the folly of rewarding A while hoping for B. *Academy of Management Executive, 9*, 7–14.
40. Beatty, R. W., & Schneier, C. E. (1975). A case for positive reinforcement. *Business Horizons, 18*, 57–66.
41. Harvey, H. W., & Sims, H. P. (1978). Some determinants of unethical decision behavior: An experiment. *Journal of Applied Psychology, 63*, 451–457.
42. Beatty, R. W., & Schneier, C. E. (1975). A case for positive reinforcement. *Business Horizons, 18*, 57–66.
43. Luthans, F., & Stajkovic, A. D. (1999). Reinforce for performance: The need to go beyond pay and even rewards. *Academy of Management Executive, 13*, 49–57.
44. Stajkovic, A. D., & Luthans, F. (1997). A meta-analysis of the effects of organizational behavior modification on task performance, 1975–1995. *Academy of Management Journal, 40*, 1122–1149.
45. Campion, M. A., & Thayer, P. W. (1987). Job design: Approaches, outcomes, and trade-offs. *Organizational Dynamics, 15*, 66–78.
46. Wilson, F. M. (1999). Rationalization and rationality: From the founding fathers to eugenics. In *Organizational behaviour: A critical introduction*. Oxford: Oxford University Press.
47. Denton, D. K. (1994). …I hate this job. *Business Horizons, 37*, 46–52.
48. Rissen, D., Melin, B., Sandsjo, L., Dohns, I., & Lundberg, U. (2002). Psychophysiological stress reactions, trapezius muscle activity, and neck and shoulder pain among female cashiers before and after introduction of job rotation. *Work & Stress, 16*, 127–137.

49. Campion, M. A., Cheraskin, L., & Stevens, M. J. (1994). Career-related antecedents and outcomes of job rotation. *Academy of Management Journal, 37*, 1518–1542.
50. Hertzberg, A., Liberti, J. M., & Paravisini, D. (2010). Information and incentives inside the firm: Evidence from loan officer rotation. *Journal of Finance, 65*, 795–828; Kane, A. A., Argote, L., & Levine, J. M. (2005). Knowledge transfer between groups via personnel rotation: Effects of social identity and knowledge quality. *Organizational Behavior and Human Decision Processes, 96*, 56–71.
51. Nalbantian, H. R. (2009, March). Making mobility matter. *Harvard Business Review, 87*(3)
52. Retrieved from https://www.digitalhrtech.com/job-rotation/.
53. Parker, S. K. (1998). Enhancing role breadth self-efficacy: The roles of job enrichment and other organizational interventions. *Journal of Applied Psychology, 83*, 835–852.
54. Campion, M. A., & McClelland, C. L. (1991). Interdisciplinary examination of the costs and benefits of enlarged jobs: A job design quasi-experiment. *Journal of Applied Psychology, 76*, 186–198.
55. Campion, M. A., & McClelland, C. L. (1993). Follow-up and extension of the interdisciplinary costs and benefits of enlarged jobs. *Journal of Applied Psychology, 78*, 339–351.
56. McEvoy, G. M., & Cascio, W. F. (1985). Strategies for reducing employee turnover. *Journal of Applied Psychology, 70*, 342–353; Locke, E. A., Sirota, D., & Wolfson, A. D. (1976). An experimental case study of the successes and failures of job enrichment in a government agency. *Journal of Applied Psychology, 61*, 701–711.
57. Locke, E. A., Sirota, D., & Wolfson, A. D. (1976). An experimental case study of the successes and failures of job enrichment in a government agency. *Journal of Applied Psychology, 61*, 701–711.
58. Cherrington, D. J., & Lynn, E. J. (1980). The desire for an enriched job as a moderator of the enrichment-satisfaction relationship. *Organizational Behavior and Human performance, 25*, 139–159; Hulin, C. L., & Blood, M. R. (1968). Job enlargement, individual differences, and worker responses. *Psychological Bulletin, 69*, 41–55.
59. Dutton, J.E., & and Wrzesniewski, A. (March, 2020). What Job Crafting Looks Like. *Harvard Business Review*. Retrieved from https://hbr.org/2020/03/what-job-crafting-looks-like.
60. Fitzpatrick, L. (2009, May 25). We're getting off the ladder. *Time, 173*(20); Wrzesniewski, A. Berg, J. M., & Dutton, J. E. (2010). Turn the job you have into the job you want. *Harvard Business Review. 88*(6), 114–117.
61. Hackman, J. R., & Oldham, G. R. (1975). Development of the job diagnostic survey. *Journal of Applied Psychology, 60*, 159–170.
62. Hu, J., Erdogan, B., Bauer, T. N., Jiang, K., Liu, S., & Li, Y. (2015). There are lots of big fish in this pond: The role of peer overqualification on task significance, perceived fit, and performance for overqualified employees. *Journal of Applied Psychology, 100*, 1228–1238; Zhou, L., Wang, M., Chang, C. H., Liu, S., Zhan. Y., & Shi, J. (2017). Commuting stress process and self-regulation at work: Moderating roles of daily task significance, family interference with work, and commuting means efficacy. *Personnel Psychology, 70*, 891–922.
63. Morgeson, F. P., Delaney-Klinger, K., & Hemingway, M. A. (2005). The importance of job autonomy, cognitive ability, and job-related skill for predicting role breadth and job performance. *Journal of Applied Psychology, 90*, 399–406; Parker, S. K., Wall, T. D., & Jackson, P. R. (1997). "That's not my job": Developing flexible employee work orientations. *Academy of Management Journal, 40*, 899–929; Parker, S. K., Williams, H. M., & Turner, N. (2006). Modeling the antecedents of proactive behavior at work. *Journal of Applied Psychology, 91*, 636–652; Parker, S. K. (2014). Beyond motivation: Job and work design for development, health, ambidexterity, and more. *Annual Review of Psychology, 65*, 661–691.
64. Gumbel, P. (2008, January 21). Galvanizing Gucci. *Fortune, 157*(1), 80–88.
65. Gajendran, R. S., Harrison, D. A., & Delaney-Klinger, K. (2015). Are telecommuters remotely good citizens? Unpacking telecommuting's effects on performance via i-deals and job resources. *Personnel Psychology, 68*, 353–393; Garnier, G. H. (1982). Context and decision making autonomy in the foreign affiliates of U.S. multinational corporations. *Academy of Management Journal, 25*, 893–908; Lyon, H. L., & Ivancevich, J. M. (1974). An exploratory investigation of organizational climate and job satisfaction in a hospital. *Academy of Management Journal, 17*, 635–648; Parker, S. K. (2003). Longitudinal effects of lean production on employee outcomes and the mediating role of work characteristics. *Journal of Applied Psychology, 88*, 620–634.
66. Kluger, A. N., & DeNisi, A. (1996). The effects of feedback interventions on performance: A historical review, a meta-analysis, and a preliminary feedback intervention theory. *Psychological Bulletin, 119*, 254–284.
67. Locke, E. A., & Latham, G. P. (1990). *A theory of goal setting and task performance*. Englewood Cliffs, NJ: Prentice-Hall.
68. Ivancevich, J. M., & McMahon, J. T. (1982). The effects of goal setting, external feedback, and self-generated feedback on outcome variables: A field experiment. *Academy of Management Journal, 25*, 359–372; Latham, G. P., & Locke, E. A. (2006). Enhancing the benefits and overcoming the pitfalls of goal setting. *Organizational Dynamics, 35*, 332–340; Umstot, D. D., Bell, C. H., & Mitchell, T. R. (1976). Effects of job enrichment and task goals on satisfaction and productivity: Implications for job design. *Journal of Applied Psychology, 61*, 379–394.
69. Pritchard, R. D., Roth, P. L., Jones, S. D., Galgay, P. J., & Watson, M. D. (1988). Designing a goal-setting system to enhance performance: A practical guide. *Organizational Dynamics, 17*, 69–78.
70. Tubbs, M. E. (1986). Goal setting: A meta-analytic examination of the empirical evidence. *Journal of Applied Psychology, 71*, 474–483.
71. Stein, N. (2000). Measuring people power. *Fortune, 142*(7), 186.
72. Mento, A. J., Steel, R. P., & Karren, R. J. (1987). A meta-analytic study of the effects of goal-setting on task performance: 1966–1984. *Organizational Behavior and Human Decision Processes, 39*, 52–83; Phillips, J. M., & Gully, S. M. (1997). Role of goal orientation, ability, need for achievement, and locus of control in the self-efficacy and goal-setting process. *Journal of Applied Psychology, 82*, 792–802; Tubbs, M. E. (1986). Goal setting: A meta-analytic examination of the empirical evidence. *Journal of Applied Psychology, 71*, 474–483; Yukl, G. A., & Latham, G. P. (1978). Interrelationships among employee participation, individual differences, goal difficulty, goal acceptance, goal instrumentality, and performance. *Personnel Psychology, 31*, 305–323.
73. Phillips, J. M., & Gully, S. M. (1997). Role of goal orientation, ability, need for achievement, and locus of control in the self-efficacy and goal-setting process. *Journal of Applied Psychology, 82*, 792-802.
74. Welsh, D. T., Baer, M. D., & Sessions, H. (2020). Hot pursuit: The affective consequences of organization-set versus self set goals for emotional exhaustion and citizenship behavior. *Journal of Applied Psychology, 105*, 166–185.
75. Shaw, K. N. (2004). Changing the goal-setting process at Microsoft. *Academy of Management Executive, 18*, 139–142.
76. Latham, G. P. (2004). The motivational benefits of goal-setting. *Academy of Management Executive, 18*, 126–129; Seijts, G. H., & Latham, G. P. (2005). Learning versus performance goals: When should each be used? *Academy of Management Executive, 19*, 124–131; Shaw, K. N. (2004). Changing the goal-setting process at Microsoft. *Academy of Management Executive, 18*, 139–142.
77. Kerr, S., & Landauer, S. (2004). Using stretch goals to promote organizational effectiveness and personal growth: General Electric and Goldman Sachs. *Academy of Management Executive, 18*, 134–138.
78. Locke, E. A. (2004). Linking goals to monetary incentives. *Academy of Management Executive, 18*, 130–133; Pritchard, R. D., Roth, P. L., Jones, S. D., Galgay, P. J., & Watson, M. D. (1988). Designing a goal-setting system to enhance performance: A practical guide. *Organizational Dynamics, 17*, 69–78; Seijts, G. H., & Latham, G. P. (2005). Learning versus performance goals: When should each be used? *Academy of Management Executive, 19*, 124–131.
79. Lepine, J. A. (2005). Adaptation of teams in response to unforeseen change: Effects of goal difficulty and team composition in terms of cognitive ability and goal orientation. *Journal of Applied Psychology, 90*, 1153–1167.
80. Make employee appraisals more productive. (2007, September). *HR Focus, 84*(9), 1, 11–15; Ryan, L. (2007, January 1). Coping with performance-review anxiety. *Business Week Online*, p. 6; Stone, D. L. (1984). The effects of feedback sequence and expertise of the rater on perceived feedback accuracy. *Personnel Psychology, 37*, 487–506; Sulkowicz, K. (2007, September 10). Straight talk at review time. *Business Week*, 16.
81. Adapted from ideas in Jackman, J. M., & Strober, M. H. (2003, April). Fear of feedback. *Harvard Business Review, 81*(4), 101–107; Wing, L., Xu, H., & Snape, E. (2007). Feedback-seeking behavior and leader-member exchange: Do supervisor-attributed motives matter? *Academy of Management Journal, 50*, 348–363; Lee, H. E., Park, H. S., Lee, T. S., & Lee, D. W. (2007). Relationships between LMX and subordinates' feedback-seeking behaviors. *Social Behavior & Personality: An International Journal, 35*, 659–674.
82. Case written by Berrin Erdogan and Talya Bauer to accompany Bauer, T. N. & Erdogan, B. (2021). *Organizational Behavior: Bridging Science and Practice (4.0)*. Boston, MA: FlatWorld. Partially based on ideas and information contained in Anonymous (August 15, 2018). Gap expands entry-level program to help make staff more diverse. *Los Angeles Times*. https://www.latimes.com/business/la-fi-gap-diversity-20180815-story.html; Fluker, D. (November 30, 2019). Meet the woman changing the diversity and inclusion status quo at Gap inc. https://www.forbes.com/sites/dominiquefluker/2019/11/30/bahja-johnson/#74d56b3178f5; *Glossy Editors* (December 4, 2019). Glossy 50: Fashion's front-runners. https://www.glossy.co/glossy-50/fashion-frontrunners; Mascarenhas, N. (April 11, 2019). Thoughts on (another) diversity panel. https://news.crunchbase.com/news/thoughts-on-another-diversity-panel/; Richards, K. (October 29, 2019). How Gap Inc.'s company-wide diversity and inclusion council is driving sales. https://www.glossy.co/fashion/how-gap-inc-s-company-wide-diversity-and-inclusion-council-is-driving-sales; Riley, J. (November 22, 2019). "Open to all" campaign partners with Yelp to release its first holiday gift guide. https://www.metroweekly.com/2019/11/open-to-all-campaign-partners-yelp-release-first-holiday-gift-guide/ ; Rivas, M. (October 31, 2019). What it's like to be a diversity officer at a major fashion brand. https://www.refinery29.com/en-us/maria-febre-gap-diversity-officer-interview; *Forbes*. (2020, May 12). Retrieved from https://www.forbes.com/companies/gap/#322e7fe33569; *Newsweek*. (2020). America's most responsible companies 2020. Retrieved from https://www.newsweek.com/americas-most-responsible-companies-2020; Refinitive. (2019, September 16). Refinitive announces the 2019 D&I index top 100 most diverse & inclusive organizations globally [Press release]. Retrieved from https://www.refinitiv.com/en/media-center/press-releases/2019/september/refinitiv-announces-the-2019-d-and-i-index-top-100-most-diverse-and-inclusive-organizations-globally.

83. Brown, H. (October 29, 2007). Gap admits possible child labor problem. Retrieved from https://abcnews.go.com/WN/story?id=3787304&page=1; Hodal, K. (June 5, 2018). Abuse is daily reality for female garment workers for Gap and H&M, says report. https://www.theguardian.com/global-development/2018/jun/05/female-garment-workers-gap-hm-south-asia.

CHAPTER 14

The Essentials of Control

Effective control procedures allows managers to monitor and regulate actions to align performance with expectations, much like pilots must manage numerous controls to complete a successful flight.

Source: Shutterstock.com

Chapter Learning Objectives

Reading this chapter will help you accomplish the following:

1. Understand what is meant by organizational control.
2. Differentiate among different levels, types, and forms of control.
3. Know the essentials of financial controls.
4. Know the essentials of nonfinancial controls.
5. Know the basics of lean control systems.
6. Craft a Balanced Scorecard for an organization or yourself.

With the planning-organizing-leading-controlling (P-O-L-C) framework, organizational controls should provide two basic functions. First, they should help managers determine if their strategy is achieving the desired results. Second, they should be an early warning system in cases where the organization is getting a little (or a lot) off track.

TABLE 14.1 The P-O-L-C Framework

Planning	Organizing	Leading	Controlling
1. Vision & Mission	1. Organization Design	1. Leadership	1. Systems/Processes
2. Strategizing	2. Culture	2. Decision Making	2. Strategic Human Resources
3. Goals & Objectives	3. Social Networks	3. Communications	

Planning	Organizing	Leading	Controlling
		4. Groups/Teams	
		5. Motivation	

14.1 Organizational Control

Learning Objectives

1. Know what is meant by organizational control.
2. Recognize that controls have costs.
3. Understand the benefits of controls.

What Is Organizational Control?

organizational control

The process by which an organization influences its subunits and members to behave in ways that lead to the attainment of organizational goals and objectives.

The fourth facet of the P-O-L-C framework, **organizational control**, refers to the processes by which an organization influences its subunits and members to behave in ways that lead to the attainment of organizational goals and objectives. When properly designed, such controls should lead to better performance because an organization is able to execute its strategy better.[1] As shown in the P-O-L-C framework figure, we typically think of or talk about control in a sequential sense, where controls (systems and processes) are put in place to make sure organizational functioning is on track. Controls can be as simple as a checklist, such as the ones commonly used by pilots, flight crews, and doctors.[2]

Organizational control typically involves four steps: (1) establish standards, (2) measure performance, (3) compare performance to standards, and then (4) take corrective action as needed. Corrective action can include changes made to performance standards—setting them higher or lower or identifying new or additional standards. Organizational controls are often most noticeable when they seem to be absent, as in the 2008 meltdown of U.S. financial markets, the crisis in the U.S. auto industry, or the lack of stricter measures to control the spread of COVID-19 around the globe.[3] As shown in these examples, effective controls are relevant to a large spectrum of organizations.

The Costs and Benefits of Organizational Controls

Organizational controls provide significant benefits, particularly when they help the firm stay on track with respect to its strategy. External stakeholders, too, such as governments, investors, and public interest groups have an interest in seeing that certain types of controls are in place. However, because controls also come at a cost, there are trade-offs between having and not having organizational controls, and even among the different forms of control.

FIGURE 14.1 Organizational Controls: Costs and Benefits

Key Costs	Key Benefits
Financial costs might include paying an accountant for an audit.	Cost and productivity control ensures that the firm functions effectively and efficiently.
Culture and reputation costs might include a damaged relationship with employees or a tarnished reputation with investors or government.	Quality control contributes to cost control (i.e., fewer defects, less waste), customer satisfaction (i.e., fewer returns), and greater sales (i.e., repeat customers and new customers).
Responsiveness costs refer to downtime between a decision and the actions required to implement it due to compliance with controls.	Opportunity recognition helps managers identify and isolate the source of positive surprises, such as a new growth market.
Poorly implemented controls exist when implementation fails or the implementation of a new control conflicts with other controls.	Managing uncertainty and complexity keeps the organization focused on its strategy and helps managers anticipate and detect negative surprises and respond opportunistically to positive surprises.
	Decentralized decision making allows the organization to be more responsive by moving decision making to those closest to customers and areas of uncertainty.

Source: Shutterstock.com

Costs

Controls can cost the organization in several areas, including (1) financial, (2) damage to culture and reputation, (3) decreased responsiveness, and (4) failed implementation. An example of financial cost is the fact that organizations are often required to perform and report the results of a financial audit. These audits are typically undertaken by external accounting firms that charge substantial fees for their services; the auditor may be a large firm like Deloitte or KPMG, or a smaller independent accounting office. Such audits are a way for banks, investors, and other key stakeholders to understand the firm's financial health. Thus, if an organization needs to borrow money from banks or has investors, it can only obtain these benefits if it incurs the monetary and staffing costs of the financial audit.

Controls can have costs in terms of organization culture and reputation. While organizations benefit from tracking employee behavior, implementing strict monitoring efforts can have undesirable cultural consequences in the form of reduced employee loyalty, greater turnover, or damage to the organization's external reputation.

Evidence of the need for controls is found in Hewlett-Packard's (HP) indictment on charges of spying on its own board of directors. In a letter to HP's board, director Tom Perkins said his accounts were "hacked" and attached a letter from AT&T explaining how the breach occurred. Records of calls made from Perkins' home phone were obtained simply with his home phone number and the last four digits of his Social Security number. His long-distance account records were obtained when someone called AT&T and pretended to be Perkins, according to the letter from AT&T.[4] HP Chairman Patricia Dunn defended this rather extreme form of control as legal, but the amount of damage to the firm's reputation from these charges led the firm to discontinue the practice. It also prompted the resignation of several directors and corporate officers.[5]

Another potential cost of having controls is that they can afford less organizational flexibility and responsiveness. Typically, controls are put in place to prevent problems, but controls can also create problems. For instance, the Federal Emergency Management Agency (FEMA) is responsible for helping people and businesses cope with the consequences of natural disasters, such as hurricanes. After Hurricane Katrina devastated communities along the U.S. Gulf Coast in 2005, FEMA found that it could not provide prompt relief to the hurricane victims because of the many levels of financial controls that it had in place.[6] Concerns with FEMA's ability to respond to natural disasters continued in 2018 when 8,000 Texans remained in temporary housing six months after Hurricane Harvey.[7]

A final area of cost, failed implementation, is needed when controls are poorly understood, so that their launch creates significant unintended, negative consequences. For example, when Hershey Foods put a new computer-based control system in place, there were so many problems with its installation that it was not able to fulfill a large percentage of its Halloween season chocolate sales that year. It did finally get the controls in working order, but the downtime created huge costs for the company in terms of inefficiencies and lost sales.[8] Some added controls may also interfere with others. For instance, a new quality control system may improve product performance but also delay product deliveries to customers.

Benefits

Although organizational controls come at some cost, most controls are valid and valuable management tools. When they are well designed and implemented, they provide at least five possible areas of benefits, including (1) improved cost and productivity control, (2) improved quality control, (3) opportunity recognition, (4) better ability to manage uncertainty and complexity, and (5) better ability to decentralize decision making.

Strong controls help the organization act efficiently and effectively by helping managers control costs and productivity levels. Costs can be controlled using budgets, where managers compare actual expenses to forecasted ones. Similarly, productivity can be controlled by comparing how much each person can produce, in terms of service or products. For instance, the productivity of a fast-food restaurant like McDonald's depends on the speed of its order takers and meal preparers. McDonald's can look across all its restaurants to identify the target speed for taking an order or wrapping a burger, then measure each store's performance on these dimensions.

Quality control is a second benefit of controls. Increasingly, quality can be quantified in terms of response time (i.e., How long did it take to prepare a burger?) or accuracy (i.e., Did the burger actually weigh one-quarter pound?). Similarly, Toyota tracks the quality of its cars according to hundreds of quantified dimensions, including the number of defects per car. Some measures of quality are qualitative, however. For instance, Toyota also tries to gauge how "delighted" each customer is with its vehicles and dealer service. One mark of quality control is the reception of the Malcolm Baldrige Performance Excellence Program award. The Baldrige award is given by the President of the United States to businesses—manufacturing and service, small and large—and to education, healthcare, and nonprofit organizations that apply and are judged to be outstanding in seven areas—leadership; strategic planning; customer and market focus; measurement, analysis, and knowledge management; human resource focus; process management; and results.[9] Controlling—how well the organization measures and analyzes its processes—is a key criterion for winning the award. The Baldrige award is given to organizations in a wide range of categories and industries, from education to ethics to manufacturing.

In efforts to reduce turnover and ensure quality, lifelike robots at the Henn-na Hotel in Japan are being used for jobs ranging from cook to concierge starting in 2018.

Source: Ned Snowman/ Shutterstock.com

The third area in which organizations can benefit from controls is opportunity recognition. For instance, when Nestlé purchased the Carnation Company for its ice cream business, it had also planned to sell off Carnation's pet food line of products. However, through its financial controls, Nestlé found that the pet food business was even more profitable than ice cream, which led to the decision to keep both.

Controls also help organizations manage uncertainty and complexity. This is a fourth area of benefit from well-designed and implemented controls. Perhaps the most easily understood example of this type of benefit is how financial controls help an organization navigate economic downturns. Without budgets and productivity controls in place, the organization might not know it has lost sales or that expenses are out of control until it is too late.

Control Criteria for the Baldrige Performance Excellence Program Award

Source: Eddie Arrossi

Measurement, Analysis, and Improvement of Organizational Performance: How do you measure, analyze, and then improve organizational performance? (45 points)

Describe how your organization measures, analyzes, aligns, reviews, and improves its performance using data and information, at all levels and in all parts of your organization. Describe how you systematically use the results of review to evaluate and improve processes.

Within your response, include answers to the following questions:

- How do you select, collect, align, and integrate data and information for tracking daily operations and for tracking overall organizational performance, including progress relative to strategic objectives and action plans? What are your key organizational performance measures, including key short-term and longer-term financial measures? How do you use these data and information to support organizational decision making and innovation?

- How do you select and ensure the effective use of key comparative data and information to support operational and strategic decision making and innovation?
- How do you keep your performance measurement system current with business needs and directions? How do you ensure that your performance measurement system is sensitive to rapid or unexpected organizational or external changes?

Performance Analysis, Review, and Improvement

- How do you review organizational performance and capabilities? What analyses do you perform to support these reviews and to ensure that the conclusions are valid? How do you use these reviews to assess organizational success, competitive performance, and progress relative to strategic objectives and action plans? How do you use these reviews to assess your organization's ability to respond rapidly to changing organizational needs and challenges in your operating environment?
- How do you translate organizational performance review findings into priorities for continuous and breakthrough improvement and into opportunities for innovation? How are these priorities and opportunities deployed to work group and functional-level operations throughout your organization to enable effective support for their decision making? When appropriate, how are the priorities and opportunities deployed to your suppliers, partners, and collaborators to ensure organizational alignment?
- How do you incorporate the results of organizational performance reviews into the systematic evaluation and improvement of key processes?

Source: National Institute of Standards and Technology. U.S. Dept. of Commerce. Image source:
https://www.nist.gov/image/baldrige-award-crystal-stage-ceremony-4-12-151jpg.

The fifth area of benefit in organizational control is related to decentralized decision making. Organization researchers have long argued that performance is best when those individuals and areas of the organization that are closest to customers and pockets of uncertainty also have the ability (i.e., the information and authority) to respond to them.[10] It would be difficult to give a McDonald's store manager information about a store's performance and possible choices if information about performance were only compiled at the city, regional, or corporate level. With store-level performance tracking (or, even better, hourly tracking of performance within a store), McDonald's gives store managers the information they need to respond to changes in local demand. Similarly, it equips McDonald's to give those managers the authority to make local decisions, track that decision-making performance, and feed it back into the control and reward systems.

Key Takeaway

This chapter introduced the basics of controls, the process by which an organization influences its subunits and members to behave in ways that lead to attaining organizational goals and objectives. When properly designed, controls lead to better performance by enabling the organization to better execute its strategy. Managers must weigh the costs and benefits of control, but some minimum level of control is essential for organizational survival and success.

Discussion Questions

1. What do properly conceived and implemented controls allow an organization to do?
2. What are four common steps in organizational control?

3. What are some of the costs of organizational controls?
4. What are some of the benefits of organizational controls?
5. How do managers determine when benefits outweigh costs?

14.2 Types and Levels of Control

Learning Objectives

1. Know the difference between strategic and operational controls.
2. Understand the different types of controls.
3. Be able to differentiate between financial and nonfinancial controls.

Strategic controls and management controls (sometimes called operating controls) are two key types of organizational controls. In this section we describe the nature and purpose of each type.

Two Levels of Control: Strategic and Operational

The analogy of a captain piloting a ship can be helpful in understanding the two key types of organizational controls. Strategic controls make sure that the ship is going in the right direction, while management and operating controls make sure the ship is in good condition before, during, and after the voyage. In the context of piloting organizations, **strategic control** is concerned with tracking the strategy as it is being implemented, detecting any problem areas or potential problem areas suggesting that the strategy is incorrect, and making any necessary adjustments.[11] Strategic controls allow managers to step back and look at the big picture and make sure all the pieces of the picture are correctly aligned.

strategic control

The process by which an organization tracks the strategy as it is being implemented, detecting any problem areas or potential problem areas that might suggest that the strategy is incorrect, and making any necessary adjustments.

Ordinarily, a significant time span occurs between initial implementation of a strategy and achievement of its intended results. For instance, a ship going from San Diego to Seattle would need a crew, supplies, fuel, and so on. The voyage might be delayed until the weather permits the captain to make the trip safely. Similarly, in larger organizations, numerous projects are undertaken, investments are made, and actions are taken to implement the new strategy at the same time. Meanwhile, the economy could be booming or perhaps falling into recession. Strategic controls are necessary to steer the firm through these events. They must provide some means of correcting direction on the basis of intermediate performance and new information.

Operational control, in contrast to strategic control, is concerned with executing the strategy. Where operational controls are imposed, they function within the framework established by the strategy. Normally these goals, objectives, and standards are established for major subsystems within the organization, such as business units, projects, products, functions, and responsibility centers.[12] Typical operational control measures include return on investment, net profit, cost, and product quality. These control measures are essentially summations of finer-grained control measures. Corrective action based on operating controls may have implications for strategic controls when they involve changes in the strategy.

operational control

A process concerned with executing the strategy.

Types of Control

Within the strategic and operational levels of control, there are several types of control. The first two types can be mapped across two dimensions: level of proactivity and outcome versus behavioral. Table 14.2 summarizes these along with examples of what such controls might look like.

Proactivity

feedforward control

The active monitoring of problems in a way that provides their timely prevention, rather than after-the-fact reaction.

Proactivity can be defined as the monitoring of problems in a way that provides their timely prevention, rather than after-the-fact reaction. In management, this is known as **feedforward control**; it addresses what can be done ahead of time to help a plan succeed. The essence of feedforward control is to see the problems coming in advance. For instance, feedforward controls include preventive maintenance on machinery and equipment and due diligence on investments.

TABLE 14.2 Types and Examples of Control

Control Proactivity	Behavioral Control	Outcome Control
Feedforward control	Organizational culture	Market demand or economic forecasts
Concurrent control	Hands-on management supervision during a project	The real-time speed of a production line
Feedback control	Qualitative measures of satisfaction	Financial measures such as profitability, sales growth

Concurrent Controls

concurrent controls

Processes that entail monitoring and adjusting ongoing activities.

The process of monitoring and adjusting ongoing activities and processes is known as **concurrent control**. Such controls are not necessarily proactive, but they can prevent problems from becoming worse. For this reason, concurrent controls are thought of as real-time controls because they deal with the present.

A fuel gauge is an example of a feedback control letting the driver know when it's time to refuel. Also helpful is the reminder arrow showing where the gas tank exists on the vehicle (in this case on the driver side).

Source: Shutterstock.com

Feedback Controls

Feedback controls involve gathering information about a completed activity, evaluating that information, and taking steps to improve similar activities in the future. This is the least proactive of controls and is generally a basis for reactions. Feedback controls permit managers to use information about past performance to bring future performance in line with planned objectives.

feedback controls

Processes that involve the gathering of information about a completed activity, evaluating that information, and taking steps to improve similar activities in the future.

Control as a Feedback Loop

Collectively, different types of control function as a feedback mechanism to help leaders and managers make adjustments in the strategy, as perhaps is reflected by changes in the planning, organizing, and leading components. This feedback loop is characterized in Figure 14.2.

FIGURE 14.2 Controls as Part of a Feedback Loop

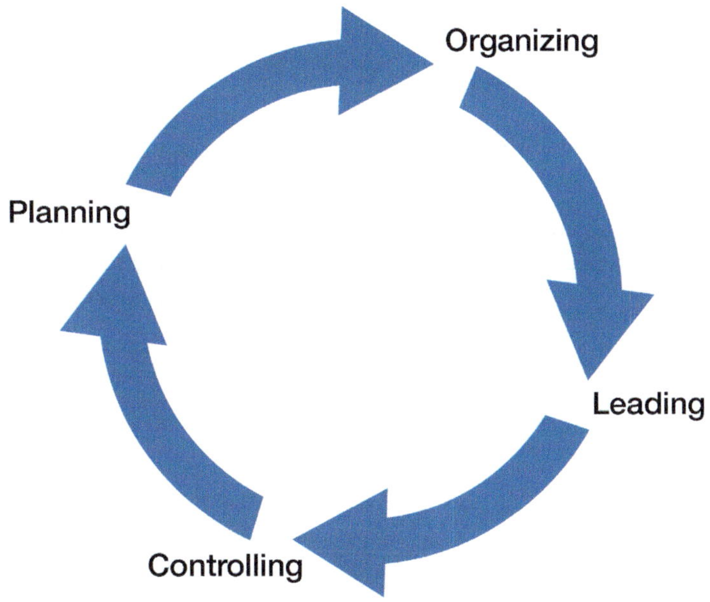

Why might it be helpful for managers to think of controls as part of a feedback loop in the P-O-L-C process? An entrepreneur writing a business plan for a completely new business would likely start with the planning component and work his or her way to the controlling component by spelling out how he or she is going to assess whether the new venture is on track. Most individuals work within an organization that is already operating, and this means that a plan is already in place. With the plan in place, managers continually face the challenge of understanding the organizing, leading, or controlling challenges facing the organization.

Music Rap-Up: Out Of Control

Twinprov perform a rap explaining different organizational controls.

View in the online reader

Outcome and Behavioral Controls

Outcome controls are generally preferable when performance can be measured through tangible performance metrics.

Behavioral controls involve the direct evaluation of managerial and employee actions, not of the results of managerial decisions. Behavioral controls are typically more appropriate when the actions of individuals can be clearly tied to the organization's performance.

The behavioral control to wear a mask to curtail the spread of COVID-19 became widely communicated but not always followed in 2020 and 2021.

Source: Shutterstock.com

outcome controls

Processes that are generally preferable when just one or two performance measures (say, return on investment or return on assets) are good gauges of a business's health.

behavioral controls

The direct evaluation of managerial and employee decision making, not of the results of managerial decisions.

FIGURE 14.3 Output Controls

Outcome controls assess measurable production and other tangible results. Often output controls emphasize "bottom-line" performance. We illustrate some outcome controls found in organizations here.

Because real estate agents are paid a percentage of the selling price when a house sells, the number of dollars generated in houses sold is an important metric. Many realty offices have designations like "five million dollar club" to recognize very productive realtors.

Within restaurants, servers can increase a key output—amount of tips received—by providing customers with fast, friendly, and high-quality service.

Grade point averages provide a tangible means to compare students for employers and graduate schools

In the movie *Elf*, the main character Buddy leaves Santa's workshop when the number of Etch-A-Sketch toys he provides is nearly nine hundred units lower than the standard pace.

To earn tenure in research-focused business schools, a professor's output generally must include publishing numerous high-quality articles in reputable scholarly journals.

Source: Shutterstock.com

FIGURE 14.4 Behavioral Controls

Behavioral controls dictate the actions of individuals. Such controls often emphasize rules and procedures. We illustrate some behavioral controls found in organizations here.

No shoes, no shirt, no paycheck. Many food service companies have strict attire requirements to make sure employees are in compliance with the rules of the Food and Drug Administration and those of local health departments.

Casual Fridays provide a welcome break in offices that enforce strict dress codes.

Many businesses require that checks are signed by two people. This prevents a dishonest employee from embezzling money.

Grading attendance is a behavioral control designed to force students to show up for class. This can be very helpful because research shows that attendance is positively related to grades. Unfortunately, however, there are no behavioral controls that force professors' lectures to be interesting.

Gotta go? Be careful not to take too much time at certain auto factories, where bathroom breaks are monitored in an effort to cut costs. Some employees of U.S. firms are limited to forty six minutes of bathroom time per shift, while Japanese automakers allow their American employees only 30 minutes per shift.

Source: Shutterstock.com

Financial and Nonfinancial Controls

Financial control involves the management of a firm's costs and expenses to control them in relation to budgeted amounts. Thus, management determines which aspects of its financial condition, such as assets, sales, or profitability, are most important, tries to forecast them through budgets, and then compares actual performance to budgeted performance. At a strategic level, total sales and indicators of profitability would be relevant strategic controls.

financial control

The management of a firm's costs and expenses to control them in relation to budgeted amounts.

One key mechanism managers rely on to control performance is the use of performance referents that serve as comparison points to understanding if performance is on target.[13] The use of multiple referents is advised, as different measures will provide different insights into the organization's functioning. In a similar manner, multiple performance measures should be utilized when individuals assess their own personal finances.

TABLE 14.3 How Organizations and Individuals Can Use Financial Performance Measures and Referents

Types of Measures	Applications for Organizations		Application for Individuals	
	Key Measure	Key Referent	Key Measure	Key Referent
Liquidity measures: Helpful for understanding if obligations can be paid when due.	Current ratio (Current assets/ Current liabilities)	A ratio of less than 1.0 suggests the firm does not have enough cash to pay its bills.	Cash in your checking account.	Do you have enough cash to cover your monthly debts?
Leverage measures: Helpful for understanding if debt level is too high. The term *leverage* refers to the extent to which borrowed money is used.	Debt-to-equity ratio	Competitors' debt-to-equity ratio. The use of debt varies across industries. Auto companies, for example, tend to have high debt-to-equity because they must build massive factories.	Debt-to-income ratio (Monthly debt payments/ Monthly income)	If you have a debt-to-income ratio higher than 40%, you may be on the verge of becoming a credit risk.
Profitability measures: Helpful for understanding how much profit, if any, is really being made.	Net income (Income after taxes)	Last year's net income. An increase shows the firm's profits are moving in the right direction	Net income (Income after taxes)	Are you making enough money to cover your yearly expenses and save for retirement?

Increasing numbers of organizations have been measuring customer loyalty, referrals, employee satisfaction, and other such performance areas that are not financial. In contrast to financial controls, **nonfinancial controls** track aspects of the organization that are not immediately financial in nature but are expected to lead to positive performance outcomes. The idea behind such nonfinancial controls is that they should provide managers with a glimpse of the organization's progress well before financial outcomes can be measured.[14] For example, GE has found that highly satisfied customers are the best predictor of future sales in many of its businesses, so it regularly tracks customer satisfaction.

nonfinancial controls

Processes that track aspects of the organization that aren't immediately financial in nature but are expected to lead to positive financial performance outcomes.

Key Takeaway

Organizational controls can take many forms. Strategic controls help managers know whether a chosen strategy is working, while operating controls contribute to successful execution of the current strategy. Within these types of strategies, controls can vary in terms of proactivity, where feedback controls were the least proactive. Outcome controls are judged by the result of the organization's activities, while behavioral controls involve monitoring how the organization's members behave on a daily basis. Financial controls are executed by monitoring costs and expenditures in relation to the organization's budget, and nonfinancial controls complement financial controls by monitoring intangibles like customer satisfaction and employee morale.

Discussion Questions

1. What is the difference between strategic and operating controls? What level of management would be most concerned with operating controls?
2. If feedforward controls are the most proactive, then why do organizations need or use feedback controls?
3. What is the difference between behavioral and outcome controls?
4. What is the difference between nonfinancial and financial controls? Is a financial control a behavioral or an outcome control?

14.3 Financial Controls

Learning Objectives

1. Understand the nature of financial controls.
2. Learn how a balance sheet works.
3. Know how an income profit and loss statement works.
4. See the sources of cash flow.

Financial controls are a key element of organizational success and survival. There are three basic financial reports that all managers should be able to understand to interpret and manage their businesses successfully: (1) the balance sheet, (2) the income/profit and loss (P&L) statement, and (3) the cash flow statement. These three reports are often referred to collectively as "the financials." Banks often require a projection of these statements in order to obtain financing.

budgeting

A listing of all planned expenses and revenues.

Financial controls provide the basis for sound management and allow managers to establish guidelines and policies that enable the business to succeed and grow. **Budgeting**, for instance, generally refers to a listing of all planned expenses and revenues. An overall budget often includes a monthly or quarterly projection of what the balance sheet and income statement will look like based on planned expenses and revenues.

The Nature of Financial Controls

Financial statements provide one of the most valuable tools to help manage financial controls. Each year, after the organization has outlined strategies to reach its goals and objectives, funds are budgeted for the necessary resources and labor. As money is spent, statements are updated to reflect how much was spent and how it was spent. Managers use these financial statements, such as an income statement or balance sheet, to monitor the progress of programs and plans. Financial statements provide management with information to monitor financial resources and activities. The income statement shows the results of the organization's operations, such as revenues, expenses, and profit or loss. The balance sheet shows what the organization is worth (assets) at a single point in time, and the extent to which those assets were financed through debt (liabilities) or owner's investment (equity).

Organizations often conduct financial audits, or formal investigations, to ensure that financial management practices follow generally accepted procedures, policies, laws, and ethical guidelines. Audits are conducted both internally by members of the company's accounting department and by outside accounting firms hired to conduct an external audit.

Personal apps such as YNAB (You Need A Budget) help apply ideas of financial controls to personal spending.

Source: Postmodern Studio/Shutterstock.com

Financial ratio analysis examines the relationship between specific figures on the financial statements to help explain the significance of those figures. By analyzing financial reports, managers are able to determine how well the business is doing and identify actions that may improve the firm's financial viability.

While actual financial performance is historical in nature, proactive managers plan ahead for the problems the business is likely to encounter and for opportunities that may arise. To do this, they use pro forma financials, which are projections; usually these are projected for three fiscal years. Being proactive requires reading and analyzing the financial statements on a regular basis. Monthly, and sometimes daily or weekly, financial analysis is common in many industries. The proactive manager has financial data available based on actual results and compares them to the budget. This process points out weaknesses in the business before they reach crisis proportions and allows the manager to make the necessary changes and adjustments before major problems develop.

A reactive manager waits to react to problems and then solves them by crisis management. This type of manager goes from crisis to crisis with little time in between to notice opportunities that may become available. The reactive manager's business is seldom prepared to take advantage of new opportunities quickly. Businesses that are managed proactively are more likely to be successful, and this result can be aided by the use of company-wide initiatives to promote proactive controls.

The Balance Sheet

The balance sheet is a snapshot of the business's financial position at a certain point in time. This can be any day of the year, but balance sheets are usually completed at the end of each month.

As shown in Table 14.4, this balance sheet is a listing of total assets (what the business owns—items of value) and total liabilities (what the business owes). The total assets are broken down into subcategories of current assets, fixed assets, and other assets. The total liabilities are broken down into subcategories of current liabilities, long-term liabilities/debt, and owner's equity.

Assets

current assets

Assets that are cash or can be readily converted to cash in the short term, such as accounts receivable or inventory.

Current assets are those assets that are cash or can be readily converted to cash in the short term, such as accounts receivable or inventory. In the balance sheet shown in Table 14.4, the current assets are cash, petty cash, accounts receivable, inventory, and supplies.

TABLE 14.4 Sample Balance Sheet

December 31, 202X			
Assets		**Liabilities**	
Current Assets		Current Liabilities	
Cash	$ 12,300	Notes Payable	$ 5,000
Petty Cash	100	Accounts Payable	35,900
		Wages Payable	14,600
Accounts Receivable	40,500	Interest Payable	2,900
Inventory	31,000	Warranty Liability	1,100
Supplies	5,300		
Total Current Assets	$ 89,200	**Total Current Liabilities**	$ 59,500
Investments	36,000	Long-Term Liabilities	
	–	Notes Payable	20,000
Property, Plant, and Equipment		Bonds Payable	400,000
Land	5,500	Total Long-Term Liabilities	420,000
Land Improvements	6,5005		
Buildings	180,000		
Equipment	201,000	**Total Liabilities**	$ 479,500
Less: Accumulated Depreciation	(56,000)		
Property, Plant, and Equipment Net	337,000		
Intangible Assets		Stockholders' Equity	
Goodwill	105,000	Common Stocks	110,000
Trade Names	200,000	Retained Earnings	229,000
Total Intangible Assets	305,000	Less: Treasury Stock	(50,000)
Other Assets	1,300		
Total Assets	$ 768,500	**Total Liability and Stockholders' Equity**	$ 768,500

Some individuals define current assets as those the business expects to use or consume within the coming fiscal year. Thus, a business's noncurrent assets would be those that have a useful life of more than one year. These include fixed assets and intangible assets.

fixed assets

Assets that are not easily converted to cash in the short term; that is, they are assets that only change over the long term. Land, buildings, equipment, vehicles, furniture, and fixtures are some examples of fixed assets.

Fixed assets are those assets that are not easily converted to cash in the short term; that is, they are assets that only change over the long term. Land, buildings, equipment, vehicles, furniture, and fixtures are some examples of fixed assets. In the Table 14.4 illustrative balance sheet, the fixed assets shown are furniture, fixtures and equipment. These fixed assets are shown less accumulated depreciation.

Intangible assets (net) may also be shown on a balance sheet. These may be goodwill, trademarks, patents, licenses, copyrights, formulas, and franchises. In this instance, net means the value of intangible assets minus amortization.

intangible assets

Assets that cannot be physically touched, or is not physical in nature.

Liabilities

Current liabilities are expenses due in the short term, usually the coming year. These are accounts payable; employment, income and sales taxes; salaries payable; federal and state unemployment insurance; and the current year's portion of multiyear debt. A comparison of the company's current assets and its current liabilities reveals its working capital. Many managers use an accounts receivable aging report and a current inventory listing as tools to help them in management of the current asset structure.

current liabilities

Liabilities coming due in the short term, usually the coming year.

Long-term debt, or liabilities, may be bank notes or loans made to purchase the business's fixed asset structure. Long-term debt/liabilities come due in a period of more than 1 year. The portion of a banknote that is not payable in the coming year is long-term debt/liability.

long-term debt

Liabilities may be bank notes or loans made to purchase the business's fixed asset structure. Long-term debt/liabilities come due in a time period of more than 1 year.

For example, a business owner may take out a bank note to buy land and a building. If the land is valued at $50,000 and the building is valued at $50,000, the business's total fixed assets are $100,000. If $20,000 is made as a down payment and $80,000 is financed with a bank note for 15 years, the $80,000 is the long-term debt.

Owner's Equity

Owner's equity refers to the amount of money the owner has invested in the firm. This amount is determined by subtracting current liabilities and long-term debt from total assets. The remaining capital/owner's equity is what the owner would have left in the event of liquidation, or the dollar amount of the total assets that the owner can claim after all creditors are paid.

The Income Profit and Loss Statement (P&L)

The profit and loss statement (P&L) shows the relation of income and expenses for a specific time interval. The income/P&L statement is expressed in a one-month format, January 1 through January 31, or a quarterly year-to-date format, January 1 through March 31. This financial statement is cumulative for a 12-month fiscal period, at which time it is closed out and a new cumulative record is started at the beginning of the new 12-month fiscal period.

The P&L statement is divided into five major categories: (1) sales or revenue, (2) cost of goods sold/cost of sales, (3) gross profit, (4) operating expenses, and (5) net income. We briefly discuss each category below.

Sales or Revenue

The sales or revenue portion of the income statement is where the retail price of the product is expressed in terms of dollars times the number of units sold. This can be product units or service units. Sales can be expressed in one category as total sales or can be broken out into more than one type of sales category—car sales, part sales, and service sales, for instance. In our example, if the company sold 20,000 books at a retail price of $25 each, the total revenues would equal $500,000. If a firm sells all of its books on credit (i.e., charged on a credit card), the company does not collect cash for these sales until the end of the month, or whenever the credit card company settles up with the firm.

Cost of Goods Sold/Cost of Sales

The cost of goods sold/sales portion of the income statement shows the cost of products purchased for resale, or the direct labor cost (service person wages) for service businesses. Cost of goods sold/sales also may include additional categories, such as freight charges cost or subcontract labor costs. These costs also may be expressed in one category as total cost of goods sold/sales or can be broken out to match the sales categories—car purchases, parts, purchases, and service salaries, for example.

TABLE 14.5 Sample Income Statement

For Year Ended December, 21, 202X	
Sales/Revenue (All on Credit):	$ 500,000
Cost of Goods Sold	380,00
Gross Profit	120,000
Operating Expenses	
Selling Expenses	35,000
Administrative Expenses	45,000
Total Operating Expenses	(80,000)
Operating Income	400,000
Interest Expense	(12,000)
Income Before Taxes	28,000
Income Tax Expense	(5,000)
Net Income	$ 23,000

Breaking out sales and cost of goods sold/sales into separate categories can have an advantage over combining all sales and costs into one category. Breaking out sales allows managers to see how much each product sold costs and the gross profit for each product. This type of analysis enables managers to make inventory and sales decisions about each product individually.

Gross Profit

The gross profit portion of the income/P&L statement notes the difference between the selling price of the product or service and what the product or service costs. The goal of any business is to sell enough units of product or service to be able to subtract the cost and have a high enough gross profit to cover operating expenses, plus yield a net income that is a reasonable return on investment. The key to operating a profitable business is to maximize gross profit.

If managers increase the retail price of a product too much above the competition, they might lose units of sales to the competition and not yield a high enough gross profit to cover expenses. However, if they decrease the retail price of the product too much below the competition, they might gain additional units of sales but not make enough gross profit per unit sold to cover expenses.

A carefully thought out pricing strategy maximizes gross profit to cover expenses and yield a positive net income. At a very basic level, this means that prices are set at a level where marginal and operating costs are covered.

Operating Expenses

The operating expense section of the income/P&L statement is a measurement of all the operating expenses of the business. There are two types of expenses, fixed and variable. Fixed expenses are those expenses that do not vary with the level of sales; thus, firms will have to cover these expenses even if sales are less than expenses. Managers have little control over these expenses once they are set. Some examples of fixed expenses are rent (contractual agreement), interest expense (note agreement), an accounting or law firm retainer for legal services of X amount per month for 12 months, and monthly charges for electricity, phone, and internet connections.

Variable expenses are those expenses that vary with the level of sales. Examples of variable expenses include bonuses, employee wages (hours per week worked), travel and entertainment expenses, and purchases of supplies. Expense control is an area where the managers can maximize net income by holding expenses to a minimum.

Net Income

The net income portion of the income/P&L statement is the bottom line. This is the measure of a firm's ability to operate at a profit. Many factors affect the outcome of the bottom line. Level of sales, pricing strategy, inventory control, accounts receivable control, ordering procedures, marketing of the business and product, expense control, customer service, and productivity of employees are just a few of these factors. The net income should be enough to allow growth in the business through reinvestment of profits and to give the owner a reasonable return on investment.

The Cash Flow Statement

The cash flow statement is the detail of cash received and cash expended for each month of the year. A projected cash flow statement helps managers determine whether the company has positive cash flow. Cash flow is probably the most immediate indicator of an impending problem, since negative cash flow will bankrupt the company if it continues for a long enough period. If the company's projections show a negative cash flow, managers might need to revisit the business plan and solve this problem.

An old joke claims, "How can I be broke if I still have checks in my checkbook (or if I still have a debit/credit card, etc.)?" While perhaps poor humor, many new managers similarly think that the only financial statement they need to manage their business effectively is an income/P&L statement; that a cash flow statement is excess detail. They mistakenly believe that the bottom-line profit is all they need to know and that if the company is showing a profit, it is going to be successful. In the long run, profitability and cash flow have a direct relationship, but profit and cash flow do not mean the same thing in the short run. A business can be operating at a loss and have a strong cash flow position. Conversely, a business can be showing an excellent profit but not have enough cash flow to sustain its sales growth.

The process of reconciling cash flow is similar to the process individuals follow in reconciling their personal bank checking accounts. The cash flow statement is composed of (1) beginning cash on hand, (2) cash receipts/deposits for the month, (3) cash paid out for the month, and (4) ending cash position.

Key Takeaway

The financial controls provide a blueprint to compare against the actual results once the business is in operation. A comparison and analysis of the business plan against the actual results can tell managers whether their business is on target. Corrections, or revisions, to policies and strategies may be necessary to achieve the business's goals. The three most important financial controls are (1) the balance sheet, (2) the income statement (sometimes called a profit and loss statement), and (3) the cash flow statement. Each gives the manager a different perspective on, and insight into how well the business is operating toward its goals. Analyzing monthly financial statements is a must since most organizations need to be able to pay their bills to stay in business.

Discussion Questions

1. What are financial controls? In your answer, describe how you would go about building a budget for an organization.
2. What is the difference between an asset and a liability?
3. What is the difference between the balance sheet and an income statement? How are the balance sheet and income statement related?
4. Why is it important to monitor an organization's cash flow?

14.4 Nonfinancial Controls

Learning Objectives

1. Become familiar with nonfinancial controls.
2. Learn about common mistakes associated with nonfinancial controls.
3. Be able to devise possible solutions to common mistakes in nonfinancial controls.

Nonfinancial controls are defined as controls where nonfinancial performance outcomes are measured. It is important to measure such outcomes because they are likely to impact long-term profitability. In this section we outline a few examples of nonfinancial controls.

Customer satisfaction is an increasingly important metric in strong nonfinancial controls.

Source: Shutterstock.com

Common Mistakes with Nonfinancial Controls

In a review of current nonfinancial control practices, Harvard professors Chris Ittner and David Larcker commented, "Tracking things like customer satisfaction and employee turnover can powerfully supplement traditional bookkeeping. Unfortunately, most companies botch the job."[15]

However, research shows that those firms that put these nonfinancial controls in place, and can validate them, earn much higher profits than those that fail to utilize such controls.[16] In this section, we will discuss common mistakes that organizations make in their control procedures.

Failure to Use Nonfinancial Controls

While poorly conceived and implemented nonfinancial controls are certainly a cost for organizations, including them in an organization's system of controls can add considerable value. For example, considering the relationship between customer satisfaction and a retail store's sales, a dissatisfied customer is hard to get back (and may have been dissatisfied enough to leave the store before even making that first purchase).

Not Linking Control to Strategy

This mistake appears to be a common one, but its root cause—failure to adapt the control system to the specific strategy of the organization—is not obvious. Growth in interest in nonfinancial controls has led to widespread adoption of such systems as the Balanced Scorecard. However, because such a system can be complex, managers tend to put them in place without tailoring them to the specific needs and characteristics of their organization.

Several things can go wrong when nonfinancial controls are not linked to the strategy. First, control systems tend to be tied to reward systems, and if managers and employees are being paid based on the achievement of certain nonstrategic, nonfinancial outcomes, then the firm's strategy and, hence, performance, could suffer. Second, if the controls are not linked to the strategy, or the linkages are unclear, then managers do not really understand which nonfinancial controls are the most important.

Failing to Validate the Links

There are two key challenges that organizations face when trying to use nonfinancial controls. First, nonfinancial controls are indirectly related to financial performance; the relationship is like a sequence of nonfinancial outcomes that cascade down to financial performance. For instance, (1) good employee recruiting leads to (2) satisfied employees, which leads to (3) an employee base that creates value, which leads to (4) satisfied customers, which leads to (5) profitable customer buying patterns, which lead to (6) good profitability. While these six nonfinancial outcomes might lead to good financial performance, it might be challenging to identify and manage the inputs to each step.

Once managers take the step of identifying these linkages, the second challenge is to show that the linkages actually exist. While more companies are putting such models in place, few are collecting the information to test and validate the actual relationships in their organization. In fact, Ittner and Larcker found that less than a quarter of the firms that they surveyed actually did any formal validation of the nonfinancial model they had developed. Consequently, a nonfinancial control that lacks validity could actually lead to poorer organizational performance than failing to use nonfinancial controls altogether.

Failing to Set Appropriate Performance Targets

The third common area of weakness in the use of nonfinancial controls is the failure to set appropriate performance targets. A firm might want to set high goals, and therefore control, for such things as customer satisfaction or employee turnover, but the cost of achieving 100% customer satisfaction or zero employee turnover may exceed their benefit financially.

Failing to set appropriate performance targets can take on another form. In such cases, instead of setting inappropriate nonfinancial controls and related targets, the organization simply has set too many.[17] This can happen when a new control system is put in place, but the old one is not removed. Just as often, it can occur because management has not made the hard choices about which nonfinancial controls are most important and invested in validating their usage.

Measurement Failure

In many cases, an inappropriate measure is used to assess whether a targeted nonfinancial control is being achieved. This can happen for a number of reasons. First, different parts of the business may assess customer satisfaction differently. This makes it very hard to consistently evaluate the relationship between customer satisfaction (a nonfinancial control) and financial performance. Second, even when a common basis for evaluation is used, the meaning may not be clear in the context of how it is measured. For example, if a firm created a simple survey of customer satisfaction, where individuals were scored on a range from 1 (dissatisfied) to 7 (satisfied), what does each individual score between 1 and 7 mean? Finally, sometimes the nonfinancial control or objective is complex. Customer or employee satisfaction, for instance, are not necessarily easily captured on a scale of 1 to 7. Imagine trying to introduce controls for leadership ability (i.e., we know if we have strong leaders, they make good choices, which eventually lead to good financial performance) or innovativeness (i.e., cool products lead to more customer enthusiasm, which eventually leads to financial performance). Such intangibles are extremely difficult to measure and to track.

Key Takeaway

Nonfinancial controls, such as those related to employee satisfaction, customer service, and so on, are an important and increasingly applied form of organizational control. While firms that use nonfinancial controls well also perform much better than firms that fail to use them, numerous managerial mistakes are made with regard to their conceptualization, implementation, or both. Beyond simply using nonfinancial controls, best practices around such controls include aligning them with the strategy, validating the links between nonfinancial controls and financial controls, setting appropriate control performance targets, and confirming the right measure of the desired control.

Discussion Questions

1. What are nonfinancial controls? Name some examples.
2. What should be the relationship between nonfinancial and financial controls?
3. What are some common mistakes made by managers with regard to nonfinancial controls?
4. What are some solutions to the common mistakes you identified?

14.5 Lean Control

Learning Objectives

1. Know what is meant by lean controls.
2. Understand the application of lean.
3. Know the five core principles of lean.

Lean control, or simply lean, has become an immensely popular business control and improvement methodology in recent years. Lean control is a highly refined example of nonfinancial controls in action. **Lean** is a system of nonfinancial controls used to improve product and service quality and decrease waste. Research suggests that up to 70% of manufacturing firms are using some form of lean in their business operations.[18] Lean was initially focused on improving manufacturing operations but is now used to improve product development, order processing, and a variety of other nonmanufacturing processes (sometimes called "lean in the office").

lean

A system of nonfinancial controls used to improve product and service quality and decrease waste.

What Is Meant by Lean Control?

Lean's popularity has both resulted from, and been driven by, an explosion in the volume of lean-related educational resources. Colleges and universities, industry trade associations, and private consulting firms routinely offer courses, seminars, and conferences to explain what lean is and how to implement lean control.

Developed by Motorola in 1986, the term Six Sigma refers to a process where, statistically, 99.99966% of products manufactured (or 3.4 defects per million operations) are free from defects.

Source: Shutterstock.com

Lean control, according to one definition, "is a process for measuring and reducing inventory and streamlining production. It is a means for changing the way a company measures plant performance. It is a knowledge-based system. It takes years of hard work, preparation, and support from upper management. Lean is so named because it purports to use much less of certain resources (space, inventory, workers, etc.) than is used by normal mass-production systems to produce comparable output." The term came into widespread use with the 1990 publication of the book *The Machine That Changed the World*, by James P. Womack, Daniel T. Jones, and Daniel Roos.[19]

This abundance of educational resources on the topic of lean is actually a mixed blessing for managers who are just now becoming interested in lean because there is no universal definition of lean and little agreement about what the truly core principles of lean are. For instance, quality programs such as Six Sigma, or even lean Six Sigma, are other titles competing for the "lean" intellectual space. Therefore, lean experts often approach the subject from differing perspectives and describe lean in different ways. Many experts strongly argue that their particular "brand" of lean is the one right way to implement and use lean.

Lean Applications

The Business Model Canvas is an often-used tool to promote lean startups.

Source: Shutterstock.com

Lean is often associated with Toyota Motor Corporation because many tools and techniques associated with the lean concept were developed by Toyota in Japan beginning in the 1950s. After World War II, Toyota's leaders were determined to make the company a full-range car and truck manufacturing enterprise, but they faced several serious challenges. The Japanese motor vehicle market was small and yet demanded a fairly wide range of vehicle types. This meant that Toyota needed to find a way to earn a profit while manufacturing a variety of vehicles in low volumes. In addition, capital was extremely scarce, which made it impossible for Toyota to make large purchases of the latest production equipment. To succeed, or even survive, Toyota needed a way to build vehicles that would require fewer resources. To achieve this goal, Toyota's leaders, principally Eiji Toyoda and Taiichi Ohno, began to create and implement the production techniques and tools that came to be known as lean.[20]

To gain the most benefits from lean, managers must be able to determine what specific lean tools and techniques will be effective in their particular business. And to make that determination, they must clearly understand what lean is designed to accomplish (its primary objectives) and what core principles lean is based on. With this understanding, managers can decide which lean tools will work well in their business, which lean tools will need to be modified or adapted to work well, and which tools are simply not appropriate.

TABLE 14.6 Savings Using Lean Control

Muda is a Japanese term for activity that is wasteful and does not add value. It is also a key concept in lean control. Waste reduction is an effective way to increase profitability. Here are the seven deadly wastes, along with their definitions.
1. **Defects** prevent the customer from accepting the product produced. The effort to create these defects is wasted. New waste management processes must be added in an effort to reclaim some value for the otherwise scrap product.
2. **Overproduction** is the production or acquisition of items before they are actually required. It is the most dangerous waste of the company because it hides the production problems. Overproduction must be stored, managed, and protected.
3. **Transportation** is a cost with no added value. In addition, each time a product is moved it stands the risk of being damaged, lost, and delayed. Transportation does not transform the product in any way that the consumer is willing to pay for.
4. **Waiting** refers to both the time spent by the workers waiting for resources to arrive and the queue for their products to empty, as well as the capital sunk in goods and services that are not yet delivered to the customer. It is often the case that there are processes to manage this waiting.
5. **Inventory** in the form of raw materials, work-in-progress, or finished goods represents a capital outlay that has not yet produced an income either by the producer or for the consumer. Any of these three items not being actively processed to add value is waste.
6. **Motion** refers to the actions performed by the producer, worker, or equipment. Motion has significance to damage, wear, and safety. It also includes the fixed assets and expenses incurred in the production process.
7. **Overprocessing** is defined as using a more expensive or otherwise valuable resource than is needed for the task or adding features that are designed for, but unneeded by the customer. There is a particular problem with this item regarding people. People may need to perform tasks that they are overqualified for to maintain their competency. This training cost can be used to offset the waste associated with overprocessing.

What are the major objectives and core principles of lean? Despite the arguments and debates that often surround attempts to define and describe lean, it is clear that the ultimate objective of lean is the avoidance of wasteful activity (dubbed **muda** in Japanese) in all business operations. As shown in Table 14.6, muda comprises *seven deadly wastes*. In the lean world, waste means any activity or condition that consumes resources but creates no value for customers. Therefore, waste includes the production of defective products that must be remade or fixed, the production of more products than the market will buy, excessive work-in-process inventories, overprocessing (processing steps that are not really needed or that add no value), unnecessary movement of people or products, and unnecessary waiting by employees.

muda

A Japanese term for activity that is wasteful and doesn't add value.

In recent years, the idea of engaging in a "lean start-up" has been used to suggest an idea where entrepreneurs eschew extensive planning and instead work to more quickly create a "minimum viable product" that customers find intriguing based on targeted research efforts.[21] The increased usage of terms such as "pivot" (where entrepreneurs make a fairly dramatic change from their initial strategy) emanate from the popularity of this lean application. This key lean application has led to the popularity of the Business Model Canvas as a tool to help entrepreneurs develop products and then rely on potential customers to help further develop and build on initial ideas.

Does your startup have an MVP? A minimum viable product is a lean application that helps early stage entrepreneurs by providing just enough value added to keep early adopters interested. A popular example is found in the success of Cards Against Humanity that was developed as a Kickstarter crowdfunding campaign.

Source: LunaseeStudios/ Shutterstock.com

The Five Core Principles of Lean

Lean methodologies are lean because they enable a business to do more with less. A lean organization uses less human effort, less equipment, less facilities space, less time, and less capital—while always coming closer to meeting customers' exact needs. Therefore, lean is not just another cost-cutting program of the kind we often see in business organizations. Lean is much more about the conservation of valuable resources than it is about cost cutting.

In their best-selling book, *Lean Thinking*, James Womack and Daniel Jones identified five core principles of lean.[22] In this section, we explain each.

1. Define Value from the Customer's Perspective

The first core principle in the Womack/Jones lean framework is that value must be defined and specified from the customer's perspective. To be meaningful, value must be defined in terms of specific products. This means that managers must understand how each specific product meets the needs of specific customers at a specific price and at a specific time.

2. Describe the Value Stream for Each Product or Service

The second core principle of lean is to describe the value stream for each product or service (or, in some cases, for groups or families of similar products). The value stream is the set of activities that the business is performing to bring a finished product to a customer. It includes both direct manufacturing activities and indirect activities such as order processing, purchasing, and materials management. Developing a detailed description or map of each value stream usually reveals huge amounts of waste. It enables managers to identify which value stream activities add value to the product, which activities add no value but cannot be immediately eliminated for various reasons, and which activities create no value and can be immediately eliminated (or at least reduced substantially).

3. Create Flow in Each Value Stream

The third essential principle of lean is embodied in the word *flow*. When a value stream has been completely described as unnecessary and non-value-adding activities have been eliminated, the basic idea of flow is to arrange the remaining activities sequentially, so that products will move smoothly and continuously from one activity to the next. However, flow means more than ease of movement. Flow is the lean principle that directly challenges the traditional model of manufacturing where people and equipment are organized and located by function, and products (and component parts) are manufactured in large batches. Lean organizations strive to improve flow by reducing the size of production batches, and in the process, they increase flexibility and lower costs.

4. Produce at the Pace (Pull) of Actual Customer Demand

Producing at the pace or pull of actual customer demand is the fourth key principle of lean. One of the greatest benefits of moving from traditional manufacturing to continuous flow production is that lead times fall dramatically. Reduced lead times and increased flexibility mean that lean organizations can respond to actual customer demand rather than attempt to predict in advance what that level of demand will be. This allows lean organizations to substantially lower both finished goods and work-in-process inventories.

5. Strive to Continuously Improve All Business Operations

The fifth core principle of lean is continuous improvement, expressed in Japanese by the word **kaizen**. Companies that implement lean adopt the mindset that it is always possible to improve any business activity, and they regularly conduct kaizen events throughout their organizations to improve specific processes or operations. Today, Toyota is recognized as one of the most "lean" business enterprises in the world.

kaizen

The Japanese term for continuous improvement.

The Lean Canvas

In the field of entrepreneurship, applications of lean can be seen in the use of the business model canvas and lean canvas.[23] Both of these models replace the traditional business plan with a streamlined tool to brainstorm and map out activities surrounding a startup or existing business. The lean canvas (displayed below) asks a series of questions about a new product or service that enable individuals to visualize potential business models without overcomplicating the approach to innovation or brainstorming new ideas. An application of this framework can be found in Airbnb where the identified problem was the challenge of finding affordable alternatives to expensive hotel options and their solution was to create an online answer to this challenge that provided a unique advantage since individual homeowners could use their personal properties at times that created a mutually beneficial match between the customer and accommodation provider.[24]

Lean applications of the Business Model Canvas provide tools for strategists and startups to develop and/or document key questions surrounding business models.

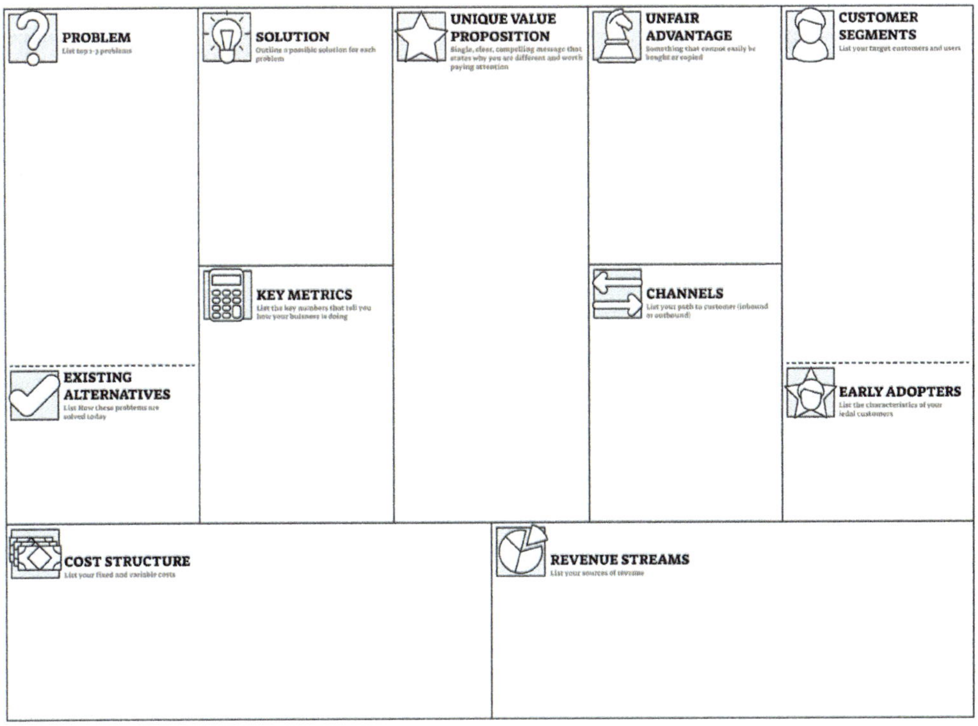

Source: Shutterstock.com

Key Takeaway

Lean control, or simply lean, is the system of nonfinancial controls used to improve product and service quality and decrease waste. While popularized through the dramatic successes of Toyota in auto manufacturing, lean processes are used to improve quality and decrease waste in most service and manufacturing industries around the world. In this section, you saw examples of the seven deadly wastes (*muda*) and the five core principles of lean, which culminate in continuous improvement, or *kaizen*.

Discussion Questions

1. What is lean control?
2. What types of industries might find lean controls valuable?
3. What does *muda* mean and what are some examples of it?
4. What are the five lean principles?
5. Pick a company you are familiar with—what would it need to do differently to comply with the five lean principles?

14.6 Crafting Your Balanced Scorecard

Learning Objectives

1. See how the Balanced Scorecard integrates nonfinancial and financial controls.
2. Be able to outline a personal Balanced Scorecard.

The Balanced Scorecard provides a tool to help balance short-term and long-term measures.

Source: Shutterstock.com

An Introduction to the Balanced Scorecard

The Balanced Scorecard was originally introduced to integrate financial and nonfinancial controls in a way that provided a balanced understanding of the determinants of firm performance. It is also a strategic performance management tool because it helps managers identify and understand the way that operating controls are tied to strategic controls, and ultimately, firm performance. In this broader sense, a **Balanced Scorecard** is a control system that translates an organization's vision, mission, and strategy into specific, quantifiable goals and to monitor the organization's performance in terms of achieving these goals.

Balanced Scorecard

A framework designed to translate an organization's vision and mission statements and overall business strategy into specific, quantifiable goals and objectives and to monitor the organization's performance in terms of achieving these goals.

According to Robert S. Kaplan and David P. Norton, the Balanced Scorecard approach "examines performance in four areas. Financial analysis, the most traditionally used performance indicator, includes assessments of measures such as operating costs and return-on-investment. Customer analysis looks at customer satisfaction and retention. Internal analysis looks at production and innovation, measuring performance in terms of maximizing profit from current products and following indicators for future productivity. Finally, learning and growth analysis explores the effectiveness of management in terms of measures of employee satisfaction and retention and information system performance."[25]

Whereas the scorecard identifies financial and nonfinancial areas of performance, the second step in the scorecard process is the development of a strategy map. The idea is to identify key performance areas in learning and growth and show how these metrics relate to internal, customer, and financial performance areas.

FIGURE 14.5 The Balanced Scorecard Hierarchy

With the scorecard and strategy map, managers can successively break broad goals down into vision, strategies, strategic initiatives, and metrics. As an example, imagine that an organization has a goal of maintaining employee satisfaction in its vision and mission statements. This would be the organization's vision in the domain of learning and growth, since employee satisfaction is indirectly related to financial performance. Strategies for achieving that learning and growth vision might include approaches such as increasing employee-management communication. Initiatives undertaken to implement the strategy could include, for example, regularly-scheduled meetings with employees. Metrics could include quantifications of employee suggestions or employee surveys. Finally, managers would want to test their assumptions about the relationship between employee satisfaction and the downstream areas such as internal, customer, and financial performance. For example, satisfied employees may be more productive and less likely to quit (internal), which leads to better products or services and customer relations (customer), which leads to lower employee recruiting and training costs and greater sales and repeat sales (financial). This sequence of causal relationships is summarized in Figure 14.6.

FIGURE 14.6 The Strategy Map: A Causal Relationship between Nonfinancial and Financial Controls

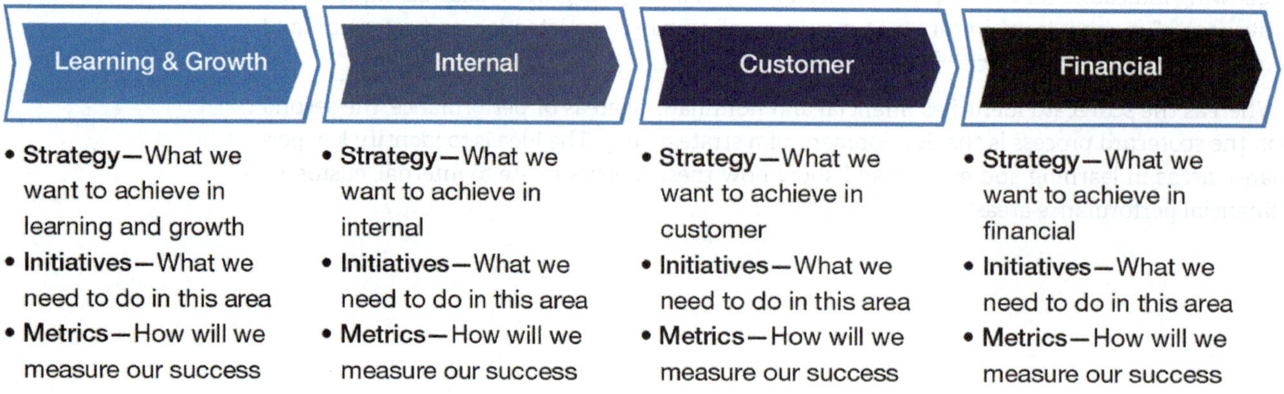

Your Personal Balanced Scorecard

Now that you have an understanding of nonfinancial and financial controls, and specific cases such as lean control systems and the Balanced Scorecard, you can consider the notion of the Balanced Scorecard for personal applications. Recall that the figure shows your position in the context of the Balanced Scorecard—it asks you to state your personal objectives, in the context of the organization's objectives. However, in developing your own Balanced Scorecard, you will be laying out a roadmap to achieve your personal and professional objectives (or mission and vision more broadly), which may overlap a lot or very little with the organization's objectives. While you can choose to focus the scorecard more narrowly on something like your career, you will be much better served by the personal Balanced Scorecard if you pursue a holistic (personal + professional) approach. For example, you may have particular personal goals about financial independence, and this would relate to other choices you might want to make about your personal and professional priorities.

Social psychologist Hubert Rampersad has sought to translate the business Balanced Scorecard into a personal balanced score by providing you with the following four suggestions.[26]

1. **Learning and growth:** your skills and learning ability. How do you learn, and how can you be successful in the future? For example, the course that you are taking in conjunction with this book may lead to a degree, be a prerequisite for other courses, and so on.
2. **Internal:** your physical health and mental state. How can you control these to create value for yourself and others? How can you remain feeling good at work as well as in your spare time? For instance, your objectives and activities related to physical and emotional fitness.
3. **Customer (external):** relations with your spouse, children, friends, employer, colleagues, and others. How do they see you?
4. **Financial:** financial stability. To what degree are you able to fulfill your financial needs? Again, do you seek financial independence, resources to fund other endeavors?

LinkedIn Learning provides a host of courses that can help improve personal learning and growth goals.

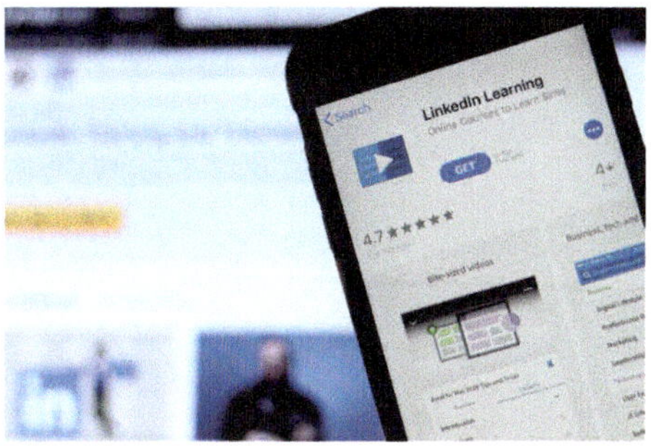

Source: Postmodern Studio/Shutterstock.com

The best way to put these suggestions into action is to work on the scorecard in several sessions, as there are a wide range of factors to consider. Your objective for the first session should be to develop your personal vision statement and list several areas of development in *learning*, *internal*, *customer*, and *financial* facets of the scorecard. You should be able to fit the scorecard on a single page for easy and frequent reference. You can use your next session with the scorecard to refine your developmental objectives and set relevant measures and near-term objectives. Post the scorecard where you can refer to it often. And, just as with organizations, if your circumstances change, then that is the critical time to revalidate or revise your personal Balanced Scorecard.

Key Takeaway

The essential components of the Balanced Scorecard can be integrated into an organization's vision, mission, and strategy and with its nonfinancial and financial controls. The components of the Balanced Scorecard need to be clearly tied to strategy and relationships among nonfinancial and financial controls. Appropriate control performance targets need to be set, and the appropriate indicators of performance used to gauge nonfinancial and financial performance. This section concluded by outlining the steps individuals might follow in building a personal Balanced Scorecard.

Discussion Questions

1. What is a Balanced Scorecard? What is the difference between a Balanced Scorecard and a simple list of nonfinancial and financial controls?
2. What roles do vision, mission, and strategy play in the development of a Balanced Scorecard?
3. What might be some of the differences between an organization's Balanced Scorecard and your personal Balanced Scorecard? What might be some of the similarities?
4. Under what circumstances should an organization's or an individual's Balanced Scorecard be revised?

14.7 Case in Point: SpaceX Mitigating Stress at Work

Source: L Galbraith/Shutterstock.com

SpaceX was founded in 2002 with the goal of reducing space transportation costs and creating the technology needed to colonize Mars. This lofty mission was the brainchild of the company's founder, Elon Musk. Musk is known for being a visionary and controversial leader with ambitious goals for his companies. In addition to his role as CEO of SpaceX, he is in leadership positions at Tesla, an electric vehicle and solar panel manufacturer; SolarCity, a solar energy services company; Neuralink, a neurotechnology company; and The Boring Company, an infrastructure and tunnel construction company.

A 2016 employee survey ranked SpaceX as having the highest stress work environment among top tech companies. Interestingly, SpaceX also ranked highest among the companies surveyed for being the most meaningful place to work. This sense of purpose is inspired by SpaceX's mission to make humans an inter-planetary species, as well as by its frequent rocket launches which serve as small but tangible milestones toward its grander mission. In addition to successfully launching astronauts into space in 2020, SpaceX plans to put astronauts on the moon by 2024. One of SpaceX's board members attributed the organization's success to the strong "meaningfulness" factor felt by its employees. After a little over 50 years of the first person stepping on the moon, SpaceX became the first private company to transport astronauts to Earth from the International Space Station when Bob Behnken and Doug Hurley made a safe water landing on SpaceX's Crew Dragon capsule on August 2, 2020.

Musk is also known for motivating his employees by making them feel like part of a larger team. He encourages senior managers to practice servant leadership, the principle of inspiring others through selflessness and helping them succeed by eliminating barriers they encounter while striving toward their goals. He is reported to expect senior leaders to work harder than those who report to them, and to make sure their teams' needs are met before their own.

Further, Musk is reported to have exceptionally high standards, be excessively demanding of his employees, and exhibit workaholic tendencies himself. In 2018, he tweeted, "There are easier places to work, but nobody ever changed the world on 40 hours a week." This type of leadership has been criticized for potentially leading to a culture of burnout.

Much like many Silicon Valley tech companies, Musk entices SpaceX employees to spend more time at work and to remain committed to the mission by providing perks such as free food and an in-house massage therapist. He also invites celebrities to give private talks, provides employee-only movie screenings, and sends employees encouraging emails and addresses them at regular all-hands gatherings. These gatherings are especially poignant when they are tied to a launch, which enables employees to celebrate the fruits of their labor.[27]

Multimedia Extension—SpaceX CEO Elon Musk on the Next Giant Leap for Mankind

View in the online reader

Case Discussion Questions

1. Would you be motivated by a company culture such as the one at SpaceX? Why or why not?
2. Do you think Musk's leadership style would work well at a company with a different type of mission?
3. What do you think are some characteristics of people who aspire to work at a place like SpaceX? Do you think this has anything to do with its stress and meaningfulness rankings?
4. Do you think SpaceX's mission or its perks are more meaningful in encouraging employees to stick around, despite the high-stress environment?
5. If leadership at SpaceX began to encourage more work-life balance for its employees, how do you think that would impact the overall performance of the organization? Please explain.

Endnotes

1. Kuratko, D. F., Ireland, R. D., & Hornsby. J. S. (2001). Improving firm performance through entrepreneurial actions: Acordia's corporate entrepreneurship strategy. *Academy of Management Executive, 15*(4), 60–71.
2. Retrieved from http://www.thehealthcareblog.com/the_health_care_blog/2007/12/pilots-use-chec.html.
3. Retrieved from https://www.reuters.com/article/us-health-coronavirus-latam/families-of-coronavirus-victims-lament-lack-of-control-in-mexico-idUSKCN25303Y.
4. Retrieved from http://i.n.com.com/pdf/ne/2006/perkins_letter.pdf.
5. Retrieved from http://news.zdnet.com/2100-9595_22-149452.html.
6. U.S. Government Printing Office. (2006, February 15). Executive summary. Select Bipartisan Committee to Investigate the Preparation for and Response to Hurricane Katrina.
7. Retrieved from https://www.texastribune.org/2018/02/27/texans-left-limbo-gov-abbott-fema-use-harvey-reinvent-disaster-respons/.
8. Hershey profits for 4Q 1999 down 11% due to SAP implementation problem, retrieved from http://www.greenspun.com/bboard/q-and-a-fetch-msg.tcl?msg_id=002SUM.
9. Retrieved from http://www.nist.gov/public_affairs/factsheet/baldfaqs.htm.
10. Galbraith, J. R. (1974). Organization design: An information processing view. *Interfaces, 4*, 28–36.
11. Venkataraman, S., & Sarasvathy, S. D. (2001). Strategy and entrepreneurship: Outlines of an untold story. In M. A. Hitt, R. E. Freeman, & J. S. Harrison (Eds.), *Handbook of strategic management* (pp. 650–668). Oxford: Blackwell.
12. Matthews, J. (1999). Strategic moves. *Supply Management, 4*(4), 36–37.
13. Short, J.C., & Palmer, T.B. (2003). Organizational performance referents: An empirical examination of their content and influences. *Organizational Behavior and Human Decision Processes, 90:* 209–224.
14. Ittner, C., & Larcker, D. F. (2003, November). Coming up short on nonfinancial performance measurement. *Harvard Business Review*, 2–8.
15. Ittner, C., & Larcker, D. F. (2003, November). Coming up short on nonfinancial performance measurement. *Harvard Business Review*, 2–8.
16. Ittner, C., & Larcker, D. F. (2003, November). Coming up short on nonfinancial performance measurement. *Harvard Business Review*, 2–8.
17. Brown, M. G. (1996). *Keeping score*. New York: Productivity Press.
18. PrintPlanet launches lean manufacturing forum. (2008, August 11). Retrieved from http://members.whattheythink.com/home/wttnews080811.cfm.
19. Womack, J. P., Jones, D. T., & Roos, D. (1990). *The machine that changed the world*. New York: Rawson Associates.
20. Retrieved from http://www.toyota.co.jp/en/history/index.html.
21. Retrieved from https://hbr.org/2013/05/why-the-lean-start-up-changes-everything.
22. Womack, J. P., & Jones, D. T. (2003). *Lean thinking*. New York: Simon & Schuster.
23. Retrieved from https://www.fastcompany.com/3034788/building-a-more-effective-way-for-startups-to-brainstorm.
24. Retrieved from https://railsware.com/blog/5-lean-canvas-examples/.
25. Kaplan, R., & Norton, D. (2001). *The strategy-focused organization*. Boston: Harvard Business School Press.
26. Rampersad, H. K. (2006). *The personal Balanced Scorecard: The way to individual happiness, personal integrity, and organizational effectiveness*. Greenwich, CT: Information Age.
27. Case written by Rachel Mattenberger, Talya Bauer, and Berrin Erdogan to accompany Bauer, T. N. & Erdogan, B. (2021). *Organizational Behavior: Bridging Science and Practice (4.0)*. Boston, MA: FlatWorld. Partially based on ideas and information contained in Dunn, M. (2020). SpaceX capsule and NASA crew make 1st splashdown in 45 years. Retrieved from https://www.stltoday.com/business/national-and-international/spacex-capsule-and-nasa-crew-make-1st-splashdown-in-45-years/article_11da7f37-d78f-5571-8534-aaa3dcbbedf7.html; Lambert, F. (2016). Tesla and SpaceX standout in tech employee survey for the most stressful and lowest paying jobs, but also most meaningful. https://electrek.co/2016/03/07/tesla-and-spacex-standout-in-tech-employee-survey-for-the-most-stressful-and-lowest-paying-jobs-but-also-most-meaningful; Umoh, R. (2017). The tactics self-made billionaire Elon Musk uses to motivate his teams. https://www.cnbc.com/2017/07/05/2-major-ways-executives-like-elon-musk-are-trying-to-stop-you-from-quitting.html; Jackson, A. (2018). Former SpaceX worker reveals 7 outrageous perks Elon Musk gives employees. https://www.businessinsider.com/spacex-worker-company-culture-2017-11; Schulte, B. (2018). Leaders who prize overwork create burnout cultures. https://www.ft.com/content/8c4cadb8-054e-11e9-bf0f-53b8511afd73; Sheetz, M. (2020, June 12). NASA's Kathy Lueders, who oversaw the SpaceX astronaut launch, will lead agency's 2024 moon effort. Retrieved from https://www.cnbc.com/2020/06/12/nasas-kathy-lueders-will-lead-2024-moon-effort-after-spacex-success.html.

CHAPTER 15

Strategic Human Resource Management

Just like chess masters who carefully maneuver their pieces to ensure victory, strategic human resource management involves positioning the organization's human resources to secure competitive advantage.

Source: Shutterstock.com

Chapter Learning Objectives

Reading this chapter will help you accomplish the following:

1. Understand the scope and changing role of strategic human resource management (SHRM) in principles of management.
2. Understand key elements in the war for talent.
3. Engage in effective selection and placement strategies.
4. Understand the roles of pay structure and pay for performance.
5. Understand the components of a high-performance work system.
6. Learn how to use the human resources Balanced Scorecard to gauge and proactively manage human capital.

Management scholars and practicing managers both argue that *the people make the place.* In today's fast-changing environment, organizations need employees who understand the organization's strategy and are empowered to execute it effectively. To achieve this goal, organizations need to follow a strategic human resource management (SHRM) approach. SHRM ensures that people are a key factor in a firm's competitive advantage. As summarized in Table 15.1, SHRM is an integral part of the control portion of the planning-organizing-leading-controlling (P-O-L-C) framework.

TABLE 15.1 The P-O-L-C Framework

Planning	Organizing	Leading	Controlling
1. Vision & Mission	1. Organization Design	1. Leadership	1. Systems/Processes
2. Strategizing	2. Culture	2. Decision Making	2. Strategic Human Resources
3. Goals & Objectives	3. Social Networks	3. Communications	
		4. Groups/Teams	
		5. Motivation	

Organizations need effective human resources (HR) practices to identify, attract, and hire the type of employees who will be most qualified to help the company achieve its goals. SHRM requires attracting the right employees to the company, identifying metrics to help employees stay on target to meet the company's goals, and rewarding individuals appropriately for their efforts so that they stay engaged and motivated. Having all these components in place—designing a high-performance work system—improves organizational performance and unleashes employee talent.

15.1 The Changing Role of Strategic Human Resource Management in Principles of Management

Learning Objectives

1. Understand how HR is becoming a strategic partner.
2. Understand the importance of an organization's human capital.
3. List the key elements of SHRM.
4. Explain the importance of focusing on outcomes.

The role of HR is changing. Previously considered a support function associated with dispersal of benefits and assurance of compliance to legal mandates, HR is now becoming a strategic partner in helping a company achieve its goals. A strategic approach to HR extends beyond historical administrative tasks such as payroll processing. Now, managers need to think more broadly and deeply about how employees will contribute to the company's success.

HR as a Strategic Partner

Strategic human resource management (SHRM) is an organizational-level approach to human resources management with a concern for the effects of such practices on firm performance. Consequently, SHRM is not just a function of the HR department—all managers and executives need to be involved, because the role of human capital (people) is so vital to a company's competitive advantage.[1] One recent research example illustrates the critical implications of considering SHRM; scholars examining over 6,000 commercial banks for over a decade of operations found that firms performed higher by keeping their staff lean if they were in stable environments, but overstaffing proved beneficial in environments where strategic change was found.[2]

strategic human resource management (SHRM)

An organizational level approach to human resources management with a concern for the effects of HRM practices on firm performance.

In addition, organizations that value their employees are more profitable than those that do not.[3] Research shows that successful organizations have several things in common, such as providing employment security, engaging in selective hiring, using self-managed teams, being decentralized, paying well, training employees, reducing status differences, and sharing information.[4] When organizations enable, develop, and motivate human capital, they improve accounting profits as well as shareholder value in the process.[5] The most successful organizations manage HR as a strategic asset and measure HR performance in terms of its strategic impact.

Demonstrating the value of human resources at the top level, former GE CEO Jack Welch personally reviewed the top 500 employees at his company every year.

Source: http://en.wikipedia.org/wiki/File:GeneralElectricSign.jpg

SHRM practices should provide answers to the following key questions:[6]

- *Competence.* To what extent does our company have the required knowledge, skills, and abilities to implement its strategy?
- *Consequence.* To what extent does our company have the right measures, rewards, and incentives in place to align people's efforts with the company strategy?
- *Governance.* To what extent does our company have the right structures, communications systems, and policies to create a high-performing organization?
- *Learning and leadership.* To what extent can our company respond to uncertainty and learn and adapt to change quickly?

The Importance of Human Capital

Employees provide an organization's **human capital**. Human capital refers to a set of skills that individuals have acquired on the job, through training and experience, which increase a person's value in the marketplace. The Society of Human Resource Management defines an organization's human capital asset as, "the collective sum of the attributes, life experience, knowledge, inventiveness, energy and enthusiasm that its people choose to invest in their work."[7] Experts have argued human capital is critical for ESG (environmental, societal, governance) performance that translates to all manners of a firm's success.[8]

human capital

The collective sum of the attributes, life experience, knowledge, inventiveness, energy, and enthusiasm that people choose to invest in their work.

Focus on Outcomes

Historically, many HR managers are more effective in the technical or operational aspects of HR than they are in the strategic ones. This trend has begun to change as managers have realized that the strategic aspects have a much larger effect on the company's success.[9] In the past, HR professionals focused on compliance to rules, such as those set by the federal government, and they tracked simple metrics like the number of employees hired or the number of hours of training delivered. The new principles of management, however, require a focus on outcomes and results, not just numbers and compliance. Just as lawyers view their key performance measure as the number of cases they have won—not just the time and effort spent working on cases—so too must HR professionals track how employees are using the skills they have learned to attain goals, versus a potentially less impactful measure such as the number of hours employees have engaged in training.[10]

John Murabito, executive vice president and head of HR and Services at Cigna, says that HR executives need to understand the company's goals and strategy and then provide employees with the skills needed. HR executives often get wrapped up in their own initiatives without understanding how their role contributes to the business. That is a concern because when it comes to the HR department, "anything that is administrative or transactional is going to get outsourced," Murabito says.[11] Indeed, the number of HR outsourcing contracts over $25 million has been increasing.[12] For example, Bank of America outsourced its HR administration to Arinso. While Arinso will provide timekeeping, payroll processing, and payroll services for 10,000 Bank of America employees outside the United States, Scotiabank signed a five-year payroll deal with Arinso for over 40,000 employees in more than 50 countries.[13] To avoid outsourcing, HR needs to stay relevant and accept accountability for its business results. In short, the people strategy needs to be fully aligned with the company's business strategy and keep the focus on outcomes.

Key Elements of HR

In high-performing companies, each element of the HR system is designed to reflect best practice and to maximize employee performance. The different parts of the HR system are strongly aligned with company goals.

Selection and Placement

When hiring, effective selection and placement involves acquainting prospective new hires with the nature of the jobs they will be expected to fulfill. This includes explaining the technical competencies needed (for example, collecting statistical data) and defining behavioral competencies. Behavioral competencies may have a customer focus, such as the ability to show empathy and support of customers' feelings and points of view, or a work management focus, such as the ability to complete tasks efficiently or to know when to seek guidance.

In addition, this process involves teaching the organization's culture by discussing the values that underpin the organization and describing the organization's "heroes." For example, are the heroes of the company people who go the extra mile to get customers to smile? Are they the people who toil through the night to develop new code? Are they the ones who can network and reach a company president to make the sale? By sharing such stories of company heroes with potential hires, managers help reinforce what makes a company unique. This, in turn, will help the job candidates determine whether they will fit into the organization's culture.

FIGURE 15.1 Key Elements of HR

Selection and Placement

Selecting the right individuals for an organization is a critical human resources task thoughtfully considered using the selection process. To tap into individuals with critical thinking skills, IBM's consulting division often asks unique interview questions such as "How many traffic lights are there in New York City?" to assess the potential employee's ability to walk through a logical process and create a reasonable estimate.

Job Design

Job design refers to the process of putting together various elements to form a job, bearing in mind organizational and individual worker requirements, as well as considerations of health, safety, and ergonomics. Workers can thank designer Robert Probst for his well-known (and often bemoaned) invention that has greatly changed how many employees engage in their day-to-day work activities—the cubicle.

Compensation and Rewards

How organizations pay employees represents one of the most tangible elements of human resource management. Such rewards can be found in real estate companies that highlight the commissions earned by their employees through membership in million dollar clubs found around the globe.

Diversity Management

Diversity goes far beyond the ideas of avoiding discrimination and involves actively appreciating and using the differing perspectives and ideas that individuals bring to the workplace. When teams include members with complementary skills, the diversity helps companies and teams come up with more creative and effective solutions. More than half of *Fortune* 500 companies now employ a chief diversity officer, or similar executive, with the charge of leveraging the power of diversity. Several international companies such as Ericsson—named after their famed inventor founder—are also well known for their global diversity management initiatives.

Source: Shutterstock.com, Roland.Magnusson_Shutterstock.com

Job Design

job design

The process of putting together various elements to form a job, bearing in mind organizational and individual worker requirements.

Job design refers to the process of putting together various elements to form a job, including organizational and individual worker requirements, as well as considerations of health, safety, and ergonomics. Job design involves training employees to have the knowledge and skills to perform all parts of their job and providing them with the authority and accountability to perform effectively.[14] Job enrichment is important for retaining employees.

Companies that allow employees growth opportunities and interesting jobs are often desirable places to work, becoming hubs for worldwide talent. For example, hospitality topped the 2020 Fortune list of best companies to work for with Hilton Hotels taking the number one spot with Kimpton Hotels & Restaurants also making the top ten.[15]

Compensation and Rewards

Organizations should carefully evaluate and pay employees based on their performance, not simply for workplace attendance. Wise companies offer rewards for skill development and organizational performance, emphasizing teamwork, collaboration, and responsibility for performance. They help employees identify new skills to develop so that they can advance and achieve higher pay and rewards. Compensation systems that include incentives, gainsharing, profit-sharing, and skill-based pay reward employees who learn new skills and put those skills to work for the organization. Employees who are trained in a broad range of skills and problem solving are more likely to grow on the job and feel more satisfaction. Such training enables them to make more valuable contributions to the company, which, in turn, gains them higher rewards and greater commitment to the company.[16] The company likewise benefits from employees' increased flexibility, productivity, and commitment.

When employees have access to information and the authority to act on that information, they are more involved in their jobs and more likely to make the right decision and take the necessary actions to further the organization's goals. Similarly, rewards need to be linked to performance, so that employees are naturally inclined to pursue outcomes that will gain them rewards and further the organization's success at the same time.

Diversity Management

Another key to successful SHRM in today's business environment is embracing diversity. In past decades, "diversity" simply meant avoiding discrimination against women, minorities, and those with disabilities in hiring. Today, diversity goes far beyond this limited definition; diversity management involves actively appreciating and using the differing perspectives and ideas that individuals bring to the workplace. Diversity is an invaluable contributor to innovation and problem-solving success. Research shows that the more diverse the group in terms of expertise, gender, age, and background, the more ability the group has to avoid the problems of groupthink.[17] Diversity helps company teams come up with more creative and effective solutions. Teams whose members have complementary skills are often more successful because members can see one another's blind spots. Members will be more inclined to make different kinds of mistakes, which means that they will be able to catch and correct those mistakes.

Decision-Making Diversity Pays Off at TIAA-CREF

Source: http://en.wikipedia.org/wiki/File:RogerWFergusonJr.jpg

Do diverse groups make better decisions? TIAA-CREF believes so. TIAA-CREF is headquartered in New York and offers financial advice, investment information, retirement plans and accounts, college savings plans, annuities, life insurance, brokerage, and trust services for over 5 million investors. In 2020, it was listed as number 81 on the *Fortune* 500 list. Researchers studying the impact on board of directors' diversity noted that diversity is a key investment criterion for TIAA-CREF because they believe a diverse board will be less beholden to management. Foremer CEO of TIAA-Cref Roger W. Ferguson Jr., believes it too. He recently proclaimed, "You get better answers if you have a diverse work force." This is a powerful statement and he cites a powerful example to make his case. Ferguson explains that executives at his Charlotte, North Carolina-based branch of the company had a "knock-down, drag-out" fight before the 2008 economic crash regarding how much of their then $430 billion portfolio should be invested in the sub-prime mortgage market. He explains that because the company is aggressive about fostering diversity, the discussion included diverse points of view that led to the decision to avoid the risk of investing heavily in the sub-prime market. He argues that such diverse points of view might have been suppressed at other organizations less focused on diversity in terms of ideas as well as more visible types of diversity such as gender or race. Researchers have reached similar conclusions, stating that "after controlling for size, industry, and other corporate governance measures, we find significant positive relationships between the fraction of women and minorities on the board and firm value."

TIAA-CREF has a long history of being recognized as a leader in valuing diversity, including being consistently recognized by *Fortune*, *Working Mother*, *Hispanic*, and *Black Enterprise* magazine as a good place to work. Their diversity program states, "Building on our success, our goal is to ensure that we continue to respect the creativity, talents, and experiences that each employee contributes regardless of age, gender, race, ethnicity, religious belief, sexual orientation, mental or physical disability, veteran status, medical condition, or family circumstance. We actively recruit and hire members of underrepresented groups for opportunities in all areas, at all levels in the organization, to achieve our objective of a highly diversified talent pool." Diversity extends to their suppliers as well. The company prefers to do business with suppliers who are in line with their diversity values in practice or because they are owned by diverse individuals.

CEO Ferguson earned a law degree and PhD in economics at Harvard University. He is a former vice chair of the U.S. Federal Reserve's board of governors and was a member of former President Barack Obama's Economic Recovery Advisory Board. Ferguson was the second African American CEO at TIAA-CREF after Clifton R. Wharton Jr., who became CEO of the company—and the first African American CEO of a major U.S. corporation—in 1987.[18] In 2021, Thasunda Brown Duckett became TIAA's third African American CEO after serving as the CEO of Chase Consumer Banking for over four years.

Key Takeaway

Human resources management is becoming increasingly important in organizations because today's knowledge economy requires employees to contribute ideas and be engaged in executing the company's strategy. HR is thus becoming a strategic partner by identifying the skills that employees need and then providing employees with the training and structures needed to develop and deploy those competencies. All the elements of HR—selection, placement, job design, and compensation—need to be aligned with the company's strategy so that the right employees are hired for the right jobs and rewarded properly for their contributions to furthering the company's goals.

Discussion Questions

1. What are the advantages of the new SHRM approach?
2. Name three elements of HR.
3. What benefits does a diverse workforce provide the company?
4. Whose responsibility is it to manage human resources in an organization?

15.2 The War for Talent

Learning Objectives

1. Define talent management.
2. Learn how to attract valuable employees.
3. Understand how to keep star employees.
4. Understand the benefits of good talent management.

war for talent

Competition between organizations to attract and retain the most able employees.

The **war for talent** refers to competition among organizations to attract and retain the most able employees. Retaining star employees is critical for many organizations as research has found that in many instances an elite number of star workers account for the vast majority of workplace outcomes.[19] In addition, agencies that track demographic trends have been warning for years that the U.S. workforce will shrink in the second and third decades of the 21st century as the baby boom generation (born 1945–1961) reaches retirement age and Millenials make up more of the workforce. Gen-Z is also catching up quickly and is now almost a quarter of the workforce.[20] As workers compete for the most desirable jobs, employers will have to compete even more fiercely to find the right talent. For example, a recent *McKinsey Quarterly* article argued the world could have a shortage of 40 million college-educated workers as soon as 2020.[21]

What Talent Management Means

Peter Cappelli of The Wharton School defines **talent management** as anticipating the need for human capital and devising a plan to meet increasing demand.[22] It goes hand in hand with **succession planning**—the process whereby an organization ensures that employees are recruited and developed to fill key roles within the company. Most companies, unfortunately, do not plan ahead for the talent they need, resulting in shortages of critical skills at some times and surpluses at others. Other companies use outdated methods of succession planning that do not accurately forecast the skills they will need in the future.

talent management

Anticipating the need for human capital and devising a plan to meet it.

succession planning

A process whereby an organization ensures that employees are recruited and developed to fill each key role within the company.

Several techniques developed to achieve productivity breakthroughs in manufacturing can be applied to talent management. For example, it is expensive to develop all talent internally; training people takes a long time and requires accurate predictions about which skill will be needed. Such predictions are increasingly difficult to make in a changing world. Therefore, rather than developing everyone internally, companies often hire talent from the outside when they need to tap specific skills. In manufacturing, this principle is known as "make or buy." In HR, the solution is to make *and* buy; that is, to train some people and to hire others from the external marketplace. In this case, "making" an employee means hiring a person who does not yet have all the needed skills to fulfill the role, but who can be trained ("made") to develop them. The key to a successful "make" decision is to distinguish between the high-potential employees who do not yet have the skills but who can learn them from employees with less potential. The "buy" decision means hiring an employee who has all the necessary skills and experience to fulfill the role from day one. The "buy" decision is useful when it is too difficult to predict exactly which skills will be needed in the future.[23]

Those born between 1997 to 2012 (sometimes referred to as Gen Z) make up 25% of the workforce.

Source: Shutterstock.com

Another principle from manufacturing that works well in talent management is to run smaller batch sizes. That is, rather than sending employees to three-year-long training programs, companies send their employees to shorter programs more frequently. With this approach, managers do not have to make the training decision so far in advance. They can wait to decide exactly which skills employees will learn closer to the time the skill is needed, thus ensuring that employees are trained in the skills they will actually use.

Attracting the Right Workers to the Organization

Winning the war for talent means more than simply attracting workers to the company. It means attracting the *right* workers—the ones who will be enthusiastic about their work. Enthusiasm for the job requires more than having a good attitude about receiving good pay and benefits—it means that an employee's goals and aspirations also match those of the company. Therefore, it is important to identify employees' preferences and mutually assess how well they align with the company's strategy. To accomplish this goal, the organization must first be clear about the type of employee it wants to hire and retain. Companies regularly engage in this process with customers—marketing executives identify specific segments of the universe of buyers to target for selling products. Red Bull, for example, targets college-age consumers, whereas SlimFast markets to adults of all ages who feel they are overweight. Both companies are selling beverages but to completely different consumer segments. Similarly, companies need to develop a profile of the type of workers they want to attract. Does a company want entrepreneurial individuals who seek autonomy and continual learning or team players who enjoy collaboration, stability, and structure? Neither employee type is inherently "better" than another, but an employee who craves autonomy may feel constrained within the very same structure in which a team player would thrive.

It is important to mutually assess how well employees' preferences align with the company's strategy. Potential employees need to know whether they will fit well into the company. One way to help prospective hires make this determination is to describe to them the "signature experience" that sets your company apart. As Tamara Erickson and Lynda Gratton define it, your company's signature experience is the distinctive practice that shows what it is really like to work at your company.[24]

Consider the signature experiences of two companies: Whole Foods and Goldman Sachs. At Whole Foods, team-based hiring is a signature experience—employees in each department vote on whether a new employee will be retained after a four-week trial period. This demonstrates to potential hires that Whole Foods is all about collaboration. In contrast, Goldman Sachs' signature experience is multiple one-on-one interviews. The story often told to prospective hires is of the MBA student who went through 60 interviews before being hired. This story signals to new hires that they need to be comfortable meeting endless new people and building networks across the company. Those who enjoy meeting and being interviewed by so many diverse people are exactly the ones who will fit into Goldman's culture. The added benefit of hiring workers who match your organizational culture and are engaged in their work is that they will be less likely to leave a company simply to earn a higher salary.

Keeping Star Employees

The war for talent stems from the approaching shortage of workers. Millions of baby boomers reaching retirement age are leaving a gaping hole in the U.S. workforce. In addition, workers are job-hopping more frequently than in the past. According to the U.S. Bureau of Labor Statistics, the average job tenure has dropped from 15 years in 1980 to 4.6 years in 2014,[25] and has since dropped to 4.1 years as of 2020 statistics.[26] Managers need to give employees reasons to stay with their company. One way to retain employees is to spend time talking about their career goals. Listening to their likes and dislikes in order to help them use the skills they like using or developing new ones they wish to acquire may go a long way in motivating employees.[27]

Managers are also advised not to be afraid to "grow" employees. Some managers want to keep their employees in their department. They fear that helping employees grow on the job will mean that employees will outgrow their job and leave.[28] In contrast, if companies help employees advance, it will be easier for the manager to move up in the organization because employees will be better able to take on the role left behind.

In some cases, employees may not be sure what career path they want. Managers can help them identify their goals by asking questions such as the following:[29]

- What assignments have you found most engaging?
- Which of your accomplishments in the last six months made you proudest?
- What makes for a great day at work?

What Employees Want

Employees want to grow and develop, stretching their capabilities. They want projects that engage their heads as well as their hearts, and they want to connect with the people and things that will help them achieve their professional goals.[30] Here are two ways to help employees reach these goals: First, connect people with mentors and help them build their networks. Research suggests that successful managers dedicate 70% more time to networking activities and 10% more time to communication than their less-successful counterparts.[31] What makes networks special? Through networks, people energize one another, learn, create, and find new opportunities for growth. Second, networks help connect people with a sense of purpose. Focusing on the need for purpose is especially important for younger workers, who rank meaningful work and challenging experiences at the top of their job search lists.[32]

As a result of a culture supporting networking, creativity, and expression, employees at 940's Kitchen & Cocktails strike a pose for National Women's Equality Day.

Source: Michael Bak, @mikebakphotography

Social Networking as a Career-Building Strategy

Source: Roman Pyshchyk/Shutterstock.com

Penelope Trunk, author of "The Brazen Careerist" column and blog (blog.penelopetrunk.com), views job hunting not as an event but as a lifestyle. She advises that in today's business environment, people change jobs so often that they need to keep their eye on the market even if they just started a new job. In her view, "the people who control their destiny most effectively leave their job when they find a better one, not when they are tossed out because of layoffs or reorganizations." This also means that social networking should be a central element in any job-search strategy. And, because many jobs are filled by knowing someone who knows about an open position, Trunk argues that it's more important to network than it is to read the want ads. Trunk evokes the principle of reciprocity when she says, "building a network is adding value to lots of people's lives so that they, in turn, will want to add value to yours." Another useful strategy is to network proactively rather than reacting to concerns about your present job or news of a possible opening. By being proactive, you will increase your chances of being in the right place at the right time.

Career networking opportunities are plentiful; regardless of where you live, you can use the internet to read blogs, subscribe to e-mail newsletters, and make friends on social networking sites. When you consider the principle of exchange, you realize that your networking possibilities are not limited to people in your chosen field—you can actually gain more by networking with those in related fields or even in jobs far removed from yours. With the exchange principle in mind, even residents of sparsely populated rural areas can network with their neighbors a few miles down the road.

Source: Adapted from Trunk, P. (2008, March 1). Take control of your career destiny. Wisconsin State Journal, B1.

Benefits of Good Talent Management

Global consulting firm McKinsey & Company conducted a study to identify links between a company's financial performance and its success in managing talent. The survey results show that there was indeed a relationship between a firm's financial performance and its global talent management practices. Three talent management practices in particular correlated highly with exceptional financial performance:

1. Creating globally consistent talent evaluation processes.
2. Achieving cultural diversity in a global setting.
3. Developing and managing global leaders.[33]

The McKinsey survey found that companies achieving scores in the top third in any of these three areas had a 70% chance of achieving financial performance in the top third of all companies.[34]

Having consistent talent evaluation means that employees around the world are evaluated on the same standards. This means that if an employee from one country transfers to another, his or her manager can be assured that the employee has been held to the same level of skills and standards. Second, having cultural diversity means having employees with knowledge about the culture of different countries, not just those with foreign language skills. This helps bring about open-mindedness across cultures. Finally, developing global leaders means rotating employees across different cultures and giving them international experience. Companies who do this best also have policies of giving managers incentives to share their employees with other units.

Key Takeaway

The coming shortage of workers makes it imperative for managers to find, hire, retain, and develop their employees. Managers first need to define the skills that the company will need for the future. Then, they can "make or buy"—that is, train or hire—employees with the needed skills. Retaining these employees requires engaging them on the job. Good talent management practices translate into improved financial performance for the company as a whole.

Discussion Questions

1. How might a manager go about identifying the skills that the company will need in the future?
2. Describe the "make or buy" option and how it can be applied to HR.
3. How would you go about attracting and recruiting talented workers to your organization? Suggest ideas you would use to retain stars and keep them happy working for you.
4. What skills might an organization like a bank need from its employees?

15.3 Effective Selection and Placement Strategies

Learning Objectives

1. Explain why a good job description benefits the employer and the applicant.
2. Describe how company culture can be used in selecting new employees.
3. Discuss the advantages and disadvantages of personnel testing.
4. Describe some considerations in international staffing and placement

Selecting the right employees and placing them in the right positions within the company is a key HR function and is vital to a company's success. Companies should devote as much care and attention to this "soft" issue as they do to financial planning, because errors will have financial impact and adverse effects on a company's strategy.

Job-Description Best Practices

An accurate and complete job description is a powerful SHRM tool that costs little to produce and can help considerably in reducing turnover. While the realistic description may discourage some applicants (often those who would not do well in the job), those who follow through with the application process are much more likely to be satisfied with the job once hired. In addition to summarizing what the worker will actually be doing all day, here are some additional suggestions for writing an effective job description:

- List the job requirements in bullet form so that job seekers can scan the posting quickly.
- Use common industry terms, which speak to knowledgeable job seekers.
- Avoid organization-specific terms and acronyms, which would confuse job seekers.
- Use meaningful job titles (not the internal job codes of the organization).
- Use key words taken from the list of common search terms (to maximize the chance that a job posting appears on a job seeker's search).
- Include information about the organization, such as a short summary and links to more detailed information.
- Highlight special intangibles and unusual benefits of the job and workplace (e.g., flextime, travel, etc.).
- Specify the job's location (and nearest large city) and provide links to local community pages (to entice job seekers with quality-of-life information).

FIGURE 15.2 Effective Selection and Placement Strategies

Selecting employees that fit with the organization's culture and values is a key HR function with the potential to impact the firm's performance. Equally important is the ability to carefully place employees within specific positions in the company. Here, we illustrate issues related to both selection and placement.

Job Description Best Practices

An accurate and complete job description is a powerful SHRM tool that costs little to produce and can help considerably in reducing turnover. Descriptions should be concise, relevant, and avoid jargon. For example, a job description for a barista (creator of coffee drinks) might say, "Prepare coffee and other hot beverages, maintain equipment, and create a hospitable atmosphere. Various part-time tasks in other areas will often be required."

Tailoring Recruitment and Selection to Match Company Culture

Managers who hire well do not just hire for skills or academic background; they ask about the potential employee's philosophy on life or how the candidate likes to spend free time to assess whether the cultural fit is right. At Google, for example, job candidates are asked questions like "If you could change the world using Google's resources, what would you build?" In fact, you can even see it in their job postings. Marissa Mayer (known as Google employee #20 and former CEO at Yahoo!) wrote a job ad that read, "You're brilliant? We're hiring. Come work at Google." Her ad got eight times more responses than their other ads.

Tools and Methods: Interviewing and Testing

Testing and interviewing are two established methods to gather information about potential employees. Interviews often include "the human being" test where candidates are simply assessed on their personability and ability to interact with others. Situational interviews focus on past experience or future situations to assess what a job candidate might do in a given situation. The rationale behind testing is to give the employer more information—information vital to assessing how well a candidate is suited to a particular job—before making the selection and placement decision. For example, behavioral traits assessments measure energy level, assertiveness, sociability, manageability, and attitude.

International Staffing and Placement

In our increasingly global economy, managers need to decide between using expatriates and hiring locals when staffing international locations. At an estimated cost of $200,000 per failed expatriate, international assignment decisions should be made with careful forethought and consideration. The challenge is to overcome the natural tendency to hire a well-known, corporate insider over an unknown local at the international site. Expatriates are useful when company-specific knowledge is important, while local hires are beneficial when large cultural issues may come into play in the day-to-day business operations. The movie (and short-lived TV show) *Outsourced* chronicles the pros and cons of each type of employee when an American manager travels to India to train his replacement, only to experience various forms of cultural shock that require him to heavily rely on the expertise of a call center worker he is hired to manage.

Source: Shutterstock.com

Tailoring Selection to Match Company Culture

Managers who hire well do not just hire for skills or academic background; they ask about the potential employee's philosophy on life or how the candidate likes to spend free time. These questions help the manager assess whether the cultural fit is right. A company in which all work is done in teams needs team players. Ask questions like, "Do you have a personal mission statement? If not, what would it be if you wrote one today?"[35] to identify potential hires' preferences. It is also important to note that research finds job candidates can be penalized when they inquire about extrinsic rewards such as pay and benefits during the selection process.[36]

At Google, for example, job candidates are asked questions like, "If you could change the world using Google's resources, what would you build?"[37] Google wants employees who will think and act on a grand scale, employees who will take on the challenges of their jobs, whatever their job may be. Take Josef Desimone, Google's former executive chef, for example. Desimone, who's worked everywhere from family-style restaurants to Michelin-caliber ones, was amazed to learn that Google had dozens of cafes for its employees. "Nobody changes the menu daily on this scale," he says. "It's unheard of." When he was hired, Desimone realized, "Wow, you hire a guy who's an expert in food and let him run with it! You don't get in his way or micromanage."[38] Google applies this approach to all positions and lets employees run with the challenge.

Traditionally, companies have built a competitive advantage by focusing on structural advantages such as economies of scale, a well-established brand, or dominance in certain market segments. Companies such as Southwest Airlines, by contrast, see its people as their advantage: "Our fares can be matched; our airplanes and routes can be copied. But we pride ourselves on our customer service," said Sherry Phelps, director of corporate employment. That's why Southwest looks for candidates who generate enthusiasm and leans toward extraverted personalities.[39] Southwest hires for attitude. Flight attendants have been known to sing and rap the safety instructions, and pilots tell jokes over the public address system.

Southwest Airlines makes clear right from the start the kind of people it wants to hire. For example, recruitment ads showed Southwest founder Herb Kelleher dressed as Elvis and read, "Work in a Place Where Elvis Has Been Spotted...The qualifications? It helps to be outgoing. Maybe even a bit off-center. And be prepared to stay awhile. After all, we have the lowest employee turnover rate in the industry." People may scoff or question why Southwest indulges in such showy activities. Phelps answers, "We do take our work seriously. It's ourselves that we don't." People who don't have a humane, can-do attitude are fired. Southwest has a probationary period during which it determines the compatibility of new hires with the culture. People may be excellent performers, but if they do not match the culture, they are let go. As Southwest's founder Kelleher once said, "People will write me and complain, 'Hey, I got terminated or put on probation for purely subjective reasons.' And I'll say, 'Right! Those are the important reasons.'"

In the United States, in all states except Montana, employees are covered under what is known as the **at-will employment doctrine**. At-will employment is "a doctrine of American law that defines an employment relationship in which either party can break the relationship with no liability, provided there was no express contract for a definite term governing the employment relationship and that the employee does not belong to a collective bargaining unit (i.e., a union)."[40] However, there are legal restrictions on how subjective the reasons for firing can be. For instance, if the organization has written hiring and firing procedures and does not follow them in selective cases, then those cases might give rise to claims of wrongful termination. Similarly, in situations where termination is clearly illegal—for example, based on age, race, religion, and so on—wrongful termination can be claimed. One recent update in hiring practices relates to 'ban the box' laws that make it illegal to ask candidates about their criminal history until a conditional job offer has been made; this practice becomes effective at the federal level in 2021 as a result of the Fair Chance to Compete for Jobs Act.[41]

The Fair Chance to Compete for Jobs Act bans potential employers from inquiring about criminal history until a conditional job offer is made.

Source: Shutterstock.com

at-will employment doctrine

A doctrine of American law that defines an employment relationship in which either party can break the relationship with no liability, provided there was no express contract for a definite term governing the employment relationship and that the employee does not belong to a collective bargaining unit (i.e., a union).

Music Rap-Up: Google Me Now

Twinprov perform a rap outlining effective strategic human resources practices.

View in the online reader

Tools and Methods: Interviewing and Testing

Interviewing and testing are two time-tested methods to learn information about a job candidate.

A detailed interview begins by asking the candidate to describe his or her work history followed by an inquiry about the person's most recent position (or the position most similar to the open position). Candidates are often asked about their previous responsibilities and major accomplishments. In-depth questions about specific job situations are also common. Called **situational interviews**, these types of interviews can focus on past experience or future situations. For example, experience-based questions are "Tell me about a major initiative you developed and the steps you used to get it adopted." Or "Describe a problem you had with someone and how you handled it." In contrast, future-oriented situational interview questions ask candidates to describe how they would handle a future hypothetical situation, such as "Suppose you came up with a faster way to do a task, but your team was reluctant to make the change. What would you do in that situation?"

situational interviews

A job interview where candidates are asked in-depth questions about specific job situations in the past or future.

In addition to what is asked, it is also important that interviewers understand what they should not ask, largely because certain questions lead to answers that may be used to discriminate. There are five particularly sensitive areas. The only times interviewers can ask about age are when it is a requirement of a job duty or if the company needs to determine whether a work permit is required. Second, it is rarely appropriate or legal to ask questions regarding race, color, national origin, or gender. Third, although candidates may volunteer religious or sexually oriented information in an interview, interviewers still need to be careful not to discriminate. Asking questions relevant to work experience or qualifications is always appropriate. Fourth, firms cannot discriminate for health or disabilities; potential employers may not ask about health or disabilities in an interview. Finally, interviewers may not ask questions about marital status, children, personal life, pregnancy, or arrest records (although employers may inquire about convictions). Certain kinds of questions could be tempting to ask if you are interviewing for a position requiring travel; however, companies can only explain the travel requirements and confirm that the requirements are acceptable.

Consulting firm interview questions such as "If you could select a song to sing on American Idol . . . what would it be?" are used to potentially tap employee creativity.

Source: Shutterstock.com

In addition to interviews, many employers use testing to select and place job applicants. Any tests given to candidates must be job related and follow guidelines set forth by the Equal Opportunity Employment Commission to be legal. For the tests to be effective, they should be developed by reputable professionals and administered by professionally qualified personnel who have had training in occupational testing in an industrial setting. The rationale behind testing is to give the employer more information before making the selection and placement decision—information vital to assessing how well a candidate is suited to a particular job. Most pre-employment assessment tests measure thinking styles, behavioral traits, and occupational interests. The results are available almost immediately after a candidate completes the roughly hour-long questionnaire. Thinking styles tests can tell the potential employer how fast someone can learn new things or how well he or she can verbally communicate. Behavioral traits assessments measure energy level, assertiveness, sociability, manageability, and attitude. For example, a high sociability score would be a desirable trait for salespeople.[42]

International Staffing and Placement

In our increasingly global economy, managers need to decide between using expatriates or hiring locals when staffing international locations. **Expatriates** are employees assigned to a foreign location on a temporary basis. On the surface, this seems a simple choice between the firm-specific expertise of the expatriate and the cultural knowledge of the local hire. In reality, companies often fail to consider the high probability and high cost of expatriates failing to adapt and perform in their international assignments.

expatriate

Employees assigned to a foreign location on a temporary basis.

Cultural issues can create misunderstandings between expatriate managers and employees, suppliers, customers, and local government officials. At an estimated cost of $200,000 per failed expatriate, international assignment decisions should be made with careful forethought and consideration. The challenge is to overcome the natural tendency to hire a well-known, corporate insider over an unknown local at the international site.

Key Takeaway

Effective selection and placement requires finding and hiring the right employees for the organization and then placing them into the jobs for which they are best suited. Providing an accurate and complete job description is a key step in the selection process. An important determination is whether the candidate's personality is a good fit for the company's culture. Interviewing is a common selection method. Situational interviews ask candidates to describe how they handled specific situations in the past (experience-based situational interviews) and how they would handle hypothetical questions in the future (future-oriented situational interviews). Other selection tools include cognitive tests, personality inventories, and behavioral traits assessments. Specific personalities may be best suited for positions that require sales, teamwork, or entrepreneurship, respectively. In our increasingly global economy, managers need to decide between using expatriates and hiring locals when staffing international locations.

Discussion Questions

1. What kind of information would you include in a job description?
2. Do you think it is important to hire employees who fit into the company culture? Why or why not?
3. List questions that you would ask in a future-oriented situational interview.
4. What requirements must employee selection tests meet?
5. If you were hiring to fill a position overseas, how would you go about selecting the best candidate?

15.4 The Roles of Pay Structure and Pay for Performance

Learning Objectives

1. Understand different pay system elements.
2. Understand the value of pay for performance plans.
3. Discuss the challenges of individual versus team-based pay.

bonus

A form of variable pay where the employee earns a one-time cash payment based on achieved objectives.

Pay can be thought of in terms of an individual's "total compensation package" that includes an individual's base salary, variable pay, share ownership, and other benefits. A **bonus**, for example, is a form of variable play. A bonus is a one-time cash payment, often awarded for exceptional performance. For example, one real estate company likely surprised many of their employees during their annual holiday party when bonuses averaged $50,000.[43] Providing employees with an annual statement of all these benefits they receive can help them understand the full value of their compensation.[44]

Indirect compensation is far more varied, including everything from legally required public protection programs such as social security to health insurance, retirement programs, paid leave, child care, or housing. Some indirect compensation elements are required by law. Examples include social security, unemployment, and disability payments. Other indirect elements are up to the employer and can offer excellent ways to provide additional benefits to employees that may benefit the employer as well. For example, a working parent may take a lower-paying job with flexible hours that will allow him or her to be home when the children get home from school. A recent graduate may be looking for stable work and a desirable place to live. Both of these individuals have different needs and, therefore, might appreciate different compensation elements.

FIGURE 15.3 Pay Systems Elements

Pay can take the form of direct or indirect compensation. Nonmonetary pay can include any benefit an employee receives from an employer or job that does not involve tangible value. This includes career and social rewards, such as job security, flexible hours and opportunity for growth, praise and recognition, task enjoyment, and friendships. Direct pay is an employee's base wage. It can be an annual salary, hourly wage, or any performance-based pay that an employee receives, such as profit-sharing bonuses. Here, we illustrate elements common to many pay systems.

Nonmonetary Pay

Includes benefits that do not involve tangible value, such as a desirable location.

Direct Pay

Employee's base wage.

Indirect pay

Everything from legally required programs to health insurance, retirement, housing, etc.

Incentive pay

A bonus paid when the specified performance objectives are met, such as the pink Cadillac given to successful Mary Kay employees.

Stock options

A right to buy a piece of the business that may be given to an employee to reward excellent service. An employee who owns a share of the business is far more likely to go the extra mile for the operation.

Bonuses

A gift given occasionally to reward exceptional performance or for special occasions. Bonuses can show an employer appreciates his or her employees and ensures that good performance or special events are rewarded.

Source: Shutterstock.com. Agia_Shutterstock.com

Setting Pay Levels

job evaluation

An evaluation of the positions in an organization to understand job design requirements and identify positions critical to strategy and firm performance.

When setting pay levels for positions, managers should make sure that the pay level is fair relative to what other employees in the position are being paid. Part of the pay level is determined by the pay at other companies. If one company pays substantially less than others, it's going to be a less desirable choice of employment unless it offers something overwhelmingly positive to offset the low pay, such as flexible hours or a fun, congenial work atmosphere. Besides these external factors, companies conduct a **job evaluation** to determine the internal value of the job—"A" positions are those on which the company's value depends, "B" positions are somewhat less important in that they do not deliver as much upside to the company, and "C" positions are those of least importance—in some cases, these are outsourced.

The most vital jobs to one company's success may not be the same as in other companies. For example, information technology companies may put top priority on their software developers and programmers, whereas for retailers such as Nordstrom, the "A" positions are those frontline employees who provide personalized service. For an airline, pilots would be a "B" job because, although they need to be well trained, investing further in their training is unlikely to increase the airline's profits. "C" positions for a retailer might include back office bill processing, while an information technology company might classify customer service as a "C" job.

When setting reward systems, it's important to pay for what the company actually hopes to achieve. Companies often say they want innovative thinking or risk taking, but they reward people who "make the numbers."[45] If companies truly want to achieve what they hope for, they need payment systems aligned with their goals. For example, if retention of star employees is important to your company, reward managers who retain top talent. At PepsiCo, for instance, one-third of a manager's bonus is tied directly to how well the manager succeeds at developing and retaining employees. Tying compensation to retention makes managers accountable for creating a culture that decreases employee turnover.[46]

Often learned at a young age, the concept of pay for performance remains one of the most effective pay structures.

Source: Shutterstock.com

Pay for Performance

pay for performance

When pay is tied directly to an individual's performance in meeting specific business goals or objectives.

Pay for performance ties pay directly to an individual's performance in meeting specific business goals or objectives. Managers (often together with the employees themselves) design performance targets to which the employee will be held accountable. The targets have accompanying metrics that enable employees and managers to track performance. The metrics can be financial indicators, or they can be indirect indicators such as customer satisfaction or speed of development. Pay-for-performance schemes often combine a fixed base salary with a variable pay component (such as bonuses or stock options) that vary with the individual's performance.

Innovative Employee Recognition Programs

In addition to regular pay structures and systems, companies often create special programs that reward exceptional employee performance. For example, the financial software company Intuit, Inc., instituted a program called Spotlight. The purpose of Spotlight is to "spotlight performance, innovation and service dedication."[47] Unlike regular salaries or year-end bonuses, Spotlight awards can be given on the spot for specific behavior that meets the reward criteria, such as filing a patent, inventing a new product, or meeting a milestone for years of service. Rewards can be cash awards of $500 to $3,000 and can be made by managers without high-level approval. In addition to cash and noncash awards, two Intuit awards feature a trip with $500 in spending money.[48]

Pay Structures for Groups and Teams

Many employers use compensation systems that reward all of the organization's employees as a group or various groups and teams within the organization. In this section, we examine these pay structures.

Gainsharing and Profit-Sharing

Gainsharing is a form of pay for performance. In gainsharing, the organization shares the financial gains with employees. Employees receive a portion of the profit achieved from their specific efforts and ideas. How much they receive is determined by their performance against the plan. With gainsharing, the organization measures their historical (baseline) performance. Then, if employees help improve the organization's performance on those measures, they share in the financial rewards achieved. This sharing is typically determined by a formula.

gainsharing

When an organization shares the financial gains with employees, such that employees receive a portion of the profit achieved from their specific efforts and ideas.

The effectiveness of a gainsharing plan depends on employees seeing a relationship between what they do and how well the organization performs. The larger the size of the organization, the harder it is for employees to see the effect of their work. Therefore, gainsharing plans are more effective in companies with fewer than 1,000 people.[49] Gainsharing success also requires the company to have good performance metrics in place so that employees can track their progress. The gainsharing plan can only be successful if employees believe and see that if they perform better, they will be paid more. The pay should be given as soon as possible after the performance so that the tie between the two is established.

While gainsharing divides a portion of cost savings or profit increases that can be directly traced back to cost saving ideas of employees, **profit-sharing** programs are those plans that provide an incentive to employees based on company profits. The assumption behind these programs is that organizations are profitable thanks to the efforts of all employees; hence employees are entitled to a portion of the profits. These programs have the intention to encourage workers to think like owners of a business.

profit-sharing

Programs that provide employees an incentive based on company profits.

When designing systems to measure performance, it is important that performance appraisals focus on quantifiable measures. Designing these measures with input from the employees helps make the measures clear and understandable to employees and increases their buy-in that the measures are reasonable.

Team-Based Pay

Many managers seek to build teams but struggle with the challenge of motivating employees to achieve the team's goals. In response to this challenge, team-based pay is becoming increasingly accepted. In 1992, only 3% of companies had team-based pay; however, the concept quickly took off. By 1999, 80% of companies had implemented this concept.

Pay Systems That Reward Both Team and Individual Performance

There are two main theories of how to reward employees. Nancy Katz characterized the theories as two opposing camps.[50] The first camp advocates rewarding individual performance through plans such as commissions-sales schemes and merit-based-pay. The claim is that this will increase employees' energy, drive, risk taking, and task identification. The disadvantages of rewarding individual performance are that employees will cooperate less, that high performers may be resented by others in the organization, and that low performers may try to undermine top performers.

The second camp believes that organizations should reward team performance, without regard for individual accomplishment. This reward system is thought to bring the advantages of increased helping and cooperation, sharing of information and resources, and mutual respect among employees. The disadvantages of team-based reward schemes are that they create a lack of drive, that low performers are "free riders," and that high performers may withdraw or act aggressively toward poorer-performing team members.

Katz sought to identify reward schemes that achieve the best of both worlds. These hybrid pay systems would reward individual and team performance, promoting excellence at both levels. Katz suggested two possible hybrid reward systems. The first system features a base rate of pay for individual performance that increases when the group reaches a target level of performance. In this reward system, individuals have a clear pay-for-performance incentive, and their rate of pay increases when the group as a whole does well. In the second hybrid, the pay-for-performance rate also increases when a target is reached. Under this reward system, however, every team member must reach a target level of performance before the higher pay rate takes effect. In contrast with the first hybrid, this reward system clearly incentivizes the better performers to aid poorer performers. Only when the poorest performer reaches the target can all team members benefit from the higher pay rate.

Key Takeaway

Compensation plans reward employees for contributing to company goals. Pay levels should reflect the value of each type of job to the company's overall success. For some companies, technical jobs are the most vital, whereas for others frontline customer service positions determine the success of the company against its competitors. Pay-for-performance plans tie an individual's pay directly to his or her ability to meet performance targets. These plans can reward individual performance or team performance or a combination of the two.

Discussion Questions

1. What factors would you consider when setting a pay level for a particular job?
2. If you were running a business, would you implement a pay-for-performance scheme? Why or why not?
3. Describe the difference between a base salary, a bonus, and a gainsharing plan.
4. Discuss the advantages and disadvantages of rewarding individual versus team performance.

15.5 Designing a High-Performance Work System

Learning Objectives

1. Define a high-performance work system.
2. Describe the role of technology in HR.
3. Describe the use of HR systems to improve organizational performance.
4. Describe succession planning and its value.

A high-performance work system (HPWS) is a set of management practices that attempt to create an environment within an organization where the employee has greater involvement and responsibility. Designing a HPWS involves putting all the HR pieces together. A HPWS is all about determining what jobs a company needs done, designing the jobs, identifying and attracting the type of employee needed to fill the job, and then evaluating employee performance and compensating them appropriately so that they stay with the company.

e-HRM

Technology is changing the way HR is done. The electronic human resource management (e-HRM) business solution is based on the idea that information technologies, including the Web, can be designed for human resources professionals and executive managers who need support to manage the workforce, monitor changes, and gather the information needed in decision making. At the same time, e-HRM can enable all employees to participate in the process and keep track of relevant information. For instance, companies provide employees with a website where they can log in; get past and current pay information, including tax forms (i.e., 1099, W-2, and so on); manage investments related to a 401(k); or opt for certain medical record-keeping services.

More generally, for example, many administrative tasks are being done online, including

- providing and describing insurance and other benefit options,
- enrolling employees for those benefits,
- enrolling employees in training programs,
- administering employee surveys to gauge their satisfaction.

Company's such as Oklahoma City based Paycom provide online payroll and other e-HRM services.

Source: ll.studio/Shutterstock.com

Many of these tasks are being done by employees themselves, which is referred to as *employee self-service*. With all the information available online, employees can access it themselves when they need it.

Part of an effective HR strategy is using technology to reduce the manual work performed by HR employees. Simple or repetitive tasks can be performed self-service through e-HRM systems that provide employees with information and lets them perform their own updates. Typical HR services that can be performed in an e-HRM system include the following:

- Answer basic compensation questions,
- Look up employee benefits information,
- Process candidate recruitment expenses,
- Receive and scan resumes into recruiting software,

- Enroll employees in training programs,
- Maintain training catalog,
- Administer tuition reimbursement,
- Update personnel files.

Organizations that have invested in e-HRM systems have found that they free up HR professionals to spend more time on the strategic aspects of their job. These strategic roles include employee development, training, and succession planning.

The Value of High-Performance Work Systems

Employees who are highly involved in conceiving, designing, and implementing workplace processes are more engaged and perform better. For example, a study analyzing 132 U.S. manufacturing firms found that companies using HPWS had significantly higher labor productivity than their competitors. The key finding was that when employees have the power to make decisions related to their performance, can access information about company costs and revenues, and have the necessary knowledge, training, and development to do their jobs—and are rewarded for their efforts—they are more productive.[51]

HPWS are used globally. For example, Fey and colleagues studied 101 foreign-based firms operating in Russia and found significant linkages between HRM practices, such as incentive-based compensation, job security, employee training, and decentralized decision making, and subjective measures of firm performance. [52]

Improving Organizational Performance

Organizations that want to improve their performance can use a combination of HR systems to get these improvements. For example, performance measurement systems help underperforming companies improve performance. The utility company Arizona Public Service used a performance measurement system to rebound from dismal financial results. The company developed 17 "critical success indicators," which it measures regularly and benchmarks against the best companies in each category. Of the 17, nine were identified as "major critical success indicators":

- Cost to produce kilowatt hour,
- Customer satisfaction,
- Fossil plants' availability,
- Operations and maintenance expenditures,
- Construction expenditures,
- Ranking as corporate citizen in Arizona,
- Safety all-injury incident rate,
- Nuclear performance,
- Shareholder value return on assets.

Each department sets measurable goals in line with these indicators, and a gainsharing plan rewards employees for meeting the indicators.

In addition, companies can use reward schemes to improve performance. Better-performing firms tend to invest in more sophisticated HRM practices, which further enhance organizational performance.[53] Currently, about 20% of firms link employee compensation to the firm's earnings.

They use reward schemes such as employee stock ownership plans, gainsharing, and profit-sharing. This trend is increasing.

Is the performance of an organization with a profit-sharing plan better than that of other firms? And, does adoption of a profit-sharing plan lead to improvement in an organization's performance? The reasons profit-sharing plans would improve organizational performance relate to motivation theory. A profit-sharing plan will likely encourage employees to monitor one another's behavior because "loafers" would erode the rewards for everyone. Moreover, profit-sharing should lead to greater information sharing, which increases the productivity and flexibility of the firm.

Researcher Michel Magnan studied 294 Canadian credit unions in the same region (controlling for regional and sector-specific economic effects). Of the firms studied, 83 had profit-sharing plans that paid the bonus in full at the end of the year. This meant that employees felt the effect of the organizational performance reward immediately, so it had a stronger motivational effect than a plan that put profits into a retirement account, where the benefit would be delayed (and essentially hidden) until retirement.

Magnan's results showed that firms with profit-sharing plans had better performance on most facets of organizational performance. They had better performance on asset growth, market capitalization, operating costs, losses on loans, and return on assets than firms without profit-sharing plans. The improved performance was especially driven by activities where employee involvement had a quick, predictable effect on firm performance, such as giving loans or controlling costs.

Another interesting finding was that when firms adopted a profit-sharing plan, their organizational performance went up. Profit-sharing plans appear to be a good turnaround tool because the firms that showed the greatest improvement were those that had not been performing well before the profit-sharing plan. Even firms that had good performance before adopting a profit-sharing plan had better performance after the profit-sharing plan.[54]

Succession Planning

Succession planning is a process whereby an organization ensures that employees are recruited and developed to fill each key role within the company. In a recent survey, HR executives and non-HR executives were asked to name their top human capital challenge. Nearly one-third of both executive groups cited succession planning,[55] but less than 20% of companies with a succession plan addressed nonmanagement positions. Slightly more than 40% of firms did not have a plan in place.

Looking across organizations, succession planning takes a number of forms (including no form at all). An absence of succession planning should be a red flag, since the competitive advantage of a growing percentage of firms is predicated on their stock of human capital and ability to manage such capital in the future. One of the overarching themes of becoming better at succession is that effective organizations become much better at developing and promoting talent from within. The figure "Levels of Succession Planning" summarizes the different levels that firms can work toward.

Succession planning is particularly important in family businesses where many businesses are unable to keep their wealth for three generations.

Source: Shutterstock.com

Levels of Succession Planning

- Level 1: No planning at all.
- Level 2: Simple replacement plan. Typically the organization has only considered what it will do if key individuals leave or become debilitated.
- Level 3: The company extends the replacement plan approach to consider lower-level positions, even including middle managers.
- Level 4: The company goes beyond the replacement plan approach to identify the competencies it will need in the future. Most often, this approach is managed along with a promote-from-within initiative.
- Level 5: In addition to promoting from within, the organization develops the capability to identify and recruit top talent externally. However, the primary source of successors should be from within, unless there are key gaps where the organization does not have key capabilities.

Dow Chemical exemplifies some best practices for succession planning:

- Dow has a comprehensive plan that addresses all levels within the organization; not just executive levels.
- CEO reviews the plan, signaling its importance.
- Managers regularly identify critical roles in the company and the competencies needed for success in those roles.
- Dow uses a grid for succession planning, plotting employees along the two dimensions of potential and performance.
- High potential employees are recommended for training and development, such as Dow Academy or an MBA.

The principles of strategic human resource management and high-performance work systems apply to nonprofit enterprises as well as for-profit companies, and the benefits of good HR practices are just as rewarding. When it comes to succession planning, nonprofits face a particularly difficult challenge of attracting workers to a field known for low pay and long hours. Often, the people attracted to the enterprise are drawn by the cause rather than by their own aspirations for promotion. Thus, identifying and training employees for leadership positions is even more important. Finally, succession planning is also considered to be especially challenging yet critical for family firms.[56]

Key Takeaway

A high-performance work system unites the social and technical systems (people and technology) and aligns them with company strategy. It ensures that all the interrelated parts of HR are aligned with one another and with company goals. Technology and structure supports employees in their ability to apply their knowledge and skills to executing company strategy. HR decisions, such as the type of compensation method chosen, can improve performance for organizations and enterprises of all types.

Discussion Questions

1. What are some ways in which HR can improve organizational performance?
2. What is the most important aspect of high performance work systems? Name three benefits of high performance work systems.

3. How does e-HRM help a company?
4. If you were designing your company's succession-planning program, what guidelines would you suggest?

15.6 Tying It All Together: Using the HR Balanced Scorecard to Gauge and Manage Your Human Capital

Learning Objectives

1. Describe how the Balanced Scorecard method can be applied to HR.
2. Learn the term "human capital."
3. Consider how your human capital might be mapped on an HR Balanced Scorecard.

The **Balanced Scorecard** helps managers define the performance categories that relate to the company's strategy. The managers then translate those categories into metrics and track performance of those metrics. Besides traditional financial measures and quality measures, companies use employee performance measures to track their people's knowledge, skills, and contribution to the company.[57]

Balanced Scorecard

A framework designed to translate an organization's vision and mission statements and overall business strategy into specific, quantifiable goals and objectives and to monitor the organization's performance in terms of achieving these goals.

The employee performance aspects of Balanced Scorecards analyze employee capabilities, satisfaction, retention, and productivity. Companies also track whether employees are motivated (for example, the number of suggestions made and implemented by employees) and whether employee performance goals are aligned with company goals.

Applying the Balanced Scorecard Method to HR

Because the Balanced Scorecard focuses on the strategy and metrics of the business, Mark Huselid and his colleagues developed the HR and Workforce Scorecard to provide a framework specific to HR. According to Huselid, the **Workforce Scorecard** identifies and measures the behaviors, skills, mind-sets, and results required for the workforce to contribute to the company's success. Specifically, as summarized in Figure 15.4, the Workforce Scorecard has four key sequential elements:[58]

Workforce Scorecard

An application of the Balanced Scorecard concept to an organization's human capital to identify and measure the behaviors, skills, mindsets, and results required for the workforce to contribute to the company's success.

1. **Workforce mindset and culture.** First, does the workforce understand the strategy, embrace it, and does it have the culture needed to support strategy execution?
2. **Workforce competencies.** Second, does the workforce, especially in the strategically important or "A" positions, have the skills it needs to execute strategy? ("A" positions are those job categories most vital to the company's success.)

3. **Leadership and workforce behaviors.** Third, are the leadership team and workforce consistently behaving in a way that will lead to attaining the company's key strategic objectives?
4. **Workforce success.** Fourth, has the workforce achieved the key strategic objectives for the business? If the organization can answer "yes" to the first three elements, then the answer should be yes here as well.[59]

FIGURE 15.4 The HR Balanced Scorecard

The HR Balanced Scorecard bridges HR best practices and the firm's comprehensive Balanced Scorecard.

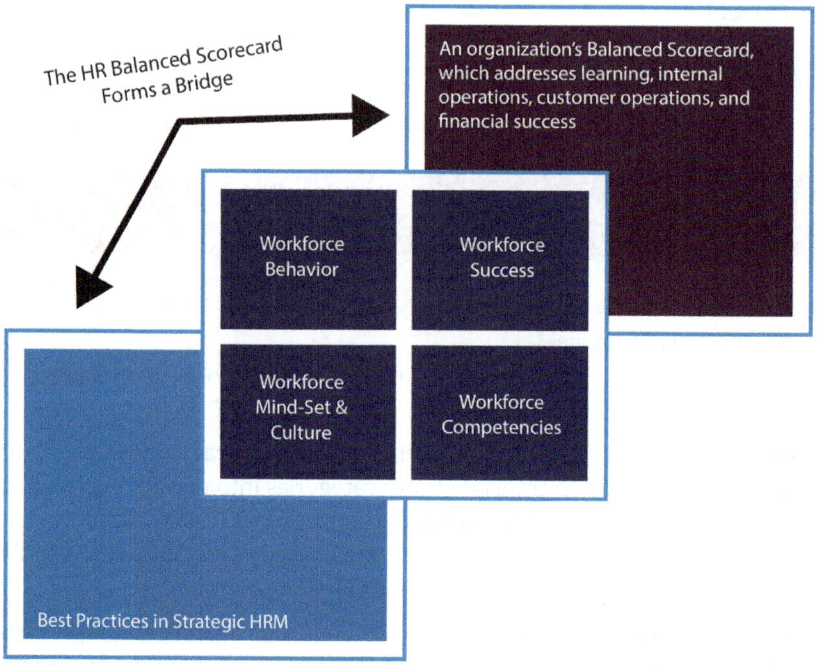

Human Capital

human capital

The collective sum of the attributes, life experience, knowledge, inventiveness, energy, and enthusiasm that its people choose to invest in their work.

Implementing the HR scorecard requires a change in perspective, from seeing people as a cost to seeing people as the company's most important asset to be managed—**human capital**. According to the Society for Human Resource Management's *Research Quarterly*, "A company's human capital asset is the collective sum of the attributes, life experience, knowledge, inventiveness, energy and enthusiasm that its people choose to invest in their work."[60] Such an asset is difficult to measure because it is intangible, and factors like "inventiveness" are subjective and open to interpretation. The challenge for managers, then, is to develop measurement systems that are more rigorous and provide a frame of reference. The metrics can range from activity-based (transactional) metrics to strategic ones. Transactional metrics are the easiest to measure and include counting the number of new people hired, fired, transferred, and promoted. The measures associated with these include the cost of each new hire, the length of time and cost associated with transferring an employee, and so forth. Typical ratios associated with transactional metrics include the training cost factor (total training cost divided by the employees trained) and training cost percentage (total training cost divided by operating expense).[61] But these transactional measures do not get at the strategic issues such as whether the right employees are being trained and whether they are remembering and using what they learned. Measuring training effectiveness requires not only devising metrics but actually changing the nature of the training.

The Bank of Montreal has taken this step. "What we're trying to do at the Bank of Montreal is to build learning into what it is that people are doing," said Jim Rush of the Bank of Montreal's Institute for Learning. "The difficulty with training as we once conceived it is that you're taken off your job, you're taken out of context, you're taken away from those things that you're currently working on, and you go through some kind of training. And then you've got to come back and begin to apply that. Well, you walk back to that environment and it hasn't changed. It's not supportive or conducive to you behaving in a different kind of way, so you revert back to the way you were, very naturally." To overcome this problem, the bank conducts training such that teams bring in specific tasks on which they are working, so that they learn by doing. This removes the gap between learning in one context and applying it in another. The bank then looks at performance indices directly related to the bottom line. "If we take an entire business unit through a program designed to help them learn how to increase the market share of a particular product, we can look at market share and see if it improved after the training."[62]

Motorola has adopted a similar approach, using action learning in its Senior Executives Program. Action learning teams are assigned a specific project by Motorola's CEO and are responsible for implementing the solutions they design. This approach not only educates the team members but also lets them implement the ideas, so they are in a position to influence the organization. In this way, the training seamlessly supports Motorola's goals.

Organizations need employees to apply the knowledge they have to activities that add value to the company. In planning and applying human capital measures, managers should use both retrospective (lagging) and prospective (leading) indicators. Lagging indicators are those that tell the company what it has accomplished (such as the Bank of Montreal's documenting the effect that training had on a business unit's performance). Leading indicators are forecasts that help an organization see where it is headed. Leading indicators include employee learning and growth indices.[63]

The Payoff

Given the complexity of what we've just discussed, some managers may be inclined to ask, "Why bother doing all this?" Research by John Lingle and William Schiemann provides a clear answer: Companies that make a concerted effort to measure intangibles such as employee performance, innovation, and change, in addition to measuring financial measures perform better. Lingle and Schiemann examined how executives measured six strategic performance areas: financial performance, operating efficiency, customer satisfaction, employee performance, innovation and change, and community/environment issues. To evaluate how carefully the measures were tracked, the researchers asked the executives, "How highly do you value the information in each strategic performance area?" and "Would you bet your job on the quality of the information on each of these areas?" The researchers found that the companies that paid the closest attention to the metrics and had the most credible information were the ones identified as industry leaders over the previous three years (74% of measurement-managed companies compared with 44% of others) and reported financial performance in the top one-third of their industry (83% compared with 52%).

The scorecard is vital because most organizations have much better control and accountability over their raw materials than they do over their workforce. For example, a retailer can quickly identify the source of a bad product, but the same retailer can't identify a poor-quality manager whose negative attitude is poisoning morale and strategic execution.[64]

Applying the Balanced Scorecard Method to Your Human Capital

Let's translate the HR scorecard to your own Balanced Scorecard of human capital. As a reminder, the idea behind the HR scorecard is that if developmental attention is given to each area, then the organization will more likely be successful. In this case, however, you use the scorecard to better understand why you may or may not be effective in your current work setting. Your scorecard will comprise four sets of answers and activities.

1. **What is your mindset and values**? Do you understand the organization's strategy and embrace it, and do you know what to do in order to implement the strategy? If you answered "no" to either of these questions, then you should consider investing some time in learning about your firm's strategy. You may need additional coursework or mentoring to understand what it takes to move the firm's strategy forward.
2. **What are your work-related competencies**? Do you have the skills and abilities to get your job done? If you have aspirations to key positions in the organization, do you have the skills and abilities for those higher roles?
3. **What are the leadership and workforce behaviors**? If you are not currently in a leadership position, do you know how consistently your leaders are behaving with regard to the achievement of strategic objectives? If you are one of the leaders, are you behaving strategically?
4. **Your success**? Can you tie your mindset, values, competencies, and behaviors to the organization's performance and success?

This simple scorecard assessment will help you understand why your human capital is helping the organization or needs additional development itself. With such an assessment in hand, you can act to help the firm succeed and identify priority areas for personal growth, learning, and development.

Key Takeaway

The Balanced Scorecard, when applied to HR, helps managers align all HR activities with the company's strategic goals. Assigning metrics to the activities lets managers track progress on goals and ensure that they are working toward strategic objectives. It adds rigor and lets managers quickly identify gaps. Companies that measure intangibles such as employee performance, innovation, and change perform better financially than companies that do not use such metrics. Rather than investing equally in training for all jobs, a company should invest disproportionately more in developing the people in the key "strategic" ("A") jobs of the company on which the company's success is most dependent.

Discussion Questions

1. List the elements of a Workforce Scorecard.
2. Discuss how human capital can be managed like a strategic asset.
3. Why is it important to align HR metrics with company strategy?
4. What kind of metrics would be most useful for HR to track?

15.7 Case in Point: People Come First at SAS

Source: Casimiro PT/Shutterstock.com

Who are your best customers? Which customers are bringing you the most profits and which are the least profitable? Companies are increasingly relying on complicated data-mining software to answer these and other questions. SAS Institute Inc. is the second largest privately held software company in the United States; of the top 100 companies from the 2018 Fortune Global 1000 list, 92 are SAS customers. Founded in 1976, SAS has its headquarters in Cary, North Carolina. The company that began as a research project designed to analyze farming data is doing extremely well by any measure. As of 2019, they had nearly 14,000 employees worldwide, were installed in 147 countries at over 83,000 locations, and reported $3.3 billion in revenue in 2018. The company is quick to attribute their success to the performance and loyalty of their workforce. This is directly correlated with how they treat their employees.

SAS, which stands for Statistical Analysis System, has perfected the art of employee management. Jenn Mann, VP for HR at SAS is quoted as saying, "SAS employees understand how important their contribution is for the company's success. Our stimulating work environment and high levels of trust provide employees with the freedom to test new ideas while maintaining a healthy work-life balance. This recognition proves yet again that happy, creative employees drive results." SAS has been ranked on *Fortune* magazine's best places to work list every year since the list was first published, including being named number 1 in 2010 and 2011. Employees seem to genuinely enjoy working at SAS and are unusually attached to the company, resulting in a turnover rate that is less than 5% in an industry where 13.5% is the norm. In fact, when Google designed their own legendary campus in California, they visited the SAS campus to get ideas.

One thing SAS does well is giving its employees opportunities to work on interesting and challenging projects. The software developers have the opportunity to develop cutting-edge software to be used around the world. The company makes an effort to concentrate its business in the areas of analytics, which add the most value and help organizations best analyze disparate data for decision making, creating opportunities for SAS workers to be challenged. Plus, the company removes obstacles for employees. Equipment, policies, rules, and meetings that could impede productivity are eliminated.

The company has a reputation as a pioneer when it comes to the perks it offers employees, but these perks are not given with a mentality of "offer everything but the kitchen sink." There is careful thinking and planning behind the choice of perks the company offers. SAS conducts regular employee satisfaction surveys, and any future benefits and perks offered are planned in response to the results. The company wants to eliminate stressors and anything that dissatisfies from people's lives. To keep employees healthy and fit, there are athletic fields; a full gym; a swimming pool where employees can swim or play inner tube water polo; and tennis, basketball, and racquetball courts on campus. Plus, the company offers free on-site health care for employees, covers dependents at their fully staffed primary medical care center, provides flexible scheduling, and offers unlimited sick leave. The company understands that employees have a life and encourages employees to work reasonable hours and then go home to their families. In fact, a famous motto in the company is, "If you are working for more than eight hours, you are just adding bugs." SAS is truly one of the industry leaders in leveraging its treatment of people for continued business success.[65]

Multimedia Extension—SAS Campus Tour

View in the online reader

Case Discussion Questions

1. SAS is involved in cutting-edge technology. Does this give it a distinct advantage in employee retention and satisfaction over, for example, a manufacturing company or a food retailer?
2. Do you feel that investing heavily in employee perks ultimately pays off for a company? Would you feel the same way during hard economic times, when the pool of highly qualified workers grows and the number of available jobs shrinks dramatically?
3. How much of an advantage does SAS have, given that the company produces analytic software to help businesses improve their functionality?
4. In addition to giving employees interesting and challenging projects, SAS also places a high level of trust in its employees. In your opinion, how do these factors contribute to employee creativity and innovation?
5. What do you think you'd like about working at SAS? What would you not potentially like?

Endnotes

1. Becker, B. E., & Huselid, M. A. (2006). Strategic human resources management: Where do we go from here? *Journal of Management, 32*, 898–925.
2. Bentley, F.S., & Kehoe, R.R. (2020). Give Them Some Slack—They're Trying to Change! The Benefits of Excess Cash, Excess Employees, and Increased Human Capital in the Strategic Change Context. *Academy of Management Journal*. https://doi.org/10.5465/amj.2018.0272.
3. Huselid, M. A. (1995). The impact of human resource management practices on turnover, productivity, and corporate financial performance. *Academy of Management Journal, 38*, 635–672; Pfeffer, J. (1998). *The human equation: Building profits by putting people first*. Boston: Harvard Business School Press; Pfeffer, J., & Veiga, J. F. (1999). Putting people first for organizational success. *Academy of Management Executive, 13*, 37–48; Welbourne, T., & Andrews, A. (1996). Predicting performance of initial public offering firms: Should HRM be in the equation? *Academy of Management Journal, 39*, 910–911.
4. Pfeffer, J., & Veiga, J. F. (1999). Putting people first for organizational success. *Academy of Management Executive, 13*, 37–48.
5. Brian, E., Becker, B. E., Huselid, M. A., & Ulrich, D. (2002). *Six key principles for measuring human capital performance in your organization*. University of Maryland Working Paper.
6. Ulrich, D. (1998). *Delivering results*. Boston: Harvard Business School Press.

7. Weatherly, L. (2003, March). Human capital—the elusive asset; measuring and managing human capital: A strategic imperative for HR. *Research Quarterly*, Society for Human Resource Management website. Retrieved from http://www.shrm.org/research/quarterly/0301capital.pdf.
8. Retrieved from https://www.forbes.com/sites/christopherskroupa/2017/10/10/human-capital-why-its-a-critical-component-for-success/#6d5a03034291; retrieved from https://www.huffingtonpost.com/entry/companies-are-made-of-people-the-importance-of-human_us_5996e927e4b03b5e472ceead.
9. Huselid, M. A., Jackson, S. E., & Schuler, R. S. (1997). Technical and strategic human resource management effectiveness as determinants of firm performance. *Academy of Management Journal, 40*, 171–188.
10. Ulrich, D. (1998). *Delivering results*. Boston: Harvard Business School Press.
11. Marquez, J. (2007, September 10). On the front line: A quintet of 2006's highest-paid HR leaders discuss how they are confronting myriad talent management challenges as well as obstacles to being viewed by their organizations as strategic business partners. *Workforce Management, 86*, 22.
12. TPI Counts 2700+ Outsourcing Contracts. (2007, December). Retrieved from http://www.sharedxpertise.org/file/230/trends--research.html.
13. HRO Europe (2006, August 23). Retrieved from http://www.hroeurope.com.
14. Lawler, E. (1992). *The ultimate advantage*. San Francisco: Jossey-Bass.
15. Retrieved from https://fortune.com/best-companies/.
16. Barnes, W. F. (2001). *The challenge of implementing and sustaining high performance work systems in the United States: An evolutionary analysis of I/N Tek and Kote*. (Doctoral dissertation, University of Notre Dame).
17. Surowiecki. J. (2005). *The wisdom of crowds*. New York: Anchor Books.
18. Based on information in Diel, S. (2010, November 4). TIAA-CREF chief Roger W. Ferguson Jr. tells Birmingham audience that diverse companies outperform others. *Birmingham News;* Reuters (2008, April 4). Chief is selected at TIAA-CREF. *New York Times;* Carter, D. A., Simkins, B. J., & Simpson, W. G. (2003). Corporate governance, board diversity, and firm value. *Financial Review*. Retrieved from https://www.tiaa-cref.org/public/about-us/employee-diversity-inclusion.
19. O'Boyle Jr., E., & Aguinis, H. (2012). The best and the rest: Revisiting the norm of normality of individual performance. *Personnel Psychology, 65*, 79–119.
20. Retrieved from https://www.inc.com/marla-tabaka/gen-z-will-make-up-24-percent-of-global-workforce-in-2020-heres-what-employers-need-to-know.html.
21. Retrieved from https://www.inc.com/jacob-morgan/the-war-for-talent-its-real-heres-why-its-happening.html.
22. Cappelli, P. (2008, March). Talent management for the 21st century, Boston. *Harvard Business Review*, 17–36.
23. Buhler, P. M. (2008, March). Managing in the new millennium; succession planning: Not just for the c suite. *Supervision, 69*(3), 19–23.
24. Erickson, T., & Gratton, L. (2007, March). What it means to work here. *Harvard Business Review*, 23–29.
25. Retrieved from http://www.toyota.co.jp/en/history/index.html.
26. Retrieved from https://www.bls.gov/news.release/tenure.nr0.htm#:~:text=Industry In January 2020, wage,years for private-sector employees.
27. Kaye, B. (2008). *Love 'em or lose 'em*. San Francisco: Barrett-Koehler.
28. Field, A. (2008, June). Do your stars see a reason to stay? *Harvard Management Update*.
29. Butler, T. (2007). *Getting unstuck*. Boston: Harvard Business School Press.
30. Deloitte Research. (2007). *Do you know where your talent is? Why acquisition and retention strategies don't work*. Geneva, Switzerland: Deloitte-Touch Research Report.
31. Luthans, F., Yodgetts, R., & Rosenkrantz, S. (1988). *Real Managers*. Cambridge: Ballinger.
32. Sheahan, P. (2006). *Generation Y: Thriving (and surviving) with generation Y at work*. Victoria, Australia: Hardie Grant Books.
33. McKinsey global-talent-management survey of over 450 executives. (2007, December). Retrieved from http://www.mckinseyquarterly.com/article_print.aspx?L2=18&L3=31&ar=2140.
34. Guthridge, M., & Komm, A. B. (1988, May). Why multinationals struggle to manage talent. *McKinsey Quarterly*, 19–25.
35. Pfeffer, J. (1998). *The human equation: Building profits by putting people first*. Boston: Harvard Business School Press.
36. Derfler-Rozin, R., & Pitesa, M. (2020). Motivation purity bias: Expression of extrinsic motivation undermines perceived intrinsic motivation and engenders bias in selection decisions. *Academy of Management Journal*. https://doi.org/10.5465/amj.2017.0617.
37. Slater, C. (2008, March). The faces and voices of Google. *Fast Company*, 37–45.
38. Slater, C. (2008, March). Josef Desimone—executive chef. *Fast Company*, 46–48.
39. Bruce, A. (1997, March). Southwest: Back to the FUNdamentals. *HR Focus, 74*(3), 11; Freiberg, K., & Freiberg, J. (2003). *Nuts! Southwest Airlines's crazy recipe for business and personal success*. Austin, TX: Bard; Hallowell, R. (1996, Winter). Southwest Airlines: A case study linking employee needs satisfaction and organizational capabilities to competitive advantage. *Human Resource Management, 35*(4), 513–529; Heskett J. L., & Hallowell, R. (1993). Southwest Airlines—1993 (A). *Harvard Business School Case*; Southwest Airlines' Herb Kelleher: Unorthodoxy at work. (1995, January). *Management Review*, 2–9; LaBarre, P. (1996, February 5). Lighten up! Blurring the line between fun and work not only humanizes organizations but strengthens the bottom line. *Industry Week, 245*(3), 53–67; Labich, K. (1994, May 2). Is Herb Kelleher America's best CEO? *Fortune*, 44–45; McNerney, D. J. (1996, August). Employee motivation: Creating a motivated workforce. *HR Focus, 73*(8), 1; Tomkins, R. (1996, November 11). HR: The seriously funny airline. *Financial Times* (33137), 14, A1–A5.
40. Rothstein, M. A., Knapp, Andria S., & Liebman, Lance. (1987). *Cases and materials on employment law* (p. 738). New York: Foundation Press.
41. Retrieved from https://www.goodhire.com/blog/ban-the-box/.
42. Mrosko, T. (2006, August). The personnel puzzle: Preemployment testing can help your bottom line. *Inside Business, 8*(8), 60–73.
43. Retrieved from https://www.cnn.com/2019/12/10/us/company-10-million-bonuses-trnd/index.html.
44. Anderson, I. (2007, August 1). Human resources: War or revolution? *Mondaq Business Briefing*, n.p.
45. Kerr, S. (1995). On the folly of rewarding A, while hoping for B. *Academy of Management Executive, 9*, 25–37.
46. Field, A. (2008, June). Do your starts see a reason to stay? *Harvard Management Update*, 5–6.
47. Hoyt, D. (2008, March). Employee recognition at Intuit; and Spotlight. Global Strategic Recognition Program. Stanford Graduate School of Business Case Study. Retrieved from http://www.globoforce.com/corporate/eng/our-customers/case-studies/intuit.html?KeepThis=true&TB_iframe=true&height=400&width=600.
48. Intuit spotlights strategic importance of global employee recognition. (2008, August 15). Retrieved from http://howtomanagehumanresources.blogspot.com/2008/08/intuit-spotlights-strategic-importance.html.
49. Lawler, E. (1992). *The ultimate advantage*. San Francisco: Jossey-Bass.
50. Katz, N. R. (1998). Promoting a healthy balance between individual achievement and team success: The impact of hybrid reward systems. Presented at the "Do Rewards Make a Difference?" Session at the Academy of Management Conference, August 9–12.
51. Konrad, A. M. (2006, March/April). Engaging employees through high-involvement work practices. *Ivey Business Journal Online*, 1–6. Retrieved from http://www.iveybusinessjournal.com.
52. Fey, C., Bjorkman, I., & Pavlovskaya, A. (2000). The effect of human resource management practices on firm performance in Russia. *International Journal of Human Resource Management, 11*, 1–18.
53. Shih, H.-A., Chiang, Y.-H., & Hsu, C.-C. (2006, August). Can high performance work systems really lead to better performance? *International Journal of Manpower, 27*(8), 741–763.
54. Magnan, M., & St-Onge, S. (1998). Profit sharing and firm performance: A comparative and longitudinal analysis. Presented at the Academy of Management Conference, August 9–12.
55. Buhler, P. M. (2008, March). Managing in the new millennium; succession planning: Not just for the c suite. *Supervision, 69*(3), 19.
56. Retrieved from http://www.forbes.com/sites/russalanprince/2015/11/03/succession-planning-a-bane-for-family-businesses/.
57. Kaplan, R., & Norton, D. (1996). *The Balanced Scorecard*. Boston: Harvard Business School Press.
58. Huselid, M., Becker, B., & Beatty, D. (2005). *The workforce scorecard: Managing human capital to execute strategy*. Boston: Harvard Business School Press.
59. Huselid, M.A., Beatty, R.W., & Becker, B.E (2005, December). "A players" or "A positions"? The strategic logic of workforce management. *Harvard Business Review*.
60. Weatherly, L. (2003, March). Human capital—the elusive asset; measuring and managing human capital: A strategic imperative for HR. *Research Quarterly*, Society for Human Resource Management. Retrieved from http://www.shrm.org/research/quarterly/0301capital.pdf.
61. Saratoga Institute—2003 SHRM National Conference, as quoted in Weatherly, L. (2003). The value of people: The challenges and opportunities of human capital measurement and reporting. *SHRM Research Quarterly, 3*, 14–25.
62. Rush, J. (1995, July). Interview backgrounder for *Fast Company*.
63. Weatherly, L. A. (2003). The value of people: The challenges and opportunities of human capital measurement and reporting. *SHRM Research Quarterly, 3*, 26–31.
64. Becker, B. E., & Huselid, M. A., (2006). Strategic human resources management: Where do we go from here? *Journal of Management, 32*, 898–925.

65. Case written by Talya Bauer and Berrin Erdogan to accompany Bauer, T. N., & Erdogan, B. (2021). *Organizational Behavior: Bridging Science and Practice (4.0).* Boston, MA: FlatWorld. Partially based on ideas and information contained in Doing well by being rather nice. (2007, December 1). *Economist.* Retrieved from http://www.financialexpress.com/news/doing-well-by-being-rather-nice/247090; Cakebread, C. (2005, July). SAS...not SOS. *Benefits Canada, 29*(7), 18; Florida, R., & Goodnight, J. (2005, July–August). Managing for creativity. *Harvard Business Review, 83*(7/8), 124–131; Fortune (2017). SAS on *Fortune* Best Companies to Work for list. http://fortune.com/best-companies/sas/; SAS (2012). SAS on *Fortune* Best Companies to Work for list in US. Retrieved from http://www.sas.com/news/preleases/2012fortuneranking.html; Karlgaard, R. (2006, October 16). Who wants to be public? *Forbes Asia, 2*(17), 22; Forbes (n.d.). America's largest private companies: 2019 ranking. Retrieved from https://www.forbes.com/largest-private-companies/list/#tab:rank; SAS. (2019). About SAS. Retrieved from https://www.sas.com/en_us/company-information/profile.html; SAS (2019). 2018 corporate social responsibility. Retrieved from https://www.sas.com/content/dam/SAS/en_us/doc/other1/csr-107835.pdf.

Index